D0164761

Clearly Visual Basic® Programming with Microsoft® Visual Basic® 2008

Diane Zak

COURSE TECHNOLOGY
CENGAGE Learning™

Australia • Brazil • Japan • Korea • Mexico • Singapore • Spain • United Kingdom • United States

COURSE TECHNOLOGY
CENGAGE Learning™

Clearly Visual Basic: Programming with Microsoft Visual Basic 2008

Diane Zak

Executive Editor: Marie Lee

Acquisitions Editor: Amy Jollymore

Managing Editor: Tricia Coia

Editorial Assistant: Patrick Frank

Marketing Manager: Bryant Chrzan

Content Project Manager: Daphne Barbas

Art Directors: Bruce Bond/Marissa Falco

Cover Designer: Cabbage Design Company

Cover Photo: Cabbage Design Company

Manufacturing Coordinator: Julio Esperas

Proofreader: Wendy Benedetto

Indexer: Alexandra Nickerson

Compositor: International Typesetting
   and Composition

© 2009 Course Technology, Cengage Learning

ALL RIGHTS RESERVED. No part of this work covered by the copyright herein may be reproduced, transmitted, stored or used in any form or by any means graphic, electronic, or mechanical, including but not limited to photocopying, recording, scanning, digitizing, taping, Web distribution, information networks, or information storage and retrieval systems, except as permitted under Section 107 or 108 of the 1976 United States Copyright Act, without the prior written permission of the publisher.

For product information and technology assistance, contact us at
Cengage Learning Customer & Sales Support, 1-800-354-9706

For permission to use material from this text or product,
submit all requests online at **cengage.com/permissions**
Further permissions questions can be emailed to
permissionrequest@cengage.com

ISBN-13: 978-1-4239-0241-6

ISBN-10: 1-4239-0241-6

Course Technology
25 Thomson Place
Boston, MA 02210
USA

Cengage Learning is a leading provider of customized learning solutions with office locations around the globe, including Singapore, the United Kingdom, Australia, Mexico, Brazil, and Japan. Locate your local office at: **international.cengage.com/region**

Cengage Learning products are represented in Canada by Nelson Education, Ltd.

For your lifelong learning solutions, visit **course.cengage.com**

Purchase any of our products at your local college store or at our preferred online store **www.ichapters.com**

Printed in Canada
1 2 3 4 5 6 7 12 11 10 09 08

TABLE OF CONTENTS

CHAPTER 22
BUILDING YOUR OWN STRUCTURE   481

CHAPTER 23
I'M SAVING FOR THE FUTURE   503

CHAPTER 24

CHAPTER 25

TABLE OF CONTENTS

CHAPTER 26
THE MISSING "LINQ"   573

CHAPTER 27
I LOVE THIS CLASS   589

APPENDIX A
DATA TYPES

INDEX

THE FOLLOWING CHAPTER, VIDEOS, AND FILES ARE AVAILABLE ELECTRONICALLY AT WWW.COURSE.COM.

CHAPTER 28
GETTING WEB-IFIED

VIDEOS
CH01-HISTORY
CH02-CONTROL STRUCTURES
CH03-PLANNING ALGORITHMS

T A B L E **O F** C O N T E N T S

CH22-STRUCTURES
CH23-TRYCATCH
CH24-LIKE OPERATOR
CH25-DATABASE 1
CH25-DATABASE 2
CH26-LINQ
CH27-CLASSES

FILES

CH3WANTMORE.PDF (ANALYZING PROBLEMS, PLANNING ALGORITHMS, DESK-CHECKING ALGORITHMS)
CH6WANTMORE.PDF (ARITHMETIC OPERATORS)
CH7WANTMORE.PDF (VARIABLES)
CH9WANTMORE.PDF (PROBLEM SPECIFICATIONS, SELECTION STRUCTURE)
CH10WANTMORE.PDF (PROBLEM SPECIFICATIONS, LOGICAL OPERATORS)
CH11WANTMORE.PDF (IF...THEN...ELSE MULTIPLE-PATH SELECTION STRUCTURE, SELECT CASE MULTIPLE-PATH SELECTION STRUCTURE)
CH12WANTMORE.PDF (NUMERIC DATA TESTING, STRING DATA TESTING)
CH13WANTMORE.PDF (DO...LOOP PRETEST, FLOWCHART)
CH14WANTMORE.PDF (DO...LOOP POSTTEST)
CH15WANTMORE.PDF (FOR...NEXT)
CH16WANTMORE.PDF (NESTED REPETITION STRUCTURES)
CH17WANTMORE.PDF (SUB PROCEDURES)
CH18WANTMORE.PDF (FUNCTION PROCEDURES)
CH19WANTMORE.PDF (SORTING ROUTINES)
CH20WANTMORE.PDF (MODULE-LEVEL MEMORY LOCATIONS)
CH21WANTMORE.PDF (TWO-DIMENSIONAL ARRAYS)

T A B L E O F C O N T E N T S

PREFACE

Clearly Visual Basic: Programming with Microsoft Visual Basic 2008 is designed for a beginning programming course. The book assumes students have no previous programming knowledge or experience. However, students should be familiar with basic Windows skills and file management. The book's primary focus is on teaching programming concepts, with a secondary focus on teaching the Visual Basic programming language. In other words, the purpose of the book is to teach students how to solve a problem that requires a computer solution. The Visual Basic language is used as a means of verifying that the solution works correctly.

ORGANIZATION AND COVERAGE

Clearly Visual Basic: Programming with Microsoft Visual Basic 2008 contains 27 chapters and one appendix. An additional chapter covering Web applications can be obtained electronically from the Course Technology Web site (*www.course.com*), and then navigating to the page for this book.

In the chapters, students with no previous programming experience learn how to analyze a problem specification and then plan and create an appropriate computer solution. Pseudocode and flowcharts are used to plan the solution, and desk-check tables are used to verify that the solution is correct before it is coded. Students code the solutions using the Visual Basic 2008 language, and then desk-check the code before it is executed. An entire chapter is devoted to teaching students how to select appropriate test data. By the end of the book, students will have learned how to write Visual Basic statements such as If...Then...Else, Select Case, Do...Loop, and For...Next. Students also will learn how to create and manipulate variables, constants, strings, sequential access files, structures, classes, and arrays. In addition, they will learn how to connect an application to a Microsoft Access database, and then use Language Integrated Query (LINQ) to query the database. LINQ is the new query language feature built into Visual Studio 2008. The text also introduces students to OOP concepts and terminology.

APPROACH

Rather than focusing on a specific programming language, *Clearly Visual Basic: Programming with Microsoft Visual Basic 2008* focuses on programming concepts that are common to all programming languages—such as input, output, selection, and repetition. Concepts are introduced, illustrated, and reinforced using simple examples and applications, which are more appropriate for a first course in programming. The concepts are spread over many short chapters, allowing students to master the material one small piece at a time. Because its emphasis is on teaching the fundamentals of programming, the book covers only the basic controls, properties, and events available in Visual Basic.

Each chapter provides the steps for creating and/or coding an application that uses the chapter's concepts. Most chapters also contain one or more *Take A Look* elements and one or more *Want More Info?* elements. The *Take A Look* elements direct students to videos that demonstrate the chapter's concepts, provide additional information about the concepts, or cover topics related to the concepts. The *Want More Info?*

elements refer students to files that contain additional examples and further explanations of a concept. Some of the files cover topics related to the concepts covered in the chapter. The *Take A Look* videos and *Want More Info?* files can be obtained electronically from the Course Technology Web site (*www.course.com*), and then navigating to the page for this book.

FEATURES

Clearly Visual Basic: Programming with Microsoft Visual Basic 2008 is an exceptional textbook because it also includes the following features:

» **Objectives.** Each chapter begins with a list of objectives so you know the topics that will be presented in the chapter. In addition to providing a quick reference to topics covered, this feature provides a useful study aid.

» **Mini-Quizzes.** Mini-Quizzes are strategically placed to test students' knowledge at various points in each chapter. Answers to the quiz questions are provided in the chapters.

» **Summary.** Each chapter contains a Summary that recaps the concepts covered in the chapter.

» **Key Terms.** Following the Summary in each chapter is a listing of the key terms (including definitions) covered in the chapter.

» **Answers to Mini-Quizzes.** Following the Key Terms in each chapter is the Answers to Mini-Quizzes section, which contains the answers to the Mini-Quizzes found in the chapter.

» **Review Questions.** Each chapter contains five Review Questions that test students' understanding of what they learned in the chapter.

» **Exercises.** Each chapter contains exercises that provide students with additional practice of the skills and concepts they learned in the chapter. The exercises are designated as TRY THIS, MODIFY THIS, INTRODUCTORY, INTERMEDIATE, ADVANCED, FIGURE THIS OUT, and SWAT THE BUGS.

»TRY THIS   » **TRY THIS Exercises.** The TRY THIS Exercises should be the first exercises students complete after reading a chapter. These exercises are similar to the application developed in the chapter, and they allow students to test their understanding of the chapter's concepts. The answers to TRY THIS exercises are provided at the end of the chapter.

»MODIFY THIS   » **MODIFY THIS Exercises.** In these exercises, students modify an existing application.

» **FIGURE THIS OUT Exercises.** These exercises require students to analyze a block of code and then answer questions about the code.

 » **SWAT THE BUGS Exercises.** The SWAT THE BUGS Exercises provide an opportunity for students to detect and correct errors in an existing application.

» **Answers to TRY THIS Exercises.** This section contains the answers to the chapter's TRY THIS Exercises.

INSTRUCTOR RESOURCES

All of the resources available with this book are provided to the instructor on a single CD-ROM. Many also can be found at the Course Technology Web site (*www.course.com*).

» **Electronic Instructor's Manual.** The Instructor's Manual that accompanies this textbook includes additional instructional material to assist in class preparation, including items such as Sample Syllabi, Chapter Outlines, Technical Notes, Lecture Notes, Quick Quizzes, Teaching Tips, Discussion Topics, and Additional Case Projects.

» **ExamView®.** This textbook is accompanied by ExamView, a powerful testing software package that allows instructors to create and administer printed, computer (LAN-based), and Internet exams. ExamView includes hundreds of questions that correspond to the topics covered in this text, enabling students to generate detailed study guides that include page references for further review. The computer-based and Internet testing components allow students to take exams at their computers, and also save time for the instructor by grading each exam automatically.

» **PowerPoint Presentations.** This book comes with Microsoft PowerPoint slides for each chapter. These are included as a teaching aid for classroom presentation, to make available to students on the network for chapter review, or to be printed for classroom distribution. Instructors can add their own slides for additional topics they introduce to the class.

» **Data Files.** Data Files are necessary for completing the chapter applications and Exercises in the book. The Data Files are provided on the Instructor Resources CD-ROM and may also be found on the Course Technology Web site at *www.course.com*.

» **Solution Files.** Solutions to the chapter applications and the end-of-chapter Review Questions and exercises are provided on the Instructor Resources CD-ROM and also may be found on the Course Technology Web site at *www.course.com*. The solutions are password protected.

» **Distance Learning.** Course Technology is proud to present online test banks in WebCT and Blackboard to provide the most complete and dynamic learning experience possible. Instructors are encouraged to make the most of the course, both online and offline. For more information on how to access the online test bank, contact your local Course Technology sales representative.

ACKNOWLEDGMENTS

Writing a book is a team effort rather than an individual one. I would like to take this opportunity to thank my team, especially Tricia Coia (Managing Editor), Daphne Barbas (Production Editor), and the Quality Assurance testers who carefully test each chapter. Thank you for your support, enthusiasm, patience, and hard work. I could not have completed this project without you. Last, but certainly not least, I want to thank the following reviewers for their invaluable ideas and comments: Anthony Basilico, Community College of Rhode Island; Albert Chan, Fayetteville State University, Michael Walton, Miami Dade College.

—*Diane Zak*

READ THIS BEFORE YOU BEGIN

TO THE USER

DATA FILES

You will need data files to complete the chapter applications and exercises in this book. Your instructor will provide the data files to you. You also can obtain the files electronically from the Course Technology Web site (*www.course.com*), and then navigating to the page for this book.

Each chapter in this book has its own set of data files, which are stored in a separate folder within the ClearlyVB folder. The files for Chapter 4 are stored in the ClearlyVB\Chap04 folder. Similarly, the files for Chapter 5 are stored in the ClearlyVB\Chap05 folder. Throughout this book, you will be instructed to open files from or save files to these folders.

You can use a computer in your school lab or your own computer to complete the chapter applications and exercises in this book.

USING YOUR OWN COMPUTER

To use your own computer to complete the material in this book, you will need the following:

» A Pentium® 4 processor, 1.6 GHz or higher, personal computer running Microsoft Windows. This book was written using Microsoft Windows Vista. It was Quality Assurance tested using Microsoft Windows Vista and Microsoft Windows XP.

» Microsoft Visual Studio 2008 installed on your computer. This book was written using Microsoft Visual Studio 2008 Professional Edition, and Quality Assurance tested using Microsoft Visual Studio 2008 Express and Professional Editions. If your book came with a copy of Microsoft Visual Studio 2008 (Express or Professional), then you may install that on your computer and use it to complete the material. You also will need to check several Visual Basic settings. Start Visual Studio 2008 (or Visual Basic 2008 Express Edition). Click Tools on the menu bar, then click Options. Expand the Projects and Solutions node in the Options dialog box, then click VB Defaults. Verify that both Option Explicit and Option Infer are set to On. Verify that Option Strict is set to Off and Option Compare is set to Binary. Click the OK button to close the Options dialog box.

FIGURES

The figures in this book reflect how your screen will look if you are using Microsoft Visual Studio 2008 Professional Edition and a Microsoft Windows Vista system. Your screen may appear slightly different in some instances if you are using another version of Microsoft Visual Studio, Microsoft Visual Basic, or Microsoft Windows.

VISIT OUR WORLD WIDE WEB SITE

Additional materials designed for this textbook might be available through the Course Technology Web site, *www.course.com*. Search this site for more details.

TO THE INSTRUCTOR

To complete the chapter applications and exercises in this book, your users must use a set of data files. These files are included on the Instructor's Resource CD. They also may be obtained electronically through the Course Technology Web site at *www.course.com*. Follow the instructions in the Help file to copy the data files to your server or standalone computer. You can view the Help file using a text editor such as WordPad or Notepad. Once the files are copied, you should instruct your users how to copy the files to their own computers or workstations.

The chapter applications and exercises in this book were Quality Assurance tested using Microsoft Visual Studio 2008 (Express and Professional) on a Microsoft Windows (Vista and XP) operating system. The book assumes that both Option Explicit and Option Infer are set to On, Option Strict is set to Off, and Option Compare is set to Binary. To verify these settings, start Visual Studio 2008 (or Visual Basic 2008 Express Edition). Click Tools on the menu bar, then click Options. Expand the Projects and Solutions node in the Options dialog box, then click VB Defaults. Verify the four Option settings, then click the OK button to close the Options dialog box.

COURSE TECHNOLOGY DATA FILES

You are granted a license to copy the data files to any computer or computer network used by individuals who have purchased this book.

1

PROGRAMMING? WHAT'S THAT?

After studying Chapter 1, you should be able to:

Define the terminology used in programming

Explain the tasks performed by a programmer

Describe the qualities of a good programmer

Understand the employment opportunities for programmers

PROGRAMMING IN A NUTSHELL

In essence, the word **programming** means *giving a mechanism the directions to accomplish a task*. If you are like most people, you've already programmed several mechanisms. For example, at one time or another, you probably programmed your digital video recorder (DVR) in order to schedule a timed-recording of a movie. You also may have programmed the speed dial feature on your cell phone. Or you may have programmed your coffee maker to begin the brewing process before you wake up in the morning. Like your DVR, cell phone, and coffee maker, a computer also is a mechanism that can be programmed. In other words, although computers appear to be amazingly intelligent machines, they still rely on human beings to give them directions. The directions given to a computer are called **computer programs** or, more simply, **programs**. The people who write the programs are called **programmers**. Programmers use a variety of special languages, called **programming languages**, to communicate with the computer. Some popular programming languages are Visual Basic, C#, C++, and Java. Later in this book, you will communicate with the computer using the Visual Basic programming language.

 To learn about the history of programming languages, view the Ch1-History video.

WHAT DOES A PROGRAMMER DO?

When a company has a problem that requires a computer solution, typically it is a programmer that comes to the rescue. The programmer might be an employee of the company; or he or she might be a freelance programmer, which is a programmer who works on temporary contracts rather than for a long-term employer. First the programmer meets with the user, which is the person (or persons) responsible for describing the problem. In many cases, this person or persons also will eventually use the solution. Depending on the complexity of the problem, the programmer may need to meet with the user several times. The purpose of the initial meetings is to determine the exact problem and to agree on the desired solution. After the programmer and user agree on the solution, the programmer begins converting the solution into a computer program. During the conversion phase, the programmer meets periodically with the user to determine whether the program fulfills the user's needs, and to refine any details of the solution. When the user is satisfied that the program does what he or she wants it to do, the programmer rigorously tests the program with sample data before releasing it to the user. In many cases, the programmer also provides the user with a manual that explains how to use the program. As this process indicates, the creation of a good computer solution to a problem—in other words, the creation of a good program—requires a great deal of interaction between the programmer and the user.

DO I HAVE WHAT IT TAKES TO BE A PROGRAMMER?

According to the 2006–07 Edition of the Occupational Outlook Handbook (OOH), published by the U.S. Department of Labor's Bureau of Labor Statistics, "When hiring programmers, employers look for people with the necessary programming skills who can think logically and pay close attention to detail. The job calls for patience, persistence, and the ability to work on exacting analytical work, especially under pressure. Ingenuity, creativity, and imagination also are particularly important when programmers design solutions and test their work for potential failures. ... Because programmers are expected to work in teams and interact directly with users, employers want programmers who are able to communicate with nontechnical personnel." If this sounds like you, then you probably have what it takes to be a programmer. But if it doesn't sound like you, it's still worth your time to understand the programming process, especially if you are planning a career in business. Knowing even a little bit about the programming process will allow you, the manager of a department, to better communicate your department's needs to a programmer. It also will give you the confidence to question the programmer when he claims that he can't make the program modification you requested. In addition, it will help you determine whether the $15,000 quote you received from a freelance programmer seems reasonable. Lastly, understanding the process a computer programmer follows when solving a problem can help you solve problems that don't need a computer solution.

EMPLOYMENT OPPORTUNITIES

But if, after reading this book, you are excited about the idea of being a computer programmer, here is some information on employment opportunities. According to the Bureau of Labor Statistics, computer programmers held about 455,000 jobs in 2004. Computer programmers are employed in almost every industry. For example, you will find large numbers of programmers working for telecommunications companies, software publishers, financial institutions, insurance carriers, educational institutions, and government agencies. The Bureau of Labor Statistics predicts that employment of programmers will grow up to 8% between 2004 and 2014. "As organizations attempt to control costs and keep up with changing technology, they will need programmers to assist in conversions to new computer languages and systems. In addition, numerous job openings will result from the need to replace programmers who leave the labor force or transfer to other occupations such as manager or systems analyst." There is a great deal of competition for programming jobs, so jobseekers will need to keep up to date with the latest programming languages and technologies. According to the OOH, median annual earnings of computer programmers were $62,890 in May 2004. The OOH also reports that, "According to the National Association of Colleges and Employers, starting salary offers for graduates with a bachelor's degree in computer science averaged $50,820 a year in 2005." You can find more information about computer programmers on the Bureau of Labor Statistics Web site at *www.bls.gov*.

SUMMARY

» You've probably already programmed—in other words, gave directions to—several mechanisms, such as your DVR, cell phone, coffee maker, digital clock, and car navigation system. The computer also is a mechanism that can accept directions from you. The directions given to a computer are called computer programs.

» Computer programs, or programs, are written by programmers using specialized languages called programming languages.

» Programmers write computer programs to solve problems that require a computer solution. For a computer program to meet the user's needs, it is essential for the programmer and user to interact during the program's planning and creation.

» Programmers must be able to think logically and be detail-oriented. They also must be patient, creative, and able to work under pressure. In addition, they must have good communication skills and be able to work well with others.

» Even non-programmers should understand the programming process.

KEY TERMS

Computer programs—the directions given to a computer; also called programs

Programmers—the people who write computer programs

Programming—giving a mechanism the directions to accomplish a task

Programming languages—the languages used by programmers to communicate with the computer

Programs—the directions given to a computer; also called computer programs

REVIEW QUESTIONS

1. The directions a programmer gives to a computer are called _____.

2. _____ is a popular programming language.

    a. C++

    b. Java

    c. Visual Basic

    d. All of the above.

3. How many times should a programmer meet with a user?

    a. once

    b. twice

    c. three times

    d. as often as necessary until the user is satisfied with the program

4. Which of the following is false?

    a. Programmers usually work alone.

    b. Programmers need good communication skills.

    c. Programmers must keep up to date with the latest programming languages and technologies.

    d. Programmers must be detail-oriented.

5. The need for programmers is expected to grow between now and the year 2014.

    a. true

    b. false

2

I AM *NOT* A CONTROL FREAK!

After studying Chapter 2, you should be able to:

Describe the three control structures

Write simple algorithms using the sequence, selection, and repetition structures

CONTROL STRUCTURES

All computer programs, no matter how simple or how complex, are written using one or more of three basic structures: sequence, selection, and repetition. These structures are called **control structures** or **logic structures**, because they control the flow of a program's logic. You will use the sequence structure in every program you write. In most programs, you also will use both the selection and repetition structures. This chapter gives you an introduction to the three control structures. It also introduces you to a computerized mechanical man named Rob, who will help illustrate the control structures. More detailed information about each structure, as well as how to implement these structures using the Visual Basic language, is provided in subsequent chapters.

THE SEQUENCE STRUCTURE

You already are familiar with the sequence structure, because you use it each time you follow a set of directions, in order, from beginning to end. A cookie recipe, for instance, provides a good example of the sequence structure. To get to the finished product (edible cookies), you need to follow each recipe instruction in order, beginning with the first instruction and ending with the last. Likewise, the **sequence structure** in a computer program directs the computer to process the program instructions, one after another, in the order listed in the program. You will find the sequence structure in every program.

You can observe how the sequence structure works by programming a mechanical man named Rob. Like a computer, Rob has a limited instruction set. In other words, Rob can understand only a specific number of instructions, also called commands. For now, you will use only three of the commands from Rob's instruction set: walk forward, turn right 90 degrees, and sit down. When told to walk forward, Rob takes one complete step forward. In other words, Rob moves his right foot forward one step, then moves his left foot to meet his right foot. For this first example, Rob is facing a chair that is two steps away from him. Your task is to write the instructions, using only the commands that Rob understands, that direct Rob to sit in the chair. Figure 2-1 shows Rob, the chair, and the instructions that will get Rob seated properly. The four instructions shown in the figure are called an **algorithm**, which is a set of step-by-step instructions that accomplish a task. For Rob to be properly seated in the chair, he must follow the instructions in order—in other words, in sequence.

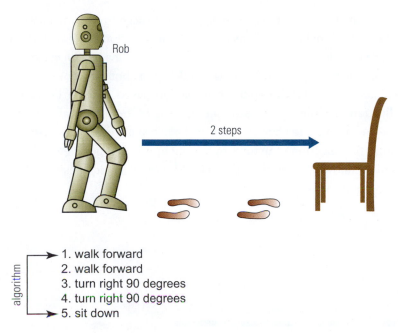

1. walk forward
2. walk forward
3. turn right 90 degrees
4. turn right 90 degrees
5. sit down

algorithm

Figure 2-1: An example of the sequence structure

THE SELECTION STRUCTURE

As with the sequence structure, you already are familiar with the **selection structure**, also called the **decision structure**. The selection structure makes a decision and then takes an appropriate action based on that decision. You use the selection structure every time you drive your car and approach an intersection. Your decision, as well as the appropriate action, is based on whether the intersection has a stop sign. If the intersection has a stop sign, you stop your car; otherwise, you proceed with caution through the intersection. When used in a computer program, the selection structure alerts the computer that a decision needs to be made, and it provides the appropriate action to take based on the result of that decision.

You can observe how the selection structure works by programming Rob, the mechanical man. In this example, assume that Rob is holding either a red or yellow balloon, and that he is facing two boxes. One of the boxes is colored yellow and the other is colored red. The two boxes are located three steps away from Rob. Your task is to have Rob drop the balloon into the appropriate box: the yellow balloon belongs in the yellow box, and the red balloon belongs in the red box. To write an algorithm to accomplish the current task, you need to use four additional instructions from Rob's instruction set: if the balloon is red, do this:, otherwise, do this:, drop the balloon in the red box, and drop the balloon in the yellow box. The additional instructions allow Rob to make a decision about the color of the balloon he is holding, and then take the appropriate action based on that decision. Figure 2-2 shows an illustration of the current example, along with the correct algorithm. Notice that the drop the balloon in the red box and drop the balloon in the yellow box instructions are indented within the selection structure. Indenting in this manner clearly indicates the instructions to be followed when the balloon is red, as well as the ones to be followed when the balloon is not red.

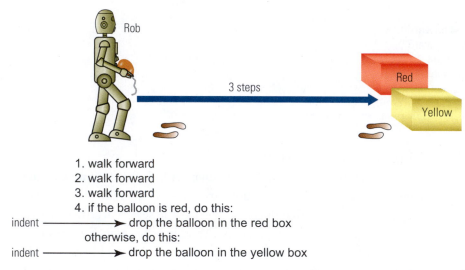

Figure 2-2: An example of the selection structure

THE REPETITION STRUCTURE

The last of the three control structures is the repetition structure. Like the sequence and selection structures, you already are familiar with the repetition structure. For example, shampoo bottles typically include the repetition structure in the directions for washing your hair. Those directions usually tell you to repeat the "apply shampoo to hair," "lather," and "rinse" steps until your hair is clean. When used in a program, the **repetition structure** directs the computer to repeat one or more instructions until some condition is met, at which time the computer should stop repeating the instructions. The repetition structure is also referred to as a **loop** or as **iteration**.

You can observe how the repetition structure works by programming Rob, the mechanical man. In this example, Rob is facing a chair that is 50 steps away from him. Your task is to write the algorithm that directs Rob to sit in the chair. If the repetition structure was not available to you, you would need to write the walk forward instruction 50 times, followed by the turn right 90 degrees instruction twice, followed by the sit down instruction. Although that algorithm would work, it is quite cumbersome to write. Imagine if Rob were 500 steps away from the chair! The best way to write the algorithm to get Rob seated in a chair that is 50 steps away from him is to use the repetition structure. To do so, however, you need to use another instruction from Rob's instruction set. In this case, you need to use the command repeat x times:, where x is the number of times you want Rob to repeat something. Figure 2-3 shows the illustration of Rob and the chair, along with the correct algorithm, which contains both the sequence and repetition structures. Notice that the instructions to be repeated—in this case, walk forward and turn right 90 degrees—are indented below their respective repeat x times: instruction. Indenting in this manner indicates that the instruction is part of the repetition structure and, therefore, needs to be repeated the specified number of times. Although both repetition structures shown in Figure 2-3 include only one instruction, a repetition structure can include many instructions.

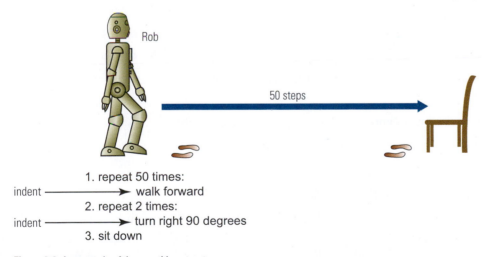

Figure 2-3: An example of the repetition structure

 It's time to view the Ch2-Control Structures video.

SUMMARY

» An algorithm is the set of step-by-step instructions that accomplish a task.

» The algorithms for all computer programs contain one or more of the following three control structures: sequence, selection, and repetition.

» The control structures, also called logic structures, are so named because they control the flow of a program's logic.

» The sequence structure directs the computer to process the program instructions, one after another, in the order listed in the program.

» The selection structure, also called the decision structure, directs the computer to make a decision, and then selects an appropriate action to take based on that decision.

» The repetition structure directs the computer to repeat one or more program instructions until some condition is met.

» The sequence structure is used in all programs. Most programs also contain both the selection and repetition structures.

KEY TERMS

Algorithm—the set of step-by-step instructions that accomplish a task

Control structures—the structures that control the flow of a program's logic; also called logic structures

Decision structure—another term for the selection structure

Iteration—another term for the repetition structure

Logic structures—another term for control structures

Loop—another term for the repetition structure

Repetition structure—the control structure that directs the computer to repeat one or more instructions until some condition is met, at which time the computer should stop repeating the instructions; also called a loop or iteration

Selection structure—the control structure that directs the computer to make a decision and then take the appropriate action based on that decision; also called the decision structure

Sequence structure—the control structure that directs the computer to process each instruction in the order listed in the program

REVIEW QUESTIONS

1. The set of instructions for adding together two numbers is an example of the
_____ structure.

    a. control

    b. repetition

    c. selection

    d. sequence

2. The recipe instruction "Beat until smooth" is an example of the _____
structure.

    a. control

    b. repetition

    c. selection

    d. sequence

3. The instruction "If it's raining outside, then take an umbrella to work" is an example
of the _____ structure.

    a. control

    b. repetition

    c. selection

    d. sequence

4. Which control structure would an algorithm use to determine whether a credit card
holder is over his credit limit?

    a. repetition

    b. selection

    c. both repetition and selection

5. A company pays a 3% annual bonus to employees who have been with the company
more than 5 years; other employees receive a 1% bonus. Which control structure
would an algorithm use to calculate every employee's bonus?

    a. repetition

    b. selection

    c. both repetition and selection

EXERCISES

Use Rob (the mechanical man) to complete Exercises 1, 3, 4, 6, and 11. Rob's instruction set is shown in Figure 2-4.

walk forward
sit down
stand up
pick the flower with your right hand
pick the flower with your left hand
drop the toy in the toy chest
turn right 90 degrees
jump over the box
throw the box out of the way
if the box is red, do this:
if the flower is white, do this:
otherwise, do this:
repeat *x* times:
repeat until you are directly in front of the chair:
repeat until you are directly in front of the toy chest:

Figure 2-4

>>TRY THIS

1. Rob is five steps away from a box, and the box is an unknown distance away from a chair, as illustrated in Figure 2-5. Using only the instructions shown in Figure 2-4, create an algorithm that directs Rob to sit in the chair. Assume that Rob must jump over the box before he can continue toward the chair. (The answers to TRY THIS Exercises are located at the end of the chapter.)

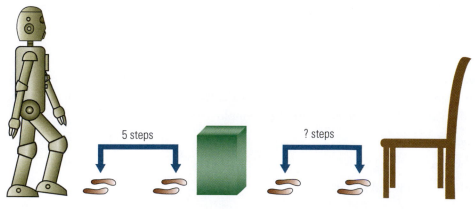

5 steps   ? steps

Figure 2-5

2. Using only the instructions shown in Figure 2-6, create an algorithm that shows the steps an instructor takes when grading a test that contains 25 questions. (The answers to TRY THIS Exercises are located at the end of the chapter.)

»TRY THIS

```
if the student's answer is not the same as the correct answer, do this:
repeat 25 times:
read the student's answer and the correct answer
mark the student's answer incorrect
```

Figure 2-6

3. Modify the answer to TRY THIS Exercise 1 as follows: Rob must jump over the box if the box is red. If the box is not red, Rob must throw the box out of the way. Use the instructions shown earlier in Figure 2-4.

»MODIFY THIS

4. Rob is facing a toy chest that is zero or more steps away from him. Rob is carrying a toy in his right hand. Using only the instructions shown earlier in Figure 2-4, create an algorithm that directs Rob to drop the toy in the toy chest.

»INTRODUCTORY

5. You have just purchased a new personal computer system. Before putting the system components together, you read the instruction booklet that came with the system. The booklet contains a list of the components that you should have received. The booklet advises you to verify that you received all of the components by matching those that you received with those on the list. If a component was received, you should cross its name off the list; otherwise, you should draw a circle around the component's name in the list. Using only the instructions shown in Figure 2-7, create an algorithm that shows the steps you should take to verify that the package contains the correct components.

»INTRODUCTORY

```
cross the component name off the list
read the component name from the list
circle the component's name on the list
search the package for the component
if the component was received, do this:
otherwise, do this:
repeat for each component name on the list:
```

Figure 2-7

6. Rob is standing in front of a flower bed that contains six flowers, as shown in Figure 2-8. Your task is to create an algorithm that directs Rob to pick the flowers as he walks to the other side of the flower bed. Rob should pick all white flowers with his right hand. Flowers that are not white should be picked with his left hand. Use the instructions shown earlier in Figure 2-4.

Rob should end up
on the other side of
the flower bed

Figure 2-8

7. A store gives a 10% discount to customers who are at least 65 years old. Using only the instructions shown in Figure 2-9, write two versions of an algorithm that prints the amount of money a customer owes. Be sure to indent the instructions appropriately.

---

assign 10% as the discount rate
assign 0 as the discount rate
calculate the amount due by subtracting the discount rate from the number 1, and then multiplying the result by the item price

if the customer's age is greater than or equal to 65, do this:
if the customer's age is less than 65, do this:
otherwise, do this:
print the amount due
read the customer's age and item price

Figure 2-9

8. Create an algorithm for making a jelly sandwich.

9. The algorithm shown in Figure 2-10 should instruct a payroll clerk on how to calculate and print the gross pay for five workers; however, some of the instructions are missing from the algorithm. Complete the algorithm. If an employee works more than 40 hours, he or she should receive time and one-half for the hours worked over 40.

» ADVANCED

---

read the employee's name, hours worked, and pay rate

_____

    calculate gross pay = hours worked times pay rate
otherwise, do this:
    calculate regular pay = pay rate times 40
    calculate overtime hours = hours worked minus 40
    calculate overtime pay = _____
    calculate gross pay = _____
print the employee's name and gross pay

Figure 2-10

10. Study the algorithm shown in Figure 2-11, and then answer the questions.

---

repeat 5 times:
    get the salesperson's name and sales amount
    calculate the bonus amount by multiplying the sales amount by 3%
    print the salesperson's name and bonus amount

Figure 2-11

    a. Which control structures are used in the algorithm shown in Figure 2-11?

    b. What will the algorithm shown in Figure 2-11 print when the user enters Mary Smith and 2000 as the salesperson's name and sales amount, respectively?

    c. How would you modify the algorithm shown in Figure 2-11 so that it also prints the salesperson's sales amount?

    d. How would you modify the algorithm shown in Figure 2-11 so that it can be used for any number of salespeople?

    e. How would you modify the algorithm shown in Figure 2-11 so that it allows the user to enter the bonus rate, and then uses that rate to calculate the bonus amount?

11. The algorithm shown in Figure 2-12 does not get Rob through the maze. Correct the algorithm.

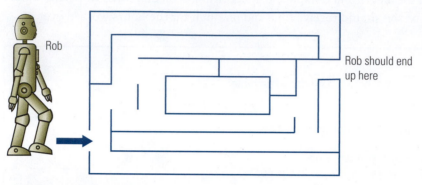

1. walk into the maze
2. turn left 90 degrees
3. repeat until you are directly in front of a wall:
     walk forward
4. turn right 90 degrees
5. repeat until you are directly in front of a wall:
     walk forward
6. turn right 90 degrees
7. repeat until you are directly in front of a wall:
     walk forward
8. turn right 90 degrees
9. repeat until you are directly in front of a wall:
     walk forward
10. turn right 90 degrees
11. repeat until you are directly in front of a wall:
     walk forward
12. turn left 90 degrees
13. repeat until you are directly in front of a wall:
     turn right 90 degrees
14. repeat until you are out of the maze:
     walk forward

Figure 2-12

ANSWERS TO "TRY THIS" EXERCISES

1. See Figure 2-13.

```
1. repeat 5 times:
       walk forward
2. jump over the box
3. repeat until you are directly in front of the chair:
       walk forward
4. repeat two times:
       turn right 90 degrees
5. sit down
```

Figure 2-13

2. See Figure 2-14.

```
repeat 25 times:
    read the student's answer and the correct answer
    if the student's answer is not the same as the correct answer, do this:
        mark the student's answer incorrect
```

Figure 2-14

3

FIRST YOU NEED TO PLAN THE PARTY

After studying Chapter 3, you should be able to:

Identify the output and input in a problem description

Plan an algorithm using pseudocode and flowcharts

Desk-check an algorithm

HOW DO PROGRAMMERS SOLVE PROBLEMS?

Figure 3-1 shows the steps that computer programmers follow when solving problems that require a computer solution.

HOW TO SOLVE A PROBLEM USING A COMPUTER

1. Analyze the problem

2. Plan the algorithm

3. Desk-check the algorithm

4. Create the user interface

5. Code the algorithm into a program

6. Desk-check the program

7. Rigorously test the program using the computer

Figure 3-1: How to solve a problem using a computer

This chapter covers the first three steps in the problem-solving process shown in Figure 3-1. The fourth step, which is to create the user interface, is covered in Chapters 4 and 5. The last three steps are explored in the remaining chapters.

STEP 1—ANALYZE THE PROBLEM

You cannot solve a problem unless you understand it, and you cannot understand a problem unless you analyze it—in other words, unless you identify its important components. The two most important components of any problem are the problem's output and its input. The **output** is the goal of solving the problem, and the **input** is the item or items needed to achieve the goal. When analyzing a problem, you always search first for the output, and then for the input. The first problem specification analyzed in this chapter is shown in Figure 3-2.

As a salesperson at J & J Sales, Addison Smith receives an annual commission, which is calculated by multiplying her annual sales by a commission rate. Addison wants a program that will both calculate and display the amount of her annual commission.

Figure 3-2: Problem specification for Addison Smith

A helpful way to identify the output is to search the problem specification for an answer to the following question: *What does the user want to see printed on paper, displayed on the screen, or stored in a file?* The answer to this question typically is stated as nouns and adjectives in the problem specification. For instance, the problem specification shown in Figure 3-2 indicates that Addison (the program's user) wants to see the amount of her annual commission displayed on the screen; therefore, the output is the annual commission. In this context, the word *annual* is an adjective, and the word *commission* is a noun.

After determining the output, you then determine the input. A helpful way to identify the input is to search the problem specification for an answer to the following question: *What information will the computer need to know to print, display, or store the output items?* As with the output, the input typically is stated as nouns and adjectives in the problem specification. When determining the input, it helps to think about the information that you would need to solve the problem manually, because the computer will need to know the same information. In this case, to determine Addison's annual commission, both you and the computer need to know her annual sales as well as the commission rate; both of these items, therefore, are the input. In this context, *annual* and *commission* are adjectives, and *sales* and *rate* are nouns. This completes the analysis step for the Addison Smith problem. Figure 3-3 summarizes the problem's output and input items.

Output: annual commission

Input: annual sales
          commission rate

Figure 3-3: Output and input items for the Addison Smith problem

Now analyze the problem specification shown in Figure 3-4.

Aiden Turner is paid every Friday. He is scheduled to receive a raise next week; however, he isn't sure of the exact raise percentage. Aiden wants a program that will both calculate and display the amount of his new weekly pay.

Figure 3-4: Problem specification for Aiden Turner

First, answer the following question: *What does the user want to see printed on paper, displayed on the screen, or stored in a file?* In this case, Aiden wants to see his new weekly pay displayed on the screen; therefore, the output is the new weekly pay. In this context, the words *new* and *weekly* are adjectives, and the word *pay* is a noun. Now answer the following question: *What information will the computer need to know to print, display, or store the output items?* To determine Aiden's new weekly pay, the computer needs to know Aiden's current weekly pay and his raise percentage; both of these items, therefore, are the input. In this context, *current*, *weekly*, and *raise* are adjectives, and *pay* and *percentage* are nouns. You have completed the analysis step for the Aiden Turner problem. The problem's output and input items are listed in Figure 3-5.

Output: new weekly pay

Input: current weekly pay
          raise percentage

Figure 3-5: Output and input items for the Aiden Turner problem

Unfortunately, analyzing real-world problems are not always as easy as analyzing the problems found in a textbook. The analysis step is the most difficult of the problem-solving steps, and it requires a lot of time, patience, and effort. If you are having trouble analyzing a problem, try reading the problem specification several times, as it is easy to miss information during the first reading. If the problem still is unclear to you, do not be shy about asking the user for more information. Remember, the more you understand a problem, the easier it will be for you to write a correct and efficient solution to the problem.

MINI-QUIZ 1

Identify the output and the input in each of the following problem specifications. (Mini-Quiz answers are located after the Key Terms section at the end of the chapter.)

1. Treyson Liverpool pays a state income tax on his yearly taxable wages. He wants a program that allows him to enter the amount of his yearly taxable wages. The program then should calculate and display the amount of his state income tax.

2. Max Jones belongs to a CD (compact disc) club that allows him to buy CDs at a much lower price than charged at his local music store. He wants to know how much he saves by buying all of his CDs through the club rather than through the music store.

3. Suman Patel saves the same amount of money each day. She wants to know the total amount she saves during a specific month.

For more examples of analyzing problems, see the Analyzing Problems section in the Ch3WantMore.pdf file.

STEP 2—PLAN THE ALGORITHM

The second step in the problem-solving process is to plan the algorithm, which is the set of instructions that, when followed, will transform the problem's input into its output. Most algorithms begin with an instruction that enters the input items into the computer. Next, you usually record instructions to process the input items to achieve the problem's output. The processing typically involves performing one or more calculations on the input items. Most algorithms end with an instruction to print, display, or store the output items. *Display*, *print*, and *store* refer to the computer screen, the printer, and a file on a disk, respectively. Figure 3-6 shows the output, input, and algorithm for the Addison Smith problem. The algorithm begins by entering the input items. It then uses the input items to calculate the output item. Notice that the algorithm states both what is to be calculated and how to calculate it. In this case, the annual commission is to be calculated by multiplying the annual sales by the commission rate. The last instruction in the algorithm displays the output item. To avoid confusion, it is important that the algorithm is consistent when referring to the input and output items. For example, if the input item is listed as "annual sales," then the algorithm should refer to the item as "annual sales," rather than using a different name, such as "sales" or "yearly sales."

Output: annual commission

Input: annual sales
         commission rate

Algorithm:
1. enter the annual sales and commission rate
2. calculate the annual commission by multiplying the annual sales by the commission rate
3. display the annual commission

Figure 3-6: Output, input, and algorithm for the Addison Smith problem

The algorithm shown in Figure 3-6 is composed of short English statements, referred to as **pseudocode**. The word *pseudocode* means *false code*. It's called false code because, although it resembles programming language instructions, pseudocode cannot be understood by a computer. Programmers use pseudocode to help them while they are planning an algorithm. It allows them to jot down their ideas using a human-readable language without having to worry about the syntax of the programming language itself. Pseudocode is not standardized; every programmer has his or her own version, but you will find some similarities among the various versions. Programmers use the pseudocode as a guide when coding the algorithm, which is the fifth step in the problem-solving process.

Besides using pseudocode, programmers also use flowcharts when planning algorithms. Unlike pseudocode, a **flowchart** uses standardized symbols to visually depict an algorithm. You can draw the flowchart symbols by hand; or, you can use the drawing or shapes feature in a word processor. You also can use a flowcharting program, such as SmartDraw or Visio. Figure 3-7 shows the Addison Smith problem's algorithm in flowchart form. The flowchart contains three different symbols: an oval, a parallelogram, and a rectangle. The symbols are connected with lines, called **flowlines**. The oval symbol is called the **start/stop symbol**. The start oval indicates the beginning of the flowchart, and the stop oval indicates the end of the flowchart. Between the start and stop ovals are two parallelograms, called input/output symbols. You use the **input/output symbol** to represent input tasks (such as getting information from the user) and output tasks (such as displaying, printing, or storing information). The first parallelogram shown in Figure 3-7 represents an input task, while the last parallelogram represents an output task. The rectangle in a flowchart is called the **process symbol** and is used to represent tasks such as calculations.

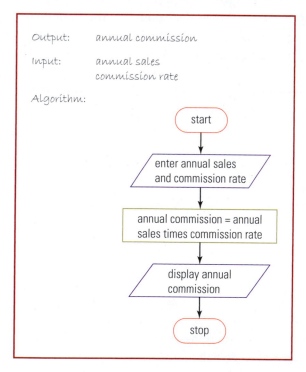

Figure 3-7: Flowchart for the Addison Smith problem's algorithm

When planning an algorithm, you do not need to create both a flowchart and pseudocode; you need to use only one of these planning tools. The tool you use is really a matter of personal preference. For simple algorithms, pseudocode works just fine. When an algorithm becomes more complex, however, the program's logic may be easier to see in a flowchart. As the old adage goes, a picture is sometimes worth a thousand words.

Figure 3-8 shows the output, input, and algorithm for the Aiden Turner problem. Here again, the algorithm begins by entering the input items. It then uses both input items to calculate the output item. Again, notice that the calculation instructions state both what is to be calculated and how to calculate it. The last instruction in the algorithm displays the output item.

Output: new weekly pay

Input: current weekly pay
           raise percentage

Algorithm:
1. enter the current weekly pay and raise percentage
2. calculate the new weekly pay by multiplying the current weekly pay by the raise percentage, and then adding the result to the current weekly pay
3. display the new weekly pay

Figure 3-8: Output, input, and algorithm for the Aiden Turner problem

Even a very simple problem can have more than one solution. For example, Figure 3-9 shows a different solution to the Aiden Turner problem. In this solution, the weekly raise is calculated in a separate instruction rather than in the instruction that calculates the new weekly pay. The weekly raise is neither an input item (because it's not provided by the user) nor an output item (because it won't be displayed, printed, or stored in a file). Instead, the weekly raise is a special item, commonly referred to as a processing item. A **processing item** represents an intermediate value that the algorithm uses when processing the input into the output. In this case, the algorithm uses the input items to calculate the weekly raise (an intermediate value), which the algorithm then uses to compute the new weekly pay. Keep in mind that not all algorithms require a processing item.

Output: new weekly pay

Processing: weekly raise

Input: current weekly pay
               raise percentage

Algorithm:
1. enter the current weekly pay and raise percentage
2. calculate the weekly raise by multiplying the current weekly pay by the raise percentage
3. calculate the new weekly pay by adding the weekly raise to the current weekly pay
4. display the new weekly pay

Figure 3-9: A different solution to the Aiden Turner problem

The solutions shown in Figures 3-8 and 3-9 produce the same result and simply represent two different ways of solving the same problem. Figure 3-10 shows Figure 3-9's algorithm in flowchart form.

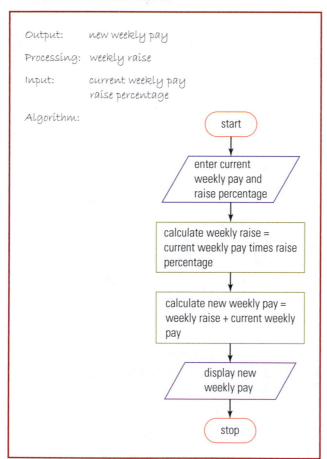

Figure 3-10: Flowchart for the Aiden Turner problem's algorithm shown in Figure 3-9

MINI-QUIZ 2

Mini-Quiz answers are located after the Key Terms section at the end of the chapter.

1. Treyson Liverpool pays a state income tax on his yearly taxable wages. He wants a program that both calculates and displays the amount of state income tax he must pay. The output is the annual state income tax. The input is the yearly taxable wages and the state income tax rate. Write the algorithm using pseudocode.

2. Rewrite Question 1's algorithm using a flowchart.

3. Max Jones belongs to a CD (compact disc) club that allows him to buy CDs at a much lower price than charged at his local music store. He wants to know how much he saves by buying all of his CDs through the club rather than through the music store. The output is the savings. The input is the number of CDs purchased, the club CD price, and the store CD price. The algorithm should use two processing items: one for the cost of buying the CDs through the club and the other for the cost of buying the CDs through the store. Write the algorithm using pseudocode.

 For more examples of planning algorithms, see the Planning Algorithms section in the Ch3WantMore.pdf file.

STEP 3—DESK-CHECK THE ALGORITHM

After analyzing a problem and planning its algorithm, you then desk-check the algorithm. The term **desk-checking** refers to the fact that the programmer reviews the algorithm while seated at his or her desk rather than in front of the computer. Desk-checking is also called **hand-tracing**, because the programmer uses a pencil and paper to follow each of the algorithm's instructions by hand. You desk-check an algorithm to verify that it is not missing any steps, and that the existing steps are correct and in the proper order. Before you begin the desk-check, you first choose a set of sample data for the input values, which you then use to manually compute the expected output values. For the Addison Smith solution, you will use input values of $85000 and .08 (8%) as Addison's annual sales and commission rate, respectively. Addison's annual commission should be $6800 ($85000 times .08); therefore, $6800 is the expected output value. You now use the sample input values to desk-check the algorithm, which should result in the expected output value. It is helpful to use a desk-check table when desk-checking an algorithm. The table should contain one column for each input item, as well as one column for each output item and one column for each processing item (if any). You can perform the desk-check using either the algorithm's pseudocode or its flowchart. Figure 3-11 shows the Addison Smith solution along with an appropriate desk-check table. (The flowchart for this solution is shown earlier in Figure 3-7.)

Output: annual commission

Input: annual sales
         commission rate

Algorithm:
1. enter the annual sales and commission rate
2. calculate the annual commission by multiplying the annual sales by the commission rate
3. display the annual commission

annual sales	commission rate	annual commission

Figure 3-11: Addison Smith solution and desk-check table

The first instruction in the algorithm is to enter the input values: $85000 for the annual sales and .08 for the commission rate. You record the results of this instruction by writing 85000 and .08 in the annual sales and commission rate columns, respectively, in the desk-check table, as shown in Figure 3-12.

annual sales	commission rate	annual commission
85000	.08	

Figure 3-12: Input values entered in the desk-check table

The second instruction in the algorithm is to calculate the annual commission by multiplying the annual sales by the commission rate. The desk-check table shows that the annual sales are 85000 and the commission rate is .08. Notice that you use the table to determine the annual sales and commission rate values; this helps to verify the accuracy of the algorithm. If, for example, the table did not show any amount in the commission rate column, you would know that your algorithm missed a step; in this case, it would have missed entering the commission rate. When you multiply the annual sales (85000) by the commission rate (.08), you get 6800. You record the number 6800 in the annual commission column, as shown in Figure 3-13.

annual sales	commission rate	annual commission
85000	.08	6800

Figure 3-13: Output value included in the desk-check table

The last instruction in the algorithm is to display the annual commission. In this case, the number 6800 will be displayed, because that is what appears in the annual commission column. Notice that this amount agrees with the manual calculation you performed prior to desk-checking the algorithm, so the algorithm appears to be correct. The only way to know for sure, however, is to test the algorithm a few more times with different input values. For the second desk-check, you will test the algorithm with annual sales of $3000 and a commission rate of .1 (10%). The annual commission should be $300. Recall that the first instruction in the algorithm is to enter the annual sales and commission rate. Therefore, you write 3000 in the annual sales column and .1 in the commission rate column, as shown in Figure 3-14. Notice that you cross out the previous values of these two items in the table before recording the new values; this is because each column should contain only one value at any time.

annual sales	commission rate	annual commission
~~85000~~	~~.08~~	~~6800~~
3000	.1	

Figure 3-14: Second set of input values included in the desk-check table

Next, you need to calculate the annual commission by multiplying the annual sales (3000) by the commission rate (.1); this results in an annual commission of 300. So you cross out the 6800 that appears in the annual commission column in the desk-check table and write 300 immediately below it, as shown in Figure 3-15. The last instruction in the algorithm is to display the annual commission. In this case, the number 300 will be displayed, which agrees with the manual calculation you performed earlier.

annual sales	commission rate	annual commission
~~85000~~	~~.08~~	~~6800~~
3000	.1	300

Figure 3-15: Results of the second desk-check included in the desk-check table

Next, you will desk-check the Aiden Turner algorithm twice, first using $400 and .03 (3%) as the current weekly pay and raise percentage, respectively, and then using $600 and .15 (15%). The new weekly pay for the first desk-check should be $412. The new weekly pay for the second desk-check should be $690. The Aiden Turner solution and completed desk-check table are shown in Figure 3-16. (The pseudocode is shown earlier in Figure 3-9.)

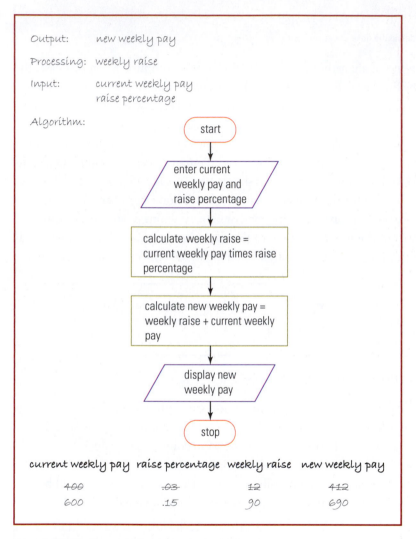

Output: new weekly pay

Processing: weekly raise

Input: current weekly pay
raise percentage

Algorithm:

start

enter current weekly pay and raise percentage

calculate weekly raise = current weekly pay times raise percentage

calculate new weekly pay = weekly raise + current weekly pay

display new weekly pay

stop

current weekly pay	raise percentage	weekly raise	new weekly pay
~~400~~	~~.03~~	~~12~~	~~412~~
600	.15	90	690

Figure 3-16: Aiden Turner solution and desk-check table

The amounts in the table agree with the manual calculations you performed earlier, so the algorithm appears to be correct. To be sure, however, you should desk-check it several more times, using both valid and invalid data. **Valid data** is data that the algorithm is expecting the user to enter. The Aiden Turner algorithm, for example, expects the user to provide positive numbers for the input values (current weekly pay and raise percentage). **Invalid data** is data that the algorithm is not expecting the user to enter. You should test an algorithm with invalid data because users sometimes make mistakes when entering data. The Aiden Turner algorithm, for instance, is not expecting the user to enter a negative value as the current weekly pay. A negative weekly pay is obviously an input error, because an employee cannot earn a negative amount for the week. In later chapters in this book, you will learn how to write algorithms that correctly handle input errors. You also will learn more about selecting good test data. For now, you can assume that the user of the program will always enter valid data.

MINI-QUIZ 3

Mini-Quiz answers are located after the Key Terms section at the end of the chapter.

1. Desk-check the following algorithm twice. First, use a yearly taxable wage of $23000 and a 3% state income tax rate. Then use a yearly taxable wage of $14000 and a 2% state income tax.

   Algorithm:
   1. enter the yearly taxable wages and state income tax rate
   2. calculate the annual state income tax by multiplying the yearly taxable wages by the state income tax rate
   3. display the annual state income tax

2. Desk-check the following algorithm twice. First, use 20, $10.50, and $14.99 as the number of CDs purchased, the club CD price, and the store CD price, respectively. Then use 5, $9.99, and $11.

   Algorithm:
   1. enter the number of CDs purchased, the club CD price, and the store CD price
   2. calculate the club cost by multiplying the number of CDs purchased by the club CD price
   3. calculate the store cost by multiplying the number of CDs purchased by the store CD price
   4. calculate the savings by subtracting the club cost from the store cost
   5. display the savings

For more examples of desk-checking algorithms, see the Desk-Checking Algorithms section in the Ch3WantMore.pdf file.

It's time to view the Ch03-Planning Algorithms video.

SUMMARY

» The first three steps in the problem-solving process are to analyze the problem, plan the algorithm, and desk-check the algorithm.

» When analyzing a problem description, the programmer first determines the output, which is the goal or purpose of solving the problem. The programmer then determines the input, which is the information needed to reach the goal. Some algorithms use intermediate values, called processing items.

» Programmers use tools, such as pseudocode and flowcharts, to organize their thoughts as they analyze problems and develop algorithms. These tools are used when coding the algorithm into a program, which is the fifth step in the problem-solving process.

» Most algorithms begin by entering some data (the input items), then processing the data (usually by performing some calculations), and then displaying, printing, or storing some data (the output items).

» The calculation instructions in an algorithm should specify what is to be calculated and how to perform the calculation.

» After completing the analysis and planning steps, a programmer then desk-checks the algorithm to determine whether it works as intended.

KEY TERMS

Desk-checking—the process of manually walking through each of the steps in an algorithm; also called hand-tracing

Flowchart—a tool that programmers use when planning an algorithm; consists of standardized symbols

Flowlines—the lines that connect the symbols in a flowchart

Hand-tracing—another term for desk-checking

Input—the items an algorithm needs to achieve the output

Input/output symbol—the parallelogram in a flowchart; used to represent input and output tasks

Invalid data—data that the algorithm is not expecting the user to enter

Output—the goal of solving a problem

Process symbol—the rectangle in a flowchart; used to represent tasks such as calculations

Processing item—an intermediate value that an algorithm uses when transforming the input into the output

Pseudocode—a tool that programmers use when planning an algorithm; consists of short English statements

Start/stop symbol—the oval in a flowchart; used to mark the beginning and end of the flowchart

Valid data—data that the algorithm is expecting the user to enter

ANSWERS TO MINI-QUIZZES

MINI-QUIZ 1

1. Output: annual state income tax

   Input: yearly taxable wages
               state income tax rate

2. Output: savings

   Input: number of CDs purchased
               club CD price
               store CD price

3. Output: total amount saved

   Input: daily savings
               number of days

MINI-QUIZ 2

1. Algorithm:
   1. enter the yearly taxable wages and state income tax rate
   2. calculate the annual state income tax by multiplying the yearly taxable wages by the state income tax rate
   3. display the annual state income tax

2. See Figure 3-17.

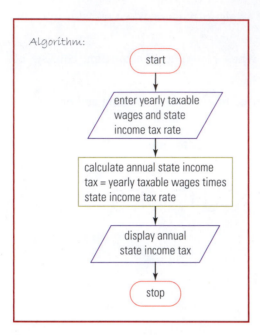

Figure 3-17

3. Algorithm:
   1. enter the number of CDs purchased, the club CD price, and the store CD price
   2. calculate the club cost by multiplying the number of CDs purchased by the club CD price
   3. calculate the store cost by multiplying the number of CDs purchased by the store CD price
   4. calculate the savings by subtracting the club cost from the store cost
   5. display the savings

MINI-QUIZ 3

1. Desk-check table

yearly taxable wages	state income tax rate	annual state income tax
~~23000~~	~~.03~~	~~690~~
14000	.02	280

2. Desk-check table

number of CDs purchased	club CD price	store CD price	club cost	store cost	savings
~~20~~	~~10.50~~	~~14.99~~	~~210~~	~~299.80~~	~~89.80~~
5	9.99	11	49.95	55	5.05

REVIEW QUESTIONS

1. Programmers refer to the items needed to reach a problem's goal as the
   _____.

   a. input   b. output

   c. processing   d. purpose

2. The calculation instructions in an algorithm should state _____.

   a. only *what* is to be calculated

   b. only *how* to calculate something

   c. both *what* is to be calculated and *how* to calculate it

   d. both *what* is to be calculated and *why* it is calculated

3. Most algorithms follow the format of _____.

   a. entering the input items, then displaying, printing, or storing the output items, and
      then processing the output items

   b. entering the input items, then processing the output items, and then displaying,
      printing, or storing the output items

   c. entering the input items, then processing the input items, and then displaying, print-
      ing, or storing the output items

   d. entering the output items, then processing the input items, and then displaying,
      printing, or storing the output items

4. In a flowchart, the _____ symbol is used to represent an instruction that gets
   information from the user.

   a. enter   b. input/output

   c. process   d. start/stop

5. When desk-checking an algorithm, you should set up a table that contains
   _____.

   a. one column for each input item and one column for each output item

   b. one column for each input item and one column for each processing item

   c. one column for each processing item and one column for each output item

   d. one column for each input item, one column for each processing item, and one col-
      umn for each output item

EXERCISES

» TRY THIS

1. Jerry Feingold wants a program that will help him calculate the amount to tip a waiter at a restaurant. The program should subtract any liquor charge from the total bill, and then calculate the tip (using a percentage) on the remainder. Desk-check your solution's algorithm using $85 as the total bill, $20 as the liquor charge, and 20% as the tip percentage. Then desk-check it using $35 as the total bill, $0 as the liquor charge, and 15% as the tip percentage. (The answers to TRY THIS Exercises are located at the end of the chapter.)

» TRY THIS

2. Party-On sells individual hot/cold cups and dessert plates for parties. Sue Chen wants a program that allows her to enter the price of a cup, the price of a plate, the number of cups purchased, and the number of plates purchased. The program should then calculate the total cost of the purchase, including the sales tax. Desk-check your solution's algorithm using $.50 as the cup price, $1 as the plate price, 35 as the number of cups, 35 as the number of plates, and 2% as the tax rate. Then desk-check it using $.25, $.75, 20, 10, and 6%. (The answers to TRY THIS Exercises are located at the end of the chapter.)

» MODIFY THIS

3. Modify the answer to TRY THIS Exercise 1 as follows. Jerry will be charging the total bill, including the tip, to his credit card. Modify the solution so that, in addition to calculating and displaying the appropriate tip, it also calculates and displays the amount charged to Jerry's credit card. Desk-check the algorithm using $50 as the total bill, $5 as the liquor charge, and 20% as the tip percentage. Then desk-check it using $15 as the total bill, $0 as the liquor charge, and 15% as the tip percentage.

» INTRODUCTORY

4. Wilma Peterson is paid by the hour. She would like a program that calculates her weekly gross pay. For this exercise, you do not need to worry about overtime pay, as Wilma never works more than 40 hours in a week. Desk-check your solution's algorithm using $10 as the hourly pay and 35 as the number of hours worked. Then desk-check it using $15 as the hourly pay and 25 as the number of hours worked.

» INTRODUCTORY

5. When Jacob Steinberg began his trip from California to Vermont, he filled his car's tank with gas and reset its trip meter to zero. After traveling 324 miles, Jacob stopped at a gas station to refuel; the gas tank required 17 gallons. Jacob wants a program that calculates his car's gas mileage at any time during the trip. The gas mileage is the number of miles his car can be driven per gallon of gas. Desk-check your solution's algorithm using 324 as the number of miles driven and 17 as the number of gallons used. Then desk-check it using 280 and 15.

» INTERMEDIATE

6. Jenna Williams is paid based on an annual salary rather than an hourly wage. She wants a program that calculates the amount of money she should receive each pay period. Desk-check your solution's algorithm twice, using your own set of data.

7. Rent A Van wants a program that calculates the total cost of renting a van. Customers pay a base fee (currently, $50) plus a charge per mile (currently, $.20). Desk-check your solution's algorithm twice, using your own set of data.

»INTERMEDIATE

8. The River Bend Hotel needs a program that calculates a customer's total bill. Each customer pays a room charge that is based on a per-night rate. For example, if the per-night rate is $55 and the customer stays two nights, the room charge is $110. Customers also may incur room service charges and telephone charges. In addition, each customer pays an entertainment tax, which is a percentage of the room charge only. Desk-check your solution's algorithm twice, using your own set of data.

»ADVANCED

9. The Paper Tree store wants a program that calculates the number of single rolls of wallpaper needed to cover a room. The salesclerk will provide the room's length, width, and ceiling height, in feet. He or she also will provide the number of square feet a single roll will cover. Desk-check your solution's algorithm twice, using your own set of data.

»ADVANCED

10. The manager of a video store wants a program that calculates the amount a customer owes when he or she returns a video. A customer can return only one video at a time. The rental fee is $3.50 for four days. Customers are charged a late fee (currently, $2) per day when the video is returned after the due date. Study the algorithm and desk-check table shown in Figure 3-18, and then answer the questions.

Output: amount due

Input: number of late days
          daily late fee

Algorithm:
1. enter the number of late days and daily late fee
2. calculate the amount due by multiplying the number of late days by the daily late fee, and then adding 3.50 to the result
3. display the amount due

number of late days	daily late fee	amount due
3	2	~~9.50~~
0	2	3.50

Figure 3-18

a. What will the algorithm shown in Figure 3-18 display when the user enters the number three as the number of late days? What will it display when the user enters the number zero as the number of late days?

b. How would you modify the solution and desk-check table to include the total late charge as a processing item?

c. How would you modify the solution from Question b to also display the total late charge?

11. Correct the following algorithm, which should calculate the average of three numbers.

Output: average

Processing: sum

Input: first number
               second number
               third number

Algorithm:

1. enter the first number, second number, and third number
2. calculate the average by dividing the sum by 3
3. display the average number

ANSWERS TO "TRY THIS" EXERCISES

1. Output: tip

   Input: total bill
                liquor charge
                tip percentage

Algorithm:

1. enter the total bill, liquor charge, and tip percentage
2. calculate the tip by subtracting the liquor charge from the total bill, and then multiplying the remainder by the tip percentage
3. display the tip

Desk-check table

total bill	liquor charge	tip percentage	tip
~~85~~	~~20~~	~~.2~~	~~13~~
35	0	.15	5.25

2. Output: total cost of purchase

Processing: total cup cost
               total plate cost
               subtotal

Input: cup price
               plate price
               number of cups
               number of plates
               sales tax rate

Algorithm:

1. enter the cup price, plate price, number of cups, number of plates, and sales tax rate
2. calculate the total cup cost by multiplying the number of cups by the cup price
3. calculate the total plate cost by multiplying the number of plates by the plate price
4. calculate the subtotal by adding together the total cup cost and total plate cost
5. calculate the total cost of purchase by multiplying the subtotal by the sales tax rate, and then adding the result to the subtotal
6. display the total cost of purchase

Desk-check table

Cup price	plate price	number of cups	number of plates	sales tax rate
~~.50~~	~~1~~	~~35~~	~~35~~	~~.02~~
.25	.75	20	10	.06

total cup cost	total plate cost	subtotal	total cost of purchase
~~17.50~~	~~35~~	~~52.50~~	~~53.55~~
5	7.50	12.50	13.25

4

I NEED A TOUR GUIDE

After studying Chapter 4, you should be able to:

Create a Visual Basic 2008 Windows application

Use the Label and PictureBox tools to add a control to a form

Set the properties of an object

Save a solution

Size and align objects using the Format menu

Lock the controls on a form

Start and end an application

Close and open an existing solution

OK, THE ALGORITHM IS CORRECT. WHAT'S NEXT?

As you learned in Chapter 3, the first three steps in the problem-solving process are to analyze the problem, plan the algorithm, and then desk-check the algorithm. When you are sure that the algorithm produces the desired results, you can move on to the fourth step, which is to create the user interface. A **user interface** is what appears on the screen, and with which you interact, while using a program. In this book, you will create the user interfaces for your programs using the tools available in Visual Basic 2008. Visual Basic 2008 is available as a stand-alone product, called Visual Basic 2008 Express Edition, or as part of Visual Studio 2008—Microsoft's newest integrated development environment. An **integrated development environment** (**IDE**) is an environment that contains all of the tools and features you need to create, run, and test your programs. In the following steps, you learn how to start either Visual Studio 2008 or Visual Basic 2008 Express Edition.

To start Visual Studio 2008 or Visual Basic 2008 Express Edition:

1. Click the **Start** button on the taskbar, then point to **All Programs**.

2. *If you are using Visual Studio 2008*, click **Microsoft Visual Studio 2008**, then click **Microsoft Visual Studio 2008**. (If the Choose Default Environment Settings dialog box appears, choose Visual Basic Development Settings, then click Start Visual Studio.) The Microsoft Visual Studio copyright screen appears momentarily, and then the Microsoft Visual Studio window opens.

   If you are using Visual Basic 2008 Express Edition, click **Microsoft Visual Basic 2008 Express Edition**. The Microsoft Visual Basic 2008 Express Edition copyright screen appears momentarily, and then the Microsoft Visual Basic 2008 Express Edition window opens.

3. Click **Window** on the menu bar, then click **Reset Window Layout**. When you are asked whether you want to restore the default window layout for the environment, click the **Yes** button. When you start the Professional Edition of Microsoft Visual Studio 2008, your screen will appear similar to Figure 4-1; however, your Recent Projects section might include some additional information. If you are using a different edition of Visual Studio, or if you are using the Express Edition of Visual Basic, your startup screen might look slightly different than the one shown in Figure 4-1. The startup screen shown in Figure 4-1 contains three windows: Toolbox, Start Page, and Solution Explorer.

Start Page window

Solution Explorer window

Toolbox window

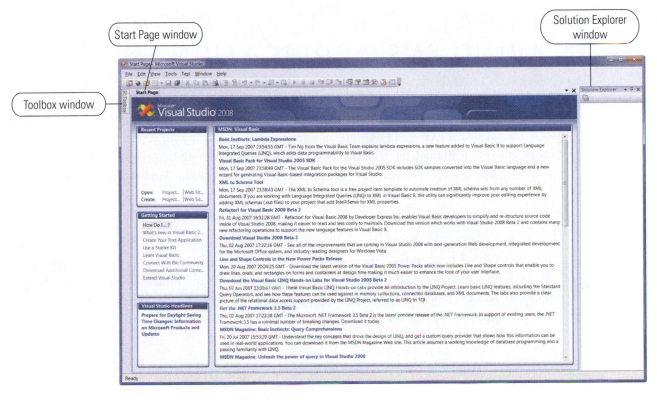

Figure 4-1: Microsoft Visual Studio 2008 Professional Edition startup screen

Included in Visual Studio 2008 are the Visual Basic, Visual C++, and Visual C# programming languages. You can use these languages to code your algorithms into programs, which is the fifth step in the problem-solving process. The combination of the user interface and the program's code is referred to as an application. You can use Visual Basic to create various types of applications, such as Windows applications and Web applications. A Windows application has a Windows user interface and runs on a desktop computer, whereas a Web application has a Web user interface and runs on a server. You also can use Visual Basic to create Smart Device applications that run on smart devices, such as Pocket PCs and Smartphones. This book focuses on Windows applications. However, Web applications are covered in a later chapter and Smart Device applications are explored in several of the Advanced Exercises in various chapters in this book.

CREATING A VISUAL BASIC WINDOWS APPLICATION

Windows applications in Visual Basic are composed of solutions, projects, and files. A solution is a container that stores the projects and files for an entire application. Although most solutions contain only one project, a solution can contain several projects. A project also is a container, but it stores only the files associated with that particular project. In the following steps, you learn how to create a Visual Basic 2008 Windows application.

To create a Visual Basic 2008 Windows application:

1. This first step is necessary so that your screen agrees with the figures and steps in this book. Click **Tools** on the menu bar, then click **Options** to open the Options dialog box. Click **Projects and Solutions**. If necessary, select the following three check boxes: **Always show Error List if build finishes with errors**, **Always show solution**, and **Save new projects when created**. If necessary, deselect the **Show Output window when build starts** check box. See Figure 4-2.

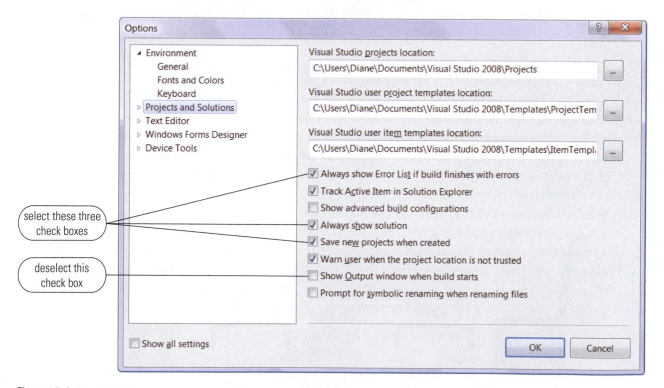

Figure 4-2: Options dialog box

2. Click the **OK** button to close the Options dialog box.

3. Click **File** on the menu bar, then click **New Project**. The New Project dialog box opens. If necessary, expand the **Visual Basic** node in the Project types list, then click **Windows**.

4. If necessary, click **Windows Forms Application** in the Visual Studio installed templates section of the Templates list.

5. Type **My Wizard Project** in the Name box.

6. Use the Browse button, which appears next to the Location box, to open the Project Location dialog box. Locate and then click the **ClearlyVB\Chap04** folder, then click the **Select Folder** button.

7. If necessary, select the **Create directory for solution** check box in the New Project dialog box.

8. Type **My Wizard Solution** in the Solution Name box. The completed New Project dialog box is shown in Figure 4-3. The drive letter will be different if you are saving to a device other than your computer's hard drive—for example, if you are saving to a flash drive. In addition, your dialog box will look different if you are using the Express Edition.

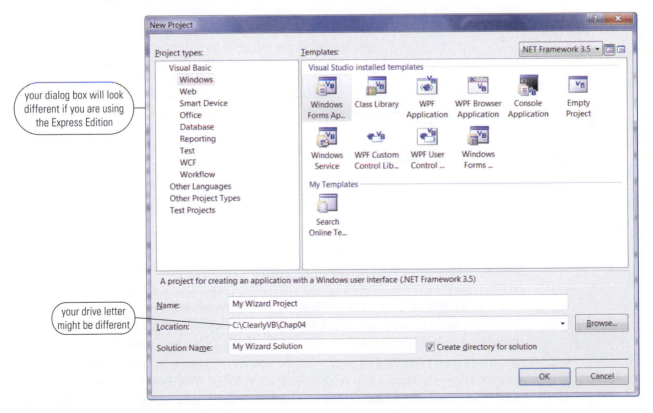

Figure 4-3: Completed New Project dialog box

9. Click the **OK** button to close the New Project dialog box. When you click the OK button, Visual Studio creates a solution and adds a Visual Basic project to the solution, as shown in Figure 4-4. The solution and project name appear in the Solution Explorer window.

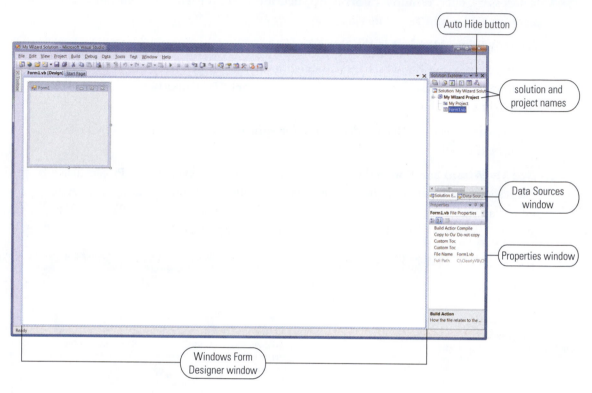

Figure 4-4: Solution and Visual Basic Project

SO MANY WINDOWS!

In addition to the Toolbox, Start Page, and Solution Explorer windows mentioned earlier, three other windows are open in the IDE shown in Figure 4-4: Windows Form Designer, Data Sources, and Properties. Having so many windows—in this case, six windows—open at the same time can be confusing, especially when you are first learning the IDE. In most cases, you will find it easier to work in the IDE if you either close or auto-hide the windows you are not currently using. The easiest way to close an open window is to click the Close button on the window's title bar. In most cases, the View menu provides an appropriate option for opening a closed window. You auto-hide a window using the Auto Hide button (shown in Figure 4-4) on the window's title bar. The Auto Hide button is a toggle button: clicking it once activates it, and clicking it again deactivates it. The Toolbox window shown in Figure 4-4 is an example of an auto-hidden window.

To close, auto-hide, and display windows in the IDE:

1. Click the **Start Page** tab to make the Start Page window the active window, then click its **Close** button.

2. Click the **Data Sources** tab, then click the **Close** button on its title bar.

3. Next, you will practice auto-hiding a window. Click the **Auto Hide** button (the vertical pushpin) on the Solution Explorer window's title bar. The Solution Explorer window is minimized and appears as a tab on the right edge of the IDE.

4. Now practice temporarily displaying a window. Place your mouse pointer on the Solution Explorer tab. The Solution Explorer window slides into view. Move your mouse pointer away from the Solution Explorer window. The window is minimized and appears as a tab again.

5. Next, you will practice permanently displaying a window. Place your mouse pointer on the Toolbox tab. When the Toolbox window slides into view, click the **Auto Hide** button (the horizontal pushpin) on its title bar. The vertical pushpin replaces the horizontal pushpin on the button. Click **Common Controls**. Figure 4-5 shows the current status of the windows in the IDE. Only the Windows Form Designer, Toolbox, and Properties windows are open in the IDE. The Solution Explorer window is auto-hidden. If the items in the Properties window do not appear in alphabetical order, click the **Alphabetical** button.

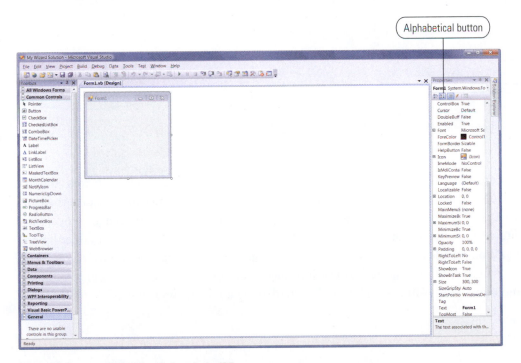

Figure 4-5: Current status of the windows in the IDE

CREATING THE USER INTERFACE

The **Windows Form Designer window** is where you create (or design) your application's user interface. The designer window shown in Figure 4-6 contains a **Windows Form object**, or form. A **form** is the foundation for the user interface in a Windows application. A form automatically includes a title bar that contains a default caption—in this case, Form1—as well as Minimize, Maximize, and Close buttons. At the top of the designer window is a tab labeled Form1.vb [Design]. [Design] identifies the window as the designer window. Form1.vb is the name of the file on your computer's hard disk (or on the device designated by your instructor or technical support person) that contains the Visual Basic instructions associated with the form.

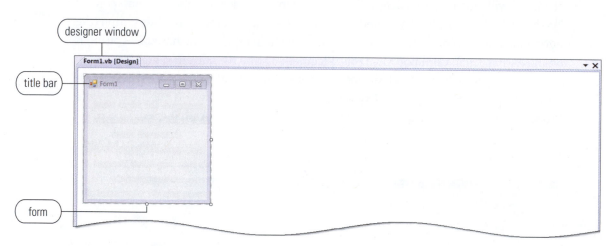

Figure 4-6: Windows Form Designer window

You create the user interface by adding objects (such as buttons, check boxes, and list boxes) to the form. The objects added to a form are called **controls**. Because the controls are graphical in nature, the user interface is often referred to as a graphical user interface, or **GUI**. You add the controls to the form using the tools contained in the **Toolbox window**. In the next set of steps, you begin creating the Wizard Application interface shown in Figure 4-7. The interface contains four controls: two picture boxes and two labels. You use a **picture box** to display an image on the form. You use **label**

controls to display text that the user is not allowed to edit while the application is running. Some label controls simply identify the contents of other controls. The label controls in Figure 4-7, for example, identify the contents of the picture boxes. Label controls also are used in an interface to display program output, such as the result of calculations. In the following steps, you also will learn how to move, delete, undelete, and size a control.

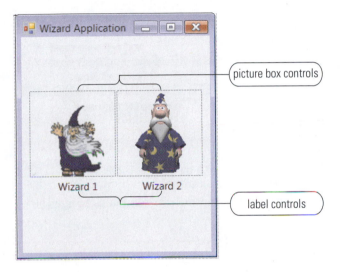

Figure 4-7: Wizard Application user interface

To begin creating the Wizard Application user interface:

1. Click the **Label** tool in the toolbox, but do not release the mouse button. Hold down the mouse button as you drag the mouse pointer to the lower-left corner of the form. As you drag the mouse pointer, you will see a solid box, as well as an outline of a rectangle and a plus box, following the mouse pointer. Notice that a blue line appears between the form's left border and the control's left border, and between the form's bottom border and the control's bottom border. The blue lines are called margin lines, because their size is determined by the contents of the control's Margin property. The purpose of the margin lines is to assist you in spacing the controls properly on a form. See Figure 4-8.

Label tool

the length of the blue lines is determined by the control's Margin property

Figure 4-8: Label tool being dragged to the form

2. Release the mouse button. A label control appears on the form, and an asterisk (*) appears on the designer window's tab to indicate that the form has been changed since the last time it was saved. See Figure 4-9.

the asterisk indicates that the form has been changed since the last time it was saved

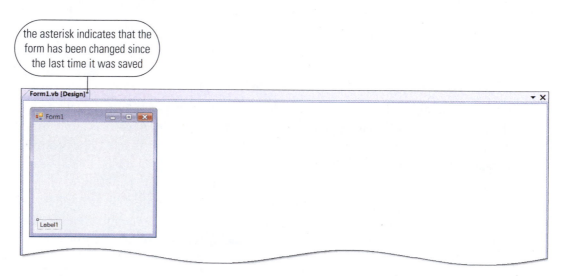

Figure 4-9: Label control added to the form

3. Now you will practice repositioning a control on the form. Place your mouse pointer on the center of the label control, then press the left mouse button and drag the control to another area of the form. (Don't worry about the exact location.) Release the mouse button.

4. Next, you will practice deleting and then restoring a control. Press the **Delete** key on your keyboard to delete the label control. Click **Edit** on the menu bar, and then click **Undo** to reinstate the label control.

5. Drag the label control back to its original location in the lower-left corner of the form.

6. Add another label control to the form. Place the label control in the center of the form.

7. Drag the Label2 control until its left border is aligned with the left border of the Label1 control, but don't release the mouse button. When the left borders of both controls are aligned, the designer displays a blue snap line, as shown in Figure 4-10. Because both controls are the same size, their right borders also are aligned.

Figure 4-10: A blue snap line appears when the borders are aligned

8. Release the mouse button.

9. Now drag the Label2 control so that the Label2 text is aligned with the Label1 text. When the text in both controls is aligned, the designer displays a pink snap line, as shown in Figure 4-11.

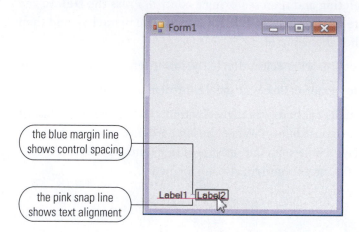

the blue margin line shows control spacing

the pink snap line shows text alignment

Figure 4-11: A pink snap line appears when the text is aligned

10. Release the mouse button.

11. Use the PictureBox tool to add two picture boxes to the form. See Figure 4-12. (You do not need to worry about the exact location of the controls in the interface.)

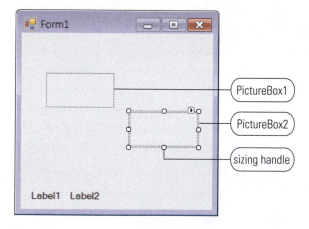

PictureBox1

PictureBox2

sizing handle

Figure 4-12: Picture boxes added to the form

12. The sizing handles on the PictureBox2 control indicate that it is selected. You can use the sizing handles to make a control bigger or smaller. Use the sizing handles to make the PictureBox2 control either bigger or smaller, then click **Edit** on the menu bar, and then click **Undo** to return the control to its original size.

13. You are finished with the Toolbox window, so you can auto-hide it. Auto-hide the Toolbox window.

To learn more about adding controls to a form, as well as sizing, moving, deleting, and undeleting the controls, view the Ch04-Controls video.

SAVE, SAVE, SAVE

It is a good practice to save the current solution every 10 or 15 minutes so that you will not lose a lot of your work if the computer loses power. You can save a solution by clicking File on the menu bar, and then clicking Save All. You also can click the Save All button on the Standard toolbar. When you save a solution, the computer saves any changes made to the files included in the solution. Saving a solution also removes the asterisk that appears on the designer window's tab.

To save the current solution:

1. Click **File** on the menu bar, then click **Save All**.

MINI-QUIZ 1

1. A _____ control displays text that the user is not allowed to edit while an application is running.

2. The _____ contains the tools you use to add objects to a form.

3. GUI stands for _____.

WHOSE PROPERTY IS IT?

Every object in a Visual Basic application has a set of attributes, called **properties**, that determine its appearance and behavior. When an object is created, a default value is assigned to each of its properties. The name and current value of each property appear in the **Properties window** when the object is selected.

To view the form's properties:

1. Click the **form** (but not a control on the form) to select it. Sizing handles appear on the form to indicate that the form is selected, and the form's properties appear in the Properties window.

2. Scroll up to the top of the Properties window. If necessary, click the **Alphabetical** button in the Properties window to display the property names in alphabetical order. Most times, it's easier to work with the Properties window when the property names are listed alphabetically.

3. Click **(Name)**, which is the third item in the Properties list, to select the form's Name property. Figure 4-13 shows a partial listing of the form's properties. (Notice that items within parentheses appear at the top of the Properties list.)

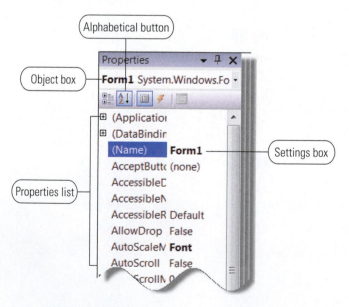

Figure 4-13: Properties window showing some of the form's properties

As indicated in Figure 4-13, the Properties window contains an Object box and a Properties list. The Object box shows the name of the selected object—in this case, Form1. The Properties list has two columns. The left column lists the names of the properties associated with the selected object. The right column contains the Settings box for each property. The Settings box displays the current value, or setting, of the property. For example, the current value of the form's Name property is Form1. Depending on the property, you can change the default value assigned to a property by selecting the property in the Properties list, and then either typing the new value in the Settings box or selecting a predefined value from a list or dialog box. Although not shown in Figure 4-13, a brief description of the selected property appears in the Description pane located at the bottom of the Properties window.

In the next set of steps, you will change the values assigned to the form's Text, StartPosition, and Font properties. The Text property controls the caption displayed both in the form's title bar and on the application's button on the taskbar while the application is running. The StartPosition property specifies the position of the form when it first appears on the screen after the application is started. The Font property determines the type, style, and size of the font used to display the text on the form. A font is the general shape of the characters in the text. Segoe UI, Tahoma, and Microsoft Sans Serif are examples of font types. Font styles include regular, bold, and italic. The numbers 9, 12, and 18 are examples of font sizes, which typically are measured in points, with one point equaling 1/72 of an inch.

To change the values assigned to some of the form's properties:

1. Scroll down the Properties list, then click **Text** in the list. Type **Wizard Application** and press **Enter**. The Wizard Application text appears in the Settings box and in the form's title bar.

2. Click **StartPosition** in the Properties list. Click the **down arrow** in the Settings box, then click **CenterScreen** to display the form in the center of the screen when the application is started.

3. Click **Font** in the Properties list, then click the **. . .** (ellipsis) button in the Settings box. Doing this opens the Font dialog box.
   For applications created for the Windows Vista environment, Microsoft recommends that you use the Segoe UI font, because it offers improved readability. Segoe is pronounced SEE-go, and UI stands for *user interface*. For most of the controls in the interface, you will use the 9-point size of the font. (Applications created for the Windows XP environment typically use the 10- or 12-point Tahoma font.) You can change the Font property for each control individually; however, an easier way is to change the form's Font property. Any control whose Font property has not been set individually will be assigned the same font as the form.

4. Click **Segoe UI** in the Font list box and click **9** in the Size list box, then click the **OK** button. The form's Font property setting changes to the new value. The Font property setting for each label control also changes to the new value. To verify that fact, click the **Label1** control, then view its Font property setting. Click the **Label2** control, then view its Font property setting.

Next, you will change the Text and Location properties of the two label controls. A label control's Text property specifies the text displayed inside the control. Its Location property controls the location of the upper-left corner of the control on the form. (Although you can simply drag a control to the desired location, you many times will be provided with the setting for the Location property so that your screen agrees with the figures in this book.)

To change two properties of each label control:

1. Click the **Label1** control to select it, then change its Text property to **Wizard 1**.

2. Click the **Location** property in the Properties list. The first number in the Settings box specifies the control's horizontal location; the second number specifies its vertical location. In other words, the first number is the location of the control's left border, and the second number is the location of its top border. Type **40, 212** and press **Enter**.

3. Click the **Label2** control. Set its Text property to **Wizard 2** and its Location property to **175, 212**.

Finally, you will change the Image and SizeMode properties of the picture boxes. The Image property specifies the name of the file containing the image to display. The SizeMode property handles how the image is displayed and can be set to Normal, StretchImage, AutoSize, CenterImage, or Zoom. The images for the Wizard application's interface are stored in the Lightning_bolts (Lightning_bolts.gif) and Wizard_appears (Wizard_appears.gif) files, which are contained in the ClearlyVB\Chap04 folder. Both image files were downloaded from the Animation Library site. You can browse and optionally download other free image files at *www.animationlibrary.com*.

To change two properties of each picture box:

1. Click the **PictureBox1** control to select it. The control's properties appear in the Properties window, and a box containing a triangle appears on the control, as shown in Figure 4-14. The box is referred to as the task box because, when you click it, it displays a list of the tasks commonly performed by the control. Each task in the list is associated with one or more properties. You can set the properties using the task list or the Properties window.

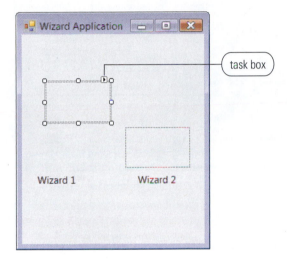

Figure 4-14: Picture box control selected on the form

2. Click the **task box** on the PictureBox1 control. A list of tasks associated with a picture box appears. Click **Choose Image**. This task is associated with the Image property in the Properties window. The Select Resource dialog box opens.

3. To include the image file within the project itself, the Project resource file radio button must be selected in the Select Resource dialog box. Verify that the Project resource file radio button is selected, then click the **Import** button. The Open dialog box opens.

4. Open the ClearlyVB\Chap04 folder, then click **Lightning_bolts** (**Lightning_bolts.gif**) in the list of filenames. Click the **Open** button. See Figure 4-15.

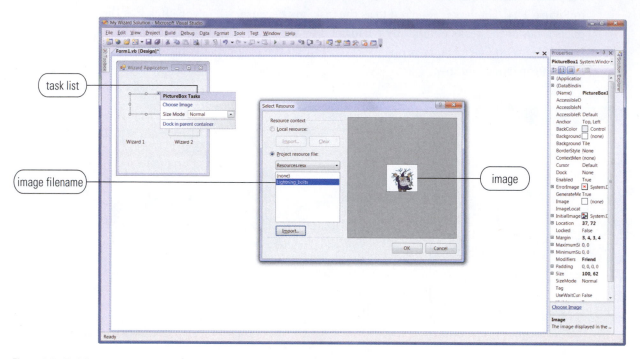

Figure 4-15: Task list and completed Select Resource dialog box

5. Click the **OK** button. A portion of the image appears in the picture box, and the Lightning_bolts filename is assigned to the control's Image property in the Properties window.

6. Click the **Size Mode** arrow in the task list box, and then click **AutoSize**. Doing this assigns the AutoSize value to the picture box control's SizeMode property in the Properties window. The AutoSize value tells the computer to automatically size the picture box to fit its contents.

7. Click the **PictureBox1** control to close its task list, then drag the picture box so that it is located above the Wizard 1 label. See Figure 4-16.

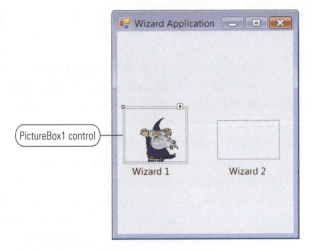

Figure 4-16: Location of PictureBox1 control

8. Click the **PictureBox2** control, then click its **task box**. Use the task list to display the image contained in the **Wizard_appears** (**Wizard_appears.gif**) file. Also use the task list to set the SizeMode property to **AutoSize**. (Don't be concerned if only a portion of the image appears in the picture box. The entire image will appear when you start the application later in this chapter.)

9. Drag the PictureBox2 control to the location shown in Figure 4-17.

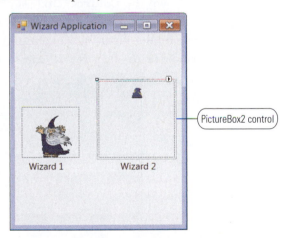

Figure 4-17: Location of PictureBox2 control

10. Auto-hide the Properties window, then save the solution by clicking the **Save All** button on the Standard toolbar. (You also can click File on the menu bar, and then click Save All.)

USING THE FORMAT MENU

The two picture boxes in the interface shown in Figure 4-17 are not the same size: PictureBox1 is smaller than PictureBox2. You can make them the same size by setting their Size properties to the same value in the Properties window. However, an easier way is to use the Format menu, which provides several options for manipulating the controls in the interface. The Align option, for example, allows you to align two or more controls by their left, right, top, or bottom borders. You can use the Make Same Size option to make two or more controls the same width and/or height. The Format menu also has a Center in Form option that centers one or more controls either horizontally or vertically on the form. Before you can use the Format menu to make the picture boxes the same size, you first must select them. The first control you select should always be the one whose size and/or location you want to match. For example, to make the size of the PictureBox1 control match the size of the PictureBox2 control, you need to select the PictureBox2 control first. The first control selected is referred to as the reference control.

To make the PictureBox1 control the same size as the PictureBox2 control:

1. The **PictureBox2** control should still be selected from the previous set of steps. Press and hold down the **Control** (**Ctrl**) key as you click the **PictureBox1** control, then release the Control key. The two picture boxes are now selected. Notice that the sizing handle on the PictureBox2 control (the reference control) is white, whereas the sizing handle on the PictureBox1 control is black. See Figure 4-18.

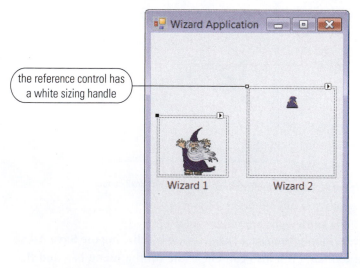

Figure 4-18: Picture boxes selected on the form

2. Click **Format** on the menu bar. Point to **Make Same Size**, and then click **Both**. The PictureBox1 control is now the same size as the PictureBox2 control.

3. Click the **form** to deselect the picture boxes.

4. Now that the PictureBox1 control is larger than its original size, the image inside it seems too small. You can make the image larger by changing the PictureBox1 control's SizeMode property from AutoSize to StretchImage. Click the **PictureBox1** control, then change its SizeMode property in the Properties list to **StretchImage**.

Now you will use the Format menu to align the top border of the PictureBox1 control with the top border of the PictureBox2 control.

To align the top borders of the two picture boxes:

1. Click the **PictureBox2** control, which is the reference control. Press and hold down the **Control** (**Ctrl**) key as you click the PictureBox1 control, then release the Control key.

2. Click **Format** on the menu bar. Point to **Align**, and then click **Tops**. The top border of the PictureBox1 control is now aligned with the top border of the PictureBox2 control.

3. Click the **form** to deselect the picture boxes.

4. Now drag the Wizard 1 label to the right so that it is centered below the PictureBox1 control. (Or, you can change the label's Location property to 50, 212.)

5. Save the solution.

 To learn more about the Format menu, view the Ch04-Format Menu video.

LOCK THEM DOWN

In the next set of steps, you will lock the controls in place on the form. Locking the controls prevents them from being moved inadvertently as you work in the IDE.

To lock the controls:

1. Right-click the **form**, then click **Lock Controls** on the context menu. Notice that a small lock appears in the upper-left corner of the form. (You also can lock the controls by clicking Format on the menu bar, and then clicking Lock Controls.) See Figure 4-19.

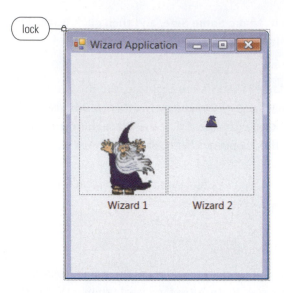

Figure 4-19: Controls locked on the form

2. Click **one of the controls** on the form. Here again, notice that a small lock appears in the upper-left corner of the control.

3. Try dragging one of the controls to a different location on the form. You will not be able to do so.

If you need to move a control after you have locked the controls in place, you can change the control's Location property setting in the Properties window. You also can unlock the control by changing its Locked property to False. To unlock all of the controls, right-click the form, and then click Lock Controls on the context menu; or use the Lock Controls option on the Format menu. The Lock Controls option on both the context menu and the Format menu is a toggle option: clicking it once activates it, and clicking it again deactivates it.

To unlock and then lock the controls:

1. Right-click the **form**, then click **Lock Controls** to unlock the controls. Notice that the small lock no longer appears in the upper-left corner of the form.

2. Right-click the **form**, then click **Lock Controls** to lock the controls.

OK, LET'S SEE THE INTERFACE IN ACTION!

Now that the user interface is complete, you can start the application to see how it will look to the user. You can start an application by clicking Debug on the menu bar, and then clicking Start Debugging; or you can simply press the F5 key on your keyboard.

To start and stop the current application:

1. Save the solution. To start the application, click **Debug** on the menu bar, and then click **Start Debugging**. (You also can press the F5 key on your keyboard.) See Figure 4-20. (Do not be concerned about any windows that appear at the bottom of your screen.)

the form's Close button

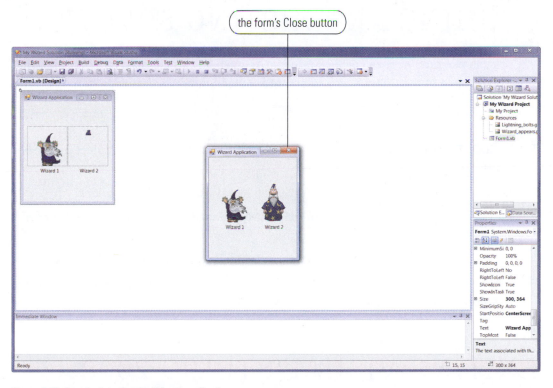

Figure 4-20: Result of starting the Wizard application

2. To stop the application, click the **Close** button on the form's title bar. (You also can click the designer window to make it the active window, then click Debug on the menu bar, and then click Stop Debugging.) When the application ends, you are returned to the IDE.

CLOSING THE CURRENT SOLUTION

When you are finished working on a solution, you should close the solution. You close a solution using the Close Solution option on the File menu. When you close a solution, all projects and files contained in the solution also are closed.

To close the current solution:

1. Click **File** on the menu bar, then click **Close Solution**.

2. Temporarily display the Solution Explorer window to verify that no solutions are open in the IDE.

OPENING AN EXISTING SOLUTION

You can use the File menu or the Start Page to open an existing solution. If a solution is already open in the IDE, it is closed before another solution is opened.

To open the Wizard Solution:

1. Click **File** on the menu bar, then click **Open Project**. The Open Project dialog box opens.

2. Locate and then open the ClearlyVB\Chap04\My Wizard Solution folder.

3. If necessary, click **My Wizard Solution** (**My Wizard Solution.sln**) in the list of filenames, and then click the **Open** button.

4. Temporarily display the Solution Explorer window to verify that the solution is open.

5. If the Windows Form Designer window is not open, right-click **Form1.vb** in the Solution Explorer window, then click **View Designer**.

EXITING VISUAL STUDIO 2008

You can exit Visual Studio using either the Close button on its title bar or the Exit option on the File menu.

To exit Visual Studio 2008:

1. Click **File** on the menu bar, then click **Exit** on the menu.

MINI-QUIZ 2

1. The name of the image file assigned to a picture box control is stored in the control's _____ property.

2. The value assigned to a label control's _____ property appears inside the control.

3. A control's Location property specifies the location of the control's _____ corner on the form.

4. To make the PictureBox2 control the same size as the PictureBox1 control, you first select the _____ control.

5. To start a Visual Basic application, click Debug, and then click _____.

SUMMARY

» The fourth step in the problem-solving process is to create the user interface.

» You can use Visual Basic to create various types of applications, such as Windows applications, Web applications, and Smart Device applications.

» Windows applications in Visual Basic are composed of solutions, projects, and files.

» You create your user interfaces by adding controls to a form in the Windows Form Designer window. You add a control using a tool from the Toolbox window.

» Label controls display text that the user is not allowed to edit while an application is running.

» You use picture boxes to display images on a form.

» A blue snap line appears when the border of one control is aligned with the border of another control. A pink snap line appears when the text in two or more controls is aligned.

» It's a good practice to save a solution every 10 or 15 minutes.

» The Properties window lists the properties of the selected object.

» The value assigned to a form's Text property appears in the form's title bar and on the application's button on the taskbar when the application is running. The value assigned to a label control's Text property appears inside the control.

» A form's StartPosition property specifies the position of the form when it first appears on the screen after the application is started.

» The Font property determines the type, style, and size of the font used to display the text on the form or inside a control. Microsoft recommends the 9-point, Segoe UI font for Windows Vista applications. Any control whose Font property has not been set individually will be assigned the same Font property value as the form.

» The value assigned to a control's Location property specifies the location of the upper-left corner of the control on the form.

» A picture box control's Image property specifies the name of the file containing the image to display. Its SizeMode property handles how the image is displayed.

» The Format menu provides options for aligning, sizing, and centering the controls on a form. The first control you select is called the reference control and is the one whose size and/or location you want to match.

» It's a good practice to lock the controls in place on the form.

» To start an application, click Debug, then click Start Debugging; or press the F5 key on your keyboard.

KEY TERMS

Controls—the objects added to a form

Form—the foundation for the user interface in a Windows application

GUI—graphical user interface

IDE—integrated development environment

Integrated development environment—an environment that contains all of the tools and features needed to create, run, and test programs; IDE

Label controls—the controls used to display text that the user is not allowed to edit while an application is running

Picture box—the control used to display an image on the form

Properties—the attributes that determine an object's appearance and behavior

Properties window—the window that displays the properties of the selected object

Toolbox window—the window that contains the tools you use to add controls to a form

User interface—what the user sees and interacts with while an application is running

Windows Form Designer window—the window you use to create, or design, the user interface

Windows Form object—the form in a Windows application

ANSWERS TO MINI-QUIZZES

MINI-QUIZ 1

1. label

2. Toolbox window

3. graphical user interface

MINI-QUIZ 2

1. Image

2. Text

3. upper-left

4. PictureBox1

5. Start Debugging

REVIEW QUESTIONS

1. A Windows form object, or form, automatically contains _____.

   a. Close, Maximize, and Minimize buttons

   b. a default caption

   c. a title bar

   d. All of the above.

2. The text "ABC Company" should appear at the top of an interface created for the ABC Company. You should display the text using a _____ control.

    a. form

    b. label

    c. picture box

    d. None of the above.

3. You use the _____ window to set the characteristics that control an object's appearance and behavior.

    a. Characteristics

    b. Designer

    c. Object

    d. Properties

4. The _____ property determines the position of a form when the application is started and the form first appears on the screen.

    a. StartPosition

    b. Location

    c. StartLocation

    d. InitialPosition

5. When aligning two or more controls, the first control selected is called the _____ control.

    a. initializer

    b. positioning

    c. reference

    d. None of the above.

EXERCISES

»TRY THIS

1. In this exercise, you create an application for the Scottsville Library. (The answers to TRY THIS Exercises are located at the end of the chapter.)

    a. Create a new Visual Basic Windows application. Assign the name Library Project to the project. Assign the name Library Solution to the solution. Save the application in the ClearlyVB\Chap04 folder.

b. Create the interface shown in Figure 4-21, using the following information. The Book_opens. gif image file for the picture box is stored in the ClearlyVB\ Chap04 folder. (The file was downloaded from the *www. animationlibrary.com* site.) Use the 9-point Segoe UI font for the form and the label. The form should appear centered on the screen when the application starts. The label should be centered horizontally on the form. The picture box's Size property should be set to 170, 140. The picture box should be centered both horizontally and vertically on the form.

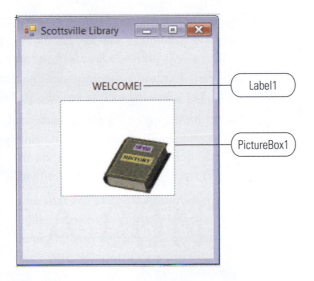

Figure 4-21

c. Lock the controls on the form. Save and then start the application. Stop the application by clicking the form's Close button, then use the File menu to close the solution.

2. In this exercise, you modify the My Wizard application created in the chapter.

MODIFY THIS

a. Use Windows to make a copy of the My Wizard Solution folder. Save the copy in the ClearlyVB\Chap04 folder. Rename the copy Modified My Wizard Solution.

b. Open the My Wizard Solution (My Wizard Solution.sln) file contained in the Modified My Wizard Solution folder. Modify the interface as follows. Move the labels to a location immediately above the picture boxes. Display the Wizard_appears image in the PictureBox1 control. Display the Lightning_bolts image in the PictureBox2 control. The PictureBox2 control should be the same size as the PictureBox1 control. The image in the PictureBox2 control should fill the control.

c. Lock the controls on the form. Save and then start the application. Stop the application by clicking the form's Close button, then use the File menu to close the solution.

3. In this exercise, you create an application for Scenic Vacations.

INTRODUCTORY

a. Create a new Visual Basic Windows application. Assign the name Scenic Project to the project. Assign the name Scenic Solution to the solution. Save the application in the ClearlyVB\Chap04 folder.

b. Create the interface shown in Figure 4-22, using the following information. The Lightsnow.gif image file for the picture box is stored in the ClearlyVB\Chap04 folder. Use the 9-point Segoe UI font for the form. Use the 18-point Segoe UI font for the label. The form should appear centered on the screen when the application starts. The label and picture box should be centered horizontally on the form.

c. Lock the controls on the form. Save and then start the application. Stop the application by clicking the form's Close button, then use the File menu to close the solution.

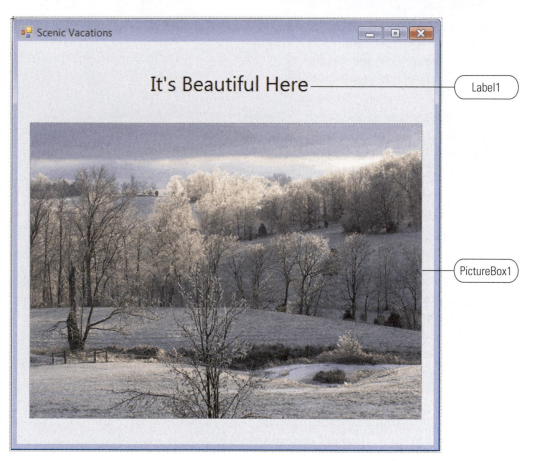

Figure 4-22

INTERMEDIATE

4. In this exercise, you download four image files that contain an up arrow, a down arrow, a left arrow, and a right arrow. You then use the files to display the arrows in an interface.

a. Download the following four files from *www.office.microsoft.com/en-us/clipart*: j0395696.gif (down arrow), j0395697.gif (left arrow), j0395698.gif (right arrow), and j0395699.gif (up arrow). Or, if you prefer, you can visit other Web sites that allow you to download image files for free. If you downloaded the image files from the

Microsoft site, they most likely will be saved to your Pictures\Microsoft Clip Organizer folder. Copy the files from that folder to the ClearlyVB\Chap04 folder.

b. Create a new Visual Basic Windows application. Assign the name Arrows Project to the project. Assign the name Arrows Solution to the solution. Save the application in the ClearlyVB\Chap04 folder.

c. Create the interface shown in Figure 4-23. The interface contains four picture boxes and four labels. Be sure to use the appropriate font. Also be sure to center the form when the application is started and the form first appears on the screen.

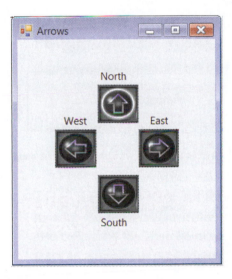

Figure 4-23

d. Lock the controls on the form. Save and then start the application. Stop the application by clicking the form's Close button, then use the File menu to close the solution.

5. In this exercise, you create an application that contains a picture box and three button controls.   **»ADVANCED**

a. Create a new Visual Basic Windows application. Assign the name Show Hide Project to the project. Assign the name Show Hide Solution to the solution. Save the application in the ClearlyVB\Chap04 folder.

b. Create the interface shown in Figure 4-24. The Lightning_bolts.gif image file for the picture box is stored in the ClearlyVB\Chap04 folder. The picture box should have a border around it; set the appropriate property.

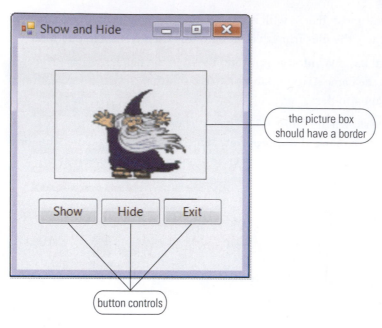

Figure 4-24

c. Lock the controls on the form. Save and then start the application. Stop the application by clicking the form's Close button, then use the File menu to close the solution.

ANSWER TO "TRY THIS" EXERCISE

1. Set the form's Font property to Segoe UI, 9pt. Set its StartPosition property to CenterScreen, and its Text property to Scottsville Library. Set the Label1 control's Text property to WELCOME!. Set the PictureBox1 control's Image property to Book_opens.gif. Set its SizeMode property to StretchImage, and its Size property to 170, 140.

5

DO IT YOURSELF DESIGNING

After studying Chapter 5, you should be able to:

Use a text box to get user input

Perform an action with a button control

Code a control's Click event procedure

Stop an application using the Me.Close() instruction

DELEGATING THE WORK

In Chapter 3, you learned how to analyze a problem, plan an appropriate algorithm, and desk-check the algorithm. Then, in Chapter 4, you learned the mechanics of creating a user interface in Visual Basic. In this chapter, you learn how to design the interface, using a problem's output and input items, as well as its algorithm. More specifically, you'll learn how to design an interface for the Addison Smith problem from Chapter 3. Figure 5-1 shows the Addison Smith problem's output, input, and algorithm. As you may remember, the algorithm calculates and displays an annual commission based on the annual sales and commission rate entered by the user.

Output: annual commission

Input: annual sales
           commission rate

Algorithm:
1. enter the annual sales and commission rate
2. calculate the annual commission by multiplying the annual sales by the commission rate
3. display the annual commission

Figure 5-1: Output, input, and algorithm for the Addison Smith problem

When designing an interface for a problem, you need to examine each step in the problem's algorithm, along with its output and input items. The first step in the Addison Smith algorithm is to enter the annual sales and commission rate, which are the two input items. Visual Basic provides many controls that allow the user to enter data; in this case, you will use two text boxes. Step 2 in the algorithm is to calculate the annual commission. The user should have control over when (and if) the calculation task is performed. This is the perfect place to use a button control, because buttons perform their tasks only when the user clicks them. Examples of buttons with which you already are familiar include the Open, Save, and OK buttons. In this case, you will assign the calculation task to a button marked Calculate Commission. The Calculate Commission button also will be assigned the "display the annual commission" task from Step 3, because the user will want to view the annual commission immediately after it has been calculated. As Figure 5-1 indicates, the annual commission is an output item. In most interfaces, output items appear in label controls, because users should not be able to edit the value of an output item while an application is running. In this case, for instance, the user should not be able to edit the annual commission after it has been calculated. Based on the information shown in Figure 5-1, the interface will use two text boxes to get the annual sales and commission rate, a button to calculate and display the annual commission, and a label to show the annual commission to the user. In addition to the controls required by the algorithm, every interface also needs a control that allows the user to end the application. In this interface, you will use a button marked Exit for this purpose. Figure 5-2 lists the controls mentioned in this section.

Control	Purpose
Label	show the annual commission
Text box	get the annual sales
Text box	get the commission rate
Button (Calculate Commission)	calculate and display the annual commission
Button (Exit)	end the application

Figure 5-2: Listing of controls

You should assign a meaningful name to each of the controls listed in Figure 5-2, because doing so will help you keep track of the various objects included in the interface. In addition, as you will learn in Chapter 6, the programmer uses an object's name to refer to the object in code. The name must begin with a letter and can contain only letters, numbers, and the underscore character. You cannot include punctuation characters or spaces in the name. There are several conventions for naming objects in Visual Basic; in this book, you will use a naming convention called Hungarian notation. Names in Hungarian notation begin with a three (or more) character ID that represents the object's type. Label control names, for example, begin with lbl. Names of buttons begin with btn, and text box names begin with txt. The remaining characters in the name represent the object's purpose. For instance, using Hungarian notation, you might assign the name lblCommission to the label that displays the annual commission. The "lbl" identifies the object as a label, and "Commission" reminds you of the label's purpose. Hungarian notation names are entered using **camel case**, which means you lowercase the ID characters and then uppercase the first letter of each word in the name. Camel case refers to the fact that the uppercase letters appear as "humps" in the name because they are taller than the lowercase letters. Figure 5-3 lists the name and purpose of each of the controls listed in Figure 5-2.

Control name	Purpose
lblCommission	show the annual commission
txtSales	get the annual sales
txtRate	get the commission rate
btnCalculate (Calculate Commission)	calculate and display the annual commission
btnExit (Exit)	end the application

Figure 5-3: Name and purpose of each control

MINI-QUIZ 1

1. It is customary to show the result of a calculation in a _____ control in the interface.

2. Using Hungarian notation, which of the following is a good name for a text box that accepts the name of a city?

   a. cityTextBox

   b. textBoxCity

   c. txtCity

   d. TxtCity

3. The three-character ID for a button control's name is _____.

Before you begin creating the Commission Calculator application, you may want to view the Ch05-Commission Calculator video. The video demonstrates all of the steps contained in this chapter. You may find it helpful to view the steps before you perform them.

To begin creating the Commission Calculator application:

1. Start Visual Studio 2008 (or Visual Basic 2008 Express Edition). Create a new Visual Basic Windows application. Assign the names Commission Calculator Project and Commission Calculator Solution to the project and solution, respectively. Save the application in the ClearlyVB\Chap05 folder.

2. Change the form's Font property to **Segoe UI, 9pt**. Change its StartPosition property to **CenterScreen**.

3. Change the form's Text property to **Commission Calculator**. Drag the form's right border until the entire Text property value can be viewed in the title bar.

4. Because a project can contain more than one form, it's a good programming practice to assign a meaningful name to each form. The names of the forms within the same project must be unique. The three-character ID for form names is frm. Change the form's Name property to **frmMain**.

5. You also will change the name of the file (on your disk) that contains the form. Right-click **Form1.vb** in the Solution Explorer window, then click **Rename**. Type **frmMain.vb** and press **Enter**.

6. Now you will begin adding the controls listed in Figure 5-3 to the form. For now, you do not have to worry about the exact location of the controls. Use the Label tool to add a label to the form. Change the label's name to **lblCommission**.

7. Use the TextBox tool to add two text boxes to the form. Name the first text box **txtSales**, and name the second text box **txtRate**.

8. Use the Button tool to add two buttons to the form. Name the first button **btnCalculate**, and name the second button **btnExit**.

9. Position the controls as shown in Figure 5-4.

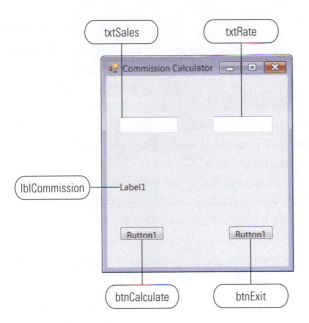

Figure 5-4: Controls added to the form

10. You will need to add descriptive identifying labels above the two text boxes; otherwise, the user won't know where to enter the input items. Add two more labels to the form. Position one of the labels above the txtSales control, and the other above the txtRate control. Use the blue snap lines to align the left border of each label with the left border of its respective text box.

11. An identifying label should be from one to three words only, with the entire label appearing on one line. It is customary in Windows applications for identifying labels to end with a colon. The colon allows some assistive technologies, which are technologies that provide assistance to individuals with disabilities, to locate the identifying labels in the interface. It also is customary to enter identifying labels using **sentence capitalization**, which means capitalizing only the first letter in the first word and in any words that are customarily capitalized. Change the Text property of the txtSales control's identifying label to **Enter sales:**. Change the Text property of the txtRate control's identifying label to **Enter rate:**.

12. The lblCommission control also needs a label to identify its contents for the user. Add another label control to the form. Position the label control above the lblCommission control, aligning both controls by their left border. Change the Text property to **Commission:**.

13. Save the solution.

14. Next, you will change each button's Text property to a value that indicates the task performed when the button is clicked. The value in a button's Text property appears on the button's face and is often referred to as the button's caption. As with identifying labels, a button's caption should be from one to three words only, with the entire caption appearing on one line. However, unlike identifying labels, a button's caption does not end with a colon and is entered using book title capitalization. With **book title capitalization**, you capitalize the first letter in each word, except for articles, conjunctions, and prepositions that do not occur at either the beginning or the end of the caption. Change the btnCalculate control's Text property to **Calculate Commission**, then drag the button's right and bottom borders until the entire caption is visible.

15. Change the btnExit control's Text property to **Exit**. Drag the button's bottom border until the button is the same height as the btnCalculate control.

16. The lblCommission control should be empty when the user interface appears on the screen. In addition, it is customary to put a border around a label that displays output, and to prevent the label from changing its size while the application is running. Click the **lblCommission** control on the form. Change its AutoSize property to **False**, and change its BorderStyle property to **FixedSingle**. Click **Text** in the Properties list. Press the **Backspace** key on your keyboard, then press **Enter**.

17. Make the lblCommission control slightly taller. Then make it the same width as its identifying label.

18. Lock the controls on the form, then save the solution. Figure 5-5 shows the current status of the interface.

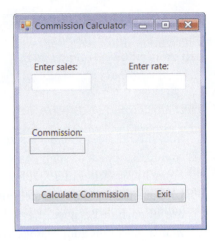

Figure 5-5: Current status of the interface

MAKING THE INTERFACE MORE USER-FRIENDLY

Looking closely at the Visual Studio menu bar shown in Figure 5-6, you will notice that the menu titles contain an underlined letter. The underlined letter is called an **access key**, and it allows the user to select a menu using the Alt key in combination with a letter or number. For example, you can select the File menu in Visual Studio by pressing Alt+F, because the letter "F" is the File menu's access key. Access keys are not case sensitive; therefore, you can select the File menu by pressing either Alt+F or Alt+f. Depending on your system's settings, the access keys may or may not appear underlined on your screen. If you do not see the underlined access keys, you can display them temporarily by pressing the Alt key. You can subsequently hide them by pressing the Alt key again. To always display access keys, click Start on the Windows Vista taskbar, click Control Panel, then click Appearance and Personalization. In the Ease of Access Center section, click Underline keyboard shortcuts and access keys, then select the Underline keyboard shortcuts and access keys check box. (You may need to scroll down to view the check box.) Click the Save button, then close the Ease of Access Center dialog box. (*To display access keys when using the Classic View in Windows Vista*, click Start, click Control Panel, double-click Ease of Access Center, click Make the keyboard easier to use, select the Underline keyboard shortcuts and access keys check box, click the Save button, then close the dialog box. *To display access keys when using the Category View in Windows XP*, click Start, click Control Panel, click Appearance and Themes, click Display, click the Appearance tab, click the Effects button, deselect the Hide underlined letters for keyboard navigation until I press the Alt key, click OK, then click OK again. Close the Appearance and Themes dialog box. *To display access keys when using the Classic View in Windows XP*, click Start, click Control Panel, double-click Display, click the Appearance tab, click the Effects button, deselect the Hide underlined letters for keyboard navigation until I press the Alt key, click OK, then click OK again. Close the Control Panel dialog box.)

Figure 5-6: Visual Studio menu bar

You should assign an access key to each control (in the interface) that can accept user input. Examples of such controls include text boxes and buttons, because the user can enter information in a text box and also can click a button. The only exceptions to this rule are the OK and Cancel buttons, which are not assigned access keys. Access keys are important because they allow a user to work with the interface even when their mouse becomes inoperative. In addition, some fast typists prefer to use access keys, because the access keys allow them to keep their hands on the keyboard. Finally, access keys are important for people with disabilities that prevent them from working with a mouse. You assign an access key by including an ampersand (&) in the control's caption or identifying label. To assign an access key to a button, you include the ampersand in the button's Text property, which is where a button's caption is stored. To assign an access key to a text box control, you include the ampersand in the Text property of the control's identifying label. (As you will learn later in this section, you also must set the identifying label's TabIndex property to a value that is one number less than the value stored in the text box's TabIndex property.) You enter the ampersand to the immediate left of the character you want to designate as the access key. Each access key in the interface should be unique. The first choice for an access key is the first letter of the caption or identifying label, unless another letter provides a more meaningful association. For example, the letter X typically is the access key for an Exit button, because the letter X provides a more meaningful association than does the letter E. If you can't use the first letter (perhaps because it already is used as the access key for another control) and no other letter provides a more meaningful association, then use a distinctive consonant in the caption or label. The last choices for an access key are a vowel or a number. In the Commission Calculator interface, four controls can accept user input: the two text boxes and the two buttons. Figure 5-7 lists the four controls along with their access keys.

Control name	Access key
txtSales	the first letter s in the Enter sales: identifying label
txtRate	the second letter r in the Enter rate: identifying label
btnCalculate	the first letter C in the Calculate Commission caption
btnExit	the letter x in the Exit caption

Figure 5-7: List of controls and their access keys

To assign access keys to the controls that can accept user input:

1. Change the Text property of the Enter sales: label to **Enter &sales:**, then change the Text property of the Enter rate: label to **Enter &rate:**.

2. Change the btnCalculate control's Text property to **&Calculate Commission**, then change the btnExit control's Text property to **E&xit**. Figure 5-8 shows the access keys in the interface. (If you do not see the access keys, press the Alt key.) Notice that the Commission: label does not have an access key. This is because the label does not identify a control that accepts user input. Instead, it identifies the lblCommission control, whose purpose is simply to show the annual commission after it has been calculated. Users cannot access the lblCommission control while the application is running; therefore, it is inappropriate to assign an access key to the control.

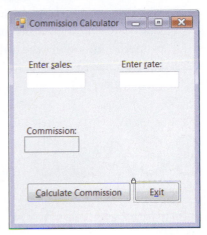

Figure 5-8: Access keys shown in the interface

In addition to assigning access keys for an interface, you also should set the interface's tab order, which is the order in which the controls receive the focus when the user presses either a Tab key or an access key. The tab order is determined by the number stored in each control's **TabIndex property**. When the interface is first created, the TabIndex values reflect the order in which each control was added to the form. The first control added to a form has a TabIndex of 0, the second control a TabIndex of 1, and so on. You can use the Properties window to reset the TabIndex property of each control so that it reflects the desired position of the control in the tab order. However, an easier way is to use the Tab Order option on the View menu. The Tab Order option is available only when the form is selected. When using the Tab Order option, you need to set the TabIndex values in numerical order, beginning with the number 0. If you make a mistake while you are performing the next set of steps, press the Esc key to remove the TabIndex information from the form, then repeat all of the steps.

To set the tab order:

1. Click the **form** to select it. Click **View** on the menu bar, then click **Tab Order**. The numbers in the blue boxes indicate the value stored in each control's TabIndex property, and reflect the order in which the controls were placed on the form. See Figure 5-9.

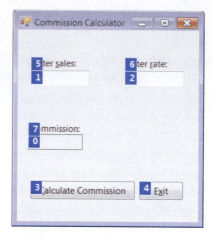

Figure 5-9: Current TabIndex values for the interface

2. Most times, the user will want to enter the sales amount first. So your initial thought might be to change the txtSales control's TabIndex value to 0. However, for a text box's access key to work properly, its identifying label must have a TabIndex value that is one number less than the text box's TabIndex value. Therefore, you will need to set the Label1 control's TabIndex to 0, and the txtSales control's TabIndex to 1. Click the **blue box that appears on top of the Enter sales: label**. The number 0 replaces the current number in the box, and the color of the box changes from blue to white to indicate that you have set the TabIndex for that control. Next, click the **blue box that appears on top of the txtSales control**. See Figure 5-10.

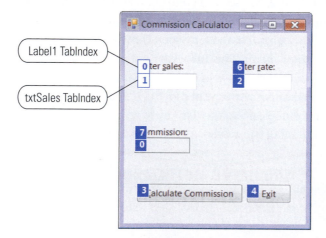

Figure 5-10: TabIndex values for the Label1 and txtSales controls

3. The user will want to enter the rate next. Here again, before setting the txtRate control's TabIndex, you will need to set the TabIndex of its identifying label. Click the **blue box that appears on top of the Enter rate: label**, then click the **blue box that appears on top of the txtRate control**. The white boxes now show TabIndex values of 2 and 3.

4. After entering the input items, the user will probably want to calculate the commission. Therefore, the next control in the tab order should be the Calculate Commission button. Click the **blue box that appears on top of the Calculate Commission button**. The white box indicates that the button's TabIndex is set to 4.

5. The only remaining control that can accept user input is the Exit button. Click the **blue box that appears on top of the Exit button** to set the button's TabIndex to 5.

6. Controls that cannot accept user input (such as the lblCommission control), and those that do not identify controls that accept user input (such as the Label2 control, which shows Commission:) should be placed at the end of the tab order. Click the **blue box that appears on top of the lblCommission control**, then click the **blue box that appears on top of the Commission: label**. When you have finished setting all of the TabIndex values, the color of the boxes will automatically change from white to blue, as shown in Figure 5-11.

Figure 5-11: Correct TabIndex values for the interface

7. Press the **Esc** key to remove the TabIndex boxes from the form, then save the solution.

8. Now test the tab order. Start the application. The insertion point appears in the txtSales text box. The insertion point indicates that the text box has the focus. When a control has the **focus**, it can accept user input. Press the **Tab** key two times. The focus moves to the txtRate control, then to the Calculate Commission button. When a button has the focus, its border is highlighted and a dotted rectangle appears around the caption. Press **Tab** two more times. The focus moves to the Exit button, and then to the txtSales control.

9. For now, test the access keys for the text boxes only. Press **Alt+r** (press and hold down the Alt key as you tap the letter r). The focus moves to the txtRate control. Press **Alt+s** to move the focus to the txtSales control.

10. Click the **Close** button on the form's title bar to close the application.

DO WHAT I TELL YOU TO DO

After creating the interface, you can begin entering the Visual Basic instructions, or **code**, that tell the controls how to respond to the user's actions. Those actions—such as clicking, double-clicking, or scrolling—are called **events**. You tell an object how to respond to an event by writing an **event procedure**, which is simply a set of Visual Basic instructions that are processed when a specific event occurs. In this chapter, you will write a Click event procedure for the Exit button, which should end the application when it is clicked. (You will code the Calculate Commission button in Chapter 6.) You enter an event procedure's code in the **Code Editor window**.

To open the Exit button's Click event procedure in the Code Editor window:

1. Right-click the **form**, then click **View Code** on the context menu. If necessary, maximize the Visual Studio window. The Code Editor window opens in the IDE, as shown in Figure 5-12. The Code Editor window already contains some Visual Basic instructions. It also contains a Class Name list box and a Method Name list box. The Class Name list box lists the names of the objects included in the user interface. The Method Name list box lists the events to which the selected object is capable of responding. You use the list boxes to select the object and event that you want to code.

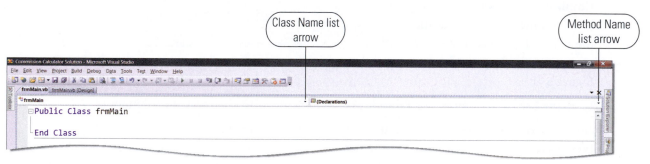

Figure 5-12: Code Editor window

2. Click the **Class Name** list arrow, then click **btnExit** in the list. Click the **Method Name** list arrow, then click **Click** in the list. A code template for the btnExit control's Click event procedure appears in the Code Editor window, as shown in Figure 5-13. The code template helps you follow the rules of the Visual Basic language, called its **syntax**. The first line in the code template is called the **procedure header**, and the last line is called the **procedure footer**.

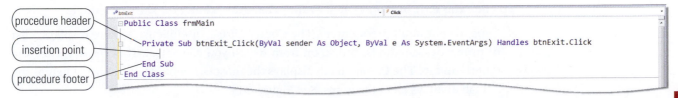

Figure 5-13: Code template for the btnExit control's Click event procedure

The procedure header begins with the two keywords Private Sub. A **keyword** is a word that has a special meaning in a programming language. Keywords appear in a different color from the rest of the code. The Private keyword indicates that the procedure can be used only within the current Code Editor window. The Sub keyword is an abbreviation of the term sub procedure. In programming terminology, a **sub procedure** is a block of code that performs a specific task. Following the Sub keyword is the name of the object, an underscore, the name of the event, and parentheses containing some text. For now, you do not have to be concerned with the text that appears between the parentheses. After the closing parenthesis is Handles btnExit.Click. This part of the procedure header indicates that the procedure handles (or is associated with) the btnExit control's Click event. It tells the computer to process the procedure when the btnExit control is clicked. The code template ends with the procedure footer, which contains the key-words End Sub. You enter your Visual Basic instructions at the location of the insertion point, which appears between the Private Sub and End Sub lines in Figure 5-13. The Code Editor automatically indents the line between the procedure header and footer. Indenting the lines within a procedure makes the instructions easier to read and is a common programming practice. When the user clicks the Exit button, it indicates that he or she wants to end the application. You can use the Me.Close() instruction to accomplish this task.

THE ME.CLOSE() INSTRUCTION

The Me.Close() instruction tells the computer to close the current form. If the current form is the only form in the application, closing it terminates the entire application. In the Me.Close() instruction, Me is a keyword that refers to the current form, and Close is one of the methods available in Visual Basic. A **method** is a predefined procedure that you can call (or invoke) when needed. For example, to close the current form when the user clicks the Exit button, you enter the Me.Close() instruction in the btnExit control's Click event procedure. Notice the empty set of parentheses after the method's name in the instruction. The parentheses are required when calling some Visual Basic methods. However, depending on the method, the parentheses may or may not be empty.

To code the Exit button's Click event procedure, then test the procedure:

1. Type **m** (but don't press Enter). The Code Editor's IntelliSense feature displays a list of properties, methods, and so on from which you can select. If necessary, click the **Common** tab. The Common tab displays the most commonly used items, whereas the All tab displays all of the items. See Figure 5-14.

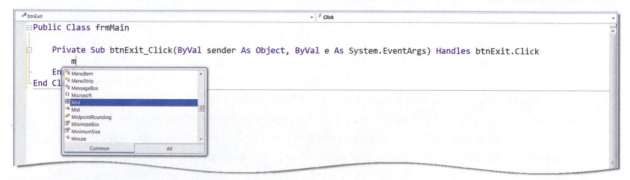

Figure 5-14: List displayed by the IntelliSense feature

Important note: If the list of choices does not appear, the IntelliSense feature may have been turned off on your computer system. To turn it on, click Tools on the menu bar, and then click Options. Expand the Text Editor node in the Options dialog box, and then click Basic. If necessary, select the Show all settings check box, then select the Auto list members check box. Click the OK button to close the Options dialog box.

2. Type **e.cl** to highlight the Close method in the list. Press **Tab** to include the Close method in the instruction, then press **Enter** to complete the instruction. The Code Editor enters the Me.Close() instruction in the procedure, as shown in Figure 5-15.

```
btnExit                                              Click
Public Class frmMain

    Private Sub btnExit_Click(ByVal sender As Object, ByVal e As System.EventArgs) Handles btnExit.Click
        Me.Close()

    End Sub
End Class
```

Figure 5-15: Completed btnExit Click event procedure

3. It's a good programming practice to test a procedure after you have coded it. This way you'll know where to look if an error occurs. Save the solution, then start the application. Click the **Exit** button. The computer processes the Me.Close() instruction contained in the button's Click event procedure, and the application ends.

4. Now test the Exit button's access key. Start the application, then press **Alt+x**. When you employ a button's access key, the computer processes any instructions contained in the button's Click event procedure. In this case, the instruction directs the computer to end the application.

5. Close the Code Editor window, then use the File menu to close the solution.

MINI-QUIZ 2

1. If a text box's TabIndex is set to 7, its identifying label's TabIndex should be set to _____.

2. If a text box's access key is the letter t, you can move the focus to the text box by pressing _____.

   a. Alt+t

   b. Ctrl+t

   c. Esc+t

   d. Shift+t

3. The first line in a procedure is called the _____.

SUMMARY

» You use a problem's input, output, and algorithm when designing the solution's interface.

» Text boxes provide an area for the user to enter data.

» Buttons are used to perform an action when clicked.

» Output items typically appear in label controls so that their values cannot be edited by the user.

» Object names in Hungarian notation begin with an ID that identifies the object's type. The rest of the name identifies the object's purpose. Object names are entered using camel case.

» Form names begin with frm. Button names begin with btn. Label names begin with lbl. Text box names begin with txt.

» Identifying labels and button captions should be from one to three words, with the entire label or caption appearing on one line. Identifying labels should end with a colon and be entered using sentence capitalization. Button captions should be entered using book title capitalization.

» To prevent a label from changing its size while the application is running, change its AutoSize property to False.

» A label's BorderStyle property determines whether the label has a border.

» You should assign an access key to each control that can accept user input.

» An interface's tab order is determined by the number stored in each control's TabIndex property.

» When an event occurs on an object, the computer processes any instructions contained in the associated event procedure.

» Event procedures, which are procedures that tell an object how to respond to an event, are entered in the Code Editor window.

» The Handles part of a procedure header indicates the object and event associated with the procedure.

» You can use the Me.Close() instruction to end an application.

KEY TERMS

Access key—the underlined character in an object's identifying label or caption; allows the user to select the object using the Alt key in combination with the underlined character

Book title capitalization—refers to capitalizing the first letter in each word, except for articles, conjunctions, and prepositions that do not occur at either the beginning or the end of the caption; button captions used this capitalization

Camel case—the case used to enter control names in Hungarian notation; using camel case, you lowercase the control's ID and then uppercase the first letter of each word in the name

Code—Visual Basic instructions

Code Editor window—the window in which you enter your Visual Basic instructions (code)

Event procedure—a set of Visual Basic instructions that tells an object how to respond to an event

Events—actions to which an object can respond; examples include clicking, double-clicking, and scrolling

Focus—when a control has the focus, it can accept user input

Keyword—a word that has a special meaning in a programming language

Method—a predefined procedure that you can call (invoke) when needed

Procedure footer—the last line in a procedure

Procedure header—the first line in a procedure

Sentence capitalization—refers to capitalizing only the first letter in the first word and in any words that are customarily capitalized; identifying labels use this capitalization

Sub procedure—a block of code that performs a specific task

Syntax—the rules of a programming language

TabIndex property—determines the position of a control in the tab order

ANSWERS TO MINI-QUIZZES

MINI-QUIZ 1

1. label

2. txtCity

3. btn

MINI-QUIZ 2

1. 6

2. a. Alt+t

3. procedure header

REVIEW QUESTIONS

1. To give the user control over when (and if) a task is performed, assign the task to a _____ control in the interface.

   a. button   b. label

   c. picture box   d. text box

2. Which of the following designates the letter Z as an access key?

    a. @ZIP code: b. &ZIP code:

    c. ˆZIP code: d. #ZIP code:

3. The computer processes a button's Click event procedure when the user _____.

    a. clicks the button

    b. employs the button's access key

    c. tabs to the button, and then presses the Enter key

    d. All of the above.

4. Which of the following appears in a procedure header and associates the procedure with the btnSave control's Click event?

    a. Handles btnSave.Click

    b. Handles Click.btnSave

    c. Header btnSave.Click

    d. Event Click.btnSave

5. Which of the following tells the computer to stop an application?

    a. Close.Me()   b. Me.Close()

    c. Me.End()   d. Me.Stop()

EXERCISES

»TRY THIS

1. In this exercise, you create an interface for the Aiden Turner problem from Chapter 3. (The answers to TRY THIS Exercises are located at the end of the chapter.)

    a. Create a new Visual Basic Windows application. Assign the name New Pay Project to the project. Assign the name New Pay Solution to the solution. Save the application in the ClearlyVB\Chap05 folder.

    b. Change the name of the form file on your disk to frmMain.vb. If necessary, change the form's name to frmMain.

    c. Create an appropriate interface using the information shown in Figure 5-16. Also include an Exit button. Be sure to assign names to the appropriate controls. Also be sure to assign access keys and set the tab order.

Output: new weekly pay

Input: current weekly pay
          raise percentage

Algorithm:
1. enter the current weekly pay and raise percentage
2. calculate the new weekly pay by multiplying the current weekly pay by the raise percentage,
    and then adding the result to the current weekly pay
3. display the new weekly pay

Figure 5-16

   d. Code the Exit button's Click event procedure so that it ends the application. You will code the algorithm in Chapter 6's Exercise 1.

   e. Save and then start the application. Test the interface's tab order and its access keys.

   f. Use the Exit button to stop the application, then use the File menu to close the solution.

2. In this exercise, you modify the New Pay interface created in Exercise 1.

»**MODIFY THIS**

   a. Use Windows to make a copy of the New Pay Solution folder. Save the copy in the ClearlyVB\Chap05 folder. Rename the copy Modified New Pay Solution.

   b. Open the New Pay Solution (New Pay Solution.sln) file contained in the Modified New Pay Solution folder. In addition to calculating and displaying the new weekly pay, Aiden Turner would now like to calculate and display his weekly raise. Modify the interface to include a label for showing the weekly raise. Be sure to also include an identifying label.

   c. Save and then start the application. Click the Exit button to stop the application, then close the solution.

3. In this exercise, you create an interface for an application that calculates a 10%, 15%, and 20% tip on a restaurant bill.

»**INTRODUCTORY**

   a. Create a new Visual Basic Windows application. Assign the name Tip Project to the project. Assign the name Tip Solution to the solution. Save the application in the ClearlyVB\Chap05 folder.

   b. Change the name of the form file on your disk to frmMain.vb. If necessary, change the form's name to frmMain.

   c. Create an appropriate interface using the information shown in Figure 5-17. Also include an Exit button. Be sure to assign names to the appropriate controls. Also be sure to assign access keys and set the tab order.

```
Output:   10% tip
          15% tip
          20% tip

Input:    restaurant bill

Algorithm:
1.  enter the restaurant bill
2.  calculate a 10% tip by multiplying the restaurant bill by 10%
3.  calculate a 15% tip by multiplying the restaurant bill by 15%
4.  calculate a 20% tip by multiplying the restaurant bill by 20%
5.  display the 10% tip, 15% tip, and 20% tip
```

Figure 5-17

    d. Code the Exit button's Click event procedure so that it ends the application. You will code the algorithm in Chapter 6's Exercise 4.

    e. Save and then start the application. Test the interface's tab order and its access keys.

    f. Use the Exit button to stop the application, then close the solution.

▶▶ INTERMEDIATE

4. In this exercise, you create an interface that calculates an annual property tax. Currently, the property tax rate is $1.02 for each $100 of a property's assessed value. However, the tax rate changes each year.

    a. Complete the algorithm shown in Figure 5-18.

```
Output:   annual property tax

Input:    assessed value
          property tax rate

Algorithm:
1.  enter _____
2.  calculate _____
3.  display _____
```

Figure 5-18

    b. Create a new Visual Basic Windows application. Assign the name Property Tax Project to the project. Assign the name Property Tax Solution to the solution. Save the application in the ClearlyVB\Chap05 folder.

    c. Change the name of the form file on your disk to frmMain.vb. If necessary, change the form's name to frmMain.

    d. Create an appropriate interface using the information from Figure 5-18. Also include an Exit button. Be sure to assign names to the appropriate controls. Also be sure to assign access keys and set the tab order.

e. Code the Exit button's Click event procedure so that it ends the application. You will code the algorithm in Chapter 6's Exercise 6.

f. Save and then start the application. Test the interface's tab order and its access keys.

g. Use the Exit button to stop the application, then close the solution.

5. In this exercise, you create an interface for RM Sales. The company divides its sales territory into four regions: North, South, East, and West. The sales manager wants an application in which he can enter each region's sales amount. The application should calculate and display the total sales, as well as the percentage of sales attributed to each region. For example, if the user enters the numbers 4000, 2000, 1000, and 3000 as the North, South, East, and West regions' sales amounts, then the total sales amount is $10000. Forty percent of the sales come from the North region, twenty percent from the South region, and so on.

»ADVANCED

a. List the output and input items, then create an appropriate algorithm.

b. Create a new Visual Basic Windows application. Assign the name Sales Project to the project. Assign the name Sales Solution to the solution. Save the application in the ClearlyVB\Chap05 folder.

c. Change the name of the form file on your disk to frmMain.vb. If necessary, change the form's name to frmMain.

d. Create an appropriate interface. Include an Exit button. Be sure to assign names to the appropriate controls. Also be sure to assign access keys and set the tab order.

e. Code the Exit button's Click event procedure so that it ends the application. You will code the algorithm in Chapter 6's Exercise 9.

f. Save and then start the application. Test the interface's tab order and its access keys.

g. Use the Exit button to stop the application, then close the solution.

6. In this exercise, you find an error in an application's code. Open the SwatTheBugs Solution (SwatTheBugs Solution.sln) file, which is contained in the ClearlyVB\Chap05\SwatTheBugs Solution folder. Start the application, then click the Exit button. Notice that the Exit button does not end the application. Locate and correct the error. (Hint: Look closely at the procedure header in the Exit button's Click event procedure.)

ANSWER TO "TRY THIS" EXERCISE

1. View the Ch05-New Pay video.

6

THE SECRET CODE

After studying Chapter 6, you should be able to:

Include a comment in the Code Editor window

Use the Val function to convert text to a number

Write expressions containing arithmetic operators

Write an assignment statement

THE FUN STARTS HERE

You completed the Addison Smith problem's interface in Chapter 5. You also coded the Exit button's Click event procedure. Now it's time to code the problem's algorithm. As you learned in Chapter 3, coding the algorithm is the fifth step in the problem-solving process. For most programmers, this is the most rewarding step, because this is where they give life to the interface. At the end of this step, the interface will change from one that the user can simply look at to one with which the user can interact. Figure 6-1 shows the Addison Smith problem's interface, and Figure 6-2 shows the problem's output, input, and algorithm.

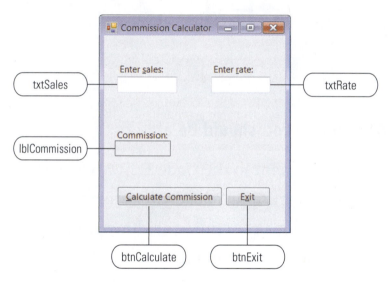

Figure 6-1: Addison Smith problem's interface

```
Output:    annual commission

Input:     annual sales
           commission rate

Algorithm:
1.  enter the annual sales and commission rate
2.  calculate the annual commission by multiplying the annual sales by the commission rate
3.  display the annual commission
```

Figure 6-2: Addison Smith problem's output, input, and algorithm

Step 1 in the algorithm is to enter the annual sales and commission rate. The user will enter the values in the two text boxes in the interface. A text box is designed to accept information from the user, and it automatically stores the information in its Text property. Therefore, no special coding is necessary for Step 1. Steps 2 and 3 are to calculate and display the annual commission. Recall that you assigned the tasks in these steps to the Calculate Commission button. The tasks should be performed when the user clicks the button. Obviously, the Calculate Commission button needs you to tell it *how* to calculate the annual commission, as well as *where* to display the calculated result, when the Click event occurs. You do this by coding the button's Click event procedure.

Before you begin coding the Calculate Commission button, you may want to view the Ch06-Commission Calculator video. The video demonstrates all of the steps contained in this chapter. You may find it helpful to view the steps before you perform them.

To open the Calculate Commission button's Click event procedure:

1. Start Visual Studio 2008 (or Visual Basic 2008 Express Edition). Open the **Commission Calculator Solution** (**Commission Calculator Solution.sln**) file, which is contained in the ClearlyVB\Chap06\Commission Calculator Solution folder. If the designer window is not open, double-click **frmMain.vb** in the Solution Explorer window.

2. Right-click the **form**, then click **View Code** on the context menu. If necessary, maximize the Visual Studio window. The Code Editor window contains the btnExit control's Click event procedure, which you coded in Chapter 5.

3. Use the Class Name and Method Name list arrows to open the code template for the btnCalculate control's Click event procedure.

It's a common programming practice to include one or more comments in a procedure. A **comment** is a message to the person reading the code and is referred to as **internal documentation**. Many programmers use comments to document a procedure's purpose, as well as to explain various sections of the procedure's code. Comments make the code more readable and easier to understand by anyone viewing it. You create a comment in Visual Basic by placing an apostrophe (') before the text that represents the comment. The computer ignores everything that appears after the apostrophe on that line. Although it is not required, some programmers use a space to separate the apostrophe from the comment itself, and they follow the comment with a blank line.

To internally document the btnCalculate Click event procedure:

1. Type **' calculates and displays the annual commission** (notice the space after the apostrophe).

2. Press **Enter** twice. See Figure 6-3.

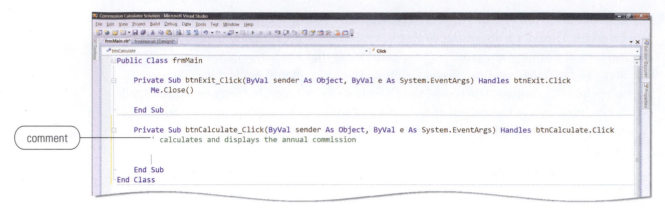

Figure 6-3: Comment entered in the procedure

First you need to tell the procedure *how* to calculate the annual commission. According to the algorithm, the annual commission is calculated by multiplying the annual sales by the commission rate. The annual sales and commission rate are stored in the Text property of the txtSales and txtRate controls, respectively. However, before you can use the Text property value in a calculation, you need to convert the value to a number. One way to do this is by using the Visual Basic Val function.

THE VAL FUNCTION

The characters entered in a text box can be numbers, letters, or special characters (such as the dollar sign, comma, or percent sign). Because of this, the value stored in a control's Text property is always treated as alphanumeric text, even when the value contains only numbers. For example, the computer treats a Text property value of 589 as three separate characters (a 5, an 8, and a 9) rather than as the number 589 (five hundred and eighty-nine). As a result, before you can use the Text property in a calculation, you must convert its alphanumeric value to a number. Visual Basic provides several ways of performing the conversion. In this chapter (and only in this chapter), you will use the Val function to convert text to numbers, because it is the easiest to learn.

A **function** is a predefined procedure that performs a specific task and then returns a value after completing the task. The **Val function**, for instance, temporarily converts one or more characters to a number, and then returns the number. (The number is stored in the computer's internal memory only while the function is processing.) The syntax of the Val function is **Val(***text***)**, where *text* is the characters you want treated as a number. The item within parentheses in the syntax is called an **argument**, and it represents information that is passed to the function while the function is processing. To temporarily convert the Text property of the txtSales control to a number, you use txtSales.Text as the *text* argument, like this:

Val(txtSales.Text). For the *text* argument to be converted to a number, it must contain only numbers and an optional period; it cannot contain a letter or a special character. When an invalid character is encountered in the *text* argument, the Val function stops the conversion process at that point. Figure 6-4 shows the numbers returned by the Val(txtSales.Text) function, using various Text property values. Notice that the function returns the number 0 when the txtSales control is empty. It also returns the number 0 when the first character in the *text* argument is invalid. However, when the invalid character occurs after the first character, the function returns the numbers previous to the invalid one.

txtSales.Text value	Number returned by the Val(txtSales.Text) function
456	456
24,500	24
$56.88	0
Abc	0
Empty text box	0

Figure 6-4: Examples of the Val function

As mentioned earlier, you can convert the txtSales control's Text property to a number using the Val(txtSales.Text) function. Likewise, you can convert the txtRate control's Text property to a number using Val(txtRate.Text). To calculate the annual commission, you multiply the sales number by the rate number. You perform the calculation using an arithmetic expression, which is an expression that contains one or more arithmetic operators.

WHO'S IN CHARGE OF THIS OPERATION?

Most programs require the computer to perform one or more calculations. You instruct the computer to perform a calculation by writing an arithmetic expression that contains one or more arithmetic operators. Figure 6-5 lists the most commonly used arithmetic operators available in Visual Basic, along with their precedence numbers. The precedence numbers indicate the order in which the computer performs the operation in an expression. Operations with a precedence number of 1 are performed before operations with a precedence number of 2, which are performed before operations with a precedence number of 3, and so on. However, you can use parentheses to override the order of precedence, because operations within parentheses always are performed before operations outside of parentheses.

Operator	Operation	Precedence number
^	exponentiation (raises a number to a power)	1
−	negation (reverses the sign of a number)	2
*, /	multiplication and division	3
\	integer division	4
Mod	modulus	5
+, −	addition and subtraction	6

Figure 6-5: Most commonly used arithmetic operators and their order of precedence

Some of the operators in Figure 6-5 have the same precedence number. For example, both the addition and subtraction operators have a precedence number of 6. When an expression contains more than one operator having the same priority, those operators are evaluated from left to right. In the expression 5 + 12 / 3 − 1, for instance, the division is performed first, then the addition, and then the subtraction. The result of the expression is the number 8, as illustrated in Figure 6-6. You can use parentheses to change the order in which the operators in an expression are evaluated. For example, the expression 5 + 12 / (3 − 1) evaluates to 11 rather than to 8, as illustrated in Figure 6-6. This is because the parentheses tell the computer to perform the subtraction operation first.

Original expression	5 + 12 / 3 − 1
The division is performed first	5 + 4 − 1
The addition is performed next	9 − 1
The subtraction is performed last	8 ─── result
Original expression	5 + 12 / (3 − 1)
The subtraction is performed first	5 + 12 / 2
The division is performed next	5 + 6
The addition is performed last	11 ─── result

Figure 6-6: Examples showing how expressions are evaluated

Two of the arithmetic operators in Figure 6-5 might be less familiar to you: the integer division operator (\) and the modulus operator (Mod). You use the **integer division operator** (\) to divide two integers (whole numbers), and then return the result as an integer. For example, the expression 211 \ 4 results in 52, which is the integer result of dividing 211 by 4. (If you use the standard division operator [/] to divide 211 by 4, the result is 52.75 rather than 52.) You might use the integer division operator in a program that determines the number of quarters, dimes, and nickels to return as change to a customer. For instance, if a customer should receive 53 cents in change, you could use the expression 53 \ 25 to determine the number of quarters to return; the expression evaluates to 2.

The modulus operator also is used to divide two numbers, but the numbers do not have to be integers; in other words, the numbers may contain a decimal place. After dividing the numbers, the **modulus operator** returns the remainder of the division. For instance, 211 Mod 4 equals 3, which is the remainder of 211 divided by 4. You can use the modulus operator to determine whether a number is even or odd. If you divide the number by 2 and the remainder is 0, the number is even; if the remainder is 1, however, the number is odd. Figure 6-7 shows examples of using arithmetic operators in expressions.

Expression	Result
2 ^ 3	8
4 * −3	−12
25 / 4	6.25
25 \ 4	6
25 Mod 4	1
7 + 6 * (5 − 2)	25

Figure 6-7: Expressions containing arithmetic operators

For more examples of using arithmetic operators, see the Arithmetic Operators section in the Ch6WantMore.pdf file.

Recall that you need to tell the btnCalculate control's Click event procedure *how* to calculate the annual commission. You can do this using the expression Val(txtSales.Text) * Val(txtRate.Text). You also need to tell the procedure *where* to display the result of the calculation. In this case, you want to display the result in the lblCommission control. To display the annual commission in the label control, you need to assign it to the control's Text property; you can accomplish this using an assignment statement, which you learn about next.

MINI-QUIZ 1

1. Write an expression to add the number 100 to the contents of the lblTotal control.

2. If the user enters $67.45 in the txtTax control, the Val(txtTax.Text) function will return the number _____.

3. If the user enters 23 in the txtTotal control, the Val(txtTotal.Text) Mod 2 expression evaluates to the number _____.

YOUR ASSIGNMENT, IF YOU CHOOSE TO ACCEPT IT

An **assignment statement** is used to assign a value to something (such as the property of a control) while an application is running. The syntax of an assignment statement is *destination = value*, where *destination* is where you want to assign (or store) the *value*. The *value* can be anything, such as numbers, letters, special characters, the property of a control, or an expression. To assign the result of the annual commission calculation to the Text property of the lblCommission control, you use lblCommission.Text as the *destination*, and the expression Val(txtSales.Text) * Val(txtRate.Text) as the *value*. The appropriate assignment statement looks like this: lblCommission.Text = Val(txtSales.Text) * Val(txtRate.Text). The equal sign in an assignment statement is referred to as the **assignment operator**. When the computer processes the assignment statement, it first performs the calculation that appears on the right side of the assignment operator. It then assigns the result of the calculation to the location that appears on the left side of the assignment operator. You can type the assignment statement into the procedure on your own; or you can use the IntelliSense feature that is built into the Code Editor. You learned about the IntelliSense feature in Chapter 5.

To code the btnCalculate control's Click event procedure, then test the procedure:

1. *If you want to type the assignment statement on your own*, type **lblCommission.text = val(txtSales.text) * val(txtRate.text)** and press **Enter**. See Figure 6-8.

   If you want to use the IntelliSense feature, type **lbl** to highlight lblCommission in the list. Now you can either press the Tab key on your keyboard to enter lblCommission in the procedure, or you can press the character that follows lblCommission in the assignment statement. In this case, the next character is the period. Type **.** (a period). The IntelliSense feature highlights the Text property in the list. (If Text is not highlighted, type the letters **te**.) Here again, you can either press the Tab key or type the next character (which is the equal sign) in the assignment statement. Type **=** (an equal sign) to include the Text property in the statement, then type **va** to highlight the Val function in the list. Type **(txts** to highlight txtSales in the list, then type **.** (a period). The Text property should be highlighted in the list. (If Text is not highlighted, type the letters **te**.) This time, press **Tab** to include the Text property in the statement, then type **)*va** to highlight the Val function in the list. Type **(txt** to highlight txtRate in the list, then type **.** (a period). The Text property should be highlighted in the list. Press **Tab**, then type **)** and press **Enter**. See Figure 6-8.

assignment
statement

```
Private Sub btnCalculate_Click(ByVal sender As Object, ByVal e As System.EventArgs) Handles btnCalculate.Click
    ' calculates and displays the annual commission

    lblCommission.Text = Val(txtSales.Text) * Val(txtRate.Text)

End Sub
```

Figure 6-8: Assignment statement entered in the procedure

2. Now test the procedure to verify that it is working correctly. Save the solution, then start the application. First, you will use a sales amount of 2000 and a commission rate of 10%. Type **2000** as the sales amount, press **Tab**, then type **.1** as the commission rate. Click the **Calculate Commission** button. The button's Click event procedure calculates and displays the annual commission, as shown in Figure 6-9.

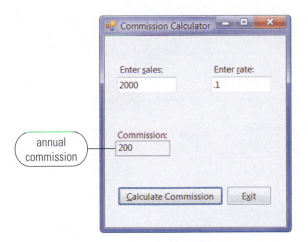

annual
commission

Figure 6-9: Annual commission shown in the interface

3. On your own, test the application using different sales and rates. Also test the application when one or both text boxes are empty.

4. When you are finished testing the application, click the **Exit** button.

Before closing the solution, you will add a few more comments in the Code Editor window. The comments will document the project's name and purpose, as well as your name and the date the project was either created or modified.

To enter additional comments in the Code Editor window:

1. Position the insertion point at the beginning of the Public Class frmMain instruction, then press **Enter** to insert a blank line above the instruction.

2. Press the **up arrow** on your keyboard to move the insertion point into the blank line. As the Class Name and Method Name list boxes indicate, the area above the Public Class line is called the **General Declarations section**.

3. Type the comments indicated in Figure 6-10; however, replace the <your name> and <current date> text with your name and the current date.

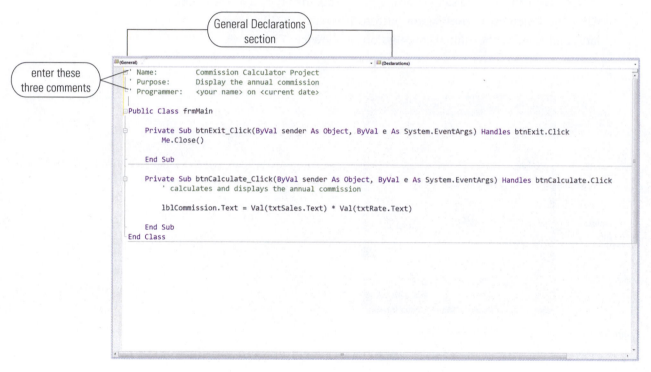

Figure 6-10: Additional comments entered in the Code Editor window

4. Save the solution. Close the Code Editor window, then close the solution.

MINI-QUIZ 2

1. Write an assignment statement that assigns the result of the Val(txtHours.Text) * Val(txtRate.Text) expression to the lblGross control.

2. Write an assignment statement that assigns, to the lblNewPrice control, the result of adding the number 5 to the contents of the txtOldPrice control.

3. The equal sign in an assignment statement is called the _____.

4. The area above the Public Class line in the Code Editor window is called the _____.

SUMMARY

» The fifth step in the problem-solving process is to code the problem's algorithm.

» When you want a procedure to make a calculation, you need to tell it how to make the calculation and where to store the result.

» You use comments to internally document a project's code. A comment begins with an apostrophe.

» The Val function temporarily converts one or more characters to a number, and then returns the number.

» You instruct a computer to perform a calculation by writing an expression that contains one or more arithmetic operators.

» Arithmetic operators having the same precedence number are evaluated from left to right in an expression.

» You can use parentheses to override the order of precedence for arithmetic operators.

» You use an assignment statement to assign a value to something while an application is running.

» When an assignment statement contains a calculation, the calculation is performed before the resulting value is assigned to its destination.

KEY TERMS

Argument—appears within parentheses after a function's name; represents information that the function uses when it is processing

Assignment operator—the equal sign in an assignment statement

Assignment statement—used in a program to assign a value to a destination (such as the property of a control)

Comment—a message entered in the Code Editor window for the purpose of internally documenting the code; begins with an apostrophe; also referred to as internal documentation

Function—a predefined procedure that performs a specific task and then returns a value after completing the task

General Declarations section—the area above the Public Class line in the Code Editor window

Integer division operator—one of the arithmetic operators; represented by the back-slash (\); returns the integer result of dividing two integers

Internal documentation—the comments entered in the Code Editor window

Modulus operator—one of the arithmetic operators; represented by the keyword Mod; divides two numbers and then returns the remainder

Val function—temporarily converts one or more characters to a number, and then returns the number

ANSWERS TO MINI-QUIZZES

MINI-QUIZ 1
1. Val(lblTotal.Text) + 100

2. 0

3. 1

MINI-QUIZ 2
1. lblGross.Text = Val(txtHours.Text) * Val(txtRate.Text)

2. lblNewPrice.Text = Val(txtOldPrice.Text) + 5

3. assignment operator

4. General Declarations section

REVIEW QUESTIONS

1. Comments in Visual Basic begin with _____.

   a. ' (apostrophe)   b. * (asterisk)

   c. ^ (caret)   d. None of the above.

2. If the user enters $5 in the txtPrice control and enters 3 in the txtQuantity control, the Val(txtPrice.Text) * Val(txtQuantity.Text) expression will evaluate to _____.

   a. 0   b. 3

   c. 15   d. None of the above.

3. If the user enters 75 in the txtNum control, which of the following changes the control's contents to –75 (a negative 75)?

   a. -txtNum.Text = Val(txtNum.Text)

   b. -txtNum.Text = txtNum.Text

   c. txtNum.Text = -Val(txtNum.Text)

   d. None of the above.

4. If the txtNum control contains the value 82, which of the following expressions evaluates to the number 4?

   a. (Val(txtNum.Text) + 6) / 22

   b. Val(txtNum.Text) Mod 6

   c. Val(txtNum.Text) \ 20

   d. All of the above.

5. The expression in which of the following assignment statements will not calculate correctly.

   a. lblTotal.Text = Val(txtSales1.Text) + Val(txtSales2.Text)

   b. lblTotal.Text = Val(txtSales1.Text + txtSales2.Text)

   c. lblTotal.Text = Val(txtRed.Text) * 2

   d. lblTotal.Text = Val(txtBlue.Text) * 1.1

EXERCISES

» TRY THIS

1. In this exercise, you code the Aiden Turner problem's algorithm from Chapter 3. You created the problem's interface in Chapter 5's TRY THIS exercise. (The answers to TRY THIS Exercises are located at the end of the chapter.)

   a. If you completed the TRY THIS exercise from Chapter 5, use Windows to copy the New Pay Solution folder from the ClearlyVB\Chap05 folder to the ClearlyVB\ Chap06 folder. If you did not complete Chapter 5's TRY THIS exercise, use Windows to change the name of the Chap06 New Pay Solution folder, which is contained in the ClearlyVB\Chap06 folder, to New Pay Solution.

   b. Open the New Pay Solution (New Pay Solution.sln) file contained in the ClearlyVB\Chap06\New Pay Solution folder. If necessary, open the designer window. Figure 6-11 shows the problem's output, input, and algorithm. Complete the application by coding its algorithm. The calculation instruction will be fairly long. You can use the line continuation character, which is the underscore (_), to break up a long instruction into two or more physical lines in the Code Editor window. Breaking up an instruction in this manner makes the instruction easier to read and understand. The line continuation character must be immediately preceded by a space, and it must appear at the end of a physical line of code. For example, to enter the assignment statement shown earlier in Figure 6-8 on two lines, you could type lblCommission.text = _ on the first line, being sure to include a space before the line continuation character. You then would press the Enter key to move the insertion point to the next line, where you would type the remainder of the assignment statement.

   Output: new weekly pay

   Input: current weekly pay
             raise percentage

   Algorithm:
   1. enter the current weekly pay and raise percentage
   2. calculate the new weekly pay by multiplying the current weekly pay by the raise percentage, and then adding the result to the current weekly pay
   3. display the new weekly pay

Figure 6-11

   c. Include comments in the Code Editor window. Save and then start the application. Test the application using various values for the current weekly pay and raise percentage. When you are finished testing the application, use the Exit button to stop the application, then use the File menu to close the solution.

2. In this exercise, you modify the Commission Calculator application created in the chapter.   **»MODIFY THIS**

   a. Use Windows to make a copy of the Commission Calculator Solution folder. Save the copy in the ClearlyVB\Chap06 folder. Rename the copy Modified Commission Calculator Solution.

   b. Open the Commission Calculator Solution (Commission Calculator Solution.sln) file contained in the Modified Commission Calculator Solution folder. Open the designer window. Currently, the application is designed to accept the decimal version of the commission rate. For example, if the rate is 6%, the application expects the user to enter .06. Modify the application so that it expects the user to enter the rate as a whole number. For example, if the rate is 6%, the user should enter 6. First, change the Enter rate: label to Enter % rate:. Next, modify the Calculate Commission button's code appropriately.

   c. Save and then start the application. Test the application using 2000 as the sales amount and 10 (for 10%) as the commission rate. The annual commission should be 200. Stop the application, then close the solution.

3. In this exercise, you code the Skate-Away Sales application.   **»INTRODUCTORY**

   a. Open the Skate Away Solution (Skate Away Solution.sln) file, which is contained in the ClearlyVB\Chap06\Skate Away Solution folder. If necessary, open the designer window.

   b. The Calculate Order button should calculate and display the total number of skateboards ordered and the total price of the order. Each skateboard costs $100. Code the button's Click event procedure.

   c. Save and then start the application. Test the application to verify that the code is working correctly, then stop the application and close the solution.

4. In this exercise, you finish coding the Tip application from Chapter 5's Exercise 3. If you did not complete Chapter 5's Exercise 3, you will need to do so before you can complete this exercise.   **»INTRODUCTORY**

   a. Use Windows to copy the Tip Solution folder from the ClearlyVB\Chap05 folder to the ClearlyVB\Chap06 folder.

   b. Open the Tip Solution (Tip Solution.sln) file contained in the ClearlyVB\Chap06\Tip Solution folder. If necessary, open the designer window. Figure 6-12 shows the problem's output, input, and algorithm. Complete the application by coding its algorithm. Include comments in the Code Editor window.

Output: 10% tip
          15% tip
          20% tip

Input: restaurant bill

Algorithm:
1. enter the restaurant bill
2. calculate a 10% tip by multiplying the restaurant bill by 10%
3. calculate a 15% tip by multiplying the restaurant bill by 15%
4. calculate a 20% tip by multiplying the restaurant bill by 20%
5. display the 10% tip, 15% tip, and 20% tip

Figure 6-12

c. Save and then start the application. Test the application to verify that the code is working correctly, then stop the application and close the solution.

»INTERMEDIATE

5. In this exercise, you create an application for the Vans & More Depot, which rents vans for company outings. Each van can transport 10 people. The application should allow the user to enter the number of people attending the outing. The application should calculate and display the number of vans that can be filled completely. It also should calculate and display the number of people who will need to find another way to get to the outing. For example, if 48 people are attending the outing, 40 of them will fit into four vans; the remaining eight people will need to arrange for their own transportation. The output for this problem is the number of vans that can be filled completely, and the number of people remaining. The input is the number of people attending the outing.

a. Write the problem's algorithm.

b. Create a new Visual Basic Windows application. Assign the name Vans Project to the project. Assign the name Vans Solution to the solution. Save the application in the ClearlyVB\Chap06 folder.

c. Change the name of the form file on your disk to frmMain.vb. If necessary, change the form's name to frmMain.

d. Create an appropriate interface. Also include an Exit button.

e. Code the Exit button's Click event procedure and the algorithm. Be sure to include comments.

f. Save and then start the application. Test the application to verify that the code is working correctly, then stop the application and close the solution.

»INTERMEDIATE

6. In this exercise, you finish coding the Property Tax application from Chapter 5's Exercise 4. If you did not complete Chapter 5's Exercise 4, you will need to do so before you can complete this exercise.

a. Use Windows to copy the Property Tax Solution folder from the ClearlyVB\Chap05 folder to the ClearlyVB\Chap06 folder.

b. Open the Property Tax Solution (Property Tax Solution.sln) file contained in the ClearlyVB\Chap06\Property Tax Solution folder. Open the designer window.

c. Code the problem's algorithm. Use comments to internally document the code.

d. Save and then start the application. Test the application to verify that the code is working correctly. (Using 104000 and 1.02, the tax is 1060.8.) Stop the application and close the solution.

7. In this exercise, you modify the application that you created in Exercise 5. In addition to renting vans, Vans & More Depot also rents cars. Each van can transport 10 people, and each car can transport five people. The modified application should calculate three values: the number of vans that can be filled, the number of cars that can be filled, and the number of people who will need to arrange other means of transportation. As an example, if 48 people are attending the outing, the company will need to rent four vans (to transport 40 people) and one car (to transport five people). The remaining three people will need to arrange for their own transportation.

   »ADVANCED

a. Use Windows to make a copy of the Vans Solution folder. Save the copy in the ClearlyVB\Chap06 folder. Rename the copy Modified Vans Solution.

b. Open the Vans Solution (Vans Solution.sln) file contained in the Modified Vans Solution folder. Make the appropriate modifications to the interface and code.

c. Save and then start the application. Test the application to verify that the code is working correctly, then stop the application and close the solution.

8. In this exercise, you create an application for Sun Projects. The company's payroll clerk wants an application that computes an employee's net pay. The clerk will enter the employee's name, hours worked, and rate of pay. For this application, you do not have to worry about overtime, because Sun Projects does not allow anyone to work more than 40 hours. The application should calculate and display the gross pay, federal withholding tax (FWT), Social Security tax (FICA), state income tax, and net pay. The FWT is calculated by multiplying the gross pay by 20%. The FICA tax is 8% of the gross pay, and the state income tax is 2% of the gross pay.

   »ADVANCED

a. List the output and input items, then create an appropriate algorithm.

b. Create a new Visual Basic Windows application. Assign the name Sun Project to the project. Assign the name Sun Solution to the solution. Save the application in the ClearlyVB\Chap06 folder.

c. Change the name of the form file on your disk to frmMain.vb. If necessary, change the form's name to frmMain.

d. Create an appropriate interface. Include an Exit button.

e. Code the Exit button's Click event procedure and the problem's algorithm.

f. Save and then start the application. Test the application to verify that the code is working correctly, then stop the application and close the solution.

9. In this exercise, you finish coding the RM Sales application from Chapter 5's Exercise 5. If you did not complete Chapter 5's Exercise 5, you will need to do so before you can complete this exercise.

a. Use Windows to copy the Sales Solution folder from the ClearlyVB\Chap05 folder to the ClearlyVB\Chap06 folder.

b. Open the Sales Solution (Sales Solution.sln) file contained in the ClearlyVB\Chap06\Sales Solution folder. Open the designer window. Code the problem's algorithm. Include appropriate comments.

c. Save and then start the application. Test the application to verify that the code is working correctly, then stop the application and close the solution.

10. A Calculate button's Click event procedure contains the lblDue.Text = Val(txtDaysLate.Text) * 2 + 3.5 statement.

a. If the user enters the number 3 in the txtDaysLate control, what will be assigned to the lblDue control when the user clicks the Calculate button?

b. If the user enters the letters AB in the txtDaysLate control, what will be assigned to the lblDue control when the user clicks the Calculate button?

c. If the txtDaysLate control is empty when the user clicks the Calculate button, what will the button's Click event procedure assign to the lblDue control?

11. In this exercise, you find an error in an application's code. Open the SwatTheBugs Solution (SwatTheBugs Solution.sln) file, which is contained in the ClearlyVB\Chap06\SwatTheBugs Solution folder. Start the application, then test the application. Notice that the code is not working correctly. Locate and correct any errors.

ANSWER TO "TRY THIS" EXERCISE

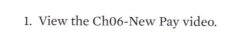

1. View the Ch06-New Pay video.

7

WHERE CAN I STORE THIS?

After studying Chapter 7, you should be able to:

Declare variables and named constants

Convert text to a numeric data type using
    the TryParse method

Understand the scope and lifetime of variables

Desk-check a program

Format a program's numeric output

USING STORAGE BINS

Inside every computer is a component called internal memory. The internal memory of a computer is composed of memory locations. It may be helpful to picture memory locations as storage bins, similar to the ones illustrated in Figure 7-1. However, unlike the storage bins in the figure, each storage bin (memory location) inside a computer can hold only one item of data at a time. The item can be a number, such as 5 or 45.89. It also can be text, which is a group of characters treated as one unit and not used in a calculation. Examples of text include your name, the part number ABN123X, the phone number 111-2345, and the Visual Basic statement Me.Close(). Some of the storage bins (memory locations) inside the computer are automatically filled with data while you use your computer. For example, when you enter the number 5 at your keyboard, the computer saves the number 5 in a memory location for you. Likewise, when you start an application, each program instruction is placed in a memory location, where it awaits processing.

Figure 7-1: Illustration of storage bins

Some of the storage bins (memory locations) inside a computer are special in that they can be reserved by a programmer for use in a program. You reserve a memory location using a Visual Basic instruction that assigns both a name and data type to the memory location. The data type indicates the type of data—for example, numeric or textual—the memory location will store. But why would a programmer need to use one of these special memory locations? In Chapter 6, you calculated Addison Smith's commission using the expression Val(txtSales.Text) * Val(txtRate.Text). Typically, programmers do not use the Text properties of controls in arithmetic expressions. One reason for this is that such expressions can get rather long and difficult to understand. Imagine writing an expression that calculates a value using the Text properties of 10 controls! And then imagine trying to understand the instruction a year after you wrote it! Instead, programmers store the Text property values in special memory locations called variables. The memory locations are called **variables** because their contents can change (vary) as the program is running. The programmer then uses the variable's name, rather than the Text property of its associated control, in the arithmetic expression. Because variable names typically are more concise than control names, using variable names in an expression makes the expression much shorter and easier to understand. Before learning how to reserve a variable in Visual Basic, you will learn how to select an appropriate data type and name for the variable.

SO, WHAT'S YOUR TYPE?

Like storage bins, variables come in different types and sizes. The type and size you use depends on the item you want the variable to store. Some variables can store a number, while others can hold text, a date, or a Boolean value (True or False). The item that a variable will accept for storage is determined by the variable's data type, which the programmer assigns to the variable when it is reserved. In this chapter, you will learn about numeric data types, which are used to reserve variables that will store numbers. The three most commonly used numeric data types available in Visual Basic are listed in Figure 7-2, along with the range of values they can store and the amount of memory needed to store each value. (You will learn about other data types in later chapters in this book. Appendix A in this book contains a complete listing of the Visual Basic data types.)

Data type	Stores	Memory required
Integer	integer Range: -2,147,483,648 to 2,147,483,647	4 bytes

Decimal	a number with a decimal place
	Range with no decimal place:
	    +/-79,228,162,514,264,337,593,543,950,335
	Range with a decimal place:
	    +/-7.9228162514264337593543950335
		16 bytes

Double	a number with a decimal place Range: +/- $4.94065645841247 \times 10^{-324}$ to +/-$1.79769313486231 \times 10^{308}$	8 bytes

Figure 7-2: Most commonly used numeric data types

As the figure indicates, variables assigned the Integer data type can store integers. An integer is a whole number, which is a number that does not contain a decimal place. Examples of integers include the numbers 0, 45, and -678. If the Text property of a control contains a whole number that you want to use in a calculation, you would assign the Text property value to an Integer variable, and then use the Integer variable in the calculation. However, if the Text property contains a number with a decimal place, and you want to use that number in a calculation, you would assign the Text property value to either a Decimal variable or a Double variable. Both data types allow variables to store numbers that have a decimal place. The differences between the two data types are in the range of numbers each type can store and the amount of memory each type needs to store the numbers. As Figure 7-2 indicates, Decimal variables take twice as much room in memory as do Double variables. However, calculations involving Decimal variables are not subject to the small rounding errors that may occur when using Double variables. In most cases, the small rounding errors do not create any problems in an application. One exception, however, is when the application performs financial calculations that require accuracy to the penny. In those cases, the Decimal data type is the best type to use.

LET'S PLAY THE NAME GAME

Every variable that a programmer uses must be assigned a name. The name should be descriptive in that it should help you remember the variable's purpose. In other words, it should describe the contents of the variable. A good variable name is one that is meaningful right after you finish a program, and also years later when you (or perhaps a co-worker) need to modify the program. A variable name must begin with a letter or an underscore. The name can contain only letters, numbers, and the underscore character. No punctuation marks or spaces are allowed in the name. In addition, the name cannot be a reserved word, such as Val. There are several conventions for naming variables in Visual Basic. In this book, you will use Hungarian notation, which is the same naming convention used for controls. Variable names in Hungarian notation begin with a three character ID that represents the variable's data type. The names of Integer variables, for example, begin with int. The remaining characters in the name represent the variable's purpose. Using Hungarian notation, you might assign the name intAge to an Integer variable that stores a person's age. Like control names, variable names are entered using camel case, which means you lowercase the ID and then uppercase the first letter of each word in the name. Figure 7-3 lists the three character ID associated with each data type listed in Figure 7-2. The figure also includes examples of variables names.

Data type	ID	Example
Integer	int	intAge
Decimal	dec	decPayRate
Double	dbl	dblPrice

Figure 7-3: Data type IDs and examples of variable names

YOU'LL NEED A RESERVATION

Now that you know how to select an appropriate name and data type for a variable, you can learn how to reserve a variable for your program to use. Reserving a variable is often referred to as declaring a variable. To declare a variable in an event procedure, where most variables are declared, you use the Visual Basic **Dim statement**. Figure 7-4 shows the Dim statement's syntax. Items in boldface in the syntax are required, while italicized items represent information that the programmer must provide. In the syntax, *variableName* and *dataType* are the name and data type, respectively, you want assigned to a memory location. The computer stores a default value in the variable when it is declared; the default value depends on the variable's data type. Integer, Decimal, and Double variables are automatically initialized to— in other words, given a beginning value of—the number 0. In addition to showing the syntax of the Dim statement, Figure 7-4 also shows several examples of declaring variables.

DECLARING A VARIABLE

<u>Syntax</u>
Dim *variableName* **As** *dataType*

<u>Examples</u>
Dim intAge As Integer
Dim decPayRate As Decimal
Dim dblPrice As Double

Figure 7-4: Syntax and examples of the Dim statement

MINI-QUIZ 1

1. Which of the three data types listed in Figure 7-2 is appropriate for storing the number of desks purchased by a customer?

2. Which of the following is not a valid name for a variable?

   a. decRate

   b. dblRate

   c. decRate_Of_Pay

   d. dblPay.Rate

3. Write a Dim statement to declare a Double variable named dblHoursWorked.

HOW MANY VARIABLES SHOULD I USE?

You use a problem's solution—in other words, its output, processing, and input information and its algorithm—to determine the variables to use when coding the application. Most times, you will use a different variable for each unique output, processing, and input item listed in the solution. The Circle Area problem's solution shown in Figure 7-5 will utilize two different variables: one to store the output item and the other one to store the input item. Looking at the algorithm, you will notice that both items are involved in calculations. The items may contain a decimal place, so you should assign their values to variables of either the Decimal or Double data type. In this case, because the values don't involve money, you'll use the Double data type. Suitable names for the two variables are dblArea and dblRadius.

Output: circle's area

Input: circle's radius

Algorithm:
1. enter the circle's radius
2. calculate the circle's area by multiplying the circle's radius by itself, and then multiplying the result by 3.141593 (which is pi rounded to six decimal places)
3. display the circle's area

Figure 7-5: Circle Area problem's solution

For more examples of using variables, see the Variables section in the Ch7WantMore.pdf file.

Before you begin coding the Circle Area application, you may want to view the Ch07-Circle Area video. The video demonstrates all of the steps contained in this chapter. You may find it helpful to view the steps before you perform them.

To open the Circle Area application, and then begin coding the application:

1. Start Visual Studio 2008 (or Visual Basic 2008 Express Edition). Open the **Circle Area Solution** (**Circle Area Solution.sln**) file, which is contained in the ClearlyVB\Chap07\Circle Area Solution folder. If necessary, open the designer window. The application's interface is shown in Figure 7-6. The user will enter the circle's radius

(the input item) in the txtRadius control. When the user clicks the Calculate button, the button's Click event procedure will use the circle's radius to calculate the circle's area (the output item). As you may remember from your math courses, the formula for calculating the area of a circle is πr^2, where π stands for pi. Before the procedure ends, it will display the circle's area in the lblArea control.

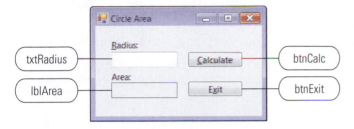

Figure 7-6: Circle Area application's interface

2. Open the Code Editor window, which contains the code for the btnExit control's Click event procedure.

3. Open the btnCalc control's Click event procedure. First, you will enter the instructions to declare the necessary variables. It is customary to enter the variable declaration statements at the beginning of the procedure. Type the comments and two Dim statements indicated in Figure 7-7, then position the insertion point as shown in the figure. The green jagged line below each variable's name indicates that the variable has been declared, but it is not used by any other statement in the procedure.

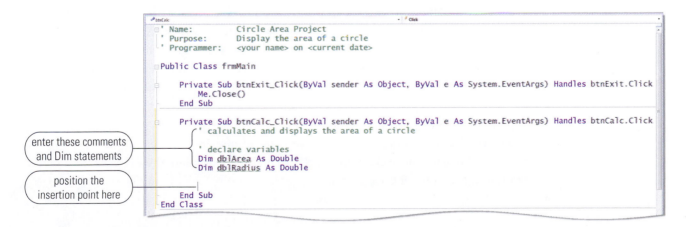

Figure 7-7: Comments and Dim statements entered in the procedure

Now you can begin coding the application's algorithm. The first step in the algorithm is to enter the circle's radius. Recall that the user enters the radius in the txtRadius control. The second step is to calculate the circle's area by multiplying the radius by itself, and then multiplying the result by 3.141593 (the value of pi rounded to six decimal places). Using what you learned in Chapter 6, you could calculate the circle's area using the expression Val(txtRadius.Text) * Val(txtRadius.Text) * 3.141593. The expression tells the computer to multiply the contents of the txtRadius control's Text property (converted temporarily to a number) by the contents of the txtRadius control's Text property (again converted temporarily to a number), and then multiply the result by the number 3.141593. However, although the Val function has been a part of the Visual Basic language since its inception, Microsoft does not guarantee that it will always be a part of the language. As a result, most programmers now use the TryParse method to convert text to numbers.

THE TRYPARSE METHOD

Every numeric data type in Visual Basic has a **TryParse method** that can be used to convert text to that numeric data type. The basic syntax of the TryParse method is *dataType*.**TryParse(***text*, *variable***)**. In the syntax, *dataType* is one of the numeric data types available in Visual Basic, such as Double, Decimal, and Integer. The *text* argument is the text you want converted to a number of the *dataType* type, and typically is the Text property of a control. The *variable* argument is the name of a numeric variable where the TryParse method can store the number. The numeric variable must have the same data type as specified in the *dataType* portion of the syntax. In other words, when using the TryParse method to convert text to a Double number, you need to provide the method with the name of a Double variable in which to store the number. The TryParse method parses the text, which means it looks at each character in the text, to determine whether the text can be converted to a number of the specified data type. If the text can be converted, the TryParse method converts the text to a number and stores the number in the variable specified in the *variable* argument. However, if the TryParse method determines that the text cannot be converted to the appropriate data type, the method assigns the number 0 to the *variable*. Figure 7-8 shows the basic syntax of the TryParse method and includes examples of using the method. (To learn more about the TryParse method, complete the FIGURE THIS OUT Exercise at the end of the chapter.)

THE BASIC SYNTAX OF THE TRYPARSE METHOD

<u>Syntax</u>

dataType.**TryParse(***text*, *variable***)**

<u>Example 1</u>

Double.TryParse(txtRadius.Text, dblRadius)

If the text entered in the txtRadius control can be converted to a Double number, the TryParse method converts the text and stores the result in the dblRadius variable; otherwise, it stores the number 0 in the dblRadius variable.

<u>Example 2</u>

Decimal.TryParse(txtSales.Text, decSales)

If the text entered in the txtSales control can be converted to a Decimal number, the TryParse method converts the text and stores the result in the decSales variable; otherwise, it stores the number 0 in the decSales variable.

<u>Example 3</u>

Integer.TryParse(txtNum.Text, intNum)

If the text entered in the txtNum control can be converted to an Integer number, the TryParse method converts the text and stores the result in the intNum variable; otherwise, it stores the number 0 in the intNum variable.

Figure 7-8: Basic syntax and examples of the TryParse method

Before entering the instruction to calculate the circle's area, you first will use the TryParse method to convert the Text property of the txtRadius control to a number. You will have the method assign the resulting number to the dblRadius variable. You then will use the dblRadius variable in the circle area calculation.

To continue coding the Circle Area application:

1. The insertion point should be positioned as shown earlier in Figure 7-7. Type ' **assign radius to a variable** and press **Enter**, then type **double.tryparse(txtRadius.text, dblRadius)** and press **Enter** twice.

2. Now you can use the dblRadius variable in the expression that calculates the circle's area. You will assign the result of the calculation to the dblArea variable. Type ' **calculate area** and press **Enter**, then type **dblArea = dblRadius * dblRadius * 3.141593** and press **Enter** twice. (You also can use dblArea = dblRadius ^ 2 * 3.141593.)

---

3. Step 3 in the algorithm (shown earlier in Figure 7-5) is to display the circle's area. Type **' display area** and press **Enter**, then type **lblArea.text = dblArea** and press **Enter**. Figure 7-9 shows the procedure's code.

```vbnet
Private Sub btnCalc_Click(ByVal sender As Object, ByVal e As System.EventArgs) Handles btnCalc.Click
    ' calculates and displays the area of a circle

    ' declare variables
    Dim dblArea As Double
    Dim dblRadius As Double

    ' assign radius to a variable
    Double.TryParse(txtRadius.Text, dblRadius)

    ' calculate area
    dblArea = dblRadius * dblRadius * 3.141593

    ' display area
    lblArea.Text = dblArea

End Sub
End Class
```

Figure 7-9: Code entered in the btnCalc control's Click event procedure

4. Save the solution.

Most variables are declared in procedures, such as event procedures. These variables are referred to as **procedure-level variables** and are said to have **procedure scope**, because they can be used only by the procedure in which they are declared. **Scope** refers to the area where a variable is recognized in an application's code. The dblRadius and dblArea variables in Figure 7-9 are procedure-level variables that can be used only by the btnCalc control's Click event procedure. When a procedure ends, its procedure-level variables are removed from the computer's internal memory. Programmers refer to the length of time a variable remains in memory as its **lifetime**. A procedure-level variable has the same lifetime as the procedure in which it is declared.

CHECK, PLEASE...I'M READY TO GO

Before testing the Circle Area application using the computer, which is Step 7 in the problem-solving process from Chapter 3, you will perform Step 6, which is to desk-check the program. You can do this using a desk-check table, similar to one that you use when desk-checking an algorithm. The desk-check table for a program will contain one column for each variable. As an example, you will desk-check the Circle Area program using radius values of 6.5 and 10. Figure 7-10 shows the completed desk-check table. On your own, desk-check the program using other values.

dblRadius	dblArea
~~6.5~~	~~132.73230425~~
10	314.1593

Figure 7-10: Desk-check table for the Circle Area program

To test the Circle Area application using the computer:

1. Start the application. Type **6.5** in the Radius text box, then click the **Calculate** button. See Figure 7-11. The button's Click event procedure tells the computer to reserve two Double variables named dblRadius and dblArea. The TryParse method in the procedure converts the 6.5 entered in the Radius text box to a number, and then stores the number in the dblRadius variable. Next, the computer multiplies the contents of the dblRadius variable by itself, and then multiplies the result by 3.141593. It then stores the result in the dblArea variable. The last statement in the procedure displays the contents of the dblArea variable in the lblArea control. When the procedure ends, the dblRadius and dblArea variables are removed from the computer's internal memory.

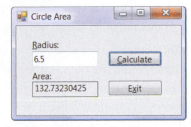

Figure 7-11: Circle's area shown in the interface

2. Change the radius from 6.5 to **10**, then click the **Calculate** button. The circle's area is 314.1593.

3. On your own, test the application using other values for the radius.

4. Click the **Exit** button to stop the application.

USING CONSTANTS TO KEEP THINGS…WELL, THE SAME

In addition to reserving (or declaring) variables in a program, you also can declare named constants. A **named constant** is a memory location whose value cannot change while the application is running. The programmer assigns a value to the named constant when it is declared. It might be helpful to picture a named constant as a locked storage bin that no one but the owner (in this case, the programmer) can open. When a named constant's value needs to be changed, the programmer must change its value in its declaration statement. Programmers use named constants to give names to constant values. After a named constant is created, the programmer then can use the constant's name (rather than its value) in the application's code. For example, rather than using the number 3.141593 in the area calculation statement shown earlier in Figure 7-9, you could assign a name (such as dblPI) to the number, and then use dblPI in the calculation statement. Named constants make code more self-documenting and easier to modify, because they allow a programmer to use meaningful words in place of values that are less clear. The named constant dblPI, for example, is much more meaningful than is the number 3.141593. Using a named constant to represent a value has another advantage: if the value changes in the future, the programmer will need to modify only the named constant's declaration statement, rather than all of the program statements that use the value.

You create a named constant using the **Const statement**. The statement's syntax is shown in Figure 7-12. In the syntax, *constantName* is the name you want assigned to the named constant. To distinguish the named constants from the variables in a program, many programmers use a modified form of Hungarian notation for the named constant names. In the modified notation, the ID characters in the name are still entered in lowercase, but the remaining part of the name is entered in uppercase—for example, dblPI. *DataType* in the syntax is the named constant's data type, and *value* is the value you want stored in the named constant. In addition to showing the Const statement's syntax, Figure 7-12 also shows examples of declaring named constants.

DECLARING A NAMED CONSTANT

Syntax

Const *constantName* **As** *dataType* = *value*

Examples

Const dblPI As Double = 3.141593

Const intMAX_HOURS As Integer = 40

Const decTAXRATE As Decimal = .05

Figure 7-12: Syntax and examples of the Const statement

To declare a named constant in the Circle Area application:

1. Position the insertion point in the blank line above the ' declare variables comment, then press **Enter**. Type **' declare named constant** and press **Enter**, then type **const dblPI as double = 3.141593** and press **Enter**. Like the variables declared in the procedure, the dblPI named constant has procedure scope and will remain in memory until the procedure ends.

2. Replace the 3.141593 in the statement that calculates the area with **dblPI**.

3. Save and then start the application. Type **2** in the Radius text box, then click the **Calculate** button. The interface shows that the area is 12.566372.

4. Click the **Exit** button to stop the application.

DRESSING UP THE OUTPUT

Many times you will want to control the number of decimal places and the special characters that appear in an application's numeric output. For example, numbers representing monetary amounts typically are displayed with either zero or two decimal places and usually include a dollar sign and a thousands separator. Similarly, numbers representing percentage amounts usually are displayed with zero or more decimal places and a percent sign. Specifying the number of decimal places and the special characters to display in a number is called **formatting**. You can format a number using the syntax *variable*.**ToString(***formatString***)**. In the syntax, *variable* is the name of a numeric variable, and ToString is a method that can be used with any of the numeric data types. The **ToString method** converts the contents of the numeric variable to text. The *formatString* argument in the syntax is a string that specifies the format you want to use. A **string** is text that is enclosed in double quotation marks. The *formatString* argument must take the form "*Axx*", where *A* is an alphabetic character called the format specifier, and *xx* is a sequence of digits called the precision specifier. The format specifier must be one of the built-in format characters. The most commonly used format characters are listed in Figure 7-13; notice that you can use either an uppercase letter or a lowercase letter as the format specifier. When used with one of the format characters listed in Figure 7-13, the precision specifier controls the number of digits that will appear after the decimal point in the formatted number. Also included in Figure 7-13 are several examples of using the ToString method.

FORMATTING A NUMBER

<u>Syntax</u>

variable.**ToString(***formatString***)**

<u>Format specifier (Name)</u>	<u>Description</u>
C or c (Currency)	displays the text with a dollar sign; if appropriate, includes a thousands separator; negative values are enclosed in parentheses
N or n (Number)	similar to the Currency format, but does not include a dollar sign, and negative values are preceded by a minus sign
F or f (Fixed-point)	same as the Number format, but does not include a thousands separator
P or p (Percent)	multiplies the value by 100 and displays the result with a percent sign; negative values are preceded by a minus sign

<u>Example 1</u>

lblCommission.Text = intCommission.ToString("C2")

if the intCommission variable contains the number 1250, the statement assigns the text $1,250.00 to the Text property of the lblCommission control

<u>Example 2</u>

lblTotal.Text = decTotal.ToString("N2")

if the decTotal variable contains the number 123.675, the statement assigns the text 123.68 to the Text property of the lblTotal control

<u>Example 3</u>

lblRate.Text = dblRate.ToString("P0")

if the dblRate variable contains the number .06, the statement assigns the text 6 % to the Text property of the lblRate control

Figure 7-13: Syntax and examples of formatting numeric output

To format the area output to include only two decimal places:

1. Change the last assignment statement from lblArea.Text = dblArea to **lblArea.Text = dblArea.ToString("N2")**. Figure 7-14 shows the btnCalc control's Click event procedure.

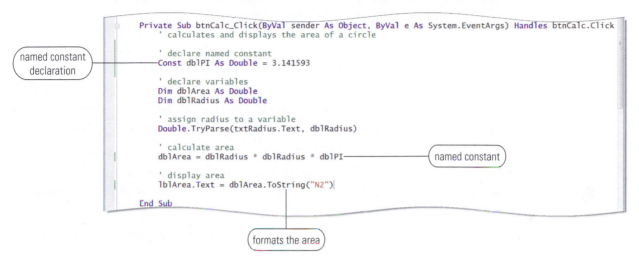

named constant declaration

```
Private Sub btnCalc_Click(ByVal sender As Object, ByVal e As System.EventArgs) Handles btnCalc.Click
    ' calculates and displays the area of a circle

    ' declare named constant
    Const dblPI As Double = 3.141593

    ' declare variables
    Dim dblArea As Double
    Dim dblRadius As Double

    ' assign radius to a variable
    Double.TryParse(txtRadius.Text, dblRadius)

    ' calculate area
    dblArea = dblRadius * dblRadius * dblPI

    ' display area
    lblArea.Text = dblArea.ToString("N2")

End Sub
```

named constant

formats the area

Figure 7-14: Completed btnCalc Click event procedure

2. Save and then start the application. Type **2** in the Radius text box, then click the **Calculate** button. The interface shows that the circle's area is 12.57.

3. Click the **Exit** button to stop the application. Close the Code Editor window, then close the solution.

MINI-QUIZ 2

1. Write the TryParse method to assign the value entered in the txtIncome control to the decIncome variable.

2. Write the statement to declare the intMINIMUM named constant whose value is 55.

3. The decSales variable contains the number 56.78. Write the assignment statement to display the value with a dollar sign and no decimal places in the lblSales control. _____.

SUMMARY

» The internal memory of a computer is composed of memory locations. Programmers can reserve some of the locations for variables and named constants.

» A memory location can store only one value at any one time.

» The value in a variable can change as the application is running, whereas the value in a named constant cannot change as the application is running.

» You use the Integer data type to store integers. The Decimal and Double data types are used to store numbers with a decimal place. The Decimal data type typically is used in calculations that involve money, because it is not subject to the small rounding errors that occur with the Double data type.

» You use the Dim statement to reserve a procedure-level variable. A procedure-level variable can be used only by the procedure in which it is declared, and it is removed from memory when the procedure ends.

» Most times, you will use a different variable for each unique output, processing, and input item listed in a problem's solution.

» Most programmers use the TryParse method, rather than the Val function, to convert text to numbers.

» You use the Const statement to declare named constants.

» You can use the ToString method to convert a number to text that contains a specific number of decimal places and optional formatting characters.

KEY TERMS

Const statement—the Visual Basic statement used to declare named constants

Dim statement— the Visual Basic statement used to declare procedure-level variables

Formatting—the process of specifying the number of decimal places and the special characters to display in a number

Lifetime—the length of time a variable remains in the computer's internal memory

Named constant—a memory location whose value cannot change while an application is running

Procedure scope—the scope of a procedure-level variable; refers to the fact that the variable can be used only by the procedure in which it is declared

Procedure-level variables—variables declared in a procedure; have procedure scope

Scope—the area where a variable is recognized in an application's code

String—text enclosed in double quotation marks

ToString method—a method used to convert the contents of a numeric variable to text; also formats the number

TryParse method—used to convert text to a numeric data type

Variables—memory locations whose contents cannot change while an application is running

ANSWERS TO MINI-QUIZZES

MINI-QUIZ 1

1. Integer

2. d. dblPay.Rate

3. Dim dblHoursWorked As Double

MINI-QUIZ 2

1. Decimal.TryParse(txtIncome.Text, decIncome)

2. Const intMINIMUM As Integer = 55

3. lblSales.Text = decSales.ToString("C0")

REVIEW QUESTIONS

1. Which of the following statements declares a variable named intNumSold?

   a. Dim intNumSold As Integer

   b. Dim As Integer intNumSold

   c. Const intNumSold As Integer

   d. None of the above.

2. If the user enters the text A34 in the txtPrice control, the TryParse(txtPrice.Text, decPrice) statement will assign _____ to the decPrice variable.

   a. A   b. A34

   c. 0   d. 34

3. Which of the following statements adds together the contents of the intScore1 and intScore2 variables, and then multiplies the sum by 2, assigning the result to the intTotal variable?

   a. intScore1 + intScore2 * 2 = intTotal

   b. (intScore1 + intScore2) * 2 = intTotal

   c. intTotal = intScore1 + intScore2 * 2

   d. None of the above.

4. Which of the following statements declares the decRATE named constant and initializes it to .15?

   a. Con decRATE As Decimal = .15

   b. Const decRATE As Decimal = .15

   c. Constant decRATE As Decimal = .15

   d. None of the above.

5. Which of the following statements formats the contents of the dblDue variable with a dollar sign and two decimal places?

   a. lblDue.Text = dblDue.ToString("C2")

   b. lblDue.Text = dblDue.ToCurrency("C2")

   c. lblDue.Text = ToString(dblDue, "C2")

   d. lblDue.Text = dblDue.ToFormat("C2")

EXERCISES

» TRY THIS

1. In this exercise, you modify the Commission Calculator application from Chapter 6 so that it uses variables and the TryParse method. (The answers to TRY THIS Exercises are located at the end of the chapter.)

   a. Open the Commission Calculator Solution (Commission Calculator Solution.sln) file contained in the ClearlyVB\Chap07\Commission Calculator Solution folder. Modify the code so that it uses variables and the TryParse method. Format the commission with a dollar sign and two decimal places.

   b. Save the solution, then start and test the application. Stop the application, then close the solution.

» TRY THIS

2. In this exercise, you code an application that calculates and displays the amount of an employee's new weekly pay. Figure 7-15 shows the output, input, and algorithm. (The answers to TRY THIS Exercises are located at the end of the chapter.)

Output: new weekly pay

Processing: weekly raise

Input: current weekly pay

Algorithm:
1. enter the current weekly pay
2. calculate the weekly raise by multiplying the current weekly pay by .03
3. calculate the new weekly pay by adding the weekly raise to the current weekly pay
4. display the new weekly pay

Figure 7-15

a. Open the New Pay Solution (New Pay Solution.sln) file contained in the ClearlyVB\Chap07\New Pay Solution folder. Code the algorithm using Decimal variables. Use a Decimal named constant for the raise rate of .03. Format the new weekly pay with a dollar sign and two decimal places.

b. Save the solution. Desk-check the program using 200 and 330 as the current weekly pay.

c. Start and then test the application. Stop the application, then close the solution.

3. In this exercise, you modify the Circle Area application created in the chapter. **»MODIFY THIS**

a. Use Windows to make a copy of the Circle Area Solution folder. Save the copy in the ClearlyVB\Chap07 folder. Rename the copy Modified Circle Area Solution.

b. Open the Circle Area Solution (Circle Area Solution.sln) file contained in the Modified Circle Area Solution folder. Modify the code so that it uses a separate calculation for the radius squared. Assign the result of the radius squared calculation to a variable, then modify the area calculation appropriately.

c. Save the solution. Start the application, then test it using 4.6 as the radius. The area should be 66.48. Stop the application, then close the solution.

4. The cashier at Jackson College wants an application that displays the total amount a **»INTRODUCTORY**
student owes for the semester, including tuition and room and board. The tuition is $100 per semester hour, and room and board is $1800 per semester. The cashier will need to enter the number of hours the student is enrolled. Use Integer named constants for the semester hour fee and the room and board fee. Use Integer variables for the input and output items, as well as for any processing items you choose to use. Format the output with a dollar sign and no decimal places.

a. List the output and input items, as well as any processing items, then create an appropriate algorithm.

b. Create a new Visual Basic Windows application. Assign the name Jackson Project to the project. Assign the name Jackson Solution to the solution. Save the application in the ClearlyVB\Chap07 folder. Change the name of the form file on your disk to frmMain.vb. If necessary, change the form's name to frmMain.

c. Create an appropriate interface. Include an Exit button. Code the Exit button's Click event procedure and the problem's algorithm. Save the solution. Desk-check the program using your own sample data.

d. Start and then test the application. Stop the application, then close the solution.

▶▶ INTRODUCTORY

5. A concert hall has three seating categories: Orchestra, Main floor, and Balcony. Orchestra seats are $25. Main floor seats are $30, and Balcony seats are $15. The manager wants an application that allows him to enter the number of tickets sold in each seating category. The application should calculate the amount of revenue generated by each seating category, as well as the total revenue.

a. List the output and input items, as well as any processing items, then create an appropriate algorithm.

b. Create a new Visual Basic Windows application. Assign the name Concert Project to the project. Assign the name Concert Solution to the solution. Save the application in the ClearlyVB\Chap07 folder. Change the name of the form file on your disk to frmMain.vb. If necessary, change the form's name to frmMain.

c. Create an appropriate interface. Include an Exit button. Code the Exit button's Click event procedure and the problem's algorithm. Save the solution. Desk-check the program using your own sample data.

d. Start and then test the application. Stop the application, then close the solution.

▶▶ INTERMEDIATE

6. In this exercise, you modify the application you created in Exercise 5. In addition to calculating and displaying the revenue for each seating category, as well as the total revenue, the application should now display the percentage of the total revenue contributed by each seating category.

a. Use Windows to make a copy of the Concert Solution folder. Save the copy in the ClearlyVB\Chap07 folder. Rename the copy Modified Concert Solution.

b. Open the Concert Solution (Concert Solution.sln) file contained in the Modified Concert Solution folder. Make the appropriate modifications to the interface and code. Use Decimal variables to store the percentages. Display the percentages with a percent sign and one decimal place.

c. Save the solution, then start and test the application. Stop the application, then close the solution.

▶▶ INTERMEDIATE

7. In this exercise, you modify the Circle Area application created in the chapter. For this exercise, the circle will represent a pizza. In addition to displaying the area of the

pizza, the modified application also will display the number of slices into which you can divide the pizza. For this exercise, use the number 14.13 as the area of a pizza slice.

a. Use Windows to make a copy of the Circle Area Solution folder. Save the copy in the ClearlyVB\Chap07 folder. Rename the copy Pizza Circle Area Solution.

b. Open the Circle Area Solution (Circle Area Solution.sln) file contained in the Pizza Circle Area Solution folder. Make the appropriate modifications to the interface and code. Display the number of slices with no decimal places.

c. Save and then start the application. Test the application using 10 as the circle's radius. The area is 314.16 and the number of slices is 22. Now test it using 6 as the radius. The area and number of slices should be 113.10 and 8. Stop the application and close the solution.

8. In this exercise, you modify the application that you created in Exercise 8 in Chapter 6. If you did not complete Chapter 6's Exercise 8, you will need to do so before you can complete this exercise.

>>**ADVANCED**

a. Use Windows to copy the Sun Solution folder from the ClearlyVB\Chap06 folder to the ClearlyVB\Chap07 folder.

b. Open the Sun Solution (Sun Solution.sln) file contained in the ClearlyVB\Chap07\Sun Solution folder. Modify the code so that it uses Decimal variables and Decimal named constants. Format the gross pay and taxes with two decimal places. Format the net pay with a dollar sign and two decimal places.

c. Save and then start the application. Test the application using 35.5 as the hours worked and 9.56 as the pay rate. The gross pay will be 339.38. The taxes will be 67.88, 27.15, and 6.79. The net pay will be $237.57. Notice that the total of the taxes and net pay differs by a penny from the gross pay. The "penny off" problem occurs because the ToString method rounds the gross pay and taxes before they are displayed. However, the amounts are not rounded when they are used to calculate the net pay. Stop the application.

d. You can fix the "penny off" problem using the Math.Round method. The method's syntax is **Math.Round(***number***,** *decimalPlaces***)**. In the syntax, *number* is the number to be rounded, and *decimalPlaces* indicates the number of decimal places to include in the rounding. For example, Math.Round(4.658, 2) evaluates to 4.66. Use the Math.Round method to fix the "penny off" problem.

e. Save and then start the application. Test the application using 35.5 as the hours worked and 9.56 as the pay rate. This time the net pay is $237.56. Stop the application, then close the solution.

»ADVANCED

9. Allen County's Property Tax Administrator wants an application that calculates the amount of property tax owed based on a property's assessed value. Seven different tax rates are involved in the calculation. Each tax rate is per $100 of assessed value. The state rate is .124, the county rate is .096, and the school rate is .557. The remaining four rates are for special services as follows: ambulance is .1, health is .038, library is .093, and soil conservation is .02. The application should display each tax as well as the total tax.

   a. List the output and input items, as well as any processing items, then create an appropriate algorithm.

   b. Create a new Visual Basic Windows application. Assign the name Allen Property Project to the project. Assign the name Allen Property Solution to the solution. Save the application in the ClearlyVB\Chap07 folder. Change the name of the form file on your disk to frmMain.vb. If necessary, change the form's name to frmMain.

   c. Create an appropriate interface. Include an Exit button. Code the Exit button's Click event procedure and the problem's algorithm. Use the Decimal data type for the variables and named constants. Display the state, county, school, ambulance, health, library, and soil conservation taxes with two decimal places. Display the total property tax with a dollar sign and two decimal places.

   d. Save the solution, then start the application. Test the application using 105000 as the assessed value. (Hint: The total property tax will be $1,079.40.)

   e. Now test the application using 121920 as the assessed value. Notice that the total of the taxes differs by a penny from the total property tax. If you add together the taxes, the total is 1253.33; however, the total property tax appears as $1,253.34. The "penny off" problem occurs because the ToString method rounds the various taxes before they are displayed. However, the tax amounts are not rounded when they are used to calculate the total tax. Stop the application.

   f. You can fix the "penny off" problem using the Math.Round method. The method's syntax is **Math.Round(***number***,** *decimalPlaces***)**. In the syntax, *number* is the number to be rounded, and *decimalPlaces* indicates the number of decimal places to include in the rounding. For example, Math.Round(4.658, 2) evaluates to 4.66. Use the Math.Round method to fix the "penny off" problem.

   g. Save and then start the application. Test the application using 121920 as the assessed value. This time the total property tax appears as $1,253.33. Stop the application, then close the solution.

10. In this exercise, you experiment with the TryParse method using different data types and values.

    a. Open the FigureThisOut Solution (FigureThisOut Solution.sln) file, which is contained in the ClearlyVB\Chap07\FigureThisOut Solution folder. Open the Code Editor window and study the code.

    b. Start the application. Enter the number 34 in the Number text box, then click the Convert button. The three TryParse methods in the code convert the number 34 to text, and then display the text in the three label controls.

    c. Enter the following values, one at a time. Click the Convert button after each entry. On a piece of paper, record the result of each TryParse method's conversion. Values: 12.55, $5.67, -4.23, (4.23), 1,457.99, 7%, 7.88-, 1 345 (notice the space after the 1), 33 (the number 33 preceded and followed by a space), 122a, and an empty text box. Stop the application, then close the solution.

11. In this exercise, you find an error in an application's code. Open the SwatTheBugs Solution (SwatTheBugs Solution.sln) file, which is contained in the ClearlyVB\Chap07\SwatTheBugs Solution folder. Start and then test the application. Notice that the code is not working correctly. Locate and correct any errors.

ANSWERS TO "TRY THIS" EXERCISES

1. See Figure 7-16.

```
Private Sub btnCalculate_Click(ByVal sender As Object, ByVal e As System.EventArgs) Handles btnCalcul
    ' calculates and displays the annual commission

    ' declare variables
    Dim decSales As Decimal
    Dim decRate As Decimal
    Dim decCommission As Decimal

    ' assign input to variables
    Decimal.TryParse(txtSales.Text, decSales)
    Decimal.TryParse(txtRate.Text, decRate)

    ' calculate and display commission
    decCommission = decSales * decRate
    lblCommission.Text = decCommission.ToString("C2")
End Sub
```

Figure 7-16

2. See Figures 7-17 and 7-18.

```
Private Sub btnCalculate_Click(ByVal sender As Object, ByVal e As System.EventArgs) Handles btnCalcul
    ' calculates and displays the new weekly pay

    ' declare named constant
    Const decRATE As Decimal = 0.03

    ' declare variables
    Dim decNewPay As Decimal
    Dim decRaise As Decimal
    Dim decCurrentPay As Decimal

    ' assign input to a variable
    Decimal.TryParse(txtCurrentPay.Text, decCurrentPay)

    ' calculate raise and new pay
    decRaise = decCurrentPay * decRATE
    decNewPay = decCurrentPay + decRaise

    ' display new pay
    lblNewPay.Text = decNewPay.ToString("C2")
End Sub
```

Figure 7-17

decRate	decNewPay	decRaise	decCurrentPay
.03	206	6	200
.03	339.90	9.90	330

Figure 7-18

8

WHAT'S WRONG WITH IT?

After studying Chapter 8, you should be able to:

Locate syntax errors using the Error List window

Locate a logic error by stepping through the code

Locate logic errors using breakpoints

Fix syntax and logic errors

THERE'S A BUG IN MY SOUP!

Congratulations on mastering the concepts of variables and named constants in Chapter 7. As you now know, you can use both types of memory locations to control the data type of numbers used in calculations. Both types of memory locations also make your code more self-documenting and easier to understand. In addition, you can use variables to store the values of processing items, which do not appear in a user interface. The only downside to variables and named constants is that their use requires additional lines of code. You may have noticed that you entered several more lines of code in Chapter 7's applications than you did in Chapter 6's applications. The amount of code you need to enter will increase as you learn new concepts throughout this book. As the amount of code increases, so does the likelihood for errors. Now would be a good time to start learning ways of finding and correcting the errors. An error in a program's code is referred to as a **bug**. The process of locating and correcting any bugs in a program is called **debugging**. Program bugs typically are caused by either syntax errors or logic errors. (You'll learn about another type of error, called a runtime error, in later chapters in this book.) Syntax errors are the easiest to find, so we'll tackle those first.

FINDING SYNTAX ERRORS

As you learned in Chapter 5, the set of rules you must follow when using a programming language is called the language's syntax. A **syntax error** occurs when you break one of the language's rules. Most syntax errors are a result of typing errors that occur when entering instructions, such as typing Me.Clse() instead of Me.Close(). The Code Editor detects most syntax errors as you enter the instructions. However, if you are not paying close attention to your computer screen, you may not notice the errors. In the next set of steps, you will observe what happens when you try to start an application that contains a syntax error.

The Ch08-Debugging video demonstrates all of the steps contained in this chapter. You may find it helpful to view the steps before you perform them. The video also shows how you can access Online Help.

To debug the Total Sales application:

1. Start Visual Studio 2008 (or Visual Basic 2008 Express Edition). Open the **Total Sales Solution** (**Total Sales Solution.sln**) file, which is contained in the ClearlyVB\ Chap08\Total Sales Solution folder. If necessary, open the designer window. The application calculates and displays the total of the sales amounts entered by the user.

2. Open the Code Editor window. Figure 8-1 shows the code entered in the btnCalc control's Click event procedure. The thin red boxes alert you that three lines of code contain a syntax error. However, you may fail to notice them if you are not paying really close attention to the code.

```vb
Private Sub btnCalc_Click(ByVal sender As Object, ByVal e As System.EventArgs) Handles btnCalc.Click
    ' calculates and displays the total sales

    ' declare variables
    Dim intNorth As Integer
    Dim intSouth As Integer
    Dim intEast As Integer
    Dim intWest As Integer
    Dim intTotal As Intger                                      ◄── syntax error

    ' assign input to variables
    Integer.TryParse(txtNorth.Text, intNorth                    ◄── syntax error
    Integer.TryParse(txtSouth.Text, intSouth)
    Integer.TryParse(txtEast.Text, intEast)
    Integer.TryParse(txtWest.Text, intWest)

    ' calculate total sales
    inTotal = intNorth + intSouth + intEast + intWest           ◄── syntax error

    ' display total sales
    lblTotal.Text = intTotal.ToString("C0")

End Sub
```

Figure 8-1: The btnCalc control's Click event procedure

3. Start the application. If the dialog box shown in Figure 8-2 appears, click the **No** button.

Microsoft Visual Studio

ⓘ There were build errors. Would you like to continue and run the last successful build?

[Yes] [No]

☐ Do not show this dialog again

Figure 8-2: Dialog box

4. The Error List window shown in Figure 8-3 opens at the bottom of the IDE. The Error List window indicates that the code contains three errors. The window provides a description of each error and the location of each error in the code. (You can change the size of the Error List window by positioning your mouse pointer on the window's top border until the mouse pointer looks like this: ⬍. Then press and hold down the left mouse button while you drag the border either up or down.)

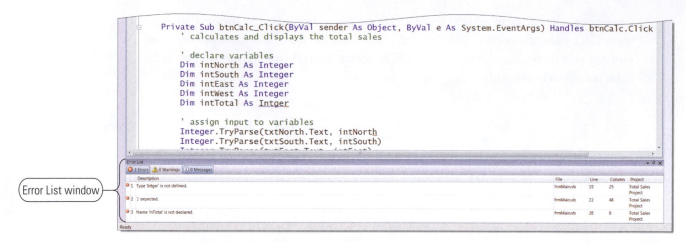

Figure 8-3: Error List window in the IDE

5. Double-click **Type 'Intger' is not defined.** in the Error List window. The Code Editor places the insertion point in the line where the error was encountered, as shown in Figure 8-4. The first error is nothing more than a typing error: the programmer meant to type Integer.

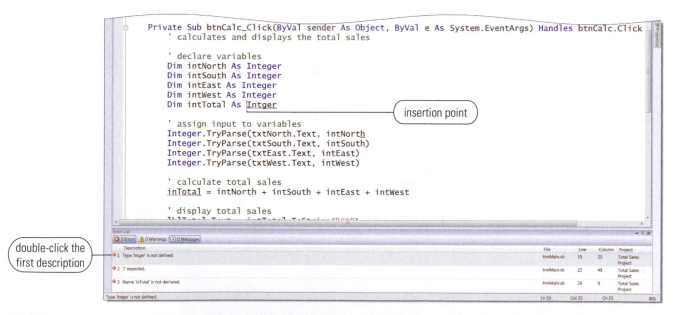

Figure 8-4: Insertion point positioned in the line containing the first error

6. You can fix the first syntax error yourself by simply typing the missing letter e; or, you can have the Code Editor correct the mistake for you. In this step, you'll see how to put the Code Editor to work. Hover your mouse pointer over the thin red box that appears

below the letter r. An Error icon (a white exclamation point in a red circle) appears along with a down arrow. (If you don't see the down arrow, hover your mouse pointer on the Error icon until the down arrow appears.) Click the **down arrow** to display a list of suggestions for fixing the error. See Figure 8-5.

```
Dim intSouth As Integer
Dim intEast As Integer
Dim intWest As Integer
Dim intTotal As Intger

' assign input to var...
Integer.TryParse(txtN...        ntNorth
Integer.TryParse(txtS...        ntSouth)
Integer.TryParse(txtEast.Text, intEast)
Integer.TryParse(txtWest.Text, intWest)
```

Error icon

Type 'Intger' is not defined.
Change 'Intger' to 'Integer'.
Change 'Intger' to 'UInteger'.
Change 'Intger' to 'IntPtr'.

Figure 8-5: List of possible solutions

7. Click **Change 'Intger' to 'Integer'.** in the list. The Code Editor changes Intger to Integer in the Dim statement and removes the error from the Error List window.

8. Double-click **')' expected.** in the Error List window. The Code Editor places the insertion point in the line containing the first TryParse method, because the ending parenthesis is missing from the statement. Hover your mouse pointer over the thin red box that appears below the letter h. When the Error icon and down arrow appear, click the **down arrow**. Click **Insert the missing ')'.** in the list. The Code Editor inserts the missing parenthesis and removes the error message from the Error List window.

9. Double-click **Name 'inTotal' is not declared.** in the Error List window. The Code Editor places the insertion point at the beginning of the statement that calculates the total sales. Hover your mouse pointer over the thin red box that appears below the letter l. When the Error icon and down arrow appear, click the **down arrow**. As the message indicates, the Code Editor cannot offer any suggestions for correcting the error. See Figure 8-6.

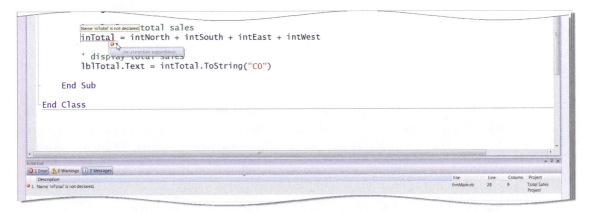

Figure 8-6: Message that appears when no correction suggestions are available

10. The error's description (Name 'inTotal' is not declared.) indicates that the Code Editor does not recognize the name inTotal. The unrecognized name appears on the left side of an assignment statement, so it belongs to something that can store information—either a control or a variable. It doesn't refer to the Text property, so it's probably the name of a variable. Looking at the beginning of the procedure, where the variables are declared, you will notice that the procedure declares a variable named intTotal. Obviously, the programmer mistyped the variable's name. Change inTotal to **intTotal** in the assignment statement, then move the insertion point to another line in the Code Editor window. When you move the insertion point, the Code Editor removes the error message from the Error List window.

11. Close the Error List window. Save and then start the application. Test the application using **2000** as the North sales, **3000** as the South sales, **1200** as the East sales, and **1800** as the West sales. The total sales are $8,000.

12. Click the **Exit** button to end the application. Close the Code Editor window, then close the solution.

LOCATING LOGIC ERRORS

As you observed in the previous section, the Code Editor makes syntax errors easy to find and correct. A much more difficult type of error to locate, and one that the Code Editor cannot detect, is a logic error. A **logic error** can occur for a variety of reasons, such as forgetting to enter an instruction or entering the instructions in the wrong order. Some logic errors occur as a result of calculation statements that are correct syntactically, but incorrect mathematically. An example of this is the dblRadiusSquared = dblRadius + dblRadius statement. The statement's syntax is correct, but it is incorrect mathematically: you square a value by multiplying it by itself, not by adding it to itself. In the remainder of this chapter, you will debug two applications that contain logic errors.

To debug the Discount application:

1. Open the **Discount Solution** (**Discount Solution.sln**) file, which is contained in the ClearlyVB\Chap08\Discount Solution folder. If necessary, open the designer window. The application calculates and displays three discount amounts, which are based on the price entered by the user.

2. Open the Code Editor window. Figure 8-7 shows the code entered in the btnCalc control's Click event procedure.

```
Private Sub btnCalc_Click(ByVal sender As Object, ByVal e As System.EventArgs) Handles btnCalc.Click
    ' calculates and displays a 10%, 20%, and
    ' 30% discount on an item's price

    ' declare variables
    Dim decPrice As Decimal
    Dim decDiscount10 As Decimal
    Dim decDiscount20 As Decimal
    Dim decDiscount30 As Decimal

    ' calculate discounts
    decDiscount10 = decPrice * 0.1
    decDiscount20 = decPrice * 0.2
    decDiscount30 = decPrice * 0.3

    ' display discounts
    lbl10.Text = decDiscount10.ToString("N2")
    lbl20.Text = decDiscount20.ToString("N2")
    lbl30.Text = decDiscount30.ToString("N2")
End Sub
```

Figure 8-7: Code entered in the btnCalc control's Click event procedure

3. Start the application. Type **100** in the Price text box, then click the **Calculate** button. The interface shows that each discount is $0.00, which is incorrect. Click the **Exit** button to stop the application.

4. You'll use the Debug menu to run the Visual Basic debugger, which is a tool that helps you locate the logic errors in your code. Click **Debug** on the menu bar. The menu's Step Into option will start your application and allow you to step through your code. It does this by executing the code one statement at a time, pausing immediately before each statement is executed. Click **Step Into**. Type **100** in the Price text box, then click the **Calculate** button. The debugger highlights the first instruction to be executed. In this case, it highlights the btnCalc_Click procedure header. In addition, an arrow points to the instruction, as shown in Figure 8-8, and the code's execution is paused. (If the interface still appears on the screen, click the Code Editor window's title bar.)

```
Private Sub btnCalc_Click(ByVal sender As Object, ByVal e As System.EventArgs) Handles btnCa
    ' calculates and displays a 10%, 20%, and
    ' 30% discount on an item's price

    ' declare variables
    Dim decPrice As Decimal
    Dim decDiscount10 As Decimal
    Dim decDiscount20 As Decimal
```

Figure 8-8: Procedure header highlighted

5. To execute the highlighted instruction, you can use either the Debug menu's Step Into option or the F8 key on your keyboard. Press the **F8** key. After the computer processes the procedure header, the debugger highlights the next statement to be processed—in this case, the decDiscount10 = decPrice * 0.1 statement—and then pauses execution of the code. (The Dim statements are skipped over because they are not considered executable by the debugger.)

6. While the execution of a procedure's code is paused, you can view the contents of controls and variables that appear in the highlighted statement, as well as in the statements above it in the procedure. Before you view the contents of a control or variable, however, you should consider the value you expect to find. Before the decDiscount10 = decPrice * 0.1 statement is processed, the decDiscount10 variable should contain its initial value, 0. (Recall that the Dim statement initializes numeric variables to 0.) Place your mouse pointer on decDiscount10 in the highlighted statement. The variable's name (decDiscount10) and current value (0D) appear in a small box, as shown in Figure 8-9. The letter D indicates that the data type of the value—in this case, 0—is Decimal. At this point, the decDiscount10 variable's value is correct.

```
Private Sub btnCalc_Click(ByVal sender As Object, ByVal e As System.EventArgs) Handles btnCa
    ' calculates and displays a 10%, 20%, and
    ' 30% discount on an item's price

    ' declare variables
    Dim decPrice As Decimal
    Dim decDiscount10 As Decimal
    Dim decDiscount20 As Decimal
    Dim decDiscount30 As Decimal

    ' calculate discounts
    decDiscount10 = decPrice * 0.1
    decDiscount20 = decPrice * 0.2
    decDiscount30 = decPrice * 0.3
```

the letter D indicates a Decimal value

Figure 8-9: Value stored in decDiscount10 before the highlighted statement is executed

7. Now consider the value you expect the decPrice variable to contain. Before the highlighted statement is processed, the decPrice variable should contain the number 100, which is the value you entered in the Price text box. Place your mouse pointer on decPrice in the highlighted statement. As Figure 8-10 shows, the decPrice variable contains 0D, which is its initial value. Consider why the variable's value is incorrect. In this case, the value is incorrect because no statement above the highlighted statement

assigns the text box's value to the decPrice variable. In other words, a statement is missing from the procedure.

```
Private Sub btnCalc_Click(ByVal sender As Object, ByVal e As System.EventArgs) Handles btnCa
    ' calculates and displays a 10%, 20%, and
    ' 30% discount on an item's price

    ' declare variables
    Dim decPrice As Decimal
    Dim decDiscount10 As Decimal
    Dim decDiscount20 As Decimal
    Dim decDiscount30 As Decimal

    ' calculate discounts
    decDiscount10 = decPrice * 0.1
    decDiscount20 = decPrice * 0.2
    decDiscount30 = decPrice * 0.3
```

Figure 8-10: Value stored in decPrice before the highlighted statement is executed

8. Click **Debug** on the menu bar, then click **Stop Debugging** to stop the debugger. Click the blank line below the last Dim statement, then press **Enter** to insert another blank line. Type **' assign price to a variable** and press **Enter**, then type **decimal. tryparse(txtPrice.text, decPrice)** and press **Enter**.

9. Save the solution. Click **Debug** on the menu bar, then click **Step Into**. Type **100** in the Price text box, then click the **Calculate** button. (If the interface still appears on the screen, click the Code Editor window's title bar.) Press **F8** to process the procedure header. The debugger highlights the Decimal.TryParse(txtPrice.Text, decPrice) statement and pauses execution of the code.

10. Before the highlighted statement is processed, the txtPrice control's Text property should contain 100, which is the value you entered in the control. Place your mouse pointer on txtPrice.Text in the highlighted statement. The box shows that the Text property contains the expected value. The 100 is enclosed in quotation marks because it is considered a string. (As you learned in Chapter 7, a string is text enclosed in quotation marks.)

11. The decPrice variable should contain its initial value, 0D. Place your mouse pointer on decPrice in the highlighted statement. The box shows that the variable contains the expected value.

12. Press **F8** to process the TryParse method. The debugger highlights the decDiscount10 = decPrice * 0.1 statement before pausing execution of the code. Place your mouse pointer on decPrice in the TryParse method, as shown in Figure 8-11. Notice that after the method is processed by the computer, the decPrice variable contains the number 100D.

```
' assign price to a variable
Decimal.TryParse(txtPrice.Text, decPrice)
                                    decPrice 100D

' calculate discounts
decDiscount10 = decPrice * 0.1
decDiscount20 = decPrice * 0.2
decDiscount30 = decPrice * 0.3
```

Figure 8-11: Value stored in decPrice after the TryParse method is executed

13. Before the highlighted statement is executed, the decDiscount10 variable should contain its initial value, and the decPrice variable should contain the value assigned to it by the TryParse method. Place your mouse pointer on decDiscount10 in the highlighted statement. The box shows that the variable contains 0D, which is correct. Place your mouse pointer on decPrice in the highlighted statement. The box shows that the variable contains 100D, which also is correct.

14. After the highlighted statement is processed, the decPrice variable should still contain 100D. However, the decDiscount10 variable should contain 10D, which is 10% of 100. Press **F8** to execute the decDiscount10 = decPrice * 0.1 statement, then place your mouse pointer on decDiscount10 in the statement. The box shows that the variable contains the expected value. On your own, verify that the decPrice variable in the statement contains the appropriate value.

15. To continue program execution without the debugger, click **Debug** on the menu bar, then click **Continue**. This time, the correct discount amounts (10.00, 20.00, and 30.00) appear in the interface.

16. Click the **Exit** button to end the application. Close the Code Editor window, then close the solution.

I'VE REACHED MY BREAKING POINT

Stepping through code one line at a time is not the only way to search for logic errors. You also can use a breakpoint to pause execution at a specific line in the code. You will learn how to set a breakpoint in the next set of steps.

To debug the Hours Worked application:

1. Open the **Hours Worked Solution** (**Hours Worked Solution.sln**) file, which is contained in the ClearlyVB\Chap08\Hours Worked Solution folder. If necessary, open the designer window. The application calculates and displays the total number of hours worked in four weeks.

2. Open the Code Editor window. Figure 8-12 shows the code entered in the btnCalculate control's Click event procedure.

```
Private Sub btnCalculate_Click(ByVal sender As Object, ByVal e As System.EventArgs) Handles btnCalcul
    ' calculates and displays the total number
    ' of hours worked during 4 weeks

    ' declare variables
    Dim dblWeek1 As Double
    Dim dblWeek2 As Double
    Dim dblWeek3 As Double
    Dim dblWeek4 As Double
    Dim dblTotal As Double

    ' assign input to variables
    Double.TryParse(txtWeek1.Text, dblWeek1)
    Double.TryParse(txtWeek2.Text, dblWeek2)
    Double.TryParse(txtWeek3.Text, dblWeek2)
    Double.TryParse(txtWeek4.Text, dblWeek4)

    ' calculate total hours worked
    dblTotal = dblWeek1 + dblWeek2 + dblWeek3 + dblWeek4

    ' display total hours worked
    lblTotal.Text = dblTotal

End Sub
```

Figure 8-12: The btnCalculate control's Click event procedure

3. Start the application. Type **1** in each of the four text boxes, then click the **Calculate** button. The interface shows that the total number of hours is 3, which is incorrect; it should be 4. Click the **Exit** button to stop the application.

4. Obviously something is wrong with the statement that calculates the total number of hours worked. Rather than having the computer pause before processing each line of code in the procedure, you will have it pause only before processing the calculation statement. You do this by setting a breakpoint on the statement. Right-click **the calculation statement**, point to **Breakpoint**, then click **Insert Breakpoint**. (You also can set a breakpoint by clicking the statement, and then using the Toggle Breakpoint option on the Debug menu.) The debugger highlights the statement and places a circle next to it, as shown in Figure 8-13.

```
    ' calculate total hours worked
    dblTotal = dblWeek1 + dblWeek2 + dblWeek3 + dblWeek4

    ' display total hours worked
    lblTotal.Text = dblTotal
```

Figure 8-13: Breakpoint set in the procedure

5. Start the application. Type **1** in each of the four text boxes, then click the **Calculate** button. The computer begins processing the code contained in the button's Click event procedure. It stops processing when it reaches the calculation statement, which it highlights. The highlighting indicates that the statement is the next one to be processed. See Figure 8-14.

```
Private Sub btnCalculate_Click(ByVal sender As Object, ByVal e As System.EventArgs) Handles
    ' calculates and displays the total number
    ' of hours worked during 4 weeks

    ' declare variables
    Dim dblWeek1 As Double
    Dim dblWeek2 As Double
    Dim dblWeek3 As Double
    Dim dblWeek4 As Double
    Dim dblTotal As Double

    ' assign input to variables
    Double.TryParse(txtWeek1.Text, dblWeek1)
    Double.TryParse(txtWeek2.Text, dblWeek2)
    Double.TryParse(txtWeek3.Text, dblWeek2)
    Double.TryParse(txtWeek4.Text, dblWeek4)

    ' calculate total hours worked
    dblTotal = dblWeek1 + dblWeek2 + dblWeek3 + dblWeek4

    ' display total hours worked
    lblTotal.Text = dblTotal

End Sub
```

Figure 8-14: Result of the computer reaching the breakpoint

6. Here again, before viewing the values contained in each variable in the highlighted statement, consider the values you expect to find. Before the calculation statement is processed, the dblTotal variable should contain its initial value (0). The other four variables should contain the number 1, which is the value you entered in each text box. Place your mouse pointer on dblTotal in the highlighted statement. The box shows that the variable's value is 0.0, which is correct. (You can verify the variable's initial value by placing your mouse pointer on dblTotal in its declaration statement.) Don't be concerned that 0.0 appears rather than 0. The .0 indicates that the value's data type is Double.

7. On your own, view the values contained in the dblWeek1, dblWeek2, dblWeek3, and dblWeek4 variables. Notice that three of the variables contain 1.0, which is correct. The dblWeek3 variable, however, contains its initial value (0.0), which is incorrect.

8. One of the TryParse methods is responsible for assigning a new value to the dblWeek3 variable. Looking closely at the four TryParse method's in the procedure, you will notice that the third one is incorrect. After converting the contents of the txtWeek3 control to a number, the method should assign the number to the dblWeek3 variable rather than to the dblWeek2 variable. Click **Debug** on the menu bar, then click **Stop Debugging**.

9. Change dblWeek2 in the third TryParse method to **dblWeek3**.

10. Now you can remove the breakpoint. Right-click the statement containing the breakpoint, point to **Breakpoint**, then click **Delete Breakpoint**.

11. Save the solution. Start the application. Enter the number **1** in each of the four text boxes, then click the **Calculate** button. The interface shows that the total number of hours is 4. On your own, test the application using other values for the hours worked in each week.

12. Click the **Exit** button to end the application. Close the Code Editor window, then close the solution.

MINI-QUIZ 1

1. When entered in a procedure, which of the following statements will result in a syntax error?

   a. Me.Clse()

   b. Integer.TryPars(txtHours.Text, intHours)

   c. Dim decRate as Decimel

   d. All of the above.

2. To step through each line of executable code, click Debug on the menu bar, then click _____.

3. When a breakpoint is set, the computer stops processing the code immediately _____ it processes the breakpoint statement.

   a. after

   b. before

SUMMARY

» In most cases, program errors (bugs) are caused by either syntax errors or logic errors. The Code Editor helps you locate and fix the syntax errors in your code. However, it cannot locate any logic errors in your code.

» Any syntax errors in an application's code are listed in the Error List window when you start the application.

» You can locate logic errors by stepping through the code. To step through code, use the Step Into option on the Debug menu, or the F8 key. You also can set breakpoints by right-clicking a line of code, pointing to Breakpoint, and then clicking Insert Breakpoint. To remove a breakpoint, right-click the breakpoint, point to Breakpoint, and then click Delete Breakpoint.

» The letter D at the end of a value indicates that the value's data type is Decimal.

» The .0 at the end of a number indicates that the number's data type is Double.

» Before viewing the value stored in a control or variable, you first should consider the value you expect to find.

KEY TERMS

Bug—an error in a program's code

Debugging—the process of locating and correcting any bugs in a program

Logic error—an error that can occur for a variety of reasons, such as forgetting to enter an instruction, entering the instructions in the wrong order, or entering a calculation statement that is incorrect mathematically

Syntax error—an error that occurs when a statement breaks one of a programming language's rules

ANSWERS TO MINI-QUIZ

MINI-QUIZ 1

1. d. All of the above.

2. Step Into

3. b. before

REVIEW QUESTIONS

1. The process of locating and fixing any errors in a program is called _____.

   a. bug-proofing

   b. bug-eliminating

   c. debugging

   d. error removal

2. While stepping through code, the debugger highlights the statement that _____.

   a. was just executed

   b. will be executed next

   c. contains the error

   d. None of the above.

3. Logic errors are listed in the Error List window.

   a. True   b. False

4. While stepping through code, you can view the contents of controls and variables that appear in the highlighted statement only.

   a. True   b. False

5. Which key is used to step through code?

   a. F8   b. F7

   c. F6   d. F5

EXERCISES

1. In this exercise, you debug an application. (The answers to TRY THIS Exercises are located at the end of the chapter.) Open the Commission Calculator Solution (Commission Calculator Solution.sln) file, which is contained in the ClearlyVB\Chap08\Commission Calculator Solution folder. Use what you learned in the chapter to debug the application. When you are finished debugging the application, close the solution.

   »TRY THIS

2. In this exercise, you debug an application. (The answers to TRY THIS Exercises are located at the end of the chapter.) Open the New Pay Solution (New Pay Solution.sln) file contained in the ClearlyVB\Chap08\New Pay Solution folder. Use what you learned in the chapter to debug the application. When you are finished debugging the application, close the solution.

   »TRY THIS

3. In this exercise, you debug an application. Open the Hawkins Solution (Hawkins Solution.sln) file, which is contained in the ClearlyVB\Chap08\Hawkins Solution folder. Use what you learned in the chapter to debug the application. When you are finished debugging the application, close the solution.

   »INTRODUCTORY

4. In this exercise, you debug an application. Open the Allenton Solution (Allenton Solution.sln) file, which is contained in the ClearlyVB\Chap08\Allenton Solution folder. Use what you learned in the chapter to debug the application. When you are finished debugging the application, close the solution.

   »INTRODUCTORY

5. In this exercise, you debug an application. Open the Martins Solution (Martins Solution.sln) file, which is contained in the ClearlyVB\Chap08\Martins Solution folder. Use what you learned in the chapter to debug the application. When you are finished debugging the application, close the solution.

   »INTERMEDIATE

6. In this exercise, you debug an application. Open the Average Score Solution (Average Score Solution.sln) file, which is contained in the ClearlyVB\Chap08\Average Score Solution folder. Use what you learned in the chapter to debug the application. When you are finished debugging the application, close the solution.

   »INTERMEDIATE

▶▶ADVANCED

7. In this exercise, you debug an application. Open the Beachwood Solution (Beachwood Solution.sln) file, which is contained in the ClearlyVB\Chap08\Beachwood Solution folder. Use what you learned in the chapter to debug the application. When you are finished debugging the application, close the solution.

▶▶ADVANCED

8. In this exercise, you debug an application. Open the Framington Solution (Framington Solution.sln) file, which is contained in the ClearlyVB\Chap08\Framington Solution folder. Use what you learned in the chapter to debug the application. When you are finished debugging the application, close the solution.

ANSWERS TO "TRY THIS" EXERCISES

The Ch08-TRYTHIS video demonstrates the answers to both TRY THIS Exercises.

9

DECISIONS, DECISIONS, DECISIONS

After studying Chapter 9, you should be able to:

Show the selection structure in both pseudocode and a flowchart

Write If...Then...Else statements

Include comparison operators in a selection structure's condition

Add a check box to an interface

SOMEONE MIGHT NEED TO MAKE A DECISION

As you learned in Chapter 2, all computer programs are written using one or more of three control structures: sequence, selection, or repetition. You used the sequence structure in the procedures you coded in the previous chapters. Recall that the instructions in each of the procedures were processed sequentially—in other words, in the order the instructions appeared in the procedure. Many times, however, the next instruction processed depends on the result of a decision that must be made. In those instances, you need to use the selection structure. The **selection structure** makes a decision and then takes an appropriate action based on that decision. But how does a programmer determine whether a problem's solution requires a selection structure? The answer to this question is by studying the problem specification. The first problem specification you will examine in this chapter involves Rob, the mechanical man from Chapter 2. The problem specification, as well as an illustration of the problem, is shown in Figure 9-1. To solve the problem, you need to get Rob from his hallway into his bedroom. You do this by directing him to take two steps forward, then open the bedroom door, and then take one step forward. The correct algorithm using the commands that Rob can understand is included in Figure 9-1. The algorithm uses only the sequence structure, because no decisions need to be made to get Rob from his initial location in the hallway to his ending location in the bedroom.

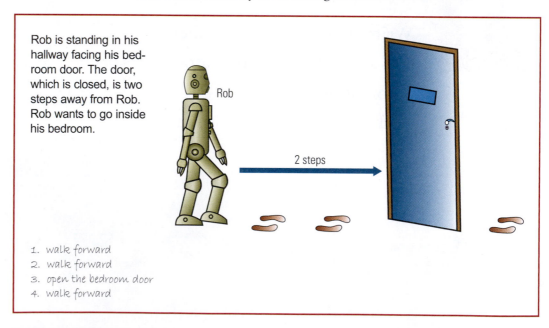

Rob is standing in his hallway facing his bedroom door. The door, which is closed, is two steps away from Rob. Rob wants to go inside his bedroom.

Rob

2 steps

1. walk forward
2. walk forward
3. open the bedroom door
4. walk forward

Figure 9-1: First problem using Rob

Now let's make a slight change to the problem specification shown in Figure 9-1. This time, Rob's bedroom door may or may not be closed. What changes will need to be made to the original algorithm shown in Figure 9-1 as a result of this minor modification? The first two instructions in the original algorithm position Rob in front of his bedroom door; Rob will still need to follow those instructions. The third instruction tells Rob to open the bedroom door. That instruction was correct for the original problem specification, which states that the bedroom door is closed. However, in the modified problem specification, the status of the bedroom door is not known: it could be closed or it could already be open. As a result, Rob will need to make a decision and then take the appropriate action based on the result. More specifically, Rob will need to determine whether the bedroom door is closed, and then open the door only if it needs to be opened. The last instruction in the original algorithm positions Rob one step inside his bedroom; Rob will still need to follow that instruction. Figure 9-2 shows the modified problem specification along with the modified algorithm. The selection structure begins with the *if the door is closed, do this:* line, and it ends with the *end if* line. Notice that the *open the door* instruction is indented within the selection structure. Indenting in this manner indicates that the instruction should be followed only when the door is closed.

Rob is standing in his hallway facing his bedroom door. The door, which may or may not be closed, is two steps away from Rob. Rob wants to go inside his bedroom.

1. walk forward
2. walk forward
3. if the door is closed, do this:
     open the door
   end if
4. walk forward

Figure 9-2: Second problem using Rob

Figure 9-3 shows another problem specification and illustration involving Rob, along with the correct algorithm. As the algorithm indicates, the problem's solution does not require Rob to make any decisions in order to accomplish his tasks. He needs simply to remove the Trash container's lid, drop the bag of trash in the container, and then replace the lid.

Rob is holding a bag of trash in his right hand. He is directly in front of two containers: one marked Trash and the other marked Recycle. A lid is on each container. Rob needs to remove the lid from the Trash container, then drop the bag of trash in the container, and then replace the lid.

Rob

Trash

Recycle

1. use your left hand to remove the lid from the Trash container
2. drop the bag of trash in the Trash container
3. use your left hand to replace the lid on the Trash container

Figure 9-3: Third problem using Rob

Figure 9-4 shows a modified version of the previous problem specification. In the modified version, you don't know whether Rob is holding a bag of trash or a bag of recyclables. Rob should drop the bag in the appropriate container. How will these changes affect the original algorithm shown in Figure 9-3? The three instructions in the original algorithm pertain to the Trash container only. Those instructions were correct for the original problem specification, which states that Rob is holding a bag of trash. However, in the modified problem specification, the contents of the bag that Rob is holding are not certain: the bag can contain either trash or recyclables. As a result, Rob will need to make a decision about the contents of the bag and then take the appropriate action based on the result. If the bag contains trash, Rob should follow the three instructions in the original algorithm. Otherwise, which means the bag contains recyclables, Rob should remove the Recycle container's lid before dropping the bag into the container and replacing the lid. Figure 9-4 shows the modified problem specification and two versions of a correct algorithm. Notice that, unlike the algorithm shown in Figure 9-2, the algorithms shown in Figure 9-4 require Rob to perform one set of instructions when the decision is true, but a different set of instructions when the decision is false. Each set of instructions is indented within the selection structure. Indenting in this manner clearly indicates the instructions to be followed when the decision is true, as well as the ones to be followed when the decision is false.

Rob is holding either a bag of trash or a bag of recyclables in his right hand. He is directly in front of two containers: one marked Trash and the other marked Recycle. A lid is on each container. Rob needs to remove the lid from the appropriate container, then drop the bag in the container, and then replace the lid.

Version 1:

```
1. if you are holding a bag of trash, do this:
       use your left hand to remove the lid from the Trash container
       drop the bag of trash in the Trash container
       use your left hand to replace the lid on the Trash container
   otherwise, do this:
       use your left hand to remove the lid from the Recycle container
       drop the bag of recyclables in the Recycle container
       use your left hand to replace the lid on the Recycle container
   end if
```

Version 2:

```
1. if you are holding a bag of recyclables, do this:
       use your left hand to remove the lid from the Recycle container
       drop the bag of recyclables in the Recycle container
       use your left hand to replace the lid on the Recycle container
   otherwise, do this:
       use your left hand to remove the lid from the Trash container
       drop the bag of trash in the Trash container
       use your left hand to replace the lid on the Trash container
   end if
```

Figure 9-4: Fourth problem using Rob

MINI-QUIZ 1

1. Rob is sitting in a chair in his living room. Next to the chair is a table. On top of the table is Rob's cell phone. Your task is to direct Rob to pick up his cell phone. Does the solution to this problem require a decision? If so, what decision needs to be made?

2. Rob is sitting in a chair in his living room. Next to the chair is a table. On top of the table is Rob's cell phone. Your task is to direct Rob to pick up his cell phone, but only when the phone rings. Does the solution to this problem require a decision? If so, what decision needs to be made?

(continued on next page)

(continued from previous page)

3. Rob is holding a red ball and is facing two boxes. One of the boxes is red and the other is yellow. Your task is to direct Rob to drop the red ball in the red box. Does the solution to this problem require a decision? If so, what decision needs to be made?

4. Rob is holding either a red ball or a yellow ball. He is facing two boxes. One of the boxes is red and the other is yellow. Your task is to direct Rob to drop the ball he is carrying in the appropriate box. Does the solution to this problem require a decision? If so, what decision needs to be made?

GOING BEYOND ROB'S PROBLEMS

Figure 9-5 shows a problem specification that doesn't involve Rob, the mechanical man. It also shows a correct algorithm for the problem. Because no decisions need to be made to solve the problem, the algorithm uses only the sequence structure.

Mary is paid a 2% bonus on her annual sales. She wants a program that both calculates and displays the amount of her bonus.

Output: bonus

Input: annual sales

Algorithm:
1. enter the annual sales
2. calculate the bonus by multiplying the annual sales by 2%
3. display the bonus

Figure 9-5: Bonus problem specification and algorithm

Consider how you would need to change the algorithm shown in Figure 9-5 if Mary is paid a 2% bonus only when she sells at least $3000 in product; otherwise, she is paid a 1.5% bonus. The modified problem specification and its algorithm are shown in Figure 9-6. Unlike the original algorithm, the modified algorithm needs to make a decision about Mary's sales amount before the bonus is calculated. Based on the result of that decision, the algorithm will assign either 2% or 1.5% as the bonus rate.

Mary is paid a 2% bonus on her annual sales when the sales are at least $3000; otherwise, she is paid a 1.5% bonus. She wants a program that both calculates and displays the amount of her bonus.

Output: bonus

Processing: bonus rate

Input: annual sales

Algorithm:
1. enter the annual sales
2. if the annual sales are at least 3000, do this:
        assign 2% as the bonus rate
    otherwise, do this:
        assign 1.5% as the bonus rate
    end if
3. calculate the bonus by multiplying the annual sales by the bonus rate
4. display the bonus

Figure 9-6: Modified bonus problem specification and its algorithm

For more experience in examining problem specifications, see the Problem Specifications section in the Ch9WantMore.pdf file.

In the next set of steps, you begin coding the algorithm shown in Figure 9-6.

To open the Bonus application, and then begin coding the application:

1. Start Visual Studio 2008 (or Visual Basic 2008 Express Edition). Open the **Bonus Solution (Bonus Solution.sln)** file, which is contained in the ClearlyVB\Chap09\Bonus Solution folder. If necessary, open the designer window. The application's interface is shown in Figure 9-7.

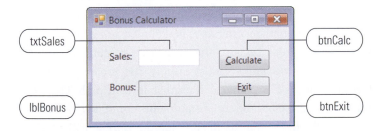

Figure 9-7: Bonus application's interface

2. Open the Code Editor window, which contains the code for the btnExit control's Click event procedure.

3. Open the btnCalc control's Click event procedure. First, you will enter the variable declaration statements. The procedure will use three Decimal variables for the input, processing, and output items. Type **' calculates and displays a bonus amount** and press **Enter** twice. Type **dim decSales as decimal** and press **Enter**. Type **dim decRate as decimal** and press **Enter**, then type **dim decBonus as decimal** and press **Enter** twice.

4. The first step in the algorithm is to enter the annual sales. The user will enter the amount in the txtSales control in the interface. The procedure will need to convert the user's entry to a number, storing the result in the decSales variable. Type **' assign sales to a variable** and press **Enter**, then type **decimal.tryparse(txtSales.text, decSales)** and press **Enter** twice.

5. Save the solution.

THE IF...THEN...ELSE STATEMENT

Step 2 in the algorithm shown in Figure 9-6 is a selection structure. You can code the selection structure in Visual Basic using the If...Then...Else statement. Figure 9-8 shows the statement's syntax. The items in square brackets in the syntax are optional. In other words, you do not always need to include the Else portion of the syntax, referred to as the Else clause, in an If...Then...Else statement. Items in boldface, however, are essential components of the statement. The keywords If, Then, and End If, for instance, must be included in the If...Then...Else statement. The keyword Else must be included only when the programmer needs to use the Else clause. Italicized items in the syntax indicate where the programmer must supply information. In the If...Then...Else statement, the programmer must supply the *condition* that the computer needs to evaluate before further processing can occur. The condition must be a Boolean expression, which is an expression that results in a Boolean value (True or False). The expressions in most conditions are formed using comparison operators. A listing of the most commonly used comparison operators is included in Figure 9-8. The operators are called **comparison operators** because they are used to compare values. Besides supplying the *condition*, the programmer must supply the statements to be processed in the If...Then...Else statement's true path and, if used, in its false path. The set of statements contained in the true path, as well as the set of statements contained in the false path, is referred to as a **statement block**. In addition to showing the If...Then...Else statement's syntax and the comparison operators, Figure 9-8 also shows examples of using comparison operators in the *condition*. Notice that the expression contained in each example's *condition* evaluates to a Boolean value—either True or False. All expressions containing a comparison operator will result in an answer of either True or False only.

IF...THEN...ELSE STATEMENT

Syntax

If *condition* **Then**

statement block containing one or more statements to be processed when the condition is true

[**Else**

statement block containing one or more statements to be processed when the condition is false]

End If

Most commonly used comparison operators

Operator	Operation
=	equal to
>	greater than
>=	greater than or equal to
<	less than
<=	less than or equal to
<>	not equal to

Example 1

```
Dim intAge As Integer
Dim decDiscount As Decimal
Integer.TryParse(txtAge.Text, intAge)
If intAge >= 65 Then
      decDiscount = .15
      lblMessage.Text = "Senior Discount"
Else
      decDiscount = .1
      lblMessage.Text = "Regular Discount"
End If
```

If the intAge variable contains a number that is greater than or equal to 65, the instructions in the true path assign .15 to the decDiscount variable and assign the string "Senior Discount" to the lblMessage control; otherwise, the instructions in the false path assign .1 to the decDiscount variable and assign the string "Regular Discount" to the lblMessage control.

Figure 9-8: If...Then...Else statement and comparison operators (*continued on next page*)

Example 2
```
Dim decOwed As Decimal
Dim decPaid As Decimal
Dim decDifference As Decimal
Decimal.TryParse(txtOwed.Text, decOwed)
Decimal.TryParse(txtPaid.Text, decPaid)
decDifference = decPaid - decOwed
If decDifference < 0 Then
      lblMessage.Text = "You still owe money"
End If
lblDifference.Text = decDifference.ToString("C2")
```

If the decDifference variable contains a number that is less than zero, the instruction in the true path assigns the string "You still owe money" to the lblMessage control.

Figure 9-8: If…Then…Else statement and comparison operators (*continued from previous page*)

The selection structure in Example 1 in Figure 9-8 tells the computer to perform one set of tasks when the condition evaluates to True, but a different set of tasks when the condition evaluates to False. In Example 2, the selection structure tells the computer to perform the one task only when the condition evaluates to True. Keep in mind that comparison operators are evaluated after any arithmetic operators in an expression. When processing the expression 7 > 3 + 5, for example, the computer first will add the number 3 to the number 5, giving 8. It then will compare the number 7 to the number 8. Because 7 is not greater than 8, the expression will evaluate to False.

To complete the btnCalc control's Click event procedure:

1. According to Step 2 in the algorithm from Figure 9-6, the selection structure's *condition* needs to compare Mary's sales amount with the number 3000. The "at least 3000" in the algorithm means that the smallest amount that qualifies for the 2% bonus is $3000. Therefore, the correct comparison operator to use in the *condition* is the >= (greater than or equal to) operator. Type ' **determine bonus rate** and press **Enter**, then type **if decSales >= 3000 then** and press **Enter**. Notice that the Code Editor automatically enters the End If line for you. It also automatically indents the current line.

2. If the value stored in the decSales variable is greater than or equal to 3000, the *condition* will evaluate to True. In that case, the bonus rate should be 2%. You will assign the bonus rate, converted to its decimal equivalent, to the decRate variable. Type **decRate = .02** and press **Enter**.

3. If the value stored in the decSales variable is not greater than or equal to 3000, the *condition* will evaluate to False. In that case, the bonus rate should be 1.5%, or .015. Type **else** and press **Enter**, then type **decRate = .015**.

4. Steps 3 and 4 in the algorithm are to calculate and then display the bonus. Click **immediately after the letter f** in the End If line, then press **Enter** twice to insert two blank lines. Type the comment and two lines of code indicated in Figure 9-9.

```
btnCalc                                        ▾  Click
    Private Sub btnCalc_Click(ByVal sender As Object, ByVal e As System.Event
        ' calculates and displays a bonus amount

        Dim decSales As Decimal
        Dim decRate As Decimal
        Dim decBonus As Decimal

        ' assign sales to a variable
        Decimal.TryParse(txtSales.Text, decSales)

        ' determine bonus rate
        If decSales >= 3000 Then
            decRate = 0.02
        Else
            decRate = 0.015
        End If

        ' calculate and display the bonus
        decBonus = decSales * decRate
        lblBonus.Text = decBonus.ToString("C2")

    End Sub
```

enter this comment and two lines of code

Figure 9-9: Completed Click event procedure for the btnCalc control

Figure 9-10 shows a desk-check table for the Bonus program. On your own, desk-check the program using other sales amounts.

decSales	decRate	decBonus (rounded to two decimal places)
~~3500.75~~	~~.02~~	~~70.02~~
500.25	.015	7.50

Figure 9-10: Completed desk-check table for the Bonus program

To test the Bonus application:

1. Save the solution, then start the application. Use the sales amounts shown in Figure 9-10, as well as your own sales amounts, to test the application.

2. When you are finished testing the application, click the **Exit** button. Close the Code Editor window, then close the solution.

EXAMINING ANOTHER PROBLEM SPECIFICATION

Figure 9-11 shows another problem specification whose solution requires a selection structure. The figure also includes a correct algorithm (in flowchart form) for the problem. In this case, the algorithm needs to determine whether the customer is an employee.

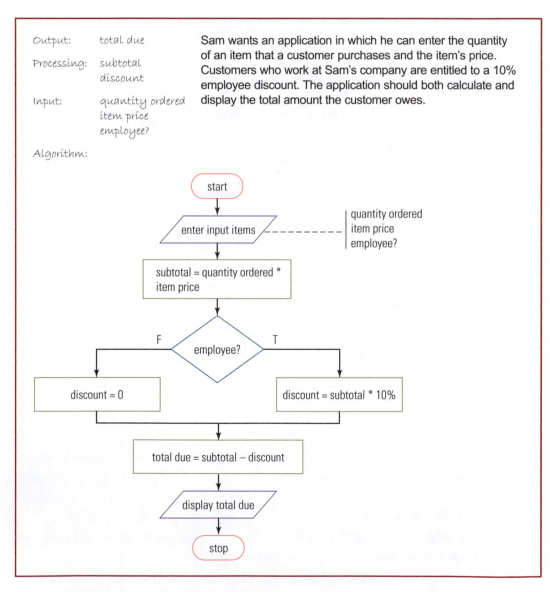

Output: total due

Processing: subtotal
               discount

Input: quantity ordered
               item price
               employee?

Algorithm:

Sam wants an application in which he can enter the quantity of an item that a customer purchases and the item's price. Customers who work at Sam's company are entitled to a 10% employee discount. The application should both calculate and display the total amount the customer owes.

Figure 9-11: Total Due problem specification and algorithm

Recall from Chapter 3 that the oval in a flowchart is the start/stop symbol, the rectangle is the process symbol, and the parallelogram is the input/output symbol. The diamond in a flowchart is called the **selection/repetition symbol**, because it is used to represent the condition in both the selection and repetition structures. In Figure 9-11's flowchart, the diamond represents the condition in a selection structure. (You will learn how to use the diamond to represent a repetition structure's condition in a later chapter.) Inside the diamond is a question whose answer is either True or False. Each diamond also has one flowline entering the symbol and two flowlines leaving the symbol. The two flowlines leading out of the diamond should be marked so that anyone reading the flowchart can distinguish the true path from the false path. You mark the flowline leading to the true path with a "T" (for True), and you mark the flowline leading to the false path with an "F" (for False). You also can mark the flowlines leading out of the diamond with a "Y" and an "N" (for Yes and No).

To open the Total Due application, and then complete the user interface and the code:

1. Open the **Total Due Solution** (**Total Due Solution.sln**) file, which is contained in the ClearlyVB\Chap09\Total Due Solution folder. If necessary, open the designer window. The application's partially completed interface appears on the screen. The user will enter the quantity ordered and the item's price in the two text boxes. The employee information will be entered using a check box, which you will add to the interface in the next step.

2. Click the **CheckBox** tool in the toolbox, then drag a check box to the form. The three-character ID used when naming check boxes is chk. Change the check box's Name property to **chkEmployee**. Change its Location property to **127, 22**. Change its Text property to **&Employee**. (The Text property of a check box should be entered using sentence capitalization, which you learned about in Chapter 5.) If the customer is an employee, the user will need to select the check box; otherwise, the check box should be unselected. You can select a check box by clicking it. When a check box is selected, clicking it again deselects it. The completed interface is shown in Figure 9-12.

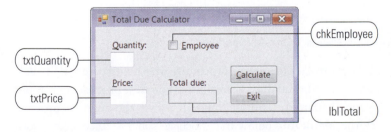

Figure 9-12: Completed interface for the Total Due application

3. Right-click the **form**, then click **Lock Controls**. Click **View** on the menu bar, then click **Tab Order**. Use the information shown in Figure 9-13 to set the tab order.

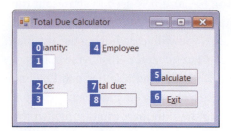

Figure 9-13: Correct TabIndex values for the interface

4. Press **Esc** to remove the TabIndex boxes from the form, then save the solution.

5. Open the Code Editor window, which contains the code for the btnExit control's Click event procedure. It also contains the partially completed Click event procedure for the btnCalc control, as shown in Figure 9-14. Notice that the procedure declares a named constant for the 10% discount rate. It also declares five variables to store the quantity ordered, item price, subtotal, discount, and total due. In addition, it assigns the quantity and price information to two of the variables. The assignment statement in the procedure displays the total due in the lblTotal control.

```
Private Sub btnCalc_Click(ByVal sender As Object, ByVal e As System.EventArgs) H
    ' calculates and displays the total amount due

    Const decDISC_RATE As Decimal = 0.1
    Dim intQuantity As Integer
    Dim decPrice As Decimal
    Dim decSubtotal As Decimal
    Dim decDiscount As Decimal
    Dim decTotal As Decimal

    ' assign quantity and price to variables
    Integer.TryParse(txtQuantity.Text, intQuantity)
    Decimal.TryParse(txtPrice.Text, decPrice)

    ' calculate subtotal, discount, and total due

    ' display total due
    lblTotal.Text = decTotal.ToString("C2")
End Sub
```

Figure 9-14: Partially completed Click event procedure for the btnCalc control

6. Missing from the btnCalc control's Click event procedure are the instructions to calculate the subtotal, discount, and total due. According to the first processing symbol shown in Figure 9-11, you calculate the subtotal by multiplying the quantity ordered by the item price. Click the **blank line** below the ' calculate subtotal, discount, and total due comment. Type **decSubtotal = intQuantity * decPrice** and press **Enter**.

7. The next symbol in the flowchart is a diamond that represents the condition in a selection structure. The selection structure's condition should determine whether the customer is an employee. Recall that the user indicates an employee by selecting the Employee check box. If the check box is not selected, it means that the customer is not an employee. You can use a check box's Checked property to determine its status: if the check box is selected, its Checked property contains the Boolean value, True; otherwise, it contains the Boolean value, False. Type **if chkEmployee.checked = true then** and press **Enter**.

8. Next, you need to code the selection structure's true path. According to the flowchart, a customer who is an employee should receive a 10% discount. Type **decDiscount = decSubtotal * decDISC_RATE** and press **Enter**. You have finished coding the true path; the false path is next.

9. According to the flowchart, a customer who is not an employee should not receive a discount. Type **else** and press **Enter**, then type **decDiscount = 0**. You have finished coding the selection structure.

10. Finally, you need to code the processing symbol located after the selection structure. The processing symbol tells you to calculate the total due by subtracting the discount from the subtotal. Click **immediately after the letter f** in the End If line, then press **Enter**. Type **decTotal = decSubtotal – decDiscount** and press **Enter**. You have finished coding the procedure. (The procedure already contains the code pertaining to the last parallelogram in the flowchart.) Figure 9-15 shows the procedure's code.

```
btnCalc                                                    Click
       Private Sub btnCalc_Click(ByVal sender As Object, ByVal e As System.EventArgs) Handles btn
           ' calculates and displays the total amount due

           Const decDISC_RATE As Decimal = 0.1
           Dim intQuantity As Integer
           Dim decPrice As Decimal
           Dim decSubtotal As Decimal
           Dim decDiscount As Decimal
           Dim decTotal As Decimal

           ' assign quantity and price to variables
           Integer.TryParse(txtQuantity.Text, intQuantity)
           Decimal.TryParse(txtPrice.Text, decPrice)

           ' calculate subtotal, discount, and total due
           decSubtotal = intQuantity * decPrice
           If chkEmployee.Checked = True Then
               decDiscount = decSubtotal * decDISC_RATE
           Else
               decDiscount = 0
           End If
           decTotal = decSubtotal - decDiscount

           ' display total due
           lblTotal.Text = decTotal.ToString("C2")
       End Sub
```

Figure 9-15: Completed Click event procedure for the btnCalc control

Figure 9-16 shows a desk-check table for the Total Due program. On your own, desk-check the program using other values for the input items.

decDISC_RATE	intQuantity	decPrice	chkEmployee.Checked
~~0.1~~	~~10~~	~~2.50~~	~~True~~
0.1	10	2.50	False

decSubtotal	decDiscount	decTotal
~~25.00~~	~~2.50~~	~~22.50~~
25.00	0	25.00

Figure 9-16: Completed desk-check table for the Total Due program

To test the Total Due application:

1. Save the solution, then start the application. Use the quantity, price, and check box information shown in Figure 9-16, as well as your own data, to test the application.

2. When you are finished testing the application, click the **Exit** button. Close the Code Editor window, then close the solution.

HEY, THAT'S NOT THE WAY *I* WOULD HAVE DONE IT

There are always several ways of solving a problem. Figure 9-17, for example, shows a different way of solving the Total Due problem from the previous section, and Figure 9-18 shows the corresponding code. Notice that this version of the solution does not use any processing items. Also notice that, unlike the selection structure shown earlier in Figure 9-11, the selection structure in Figure 9-17 contains an instruction in its true path only. The instruction multiplies the total due by 90%, because that is the amount the employee would owe after getting the 10% discount.

Sam wants an application in which he can enter the quantity of an item that a customer purchases and the item's price. Customers who work at Sam's company are entitled to a 10% employee discount. The application should both calculate and display the total amount the customer owes.

Output: total due

Input: quantity ordered
            item price
            employee?

Algorithm:

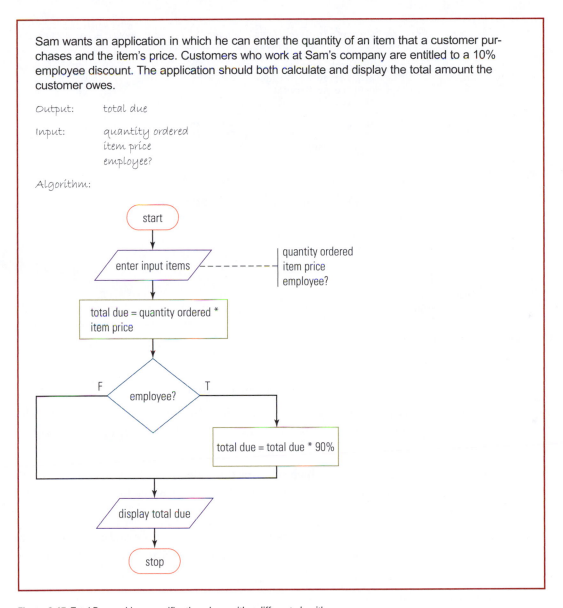

Figure 9-17: Total Due problem specification along with a different algorithm

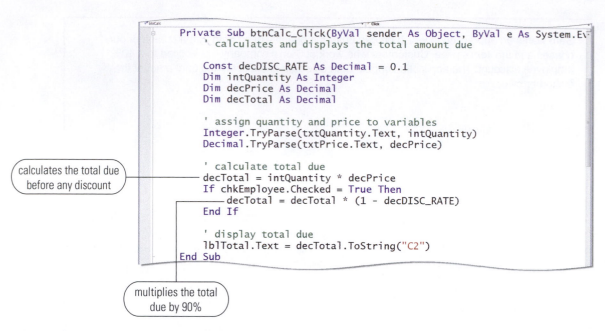

```
Private Sub btnCalc_Click(ByVal sender As Object, ByVal e As System.Ev
    ' calculates and displays the total amount due

    Const decDISC_RATE As Decimal = 0.1
    Dim intQuantity As Integer
    Dim decPrice As Decimal
    Dim decTotal As Decimal

    ' assign quantity and price to variables
    Integer.TryParse(txtQuantity.Text, intQuantity)
    Decimal.TryParse(txtPrice.Text, decPrice)

    ' calculate total due
    decTotal = intQuantity * decPrice
    If chkEmployee.Checked = True Then
        decTotal = decTotal * (1 - decDISC_RATE)
    End If

    ' display total due
    lblTotal.Text = decTotal.ToString("C2")
End Sub
```

calculates the total due before any discount

multiplies the total due by 90%

Figure 9-18: Code corresponding to Figure 9-17's algorithm

To code the Total Due—Version 2 application, and then test it:

1. Open the **Total Due Solution** (**Total Due Solution.sln**) file, which is contained in the ClearlyVB\Chap09\Total Due Solution—Version 2 folder. If necessary, open the designer window.

2. Open the Code Editor window, which contains the code for the btnExit control's Click event procedure. Open the btnCalc control's Click event procedure, then enter the code shown in Figure 9-18.

3. Save the solution, then start the application. Use the quantity, price, and check box information shown earlier in Figure 9-16, as well as your own data, to test the application.

4. When you are finished testing the application, click the **Exit** button. Close the Code Editor window, then close the solution.

Figure 9-19 shows still a different way of solving the Total Due problem, and Figure 9-20 shows the corresponding code.

Sam wants an application in which he can enter the quantity of an item that a customer purchases and the item's price. Customers who work at Sam's company are entitled to a 10% employee discount. The application should both calculate and display the total amount the customer owes.

Output: total due

Processing: discount

Input: quantity ordered
               item price
               employee?

Algorithm:
1. enter the quantity ordered, item price, and employee? items
2. calculate the total due by multiplying the quantity ordered by the item price
3. if employee?, do this:
       calculate the discount by multiplying the total due by 10%
       subtract the discount from the total due
   end if
4. display the total due

Figure 9-19: A different way of solving the Total Due problem

```
Private Sub btnCalc_Click(ByVal sender As Object, ByVal e As System.EventArgs
    ' calculates and displays the total amount due

    Const decDISC_RATE As Decimal = 0.1
    Dim intQuantity As Integer
    Dim decPrice As Decimal
    Dim decTotal As Decimal

    ' assign quantity and price to variables
    Integer.TryParse(txtQuantity.Text, intQuantity)
    Decimal.TryParse(txtPrice.Text, decPrice)

    ' calculate total due
    decTotal = intQuantity * decPrice
    If chkEmployee.Checked = True Then
        Dim decDiscount As Decimal
        decDiscount = decTotal * decDISC_RATE
        decTotal = decTotal - decDiscount
    End If

    ' display total due
    lblTotal.Text = decTotal.ToString("C2")
End Sub
```

block variable

Figure 9-20: Code corresponding to Figure 9-19's algorithm

Study closely the instructions in the selection structure's true path shown in Figure 9-20. The first instruction, Dim decDiscount As Decimal, declares a variable named decDiscount. Like the variables declared at the beginning of a procedure, variables declared within a statement block in a selection structure remain in memory until the procedure ends. However, unlike variables declared at the beginning of a procedure, variables declared within a statement block have block scope rather than procedure scope. A variable that has procedure scope can be used anywhere within the procedure, whereas a variable that has **block scope** can be used only within the statement block in which it is declared. In this case, for example, the intQuantity, decPrice, and decTotal variables (and also the decDISC_RATE named constant) can be used anywhere within the btnCalc control's Click event procedure, but the decDiscount variable can be used only within the If...Then...Else statement's true path. You may be wondering why the decDiscount variable was not declared at the beginning of the procedure, along with the other variables. Although there is nothing wrong with declaring all variables at the beginning of a procedure, the decDiscount variable is necessary only when the discount needs to be calculated, so many programmers would prefer to create the variable only if it is necessary to do so. This is because fewer unintentional errors occur in applications when the variables are declared using the minimum scope needed. In this case, the minimum scope for the decDiscount variable is block scope, because only the selection structure's true path uses the variable. A variable declared within a statement block is called a **block variable**.

To code the Total Due—Version 3 application, and then test it:

1. Open the **Total Due Solution** (**Total Due Solution.sln**) file, which is contained in the ClearlyVB\Chap09\Total Due Solution—Version 3 folder. If necessary, open the designer window.

2. Open the Code Editor window, which contains the code for the btnExit control's Click event procedure. Open the btnCalc control's Click event procedure, then enter the code shown in Figure 9-20.

3. Save the solution, then start the application. Use the quantity, price, and check box information shown earlier in Figure 9-16, as well as your own data, to test the application.

4. When you are finished testing the application, click the **Exit** button. Close the Code Editor window, then close the solution.

MINI-QUIZ 2

1. Write an If...Then...Else statement that displays the string "Overtime pay" in the lblMsg control when the number of hours contained in the decHours variable is greater than 40.

2. Modify the If...Then...Else statement from Question 1 so that it displays the string "Regular pay only" when the selection structure's condition evaluates to False.

3. What is the scope of a variable declared in a selection structure's false path?

   a. the entire application

   b. the procedure containing the selection structure

   c. the entire selection structure

   d. only the selection structure's false path

For more examples of selection structures, see the Selection Structure section in the Ch9WantMore.pdf file.

It's time to view the Ch09-Selection Structure video.

SUMMARY

» The selection structure is one of the three control structures. It is used when you need the computer to make a decision and then take an appropriate action.

» Studying the problem specification will help you determine whether a solution requires a selection structure.

» You should indent the instructions in a selection structure's true path and in its false path. The set of instructions in each path is called a statement block.

» You can use the If...Then...Else statement to code the selection structure in Visual Basic. The statement's condition must contain an expression that evaluates to a Boolean value, either True or False. You will find comparison operators in most conditions.

» An expression containing a comparison operator will always evaluate to either True or False.

» In a flowchart, the selection structure's condition is represented by a diamond, which is called the selection/repetition symbol. The diamond should contain a question or comparison that evaluates to either True or False only. The two flowlines leading out of the diamond should indicate the true path and the false path.

» The three-character ID used when naming check boxes is chk. When a check box is selected, its Checked property contains the Boolean value, True; otherwise, it contains the Boolean value, False.

» There are many ways to solve the same problem.

» A block variable has block scope, which means it can be used only within the block in which it is declared.

KEY TERMS

Block scope—the scope of a block variable; refers to the fact that the variable can be used only within the statement block in which it is declared

Block variable—a variable declared within a statement block; the variable has block scope

Comparison operators—the operators used to compare values in a selection structure's condition

Selection/repetition symbol—the diamond in a flowchart

Selection structure—the structure used in a program to indicate that a decision needs to be made, and an appropriate action needs to be taken based on the result

Statement block—the set of instructions in a selection structure's true path, and the set of instructions in its false path

ANSWERS TO MINI-QUIZZES

MINI-QUIZ 1

1. The solution does not require a decision.

2. The solution requires a decision about whether the phone is ringing.

3. The solution does not require a decision.

4. The solution requires a decision about the color of the ball.

MINI-QUIZ 2

1. If decHours > 40 Then
       lblMsg.Text = "Overtime pay"
   End if

2. If decHours > 40 Then
       lblMsg.Text = "Overtime pay"
   Else
       lblMsg.Text = "Regular pay only"
   End if

3. d. only the selection structure's false path

REVIEW QUESTIONS

1. Which of the following conditions will evaluate to True when the intPopulation variable contains the value 56000?

   a. If intPopulation = 56000 Then

   b. If intPopulation <> 0 Then

   c. If intPopulation > 1 Then

   d. All of the above.

2. Which of the following conditions will evaluate to True when the chkShipping check box is not selected?

   a. If chkShipping.Check = False Then

   b. If chkShipping.Checked = False Then

   c. If chkShipping.Checked = No Then

   d. If chkShipping.Check = No Then

3. Which of the following has the smallest scope?

   a. A variable declared at the beginning of a procedure.

   b. A variable declared within a selection structure's true path.

   c. A variable declared within a selection structure's false path.

   d. Both b and c.

4. Which of the following is used to represent the selection structure's condition in a flowchart?

   a. diamond   b. oval

   c. parallelogram   d. rectangle

5. If the decRate variable contains the value .25, the condition decRate > 1 will evaluate to
_____ .

    a. False   b. No

    c. True   d. Yes

EXERCISES

»TRY THIS

1. In this exercise, you calculate either the sum of or the difference between two integers
entered by the user. (The answers to TRY THIS Exercises are located at the end of the
chapter.)

    a. Open the AddSub Solution (AddSub Solution.sln) file contained in the ClearlyVB\
Chap09\AddSub Solution folder. If the user wants to subtract the two integers, he
or she will need to select the Subtraction check box. If the check box is not selected,
the integers should be added. List the output and input items, as well as any processing items, then create an appropriate algorithm.

    b. Code the btnCalc control's Click event procedure. Save the solution, then start and
test the application. Stop the application, then close the solution.

»TRY THIS

2. In this exercise, you code an application that calculates and displays the amount of an
employee's new weekly pay. Figure 9-21 shows the output, processing, input, and algorithm. (The answers to TRY THIS Exercises are located at the end of the chapter.)

```
Output:      new weekly pay

Processing:  raise rate
             weekly raise

Input:       pay code
             current weekly pay

Algorithm:
1. enter the pay code and current weekly pay
2. if the pay code is 1, do this:
      assign .03 as the raise rate
   otherwise, do this:
      assign .05 as the raise rate
   end if
3. calculate the weekly raise by multiplying the current weekly pay by the raise rate
4. calculate the new weekly pay by adding the weekly raise to the current weekly pay
5. display the new weekly pay
```

Figure 9-21

a. Open the New Pay Solution (New Pay Solution.sln) file contained in the ClearlyVB\Chap09\New Pay Solution folder. Code the algorithm using Decimal variables for everything but the pay code. Format the new weekly pay with a dollar sign and two decimal places.

b. Save the solution. Desk-check the program using 1 as the pay code and 200 as the current weekly pay. Then desk-check the program using 3 as the pay code and 200 as the current weekly pay.

c. Start and then test the application. Stop the application, then close the solution.

3. In this exercise, you modify one of the Total Due applications completed in the chapter. **»MODIFY THIS**

a. Use Windows to make a copy of the Total Due Solution folder. Save the copy in the ClearlyVB\Chap09 folder. Rename the copy Modified Total Due Solution.

b. Open the Total Due Solution (Total Due Solution.sln) file contained in the Modified Total Due Solution folder. Currently, the selection structure determines whether the check box is selected. Modify the selection structure so that it determines whether the check box is not selected.

c. Save the solution. Start and then test the application. Stop the application, then close the solution.

4. Computer Haven offers programming seminars to companies. The price per person depends on the number of people the company registers. If the company registers from 1 to 10 people, the price per person is $100. If the company registers more than 10 people, the price per person is $80. Computer Haven wants an application that calculates the total amount a company owes. **»INTRODUCTORY**

a. List the output and input items, as well as any processing items, then create an appropriate algorithm.

b. Create a new Visual Basic Windows application. Assign the name Seminar Project to the project. Assign the name Seminar Solution to the solution. Save the application in the ClearlyVB\Chap09 folder. Change the name of the form file on your disk to frmMain.vb. If necessary, change the form's name to frmMain.

c. Create an appropriate interface. Include an Exit button. Code the Exit button's Click event procedure and the problem's algorithm. Save the solution. Desk-check the program using your own sample data.

d. Start and then test the application. Stop the application, then close the solution.

»INTRODUCTORY

5. Tea Time Company wants an application that allows the clerk to enter the number of pounds of tea ordered, the price per pound, and whether the customer should be charged the $15 shipping fee. Use a check box for the shipping information. The application should calculate the total due.

   a. List the output and input items, as well as any processing items, then create an appropriate algorithm.

   b. Create a new Visual Basic Windows application. Assign the name Tea Time Project to the project. Assign the name Tea Time Solution to the solution. Save the application in the ClearlyVB\Chap09 folder. Change the name of the form file on your disk to frmMain.vb. If necessary, change the form's name to frmMain.

   c. Create an appropriate interface. Include an Exit button. Code the Exit button's Click event procedure and the problem's algorithm. Save the solution. Desk-check the program using your own sample data.

   d. Start and then test the application. Stop the application, then close the solution.

»INTERMEDIATE

6. Marcy's Department Store is having a BoGoHo (Buy One, Get One Half Off) sale. Create an application that allows the user to enter the prices of two items. The application should both calculate and display the total owed. The half-off should always be taken on the item having the lowest price. For example, if one item costs $24.99 and the other item costs $12.50, the half-off would be taken on the $12.50 item. (In other words, the item would cost $6.25.) Name the solution, project, and form file Marcy Solution, Marcy Project, and frmMain.vb, respectively. Save the application in the ClearlyVB\Chap09 folder. Code the application. Save the solution, then start and test the application. Stop the application, then close the solution.

»INTERMEDIATE

7. Allenton Water Department wants an application that calculates a customer's water bill. The clerk will enter the current meter reading and the previous meter reading. The application should calculate and display the number of gallons of water used and the total charge for the water. The charge for water is $1.75 per 1000 gallons, or .00175 per gallon. Make the calculations only when the current meter reading is greater than or equal to the previous meter reading; otherwise, display -1 as the number of gallons used and the total charge. Name the solution, project, and form file Allenton Solution, Allenton Project, and frmMain.vb, respectively. Save the application in the ClearlyVB\Chap09 folder. Code the application. Save the solution, then start and test the application. Stop the application, then close the solution.

8. In this exercise, you modify the application from Chapter 7's Exercise 8. If you did not complete Chapter 7's Exercise 8, you will need to do so before you can complete this exercise. **»ADVANCED**

 a. Use Windows to copy the Sun Solution folder from the ClearlyVB\Chap07 folder to the ClearlyVB\Chap09 folder.

 b. Open the Sun Solution (Sun Solution.sln) file contained in the ClearlyVB\Chap09\ Sun Solution folder. Modify the code so that it pays the employee time and one-half for any hours worked over 40.

 c. Save and then start the application. Test the application using 35.5 as the hours worked and 9.56 as the pay rate. The net pay will be $237.56. Now test the application using 44 as the hours worked and 9.56 as the pay rate. The net pay will be $307.83. Stop the application, then close the solution.

9. Ned's Health Club wants an application that calculates and displays a member's monthly dues. Each member is charged a basic fee of $25 per month; however, there are additional monthly charges for golf, racquetball, and tennis. The additional monthly charges are $5 for racquetball, $10 for golf, and $20 for tennis. The interface should include three check boxes for the additional charge information. Use a text box for the member's name and a label to display the monthly dues. Name the solution, project, and form file Health Solution, Health Project, and frmMain.vb, respectively. Save the application in the ClearlyVB\Chap09 folder. Code the application. Save the solution, then start and test the application. Stop the application, then close the solution. **»ADVANCED**

10. Open the FigureThisOut Solution (FigureThisOut Solution.sln) file, which is contained in the ClearlyVB\Chap09\FigureThisOut Solution folder. Start the application. Enter 2 as the first number and 5 as the second number, then click the Display button. Enter 7 as the first number and 6 as the second number, then click the Display button. Stop the application. Open the Code Editor window and study the btnDisplay control's Click event procedure. What task is performed by the procedure? What is the purpose of the selection structure? What is the purpose of the block variable? Why is the variable necessary? Close the solution.

11. In this exercise, you find an error in an application's code. Open the SwatTheBugs Solution (SwatTheBugs Solution.sln) file, which is contained in the ClearlyVB\ Chap09\SwatTheBugs Solution folder. Open the Code Editor window and study the code. Start and then test the application. Notice that the code is not working correctly. Locate and correct any errors.

ANSWERS TO "TRY THIS" EXERCISES

1. See Figures 9-22 and 9-23.

Output: answer

Input: first integer
        second integer
        subtraction?

Algorithm:
1. enter the first integer, second integer, and subtraction? items
2. if subtraction?, do this:
    calculate the answer by subtracting the second integer from the first integer
  otherwise, do this:
    calculate the answer by adding the second integer to the first integer
  end if
3. display the answer

Figure 9-22

```
Private Sub btnCalc_Click(ByVal sender As Object, ByVal e As System.EventArgs
    ' calculates either the sum of or the difference between two numbers

    Dim intNum1 As Integer
    Dim intNum2 As Integer
    Dim intAnswer As Integer

    ' assign numbers to variables
    Integer.TryParse(txtNum1.Text, intNum1)
    Integer.TryParse(txtNum2.Text, intNum2)

    ' calculate and display the difference or sum
    If chkSubtract.Checked = True Then
        intAnswer = intNum1 - intNum2
    Else
        intAnswer = intNum1 + intNum2
    End If
    lblAnswer.Text = intAnswer
End Sub
```

Figure 9-23

2. See Figures 9-24 and 9-25.

intCode	decCurrentPay	decRate	decRaise	decNewPay
~~1~~	~~200~~	~~.03~~	~~6~~	~~206~~
3	200	.05	10	210

Figure 9-24

```
Private Sub btnCalculate_Click(ByVal sender As Object, ByVal e As System.EventAr(
    ' calculates and displays the new weekly pay

    Dim intCode As Integer
    Dim decCurrentPay As Decimal
    Dim decRate As Decimal
    Dim decRaise As Decimal
    Dim decNewPay As Decimal

    ' assign input to variables
    Integer.TryParse(txtCode.Text, intCode)
    Decimal.TryParse(txtCurrentPay.Text, decCurrentPay)

    ' calculate raise and new pay
    If intCode = 1 Then
        decRate = 0.03
    Else
        decRate = 0.05
    End If
    decRaise = decCurrentPay * decRate
    decNewPay = decCurrentPay + decRaise

    ' display new pay
    lblNewPay.Text = decNewPay.ToString("C2")
End Sub
```

Figure 9-25

10

TIME TO LEAVE THE NEST

After studying Chapter 10, you should be able to:

Nest selection structures

Include logical operators in a selection structure's condition

NESTED SELECTION STRUCTURES

As you learned in Chapter 9, you use the selection structure to make a decision and then select the appropriate path—either the true path or the false path—based on the result. Both paths in a selection structure can include instructions that declare variables, perform calculations, and so on. Both paths also can include other selection structures. When either a selection structure's true path or its false path contains another selection structure, the inner selection structure is referred to as a **nested selection structure**, because it is contained (nested) within the outer selection structure. You use a nested selection structure when more than one decision must be made before the appropriate action can be taken. Similar to the initial examples of selection structures in Chapter 9, the first examples of nested selection structures will involve Rob, the mechanical man. The first problem specification and its algorithm are shown in Figure 10-1. (The problem specification and algorithm are from Figure 9-4 in Chapter 9. Figure 9-3 shows an illustration of Rob and the containers.) The algorithm requires a selection structure, but not a nested one. This is because only one decision—whether Rob is holding a bag of trash—is necessary.

Rob is holding either a bag of trash or a bag of recyclables in his right hand. He is directly in front of two containers: one marked Trash and the other marked Recycle. A lid is on each container. Rob needs to remove the lid from the appropriate container, then drop the bag in the container, and then replace the lid.

1. if you are holding a bag of trash, do this:
      use your left hand to remove the lid from the Trash container
      drop the bag of trash in the Trash container
      use your left hand to replace the lid on the Trash container
   otherwise, do this:
      use your left hand to remove the lid from the Recycle container
      drop the bag of recyclables in the Recycle container
      use your left hand to replace the lid on the Recycle container
   end if

Figure 10-1: First problem using Rob

Now let's make a slight change to the problem specification shown in Figure 10-1. This time, the status of the lids on both containers is not known: the lids could be on or off. Consider the changes you will need to make to the original algorithm shown in Figure 10-1. The first instruction in the original algorithm represents the selection structure's condition. In this case, the condition tells Rob to make a decision about the bag he is holding; Rob still will need to make this decision. The next three instructions tell Rob what to do when the condition is true, which is when he is holding a bag of trash. The first instruction in the true path tells Rob to remove the lid from the Trash container. That instruction was correct for the original problem specification, where you knew the lid was on the Trash container.

However, in the modified problem specification, you don't know the status of the lid. Therefore, before instructing Rob to remove the lid, you need to tell him to make a decision about the lid's status, and only remove the lid if it's on the container. The last two instructions in the true path tell Rob to drop the bag of trash in the Trash container and then replace the lid; Rob still will need to follow both instructions. Next, let's look at the false path of the selection structure in the original algorithm. The first instruction in the false path tells Rob to remove the lid from the Recycle container. Here again, Rob first will need to determine whether it's necessary to remove the lid. The last two instructions in the false path tell Rob to drop the bag of recyclables in the Recycle container and then replace the lid; Rob still will need to follow both instructions. Figure 10-2 shows the modified problem specification along with the modified algorithm, which contains an outer selection structure and two nested selection structures. The outer selection structure begins with the *if you are holding a bag of trash, do this:* line, and it ends with the last *end if* line. The *otherwise, do this:* line belongs to the outer selection structure. Notice that the instructions in both the true and false paths are indented within the outer selection structure. Indenting in this manner clearly indicates the instructions to be followed when Rob is holding a bag of trash, as well as the ones to be followed when the bag does not contain trash. One of the nested selection structures appears in the outer selection structure's true path, and the other appears in its false path. The nested selection structure in the true path begins with the *if the lid is on the Trash container, do this:* line and it ends with the first *end if* line. The instruction between both lines is indented to clearly indicate that it is part of the nested selection structure. The nested selection structure in the false path begins with the *if the lid is on the Recycle container, do this:* line and it ends with the second *end if* line. Here again, the instruction between both lines is indented within the nested selection structure.

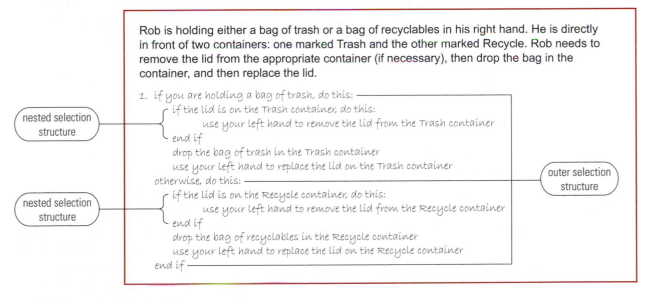

Figure 10-2: Second problem using Rob

Figure 10-3 shows another problem specification involving Rob, along with the correct algorithm. As the algorithm indicates, the problem's solution requires Rob to make only one decision in order to accomplish his task. In this case, he needs to determine the clerk's response as to whether the store accepts the Discovery card.

Rob is at a store's checkout counter, waiting to pay for the items he is purchasing. He'd like to use his Discovery card to pay the bill, but he's not sure whether the store accepts the card. If the store doesn't accept the Discovery card, Rob will need to pay cash for the items he is purchasing.

1. ask the clerk whether the store accepts the Discovery card
2. if the clerk indicates that the store accepts the Discovery card, do this:
        use your Discovery card to pay the bill
    otherwise, do this:
        use cash to pay the bill
    end if

Figure 10-3: Third problem using Rob

Now let's change the problem specification shown in Figure 10-3. This time, Rob would like to use either his Discovery card or his Vita card, but he prefers to use his Discovery card. If the store does not take either card, Rob will need to pay cash for the items he is purchasing. Let's look at each line in the original algorithm shown in Figure 10-3 to determine the changes you will need to make. Rob still will need to ask the clerk whether the store accepts the Discovery card; if it does, Rob should use his Discovery card to pay the bill. Therefore, the first three lines in the original algorithm do not need to be changed. The next line in the algorithm is the *otherwise, do this:* line. The modified algorithm still will need this line to indicate that there are tasks to be performed when the store does not accept the Discovery card. The next line in the original algorithm tells Rob to use cash to pay his bill. That instruction was correct for the original problem specification, which gave Rob only two payment choices: either Discovery or cash. However, in the modified problem specification, Rob has three payment choices: Discovery, Vita, or cash. Before instructing Rob to pay with cash, you need to tell him to inquire whether the store accepts the Vita card; if it does, Rob should use his Vita card to pay the bill. Rob should be instructed to use cash only when the store does not accept either charge card. Figure 10-4 shows the modified problem specification along with its algorithm. The algorithm contains an outer selection structure and a nested selection structure. The outer selection structure begins with the *if the clerk indicates that the store accepts the Discovery card, do this:* line, and it ends with the last *end if* line. The first *otherwise, do this:* line belongs to the outer selection structure. Notice that the instructions in the outer selection structure's true and false paths are indented. The nested selection structure, which appears in the outer selection structure's false path, begins with the *if the clerk indicates that the store accepts the Vita card, do this:* line and it ends with the first *end if* line. The indented *otherwise, do this:* line belongs to the nested selection structure.

For clarity, the instruction in the nested selection structure's true path, as well as the instruction in its false path, is indented within the structure.

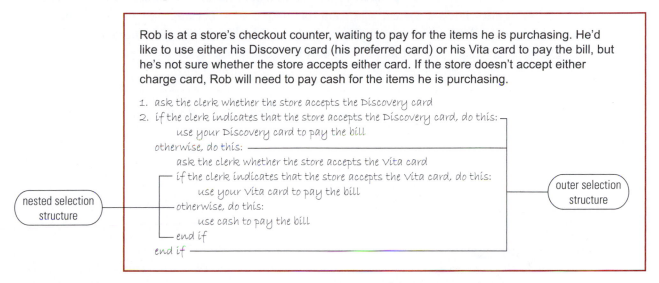

Rob is at a store's checkout counter, waiting to pay for the items he is purchasing. He'd like to use either his Discovery card (his preferred card) or his Vita card to pay the bill, but he's not sure whether the store accepts either card. If the store doesn't accept either charge card, Rob will need to pay cash for the items he is purchasing.

1. ask the clerk whether the store accepts the Discovery card
2. if the clerk indicates that the store accepts the Discovery card, do this:
   use your Discovery card to pay the bill
   otherwise, do this:
   ask the clerk whether the store accepts the Vita card
   if the clerk indicates that the store accepts the Vita card, do this:
   use your Vita card to pay the bill
   otherwise, do this:
   use cash to pay the bill
   end if
end if

nested selection structure

outer selection structure

Figure 10-4: Fourth problem using Rob

MINI-QUIZ 1

1. Rob is sitting in a chair in his living room. Next to the chair is a table. On top of the table is Rob's cell phone. Your task is to direct Rob to answer his cell phone, but only when the phone rings. Does the solution to this problem require a nested selection structure? If so, what decision needs to be made by the nested selection structure's condition?

2. Rob is sitting in a chair in his living room. Next to the chair is a table. On top of the table is Rob's cell phone. Your task is to direct Rob to answer his cell phone, but only when the phone rings. If the caller is a telemarketer, Rob should hang up the phone. Does the solution to this problem require a nested selection structure? If so, what decision needs to be made by the nested selection structure's condition?

3. Rob is holding either a red ball or a yellow ball. He is facing two boxes. One of the boxes is red and the other is yellow. Your task is to direct Rob to drop the ball he is carrying in the appropriate box, but only if the box is not already full. How many nested selection structures does this problem require? What decision needs to be made by each nested selection structure's condition?

PUTTING ROB'S PROBLEMS ASIDE

Figure 10-5 shows a problem specification that doesn't involve Rob, the mechanical man. It also shows a correct algorithm for the problem. Because only one decision—in this case, whether the user wants to perform subtraction—needs to be made to solve the problem, the algorithm requires only one selection structure.

Jennifer wants an application that calculates either the sum of or the difference between the two integers she enters.

Output: answer

Input: first integer
            second integer
            subtraction?

Algorithm:
1. enter the first integer, second integer, and subtraction? items
2. if subtraction?, do this:
        calculate the answer by subtracting the second integer from the first integer
    otherwise, do this:
        calculate the answer by adding the second integer to the first integer
    end if
3. display the answer

Figure 10-5: Math problem specification and algorithm

Consider how you would need to change the algorithm shown in Figure 10-5 if, when performing subtraction, Jennifer wants the application to always subtract the smaller integer from the larger one. The modified problem specification and its algorithm are shown in Figure 10-6. Unlike the original algorithm, the modified algorithm needs to make two decisions. The first decision determines whether the user wants to perform subtraction; if she does, a second decision needs to be made. The second decision determines whether the first integer is greater than the second integer.

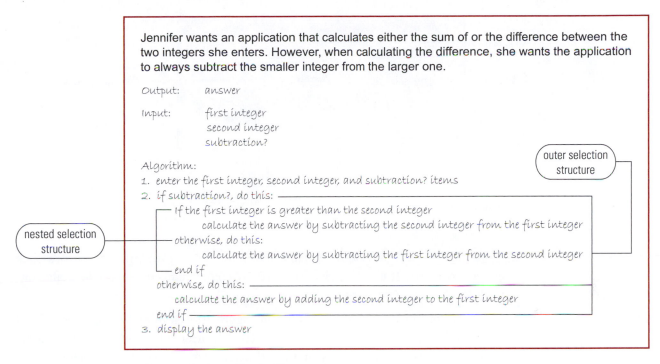

Jennifer wants an application that calculates either the sum of or the difference between the two integers she enters. However, when calculating the difference, she wants the application to always subtract the smaller integer from the larger one.

Output: answer

Input: first integer
            second integer
            subtraction?

Algorithm:
1. enter the first integer, second integer, and subtraction? items
2. if subtraction?, do this:
        If the first integer is greater than the second integer
            calculate the answer by subtracting the second integer from the first integer
        otherwise, do this:
            calculate the answer by subtracting the first integer from the second integer
        end if
    otherwise, do this:
        calculate the answer by adding the second integer to the first integer
    end if
3. display the answer

nested selection structure

outer selection structure

Figure 10-6: Modified math problem specification and its algorithm

For more experience in examining problem specifications, see the Problem Specifications section in the Ch10WantMore.pdf file.

In the next set of steps, you will code the algorithm shown in Figure 10-6.

To open the AddSub application, and then code the btnCalc control's Click event procedure:

1. Start Visual Studio 2008 (or Visual Basic 2008 Express Edition). Open the **AddSub Solution** (**AddSub Solution.sln**) file, which is contained in the ClearlyVB\Chap10\ AddSub Solution folder. If necessary, open the designer window. The application's interface is shown in Figure 10-7.

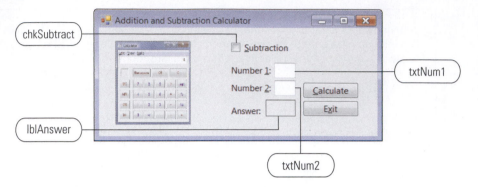

Figure 10-7: AddSub application's interface

2. Open the Code Editor window, which contains the code for the btnExit control's Click event procedure. It also contains the partially completed code for the btnCalc control's Click event procedure.

3. The first step in the algorithm shown in Figure 10-6 is to enter the integers and whether the user wants to perform subtraction. The user will enter the integers in the txtNum1 and txtNum2 controls, and use the Subtraction check box to indicate subtraction. The btnCalc control's Click event procedure already contains the code to declare the necessary variables, as well as to assign the integers to variables. According to Step 2 in the algorithm, the outer selection structure's condition needs to determine whether the user wants to perform subtraction. This can be determined using the Subtraction check box's Checked property. Click the **blank line** below the ' calculate and display the difference or sum comment in the btnCalc control's Click event procedure. Type **if chkSubtract.checked** = **true then** and press **Enter**.

4. If the Subtraction check box is selected, a nested selection structure should determine whether the first integer is greater than the second integer. Type **if intNum1 > intNum2 then** and press **Enter**.

5. According to the algorithm, if the first integer is greater than the second integer, the nested selection structure's true path should calculate the answer by subtracting the second integer from the first integer. Type **intAnswer** = **intNum1 – intNum2** and press **Enter**.

6. If the first integer is not greater than the second integer, the nested selection structure's false path should calculate the answer by subtracting the first integer from the second integer. Type **else** and press **Enter**, then type **intAnswer** = **intNum2 – intNum1**. You have finished coding the nested selection structure and the true path of the outer selection structure. However, you still need to code the outer selection structure's false path.

7. If the Subtraction check box is not selected, it means that the user wants addition. Therefore, the outer selection structure's false path should add together both integers. Click **after the letter f** in the first End If line, then press **Enter** to insert a blank line. Type **else** and press **Enter**, then type **intAnswer = intNum2 + intNum1**. Figure 10-8 shows the code entered in the procedure.

```
Private Sub btnCalc_Click(ByVal sender As Object, ByVal e As System.EventArgs
    ' calculates either the sum of or the difference between two numbers

    Dim intNum1 As Integer
    Dim intNum2 As Integer
    Dim intAnswer As Integer

    ' assign numbers to variables
    Integer.TryParse(txtNum1.Text, intNum1)
    Integer.TryParse(txtNum2.Text, intNum2)

    ' calculate and display the difference or sum
    If chkSubtract.Checked = True Then
        If intNum1 > intNum2 Then
            intAnswer = intNum1 - intNum2
        Else
            intAnswer = intNum2 - intNum1
        End If
    Else
        intAnswer = intNum1 + intNum2
    End If
    lblAnswer.Text = intAnswer
End Sub
```

nested selection structure

outer selection structure

Figure 10-8: Code entered in the btnCalc control's Click event procedure

8. Save the solution, then start the application. Type **22** in the Number 1 text box and type **12** in the Number 2 text box, then click the **Calculate** button. The btnCalc control's Click event procedure adds together both integers and displays the sum (34) in the Answer label.

9. Click the **Subtraction** check box, then click the **Calculate** button. The btnCalc control's Click event procedure subtracts the smaller integer (12) from the larger integer (22), and then displays the difference (10) in the Answer label.

10. Change the contents of the Number 1 text box to **5**, then click the **Calculate** button. The btnCalc control's Click event procedure subtracts the smaller integer (5) from the larger integer (12), and then displays the difference (7) in the Answer label. See Figure 10-9.

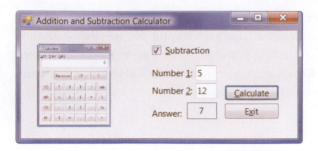

Figure 10-9: Difference displayed in the interface

11. Click the **Exit** button to stop the application.

Jennifer thinks that the interface shown in Figure 10-9 might be misleading, because it looks as though the answer (7) is the result of subtracting the number 12 from the number 5. She has asked you to modify the application to make it obvious that the answer is the result of subtracting the smaller integer from the larger integer—in this case, subtracting 5 from 12. You can do this by swapping the contents of both text boxes when the smaller integer appears in the Number 1 text box. You swap the values by assigning the first integer (which the user enters in the Number 1 text box) to the Number 2 text box, and assigning the second integer (which the user enters in the Number 2 text box) to the Number 1 text box. But where do you enter the swapping instructions? Study the algorithm shown earlier in Figure 10-6. Locate the instructions that are followed when the user wants to perform subtraction; you will need to enter the swapping instructions somewhere in that location. In this case, the instructions in the nested selection structure are followed when the Subtraction check box is selected. Now consider where (in the nested selection structure) to enter the swapping instructions. If the nested selection structure's condition evaluates to True, it means that the Number 1 text box already contains the larger integer; so no swap is necessary in the nested selection structure's true path. However, if the nested selection structure's condition evaluates to False, it means that the number in the Number 1 text box is not larger than the number in the Number 2 text box; the numbers in both text boxes should be swapped at this point. Figure 10-10 shows the first modification to the algorithm from Figure 10-6.

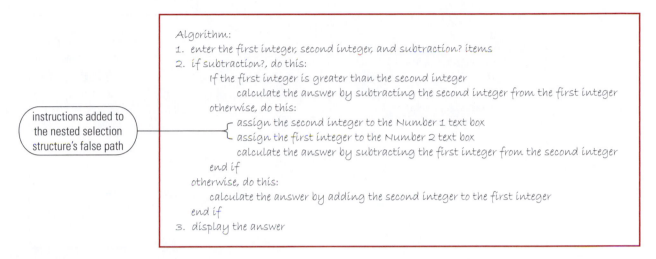

Algorithm:
1. enter the first integer, second integer, and subtraction? items
2. if subtraction?, do this:
      If the first integer is greater than the second integer
            calculate the answer by subtracting the second integer from the first integer
      otherwise, do this:
            assign the second integer to the Number 1 text box
            assign the first integer to the Number 2 text box
            calculate the answer by subtracting the first integer from the second integer
      end if
   otherwise, do this:
      calculate the answer by adding the second integer to the first integer
   end if
3. display the answer

instructions added to
the nested selection
structure's false path

Figure 10-10: First modification to the algorithm from Figure 10-6

When comparing two numbers, keep in mind that the first number can be greater than, less than, or equal to the second number. Study the comparison made in the nested selection structure's condition in Figure 10-10. If the condition is True, it means that the first integer (entered in the Number 1 text box) is the larger of the two integers, so the answer can be calculated by subtracting the second integer from the first integer. However, if the condition is False, it doesn't necessarily mean that the first integer (entered in the Number 1 text box) is less than the second integer (entered in the Number 2 text box); both integers could be equal. The modified algorithm in Figure 10-10 will swap the text box values, as well as calculate the answer, when the first integer is either less than or equal to the second integer. Although you could leave the algorithm as is, there is no reason to swap the text box values when both integers are equal. You can fix the algorithm by including the "equal to" comparison in the nested selection structure's condition, as shown in the final algorithm in Figure 10-11. In the final algorithm, the nested selection structure's condition determines whether the first integer is greater than or equal to the second integer. If the condition is True, the answer is calculated by subtracting the second integer from the first integer. If the condition is False, the text box values are swapped and the answer is calculated by subtracting the first integer from the second integer.

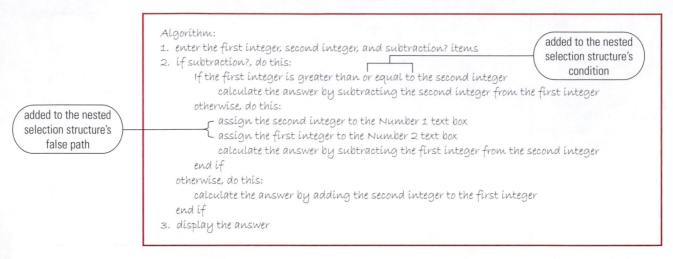

Figure 10-11: Final algorithm for the math problem

To modify the btnCalc control's Click event procedure:

1. Change the nested selection structure's condition to **intNum1 >= intNum2**.

2. Click **after the e** in the nested selection structure's Else line, then press **Enter** to insert a blank line in the nested selection structure's false path. Type **txtNum1.text = intNum2** and press **Enter**, then type **txtNum2.text = intNum1**. See Figure 10-12.

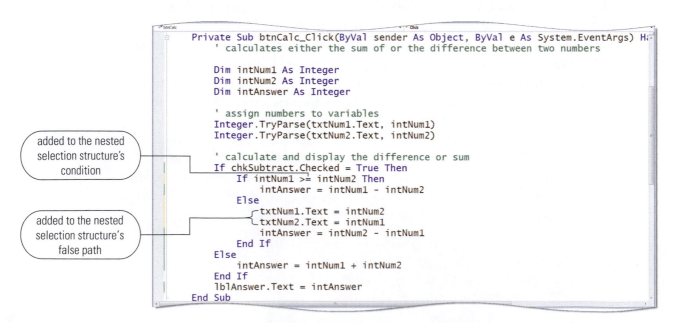

Figure 10-12: Completed Click event procedure for the btnCalc control

3. Save the solution, then start the application. Type **22** in the Number 1 text box and type **12** in the Number 2 text box, then click the **Calculate** button. The btnCalc control's Click event procedure adds together both integers and displays the sum (34) in the Answer label.

4. Click the **Subtraction** check box, then click the **Calculate** button. The btnCalc control's Click event procedure subtracts the smaller integer (12) from the larger integer (22), and then displays the difference (10) in the Answer label.

5. Change the contents of the Number 1 text box to **5**, then click the **Calculate** button. The btnCalc control's Click event procedure swaps the values in the text boxes. It then subtracts the smaller integer (5) from the larger integer (12), and displays the difference (7) in the Answer label. See Figure 10-13.

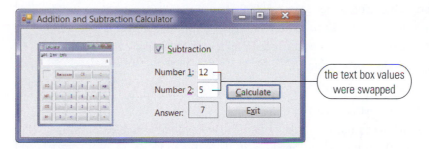

Figure 10-13: Interface showing that the values were swapped

6. Click the **Exit** button. Close the Code Editor window, then close the solution.

THAT'S WAY TOO LOGICAL FOR ME

In Chapter 9, you learned how to include comparison operators in an If...Then...Else statement's condition. You also can include logical operators in the condition. **Logical operators**, sometimes referred to as **Boolean operators**, allow you to combine two or more conditions into one compound condition. Figure 10-14 lists two of the logical operators available in Visual Basic, along with their order of precedence. The figure also contains examples of using logical operators in the If...Then...Else statement's condition. Like expressions containing comparison operators, expressions containing logical operators always evaluate to a Boolean value. Keep in mind that logical operators are always evaluated after any comparison operators in an expression.

Operator	Operation	Precedence number
AndAlso	all conditions must be True for the compound condition to be True	1
OrElse	only one of the conditions needs to be True for the compound condition to be True	2

Example 1

If intPopulation > 25000 AndAlso intPopulation <= 50000 Then

The compound condition evaluates to True when the intPopulation variable contains a number that is greater than 25000 but less than or equal to 50000; otherwise, it evaluates to False.

Example 2

If chkBonus.Checked = True AndAlso decSales > 50000 Then

The compound condition evaluates to True when the chkBonus control is selected and, at the same time, the decSales variable contains a value that is greater than 50000; otherwise, it evaluates to False.

Example 3

If intPayCode = 1 OrElse intPayCode = 2 Then

The compound condition evaluates to True when the intPayCode variable contains either the number 1 or the number 2; otherwise, it evaluates to False.

Example 4

If intRating = 5 OrElse decSales <= 2500 Then

The compound condition evaluates to True when either the intRating variable contains the number 5 or the decSales variable contains a value that is less than or equal to 2500; otherwise, it evaluates to False.

Figure 10-14: Listing and examples of logical operators

So far in this book, you have learned about arithmetic operators (Chapter 6), comparison operators (Chapter 9), and logical operators. If an expression contains logical operators, comparison operators, and arithmetic operators, the arithmetic operators are evaluated first, followed by the comparison operators, followed by the logical operators. As a result, when the computer processes the expression 12 > 0 AndAlso 12 < 10 * 2, it evaluates the arithmetic operator (*) first, followed by the two comparison operators (> and <), followed by the logical operator (AndAlso). The expression evaluates to True, as shown in Figure 10-15.

Evaluation steps	Result
Original expression	12 > 0 AndAlso 12 < 10 * 2
10 * 2 is evaluated first	12 > 0 AndAlso 12 < 20
12 > 0 is evaluated second	True AndAlso 12 < 20
12 < 20 is evaluated third	True AndAlso True
True AndAlso True is evaluated last	True

Figure 10-15: Evaluation steps for an expression containing arithmetic, comparison, and logical operators

Study the problem specification and algorithm shown in Figure 10-16. The selection structure in the algorithm makes a decision regarding the employee's hours. More specifically, it determines whether the hours are within the acceptable range. In this case, the acceptable range is greater than or equal to 0 but less than or equal to 40. Now compare the selection structure in the algorithm with the code shown in Figure 10-17. Notice that the *if the hours worked are greater than or equal to 0 but less than or equal to 40, do this:* line is coded as If decHours >= 0 AndAlso decHours <= 40 Then in Visual Basic.

ABC Company wants an application that displays an employee's gross pay. All employees earn $8.35 per hour. The payroll clerk will enter the number of hours worked, which should be greater than or equal to 0 but less than or equal to 40.

Output: gross pay

Input: hours worked

Algorithm:
1. enter the hours worked
2. if the hours worked are greater than or equal to 0 but less than or equal to 40, do this:
        calculate the gross pay by multiplying the hours worked by 8.35
        display the gross pay
   otherwise, do this:
        display an error message
   end if

Figure 10-16: Gross pay problem specification and algorithm

```
Private Sub btnCalc_Click(ByVal sender As Object, ByVal e As System.Ev
    ' calculates and displays a gross pay amount

    Dim decHours As Decimal
    Dim decGross As Decimal

    ' calculate and display gross pay, or display an error message
    Decimal.TryParse(txtHours.Text, decHours)
    If decHours >= 0 AndAlso decHours <= 40 Then
        decGross = decHours * 8.35
        lblGross.Text = decGross.ToString("C2")
    Else
        lblGross.Text = "Incorrect hours"
    End If
End Sub
```

selection structure

Figure 10-17: Code corresponding to Figure 10-16's algorithm

To complete the Gross Pay application's code:

1. Open the **Gross Pay Solution** (**Gross Pay Solution.sln**) file, which is contained in the ClearlyVB\Chap10\Gross Pay Solution folder. If necessary, open the designer window.

2. Open the Code Editor window, which contains the code for the btnExit control's Click event procedure. In the partially completed btnCalc control's Click event procedure, enter the selection structure shown in Figure 10-17.

3. Save the solution, then start the application. Type **20** in the Hours worked text box, then click the **Calculate** button. Because the hours are within the acceptable range, the btnCalc control's Click event procedure calculates the gross pay and displays the result ($167.00) in the Gross pay label.

4. Type **45** in the Hours worked text box, then click the **Calculate** button. In this case, the hours worked are not within the acceptable range, so the btnCalc control's Click event procedure displays the "Incorrect hours" message in the Gross pay label. See Figure 10-18.

Figure 10-18: Error message displayed in the interface

5. Click the **Exit** button. Close the Code Editor window, then close the solution.

For more examples of logical operators, see the Logical Operators section in the Ch10WantMore.pdf file.

MINI-QUIZ 2

1. Which of the following conditions determines whether the intQuantity variable contains a number that is less than 0 or greater than 1000?

    a. intQuantity < 0 AndAlso intQuantity > 1000

    b. intQuantity < 0 OrElse intQuantity > 1000

    c. intQuantity < 0 AndAlso > 1000

    d. intQuantity < 0 OrElse > 1000

2. Which of the following conditions determines whether the decPrice variable contains a number that is greater than 15.45 but less than 25.75?

    a. decPrice < 15.45 AndAlso decPrice < 25.75

    b. decPrice > 15.45 OrElse < 25.75

    c. decPrice > 15.45 AndAlso decPrice < 25.75

    d. decPrice > 15.45 OrElse decPrice < 25.75

3. Which of the following conditions determines whether both check boxes are selected?

    a. chkDiscount.Checked = True AndAlso chkCoupon.Checked = True

    b. chkDiscount.Checked = True OrElse chkCoupon.Checked = True

    c. chkDiscount.Selected = True AndAlso chkCoupon.Selected = True

    d. chkDiscount.Selected = True OrElse chkCoupon.Selected = True

4. The expression 6 + 3 > 7 AndAlso 8 < 4 will evaluate to _____.

    a. True   b. False

It's time to view the Ch10-Nested Selection Structure video.

SUMMARY

» Both paths in a selection structure can include other selection structures, called nested selection structures.

» Nested selection structures are used when more than one decision must be made before the appropriate action can be taken.

» When comparing two numbers, keep in mind that the first number can be greater than, less than, or equal to the second number.

» You can include logical operators in an If...Then...Else statement's condition. The logical operators allow you to combine two or more conditions into one compound condition.

» When the AndAlso logical operator is used to combine conditions, all of the conditions must be True for the compound condition to be True. When the OrElse logical operator is used to combine conditions, only one of the conditions needs to be True for the compound condition to be True.

» The AndAlso operator has a higher precedence than the OrElse operator.

» Arithmetic operators in an expression are evaluated first, followed by comparison operators, followed by logical operators.

KEY TERMS

Boolean operators—another term for logical operators

Logical operators—the operators used to combine two or more conditions into one compound condition; examples are the AndAlso and OrElse operators; also referred to as Boolean operators

Nested selection structure—a selection structure contained within another selection structure

ANSWERS TO MINI-QUIZZES

MINI-QUIZ 1

1. The solution does not require a nested selection structure.

2. The solution requires a nested selection structure whose condition determines whether the caller is a telemarketer.

3. The solution requires two nested selection structures. The condition in one of the nested selection structures should determine whether the red box is full. The condition in the other nested selection structure should determine whether the yellow box is full.

MINI-QUIZ 2

1. b. intQuantity < 0 OrElse intQuantity > 1000

2. c. decPrice > 15.45 AndAlso decPrice < 25.75

3. a. chkDiscount.Checked = True AndAlso chkCoupon.Checked = True

4. b. False

REVIEW QUESTIONS

1. Which of the following expressions will evaluate to True?

   a. 7 > 4 AndAlso 6 <> 3   b. 9 + 3 < 20 OrElse 8 > 9

   c. 67 Mod 2 = 1   d. All of the above.

2. If the intUnits and decPrice variables contain the numbers 5 and 12.45, the intUnits > 0 AndAlso intUnits < 10 OrElse decPrice > 25 expression will evaluate to _____.

   a. True   b. False

3. If the intUnits and decPrice variables contain the numbers 5 and 12.45, the intUnits > 0 AndAlso decPrice > 0 AndAlso decPrice < 10 expression will evaluate to _____.

   a. True   b. False

4. Which of the operators in the expression 6 + 7 * 3 > 25 − 2 will be evaluated first?

   a. +   b. *

   c. >   d. −

5. The expression in Question 4 will evaluate to _____.

   a. True   b. False

EXERCISES

»TRY THIS

1. In this exercise, you modify one of the Total Due applications created in Chapter 9. (The answers to TRY THIS Exercises are located at the end of the chapter.)

   a. Use Windows to copy the Total Due Solution folder from the ClearlyVB\Chap09 folder to the ClearlyVB\Chap10 folder.

   b. Open the Total Due Solution (Total Due Solution.sln) file contained in the ClearlyVB\Chap10\Total Due Solution folder. Open the designer window, then open the Code Editor window. Modify the btnCalc control's Click event procedure so that it calculates the 10% discount not only for employees, but for any customer whose quantity ordered is 10 or more.

   c. Save the solution, then start and test the application. Stop the application, then close the solution.

»TRY THIS

2. In this exercise, you modify one of the Total Due applications created in Chapter 9. (The answers to TRY THIS Exercises are located at the end of the chapter.)

   a. Use Windows to copy the Total Due Solution—Version 2 folder from the ClearlyVB\Chap09 folder to the ClearlyVB\Chap10 folder.

   b. Open the Total Due Solution (Total Due Solution.sln) file contained in the ClearlyVB\Chap10\Total Due Solution—Version 2 folder. Open the designer window, then open the Code Editor window. Sam's company now gives a 12% discount to employees. Customers who are not employees, but who have ordered more than 20 items, receive a 5% discount. Modify the btnCalc control's Click event procedure.

   c. Save the solution, then start and test the application. Stop the application, then close the solution.

»MODIFY THIS

3. In this exercise, you modify the Gross Pay application coded in the chapter.

   a. Use Windows to make a copy of the Gross Pay Solution folder. Save the copy in the ClearlyVB\Chap10 folder. Rename the copy Modified Gross Pay Solution.

   b. Open the Gross Pay Solution (Gross Pay Solution.sln) file contained in the Modified Gross Pay Solution folder. Currently, the selection structure's condition determines whether the hours worked are in the acceptable range. Modify the condition so that it determines whether the hours worked are not in the acceptable range, then make the appropriate modifications to the instructions within the selection structure.

   c. Save the solution. Start and then test the application. Stop the application, then close the solution.

4. Professor Jones wants an application that both calculates and displays a student's average score on two tests.

» INTRODUCTORY

   a. Open the Jones Solution (Jones Solution.sln) file, which is contained in the ClearlyVB\Chap10\Jones Solution folder.

   b. Open the Code Editor window. Code the btnCalc control's Click event procedure. The procedure should verify that each score is valid. To be valid the score must be greater than or equal to zero. Display an appropriate message in the lblMessage control when one or more scores are not valid; otherwise, calculate and display the average score.

   c. Save the solution. Start and then test the application. Stop the application, then close the solution.

5. Geriatric Medical Supplies pays each salesperson a 3% bonus on his or her annual sales. In addition, any salesperson who has been with the company for more than 10 years receives an additional bonus. The additional bonus is $100 for each year the employee has been with the company. The company wants an application that both calculates and displays a salesperson's total bonus.

» INTRODUCTORY

   a. List the output and input items, as well as any processing items, then create an appropriate algorithm. The algorithm should verify that the sales amount entered by the user is not less than zero. If it is less than zero, display an appropriate error message.

   b. Create a new Visual Basic Windows application. Assign the name Geriatric Project to the project. Assign the name Geriatric Solution to the solution. Save the application in the ClearlyVB\Chap10 folder. Change the name of the form file on your disk to frmMain.vb. If necessary, change the form's name to frmMain.

   c. Create an appropriate interface. Include an Exit button. Code the Exit button's Click event procedure and the problem's algorithm. Save the solution. Desk-check the program using your own sample data.

   d. Start and then test the application. Stop the application, then close the solution.

6. Small Loans Inc wants an application that displays the maximum amount a customer can borrow. Use the following rules to determine the amount. A customer whose annual salary is at least $35000 can borrow up to 25% of their salary, but only if they have been employed at their current job for at least 5 years. If they have been employed less than 5 years, they can borrow only a maximum of 20% of their salary. Customers who earn less than $35000 per year can borrow up to 5% of their salary. Name the solution, project, and form file Loans Solution, Loans Project, and frmMain.vb, respectively. Save the application in the ClearlyVB\Chap10 folder. Code the application. Save the solution, then start and test the application. Stop the application, then close the solution.

» INTERMEDIATE

»INTERMEDIATE

7. In this exercise, you modify one of the Total Due applications created in Chapter 9.

   a. Use Windows to copy the Total Due Solution—Version 3 folder from the ClearlyVB\ Chap09 folder to the ClearlyVB\Chap10 folder.

   b. Open the Total Due Solution (Total Due Solution.sln) file contained in the ClearlyVB\Chap10\Total Due Solution—Version 3 folder. Open the designer window, then open the Code Editor window. Sam's company now gives a 15% discount to employees. Customers who are not employees, but who have ordered more than 10 items, receive an 8% discount. Modify the btnCalc control's Click event procedure.

   c. Save the solution, then start and test the application. Stop the application, then close the solution.

»ADVANCED

8. In this exercise, you modify the application from Chapter 9's Exercise 9. If you did not complete Chapter 9's Exercise 9, you will need to do so before you can complete this exercise.

   a. Use Windows to copy the Health Solution folder from the ClearlyVB\Chap09 folder to the ClearlyVB\Chap10 folder.

   b. Open the Health Solution (Health Solution.sln) file contained in the ClearlyVB\ Chap10\Health Solution folder. Modify the code so that it gives the member a 10% discount on his monthly dues when he signs up for all three of the additional activities (golf, racquetball, and tennis).

   c. Save the solution, then start and test the application. Stop the application, then close the solution.

»ADVANCED

9. Johnson Supply wants an application that displays the price of an order, based on the number of units ordered and the customer's status (either wholesaler or retailer). Use a check box to indicate that the customer is a wholesaler. The price per unit is shown in the following chart. Name the solution, project, and form file Johnson Solution, Johnson Project, and frmMain.vb, respectively. Save the solution in the ClearlyVB\Chap10 folder. Code the application, then start and test it. Stop the application, then close the solution.

Wholesaler		Retailer	
Number of units	Price per unit ($)	Number of units	Price per unit ($)
1–4	10	1–3	15
5 and over	9	4–8	14
		9 and over	12

10. Open the FigureThisOut Solution (FigureThisOut Solution.sln) file, which is contained in the ClearlyVB\Chap10\FigureThisOut Solution folder. Open the Code Editor window and study the btnDisplay control's Click event procedure. What task is performed by the procedure? What are the rules for charging the various fees?

In other words, who is charged $10? Who is charged $5, and who is charged $20? You will test the application to verify that your answers are correct. Start the application. Enter 21 as the age and then click the Display Fee button. Select the Member check box, then click the Display Fee button. Now enter 66 as the age, then click the Display Fee button. Stop the application, then close the solution.

11. In this exercise, you find an error in an application's code. Open the SwatTheBugs Solution (SwatTheBugs Solution.sln) file, which is contained in the ClearlyVB\ Chap10\SwatTheBugs Solution folder. The application should calculate an 8% bonus on a salesperson's sales. However, a salesperson having a sales code of 5 receives an additional $150 bonus when his sales are at least $10000; otherwise, he receives an additional $125 bonus. Open the Code Editor window and study the code. Start and then test the application. Notice that the code is not working correctly. Locate and correct any errors.

ANSWERS TO "TRY THIS" EXERCISES

1. To modify the Total Due application, change the selection structure's condition to chkEmployee.Checked = True OrElse intQuantity >= 10.

2. See Figure 10-19.

```vb
Private Sub btnCalc_Click(ByVal sender As Object, ByVal e As System.EventArgs) Handle
    ' calculates and displays the total amount due

    Const decEMP_DISC_RATE As Decimal = 0.12
    Const decNON_EMP_DISC_RATE As Decimal = 0.05
    Dim intQuantity As Integer
    Dim decPrice As Decimal
    Dim decTotal As Decimal

    ' assign quantity and price to variables
    Integer.TryParse(txtQuantity.Text, intQuantity)
    Decimal.TryParse(txtPrice.Text, decPrice)

    ' calculate total due
    decTotal = intQuantity * decPrice
    If chkEmployee.Checked = True Then
        decTotal = decTotal * (1 - decEMP_DISC_RATE)
    Else
        If intQuantity > 20 Then
            decTotal = decTotal * (1 - decNON_EMP_DISC_RATE)
        End If
    End If

    ' display total due
    lblTotal.Text = decTotal.ToString("C2")
End Sub
```

Figure 10-19

11

SO MANY PATHS...
SO LITTLE TIME

After studying Chapter 11, you should be able to:

Code a multiple-path selection structure using If/ElseIf/Else

Declare a variable using the String data type

Convert a string to uppercase or lowercase

Code a multiple-path selection structure using Select Case

Include a radio button in an interface

MULTIPLE-PATH SELECTION STRUCTURES

At times, you may need to create a selection structure that can choose from several alternatives. Such selection structures are referred to as either **multiple-path selection structures** or **extended selection structures**. Figure 11-1 contains a problem specification that requires a multiple-path selection structure. The figure also contains an appropriate algorithm. The multiple-path selection structure begins with the *if the code is 1, do this:* line, and it ends with the last *end if* line.

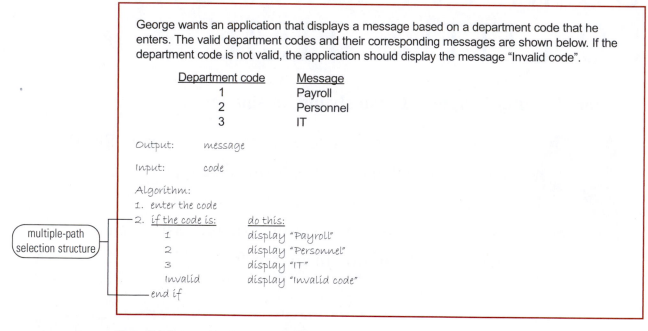

Figure 11-1: Department code problem specification and algorithm

Figure 11-2 shows two ways of coding the multiple-path selection structure from Figure 11-1. Version 1 uses nested If...Then...Else statements, which you learned about in Chapter 10. Version 2 uses another form of the If...Then...Else statement, called **If/ElseIf/Else**. Although both versions of the code produce the same result, Version 2 is a much more convenient way of coding a multiple-path selection structure.

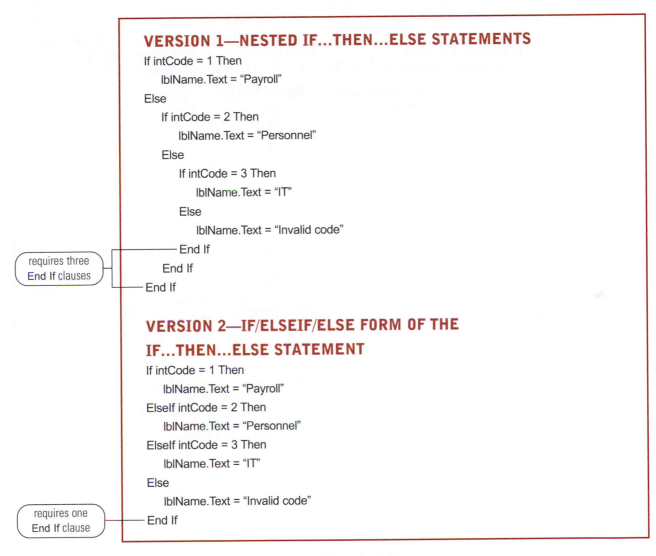

VERSION 1—NESTED IF...THEN...ELSE STATEMENTS

```
If intCode = 1 Then
    lblName.Text = "Payroll"
Else
    If intCode = 2 Then
        lblName.Text = "Personnel"
    Else
        If intCode = 3 Then
            lblName.Text = "IT"
        Else
            lblName.Text = "Invalid code"
        End If
    End If
End If
```

requires three End If clauses

VERSION 2—IF/ELSEIF/ELSE FORM OF THE IF...THEN...ELSE STATEMENT

```
If intCode = 1 Then
    lblName.Text = "Payroll"
ElseIf intCode = 2 Then
    lblName.Text = "Personnel"
ElseIf intCode = 3 Then
    lblName.Text = "IT"
Else
    lblName.Text = "Invalid code"
End If
```

requires one End If clause

Figure 11-2: Two versions of the code for the multiple-path selection structure

Figure 11-3 shows another problem description that requires a multiple-path selection structure. In this case, the selection structure must determine the membership type before it can display the correct fee. The figure also includes an appropriate algorithm in flowchart form.

Fitness For Good health club wants an application that displays a member's monthly fee, which is based on a code entered by the user. The code corresponds to the membership type, as shown below. If the user enters an invalid code, display 0 (zero) as the monthly fee.

Code	Membership type	Monthly fee
S	Single	40
F	Family	50
S65	Single Senior	30
C65	Couple Senior	35

Output: fee

Input: code

Algorithm:

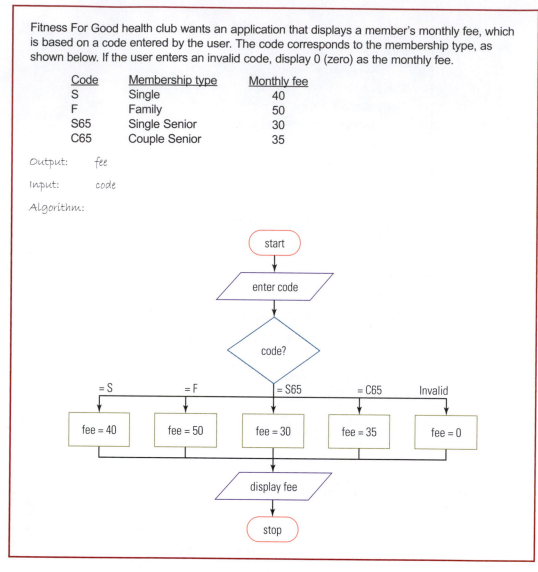

Figure 11-3: Fitness For Good problem specification and algorithm

In the next set of steps, you will code the algorithm shown in Figure 11-3.

To open the Fitness For Good application, and then code and test the btnDisplay control's Click event procedure:

1. Start Visual Studio 2008 (or Visual Basic 2008 Express Edition). Open the **Fitness Solution (Fitness Solution.sln)** file, which is contained in the ClearlyVB\Chap11\

Fitness Solution-If folder. If necessary, open the designer window. The application's interface is shown in Figure 11-4.

Figure 11-4: Fitness For Good application's interface

2. Open the Code Editor window, which contains the code for the btnExit control's Click event procedure. It also contains the partially completed Click event procedure for the btnDisplay control.

3. The btnDisplay control's Click event procedure will use an Integer variable to store the monthly fee. Click the **blank line** below the last Const statement, then type **dim intFee as integer** and press **Enter**.

4. The procedure also will use a variable to store the code that represents the membership type: S, F, S65, or C65. You can't declare the variable using any of the data types you learned about in Chapter 7, which are the Integer, Decimal, and Double data types. This is because variables declared with those data types can store numbers only, and each code contains a letter. Instead, you declare the variable using a data type called String. The **String data type** can store alphanumeric text, which is text that may contain letters, numbers, or special characters. Examples of alphanumeric text include the membership codes "F" and "S65", as well as the phone number "111-2222". The three-character ID used when naming String variables (and String named constants) is str. Type **dim strCode as string** and press **Enter** twice.

5. Now use the flowchart shown in Figure 11-3 to code the procedure. The first symbol below the Start oval is the "enter code" parallelogram. The user will enter the code in the txtCode control. You will assign the control's Text property to the strCode variable. Recall that the value stored in the Text property is treated as alphanumeric text; therefore, you can simply assign the value to the variable. Type **' assign code to a variable** and press **Enter**, then type **strCode = txtCode.text** and press **Enter** twice.

6. Next is a multiple-path selection structure that uses the code to determine the appropriate fee. Type **' determine fee** and press **Enter**, then enter the multiple-path selection structure shown in Figure 11-5. Be sure to type the codes using uppercase letters.

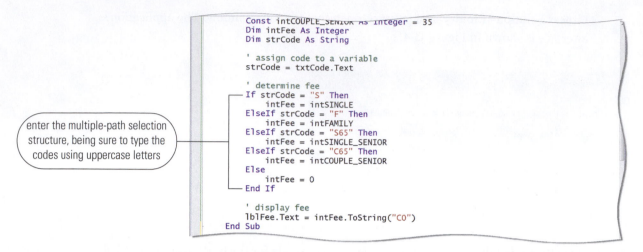

```
Const intCOUPLE_SENIOR As Integer = 35
Dim intFee As Integer
Dim strCode As String

' assign code to a variable
strCode = txtCode.Text

' determine fee
If strCode = "S" Then
    intFee = intSINGLE
ElseIf strCode = "F" Then
    intFee = intFAMILY
ElseIf strCode = "S65" Then
    intFee = intSINGLE_SENIOR
ElseIf strCode = "C65" Then
    intFee = intCOUPLE_SENIOR
Else
    intFee = 0
End If

' display fee
lblFee.Text = intFee.ToString("C0")
End Sub
```

enter the multiple-path selection structure, being sure to type the codes using uppercase letters

Figure 11-5: Multiple-path selection structure entered in the procedure

7. Save the solution, then start the application. Test the application's code by displaying the Single Senior membership fee, which should be $30. Type **S65** (be sure to type an uppercase letter S) as the code, then click the **Display Fee** button. The correct fee ($30) appears in the Monthly fee box.

8. Now display the Couple Senior membership fee. Change the code to **C65** (be sure to type an uppercase letter C), then click the **Display Fee** button. The correct amount ($35) appears as the monthly fee.

9. Next, display the fee for a Family membership. Change the code to the uppercase letter **F**, then click the **Display Fee** button. The correct amount ($50) appears as the monthly fee.

10. Finally, display the Single membership fee, which should be $40. Change the code to a lowercase letter **s**, then click the **Display Fee** button. The Monthly fee box shows $0, which is incorrect. You learn how to fix this problem in the next section.

11. Click the **Exit** button to end the application.

DON'T BE SO SENSITIVE

As is true in most programming languages, string comparisons in Visual Basic are case sensitive, which means that the uppercase version of a letter is not the same as its lowercase counterpart. So, although a human being recognizes S and s as simply two different ways of writing the same letter, a computer does not make this connection between both letters. To a computer, an S is entirely different from an s, and both characters have no relation to each other. This is because each character on the computer keyboard is stored differently in the computer's internal memory. The uppercase letter S, for example, is stored using a Unicode value of 83, whereas the lowercase letter s is stored using a Unicode value of 115. Unicode is the universal coding scheme for characters. It assigns a unique numeric value to each character used in the written languages of the world. (For more information, see The Unicode Standard at *www.unicode.org*.) As a result, the strCode = "S" condition in the multiple-path selection structure evaluates to False when the strCode variable contains the lowercase letter s; therefore, the selection structure assigns the number 0 to the intFee variable. Before using a string in a comparison, you can convert it to either uppercase or lowercase, and then use the converted string in the comparison. You use the **ToUpper method** to convert a string to uppercase, and the **ToLower method** to convert a string to lowercase. Figure 11-6 shows the syntax of both methods and includes examples of using the methods. In each syntax, *string* typically is either the name of a String variable or the Text property of an object. Both methods temporarily convert the *string* to the specified case. You also can use the methods to permanently convert the contents of a String variable to uppercase or lowercase; the same is true for the value stored in a control's Text property. You do this using an assignment statement, as illustrated in Example 3. When using the ToUpper method in a comparison, be sure that everything you are comparing is uppercase. In other words, the clause If strLetter.ToUpper = "p" Then will not work correctly: the condition will always evaluate to False, because the uppercase version of a letter will never be equal to its lowercase counterpart. Likewise, when using the ToLower method in a comparison, be sure that everything you are comparing is lowercase. The ToUpper and ToLower methods affect only characters that represent letters of the alphabet, as these are the only characters that have uppercase and lowercase forms.

CONVERTING A STRING TO UPPERCASE OR LOWERCASE

Syntax

string.**ToUpper**
string.**ToLower**

Example 1

If txtCode.Text.ToUpper = "F" Then
compares the uppercase version of the string stored in the txtCode's Text property with the uppercase letter "F"

Figure 11-6: Syntax and examples of the ToUpper and ToLower methods (*continued on next page*)

Example 2

If txtCity.Text.ToLower = "reno" Then
compares the lowercase version of the string stored in the txtCity's Text property with the lowercase letters "reno"

Example 3

strName = strName.ToUpper
txtState.Text = txtState.Text.ToLower
changes the contents of the strName variable to uppercase, and changes the contents of the txtState's Text property to lowercase

---

Figure 11-6: Syntax and examples of the ToUpper and ToLower methods (*continued from previous page*)

To fix the code shown earlier in Figure 11-5, you will use the ToUpper method to convert the user input to uppercase. One way to accomplish this is by appending the ToUpper method to the end of the strCode = txtCode.Text statement, like this: strCode = txtCode.Text.ToUpper. When processing the strCode = txtCode.Text.ToUpper statement, the computer first makes a temporary copy of the string entered in the txtCode control. It then converts the copy to uppercase, storing the result in the strCode variable. Finally, it removes the copy from its internal memory. You also can convert the user input to uppercase in the selection structure. You would do this by appending the ToUpper method to the strCode variable in each of the four conditions, like this: strCode.ToUpper. However, keep in mind that each time a condition in the selection structure is evaluated, the computer will have to make a temporary copy of the user input, then convert the copy to uppercase, and then compare the copy to the membership code. It's easier for the programmer, and more efficient for the computer, to convert the user input to uppercase in the statement that assigns the input to the strCode variable.

To fix the string comparison problem noted in the previous set of steps:

1. Change the strCode = txtCode.Text statement to **strCode = txtCode.Text.ToUpper**.

2. Save the solution, then start the application. First, display the Single membership fee, which should be $40. Type **s** as the code, then click the **Display Fee** button. The correct fee appears in the Monthly fee box.

3. Next, display the Couple Senior membership fee. Change the code to **c65**, then click the **Display Fee** button. The correct fee ($35) appears in the Monthly fee box.

4. Now test the application using an invalid code; the Monthly fee box should show $0. Change the code to **x**, then click the **Display Fee** button. The correct amount appears in the Monthly fee box.

5. Click the **Exit** button to end the application. Close the Code Editor window, then close the solution.

For more examples of using the If...Then...Else statement to code a multiple-path selection structure, see the If...Then...Else Multiple-Path Selection Structure section in the Ch11WantMore.pdf file.

MINI-QUIZ 1

1. Write a multiple-path selection structure that determines the appropriate discount rate based on a promotion code entered by the user. The user's entry is stored in the intPromoCode variable. The valid promotion codes are 1, 2, 3, and 4. The corresponding discount rates are 2%, 5%, 10%, and 25%, respectively. Assign the discount rate (converted to decimal) to the decRate variable. If the user enters an invalid promotion code, assign the number 0 to the decRate variable. Use the If/ElseIf/Else form of the If...Then...Else statement.

2. Write a statement that assigns the contents of the txtId control, in uppercase, to the strId variable.

3. Write a multiple-path selection structure that displays both the first name and last name corresponding to an ID entered by the user. The ID is stored in the strId variable from Question 2. Display the first name in the lblFirst control. Display the last name in the lblLast control. The valid IDs are "12A", "45B", "67X", and "78Y". The corresponding names are Jerry Jones, Mark Smith, Jill Batist, and Cheryl Sworski. If the user enters an invalid ID, assign a question mark to both the lblFirst and lblLast controls. Use the If/ElseIf/Else form of the If...Then...Else statement.

WHAT'S THE NEXT CASE ON THE DOCKET?

The If...Then...Else statement is not the only statement you can use to code a multiple-path selection structure in Visual Basic; you also can use the **Select Case statement**. Figure 11-7 shows the Select Case statement's syntax. It also shows how to use the statement to code a multiple-path selection structure that displays a message corresponding to a letter grade. The Select Case statement begins with the keywords Select Case, followed by a *selectorExpression*. The *selectorExpression* can contain any combination of variables, constants, methods, operators, or properties. In the example in Figure 11-7, the *selectorExpression* is a String variable named strGrade. The Select Case statement ends with the End Select clause. Between the Select Case and End Select clauses are the individual Case clauses. Each Case clause represents a different path that the computer can follow. It is customary to indent each Case clause, as well as the instructions within each Case clause, as shown in the figure. You can have as many Case clauses as necessary in a Select Case statement. However, if the Select Case statement includes a Case Else clause, the Case Else clause must be the last clause in the statement. Each of the individual Case clauses, except the Case Else clause, must contain an *expressionList*, which can include one or more expressions. To include more than one expression in an *expressionList*, you separate each expression with a comma, as in the *expressionList* Case "D", "F". The *selectorExpression* needs to match only one of the expressions listed in an *expressionList*. The data type of the expressions must be compatible with the data type of the *selectorExpression*. If the *selectorExpression* is numeric, the expressions in the Case clauses should be numeric. Likewise, if the *selectorExpression* is a string, the expressions should be strings. In the example in Figure 11-7, the *selectorExpression* (strGrade) is a string, and so are the expressions: "A", "B", "C", "D", and "F".

SELECT CASE STATEMENT

Syntax

Select Case *selectorExpression*
    Case *expressionList1*
        instructions for the first Case
   [**Case** *expressionList2*
        instructions for the second Case]

Figure 11-7: Syntax and an example of the Select Case statement (*continued on next page*)

```
        [Case expressionListN
                instructions for the Nth case]
        [Case Else
                instructions for when the selectorExpression does not match any of the
                expressionLists]
End Select

Example

Dim strGrade As String = txtGrade.Text.ToUpper
Select Case strGrade
    Case "A"
        lblMsg.Text = "Excellent"
    Case "B"
        lblMsg.Text = "Above Average"
    Case "C"
        lblMsg.Text = "Average"
    Case "D", "F"
        lblMsg.Text = "Below Average"
    Case Else
        lblMsg.Text = "Error"
End Select
```

Figure 11-7: Syntax and an example of the Select Case statement (*continued from previous page*)

When processing the Select Case statement, the computer first compares the value of the *selectorExpression* with the values listed in *expressionList1*. If a match is found, the computer processes the instructions for the first Case, stopping when it reaches either another Case clause or the End Select clause; it then skips to the instruction following the End Select clause. If a match is not found in *expressionList1*, the computer skips to the second Case clause, where it compares the *selectorExpression* with the values listed in *expressionList2*. If a match is found, the computer processes the instructions for the second Case clause and then skips to the instruction following the End Select clause. If a match is not found, the computer skips to the third Case clause, and so on. If the *selectorExpression* does not match any of the values listed in any of the *expressionLists*, the computer processes the instructions listed in the Case Else clause (if there is one), and then skips to the instruction following the End Select clause. Keep in mind that if the *selectorExpression* matches a value in more than one Case clause, only the instructions in the first match are processed.

To code the Fitness For Good application using the Select Case statement:

1. Open the **Fitness Solution** (**Fitness Solution.sln**) file, which is contained in the ClearlyVB\Chap11\Fitness Solution-Select Case folder. If necessary, open the designer window. The application's interface (shown earlier in Figure 11-4) appears on the screen.

2. Open the Code Editor window. In the btnDisplay control's Click event procedure, enter the Select Case statement shown in Figure 11-8.

```
' assign code to a variable
strCode = txtCode.Text.ToUpper

' determine fee
Select Case strCode
    Case "S"
        intFee = intSINGLE
    Case "F"
        intFee = intFAMILY
    Case "S65"
        intFee = intSINGLE_SENIOR
    Case "C65"
        intFee = intCOUPLE_SENIOR
End Select

' display fee
lblFee.Text = intFee.ToString("C0")
```

enter the Select Case statement

Figure 11-8: Select Case statement entered in the btnDisplay control's Click event procedure

3. Save the solution, then start the application.

4. Type **f** as the code, then click the **Display Fee** button. The strCode = txtCode.Text.ToUpper statement in the button's Click event procedure assigns the uppercase letter F to the strCode variable. The Select Case statement is processed next. When processing the statement, the computer first compares the contents of the strCode variable (F) to the first Case clause's *expressionList*: "S". F does not equal S, so the computer skips to the second Case clause, where it compares the contents of the strCode variable (F) to the string "F". F equals F, so the computer processes the intFee = intFAMILY assignment statement in the second Case clause. It then skips to the instruction following the End Select clause. The

instruction displays the contents of the intFee variable (converted to Currency with zero decimal places) in the lblFee control; in this case, it displays $50.

5. On your own, test the application using the following codes: **S**, **s65**, **C65**, and **x**. The monthly fees should be $40, $30, $35, and $0.

6. Click the **Exit** button to end the application. Close the Code Editor window, then close the solution.

SPECIFYING A RANGE OF VALUES IN A CASE CLAUSE'S EXPRESSIONLIST

You also can specify a range of values in a Case clause's *expressionList*, such as the values 1 through 4 or values greater than 10. You do this using either the keyword To or the keyword Is. You use the To keyword when you know both the upper and lower bounds of the range, and you use the Is keyword when you know only one end of the range (either the upper or lower end). To illustrate this concept, the price of an item sold by ABC Corporation depends on the number of items ordered, as shown in Figure 11-9. The figure also shows the Select Case statement that will assign the appropriate price to the intPrice variable. According to the price chart, the price for 1 to 5 items is $25 each. Therefore, you could write the first Case clause as Case 1, 2, 3, 4, 5. However, a more convenient way of writing that range of numbers is to use the keyword To, but you must follow this syntax to do so: **Case** *smallest value in the range* **To** *largest value in the range*. For instance, the expression 1 To 5 in the first Case clause specifies the range of numbers from 1 to 5, inclusive. The expression 6 To 10 in the second Case clause specifies the range of numbers from 6 to 10, inclusive. Notice that both Case clauses state both the lower (1 and 6) and upper (5 and 10) ends of each range. The third Case clause, Case Is > 10, contains the Is keyword rather than the To keyword. Recall that you use the Is keyword when you know only one end of the range of values—either the upper end or the lower end. In this case you know only the lower end of the range, 10. You always use the Is keyword in combination with one of the following comparison operators: =, <, <=, >, >=, <>. The Case Is > 10 clause specifies all numbers greater than the number 10. Because intNumOrdered is an Integer variable, you also can write this Case clause as Case Is >= 11. The Case Else clause in the example is processed only when the intNumOrdered variable contains a value that is not included in any of the previous Case clauses—more specifically, a zero or a negative number.

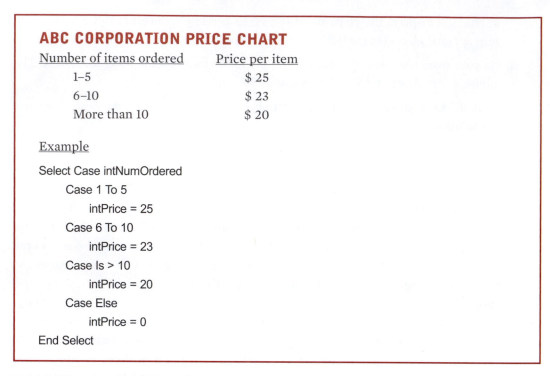

ABC CORPORATION PRICE CHART

Number of items ordered	Price per item
1–5	$ 25
6–10	$ 23
More than 10	$ 20

Example

```
Select Case intNumOrdered
    Case 1 To 5
        intPrice = 25
    Case 6 To 10
        intPrice = 23
    Case Is > 10
        intPrice = 20
    Case Else
        intPrice = 0
End Select
```

Figure 11-9: Example of using the To and Is keywords in a Select Case statement

To code the ABC Corporation application, then test the application:

1. Open the **ABC Solution** (**ABC Solution.sln**) file, which is contained in the ClearlyVB\ Chap11\ABC Solution folder. If necessary, open the designer window. The application's interface is shown in Figure 11-10.

Figure 11-10: User interface for the ABC Corporation application

2. Open the Code Editor window. In the btnDisplayPrice control's Click event procedure, enter the Select Case statement shown in Figure 11-11.

enter the Select Case statement

```
Private Sub btnDisplayPrice_Click(ByVal sender As Object, ByVal e As Syst
    ' displays the price per item

    Dim intNumOrdered As Integer
    Dim intPrice As Integer

    ' assign number ordered to a variable
    Integer.TryParse(txtNumOrdered.Text, intNumOrdered)

    ' determine the price per item, then display the price
    Select Case intNumOrdered
        Case 1 To 5
            intPrice = 25
        Case 6 To 10
            intPrice = 23
        Case Is > 10
            intPrice = 20
        Case Else
            intPrice = 0
    End Select
    lblPrice.Text = intPrice.ToString("C2")
End Sub
```

Figure 11-11: Select Case statement entered in the btnDisplayPrice control's Click event procedure

3. Save the solution, then start the application.

4. Type **4** as the number ordered, then click the **Display Price** button. The Integer. TryParse(txtNumOrdered.Text, intNumOrdered) statement in the button's Click event procedure assigns the number ordered to the intNumOrdered variable. The Select Case statement is processed next. When processing the statement, the computer first compares the contents of the intNumOrdered variable (4) to the first Case clause's *expressionList*: the range 1 To 5. The number 4 is included in that range, so the computer assigns the number 25 to the intPrice variable. It then skips to the instruction following the End Select clause. The instruction displays the contents of the intPrice variable (converted to Currency with two decimal places) in the lblPrice control; in this case, it displays $25.00.

5. On your own, test the application using the following numbers: **10, -3, 12**, and **x**. The prices should be $23.00, $0.00, $20.00, and $0.00.

6. Click the **Exit** button to end the application. Close the Code Editor window, then close the solution.

For more examples of using the Select Case statement to code a multiple-path selection structure, see the Select Case Multiple-Path Selection Structure section in the Ch11WantMore.pdf file.

USING RADIO BUTTONS

The If/ElseIf/Else and Case forms of the selection structure are often used when coding interfaces that contain radio buttons. A **radio button** is created using the RadioButton tool in the toolbox, and it allows you to limit the user to only one choice in a group of two or more related but mutually exclusive choices. Figure 11-12 shows a sample run of the Gentry Supplies application, which uses radio buttons in its interface. Notice that each radio button is labeled so the user knows its purpose. You enter the label using sentence capitalization in the radio button's Text property. Each radio button also has a unique access key that allows the user to select the button using the keyboard.

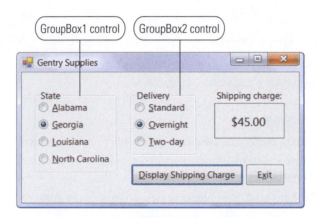

Figure 11-12: Sample run of the Gentry Supplies application

Two groups of radio buttons appear in the Gentry Supplies interface: one group contains the four state radio buttons and the other contains the three delivery radio buttons. To include two groups of radio buttons in an interface, at least one of the groups must be placed within a container, such as a group box control. Otherwise, the radio buttons are considered to be in the same group and only one can be selected at any one time. In this case, the radio buttons pertaining to the state choice are contained in the GroupBox1 control, and the radio buttons pertaining to the delivery choice are contained in the GroupBox2 control. You create a group box using the GroupBox tool in the toolbox. Placing each group of radio buttons in a separate group box allows the user to select one button from each group. Keep in mind that the minimum number of radio buttons in a group is two, because the only way to deselect a radio button is to select another radio button. The recommended maximum number of radio buttons in a group is seven. It is customary in Windows applications to have one of the radio buttons in each group already selected when the user interface first appears. The selected button is called the **default radio button** and is either the radio button that represents the user's most likely choice or the first radio button in the group. You designate a radio button as the default radio button by setting the button's Checked property to the Boolean value True. When you set the Checked property to True in the Properties window, a black dot appears inside the button's circle to indicate that the button is selected.

When the user clicks the Display Shipping Charge button in the Gentry Supplies interface, the button's Click event procedure should display the appropriate shipping charge. The shipping charges are shown in Figure 11-13.

State	Standard delivery charge
Alabama	20
Georgia	35
Louisiana	30
North Carolina	28
Overnight delivery	add $10 to the standard delivery charge
Two-day delivery	add $5 to the standard delivery charge

Figure 11-13: Gentry Supplies shipping chart

To code the Gentry Supplies application, then test the application:

1. Open the **Gentry Supplies Solution** (**Gentry Supplies Solution.sln**) file, which is contained in the ClearlyVB\Chap11\Gentry Supplies Solution folder. If necessary, open the designer window.

2. Open the Code Editor window. In the btnDisplay control's Click event procedure, enter the two selection structures shown in Figure 11-14. Notice that the code uses the Checked property to determine the radio button selected in the State group, as well as the radio button selected in the Delivery group.

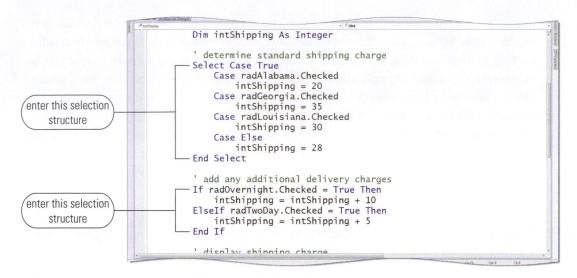

Figure 11-14: Selection structures entered in the btnDisplay control's Click event procedure

3. Save the solution, then start the application. Click the **Georgia** radio button, then click the **Overnight** radio button. Click the **Display Shipping Charge** button. The shipping charge is $45.00, as shown earlier in Figure 11-12.

4. On your own, display the shipping charge for a two-day delivery to Alabama, a standard delivery to North Carolina, an overnight delivery to North Carolina, and an overnight delivery to Louisiana. The shipping charges should be $25.00, $28.00, $38.00, and $40.00.

5. Click the **Exit** button to end the application. Close the Code Editor window, then close the solution.

To learn how to add a group box and radio button to a form, view the Ch11-Group Box and Radio Button video.

MINI-QUIZ 2

1. Rewrite Question 1 from Mini-Quiz 1 using the Select Case statement.

2. Rewrite Question 3 from Mini-Quiz 1 using the Select Case statement.

3. Which of the following Case clauses specifies integers from 10 through 20, inclusive?

   a. Case Is 10 To 20

   b. Case Is >= 10 AndAlso <= 20

   c. Case 20 To 10

   d. None of the above.

4. A form contains three radio buttons: January, February, and March. The radio buttons are named radJanuary, radFebruary, and radMarch. Write a multiple-path selection structure that displays the birthstone corresponding to the selected radio button. The birthstones for the three months are Garnet, Amethyst, and Aquamarine. Display the birthstone in the lblBirthstone control. Use the Select Case statement.

SUMMARY

» The solutions to some problems require a multiple-path (or extended) selection structure.

» You can code a multiple-path selection structure using either the If...Then...Else statement or the Select Case statement.

» String comparisons in Visual Basic are case sensitive.

» Each character on the computer keyboard is associated with a unique Unicode value.

» Before using a string in a comparison, you can convert it (temporarily) to either uppercase or lowercase using the ToUpper or ToLower methods, respectively.

» The data type of the expressions in a Select Case statement must be compatible with the data type of the statement's *selectorExpression*.

» You can use the To or Is keywords to specify a range of values in a Select Case statement. You use the To keyword when you know both the upper and lower bounds of the range. You use the Is keyword when you know only one end of the range (either the upper or lower end).

» You can use a radio button to limit the user to one choice from a group of two or more related but mutually exclusive choices.

» To include two groups of radio buttons in an interface, at least one of the groups must be placed within a container, such as a group box control.

» It is customary to have one radio button in each group of radio buttons selected when the user interface first appears.

» The Boolean value stored in a radio button's Checked property determines whether the radio button is selected (True) or unselected (False).

KEY TERMS

Default radio button—the radio button that is automatically selected when an interface first appears

Extended selection structures—selection structures that have several alternatives from which to choose; also called multiple-path selection structures

If/ElseIf/Else—a form of the If...Then...Else statement; provides a convenient way of coding a multiple-path selection structure

Multiple-path selection structures—selection structures that have several alternatives from which to choose; also called extended selection structures

Radio button—a control that limits the user to only one choice in a group of two or more related but mutually exclusive choices

Select Case statement—like the If...Then..Else statement, this statement can be used to code a multiple-path selection structure

String data type—the data type for storing alphanumeric text

ToLower method—used to convert a string, temporarily, to lowercase

ToUpper method—used to convert a string, temporarily, to uppercase

ANSWERS TO MINI-QUIZZES

MINI-QUIZ 1

1. ```
   If intPromoCode = 1 Then
       decRate = .02
   ElseIf intPromoCode = 2 Then
       decRate = .05
   ElseIf intPromoCode = 3 Then
       decRate = .1
   ElseIf intPromoCode = 4 Then
       decRate = .25
   Else
       decRate = 0
   End If
   ```

2. ```
   strId = txtId.Text.ToUpper
   ```

3. ```
   If strId = "12A" Then
       lblFirst.Text = "Jerry"
       lblLast.Text = "Jones"
   ElseIf strId = "45B" Then
       lblFirst.Text = "Mark"
       lblLast.Text = "Smith"
   ElseIf strId = "67X" Then
       lblFirst.Text = "Jill"
       lblLast.Text = "Batist"
   ElseIf strId = "78Y" Then
       lblFirst.Text = "Cheryl"
       lblLast.Text = "Sworski"
   Else
       lblFirst.Text = "?"
       lblLast.Text = "?"
   End If
   ```
   ```

MINI-QUIZ 2

1. Select Case intPromoCode
       Case 1
           decRate = .02
       Case 2
           decRate = .05
       Case 3
           decRate = .1
       Case 4
           decRate = .25
       Case Else
           decRate = 0
   End Select

2. Select Case strId
       Case "12A"
           lblFirst.Text = "Jerry"
           lblLast.Text = "Jones"
       Case "45B"
           lblFirst.Text = "Mark"
           lblLast.Text = "Smith"
       Case "67X"
           lblFirst.Text = "Jill"
           lblLast.Text = "Batist"
       Case "78Y"
           lblFirst.Text = "Cheryl"
           lblLast.Text = "Sworski"
       Case Else
           lblFirst.Text = "?"
           lblLast.Text = "?"
   End Select

3. d. None of the above.

4. Select Case True
       Case radJanuary.Checked
           lblBirthstone.Text = "Garnet"
       Case radFebruary.Checked
           lblBirthstone.Text = "Amethyst"
       Case Else
           lblBirthstone.Text = "Aquamarine"
   End Select

REVIEW QUESTIONS

1. Which of the following calculates a 5% discount when the units sold are from 1 through 100, a 7% discount when the units sold are from 101 through 200, and a 10% discount when the units sold are over 200? If the number of units sold is less than or equal to 0, the discount should be 0. The number of units sold is stored in the intUnits variable. Each unit costs $100.

   a. If intUnits > 0 AndAlso intUnits < 101 Then
   >   decDiscount = (intUnits * 100) * .05
   > ElseIf intUnits > 100 AndAlso intUnits < 201 Then
   >   decDiscount = (intUnits * 100) * .07
   > ElseIf intUnits > 200 Then
   >   decDiscount = (intUnits * 100) * .1
   > Else
   >   decDiscount = 0
   > End If

   b. Select Case intUnits
   >   Case 1 To 100
   >   decDiscount = (intUnits * 100) * .05
   >   Case 101 To 200
   >   decDiscount = (intUnits * 100) * .07
   >   Case > 200
   >   decDiscount = (intUnits * 100) * .1
   >   Case Else
   >   decDiscount = 0
   > End Case

   c. Select Case intUnits
   >   Case < 1
   >   decDiscount = 0
   >   Case 1 To 100
   >   decDiscount = (intUnits * 100) * .05
   >   Case 101 To 200
   >   decDiscount = (intUnits * 100) * .07
   >   Case Else
   >   decDiscount = (intUnits * 100) * .1
   > End Case

   d. All of the above.

2. Which of the following assigns the contents of the txtState control, in uppercase, to the strState variable?

a. If strState = txtState.Text.ToUpper Then

b. strState.ToUpper = txtState.Text

c. strState = txtState.Text.ToUpper

d. All of the above.

3. Which of the following Case clauses will be processed when the intNum variable contains one of the following integers: 5, 6, 7, 8, or 9?

a. Case >= 5 AndAlso <= 9   b. Case 5 To 9

c. Case 9 To 5   d. All of the above.

4. Which of the following determines whether the radAddition radio button is selected?

a. If radAddition.Checked = True Then

b. If radAddition.Checked = Yes Then

c. If radAddition.Selected = On

d. If radAddition.Selected = True

5. The minimum number of radio buttons in a group is _____.

a. one

b. two

c. three

d. There is no minimum number of radio buttons in a group.

EXERCISES

»TRY THIS

1. In this exercise, you modify the code shown in Version 2 in Figure 11-2. (The answers to TRY THIS Exercises are located at the end of the chapter.)

a. Open the Department Solution (Department Solution.sln) file, which is contained in the ClearlyVB\Chap11\Department Solution folder. Open the Code Editor window. Replace the selection structure in the btnDisplay control's Click event procedure with a Select Case statement.

b. Save the solution, then start and test the application. Stop the application, then close the solution.

2. In this exercise, you modify the selection structure in an existing application. (The answers to TRY THIS Exercises are located at the end of the chapter.)

» TRY THIS

a. Open the Total Due Solution (Total Due Solution.sln) file, which is contained in the ClearlyVB\Chap11\Total Due Solution folder. Open the Code Editor window. Change the outer If...Then...Else statement in the btnCalc control's Click event procedure to a Select Case statement.

b. Save the solution, then start and test the application. Stop the application, then close the solution.

3. In this exercise, you modify one of the Fitness For Good applications coded in the chapter.

» MODIFY THIS

a. Use Windows to make a copy of the Fitness Solution-Select Case folder. Save the copy in the ClearlyVB\Chap11 folder. Rename the copy Modified Fitness Solution-Select Case.

b. Open the Fitness Solution (Fitness Solution.sln) file contained in the Modified Fitness Solution-Select Case folder. The health club has added an additional membership type. The monthly fee for the new Child membership type is $5. Make the appropriate modifications to both the interface and the code.

c. Save the solution. Start and then test the application. Stop the application, then close the solution.

4. The owner of Harry's Car Sales pays each salesperson a commission based on his or her monthly sales. The sales ranges and corresponding commission rates are shown in Figure 11-15.

» INTRODUCTORY

Monthly sales	Commission rate
$0–$19,999.99	4%
$20,000–$29,999.99	5%
$30,000–$39,999.99	6%
$40,000–$49,999.99	7%
$50,000 or more	9%
Less than $0	0%

Figure 11-15: Sales and commission chart

a. Open the Harry Car Solution (Harry Car Solution.sln) file, which is contained in the ClearlyVB\Chap11\Harry Car Solution folder. Open the Code Editor window. Code the btnCalc control's Click event procedure so that it both calculates and displays a salesperson's commission. Use the If/ElseIf/Else form of the If...Then...Else statement.

b. Save the solution. Start and then test the application. Stop the application, then close the solution.

c. Use Windows to make a copy of the Harry Car Solution folder. Save the copy in the ClearlyVB\Chap11 folder. Rename the copy Modified Harry Car Solution.

d. Open the Harry Car Solution (Harry Car Solution.sln) file contained in the Modified Harry Car Solution folder. Change the selection structure in the btnCalc control's Click event procedure to a Select Case statement.

e. Save the solution. Start and then test the application. Stop the application, then close the solution.

» INTRODUCTORY

5. The owner of Concerts For All wants an application that displays the price of a concert ticket. The ticket price is based on the seat location. Box seats are $75. Pavilion seats are $30, and lawn seats are $21. However, at times, the owner offers a 10% discount on the ticket price. Use radio buttons for the seat locations, and use a check box for the 10% discount.

a. List the output and input items, as well as any processing items, then create an appropriate algorithm using a flowchart.

b. Create a new Visual Basic Windows application. Name the solution, project, and form file Concerts Solution, Concerts Project, and frmMain.vb, respectively. Save the application in the ClearlyVB\Chap11 folder. If necessary, change the form's name to frmMain.

c. Create an appropriate interface. Include an Exit button. Code the Exit button's Click event procedure and the problem's algorithm. Save the solution.

d. Start and then test the application. Stop the application, then close the solution.

» INTERMEDIATE

6. Jack Jefferson, a teacher at Alvaton Elementary School, wants an application that helps his students learn the capitals of 10 states. Create the interface shown in Figure 11-16. If the selected capital corresponds to the selected state, display the message "Correct" in the Result box; otherwise, display the message "Try again". Name the solution, project, and form file State Capital Solution, State Capital Project, and frmMain.vb, respectively. Save the application in the ClearlyVB\Chap11 folder. Code the application. Save the solution, then start and test the application. Stop the application, then close the solution.

Figure 11-16: State Capitals interface

7. In this exercise, you create an application that converts US Dollars to a different currency. The currencies and exchange rates are listed in Figure 11-17. The application should allow the user to enter the number of US Dollars, and also select the desired currency from a group of radio buttons. Name the solution, project, and form file Currency Solution, Currency Project, and frmMain.vb, respectively. Save the application in the ClearlyVB\Chap11 folder. Code the application. Save the solution, then start and test the application. Stop the application, then close the solution.

» INTERMEDIATE

Currency	Exchange rate
Canada Dollar	1.01615
Eurozone Euro	.638490
India Rupee	40.1798
Japan Yen	104.390
Mexico Peso	10.4613
South Africa Rand	7.60310
United Kingdom Pound	.504285

Figure 11-17: Currencies and exchange rates

»ADVANCED

8. In this exercise, you create an application for Willow Health Club. The application displays the number of daily calories needed to maintain a member's current weight. The formulas for calculating the number of daily calories are shown in Figure 11-18.

Moderately active female: total daily calories = weight multiplied by 12 calories per pound
Relatively inactive female: total daily calories = weight multiplied by 10 calories per pound
Moderately active male: total daily calories = weight multiplied by 15 calories per pound
Relatively inactive male: total daily calories = weight multiplied by 13 calories per pound

Figure 11-18: Formulas for calculating the daily calories

a. List the output and input items, as well as any processing items, then create an appropriate algorithm using pseudocode.

b. Create a new Visual Basic Windows application. Name the solution, project, and form file Willow Solution, Willow Project, and frmMain.vb, respectively. Save the application in the ClearlyVB\Chap11 folder. If necessary, change the form's name to frmMain.

c. Create an appropriate interface. Include an Exit button. Code the Exit button's Click event procedure and the problem's algorithm. Save the solution.

d. Start and then test the application. Stop the application, then close the solution.

»ADVANCED

9. Shopper Haven wants an application that displays the number of reward points a customer earns each month. The reward points are based on the customer's membership type and total monthly purchase amount, as shown in Figure 11-19.

Membership type	Total monthly purchase	Reward points
Standard	0–74.99	5% of the total monthly purchase
	75–149.99	7.5% of the total monthly purchase
	150 and over	10% of the total monthly purchase
Plus	0–149.99	6% of the total monthly purchase
	150 and over	13% of the total monthly purchase
Premium	0–199.99	4% of the total monthly purchase
	200 and over	15% of the total monthly purchase

Figure 11-19: Reward points chart

a. List the output and input items, as well as any processing items, then create an appropriate algorithm using pseudocode.

b. Create a new Visual Basic Windows application. Name the solution, project, and form file Shopper Solution, Shopper Project, and frmMain.vb, respectively. Save the application in the ClearlyVB\Chap11 folder. If necessary, change the form's name to frmMain.

c. Create an appropriate interface. Include an Exit button. Code the Exit button's Click event procedure and the problem's algorithm. Display the reward points as whole numbers. Save the solution.

d. Start and then test the application. Stop the application, then close the solution.

10. Open the FigureThisOut Solution (FigureThisOut Solution.sln) file, which is contained in the ClearlyVB\Chap11\FigureThisOut Solution folder. Open the Code Editor window and study the btnDisplay control's Click event procedure. What task is performed by the procedure? What are the rules for charging the various rates? Test the application to verify that your answers are correct. Stop the application, then close the solution.

11. In this exercise, you find an error in an application's code. Open the SwatTheBugs Solution (SwatTheBugs Solution.sln) file, which is contained in the ClearlyVB\Chap11\ SwatTheBugs Solution folder. The application should display a shipping charge that is based on the total price entered by the user. If the total price is less than $1, the shipping charge is $0. If the total price is greater than or equal to $1 but less than $100, the shipping charge is $5. If the total price is greater than or equal to $100 but less than $501, the shipping charge is $10. If the total price is greater than or equal to $501 but less than $1001, the shipping charge is $12. If the total price is greater than or equal to $1001, the shipping charge is $14. Start the application. Test the application using the following total prices: 100, 501, 1500, 500.75, 30, and 1000.33. Notice that the application does not display the correct shipping charge for some of these total prices. Open the Code Editor window and study the code. Locate and correct the errors in the code. Save the solution, then start and test the application.

ANSWERS TO "TRY THIS" EXERCISES

1. To modify the btnDisplay control's Click event procedure, change the If...Then...Else statement to:

```
Select Case intCode
    Case 1
        lblName.Text = "Payroll"
    Case 2
        lblName.Text = "Personnel"
    Case 3
        lblName.Text = "IT"
    Case Else
        lblName.Text = "Invalid code"
End Select
```

2. To modify the btnCalc control's Click event procedure, change the outer If...Then...Else statement to:

```
Select Case chkEmployee.Checked
    Case True
        decTotal = decTotal * (1 - decEMP_DISC_RATE)
    Case Else
        If intQuantity > 20 Then
            decTotal = decTotal * (1 - decNON_EMP_DISC_RATE)
        End If
End Select
```

12

TESTING, TESTING...1, 2, 3

After studying Chapter 12, you should be able to:

Select appropriate test data for an application

Prevent the entry of unwanted characters in a text box

Create a message box with the MessageBox.Show method

Trim leading and trailing spaces from a string

WILL YOUR APPLICATION PASS THE TEST?

As you learned in Chapter 3, the last step in the problem-solving process is to rigorously test the program before releasing it to the user. You test the program using a computer along with a set of sample data that includes both valid and invalid data. Valid data is data that the program is expecting the user to enter. You test with valid data to ensure that the program produces the correct results. Invalid data, on the other hand, is data that the program is not expecting the user to enter. Invalid data typically is the result of the user making a typing error, entering the data in an incorrect format, or neglecting to make a required entry. You test with invalid data to ensure that the program does not display erroneous results or end abruptly because of an input error. Figure 12-1 lists some guidelines for selecting appropriate test data for an application. You will use these guidelines to test several applications in this chapter. (Additional guidelines will be added to the list in subsequent chapters.)

GUIDELINES FOR SELECTING TEST DATA

1. Test the application without entering any data.

2. If the application's code expects a text box to contain a number, use both valid and invalid values for the text box. Typically, you should include the number 0 in the test data, as well as positive and negative integers, positive and negative non-integers, and alphanumeric text.

3. If the application's code contains a selection structure, use values that will test each path. If a condition contains a range of values, the test data should include the lowest and highest values in the range, as well as a value within the range. If a condition compares strings, include uppercase text and lowercase text in the test data.

Figure 12-1: Guidelines for selecting an application's test data

THE ONLY COOKIES-VERSION 1 APPLICATION

Figure 12-2 shows the interface for the Only Cookies-Version 1 application. The interface provides a text box for entering the number of pounds of cookies ordered; the number of pounds may contain a decimal place. Each pound of cookies costs $5. When the user clicks the Calculate button, the button's Click event procedure calculates and displays the total price of the order. The Click event procedure is shown in Figure 12-3. Notice that the procedure uses an Integer named constant for the pound price, and two Decimal variables for the pounds ordered and the total price.

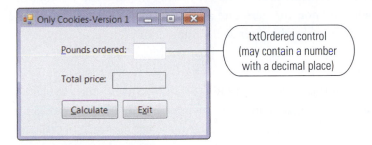

Figure 12-2: Interface for the Only Cookies-Version 1 application

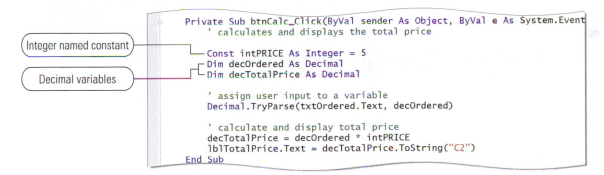

Figure 12-3: Calculate button's Click event procedure in the Only Cookies-Version 1 application

Before testing the Only Cookies-Version 1 application, you will use the guidelines from Figure 12-1, as well as the interface and code shown in Figures 12-2 and 12-3, to create a set of test data. You will record the test data in a testing chart, along with the expected results. The first guideline is to test the application without entering any data. As the interface and code indicate, only one item of data is entered by the user in this application: the number of pounds of cookies ordered. If the user clicks the Calculate button without entering a value in the Pounds ordered box, the procedure should display $0.00 in the Total price box. (The "C2" *formatString* in the procedure's code formats the total price with a dollar sign and two decimal places.) In the testing chart, you record "No data entered" and $0.00, as shown in Figure 12-4.

Test data	Expected result
No data entered	$0.00

Figure 12-4: First entry in the application's testing chart

The Only Cookies-Version 1 application expects the user to enter a number in the Pounds ordered text box. Therefore, according to the second guideline in Figure 12-1, you should test the application by entering both valid and invalid values in the text box. As the guideline indicates, typical values used for testing include the number 0, positive and negative integers and non-integers, and alphanumeric text. Begin by making a list of valid values that the user might enter as the number of pounds ordered. For example, the user might enter the number 0 or the positive integers 10 and 25; or he might enter the positive non-integer 4.5. The expected results are $0.00, $50.00, $125.00, and $22.50. (Recall that the price per pound is $5.) If the user wants to calculate a refund, he also might enter a negative number, such as the negative integer -3 or the negative non-integer -6.5. The expected results using these values are ($15.00) and ($32.50). You record the test data, along with the expected results, in the testing chart, as shown in Figure 12-5.

Test data	Expected result
No data entered	$0.00
Valid values:	
0	$0.00
10	$50.00
25	$125.00
4.5	$22.50
-3	($15.00)
-6.5	($32.50)

Figure 12-5: Valid values entered in the application's testing chart

Now consider values that the user might enter by mistake. In the current application, the user might inadvertently enter the letter x, the # symbol, or 3O (the number 3 followed by the uppercase letter O). If the user enters an invalid value, the application should display $0.00 in the Total price box. Figure 12-6 shows the invalid values and their expected results entered in the testing chart. Notice that the test data contains the number 0, positive and negative integers and non-integers, and alphanumeric text.

Test data	Expected result
No data entered	$0.00
Valid values:	
0	$0.00
10	$50.00
25	$125.00
4.5	$22.50
-3	($15.00)
-6.5	($32.50)
Invalid values:	
x, #, 30	$0.00

Figure 12-6: Testing chart for the Only Cookies-Version 1 application

The third guideline in Figure 12-1 pertains to selection structures. You can skip the third guideline because the application's code does not contain a selection structure. In this first set of steps, you will test the application using the test data and expected results listed in Figure 12-6.

To test the Only Cookies-Version 1 application:

1. Start Visual Studio 2008 (or Visual Basic 2008 Express Edition). Open the **Only Cookies Solution** (**Only Cookies Solution.sln**) file, which is contained in the ClearlyVB\ Chap12\Only Cookies Solution-Version 1 folder. If necessary, open the designer window.

2. Start the application. First, test the application without entering any data. Click the **Calculate** button. The expected result, $0.00, appears in the Total price box.

3. Type **0** in the Pounds ordered box, then click the **Calculate** button. The expected result, $0.00, appears in the Total price box. Change the number of pounds ordered to **10**, then click the **Calculate** button. $50.00 appears in the Total price box, which is correct.

4. On your own, test the application using the following valid values: **25**, **4.5**, **-3**, and **-6.5**. The total prices should agree with the corresponding results listed in Figure 12-6.

5. Change the number of pounds ordered to **x**, then click the **Calculate** button. The TryParse method in the button's Click event procedure cannot convert the letter x to the Decimal data type, so it assigns the number 0 to the decOrdered variable. The decTotalPrice = decOrdered * intPRICE statement calculates the total price (0). The last assignment statement in the procedure formats the total price with a dollar sign and two decimal places, and then displays the result shown in the testing chart—$0.00.

6. On your own, test the application using the following two invalid values: **#** and **3O** (be sure to type the uppercase letter O rather than the number 0). The results should agree with the ones listed in Figure 12-6.

7. Click the **Exit** button, then close the solution.

THE ONLY COOKIES-VERSION 2 APPLICATION

Figure 12-7 shows the interface for the Only Cookies-Version 2 application. Except for the title bar text, the interface is identical to the one in the Only Cookies-Version 1 application. However, in this version of the application, the number of pounds entered in the Pounds ordered text box must be an integer. Each pound of cookies still costs $5. Figure 12-8 shows the Calculate button's Click event procedure, which calculates and displays the total price of the order. Notice that in this version of the application, the Click event procedure uses Integer variables (rather than Decimal variables) for the pounds ordered and total price.

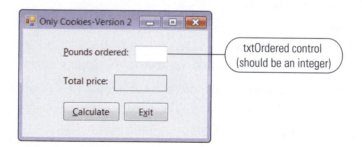

Figure 12-7: Interface for the Only Cookies-Version 2 application

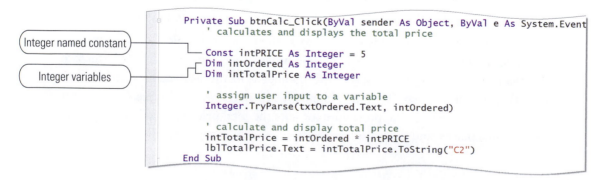

Figure 12-8: Calculate button's Click event procedure in the Only Cookies-Version 2 application

Figure 12-9 shows the testing chart for the Only Cookies-Version 2 application. Comparing this testing chart with the one shown earlier in Figure 12-6, you will notice that the two non-integer values (4.5 and -6.5) now appear in the Invalid values section. This is because the Only Cookies-Version 2 application expects the user to enter an integer in the Pounds ordered text box.

Test data	Expected result
No data entered	$0.00
Valid values:	
0	$0.00
10	$50.00
25	$125.00
-3	($15.00)
Invalid values:	
x, #, 3O	$0.00
4.5	$0.00
-6.5	$0.00

Figure 12-9: Testing chart for the Only Cookies-Version 2 application

To test the Only Cookies-Version 2 application:

1. Open the **Only Cookies Solution** (**Only Cookies Solution.sln**) file, which is contained in the ClearlyVB\Chap12\Only Cookies Solution-Version 2 folder. If necessary, open the designer window.

2. Start the application. First, test the application without entering any data. Click the **Calculate** button. The expected result, $0.00, appears in the Total price box.

3. On your own, test the application using the following values: **0, 10, 25, -3, x, #,** and **3O** (be sure to type the uppercase letter O rather than the number 0). The total prices should agree with the corresponding results listed in Figure 12-9.

4. Change the number of pounds ordered to **4.5**, then click the **Calculate** button. The TryParse method in the button's Click event procedure cannot convert the non-integer 4.5 to the Integer data type, so it assigns the number 0 to the intOrdered variable. When the intOrdered variable contains the number 0, the total price will be 0 and the procedure will display $0.00 in the Total price box. See Figure 12-10. Although the total price agrees with the expected result, it is very misleading because it indicates that the cookies are free of charge. You will learn one way to fix this problem in the next section.

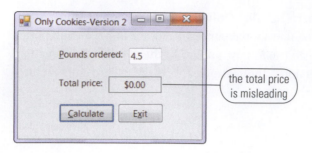

Figure 12-10: Result of entering a non-integer in the text box

5. Change the number of pounds ordered to **-6.5**, then click the **Calculate** button. $0.00 appears in the Total price box. Here again, the total price is misleading. Click the **Exit** button.

STOP! THIS IS A RESTRICTED AREA!

The Only Cookies-Version 2 application expects the user to enter the number of pounds as an integer. The number of pounds should not contain any letters, periods, or special characters. Unfortunately, you can't stop the user from trying to enter an inappropriate character into a text box. However, you can prevent the text box from accepting the character; you do this by coding the text box's KeyPress event procedure. A control's **KeyPress event** occurs each time the user presses a key while the control has the focus. When the KeyPress event occurs, a character corresponding to the pressed key is sent to the KeyPress event's e parameter, which appears between the parentheses in the event's procedure header. For example, when the user presses the period while entering data into a text box, the text box's KeyPress event occurs and a period is sent to the event's e parameter. Similarly, when the Shift key along with a letter is pressed, the uppercase version of the letter is sent to the e parameter. To prevent a text box from accepting an inappropriate character, you first use the e parameter's **KeyChar property** to determine the pressed key. (KeyChar stands for "key character.") You then use the e parameter's **Handled property** to cancel the pressed key if it is an inappropriate one. Figure 12-11 shows examples of using the KeyChar and Handled properties in the KeyPress event procedure. Notice that you refer to the Backspace key on your keyboard using the **ControlChars.Back constant**. The Backspace key is necessary for editing the text box entry.

PREVENTING A TEXT BOX FROM ACCEPTING CERTAIN CHARACTERS

Example 1

```
Private Sub txtRegistered_KeyPress(ByVal sender As Object, _
    ByVal e As System.Windows.Forms.KeyPressEventArgs) _
    Handles txtRegistered.KeyPress
    ' allows the text box to accept only the letters
    ' Y, y, N, and n and the Backspace key for editing

    If e.KeyChar <> "Y" AndAlso e.KeyChar <> "y" _
        AndAlso e.KeyChar <> "N" AndAlso e.KeyChar <> "n" _
        AndAlso e.KeyChar <> ControlChars.Back Then
            e.Handled = True
    End If
End Sub
```

Example 2

```
Private Sub txtOrdered_KeyPress(ByVal sender As Object, _
    ByVal e As System.Windows.Forms.KeyPressEventArgs) _
    Handles txtOrdered.KeyPress
    ' allows the text box to accept only numbers, the hyphen,
    ' and the Backspace key for editing

    If (e.KeyChar < "0" OrElse e.KeyChar > "9") _
        AndAlso e.KeyChar <> "-" _
        AndAlso e.KeyChar <> ControlChars.Back Then
            e.Handled = True
    End If
End Sub
```

Figure 12-11: How to prevent a text box from accepting certain characters

In the next set of steps, you will modify the Only Cookies-Version 2 application by entering code in the txtOrdered control's KeyPress event procedure. The code will prevent the text box from accepting any character other than a number, the hyphen, and the Backspace key. Whenever you make a change to an application's code, you should retest the application using the test data listed in the testing chart. Figure 12-12 shows the testing chart for the modified Only Cookies-Version 2 application.

Test data	Expected result
No data entered	$0.00
Valid values: 0 10 25 -3	 $0.00 $50.00 $125.00 ($15.00)
Invalid values: x, #, 30, 4.5, -6.5	 not allowed in the text box

Figure 12-12: Testing chart for the modified Only Cookies-Version 2 application

To modify the Only Cookies-Version 2 application, then test the application:

1. Open the Code Editor window. Open the code template for the txtOrdered control's KeyPress event procedure. Enter the comments and five lines of code shown in Example 2 in Figure 12-11.

2. Start the application. On your own, test the application without entering any data, then test it using the following values: **0**, **10**, **25**, and **-3**.

3. Now test the application using the following values: **x**, **#**, and **3O** (be sure to type the uppercase letter O rather than the number 0), **4.5**, and **-6.5**. You will not be able to enter the letter x, the # symbol, the uppercase letter O, or the period.

4. Click the **Exit** button. Close the Code Editor window, then close the solution.

For more examples of applications that require numeric data, see the Numeric Data Testing section in the Ch12WantMore.pdf file.

MINI-QUIZ 1

1. What is the first guideline for selecting test data?

2. If the txtSales control contains the number 345.78, the Integer.TryParse (txtSales.Text, intSales) statement will assign _____ to the intSales variable.

3. When the user types the number 9 in a text box, the 9 is sent to the KeyPress event's _____ parameter.

THE SHADY HOLLOW HOTEL- VERSION 1 APPLICATION

The daily rate for a Standard room at Shady Hollow Hotel is $90. The daily rate for a Deluxe room is $115, and the daily rate for a Suite is $130. Figure 12-13 shows the interface for the Shady Hollow Hotel-Version 1 application. The interface uses radio buttons for the room type selection. When the user clicks the Display Rate button, its Click event procedure displays the daily rate in the interface. The Click event procedure is shown in Figure 12-14.

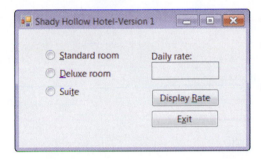

Figure 12-13: Interface for the Shady Hollow Hotel-Version 1 application

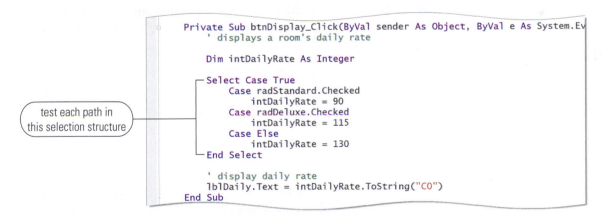

```
Private Sub btnDisplay_Click(ByVal sender As Object, ByVal e As System.Ev
    ' displays a room's daily rate

    Dim intDailyRate As Integer

    Select Case True
        Case radStandard.Checked
            intDailyRate = 90
        Case radDeluxe.Checked
            intDailyRate = 115
        Case Else
            intDailyRate = 130
    End Select

    ' display daily rate
    lblDaily.Text = intDailyRate.ToString("C0")
End Sub
```

test each path in this selection structure

Figure 12-14: Display Rate button's Click event procedure in the Shady Hollow Hotel-Version 1 application

Before testing the Shady Hollow Hotel-Version 1 application, you will use the guidelines from Figure 12-1, as well as the interface and code shown in Figures 12-13 and 12-14, to create a set of test data. The first guideline is to test the application without entering any data. If no radio buttons are selected, the Daily rate box should show $0. The second guideline pertains to numbers entered in a text box; you can skip this guideline because the application does not use any text boxes. The third guideline covers selection structures. The application's code contains one selection structure, which is located in the Display Rate button's Click event procedure. According to the third guideline, you need to test each path in the selection structure. The first path's condition (radStandard.Checked) will evaluate to True when the Standard room radio button is selected; when the condition is True, $90 should appear in the Daily rate box. The second path's condition (radDeluxe.Checked) will evaluate to True when the Deluxe room radio button is selected; when this condition is True, $115 should appear in the Daily rate box. The third path, which is the Case Else path, is processed when the other two path conditions evaluate to False. When the Case Else path is processed, $130 should appear in the Daily rate box. Figure 12-15 shows the application's testing chart.

Test data	Expected result
No data entered	$0
Standard room radio button selected	$90
Deluxe room radio button selected	$115
Suite radio button selected	$130

Figure 12-15: Testing chart for the Shady Hollow Hotel-Version 1 application

To test the Shady Hollow Hotel-Version 1 application:

1. Open the **Shady Hollow Solution (Shady Hollow Solution.sln)** file, which is contained in the ClearlyVB\Chap12\Shady Hollow Solution-Version 1 folder. If necessary, open the designer window.

2. Start the application. First, test the application without entering any data. Click the **Display Rate** button. The Daily rate box shows $130, which is the daily rate for a Suite. The $130 rate is not correct, because the Suite radio button is not selected in the interface. Click the **Exit** button to end the application.

3. Open the Code Editor window. Locate the btnDisplay control's Click event procedure. Notice that the Suite rate is assigned in the Case Else clause, which is processed when the Standard room and Deluxe room radio buttons are not selected. In other words, it's processed when the Suite radio button is selected (which is correct) and also when no radio button is selected (which is incorrect). You can fix the problem by changing the Case Else clause to Case radSuite.Checked; doing this tells the computer to display $130 only when the Suite radio button is selected. You also can fix the problem by designating one of the radio buttons as the default radio button. Designating a default radio button ensures that a radio button is automatically selected when the interface first appears; it also is a common practice in Windows applications, as you learned in Chapter 11.

4. Close the Code Editor window. Click the **Standard room** radio button, then set its Checked property to **True**.

5. Save the solution, then start the application. Notice that the Standard room radio button is automatically selected. Click the **Display Rate** button. The Daily rate box shows $90, which is the correct Standard room rate.

6. Click the **Deluxe room** radio button, then click the **Display Rate** button. The Daily rate box shows $115, which is correct. Click the **Suite** radio button, then click the **Display Rate** button. The Daily rate box shows the correct rate, $130. Click the **Standard room** radio button, then click the **Display Rate** button. The correct rate appears in the Daily rate box.

7. Click the **Exit** button, then close the solution.

Figure 12-16 shows the modified testing chart for the Shady Hollow Hotel-Version 1 application.

Test data	Expected result
No data entered	$90 (Standard radio button is the default radio button)
Standard room radio button selected	$90
Deluxe room radio button selected	$115
Suite radio button selected	$130

Figure 12-16: Modified testing chart for the Shady Hollow Hotel-Version 1 application

THE SHADY HOLLOW HOTEL-VERSION 2 APPLICATION

Shady Hollow Hotel is being renovated and now offers only two types of rooms: Standard and Deluxe. The daily rate for a Standard room is $90; the daily rate for a Deluxe room is $115. Figure 12-17 shows the interface for the Shady Hollow Hotel-Version 2 application. The interface uses a text box for the room type selection—either S for Standard or D for Deluxe. When the user clicks the Display Rate button, its Click event procedure displays the daily rate in the Daily rate box. The Click event procedure is shown in Figure 12-18.

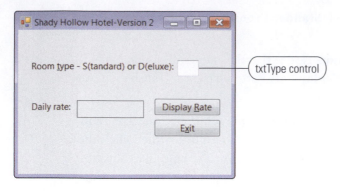

Figure 12-17: Interface for the Shady Hollow Hotel-Version 2 application

assigns the contents of the text box, in uppercase, to the variable

test each path in this selection structure

```
Private Sub btnDisplay_Click(ByVal sender As Object, ByVal e As System.Ev
    ' displays a room's daily rate

    Dim strType As String
    Dim intDailyRate As Integer

    ' assign room type to a variable
    strType = txtType.Text.ToUpper

    If strType = "S" Then
        intDailyRate = 90
    ElseIf strType = "D" Then
        intDailyRate = 115
    End If

    ' display daily rate
    lblDaily.Text = intDailyRate.ToString("C0")
End Sub
```

Figure 12-18: Display Rate button's Click event procedure in the Shady Hollow Hotel-Version 2 application

Before testing the Shady Hollow Hotel-Version 2 application, you will create a set of test data. Recall that the first guideline in Figure 12-1 is to test the application without entering any data. This application requires the user to enter only one item of data: the room type. If the user clicks the Display Rate button without entering the room type, the procedure should display $0 in the Daily rate box. The second guideline in Figure 12-1 pertains to numbers entered in a text box. In this application, the user will be entering a string (rather than a number) in the txtType control; therefore, you can skip the second guideline. The third guideline covers selection structures. The only selection structure in the application's code is located in the Display Rate button's Click event procedure. According to the third guideline, you need to test each path in the selection structure. If the path condition compares strings, you should include uppercase and lowercase text in the test data. Begin by making a list of valid values that the user might enter as the room type. In this case, the user might enter any of the following letters: S, s, D, or d. The expected results are $90, $90, $115, and $115. Now consider values that the user might enter by mistake. In the current application, the user might inadvertently enter the letter a, the $, or even the number 9. If the user enters an invalid value, the application should display $0 in the Daily rate box. Figure 12-19 shows the application's testing chart.

Test data	Expected result
No data entered	$0

Valid values:
  S, s
  D, d
	
	$90
	$115

Invalid values: a, $, 9	 $0

Figure 12-19: Testing chart for the Shady Hollow Hotel-Version 2 application

To test the Shady Hollow Hotel-Version 2 application:

1. Open the **Shady Hollow Solution** (**Shady Hollow Solution.sln**) file, which is contained in the ClearlyVB\Chap12\Shady Hollow Solution-Version 2 folder. If necessary, open the designer window.

2. Start the application. First, test the application without entering any data. Click the **Display Rate** button. The expected result, $0, appears in the Daily rate box.

3. On your own, test the application using the following values: **S, a, D, $, s, d**, and **9**. The results should be $90, $0, $115, $0, $90, $115, and $0.

4. Click the **Exit** button.

I NEED TO TELL YOU SOMETHING

As you observed in the previous set of steps, $0 appears in the Daily rate box when the room type is either missing or invalid. In situations such as this, many programmers also display a message alerting the user of the input error. You can display the message either in a label control in the interface or in a message box; most programmers use a message box. You create a message box using the **MessageBox.Show method**. The basic syntax of the method is shown in Figure 12-20 along with an example of using the method. You enter the message in the method's *message* argument. Typically, the message is entered using sentence capitalization. The text in the *titleBarText* argument appears in the form's title bar. In most cases, the *titleBarText* is the name of the application and is entered using book title capitalization. The MessageBoxButtons.OK and MessageBoxIcon.Information arguments display an OK button and an Information icon in the message box, as illustrated in Figure 12-21. The user closes the message box by clicking the OK button. (You will learn more about the MessageBox.Show method in a subsequent chapter.)

THE BASIC SYNTAX OF THE MESSAGEBOX.SHOW METHOD

<u>Syntax</u>

MessageBox.Show(*message*, *titleBarText*, **MessageBoxButtons.OK,**
MessageBoxIcon.Information)

<u>Example</u>

MessageBox.Show("The message appears here", "The titleBarText appears here", _
          MessageBoxButtons.OK, MessageBoxIcon.Information)

Figure 12-20: Basic syntax and an example of the MessageBox.Show method

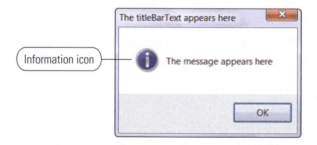

Figure 12-21: Message box created by the example in Figure 12-20

To modify the Shady Hollow Hotel-Version 2 application:

1. Open the Code Editor window. Locate the btnDisplay control's Click event procedure. Modify the If...Then...Else statement as indicated in Figure 12-22.

```
If strType = "S" Then
    intDailyRate = 90
ElseIf strType = "D" Then
    intDailyRate = 115
Else
    MessageBox.Show("Please enter a valid room type", _
                    "Shady Hollow Hotel", _
                    MessageBoxButtons.OK, MessageBoxIcon.Information)
End If
```

enter the Else clause and the MessageBox.Show method

Figure 12-22: Modified If...Then...Else statement

2. Save the solution.

As mentioned earlier, you should retest the application whenever you make a change to its code. Figure 12-23 shows the modified testing chart for the Shady Hollow Hotel-Version 2 application.

Test data	Expected result
No data entered	message, $0
Valid values: S, s D, d	$90 $115
Invalid values: a, $, 9	message, $0

Figure 12-23: Modified testing chart for the Shady Hollow Hotel-Version 2 application

To test the modified Shady Hollow Hotel-Version 2 application:

1. Start the application. Click the **Display Rate** button. A message box appears on the screen, as shown in Figure 12-24.

Figure 12-24: Message box

2. Click the **OK** button to close the message box. $0 appears in the Daily rate box.

3. On your own, test the application using the valid and invalid values shown in Figure 12-23. The results should agree with the ones listed in the figure.

4. Click the **Exit** button.

JUST WHEN YOU THOUGHT IT WAS SAFE

When you are satisfied that an application is functioning correctly, you can release it to the user. However, keep this fact in mind: no matter how thoroughly you test an application, chances are it still will contain some errors, called **bugs**. This is because it's almost impossible to create a set of test data that covers every possible scenario the application will encounter. Typically, the number of bugs is directly related to the size and complexity of the application. In other words, large and complex applications usually have more errors than do small and simple ones. Because of this, most large and complex applications are beta tested by volunteers before being sold in the marketplace. Beta testers are encouraged to use the application as often as possible, because some bugs surface only after months of use. When a beta tester finds a bug in the application, she submits a bug report to the programmer. Although the Shady Hollow Hotel-Version 2 application is small and very simple, it contains a minor bug.

To locate the bug in the Shady Hollow Hotel-Version 2 application:

1. Start the application. When entering data in a text box, it is not uncommon for a user to inadvertently include a space character at the end of the entry. Type the letter **d**, then press the **spacebar** on your keyboard. Click the **Display Rate** button. The message "Please enter a valid room type" appears in a message box. At this point, the user most certainly is thinking, "But I *did* enter a valid room type: d." It's doubtful that the user remembers pressing the spacebar, because it's usually done unconsciously.

2. Click the **OK** button to close the message box. $0 appears in the Daily rate box, as shown in Figure 12-25. The interface adds to the user's confusion, because it appears that the daily rate for a Deluxe room is $0. (It's not obvious that a space character follows the letter d in the text box.)

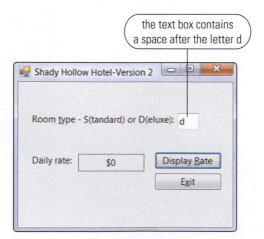

Figure 12-25: Result of including a space after the room type

3. Click the **Exit** button.

There are several ways to fix the bug in the application. For example, you can change the txtType control's MaxLength property to 1; doing this limits the text box entry to one character only. You learned about the MaxLength property in Chapter 4. You also can use the txtType control's KeyPress event to prevent the text box from accepting the space character. You learned about the KeyPress event earlier in this chapter. In addition, you can use the **Trim method** to remove any spaces that appear before and after the room type. Figure 12-26 shows the basic syntax of the Trim method and includes examples of using the method. In the syntax, *string* typically is either the Text property of a control or the name of a String variable. When the computer processes the Trim method, it makes a temporary copy of the *string* in memory, and then performs the necessary trimming on the copy only. In other words, the method does not remove any spaces from the original *string*. To remove the spaces from the original *string*, you must assign the result of the Trim method to the *string*, as shown in Example 2.

THE BASIC SYNTAX OF THE TRIM METHOD

<u>Syntax</u>

string.**Trim**

<u>Example 1</u>

strName = txtName.Text.Trim

assigns the contents of the txtName control, excluding any leading and trailing spaces, to the strName variable

<u>Example 2</u>

txtCity.Text = txtCity.Text.Trim

removes any leading and trailing spaces from the txtCity control

---

Figure 12-26: Basic syntax and examples of the Trim method

To include the Trim method in the Shady Hollow Hotel-Version 2 application:

1. In the statement that assigns the contents of the txtType control to the strType variable, change txtType.Text.ToUpper to **txtType.Text.ToUpper.Trim**.

2. Save the solution, then start the application. Type the letter **d**, then press the **spacebar** on your keyboard. Click the **Display Rate** button. The daily rate for a Deluxe room, $115, appears in the Daily rate box. Click the **Exit** button.

Figure 12-27 shows the final testing chart for the Shady Hollow Hotel-Version 2 application.

Test data	Expected result
No data entered	message, $0
Valid values: S, s, one or more spaces before and/or after these letters D, d, one or more spaces before and/or after these letters	$90 $115
Invalid values: a, $, 9, one or more spaces	message, $0

Figure 12-27: Final testing chart for the Shady Hollow Hotel-Version 2 application

To retest the Shady Hollow Hotel-Version 2 application:

1. Start the application. On your own, test the application using the test data shown in Figure 12-27.

2. Click the **Exit** button. Close the Code Editor window, then close the solution.

For more examples of applications that require string data, see the String Data Testing section in the Ch12WantMore.pdf file.

MINI-QUIZ 2

1. You want a message box that contains the "You win!" message. The "Game Over" text should appear in the message box's title bar. The message box should contain an OK button and an Information icon. Write the appropriate MessageBox.Show method.

2. Write the statement to remove any leading and/or trailing spaces from the txtState control.

3. Write a statement that first removes any leading and/or trailing spaces from the strDept variable and then changes the contents of the variable to uppercase.

It's time to view the Ch12-Testing video.

SUMMARY

» You should thoroughly test a program, using both valid and invalid data, before releasing the program to the user.

» The guidelines for selecting test data are listed in Figure 12-1 in the chapter.

» You can use a testing chart to record the test data and the expected results.

» You can prevent a text box from accepting a character by coding the text box's KeyPress event procedure. The KeyPress event occurs each time a key is pressed when the text box has the focus. A character corresponding to the pressed key is sent to the event's e parameter. You use the e parameter's KeyChar property to determine the pressed key. You cancel the key by setting the e parameter's Handled property to True.

» Whenever you make a change to an application's code, you should retest the application using the data listed in its testing chart.

» You can use the MessageBox.Show method to display a message to the user while an application is running.

» The Trim method makes a temporary copy of a string. It then performs the necessary trimming on the copy only.

KEY TERMS

Bugs—the errors in an application's code

ControlChars.Back constant—represents the Backspace key on a keyboard

Handled property—a property of the KeyPress event procedure's e parameter; used to cancel the key pressed by the user

KeyChar property—a property of the KeyPress event procedure's e parameter; stores the character associated with the key pressed by the user

KeyPress event—occurs each time the user presses a key while the control has the focus

MessageBox.Show method—displays a message box that contains a message, title bar text, a button, and an icon; allows the application to communicate with the user while it is running

Trim method—removes spaces from both the beginning and end of a string

ANSWERS TO MINI-QUIZZES

MINI-QUIZ 1

1. Test the application without entering any data.

2. 0

3. e

MINI-QUIZ 2

1. MessageBox.Show("You win!", "Game Over", _
        MessageBoxButtons.OK, MessageBoxIcon.Information)

2. txtState.Text = txtState.Text.Trim

3. strDept = strDept.Trim.ToUpper

REVIEW QUESTIONS

1. The _____ constant refers to the Backspace key on your keyboard.

   a. Control.Back   b. Control.Backspace

   c. ControlKey.Back   d. None of the above.

2. Which of the following statements can be used in a text box's KeyPress event to cancel the key pressed by the user?

   a. e.Cancel = True   b. e.Handled = True

   c. e.KeyChar = True   d. None of the above.

3. Which of the following determines whether the user pressed the $ (dollar sign) key?

   a. If ControlChars.DollarSign = True Then

   b. If e.KeyChar = Chars.DollarSign Then

   c. If e.KeyChar = "$" Then

   d. If KeyChar.ControlChars = "$" Then

4. Which of the following creates a message box that displays an OK button, an Information icon, "Hatfield Sales" in the title bar, and the "Please enter a sales amount" message?

   a. MessageBox.Show("Please enter a sales amount", "Hatfield Sales", _
      MessageBoxButtons.OK, MessageBoxIcon.Information)

   b. MessageBox.Display("Hatfield Sales", "Please enter a sales amount", _
      MessageBox.OKButton, MessageBox.InformationIcon)

   c. Message.Show("Please enter a sales amount", "Hatfield Sales", _
      MessageButtons.OK, MessageIcon.Information)

   d. MessageBox.Show("Hatfield Sales", "Please enter a sales amount", _
      MessageBoxButtons.OK, MessageBoxIcon.Information)

5. If a condition contains a range of values, the test data should include _____.

   a. the lowest value in the range

   b. the highest value in the range

   c. a value within the range

   d. All of the above.

EXERCISES

1. In this exercise, you create a testing chart for an application. You then use the data in the chart to test the application. (The answers to TRY THIS Exercises are located at the end of the chapter.)

   »TRY THIS

   a. Open the Shady Hollow Solution (Shady Hollow Solution.sln) file, which is contained in the ClearlyVB\Chap12\Shady Hollow Solution-Version 3 folder. Open the Code Editor window and review the existing code. Use the guidelines in Figure 12-1, as well as the application's interface and code, to create a testing chart for the application.

   b. Start and test the application. Stop the application, then close the solution.

2. In this exercise, you create a testing chart for an application. You then use the data in the chart to test the application. (The answers to TRY THIS Exercises are located at the end of the chapter.)

   »TRY THIS

   a. Open the Bonus Solution (Bonus Solution.sln) file, which is contained in the ClearlyVB\Chap12\Bonus Solution folder. Open the Code Editor window and review the existing code. Use the guidelines in Figure 12-1, as well as the application's interface and code, to create a testing chart for the application.

   b. Start and then test the application. Stop the application, then close the solution.

»MODIFY THIS

3. In this exercise, you modify an existing application.

    a. Open the Shady Hollow Solution (Shady Hollow Solution.sln) file, which is contained in the Shady Hollow Solution-Version 4 folder. Change the txtType control's MaxLength property to 1. The txtType control should accept only the Backspace key and the letters S, s, D, and d. Make the appropriate modifications to the code.

    b. Save the solution. Start and then test the application. Stop the application, then close the solution.

»INTRODUCTORY

4. Open the Department Solution (Department Solution.sln) file, which is contained in the ClearlyVB\Chap12\Department Solution folder. Change the text box's MaxLength property to 1. Change its CharacterCasing property to Upper. Open the Code Editor window. The text box should accept only the Backspace key and the letters A, a, B, and b. If the user clicks the Display button without entering a code, the selection structure should display the text "Not available" in the lblName control. It also should display the "Please enter a code" message in a message box, the text "Department Codes" in the title bar, an OK button, and an Information icon. Make the appropriate modifications to the code. Save the solution. Start and then test the application. Stop the application, then close the solution.

»INTRODUCTORY

5. Open the Sales Tax Solution (Sales Tax Solution.sln) file, which is contained in the ClearlyVB\Chap12\Sales Tax Solution folder. Open the Code Editor window and review the existing code. The text box should accept only numbers, the period, and the Backspace key; make the appropriate modifications to the code. Use the guidelines in Figure 12-1, as well as the application's interface and code, to create a testing chart for the application. Start and then test the application. Stop the application, then close the solution.

»INTERMEDIATE

6. Open the Gross Pay Solution (Gross Pay Solution.sln) file, which is contained in the ClearlyVB\Chap12\Gross Pay Solution folder. Open the Code Editor window and review the existing code. Both text boxes should accept only numbers, the period, and the Backspace key; make the appropriate modifications to the code. Use the guidelines in Figure 12-1, as well as the application's interface and code, to create a testing chart for the application. Start and then test the application. Stop the application, then close the solution.

»INTERMEDIATE

7. Open the ABC Solution (ABC Solution.sln) file, which is contained in the ClearlyVB\Chap12\ABC Solution folder. Open the Code Editor window and review the existing code. Modify the code so that the text box accepts only numbers and the Backspace key. Use the guidelines in Figure 12-1, as well as the application's interface and code, to create a testing chart for the application. Start and then test the application. Stop the application and make any needed changes to the code and testing chart. Start and then test the application again. Stop the application, then close the solution.

»ADVANCED

8. Open the Average Solution (Average Solution.sln) file, which is contained in the ClearlyVB\Chap12\Average Solution folder. Open the Code Editor window and review the existing code. Start and then test the application, using the testing information

included in the btnCalc control's Click event procedure. Notice that the code does not always produce the expected result. Stop the application and make the necessary changes to the code. (Hint: To determine whether a text box is empty, compare its Text property to the String.Empty constant.) Start and then test the application again. Stop the application, then close the solution.

9. Open the Total Due Solution (Total Due Solution.sln) file, which is contained in the ClearlyVB\Chap12\Total Due Solution folder. Open the Code Editor window and review the existing code. Create a testing chart for the application. Start and then test the application. Stop the application and make any needed changes to the code. Start and then test the application again. Stop the application, then close the solution.

10. Open the FigureThisOut Solution (FigureThisOut Solution.sln) file, which is contained in the ClearlyVB\Chap12\FigureThisOut Solution folder. Open the Code Editor window and study the existing code. Start the application. Enter the number 1,200 (be sure to type the comma) in both text boxes, then click the Calculate button. The answers, which should be the same, appear in the two label controls. Why are the answers different? How can you fix the problem? Stop the application. Fix the problem, then save the solution. Start and then test the application. Stop the application, then close the solution.

11. In this exercise, you find an error in an application's code. Open the SwatTheBugs Solution (SwatTheBugs Solution.sln) file, which is contained in the ClearlyVB\Chap12\SwatTheBugs Solution folder. Create a testing chart. Start and then test the application. Be sure to verify that the KeyPress procedure works correctly. Stop the application. Locate and correct the errors in the code. Save the solution, then start and test the application. Stop the application, then close the solution.

ANSWERS TO "TRY THIS" EXERCISES

1. See Figure 12-28.

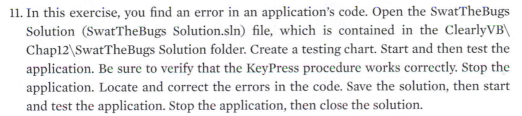

Test data	Expected result
No data entered	$90 (Standard radio button is the default radio button)

Gold Club member check box not selected
    Standard room radio button selected
    Deluxe room radio button selected
    Suite radio button selected
	$90
	$115
	$130

Gold Club member check box selected
    Standard room radio button selected
    Deluxe room radio button selected
    Suite radio button selected
	$80
	$105
	$120

Figure 12-28

2. See Figure 12-29. Some of the values listed in the first column in your testing chart may be different from those shown in the figure. However, your values should include 0, a negative integer, a negative non-integer, a positive integer, a positive non-integer, and alphanumeric text. Your values should test each path in the selection structure. Recall that when a condition contains a range of values, the test data should include the lowest and highest values in the range, as well as a value within the range. Therefore, your values should include the numbers 100 and 5000 (which are the lowest and highest values in the first condition), as well as a number within that range. Your values also should include the number 5000.01 (which is the lowest value in the second condition), as well as another number that would make the second condition evaluate to True.

Test data	Expected result
No data entered	$0.00
Valid values:	
0	$0.00
100	$5.00
2500.75	$125.04
5000	$250.00
5000.01	$500.00
12000	$1,200.00
10	$0.00
-5	$0.00
-6.5	$0.00
Invalid values:	
x, $6, 3A	$0.00

Figure 12-29

13

HOW LONG CAN THIS GO ON?

After studying Chapter 13, you should be able to:

Write a pretest loop using the Do...Loop statement

Utilize counter and accumulator variables

Refresh the screen

Delay program execution

Show a pretest loop in both pseudocode and a flowchart

Display a dialog box using the InputBox function

OVER AND OVER AGAIN

Recall that all computer programs are written using one or more of three control structures: sequence, selection, or repetition. You learned about the sequence and selection structures in previous chapters. This chapter provides an introduction to the repetition structure. Programmers use the **repetition structure**, referred to more simply as a **loop**, when they need the computer to repeatedly process one or more program instructions until some condition is met, at which time the repetition structure ends. A repetition structure can be either a pretest loop or a posttest loop. In both types of loops, the condition is evaluated with each repetition (or iteration) of the loop. In a **pretest loop**, the loop condition is evaluated *before* the instructions within the loop are processed. In a **posttest loop**, the evaluation occurs *after* the instructions within the loop are processed. Depending on the result of the evaluation, the instructions in a pretest loop may never be processed. The instructions in a posttest loop, however, always will be processed at least once. Of the two types of loops, the pretest loop is the most commonly used. You will learn about pretest loops in this chapter and in Chapter 15; posttest loops are covered in Chapter 14.

The programmer determines whether a problem's solution requires a repetition structure by studying the problem specification. The first problem specification you will examine in this chapter involves Rob, the mechanical man from Chapter 2. The problem specification, along with an illustration of the problem, is shown in Figure 13-1. The figure also includes the correct algorithm using the commands that Rob can understand. The algorithm uses only the sequence structure, because no decisions need to be made and no instructions need to be repeated.

Rob is sitting at a table in a bookstore. He needs to sign a copy of his bestselling book on Robotics for a customer.

Rob

1. accept the book from the customer
2. place the book on the table
3. open the front cover of the book
4. sign your name on the first page
5. close the book
6. return the book to the customer
7. thank the customer

Figure 13-1: First problem using Rob

Now let's change the problem specification slightly. Rob is still sitting at a table in the bookstore; but this time, he's there for a book signing. The store has just opened and there's already a long line of customers. Rob doesn't want to disappoint his fans, so he plans on staying until every book is signed. Consider how this change will affect the original algorithm shown in Figure 13-1. The original algorithm contains the instructions for signing only one customer's book. In the modified algorithm, Rob will need to repeat the same instructions for every customer. Figure 13-2 shows the modified problem specification along with the modified algorithm. The repetition structure begins with the *repeat for each customer:* line, and it ends with the *end repeat* line. The instructions between both lines are indented to indicate that they are part of the repetition structure and, therefore, need to be followed for each customer.

Rob is sitting at a table in a bookstore, attending his book signing. He needs to sign a copy of his bestselling book on Robotics for each customer.

```
1. repeat for each customer:
       accept the book from the customer
       place the book on the table
       open the front cover of the book
       sign your name on the first page
       close the book
       return the book to the customer
       thank the customer
   end repeat
```

Figure 13-2: Second problem using Rob

Figure 13-3 shows another problem specification and algorithm involving Rob. To solve the problem, you need to get Rob from his hallway into his bedroom. Notice that the algorithm contains both the sequence and selection structures. The first instruction positions Rob directly in front of his bedroom door. The second instruction determines whether the bedroom door is closed, and then takes the appropriate action based on the result. The last instruction walks Rob into the bedroom.

Rob is standing in his hallway facing his bedroom door. The door, which may or may not be closed, is one step away from Rob. Rob wants to go inside his bedroom.

```
1. walk forward
2. if the door is closed, do this:
       open the door
   end if
3. walk forward
```

Figure 13-3: Third problem using Rob

Figure 13-4 shows a modified version of the previous problem specification; in this version, Rob is 10 steps away from the door. How could you rewrite the original algorithm to reflect this minor change? One way is by adding nine more *walk forward* instructions to the original algorithm; however, that would be quite cumbersome to write. Imagine if Rob were 500 steps from the door! A better way to modify the original algorithm is by adding a repetition structure to it, as shown in the modified algorithm in Figure 13-4. The repetition structure, which begins with the *repeat 10 times:* line and ends with the *end repeat* line, directs Rob to walk forward 10 times.

Rob is standing in his hallway facing his bedroom door. The door, which may or may not be closed, is 10 steps away from Rob. Rob wants to go inside his bedroom.

1. repeat 10 times:
      walk forward
   end repeat
2. if the door is closed, do this:
      open the door
   end if
3. walk forward

Figure 13-4: Fourth problem using Rob

Figure 13-5 shows a modified version of the previous problem specification. In this version, the number of steps between Rob and the door is unknown. He might be 10 steps away or 500 steps away; or, Rob might already be directly in front of the door. How will this affect the algorithm shown in Figure 13-4? The repetition structure in the algorithm will need to be changed because the number of steps between Rob and the door is no longer known. Rather than telling Rob to repeat the *walk forward* instruction 10 times, the repetition structure will need to tell him to repeat the instruction until he is directly in front of the door. Once Rob is positioned correctly, he still will need to follow the second and third instructions in the algorithm. The modified algorithm is included in Figure 13-5. The repetition structure begins with the *repeat until you are directly in front of the door:* line, and it ends with the *end repeat* line.

Rob is standing in his hallway facing his bedroom door. The door, which may or may not be closed, is an unknown number of steps away from Rob. Rob wants to go inside his bedroom.

```
1.  repeat until you are directly in front of the door:
        walk forward
    end repeat
2.  if the door is closed, do this:
        open the door
    end if
3.  walk forward
```

Figure 13-5: Fifth problem using Rob

The repetition structure in Figure 13-5's algorithm ends when Rob is standing directly in front of his bedroom door. If Rob is 10 steps away from the door, the repetition structure directs him to walk forward 10 times before determining whether the door is closed. Similarly, if Rob is 500 steps away from the door, the repetition structure directs him to walk forward 500 times. If Rob is directly in front of the door, the walk forward instruction in the repetition structure is bypassed.

MINI-QUIZ 1

1. Rob is sitting in a chair in his living room. Next to the chair is a table. On top of the table is Rob's cell phone. Your task is to direct Rob to pick up his cell phone. Does the solution to this problem require a repetition structure? If so, what needs to be repeated?

2. Rob is sitting in a chair in his living room. At the other end of the room is a table. On top of the table is Rob's cell phone. Your task is to direct Rob to pick up his cell phone, but only when the phone rings. Does the solution to this problem require a repetition structure? If so, what needs to be repeated?

3. Rob wants to write down, on a piece of paper, the name of each book in his personal library. The loop in the solution can begin with repeat for _____.

THE DO...LOOP STATEMENT

Before solving real-world problems that require a repetition structure, you will learn about the Do...Loop statement, which is one of three statements used to code a repetition structure in Visual Basic. (The other two statements, For...Next and For Each...Next, are covered in subsequent chapters.) You can use the Do...Loop statement to code both a pretest loop and a posttest loop. As mentioned earlier, this chapter covers pretest loops. Figure 13-6 shows the syntax of the Do...Loop statement when used to code a pretest loop. The statement begins with the Do clause and ends with the Loop clause. Between both clauses, you enter the instructions you want the computer to repeat. The {While | Until} portion of the syntax indicates that you can select only one of the keywords appearing within the braces—either While or Until. You do not type the braces or the pipe symbol (|) when entering the Do...Loop statement. You follow the While or Until keyword with a *condition*, which can contain variables, constants, properties, methods, or operators. Like the *condition* in the If...Then...Else statement, the *condition* in the Do...Loop statement must evaluate to a Boolean value—either True or False. The *condition* determines whether the computer processes the loop instructions. The keyword While indicates that the loop instructions should be processed *while* the condition is true. The keyword Until, on the other hand, indicates that the loop instructions should be processed *until* the condition becomes true. Also included in Figure 13-6 are two examples of pretest loops. Both examples produce the same result, which is to display the numbers 1, 2, and 3 in message boxes.

DO...LOOP STATEMENT

Syntax for coding a pretest loop

Do {While | Until} *condition*

> *instructions to be processed either while the condition is true or until the condition becomes true*

Loop

Example 1

```
intNumber = 1
Do While intNumber <= 3
    MessageBox.Show(intNumber.ToString)
    intNumber = intNumber + 1
Loop
```

Figure 13-6: Syntax and examples of the Do…Loop statement for a pretest loop (*continued on next page*)

Example 2

```
intNumber = 1
Do Until intNumber > 3
    MessageBox.Show(intNumber.ToString)
    intNumber = intNumber + 1
Loop
```

Figure 13-6: Syntax and examples of the Do…Loop statement for a pretest loop (*continued from previous page*)

Both examples in Figure 13-6 begin by assigning the number 1 to an Integer variable named intNumber. The intNumber variable is called a **counter variable**, because it is used to count something. Repetition structures use counter variables to count such things as the number of employees paid in a week or the number of positive numbers entered by the user. The repetition structures in Figure 13-6 use the intNumber counter variable to keep track of the number of times the loop instructions are processed. Counter variables are always numeric variables and are typically assigned a beginning value of either 0 or 1, depending on the value required by the application. The assignment is done outside the loop, because it needs to be performed only once. Counter variables also must be updated. **Updating**, also called **incrementing**, means adding a number to the value stored in the counter variable. The number can be positive or negative, integer or non-integer. A counter variable is always incremented by a constant value, usually the number 1. You update the counter variable within the loop, because the updating task must be performed each time the loop instructions are processed. In both examples in Figure 13-6, the counter variable is updated by the intNumber = intNumber + 1 statement within the loop.

The Do clause in Example 1 in Figure 13-6 tells the computer to repeat the loop instructions *while* the value in the intNumber variable is less than or equal to 3. The Do clause in Example 2, on the other hand, tells the computer to repeat the loop instructions *until* the value in the intNumber variable is greater than 3. As mentioned earlier, both examples produce the same result; both simply represent two different ways of saying the same thing. Figure 13-7 describes the way the computer processes the code shown in Example 1. Notice that the loop ends when the counter variable, intNumber, contains the number 4.

Processing steps for Example 1
1. The intNumber variable is assigned the number 1.
2. The Do clause, which marks the beginning of the loop, checks whether the value in the intNumber variable is less than or equal to 3. It is.
3. The loop instructions display the contents of the intNumber variable (1) and then add 1 to the variable's value, giving 2.
4. The Loop clause, which marks the end of the loop, returns processing to the Do clause.
5. The Do clause checks whether the value in the intNumber variable is less than or equal to 3. It is.
6. The loop instructions display the contents of the intNumber variable (2) and then add 1 to the variable's value, giving 3.
7. The Loop clause returns processing to the Do clause.
8. The Do clause checks whether the value in the intNumber variable is less than or equal to 3. It is.
9. The loop instructions display the contents of the intNumber variable (3) and then add 1 to the variable's value, giving 4.
10. The Loop clause returns processing to the Do clause.
11. The Do clause checks whether the value in the intNumber variable is less than or equal to 3. It isn't, so the computer stops processing the Do...Loop statement. Processing continues with the statement following the Loop clause.

Figure 13-7: Processing steps for the pretest loop shown in Example 1 in Figure 13-6

For more examples of using the Do...Loop statement to code a pretest loop, see the Do...Loop Pretest section in the Ch13WantMore.pdf file.

MY DREAM CAR-VERSION 1 APPLICATION

Figure 13-8 shows the interface for the My Dream Car-Version 1 application. You will use a repetition structure to make the I WANT THIS CAR! message blink several times when the user clicks the Click Me button.

Figure 13-8: Interface for the My Dream Car-Version 1 application

You make a control blink using code that changes the control's Visible property while the application is running. The way the property is changed depends on its initial setting. If the Visible property is set to True in the Properties window, the code will need to set the property to False and then back to True for each blink. On the other hand, if the Visible property's initial setting is False, the code must switch the property to True and then back to False for each blink. In the My Dream Car-Version 1 application, the lblMessage control's Visible property is set to False in the Properties window. Therefore, to make the control blink once, the code will need to set the Visible property twice: first to True and then to False. Similarly, to make the control blink twice, the code needs to set the Visible property four times: first to True, then to False, then to True, and finally to False. The Click Me button's Click event procedure will make the control blink 10 times, so it will need to set the Visible property 20 times, alternating between the True and False settings. You will use a counter variable to keep track of the number of times the Visible property is set.

Switching the Visible property isn't all that is necessary to make a control blink. Because the computer will process the switching instructions so rapidly, you won't even notice that the control is blinking. To actually see the control blink, you will need to both refresh the interface and delay program execution each time you change the Visible property's setting. You refresh the interface using the form's Refresh method. The **Refresh method** will ensure that any code appearing before it that affects the interface's appearance is processed. The Refresh method's syntax is **Me.Refresh()**, where Me refers to the current form. You can delay program execution using the **Sleep method** in the following syntax: **System.Threading.Thread.Sleep(***milliseconds***)**. The *milliseconds* argument is the number of milliseconds to suspend the program. A millisecond is 1/1000 of a second; in other words, there are 1000 milliseconds in a second. Figure 13-9 shows the algorithm for the Click Me button's Click event procedure.

```
1.  assign 1 to a counter variable
2.  repeat while the counter variable's value is less than or equal to 20:
        if the lblMessage control's Visible property is set to True
            set the property to False
        else
            set the property to True
        end if
        refresh the interface
        delay program execution for 1/4 second
        add 1 to the counter variable
    end repeat
```

Figure 13-9: Algorithm for the Click Me button's Click event procedure in Version 1

Before you begin coding the My Dream Car-Version 1 application, you may want to view the Ch13-My Dream Car video. The video demonstrates the steps contained in the following section, and also shows a different way of coding the application. It also shows you how to stop an infinite (endless) loop.

To open the My Dream Car-Version 1 application, and then code and test the application:

1. Start Visual Studio 2008 (or Visual Basic 2008 Express Edition). Open the **Car Solution** (**Car Solution.sln**) file, which is contained in the ClearlyVB\Chap13\Car Solution-Version 1 folder. If necessary, open the designer window.

2. Open the Code Editor window, which contains the code for the btnExit control's Click event procedure. Open the btnClickMe control's Click event procedure. Type **' blinks the lblMessage control** and press **Enter** twice.

3. First, declare a counter variable that will keep track of the number of times the loop instructions are processed. Type **' declare counter variable** and press **Enter**, then type **dim intCount as integer** and press **Enter** twice.

4. The first step in the algorithm is to assign the number 1 to the counter variable. Type **' begin counting** and press **Enter**, then type **intCount = 1** and press **Enter**.

5. The second step in the algorithm is a repetition structure that repeats its instructions while the counter variable's value is less than or equal to 20. Type **do while intCount <= 20** and press **Enter**. Notice that the Code Editor automatically enters the Loop clause for you. It also automatically indents the current line.

6. The first instruction in the loop is a selection structure that determines the current value of the lblMessage control's Visible property, and then takes the appropriate action based on the result. Type the following selection structure.

    If lblMessage.Visible = False Then
        lblMessage.Visible = True
    Else
        lblMessage.Visible = False
    End If

7. The remaining loop instructions refresh the interface, delay program execution for a quarter of a second, and update the counter variable. Type the comment and three lines of code indicated in Figure 13-10.

```
Private Sub btnClickMe_Click(ByVal sender As Object, ByVal e As System
    ' blinks the lblMessage control

    ' declare counter variable
    Dim intCount As Integer

    ' begin counting
    intCount = 1
    Do While intCount <= 20
        If lblMessage.Visible = False Then
            lblMessage.Visible = True
        Else
            lblMessage.Visible = False
        End If
        Me.Refresh()
        System.Threading.Thread.Sleep(250)
        ' update the counter variable
        intCount = intCount + 1
    Loop
End Sub
```

enter this comment and three lines of code

Figure 13-10: Completed Click event procedure for the btnClickMe control in Version 1

8. Save the solution, then start the application. Click the **Click Me** button. The lblMessage control blinks 10 times. Click the **Exit** button. Close the Code Editor window, then close the solution.

FLOWCHARTING THE CLICK ME BUTTON'S CLICK EVENT PROCEDURE

As you learned in Chapter 3, some programmers use flowcharts rather than pseudocode when planning algorithms. The flowchart for the Click Me button's Click event procedure is shown in Figure 13-11. (The pseudocode is shown in Figure 13-9.)

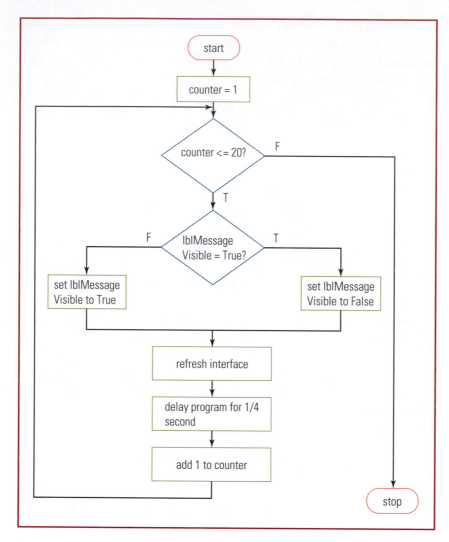

Figure 13-11: Algorithm (in flowchart form) for the Click Me button's Click event procedure in Version 1

The loop condition is represented by a diamond in a flowchart. As with the selection structure diamond, the repetition structure diamond contains a question whose answer is either True or False. The answer determines whether the instructions within the loop are processed. Like the selection structure diamond, the repetition structure diamond has one flowline entering the symbol and two flowlines leaving the symbol. The two flowlines leading out of the diamond should be marked so that anyone reading the flowchart can distinguish the true path from the false path. You mark the flowline leading to the true path with a "T" (for True), and you mark the flowline leading to the false path with an "F" (for False). You also can mark the flowlines leading out of a repetition diamond with a "Y" and an "N" (for Yes and No). In the flowchart shown in Figure 13-11, the flowline entering the repetition diamond, as well as the symbols and flowlines within the repetition structure's True path, form a circle or loop. It is this loop, or circle, that distinguishes the repetition structure from the selection structure in a flowchart.

For more examples of flowcharts, see the Flowchart section in the Ch13WantMore.pdf file.

MY DREAM CAR-VERSION 2 APPLICATION

Except for the title bar text, the interface for the My Dream Car-Version 2 application appears identical to the one shown earlier in Figure 13-8. However, in this version, the lblMessage control's Visible property is set to True in the Properties window, and the picCar control's Visible property is set to False. When the user clicks the Click Me button, the button's Click event procedure will position the picCar control off the left edge of the form. This can be accomplished by setting the control's Left property to a negative number; you will use -750. The Click event procedure then will set the control's Visible property to True, and then slowly drag the control to the center of the form. You can drag the control by including, in a loop, an instruction that increments the control's Left property value; in this case, you will increment the value by 15. You will include the Refresh and Sleep methods within the loop to prevent the computer from processing the dragging instructions too rapidly. The loop will stop when the Left property value is greater than 70. Why 70? Currently, the picCar control is centered horizontally on the form. If you check its Location property, you will notice that its X value, which determines its horizontal position on the form, is set to 74 (your property value may differ slightly). Figure 13-12 shows the algorithm for the Click Me button's Click event procedure.

1. position the picCar control off the left edge of the form by setting its Left property to -750
2. set the picCar control's Visible property to True
3. repeat until the value in the picCar control's Left property is greater than 70:
     reposition the picCar control by adding 15 to its Left property
     refresh the interface
     delay program execution for 1/4 second
   end repeat

Figure 13-12: Algorithm for the Click Me button's Click event procedure in Version 2

To open the My Dream Car-Version 2 application, and then code and test the application:

1. Open the **Car Solution** (**Car Solution.sln**) file, which is contained in the ClearlyVB\Chap13\Car Solution-Version 2 folder. If necessary, open the designer window.

2. Open the Code Editor window, which contains the code for the btnExit control's Click event procedure. Open the btnClickMe control's Click event procedure. Type '**drags the picCar control to the center of the form** and press **Enter** twice.

3. The first two steps in the algorithm are to position the picCar control off the left edge of the form and set the control's Visible property to True. Type '**position picCar control off the left edge of the form** and press **Enter**, then type **picCar.left = -750** and press **Enter**. Type '**show the picCar control** and press **Enter**, then type **picCar.visible = true** and press **Enter** twice.

4. The third step in the algorithm is a repetition structure that repeats its instructions until the value in the picCar control's Left property is greater than 70. Type **do until picCar.Left > 70** and press **Enter**.

5. The first loop instruction repositions the picCar control by adding 15 to its Left property. The remaining loop instructions refresh the interface and delay program execution for a quarter of a second. Type the comment and three lines of code indicated in Figure 13-13.

```
Private Sub btnClickMe_Click(ByVal sender As Object, ByVal e As System
    ' drags the picCar control to the center of the form

    ' position picCar control off the left edge of the form
    picCar.Left = -750
    ' show the picCar control
    picCar.Visible = True

    Do Until picCar.Left > 70
        ' move the picCar control
        picCar.Left = picCar.Left + 15
        Me.Refresh()
        System.Threading.Thread.Sleep(250)
    Loop
End Sub
```

enter this comment and three lines of code

Figure 13-13: Completed Click event procedure for the btnClickMe control in Version 2

6. Save the solution, then start the application. Click the **Click Me** button. The car image is dragged from the left edge to the center of the form. Click the **Exit** button. Close the Code Editor window, then close the solution.

MINI-QUIZ 2

1. Write a Visual Basic Do clause that processes the loop instructions as long as the value in the intQuantity variable is greater than the number 0. Use the While keyword.

2. Rewrite the Do clause from Question 1 using the Until keyword.

3. Write an assignment statement that increments the intNumEmployees counter variable by 1.

4. Write the statement to pause program execution for 1 second.

THE SALES EXPRESS APPLICATION

Figure 13-14 shows a problem specification whose solution requires a repetition structure. It also shows a correct algorithm for the problem. The algorithm uses a counter variable to keep track of the number of sales amounts entered by the sales manager. It uses an accumulator variable to total the sales amounts. An **accumulator variable** is a numeric variable used for accumulating (adding together) something. Repetition structures use accumulator variables to tally information such as the total dollar amount of a week's payroll. The repetition structure in Figure 13-14 uses the accumulator variable to total the sales amounts entered by the user. Like counter variables, accumulator variables are assigned a value outside the loop; in almost all cases, the value is 0. Also like counter variables, accumulator variables are updated within the loop. However, unlike counter variables, accumulator variables are incremented by an amount that varies (rather than by a constant value). In the Sales Express algorithm, the accumulator variable is incremented by the sales amount entered by the sales manager. The algorithm uses the values in the accumulator and counter variables to calculate the average sales amount.

The sales manager of Sales Express wants an application that allows him to enter the amount of each salesperson's sales, one at a time. After all of the sales amounts have been entered, the application should both calculate and display the average sales amount.

Output: average sales amount

Processing: sales counter variable (start at 0)
              sales accumulator variable (start at 0)

Figure 13-14: Sales Express application's problem specification and algorithm (*continued on next page*)

Input: sales amount (for each salesperson)

Algorithm:
1. assign 0 to the sales counter and sales accumulator variables
2. enter a sales amount
3. repeat until there are no more sales amounts to enter:
        add the sales amount to the sales accumulator variable
        add 1 to the sales counter variable
        enter a sales amount
    end repeat
4. calculate the average sales amount by dividing the sales accumulator variable by the sales
    counter variable
5. display the average sales amount

Figure 13-14: Sales Express application's problem specification and algorithm (*continued from previous page*)

Notice that *enter a sales amount* appears twice in the algorithm: immediately above the loop and also within the loop. The *enter a sales amount* entry above the loop is referred to as the **priming read**, because it is used to prime (prepare or set up) the loop. In this case, the priming read gets only the first salesperson's sales amount from the user. Because the loop in Figure 13-14 is a pretest loop, the first value determines whether the loop instructions are processed at all. The *enter a sales amount* entry within the loop gets the sales amounts for the remaining salespeople (if any) from the user.

To open the Sales Express application, and then begin coding the application:

1. Open the **Sales Express Solution** (**Sales Express Solution.sln**) file, which is contained in the ClearlyVB\Chap13\Sales Express Solution folder. If necessary, open the designer window.

2. Open the Code Editor window, which contains the code for the btnExit control's Click event procedure. Open the btnCalc control's Click event procedure. Type **' calculates and displays the average sales amount** and press **Enter** twice.

3. First, declare the necessary variables. The procedure requires four variables for the output, processing, and input items. Enter the following declaration statements and comments. Press **Enter** twice after typing the last declaration statement.

```
Dim intNumSales As Integer     ' counter
Dim decTotalSales As Decimal   ' accumulator
Dim decSales As Decimal
Dim decAverage As Decimal
```

4. The first step in the algorithm is to assign the number 0 to the counter and accumulator variables. Type **intNumSales = 0** and press **Enter**, then type **decTotalSales = 0** and press **Enter**.

5. The second step is to enter the sales amount. You will accomplish this task using the InputBox function. Save the solution.

THE INPUTBOX FUNCTION

The **InputBox function** displays one of the standard dialog boxes available in Visual Basic; an example is shown in Figure 13-15. The dialog box contains a message, an OK button, a Cancel button, and an input area where the user can enter information. The value returned by the InputBox function depends on whether the user clicks the OK button, Cancel button, or Close button. If the user clicks the OK button, the InputBox function returns the value contained in the input area of the dialog box; this value is always treated as a string. However, if the user clicks either the Cancel button in the dialog box or the Close button on the dialog box's title bar, the InputBox function returns an empty string. The empty string is represented by the **String.Empty constant** in Visual Basic.

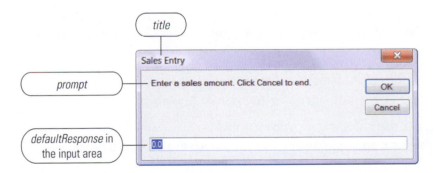

Figure 13-15: Example of a dialog box created by the InputBox function

The message in the dialog box should prompt the user to enter the appropriate information in the input area. The user then needs to click either the OK button or the Cancel button to continue working in the application. Figure 13-16 shows the basic syntax of the InputBox function and includes several examples of using the function. In the syntax, *prompt* is the message to display inside the dialog box, *title* is the text to display in the dialog box's title bar, and *defaultResponse* is the text you want displayed in the input area of the dialog box. In the dialog box shown in Figure 13-15, "Enter a sales amount. Click Cancel to end." is the *prompt*, "Sales Entry" is the *title*, and "0.0" is the *defaultResponse*. When entering the InputBox function in the Code

Editor window, the *prompt*, *title*, and *defaultResponse* arguments must be enclosed in quotation marks, unless that information is stored in a String named constant or String variable. The Windows standard is to use sentence capitalization for the *prompt*, but book title capitalization for the *title*. The capitalization (if any) you use for the *defaultResponse* depends on the text itself. The *title* and *defaultResponse* arguments are optional, as indicated by the square brackets in the syntax. If you omit the *title* argument, the project name appears in the title bar. If you omit the *defaultResponse* argument, a blank input area appears when the dialog box opens. In most cases, you assign the value returned by the InputBox function to a String variable, as indicated in the examples in Figure 13-16.

INPUTBOX FUNCTION

<u>Syntax</u>

InputBox(*prompt*[**,** *title*][**,** *defaultResponse*]**)**

<u>Example 1</u>

strName = InputBox("Enter your first name:", "Name Entry")
Displays a dialog box that shows "Enter your first name:" as the message, "Name Entry" in the title bar, and an empty input area. Assigns the user's response to a String variable named strName.

<u>Example 2</u>

strState = InputBox("State name:", "State", "Alaska")
Displays a dialog box that shows "State name:" as the message, "State" in the title bar, and "Alaska" in the input area. Assigns the user's response to a String variable named strState.

<u>Example 3</u>

Const strPROMPT As String = "Enter the rate:"
Const strTITLE As String = "Rate"
strRate = InputBox(strPROMPT, strTITLE, ".00")
Displays a dialog box that shows the contents of the strPROMPT constant as the message, the contents of the strTITLE constant in the title bar, and ".00" in the input area. Assigns the user's response to a String variable named strRate.

Figure 13-16: Syntax and examples of the InputBox function

To continue coding the application:

1. First, create named constants for the InputBox function's *prompt* and *title* arguments. Click the **blank line** above the first Dim statement, then press **Enter** to insert a blank line. Type **const strPROMPT as string** = _ and press **Enter**. Press **Tab**, then type **"Enter a sales amount. Click Cancel to end."** and press **Enter**. Type **const strTITLE as string** = **"Sales Entry"** and press **Enter**.

2. Now create a String variable to store the value returned by the InputBox function. Type **dim strInputSales as string** and press **Enter**.

3. Next, enter the InputBox function in the procedure. Store the function's return value in the strInputSales variable. Click the **blank line** below the decTotalSales = 0 statement. Type **'** **get the first sales amount** and press **Enter**, then type **strInputSales = inputbox(strPROMPT, strTITLE, "0.0")** and press **Enter**.

4. Step 3 in the algorithm is a loop that repeats its instructions until there are no more sales amounts to enter. The user indicates that she has finished entering data by clicking the Cancel button in the dialog box. Recall that when the Cancel button is clicked, the InputBox function returns the empty string. Type **do until strInputSales = String.Empty** and press **Enter**.

5. The first instruction in the loop increments the accumulator variable by the sales amount. Before you can do this, you need to convert the sales amount stored in the strInputSales variable to the Decimal data type. Type **decimal.tryparse(strInputSales, decSales)** and press **Enter**, then type **decTotalSales = decTotalSales + decSales** and press **Enter**.

6. The next instruction in the loop increments the counter variable by 1. Type **intNumSales = intNumSales + 1** and press **Enter**.

7. The last instruction in the loop is to enter another sales amount. Type **'** **get another sales amount** and press **Enter**, then type **strInputSales = inputbox(strPROMPT, strTITLE, "0.0")**.

8. Steps 4 and 5 in the algorithm are to calculate and display the average sales amount. As the algorithm indicates, both tasks are performed after the loop has finished processing. Click **after the letter p** in the Loop clause, then press **Enter** twice to insert two blank lines. Type **decAverage = decTotalSales / intNumSales** and press **Enter**, then type **lblAverage.text = decAverage.tostring("C2")** and press **Enter**.

9. Save the solution. Figure 13-17 shows the code entered in the procedure.

```
Private Sub btnCalc_Click(ByVal sender As Object, _
    ByVal e As System.EventArgs) Handles btnCalc.Click
    ' calculates and displays the average sales amount

    Const strPROMPT As String = _
        "Enter a sales amount. Click Cancel to end."
    Const strTITLE As String = "Sales Entry"
    Dim strInputSales As String

    Dim intNumSales As Integer        ' counter
    Dim decTotalSales As Decimal      ' accumulator
    Dim decSales As Decimal
    Dim decAverage As Decimal

    intNumSales = 0
    decTotalSales = 0
    ' get the first sales amount
    strInputSales = InputBox(strPROMPT, strTITLE, "0.0")      ← priming read
    Do Until strInputSales = String.Empty
        Decimal.TryParse(strInputSales, decSales)
        decTotalSales = decTotalSales + decSales
        intNumSales = intNumSales + 1
        ' get another sales amount
        strInputSales = InputBox(strPROMPT, strTITLE, "0.0")  ← matching read
    Loop

    decAverage = decTotalSales / intNumSales
    lblAverage.Text = decAverage.ToString("C2")

End Sub
```

Figure 13-17: Code entered in the btnCalc control's Click event procedure

Keep in mind that any code containing a priming read must also include a matching read within the loop. The matching read provides the way to end the loop. The result of forgetting to enter the matching read is an infinite (endless) loop. To stop an endless loop, click Debug on the menu bar, then click Stop Debugging.

Figure 13-18 shows a sample testing chart for the Sales Express application. At times, you may not be sure of the expected result when testing with an invalid value. In those cases, you can wait until *after* testing the application to complete the Expected result entry. However, after determining the result, don't simply enter it in the chart; rather, study the code to understand why it generated that result.

Test data	Expected result
No data entered	$0.00
Valid values: 0 25.67 100, 75.50, 30.25 -5 78.56, -4	 $0.00 $25.67 $68.58 ($5.00) $37.28
Invalid values: Empty input area x, $5	

Figure 13-18: Testing chart for the Sales Express application

To test the application:

1. Start the application, then click the **Calculate** button. The dialog box shown earlier in Figure 13-15 opens. Click the **Cancel** button in the dialog box; doing so results in a run-time error. A **runtime error** is an error that occurs while an application is running. The Code Editor highlights the statement where the error was encountered, and it displays a help box that provides information pertaining to the error. In this case, the Code Editor highlights the decAverage = decTotalSales / intNumSales statement, and the help box indicates that the statement is attempting to divide by zero.

2. Place your mouse pointer on intNumSales in the highlighted statement, as shown in Figure 13-19. The variable contains the number 0, because no sales amounts were entered.

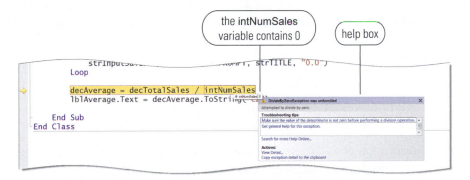

Figure 13-19: Result of the runtime error caused by dividing by zero

3. Click **Debug** on the menu bar, then click **Stop Debugging**.

4. Before using a variable as the divisor in an expression, you always should verify that the variable does not contain the number 0 because, as in math, division by zero is not mathematically possible. Click the **blank line** below the Loop clause, then press **Enter** to insert a blank line. Enter the selection structure shown in Figure 13-20. (You will need to move the calculation statement to the selection structure's true path.)

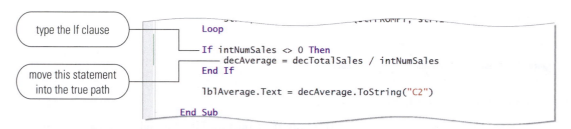

type the If clause

move this statement into the true path

```
                                          Loop

                                          If intNumSales <> 0 Then
                                              decAverage = decTotalSales / intNumSales
                                          End If

                                          lblAverage.Text = decAverage.ToString("C2")

                                      End Sub
```

Figure 13-20: Selection structure entered in the procedure

5. Save the solution, then start the application. Click the **Calculate** button, then click the **Cancel** button in the dialog box. $0.00 appears in the Average sales amount box, which is correct.

6. Click the **Calculate** button. Type **25.67** in the dialog box, then press **Enter** to select the OK button. Now click the **Cancel** button in the dialog box to indicate that you have no more sales amounts to enter. The average sales amount is $25.67, which is correct.

7. Click the **Calculate** button. Type **100** and press **Enter**, then type **75.50** and press **Enter**. Type **30.25** and press **Enter**, then click the **Cancel** button. The average sales amount is $68.58, which is correct.

8. Click the **Calculate** button. Type **-5** and press **Enter**, then click the **Cancel** button. ($5.00) appears in the Average sales amount box, which is the expected result.

9. Click the **Calculate** button. Type **78.56** and press **Enter**, then type **-4** and press **Enter**. Click the **Cancel** button. The average sales amount is $37.28, which is correct.

10. Now test the application with the invalid values listed in the testing chart. Click the **Calculate** button. Press the **Backspace** key to delete the 0.00 in the dialog box, then press **Enter**. Because the input area does not contain a value, the InputBox function returns the empty string. As a result, the loop ends and the procedure displays $0.00 as the average sales amount.

11. Click the **Calculate** button. Type **x** and press **Enter**, then type **$5** and press **Enter**. Click the **Cancel** button. $0.00 appears in the Average sales amount box. Why $0.00?

The TryParse method converts the letter x to the number 0 and stores the result in the decSales variable. The variable's value is then added to the accumulator variable, giving 0. Next, the counter variable is incremented by 1, giving 1. The InputBox function then prompts you to enter another sales amount. Because the TryParse method does not recognize the $, it converts your $5 entry to the number 0 and stores the result in the decSales variable. The variable's value is added to the accumulator variable, giving 0. Next, the counter variable is incremented by 1, giving 2. The InputBox function then prompts you to enter another sales amount. When you click the Cancel button, the loop ends and the average sales amount is calculated by dividing the accumulator variable's value (0) by the counter variable's value (2); the result is 0. The formatted result appears in the lblAverage control. The $0.00 is an acceptable value to display when the user enters a letter or a special character along with a number.

12. Click the **Exit** button to end the application. Close the Code Editor window, then close the solution.

MINI-QUIZ 3

1. Write an assignment statement to increment the intTotalNum accumulator variable by the contents of the intNum variable.

2. The empty string in Visual Basic is represented by the _____ named constant.

3. Write a statement that assigns the InputBox function's return value to the strItem variable. The text "Item Name" should appear in the dialog box's title bar. The "Enter the item:" message should appear inside the dialog box. The input area should be empty.

SUMMARY

» You use a repetition structure, or loop, to repeatedly process one or more program instructions.

» A loop can be either a pretest loop or a posttest loop. Pretest loops are more commonly used. The condition in a pretest loop is evaluated *before* the loop instructions are processed. The condition in a posttest loop is evaluated *after* the loop instructions are processed.

» You can use the Do...Loop statement to code a pretest loop in Visual Basic. To process the loop instructions *while* a condition is true, you use the While keyword. You use the Until keyword to process the loop instructions *until* a condition becomes true.

» Counter and accumulator variables should be assigned a value outside the loop, but updated within the loop. Counter variables are updated by a constant value, whereas accumulator variables are updated by an amount that varies.

» The loop condition is represented by a diamond in a flowchart.

» The priming read, which appears above the loop, gets only the first input item from the user.

» You can use the InputBox function to display a dialog box that contains a message, an OK button, a Cancel button, and an input area. The function always returns a string.

» If a variable is used as the divisor in an expression, always verify that the variable does not contain the number 0 before the expression is processed by the computer.

KEY TERMS

Accumulator variable—a numeric variable used for accumulating (adding together) something

Counter variable—a numeric variable used for counting something

Incrementing—another term for updating

InputBox function—displays a dialog box containing a message, OK and Cancel buttons, and an input area

Loop—another term for the repetition structure

Posttest loop— a loop whose condition is evaluated *after* the instructions within the loop are processed

Pretest loop—a loop whose condition is evaluated *before* the instructions within the loop are processed

Priming read—the input instruction that appears above the loop that it controls; determines whether the loop instructions will be processed the first time

Refresh method—used to refresh (redraw) the interface

Repetition structure—one of the three programming structures; used to repeatedly process one or more program instructions either while a condition is true or until a condition becomes true; also called a loop

Runtime error—an error that occurs while an application is running

Sleep method—used to delay program execution

String.Empty constant—represents the empty string in Visual Basic

Updating—adding a number to the value stored in a counter or accumulator variable; also called incrementing

ANSWERS TO MINI-QUIZZES

MINI-QUIZ 1

1. The solution does not require a repetition structure.

2. The solution requires a repetition structure. The walk forward instruction will need to be repeated until Rob is directly in front of the table.

3. each book in your personal library

MINI-QUIZ 2

1. Do While intQuantity > 0

2. Do Until intQuantity <= 0

3. intNumEmployees = intNumEmployees + 1

4. System.Threading.Thread.Sleep(1000)

MINI-QUIZ 3

1. intTotalNum = intTotalNum + intNum

2. String.Empty

3. strItem = InputBox("Enter the item:", "Item Name")

REVIEW QUESTIONS

1. Which of the following Do clauses stops the loop when the value in the intAge variable is less than the number 0?

   a. Do While intAge >= 0   b. Do Until intAge <= 0

   c. Do Until intAge >= 0   d. None of the above.

2. How many times will the MessageBox.Show method in the following code be processed?

```
intCounter = 0
Do While intCounter > 3
    MessageBox.Show("Hello")
    intCounter = intCounter + 1
Loop
```

a. 0   b. 1

c. 3   d. 4

3. When the user clicks the Cancel button in an InputBox function's dialog box, the function returns _____.

a. the number 0

b. the empty string

c. an error message

d. None of the above.

4. Which of the following statements creates a dialog box that prompts the user for the name of a city, and then assigns the user's response to the strCity variable?

a. InputBox("Enter the city name:", "City", strCity)

b. InputBox("Enter the city name:", strCity)

c. strCity = InputBox("Enter the city name:", "City")

d. None of the above.

5. How many times will the MessageBox.Show method in the following code be processed?

```
intCounter = 0
Do Until intCounter > 3
    MessageBox.Show("Hello")
    intCounter = intCounter + 1
Loop
```

a. 0   b. 1

c. 3   d. 4

EXERCISES

1. In this exercise, you modify the My Dream Car-Version 1 application coded in the chapter. (The answers to TRY THIS Exercises are located at the end of the chapter.)

   a. Use Windows to make a copy of the Car Solution-Version 1 folder. Save the copy in the ClearlyVB\Chap13 folder. Rename the copy Car Solution-Version 3.

   b. Open the Car Solution (Car Solution.sln) file contained in the ClearlyVB\Chap13\Car Solution-Version 3 folder. Change Version 1 in the title bar to Version 3.

   c. Open the Code Editor window. Change the Do clause so that it uses the Until keyword rather than the While keyword. Save the solution. Start and then test the application. Stop the application.

   d. Rather than having the counter variable count up from 1, have it count down from 20. Make the appropriate modifications to the code. Save the solution. Start and then test the application. Stop the application, then close the solution.

2. In this exercise, you code an application that calculates sales tax amounts. (The answers to TRY THIS Exercises are located at the end of the chapter.)

   a. Open the Sales Tax Solution (Sales Tax Solution.sln) file, which is contained in the ClearlyVB\Chap13\Sales Tax Solution folder. The application should allow the user to enter zero or more sales amounts. After a sales amount is entered, the application should display the amount of a 6% sales tax. Display the sales tax in a message box before asking the user to enter another sales amount. Code the Calculate Sales Tax button's Click event procedure.

   b. Save the solution. Start and then test the application. Stop the application, then close the solution.

3. In this exercise, you modify the Sales Express application coded in the chapter.

   a. Use Windows to make a copy of the Sales Express Solution folder. Save the copy in the ClearlyVB\Chap13 folder. Rename the copy Modified Sales Express Solution.

   b. Open the Sales Express Solution (Sales Express Solution.sln) file contained in the Modified Sales Express Solution folder. Open the Code Editor window. Change the Do clause so that it uses the While keyword rather than the Until keyword.

   c. If the counter variable contains the number 0, display a message informing the user that no sales amounts were entered. Display the message in a message box.

   d. After displaying the average sales amount, blink the lblAverage control 5 times.

   e. Save the solution. Start and then test the application. Stop the application, then close the solution.

»TRY THIS

»TRY THIS

»MODIFY THIS

»INTRODUCTORY

4. Open the Average Score Solution (Average Score Solution.sln) file, which is contained in the ClearlyVB\Chap13\Average Score Solution folder. The application should allow the user to enter 5 test scores. It then should both calculate and display the average test score. If the average test score is greater than 80, blink the lblAverage control 6 times. Code the Calculate button's Click event procedure. Save the solution. Start and then test the application. Stop the application, then close the solution.

»INTRODUCTORY

5. Open the Weekly Pay Solution (Weekly Pay Solution.sln) file, which is contained in the ClearlyVB\Chap13\Weekly Pay Solution folder. The application should allow the user to enter zero or more weekly pay amounts. It then should display the number of amounts entered and the sum of the amounts entered. Code the Calculate button's Click event procedure. After displaying the sum, the procedure should change the lblSum control's ForeColor property from Color.Black to Color.Red and back again; do this several times. Save the solution. Start and then test the application. Stop the application, then close the solution.

»INTERMEDIATE

6. Effective January 1st of each year, Gabriela receives a 5% raise on her previous year's salary. She wants a program that both calculates and displays the amount of her raises for the next 3 years. Display the raise amounts in message boxes. Display her total salary for the 3 years in a label control.

   a. List the output and input items, as well as any processing items, then create an appropriate algorithm using pseudocode.

   b. Create a new Visual Basic Windows application. Name the solution, project, and form file Raise Solution, Raise Project, and frmMain.vb, respectively. Save the application in the ClearlyVB\Chap13 folder. If necessary, change the form's name to frmMain.

   c. Create an appropriate interface. Include a text box for entering the initial salary amount. Also include an Exit button. Code the Exit button's Click event procedure and the problem's algorithm. Save the solution.

   d. Start and then test the application. (Hint: For an annual salary of 10000, the raise amounts are $500.00, $525.00, and $551.25. The total salary is $33,101.25.) Stop the application, then close the solution.

»INTERMEDIATE

7. In this exercise, you display the sum of the even integers between and including two numbers entered by the user.

   a. Open the Sum Even Solution (Sum Even Solution.sln) file, which is contained in the ClearlyVB\Chap13\Sum Even Solution folder. The interface provides text boxes for the user to enter two numbers, which should be integers. Code the application so each text box accepts only numbers and the Backspace key.

b. The Display button's Click event procedure should display the sum of the even numbers between the two integers entered by the user. If the user's entry is even, it should be included in the sum. For example, if the user enters the integers 2 and 7, the procedure should display 12 (2 + 4 + 6). If the user enters the integers 2 and 8, the procedure should display 20 (2 + 4 + 6 + 8). Code the Display button's Click event procedure.

c. Save the solution. Start and then test the application. Stop the application, then close the solution.

8. In this exercise, you create an application for Premium Paper. The application allows the sales manager to enter the company's income and expense amounts. The number of income and expense amounts may vary each time the application is started. For example, the user may enter 5 income amounts and 3 expense amounts. Or, he or she may enter 20 income amounts and 30 expense amounts. The application should calculate and display the company's total income, total expenses, and profit (or loss). Use the InputBox function to get the individual income and expense amounts. If the company experienced a loss, display the amount of the loss using a red font; otherwise, display the profit using a black font. (Hint: Change the label control's ForeColor property to Color.Red or Color.Black.)

» **ADVANCED**

a. List the output and input items, as well as any processing items, then create an appropriate algorithm using pseudocode.

b. Create a new Visual Basic Windows application. Name the solution, project, and form file Premium Solution, Premium Project, and frmMain.vb, respectively. Save the application in the ClearlyVB\Chap13 folder. If necessary, change the form's name to frmMain.

c. Design an appropriate interface. Use label controls to display the total income, total expenses, and profit (loss). Display the calculated amounts with a dollar sign and two decimal places.

d. Code the application. Keep in mind that the income and expense amounts may contain decimal places.

e. Save the solution. Start and then test the application. Stop the application, then close the solution.

9. In this exercise, you modify the Sales Express application coded in the chapter.

» **ADVANCED**

a. Use Windows to make a copy of the Sales Express Solution folder. Save the copy in the ClearlyVB\Chap13 folder. Rename the copy Advanced Sales Express Solution.

b. Open the Sales Express Solution (Sales Express Solution.sln) file contained in the ClearlyVB\Chap13\Sales Express Solution folder. Modify the user interface so that it can display the number of sales amounts entered by the user.

c. Open the Code Editor window. If the user enters a sales amount that is not greater than 0, do not include the sales amount in the average; use a message box to display an appropriate message to the user. In addition to displaying the average sales amount, the application also should display the number of sales amounts entered. Make the appropriate modifications to the application's code. Save the solution. Start and then test the application. Stop the application, then close the solution.

10. Open the FigureThisOut Solution (FigureThisOut Solution.sln) file, which is contained in the ClearlyVB\Chap13\FigureThisOut Solution folder. Open the Code Editor window and study the existing code. Use a chart similar to the one in Figure 13-7 to describe the way the Calculate button's code will be processed. Start and then test the application. Stop the application, then close the solution.

11. In this exercise, you find an error in an application's code. Open the SwatTheBugs Solution (SwatTheBugs Solution.sln) file, which is contained in the ClearlyVB\Chap13\SwatTheBugs Solution folder. The application should drag the picture box up and then down again on the form. Start the application, then click the Up and Down button. Notice that the application is not working correctly. Click the Exit button. Open the Code Editor window. Locate and correct any errors in the code. Save the solution, then start and test the application again. Stop the application, then close the solution.

ANSWERS TO "TRY THIS" EXERCISES

1. For Step c, change the Do clause to Do Until intCount > 20. For Step d, change the intCount = 1 statement to intCount = 20. Also change the Do clause to Do Until intCount < 1, and change the intCount = intCount + 1 statement to intCount = intCount - 1.

2. See Figure 13-21.

```
Private Sub btnCalc_Click(ByVal sender As Object, _
    ByVal e As System.EventArgs) Handles btnCalc.Click
    ' calculates and displays sales tax amounts

    Const strPROMPT As String = _
            "Enter a sales amount. Click Cancel to end."
    Const strTITLE As String = "Sales Entry"
    Const decTAX_RATE As Decimal = 0.06
    Dim strInputSales As String
    Dim decSales As Decimal
    Dim decTax As Decimal

    ' get the first sales amount
    strInputSales = InputBox(strPROMPT, strTITLE, "0.0")
    Do Until strInputSales = String.Empty
            Decimal.TryParse(strInputSales, decSales)
            decTax = decSales * decTAX_RATE
            MessageBox.Show(decTax.ToString("C2"), _
                            "Sales Tax", MessageBoxButtons.OK, _
                            MessageBoxIcon.Information)
            ' get another sales amount
            strInputSales = InputBox(strPROMPT, strTITLE, "0.0")
    Loop
End Sub
```

Figure 13-21

14

DO IT, THEN ASK PERMISSION

After studying Chapter 14, you should be able to:

Write a posttest loop using the Do...Loop statement

Show a posttest loop in both pseudocode and a flowchart

Concatenate strings

TESTING AFTER THE FACT

Recall that a repetition structure can be either a pretest loop or a posttest loop. The difference between both types of loops pertains to when the loop condition is evaluated. Unlike the pretest loop condition, which is evaluated *before* the instructions within the loop are processed, the posttest loop condition is evaluated *after* the instructions within the loop are processed. As a result, the instructions in a pretest loop may never be processed, but the instructions in a posttest loop always will be processed at least once. You learned about pretest loops in Chapter 13; this chapter covers posttest loops. Although most programmers use pretest loops, it is essential to understand the way posttest loops work. You may encounter a situation where a posttest loop is the better choice. Or, you may encounter a posttest loop in another programmer's code that you are either modifying or debugging. The posttest loop might even be the cause of the code not working correctly.

The problem specification and algorithms shown in Figure 14-1 will help clarify the difference between pretest and posttest loops. The first algorithm uses a pretest loop; the other algorithm uses a posttest loop. (The problem specification and pretest loop algorithm are from Figure 13-5 in Chapter 13.) The purpose of the loop in each algorithm is to position Rob directly in front of his bedroom door. Compare the first and last lines in the pretest loop with the first and last lines in the posttest loop. More specifically, notice the location of the loop condition—in this case, until you are directly in front of the bedroom door. In the pretest loop, the condition appears in the first line; this indicates that Rob should evaluate it *before* he follows the instructions in the loop. In the posttest loop, the condition appears in the last line, indicating that Rob should evaluate it only *after* following the instructions in the loop.

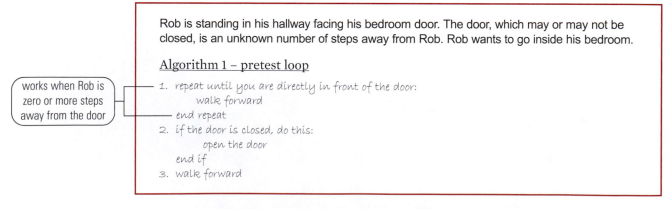

Rob is standing in his hallway facing his bedroom door. The door, which may or may not be closed, is an unknown number of steps away from Rob. Rob wants to go inside his bedroom.

Algorithm 1 – pretest loop

works when Rob is zero or more steps away from the door

1. repeat until you are directly in front of the door:
       walk forward
   end repeat
2. if the door is closed, do this:
       open the door
   end if
3. walk forward

Figure 14-1: Rob algorithms containing pretest and posttest loops (*continued on next page*)

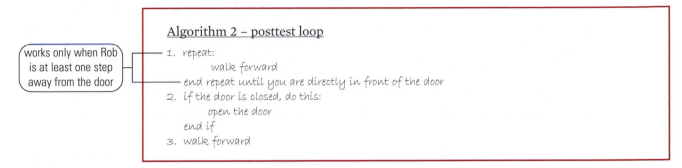

Figure 14-1: Rob algorithms containing pretest and posttest loops (*continued from previous page*)

As Figure 14-1 indicates, the pretest loop in Algorithm 1 will work when Rob is zero or more steps away from his bedroom door. The posttest loop in Algorithm 2, however, will work only when Rob is at least one step away from the door. To understand why the loops are not interchangeable, you will test them. For the first test, Rob is one step away from the door. In the pretest loop, the loop condition checks Rob's current location. Rob is not directly in front of his bedroom door, so he is told to walk forward and the loop condition is evaluated again. Rob is now positioned correctly in front of the door, so the loop ends and Rob continues to Step 2 in the algorithm. The posttest loop, on the other hand, instructs Rob to walk forward, which places him directly in front of his bedroom door. The loop condition is evaluated next. The condition checks whether Rob is positioned correctly; he is, so the loop ends and Rob continues to Step 2 in the algorithm. Notice that, when Rob is one step away from the door, the pretest and posttest loops produce the same result; both position Rob in front of the door. For the second test, Rob is directly in front of his bedroom door. The condition in the pretest loop checks Rob's current location. Rob is already positioned correctly, so the walk forward instruction is bypassed and the loop ends. The posttest loop, on the other hand, instructs Rob to walk forward before the loop condition is evaluated. If Rob walks forward, he will bump into the door. Obviously, the posttest loop in Algorithm 2 does not work correctly when Rob starts out directly in front of his bedroom door. You can fix this problem by adding a selection structure to the algorithm, as shown in Figure 14-2.

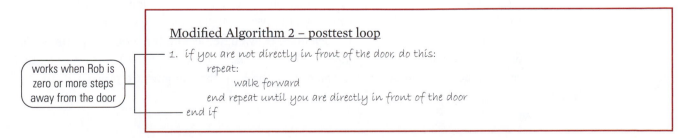

Figure 14-2: Selection structure added to Algorithm 2 from Figure 14-1 (*continued on next page*)

> 2. if the door is closed, do this:
>   open the door
>   end if
> 3. walk forward

Figure 14-2: Selection structure added to Algorithm 2 from Figure 14-1 (*continued from previous page*)

The posttest loop in Figure 14-2 is identical to the posttest loop in Figure 14-1, except it is processed only when Rob is not directly in front of his bedroom door. First, test the algorithm with Rob one step away from the door. The algorithm in Figure 14-2 begins with a selection structure whose condition checks Rob's initial location. He's not directly in front of the door, so the posttest loop instructs him to *walk forward*. The loop condition is evaluated next. At this point, Rob is positioned correctly; so the loop ends, and so does the selection structure. Rob now continues to Step 2 in the algorithm. For the second test, Rob is directly in front of his bedroom door. Here again, the condition in the selection structure checks Rob's initial location. In this case, Rob is already in front of his bedroom door, so the entire posttest loop is bypassed and Rob continues to Step 2 in the algorithm. Although the modified algorithm works correctly, most programmers prefer to use a pretest loop (rather than a posttest loop with a selection structure) because it is easier to write and understand. Posttest loops should be used only when their instructions must be processed at least once.

MORE ON THE DO...LOOP STATEMENT

In Chapter 13, you learned how to use the Do...Loop statement to code a pretest loop. The statement also is used to code a posttest loop; the syntax for doing this is shown in Figure 14-3. Comparing the statement's posttest syntax with its pretest syntax (shown in Figure 13-6 in Chapter 13), you will notice one difference: the location of the {While | Until} *condition* section. In the pretest syntax, the {While | Until} *condition* section is part of the Do clause and indicates that the *condition* is evaluated *before* the loop instructions are processed. In the posttest syntax, on the other hand, it's part of the Loop clause, indicating that the *condition* is evaluated *after* the loop instructions are processed. In the posttest syntax, the only purpose of the Do clause is to mark the beginning of the loop. Figure 14-3 also shows how to write the pretest loops from Figure 13-6 as posttest loops. Like the pretest loops, both posttest loops display the numbers 1, 2, and 3 in message boxes.

DO...LOOP STATEMENT

<u>Syntax for coding a posttest loop</u>

Do

    instructions to be processed either while the condition is true or until the condition becomes true

Loop {While | Until} *condition*

<u>Example 1</u>

```
intNumber = 1
Do
    MessageBox.Show(intNumber.ToString)
    intNumber = intNumber + 1
Loop While intNumber <= 3
```

<u>Example 2</u>

```
intNumber = 1
Do
    MessageBox.Show(intNumber.ToString)
    intNumber = intNumber + 1
Loop Until intNumber > 3
```

Figure 14-3: Syntax and examples of the Do...Loop statement for a posttest loop

PSEUDOCODE AND FLOWCHART FOR A POSTTEST LOOP

Figure 14-4 shows the pseudocode and flowchart for Example 2 in Figure 14-3. Not surprisingly, the repetition diamond appears at the bottom of the loop in a posttest loop. (Recall that it appears at the top of the loop in a pretest loop.) The loop in the figure is formed by all of the symbols and flowlines in the loop's False path.

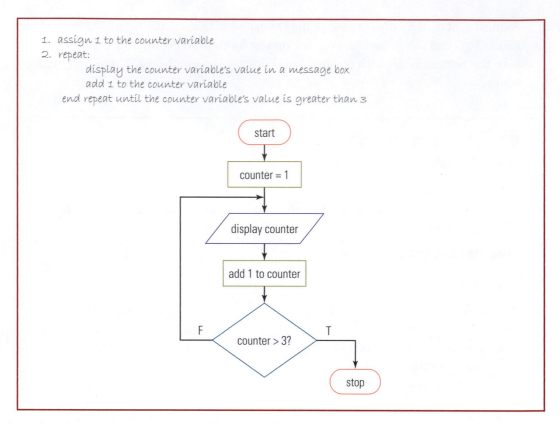

1. assign 1 to the counter variable
2. repeat:
   display the counter variable's value in a message box
   add 1 to the counter variable
   end repeat until the counter variable's value is greater than 3

Figure 14-4: Pseudocode and flowchart for Example 2 in Figure 14-3

THE GOOD MORNING APPLICATION

In this first set of steps, you will finish coding an application that displays the message "Good Morning!" in a label control. The number of times to display the message will be entered in a text box.

To open the Good Morning application, and then code and test the application:

1. Start Visual Studio 2008 (or Visual Basic 2008 Express Edition). Open the **Good Morning Solution** (**Good Morning Solution.sln**) file, which is contained in the ClearlyVB\Chap14\Good Morning Solution folder. If necessary, open the designer window. The application's interface is shown in Figure 14-5.

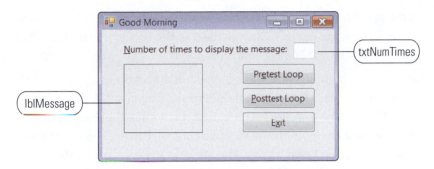

Figure 14-5: Good Morning application's user interface

2. Open the Code Editor window. Locate the btnPretest control's Click event procedure. The procedure will use a pretest loop to repeat the loop instructions until the value in the counter variable (intCounter) is greater than the value in the intNumTimes variable. Change the Do clause to **Do Until intCounter > intNumTimes**. The first instruction in the loop displays the "Good Morning!" message in the lblMessage control. The instruction contains two new items that will be explained in the next section: the ampersand (used to concatenate strings) and the ControlChars.NewLine constant (used to start a new line). The second instruction in the loop increments the counter variable by 1.

3. Next, locate the btnPosttest control's Click event procedure. This procedure will use a posttest loop to repeat the loop instructions until the value in the counter variable (intCounter) is greater than the value in the intNumTimes variable. Change the Loop clause to **Loop Until intCounter > intNumTimes**.

4. Save the solution, then start the application. First, test the Pretest Loop button's code. Type **4** in the text box, then click the **Pretest Loop** button. The "Good Morning!" message appears 4 times in the lblMessage control. Each message appears on a separate line in the control, as shown in Figure 14-6.

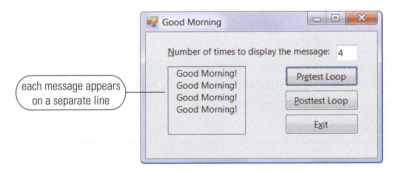

Figure 14-6: Good Morning! messages displayed in the lblMessage control

5. Change the 4 in the text box to **2**, then click the **Pretest Loop** button. The message appears twice in the lblMessage control. Change the 2 in the text box to **0**, then click the **Pretest Loop** button. The lblMessage control is empty.

6. Now test the Posttest Loop button's code. Change the 0 in the text box to **4**, then click the **Posttest Loop** button. The "Good Morning!" message appears 4 times in the lblMessage control. Change the 4 in the text box to **2**, then click the **Posttest Loop** button. The message appears twice in the lblMessage control. Change the 2 in the text box to **0**, then click the **Posttest Loop** button. The message appears in the lblMessage control, even though the control should be empty.

7. Click the **Exit** button.

Figure 14-7 shows the pretest and posttest loops in the Good Morning application. It also describes the way the computer processes the code in each loop when the user enters the number 0. As indicated in the figure, the pretest loop instructions are not processed when the text box contains the number 0; the posttest loop instructions, however, are processed one time.

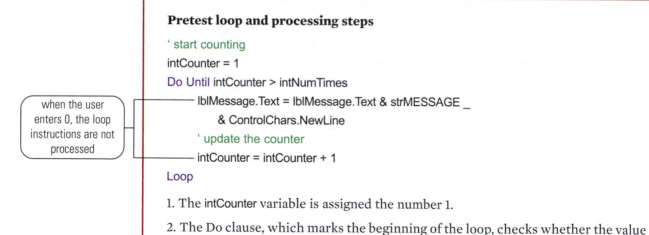

Pretest loop and processing steps

```
' start counting
intCounter = 1
Do Until intCounter > intNumTimes
        lblMessage.Text = lblMessage.Text & strMESSAGE _
            & ControlChars.NewLine
    ' update the counter
        intCounter = intCounter + 1
Loop
```

when the user enters 0, the loop instructions are not processed

1. The intCounter variable is assigned the number 1.

2. The Do clause, which marks the beginning of the loop, checks whether the value in the intCounter variable (1) is greater than the value in the intNumTimes variable (0). It is, so the loop ends. Processing continues with the statement following the Loop clause.

Figure 14-7: Pretest and posttest loops and processing steps (*continued on next page*)

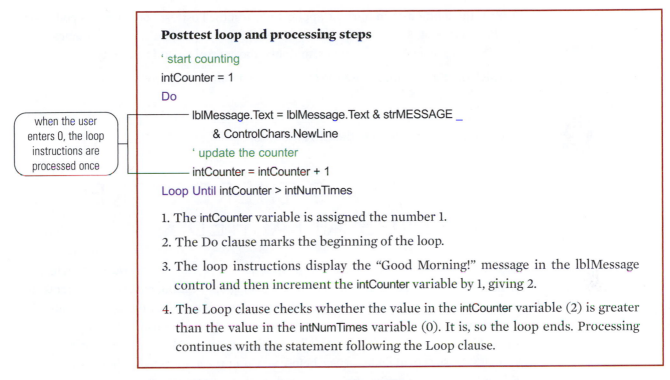

Posttest loop and processing steps

```
' start counting
intCounter = 1
Do
        lblMessage.Text = lblMessage.Text & strMESSAGE _
            & ControlChars.NewLine
        ' update the counter
        intCounter = intCounter + 1
Loop Until intCounter > intNumTimes
```

when the user enters 0, the loop instructions are processed once

1. The intCounter variable is assigned the number 1.

2. The Do clause marks the beginning of the loop.

3. The loop instructions display the "Good Morning!" message in the lblMessage control and then increment the intCounter variable by 1, giving 2.

4. The Loop clause checks whether the value in the intCounter variable (2) is greater than the value in the intNumTimes variable (0). It is, so the loop ends. Processing continues with the statement following the Loop clause.

Figure 14-7: Pretest and posttest loops and processing steps (*continued from previous page*)

You can fix the problem in the Posttest Loop button's code by placing the posttest loop in a selection structure. The selection structure's condition will compare the value stored in the intNumTimes variable with the number 0. The posttest loop will be processed only when the variable does not contain the number 0; otherwise, the loop will be skipped over.

To fix the problem in the Posttest Loop button's code:

1. Modify the btnPosttest control's Click event procedure by adding the selection structure shown in Figure 14-8.

```
    ' start counting
    intCounter = 1
    If intNumTimes <> 0 Then
        Do
            lblMessage.Text = lblMessage.Text & strMESSAGE _
                & ControlChars.NewLine
            ' update the counter
            intCounter = intCounter + 1
        Loop Until intCounter > intNumTimes
    End If
End Sub
```

place the posttest loop inside a selection structure

Figure 14-8: Selection structure added to the btnPosttest control's Click event procedure

2. Save the solution, then start the application. Test the Posttest Loop button's code using the numbers **4**, **2**, and **0**. The "Good Morning!" message should appear 4 times in the lblMessage control, then 2 times, and then the control should be empty.

3. Click the **Exit** button. Close the Code Editor window, then close the solution.

 For more examples of using the Do...Loop statement to code a posttest loop, see the Do...Loop Posttest section in the Ch14WantMore.pdf file.

BUT THEY SAID THERE WERE NO STRINGS ATTACHED

The lblMessage.Text = lblMessage.Text & strMESSAGE & ControlChars.NewLine statement, which appears in both loops in the Good Morning application, contains two items that were not covered in the previous chapters: the concatenation operator and the ControlChars.NewLine constant. You use the **concatenation operator**, which is the ampersand (**&**), to concatenate (connect or link) strings together. When concatenating strings, you must be sure to include a space before and after the ampersand; otherwise, the Code Editor will not recognize the ampersand as the concatenation operator. Figure 14-9 shows examples of string concatenation.

CONCATENATING STRINGS

Variables	Contents
strFirstName	Lucretia
strLastName	Jackson
intAge	30

Concatenated string	Result
strFirstName & strLastName	LucretiaJackson
strFirstName & " " & strLastName	Lucretia Jackson
strLastName & ", " & strFirstName	Jackson, Lucretia
"She is " & intAge.ToString & "!"	She is 30!

Figure 14-9: Examples of concatenating strings

The concatenation operator appears twice in the lblMessage.Text = lblMessage.Text & strMESSAGE & ControlChars.NewLine statement. The statement concatenates three strings: the contents of the lblMessage control, the contents of the strMESSAGE constant, and the ControlChars.NewLine constant. The **ControlChars.NewLine constant** represents the Enter key on your keyboard and is used to create a new line. In this case, it creates a new line in the lblMessage control. The ControlChars.NewLine constant is the reason that each message appears on a separate line in the label control, as shown earlier in Figure 14-6.

MINI-QUIZ 1

1. Write a Visual Basic Loop clause that processes the loop instructions as long as the value in the intQuantity variable is greater than the number 0. Use the While keyword.

2. Rewrite the Loop clause from Question 1 using the Until keyword.

3. Write an assignment statement that concatenates the message "My favorite city is " with the contents of the strCity variable, and then assigns the result to the lblCity control.

It's time to view the Ch14-Stepping Through a Loop video.

SUMMARY

» The instructions in a posttest loop will always be processed at least once.

» You use the Do...Loop statement to code a posttest loop in Visual Basic. The Do clause simply marks the beginning of the loop. The Loop clause contains either the While keyword or the Until keyword, followed by the loop condition.

» You concatenate strings using the concatenation operator, which is the ampersand (&). The concatenation operator must be both preceded and followed by a space.

» The Enter key on your keyboard is represented by the ControlChars.NewLine constant.

KEY TERMS

&—the concatenation operator in Visual Basic

Concatenation operator—the ampersand (&); used to concatenate strings

ControlChars.NewLine constant—a Visual Basic constant that represents the Enter key on your keyboard; creates a new line

ANSWERS TO MINI-QUIZ

MINI-QUIZ 1

1. Loop While intQuantity > 0

2. Loop Until intQuantity <= 0

3. lblCity.Text = "My favorite city is " & strCity

REVIEW QUESTIONS

1. Which of the following Loop clauses stops the loop when the value in the intAge variable is less than the number 0?

   a. Loop While intAge >= 0

   b. Loop Until intAge <= 0

   c. Loop Until intAge >= 0

   d. None of the above.

2. How many times will the MessageBox.Show method in the following code be processed?

   intCounter = 0

   Do

      MessageBox.Show("Hello")

      intCounter = intCounter + 1

   Loop While intCounter > 3

   a. 0   b. 1

   c. 3   d. 4

3. What is the value in the intCounter variable when the loop in Review Question 2 ends?

a. 0   b. 1

c. 3   d. 4

4. How many times will the MessageBox.Show method in the following code be processed?

```
intCounter = 0

Do

    MessageBox.Show("Hello")

    intCounter = intCounter + 1

Loop Until intCounter > 3
```

a. 0   b. 1

c. 3   d. 4

5. The strCity variable contains the string "Boston" and the strState variable contains the string "MA". Which of the following will display the string "Boston, MA" (the city, a comma, a space, and the state) in the lblAddress control?

a. lblAddress.Text = "strCity" & ", " & "strState"

b. lblAddress.Text = strCity $ ", " $ strState

c. lblAddress.Text = strCity & ", " & strState

d. lblAddress.Text = "strCity," & "strState"

EXERCISES

1. Show the processing steps for the code in Example 1 in Figure 14-3. Use Figure 14-7 as a guide. (The answers to TRY THIS Exercises are located at the end of the chapter.)   **»TRY THIS**

2. In this exercise, you modify the My Dream Car-Version 1 application from Chapter 13. (The answers to TRY THIS Exercises are located at the end of the chapter.) Open the Car Solution (Car Solution.sln) file contained in the ClearlyVB\Chap14\Car Solution-Version 1 folder. Open the Code Editor window. Change the pretest loop to a posttest loop. Use the Until keyword. Save the solution. Start and then test the application. Stop the application, then close the solution.   **»TRY THIS**

》MODIFY THIS

3. In this exercise, you modify the Good Morning application coded in the chapter.

   a. Use Windows to make a copy of the Good Morning Solution folder. Save the copy in the ClearlyVB\Chap14 folder. Rename the copy Modified Good Morning Solution.

   b. Open the Good Morning Solution (Good Morning Solution.sln) file contained in the Modified Good Morning Solution folder. Open the designer window.

   c. Open the Code Editor window. Rather than having the pretest loop count up from 1, you will have it count down from the number of times entered by the user. Change the intCounter = 1 statement in the btnPretest control's Click event procedure to intCounter = intNumTimes. Make the necessary modifications to the code to accommodate this change.

   d. Save the solution. Start and then test the Pretest Loop button's code. Stop the application.

   e. The Posttest Loop button should display the intCounter variable's value, 1 space, and the "Good Morning!" message on the same line in the lblMessage control. Modify the btnPosttest control's Click event procedure.

   f. Save the solution. Start and then test the Posttest Loop button's code. Stop the application, then close the solution.

》INTRODUCTORY

4. Open the Average Score Solution (Average Score Solution.sln) file, which is contained in the ClearlyVB\Chap14\Average Score Solution folder. The application should allow the user to enter 5 test scores; use a posttest loop. It then should both calculate and display the average test score. If the average test score is greater than 80, blink the lblAverage control 6 times; use a posttest loop. Code the Calculate button's Click event procedure. Save the solution. Start and then test the application. Stop the application, then close the solution.

》INTERMEDIATE

5. In this exercise, you create an application that displays a multiplication table in a label control. A sample run of the application is shown in Figure 14-10. The multiplication table multiplies the number entered in the text box by the numbers 1 through 9, and shows the product.

   a. List the output and input items, as well as any processing items, then create an appropriate algorithm using pseudocode.

   b. Create a new Visual Basic Windows application. Name the solution, project, and form file Multiplication Solution, Multiplication Project, and frmMain.vb, respectively. Save the application in the ClearlyVB\Chap14 folder. If necessary, change the form's name to frmMain.

c. Create the interface shown in Figure 14-10. Code the application using a posttest loop in the Display Table button's Click event procedure.

d. Save the solution. Start and then test the application. Stop the application, then close the solution.

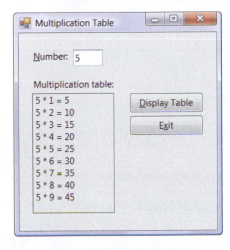

Figure 14-10: Multiplication Table interface

6. In this exercise, you modify the Sales Express application from Chapter 13. Open the Sales Express Solution (Sales Express Solution.sln) file, which is contained in the ClearlyVB\Chap14\Sales Express Solution folder. Open the Code Editor window. Change the pretest loop in the btnCalc control's Click event procedure to a posttest loop. Make the necessary modifications to the code. Save the solution, then start and test the application. Stop the application, then close the solution.

7. Open the FigureThisOut Solution (FigureThisOut Solution.sln) file, which is contained in the ClearlyVB\Chap14\FigureThisOut Solution folder. Open the Code Editor window and study the existing code. Change the intCount = 1 statement to intCount = 0. What additional changes will need to be made to the code as a result of starting the counter at 0 rather than at 1? Make the necessary changes. Start and then test the application. Stop the application, then close the solution.

8. In this exercise, you find an error in an application's code. Open the SwatTheBugs Solution (SwatTheBugs Solution.sln) file, which is contained in the ClearlyVB\Chap14\SwatTheBugs Solution folder. Start and then test the application by trying to enter three sale amounts. Notice that the application is not working correctly. Click the Exit button. Open the Code Editor window. Locate and correct any errors in the code. Save the solution, then start and test the application again. Stop the application, then close the solution.

»**ADVANCED**

ANSWERS TO "TRY THIS" EXERCISES

1. See Figure 14-11.

1. The intNumber variable is assigned the number 1.
2. The Do clause marks the beginning of the loop.
3. The loop instructions display the intNumber variable's value (1) in a message box and then increment the variable by 1, giving 2.
4. The Loop clause checks whether the value in the intNumber variable (2) is less than or equal to 3. It is, so processing returns to the Do clause.
5. The Do clause marks the beginning of the loop.
6. The loop instructions display the intNumber variable's value (2) in a message box and then increment the variable by 1, giving 3.
7. The Loop clause checks whether the value in the intNumber variable (3) is less than or equal to 3. It is, so processing returns to the Do clause.
8. The Do clause marks the beginning of the loop.
9. The loop instructions display the intNumber variable's value (3) in a message box and then increment the variable by 1, giving 4.
10. The Loop clause checks whether the value in the intNumber variable (4) is less than or equal to 3. It's not, so the loop ends. Processing continues with the statement following the Loop clause.

Figure 14-11

2. Change the Do While intCount <= 20 clause to Do, and change the Loop clause to Loop Until intCount > 20.

15

LET ME COUNT THE WAYS

After studying Chapter 15, you should be able to:

Code a pretest loop using the For...Next statement

Play an audio file while an application is running

Calculate a periodic payment using the Financial.Pmt method

WHEN WILL IT STOP?

A loop whose instructions you want processed a precise number of times is often referred to as a **counter loop**, because it uses a counter variable to keep track of the number of times the loop instructions are processed. A counter loop can be either a pretest loop or a posttest loop. You code a posttest counter loop using the Do...Loop statement. A pretest counter loop, on the other hand, can be coded using either the Do...Loop statement or the For...Next statement. However, the For...Next statement provides a more convenient way to code that type of loop, because it takes care of initializing and updating the counter variable, as well as evaluating the loop condition. The For...Next statement's syntax is shown in Figure 15-1, along with the tasks the computer performs when processing the statement. The statement begins with the For clause and ends with the Next clause. Between the two clauses, you enter the instructions you want the computer to repeat. *Counter*, which appears in both the For and Next clauses, is the name of the counter variable, which must be a numeric variable. Although, technically, you do not need to specify the counter variable's name in the Next clause, doing so is highly recommended because it makes your code more self-documenting. You can use the As *dataType* portion of the For clause to declare the counter variable. When you declare a variable in the For clause, the variable has block scope and can be used only within the For...Next loop. The variable is removed from the computer's internal memory when the loop ends. (You learned about block scope in Chapter 9.) Alternatively, you can declare the counter variable in a Dim statement, as long as the Dim statement appears somewhere above the For...Next statement. As you know, when a variable is declared in a Dim statement at the beginning of a procedure, it has procedure scope and can be used by the entire procedure. When deciding where to declare the counter variable, keep in mind that if a variable is needed only by the For...Next statement, then it is a better programming practice to declare the variable in the For clause. As you learned in Chapter 9, fewer unintentional errors occur in applications when the variables are declared using the minimum scope needed. Block variables have a smaller scope than do procedure-level variables. The *startValue*, *endValue*, and *stepValue* items in the syntax determine the number of times the loop instructions are processed. The *startValue* tells the computer where to begin counting, and the *endValue* tells the computer when to stop counting. The *stepValue* tells the computer how much to count by—in other words, how much to add to the counter variable each time the loop is processed. If you omit the *stepValue*, a *stepValue* of positive 1 is used. The *startValue*, *endValue*, and *stepValue* must be numeric and can be either positive or negative, integer or non-integer. The example in Figure 15-1 uses the

For...Next statement to display (in message boxes) integers from 10 (the *startValue*) through 13 (the *endValue*) in increments of 1 (the *stepValue*).

FOR...NEXT STATEMENT

<u>Syntax</u>

For *counter* [**As** *dataType*] = *startValue* **To** *endValue* [**Step** *stepValue*]

   [*statements*]

Next *counter*

<u>Processing tasks</u>

1. If the counter variable is declared in the For clause, the computer creates and initializes the variable to the *startValue*; otherwise, it just performs the initialization task. This is done only once, at the beginning of the loop.

2. The computer evaluates the loop condition by comparing the value in the counter variable with the *endValue*. If the *stepValue* is positive, the comparison determines whether the counter variable's value is greater than the *endValue*. If the *stepValue* is negative, on the other hand, the comparison determines whether the counter variable's value is less than the *endValue*.

3. If the loop condition evaluates to True, the computer stops processing the loop; processing continues with the statement following the Next clause. If the loop condition evaluates to False, on the other hand, the computer processes the instructions within the loop and then task 4 is performed. Notice that the computer evaluates the loop condition *before* processing the instructions within the loop.

4. Task 4 is performed only when the loop condition evaluates to False. In this task, the computer adds the *stepValue* to the contents of the counter variable. It then repeats tasks 2, 3, and 4 until the loop condition evaluates to True.

<u>Example</u>

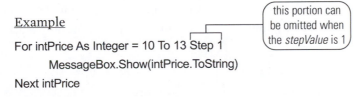

this portion can be omitted when the *stepValue* is 1

```
For intPrice As Integer = 10 To 13 Step 1
    MessageBox.Show(intPrice.ToString)
Next intPrice
```

Figure 15-1: Syntax and an example of the For…Next statement

Figure 15-2 describes the way the computer processes the code shown in the example in Figure 15-1. Notice that the computer processes the loop instruction four times and displays the numbers 10, 11, 12, and 13 (one at a time) in message boxes. The loop stops when the counter variable, intPrice, contains the number 14.

Processing steps for the example in Figure 15-1

1. The computer creates the intPrice variable and initializes it to 10.
2. The computer checks whether the value in the intPrice variable is greater than 13. It's not, so the computer displays the number 10 in a message box and then adds 1 to the contents of the intPrice variable, giving 11.
3. The computer again checks whether the value in the intPrice variable is greater than 13. It's not, so the computer displays the number 11 in a message box and then adds 1 to the contents of the intPrice variable, giving 12.
4. The computer again checks whether the value in the intPrice variable is greater than 13. It's not, so the computer displays the number 12 in a message box and then adds 1 to the contents of the intPrice variable, giving 13.
5. The computer again checks whether the value in the intPrice variable is greater than 13. It's not, so the computer displays the number 13 in a message box and then adds 1 to the contents of the intPrice variable, giving 14.
6. The computer again checks whether the value in the intPrice variable is greater than 13. It is, so the computer stops processing the For…Next loop. Processing continues with the statement following the Next clause.

Figure 15-2: Processing steps for the example in Figure 15-1

For more examples of using the For..Next statement to code a pretest counter loop, see the For…Next section in the Ch15WantMore.pdf file.

SPACESHIP-VERSION 1 APPLICATION

Figure 15-3 shows the interface for the Spaceship-Version 1 application. (The spaceship image is from the Microsoft Office Clip Art collection, which is available at *http://office.microsoft.com*.) In the Go button's Click event procedure, you will include a For…Next statement that displays the numbers 1, 2, and 3 in the lblCountToBlastOff control.

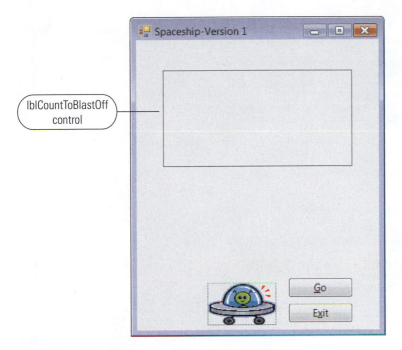

lblCountToBlastOff control

Figure 15-3: Interface for the Spaceship-Version 1 application

Before you begin coding the Spaceship-Version 1 application, you may want to view the Ch15-Spaceship video. The video demonstrates the steps contained in the following section. It also demonstrates the steps needed to code the Spaceship-Version 2 application.

To open the Spaceship-Version 1 application, and then code and test the application:

1. Start Visual Studio 2008 (or Visual Basic 2008 Express Edition). Open the **Spaceship Solution** (**Spaceship Solution.sln**) file, which is contained in the ClearlyVB\Chap15\ Spaceship Solution-Version 1 folder. If necessary, open the designer window.

2. Open the Code Editor window. Locate the btnGo control's Click event procedure. See Figure 15-4. The procedure starts the spaceship at the bottom of the form. It then removes the border from the lblCountToBlastOff control and also sets the control's Visible property to True. Next, the procedure displays the "Blast Off!" message in the lblCountToBlastOff control; it then pauses program execution for a short time before hiding the control. The Do...Loop statement drags the spaceship to the top of the form.

```
Private Sub btnGo_Click(ByVal sender As Object, ByVal e As System.EventArgs) Hand
    ' drags the spaceship from the bottom to the top of the form

    ' start the spaceship at the bottom of the form
    picSpaceship.Top = 355
    ' remove the border from the label control
    ' then show the control
    lblCountToBlastOff.BorderStyle = BorderStyle.None
    lblCountToBlastOff.Visible = True

    ' count up from 1 to 3, pausing execution after each number


    ' display the "Blast Off!" message, then pause execution
    lblCountToBlastOff.Text = "Blast Off!"
    Me.Refresh()
    System.Threading.Thread.Sleep(500)

    ' hide the label control
    lblCountToBlastOff.Visible = False

    ' drag the spaceship to the top of the form
    Do While picSpaceship.Top > 0
        picSpaceship.Top = picSpaceship.Top - 100
        Me.Refresh()
        System.Threading.Thread.Sleep(100)
    Loop
End Sub
```

Figure 15-4: Go button's Click event procedure in the Spaceship-Version 1 application

3. Start the application, then click the **Go** button. The "Blast Off!" message appears in the label control and then the spaceship is dragged to the top of the form. Click the **Exit** button.

4. Click the **blank line** below the ' count up from 1 to 3, pausing execution after each number comment. Type **for intCount as integer = 1 to 3** and press **Enter**. Notice that the Code Editor automatically enters the Next clause for you.

5. First display the counter variable's value in the lblCountToBlastOff control. Type **lblCountToBlastOff.text = intCount.tostring** and press **Enter**.

6. Now refresh the screen and pause program execution for a half of a second so that the user can view the current number in the lblCountToBlastOff control. Type **me.refresh()** and press **Enter**, then type **system.threading.thread.sleep(500)**.

7. Change the Next clause to **Next intCount**, then save the solution.

8. Start the application, then click the **Go** button. The numbers 1, 2, and 3 appear (one at a time) in the label control, followed by the "Blast Off!" message. The spaceship is then dragged to the top of the form.

9. Click the **Exit** button. Close the Code Editor window, then close the solution.

SPACESHIP-VERSION 2 APPLICATION

In this version of the Spaceship application, the For...Next statement in the Go button's Click event procedure will display the numbers 3, 2, and 1 in the lblCountToBlastOff control.

To open the Spaceship-Version 2 application, and then code and test the application:

1. Open the **Spaceship Solution** (**Spaceship Solution.sln**) file, which is contained in the ClearlyVB\Chap15\Spaceship Solution-Version 2 folder. If necessary, open the designer window. Except for the title bar text, the interface is identical to the one shown earlier in Figure 15-3.

2. Open the Code Editor window. Locate the btnGo control's Click event procedure, which contains the same code shown earlier in Figure 15-4. The only difference is in the fifth comment: in this procedure, the comment contains the text "count down from 3 to 1" rather than "count up from 1 to 3."

3. Enter the For...Next statement shown in Figure 15-5. Notice that the *stepValue* is a negative number, which is a requirement for the loop to be processed when the *startValue* is greater than the *endValue*.

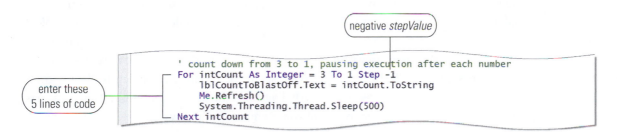

negative *stepValue*

```
' count down from 3 to 1, pausing execution after each number
For intCount As Integer = 3 To 1 Step -1
    lblCountToBlastOff.Text = intCount.ToString
    Me.Refresh()
    System.Threading.Thread.Sleep(500)
Next intCount
```

enter these 5 lines of code

Figure 15-5: For...Next statement entered in the Go button's Click event procedure in the Spaceship-Version 2 application

4. Save the solution. Start the application, then click the **Go** button. The numbers 3, 2, and 1 appear (one at a time) in the label control, followed by the "Blast Off!" message. The spaceship is then dragged to the top of the form. Click the **Exit** button.

MINI-QUIZ 1

1. Write a Visual Basic For clause that creates a counter variable named intX and initializes it to 10. While the loop is processing, the counter variable should have values of 10, 12, 14, 16, 18, and 20. The loop should stop when the variable's value is 22.

2. Rewrite the For clause from Question 1 so that it initializes the counter variable to 30 and stops the loop when the variable's value is less than 0.

3. If the *startValue* is greater than the *endValue*, the *stepValue* must be a _____ number for the loop to be processed.

   a. negative   b. positive

HEY, TURN THAT NOISE DOWN!

You can make the Spaceship-Version 2 application more exciting by having it play the Rising Zap sound immediately before the spaceship blasts off. The Rising Zap sound is stored in an audio file named j0388399.wav; the file is contained in the current project's bin\Debug folder. (The audio file is from the Microsoft Office Clip Art collection, which is available at *http://office.microsoft.com*.) To have an application play an audio file while it is running, you use the syntax **My.Computer.Audio.Play(***fileName***)**. The My in the syntax refers to Visual Basic's **My feature**—a feature that exposes a set of commonly used objects to the programmer. One of the objects exposed by the My feature is the My.Computer object; not surprisingly, the My.Computer object refers to your computer. The My.Computer object provides access to other objects, such as your computer's Audio object. To have the Audio object play an audio file, you use its Play method. (If the audio file is not in the project's bin\Debug folder, you will need to include the path to the file in the *fileName* argument.)

To finish coding the Go button's Click event procedure, and then test the procedure:

1. Click the blank line below the Next intCount clause in the btnGo control's Click event procedure, then press **Enter** to insert a blank line. Type **' play an audio file** and press **Enter**. Type **my.computer.audio.play("j0388399.wav")** and press **Enter**.

2. Save the solution. Start the application, then click the **Go** button. The numbers 3, 2, and 1 appear (one at a time) in the label control, followed by the "Blast Off!" message. The spaceship is then dragged to the top of the form, and then you hear the Rising Zap sound. Click the **Exit** button.

3. It would be better if the Rising Zap sound played *before* the spaceship took off. You can accomplish this by pausing the program before the Do...Loop statement begins its processing. Click the **blank line** above the ' drag the spaceship to the top of the form comment, then press **Enter** to insert a blank line. Type **me.refresh()** and press **Enter**, then type **system.threading.thread.sleep(500)** and press **Enter**.

4. Save the solution. Start the application, then click the **Go** button. The numbers 3, 2, and 1 appear (one at a time) in the label control, followed by the "Blast Off!" message. The Rising Zap sound begins playing as the spaceship starts its journey to the top of the form.

5. Click the **Exit** button. Close the Code Editor window, then close the solution.

THE MONTHLY PAYMENT CALCULATOR APPLICATION

Figure 15-6 shows the interface for the Monthly Payment Calculator application, which displays monthly payments on a loan. The interface provides text boxes for the user to enter the principal and term. The principal is the amount of the loan, and the term is the number of years the borrower has to pay off the loan. The application will calculate the monthly payments using annual interest rates of 4% through 7%. It will display the annual interest rates and monthly payments in the lblPayments control. Figure 15-7 shows the application's output, processing, and input items, as well as its algorithm.

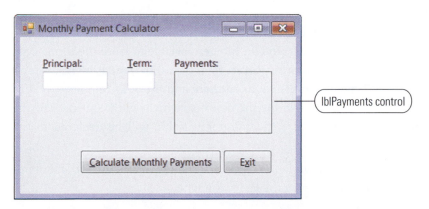

Figure 15-6: User interface for the Monthly Payment Calculator application

---

Output: monthly payment (for each annual interest rate)

Processing: annual interest rate (counter that counts from 4% through 7% in increments of 1%)

Input: principal
               term (in years)

Algorithm:
1. enter the principal and term
2. remove any previous monthly payments from the Payments box
3. repeat for annual interest rates from 4% through 7% in increments of 1%
        calculate the current monthly payment using the principal, term, and current annual
        interest rate
        display the current annual interest rate and the current monthly payment in the
        Payments box
   end repeat

Figure 15-7: Output, processing, input, and algorithm for the Monthly Payment Calculator application

To open the Monthly Payment Calculator application, and then begin coding the application:

1. Open the **Monthly Payment Solution** (**Monthly Payment Solution.sln**) file, which is contained in the ClearlyVB\Chap15\Monthly Payment Solution folder. If necessary, open the designer window.

2. Open the Code Editor window, then open the code template for the btnCalc control's Click event procedure. Type **' calculates and displays monthly payment amounts** and press **Enter** twice.

3. First, declare the necessary variables. You will use Decimal variables to store the principal and monthly payment amounts, and an Integer variable to store the term. Type **dim decPrincipal as decimal** and press **Enter**, then type **dim decPayment as decimal** and press **Enter**. Type **dim intTerm as integer** and press **Enter** twice. Notice that you are not declaring a variable for the counter, which will keep track of the annual interest rates; this is because the counter variable will be declared in the For...Next statement.

4. Next, assign the input items to variables. Enter the following comment and statements. Press **Enter** twice after typing the last statement.

    ' assign input to variables
    Decimal.TryParse(txtPrincipal.Text, decPrincipal)
    Integer.TryParse(txtTerm.Text, intTerm)

5. Before displaying the rates and payments in the lblPayments control, the procedure should remove any previous information from the control. Type **' clear label control** and press **Enter**, then type **lblPayments.text = string.empty** and press **Enter** twice.

6. Step 3 in the algorithm is a pretest loop whose instructions you want processed a precise number of times—in this case, from 4% through 7% in increments of 1%. You will use the For...Next statement to code this counter loop. Type **' calculate and display the monthly payments** and press **Enter**. Type **for decRate as decimal = .04 to .07 step .01** and press **Enter**. Notice that the For...Next statement's *startValue*, *endValue*, and *stepValue* can include decimal places, and that the counter variable's data type is Decimal.

7. Change the Next clause to **Next decRate**, then save the solution.

THE FINANCIAL.PMT METHOD

According to the algorithm shown in Figure 15-7, the first instruction in the loop should calculate the monthly payment using the principal, term, and current annual interest rate. The mathematical formula for calculating a periodic payment on a loan is rather complex, so Visual Basic provides a method that performs the calculation for you; the method is called the **Financial.Pmt method**. ("Pmt" stands for "Payment.") Figure 15-8 shows the method's basic syntax and lists the meaning of each of the three arguments included in the syntax. The *Rate* and *NPer* (number of periods) arguments must be expressed using the same units. If *Rate* is a monthly interest rate, then *NPer* must specify the number of monthly payments. Likewise, if *Rate* is an annual interest rate, then *NPer* must specify the number of annual payments. Figure 15-8 also includes examples of using the Financial.Pmt method. Example 1 calculates the annual payment for a loan of $9,000 for 3 years at 5% interest. As the example indicates, the annual payment returned by the Financial.Pmt method and rounded to the nearest cent is -3,304.88. This means that if you borrow $9,000 for 3 years at 5% interest, you will need to make three annual payments of $3,304.88 to pay off the loan. Notice that the Financial.Pmt method returns a negative number. To change the negative number to a positive number, you can precede the method with the negation operator, like this: -Financial.Pmt(.05, 3, 9000). As you learned in Chapter 6, the negation operator reverses the sign of a number: a negative number preceded by the negation operator becomes a positive number, and a positive number preceded by the negation operator becomes a negative number. The Financial.Pmt method in Example 2 in Figure 15-8 calculates the monthly payment for a loan of $12,000 for 5 years at 6% interest. In this example, the *Rate* and *NPer* arguments are expressed in monthly terms rather than in annual terms. The monthly payment for this loan, rounded to the nearest cent and changed to a positive number, is 231.99. (The Financial.Pmt method also can be used to calculate a periodic payment on an investment rather than on a loan. You learn how to do this in Computer Exercise 7.)

USING THE BASIC SYNTAX OF THE FINANCIAL.PMT METHOD
Syntax

Financial.Pmt(*Rate***,** *NPer***,** *PV***)**

Argument	Meaning
Rate	interest rate per period
NPer	total number of payment periods (the term)
PV	present value of the loan; in other words, the loan amount

Example 1 - Calculates the annual payment for a loan of $9,000 for 3 years at 5% interest. *Rate* is .05, *NPer* is 3, and *PV* is 9000.

Method: Financial.Pmt(.05, 3, 9000)

Annual payment (rounded to the nearest cent):   -3,304.88

Example 2 - Calculates the monthly payment for a loan of $12,000 for 5 years at 6% interest. *Rate* is .06/12, *NPer* is 5 * 12, and *PV* is 12000.

Method: -Financial.Pmt(.06 / 12, 5 * 12, 12000)

Monthly payment (rounded to the nearest cent and changed to a positive number): 231.99

Figure 15-8: Syntax and examples of the Financial.Pmt method

To continue coding the btnCalc control's Click event procedure, then test the application:

1. Click the **blank line** above the Next decRate clause. In this application, you will use the expression decRate / 12 as the Financial.Pmt method's *Rate* argument, and intTerm * 12 as its *NPer* argument. It is necessary to divide the annual interest rate by 12 to get a monthly rate, because you want to display monthly payments rather than annual payments. Similarly, you need to multiply the number of years by 12 to get the number of monthly payments. The method's *PV* argument will be decPrincipal. Type **decPayment = -financial.pmt(decRate/12, intTerm * 12, decPrincipal)** and press **Enter**. (Be sure to type the hyphen before the Financial.Pmt method.)

2. The next instruction in the loop should display both the current annual interest rate and the current monthly payment in the lblPayments control. You can do this using string concatenation, which you learned about in Chapter 14. You will separate the rate from the payment using the following characters: " -> " (a space, hyphen, greater than sign, space). Type the lines of code indicated in Figure 15-9.

```
Private Sub btnCalc_Click(ByVal sender As Object, ByVal e As System.EventArgs
    ' calculates and displays monthly payment amounts

    Dim decPrincipal As Decimal
    Dim decPayment As Decimal
    Dim intTerm As Integer

    ' assign input to variables
    Decimal.TryParse(txtPrincipal.Text, decPrincipal)
    Integer.TryParse(txtTerm.Text, intTerm)

    ' clear label control
    lblPayments.Text = String.Empty

    ' calculate and display the monthly payments
    For decRate As Decimal = 0.04 To 0.07 Step 0.01
        decPayment = -Financial.Pmt(decRate / 12, intTerm * 12, decPrincipal)
        lblPayments.Text = lblPayments.Text & decRate.ToString("P0") _
            & " -> " & decPayment.ToString("C2") _
            & ControlChars.NewLine
    Next decRate
End Sub
```

enter these 3 lines of code

Figure 15-9: Additional code entered in the btnCalc control's Click event procedure

3. The instructions in the For...Next loop in Figure 15-9 will be processed four times, using rates of 4%, 5%, 6%, and 7%. Save the solution, then start the application. First, display the monthly payments for a loan of $12,000 for 5 years. Type **12000** in the Principal box, then type **5** in the Term box. Click the **Calculate Monthly Payments** button. The four rates and monthly payments appear in the interface, as shown in Figure 15-10.

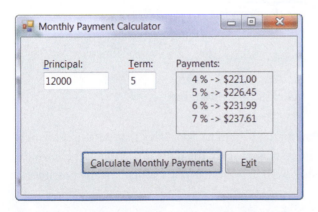

Figure 15-10: Rates and monthly payments shown in the interface

4. Remove the entries from the Principal and Term boxes, then click the **Calculate Monthly Payments** button; doing this results in a runtime error, also referred to as an **exception**. The Code Editor highlights the statement where the error was encountered, and it displays a help box that provides information pertaining to the error.

In this case, the Code Editor highlights the statement containing the Financial.Pmt method, and the help box indicates that the *NPer* argument does not contain a valid value.

5. Position your mouse pointer on intTerm in the highlighted statement, as shown in Figure 15-11. The variable contains the number 0, because no term was entered in the Term box.

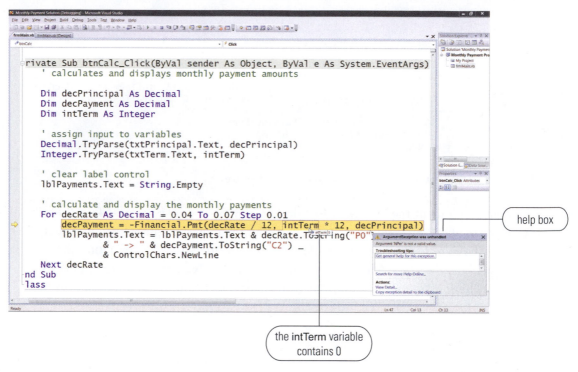

Figure 15-11: Result of the runtime error caused by an invalid *NPer* value

6. Click **Debug** on the menu bar, then click **Stop Debugging**.

As mentioned earlier, the Financial.Pmt method contains a complex mathematical formula for calculating a periodic payment. The term appears in the divisor portion of the formula; therefore, its value cannot be 0, because division by zero is not mathematically possible.

To complete the btnCalc control's Click event procedure, then test the application:

1. Click the **blank line** above the ' calculate and display the monthly payments comment, then press **Enter** to insert a blank line. Type **' determine whether the term is valid** and press **Enter**. Type the selection structure shown in Figure 15-12. You will need to move the comment and For...Next statement into the selection structure's false path.

```
                    ' clear label control
                    lblPayments.Text = String.Empty

                    ' determine whether the term is valid
                    If intTerm = 0 Then
                        MessageBox.Show("Please enter a valid term.", _
                                        "Monthly Payment Calculator", _
                                        MessageBoxButtons.OK, MessageBoxIcon.Information)
                    Else
                        ' calculate and display the monthly payments
                        For decRate As Decimal = 0.04 To 0.07 Step 0.01
                            decPayment = -Financial.Pmt(decRate / 12, intTerm * 12, decPrincipal)
                            lblPayments.Text = lblPayments.Text & decRate.ToString("P0") _
                                        & " -> " & decPayment.ToString("C2") _
                                        & ControlChars.NewLine
                        Next decRate
                    End If
                End Sub
```

enter this selection structure

Figure 15-12: Selection structure entered in the procedure

2. Save the solution, then start the application. Click the **Calculate Monthly Payments** button. The message "Please enter a valid term." appears in a message box. Click the **OK** button to close the message box.

3. Type **12000** in the Principal box, then type **5** in the Term box. Click the **Calculate Monthly Payments** button. The rates and monthly payments appear in the interface, as shown earlier in Figure 15-10.

4. Click the **Exit** button. Close the Code Editor window, then close the solution.

MINI-QUIZ 2

1. Write a Visual Basic statement to play an audio file named Giggle.wav.

2. For the Financial.Pmt method to display an annual payment, you will need to _____.

   a. divide the annual interest rate by 12

   b. multiply the annual interest rate by 12

   c. use the annual interest rate

3. You can use the _____ operator to change a negative number, such as the number returned by the Financial.Pmt method, to a positive number.

SUMMARY

» The For...Next statement provides a convenient way to code a counter loop. The loop is a pretest loop, because the condition is evaluated *before* the instructions in the loop are processed.

» A variable declared in a For clause has block scope and can be used only by the For...Next loop.

» The For...Next statement's counter variable must be numeric. Its *startValue*, *endValue*, and *stepValue* can be positive or negative numbers, integers or non-integers. If the *stepValue* is positive, the loop condition checks whether the counter variable's value is greater than the *endValue*. If the *stepValue* is negative, the loop condition checks whether the counter variable's value is less than the *endValue*.

» You can use the syntax My.Computer.Audio.Play(*fileName*) to play an audio file while an application is running.

» You can use the Financial.Pmt method to calculate a periodic payment on a loan or investment.

KEY TERMS

Counter loop—a loop that uses a counter variable to process the loop instructions a precise number of times

Exception—another term for a runtime error

Financial.Pmt method—can be used to calculate and return a periodic payment on a loan or investment

My feature—a Visual Basic feature that exposes a set of commonly used objects to the programmer

ANSWERS TO MINI-QUIZZES

MINI-QUIZ 1

1. For intX As Integer = 10 To 20 Step 2

2. For intX As Integer = 30 To 0 Step -2

3. a. negative

MINI-QUIZ 2

1. My.Computer.Audio.Play("Giggle.wav")

2. c. use the annual interest rate

3. negation (or -)

REVIEW QUESTIONS

1. A For...Next statement contains the following For clause: For intX As Integer = 2 To 11 Step 2. What value is stored in the intX variable when the statement ends?

   a. 11

   b. 12

   c. 13

   d. None of the above.

2. How many times will the MessageBox.Show method in the following code be processed?

   ```
   For intCounter As Integer = 4 To 11 Step 3

       MessageBox.Show("Hello")

   Next intCounter
   ```

   a. 3

   b. 4

   c. 5

   d. None of the above.

3. What is the value in the intCounter variable when the loop in Review Question 2 ends?

   a. 11   b. 12

   c. 13   d. 14

4. Which of the following calculates an annual payment on a $50,000 loan? The term is 10 years and the annual interest rate is 3%.

   a. -Financial.Pmt(.03 / 12, 10, 50000)

   b. -Financial.Pmt(.03 / 12, 10 * 12, 50000)

   c. -Financial.Pmt(.03, 10 * 12, 50000)

   d. -Financial.Pmt(.03, 10, 50000)

5. Which of the following calculates a monthly payment on a $50,000 loan? The term is 10 years and the annual interest rate is 3%.

   a. -Financial.Pmt(.03 / 12, 10, 50000)

   b. -Financial.Pmt(.03 / 12, 10 * 12, 50000)

   c. -Financial.Pmt(.03, 10 * 12, 50000)

   d. -Financial.Pmt(.03, 10, 50000)

EXERCISES

» TRY THIS

1. List the processing steps for the following code. Use Figure 15-2 as a guide. (The answers to TRY THIS Exercises are located at the end of the chapter.)

```
For decX As Decimal = 6.5 To 8.5
    MessageBox.Show(decX.ToString)
Next decX
```

» TRY THIS

2. In this exercise, you code an application that allows the user to enter two integers. The application then displays all of the odd numbers from the first integer to the second integer, and all of the even numbers from the first integer to the second integer. (The answers to TRY THIS Exercises are located at the end of the chapter.)

   a. Open the OddEven Solution (OddEven Solution.sln) file, which is contained in the ClearlyVB\Chap15\OddEven Solution folder. Open the Code Editor window. Code the application using the For...Next statement. If the integer in the txtNum1 control is greater than the integer in the txtNum2 control, the *stepValue* should be a negative number 1; otherwise, it should be a positive number 1.

   b. Save the solution, then start the application. Test the application by entering the integers 6 and 25. The application should display the following odd numbers: 7, 9, 11, 13, 15, 17, 19, 21, 23, and 25. It also should display the following even numbers: 6, 8, 10, 12, 14, 16, 18, 20, 22, and 24.

   c. Now test the application by entering the integers 25 and 6. The application should display the following odd numbers: 25, 23, 21, 19, 17, 15, 13, 11, 9, and 7. It also should display the following even numbers: 24, 22, 20, 18, 16, 14, 12, 10, 8, and 6. Stop the application, then close the solution.

3. In this exercise, you modify the My Dream Car-Version 1 application coded in Chapter 14. Open the Car Solution (Car Solution.sln) file, which is contained in the ClearlyVB\ Chap15\Car Solution-Version 1 folder. Open the Code Editor window. Locate the btnClickMe control's Click event procedure. Change the procedure's code so that it uses the For...Next statement rather than the Do...Loop statement. Save the solution. Start and then test the application. Stop the application, then close the solution.

» **MODIFY THIS**

4. Open the New Salary Solution (New Salary Solution.sln) file, which is contained in the ClearlyVB\Chap15\New Salary Solution folder. The application allows the user to enter his or her current salary. The Calculate button's Click event procedure should calculate the new salary amounts using rates of 2% through 6% in increments of .5%. Display the rates and salary amounts in the lblNewSalary control. Save the solution. Start and then test the application. Stop the application, then close the solution.

» **INTRODUCTORY**

5. In this exercise, you code an application that displays the quarterly payments on a loan.

» **INTRODUCTORY**

   a. Open the Quarterly Payment Solution (Quarterly Payment Solution.sln) file, which is contained in the ClearlyVB\Chap15\Quarterly Payment Solution folder. The interface allows the user to enter the principal and the rate (as a decimal number).

   b. Open the Code Editor window. Both text boxes should accept only numbers, the period, and the Backspace key. Code the appropriate event procedures.

   c. The Calculate Quarterly Payments button should calculate the quarterly payments using the principal and rate entered by the user, and terms of 2, 3, 4, and 5 years. If the rate is entered as an integer (which means it's greater than or equal to 1), convert the integer to its decimal equivalent by dividing it by 100. Display the terms and quarterly payments in the lblPayments control.

   d. Save the solution. Start and then test the application. Stop the application, then close the solution.

6. In this exercise, you modify the Spaceship-Version 1 application coded in the chapter.

» **INTERMEDIATE**

   a. Use Windows to make a copy of the Spaceship Solution-Version 1 folder. Save the copy in the ClearlyVB\Chap15 folder. Rename the copy Modified Spaceship Solution-Version 1.

   b. Open the Spaceship Solution (Spaceship Solution.sln) file contained in the Modified Spaceship Solution-Version 1 folder. Open the designer window, then open the Code Editor window. Modify the Go button's Click event procedure so that it uses a For...Next statement (rather than a Do...Loop statement) to drag the spaceship to the top of the form.

   c. Save the solution. Start and then test the application. Stop the application, then close the solution.

INTERMEDIATE

7. In this exercise, you learn how to use the Financial.Pmt method to calculate a periodic payment on an investment (rather than on a loan).

   a. Open the Investment Solution (Investment Solution.sln) file, which is contained in the ClearlyVB\Chap15\Investment Solution folder. The application should calculate the amount you need to save each month to accumulate $40,000 at the end of 20 years, assuming a 6% interest rate. You can calculate this amount using the syntax **Financial.Pmt(***Rate*, *NPer*, *PV*, *FV***)**. The *Rate* argument is the interest rate per period, and the *NPer* argument is the total number of payment periods. The *PV* argument is the present value of the investment, which is 0 (zero). The *FV* argument is the future value of the investment. The future value is the amount you want to accumulate.

   b. Open the Code Editor window and code the btnCalc control's Click event procedure. Display the monthly amount as a positive number. Save the solution, then start and test the application. (The answer should be $86.57.) Stop the application.

   c. Modify the application to allow you to enter any future value. Use the InputBox function. Save the solution, then start and test the application. Stop the application, then close the solution.

ADVANCED

8. In this exercise, you create an application that displays a monthly payment on a loan of $3000 for 1 year at 7% interest. The application also should display the amount applied to the loan's principal each month, and the amount that represents interest. The application will use the Financial.Pmt method, which you learned about in the chapter, to calculate the monthly payment. It also will use the Financial.PPmt method to calculate the portion of the payment applied to the principal each month. The method's syntax is **Financial.PPmt(***Rate*, *Per*, *NPer*, *PV***)**, where *Rate* is the interest rate, *NPer* is the number of payment periods, and *PV* is the present value of the loan. The *Per* argument is the payment period in which you are interested and must be from 1 through *NPer*.

   a. List the output and input items, as well as any processing items, then create an appropriate algorithm using pseudocode.

   b. Create a new Visual Basic Windows application. Name the solution, project, and form file Principal and Interest Solution, Principal and Interest Project, and frmMain.vb, respectively. Save the application in the ClearlyVB\Chap15 folder. If necessary, change the form's name to frmMain.

   c. Create the interface shown in Figure 15-13. Set the text box's Font property to Courier New, 9 pt. Set its Multiline and ReadOnly properties to True, and its ScrollBars property to Vertical.

   d. Code the application using a For...Next statement to keep track of the Financial.PPmt method's *Per* argument. The *Per* values will be from 1 through 12.

e. Save the solution, then start and test the application. (Hint: The monthly payment should be $259.58. In the first month, 242.08 is applied to the principal, and 17.50 is interest.) Stop the application, then close the solution.

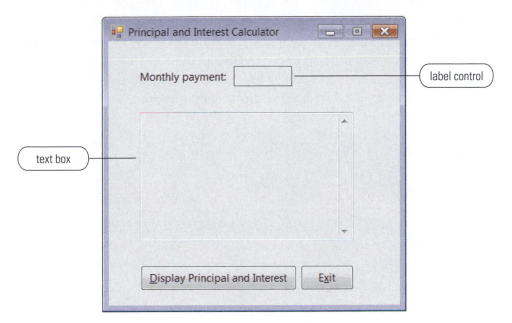

Figure 15-13: Principal and Interest Calculator interface

9. In this exercise, you create an application for the accountant at Sonheim Manufacturing Company. The application will display an asset's annual depreciation schedule. The accountant will enter the asset's cost, useful life (in years), and salvage value (which is the asset's value at the end of its useful life). The application should use the double-declining balance method to calculate the annual depreciation amounts; you can calculate the amounts using the Financial.DDB method. The method's syntax is **Financial.DDB(**cost, *salvage*, *life*, *period*), where *period* is the period for which you want the depreciation amount calculated.

     » **ADVANCED**

a. List the output and input items, as well as any processing items, then create an appropriate algorithm using pseudocode.

b. Create a new Visual Basic Windows application. Name the solution, project, and form file Sonheim Solution, Sonheim Project, and frmMain.vb, respectively. Save the application in the ClearlyVB\Chap15 folder. If necessary, change the form's name to frmMain.

c. Create the interface shown in Figure 15-14. Set the txtSchedule control's Multiline and ReadOnly properties to True, and its ScrollBars property to Vertical.

d. Code the application using a For...Next statement to keep track of the Financial.DDB method's *period* argument. The *period* values will be from 1 through the value in the *life* argument. The cost, life, and salvage text boxes should accept numbers and the Backspace key. The cost and salvage text boxes also should accept the period.

e. Save the solution, then start the application. Enter 1000, 4, and 100 as the cost, life, and salvage value, respectively. Click the Display Depreciation Schedule button. The annual depreciation amounts for the four years should be 500.00, 250.00, 125.00, and 25.00. Stop the application, then close the solution.

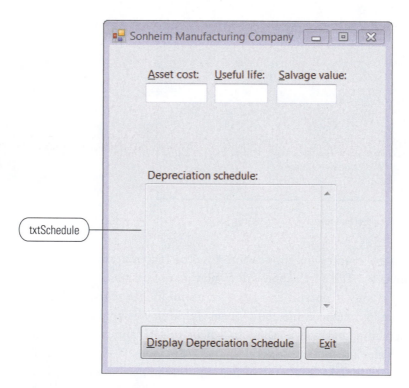

Figure 15-14: Sonheim Manufacturing interface

10. Open the FigureThisOut Solution (FigureThisOut Solution.sln) file, which is contained in the ClearlyVB\Chap15\FigureThisOut Solution folder. Open the Code Editor window and study the existing code. The btnCalc control's Click event procedure gets four test scores from the user and then calculates and displays the number of test scores entered and the average test score. Start the application, then click the Calculate button. Type 100 and press Enter, then type 85 and press Enter. Click the

Cancel button. Notice that the InputBox function's dialog box appears again. Click the Cancel button. Does the application display the correct number of scores entered and the correct average? Research the For...Next statement, looking for a way to stop the loop prematurely. Modify the btnCalc control's Click event procedure so the loop stops when the user clicks the Cancel button. Start and then test the application. Stop the application, then close the solution.

11. In this exercise, you find an error in an application's code. Open the SwatTheBugs Solution (SwatTheBugs Solution.sln) file, which is contained in the ClearlyVB\ Chap15\SwatTheBugs Solution folder. Start and then test the application. Notice that the application is not working correctly. Click the Exit button. Open the Code Editor window. Locate and correct any errors in the code. Save the solution, then start and test the application again. Stop the application, then close the solution.

ANSWERS TO "TRY THIS" EXERCISES

1. See Figure 15-15.

1. The computer creates the decX variable and initializes it to 6.5.
2. The computer checks whether the value in the decX variable is greater than 8.5. It's not, so the computer displays the number 6.5 in a message box, and then adds 1 to the contents of the decX variable, giving 7.5.
3. The computer again checks whether the value in the decX variable is greater than 8.5. It's not, so the computer displays the number 7.5 in a message box, and then adds 1 to the contents of the decX variable, giving 8.5.
4. The computer again checks whether the value in the decX variable is greater than 8.5. It's not, so the computer displays the number 8.5 in a message box, and then adds 1 to the contents of the decX variable, giving 9.5.
5. The computer again checks whether the value in the decX variable is greater than 8.5. It is, so the computer stops processing the For...Next loop. Processing continues with the statement following the Next clause.

Figure 15-15

2. See Figure 15-16.

```vb
Private Sub btnDisplay_Click(ByVal sender As Object, _
    ByVal e As System.EventArgs) Handles btnDisplay.Click
    ' displays the odd and even numbers from one integer to another

    Dim intNum1 As Integer
    Dim intNum2 As Integer
    Dim intStep As Integer

    Integer.TryParse(txtNum1.Text, intNum1)
    Integer.TryParse(txtNum2.Text, intNum2)

    ' determine stepValue
    If intNum1 > intNum2 Then
        intStep = -1
    Else
        intStep = 1
    End If

    lblOdd.Text = String.Empty
    lblEven.Text = String.Empty

    For intNumber As Integer = intNum1 To intNum2 Step intStep
        If intNumber Mod 2 = 0 Then
            lblEven.Text = lblEven.Text & intNumber.ToString _
                & ControlChars.NewLine
        Else
            lblOdd.Text = lblOdd.Text & intNumber.ToString _
                & ControlChars.NewLine
        End If
    Next intNumber
End Sub
```

Figure 15-16

16

I'M ON THE INSIDE; YOU'RE ON THE OUTSIDE

After studying Chapter 16, you should be able to:

Nest repetition structures

Utilize a text box's Multiline, ReadOnly, and

ScrollBars properties

ONE LOOP WITHIN ANOTHER LOOP

Like selection structures, repetition structures can be nested. In other words, you can place one repetition structure (called the nested or inner repetition structure) within another repetition structure (called the outer repetition structure). Both repetition structures can be pretest loops, or both can be posttest loops. Or, one can be a pretest loop and the other a posttest loop. A programmer determines whether a problem's solution requires a nested repetition structure by studying the problem specification. Figure 16-1 shows a problem specification and algorithm from Chapter 13. The algorithm requires a repetition structure because the instructions for signing a book need to be repeated for every customer. However, the algorithm does not require a nested repetition structure. This is because all of the instructions within the repetition structure should be followed only once per customer.

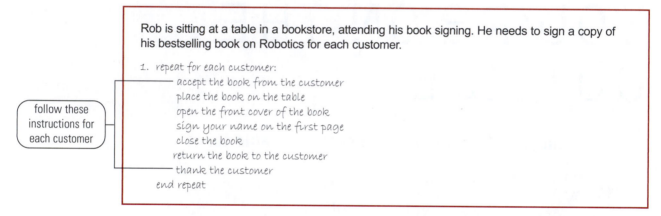

Figure 16-1: Problem specification and algorithm for signing one book for each customer

Now consider the possibility that a customer may have more than one book for Rob to sign. It's even possible that a customer, not knowing about the book signing in advance, has left his book at home and is standing in line for the sole purpose of meeting Rob. What changes will need to be made to the algorithm shown in Figure 16-1? The current instructions within the repetition structure still must be repeated for each customer. In addition, however, all but the last instruction in the loop (the thank the customer instruction) must be repeated for each of the customer's books. You will need to use a nested repetition structure to include this additional task in the algorithm. Rob will thank the customer only after all of the customer's books have been signed, so the thank the customer instruction should not be part of the nested loop. Figure 16-2 shows the modified algorithm, which contains an outer repetition structure and a nested repetition structure. The outer repetition structure begins with the repeat for each customer: line and it ends with the last end repeat line. The nested repetition structure begins with the repeat for each of the customer's books: line and it ends with the first end repeat line. All of the instructions will be followed for each customer; however, six instructions also will be followed for each book the customer wants signed.

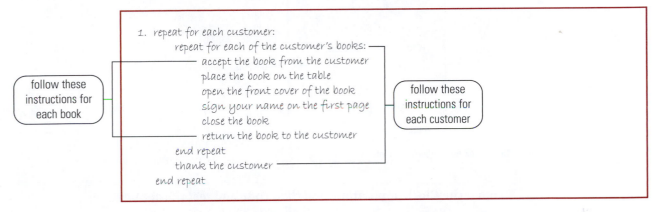

Figure 16-2: Problem specification and algorithm for signing zero or more books for each customer

CLOCK APPLICATION

A clock uses nested repetition structures to keep track of the time. For example, consider a clock's hour and minute hands only. The minute hand is controlled by the inner (nested) loop, whereas the hour hand is controlled by the outer loop. The minute hand on a clock moves one position, clockwise, for every minute that has elapsed. After the minute hand moves 60 positions, the hour hand moves one position, also clockwise. The minute hand then begins its journey around the clock again. Figure 16-3 shows the logic used by a clock's hour and minute hands. Notice that the entire nested loop is contained within the outer loop; this must be true for the loop to be nested and for it to work correctly.

```
1. repeat for hours from 0 through 23 in increments of 1
      repeat for minutes from 0 through 59 in increments of 1
            move minute hand 1 position, clockwise
      end repeat
      move hour hand 1 position, clockwise
   end repeat
```

Figure 16-3: Logic used by a clock's hour and minute hands

Figure 16-4 shows the interface for the Clock application. (The clock image is from the Microsoft Office Clip Art collection, which is available at *http://office.microsoft.com.*) In the Start button's Click event procedure, you will have an outer loop display the number of hours, and a nested loop display the number of minutes.

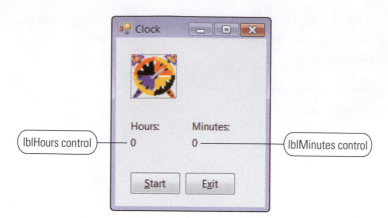

Figure 16-4: Clock application's user interface

To open the Clock application, and then code and test the application:

1. Start Visual Studio 2008 (or Visual Basic 2008 Express Edition). Open the **Clock Solution** (**Clock Solution.sln**) file, which is contained in the ClearlyVB\ Chap16\Clock Solution folder. If necessary, open the designer window.

2. Open the Code Editor window, then open the code template for the btnStart control's Click event procedure. Type **' displays hours and minutes** and press **Enter** twice.

3. For simplicity in watching the hours tick away in the interface, you will display hour values from 0 through 3 rather than from 0 through 23. Type **for intHours as integer = 0 to 3** and press **Enter**, then type **lblHours.text = intHours.tostring** and press **Enter**.

4. You also will display minute values from 0 through 9 rather than from 0 through 59. Type **for intMinutes as integer = 0 to 9** and press **Enter**, then type **lblMinutes.text = intMinutes.tostring** and press **Enter**.

5. You will need to refresh the interface and then pause program execution to see each of the hour and minute values in the interface. Type **me.refresh()** and press **Enter**, then type **system.threading.thread.sleep(500)** to pause program execution for a half of a second.

6. Change the nested Next clause to **Next intMinutes**, and change the outer Next clause to **Next intHours**. See Figure 16-5.

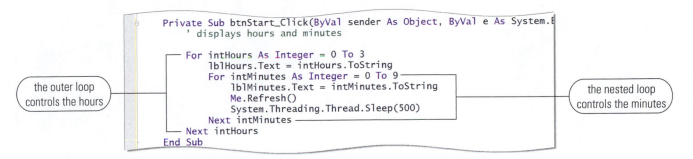

```
Private Sub btnStart_Click(ByVal sender As Object, ByVal e As System.E
    ' displays hours and minutes

    For intHours As Integer = 0 To 3
        lblHours.Text = intHours.ToString
        For intMinutes As Integer = 0 To 9
            lblMinutes.Text = intMinutes.ToString
            Me.Refresh()
            System.Threading.Thread.Sleep(500)
        Next intMinutes
    Next intHours
End Sub
```

the outer loop controls the hours

the nested loop controls the minutes

Figure 16-5: Start button's Click event procedure

7. Save the solution. Start the application, then click the **Start** button. The number 0 appears in the lblHours control, and the numbers 0 through 9 appear (one at a time) in the lblMinutes control. Notice that the number of hours is increased by 1 when the number of minutes changes from 9 to 0. (On a real digital clock, the hour value is updated when the number of minutes changes from 59 to 0.) When the procedure ends, the lblHours and lblMinutes controls contain the numbers 3 and 9, respectively. (If you want to end the procedure prematurely, click the form in the designer window, then click Debug on the menu bar, and then click Stop Debugging.)

8. Click the **Exit** button. Close the Code Editor window, then close the solution.

For more examples of nested repetition structures, see the Nested Repetition Structures section in the Ch16WantMore.pdf file.

The Ch16-Nested Loops video demonstrates nested loops by stepping through the code.

REVISITING THE MONTHLY PAYMENT CALCULATOR APPLICATION

Figure 16-6 shows the output, processing, and input items, as well as the algorithm, for the Monthly Payment Calculator application from Chapter 15. The application calculates and displays the monthly payments on a loan. The payments are calculated using the principal and term entered by the user, along with a loop that varies the annual interest rates from 4% through 7%.

Output: monthly payment (for each annual interest rate)

Processing: annual interest rate (counter that counts from 4% through 7% in increments of 1%)

Input: principal
               term (in years)

Algorithm:
1. enter the principal and term
2. remove any previous monthly payments from the Payments box
3. repeat for annual interest rates from 4% through 7% in increments of 1%
      calculate the current monthly payment using the principal, term, and current annual
      interest rate
      display the current annual interest rate and the current monthly payment in the
      Payments box
   end repeat

Figure 16-6: Planning information for the Monthly Payment Calculator application from Chapter 15

Now let's say you are asked to modify the application so that, rather than having the user enter the term, it automatically uses terms of 2 through 5 years. What changes would need to be made to the algorithm shown in Figure 16-6? Obviously, you would change the first instruction to enter the principal. The second instruction, which clears the contents of the Payments box, would still be necessary. Step 3's repetition structure contains the instructions to calculate and display the monthly payments. Currently, the instructions are repeated for annual interest rates from 4% through 7%. The instructions also need to be repeated for terms from 2 through 5 years. You can accomplish this task by including an additional loop in the algorithm. You can either nest the term loop within the rate loop, or nest the rate loop within the term loop. But how do you determine the nested loop? If you want to display the monthly payments by term within rate—for example, display the payments for 2 through 5 years using a 4% rate, followed by the payments for 2 through 5 years using a 5% rate, and so on—you would nest the term loop within the rate loop. However, if you want to display the monthly payments by rate within term— for example, display the 2-year payments for 4% through 7%, followed by the 3-year payments for 4% through 7%, and so on—you would nest the rate loop within the term loop.

Figure 16-7 shows the planning information for the modified Monthly Payment Calculator application. The algorithm will display the monthly payments by rate within term.

```
Output:        monthly payment (for each annual interest rate within each term)

Processing:    annual interest rate (counter that counts from 4% through 7% in increments of 1%)
               term (counter that counts from 2 years through 5 years in increments of 1 year)

Input:         principal

Algorithm:
1.  enter the principal
2.  remove any previous monthly payments from the Payments box
3.  repeat for terms from 2 years through 5 years in increments of 1 year
        display the term in the Payments box
        repeat for annual interest rates from 4% through 7% in increments of 1%
            calculate the current monthly payment using the principal, term, and current
            annual interest rate
            display the current annual interest rate and the current monthly payment in the
            Payments box
        end repeat
        display a blank line in the Payments box to separate the current term's information from
        the next term's information
    end repeat
```

Figure 16-7: Planning information for the modified Monthly Payment Calculator application

To open the Monthly Payment Calculator application, and then code the application:

1. Open the **Monthly Payment Solution** (**Monthly Payment Solution.sln**) file, which is contained in the ClearlyVB\Chap16\Monthly Payment Solution-Version 1 folder. If necessary, open the designer window. The application's user interface is shown in Figure 16-8. The user will enter the principal in the txtPrincipal control. When the user clicks the Calculate Monthly Payments button, the payments will appear in the txtPayments control.

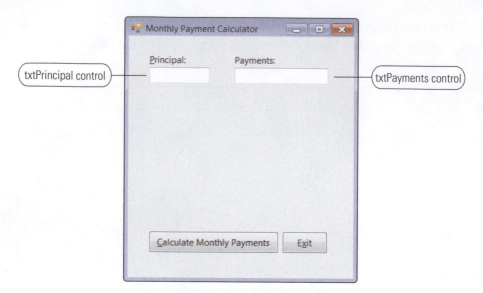

Figure 16-8: User interface for the Monthly Payment Calculator application

You may be wondering why the interface uses a text box rather than a label control to display the monthly payments. Although you can display a great deal of information in both types of controls, a text box can have scroll bars, which allow you to view any information not currently showing in the control. However, for a text box to include scroll bars, its ScrollBars and Multiline properties must be set appropriately. The **ScrollBars property** indicates whether any scroll bars appear on the text box. To include scroll bars, you need to change the property's setting from None to either Horizontal, Vertical, or Both. A text box's **Multiline property** specifies whether the text can span more than one line in the control. For a text box to contain scroll bars, its Multiline property must be set to True.

2. Click the **txtPayments control**. Change the control's Multiline property to **True**, and change its ScrollBars property to **Vertical**. A vertical scroll bar appears on the right side of the text box.

As you know, users cannot edit the contents of a label control while the application is running; however, they can edit the contents of a text box. In this application, however, the user should not be allowed to change the payments displayed in the txtPayments control. You can prevent the user from editing the contents of a text box by setting the text box's **ReadOnly property** to True.

3. Change the txtPayments control's ReadOnly property to **True**. Notice that the text box is now colored gray rather than white.

4. To display more monthly payments in the control, set the txtPayments control's Size property to **155, 240**. Save the solution.

5. Open the Code Editor window, then open the code template for the btnCalc control's Click event procedure. Type **' calculates and displays monthly payment amounts** and press **Enter**, then type **' using terms of 2 through 5 years and rates from 4% through 7%** and press **Enter** twice.

6. First, declare Decimal variables to store the principal and monthly payment amounts. Type **dim decPrincipal as decimal** and press **Enter**, then type **dim decPayment as decimal** and press **Enter** twice. Notice that you are not declaring variables to store the annual interest rates and terms; this is because the variables will be declared in the For...Next statements.

7. Next, assign the principal to a variable. Type **' assign principal to a variable** and press **Enter**, then type **decimal.tryparse(txtPrincipal.text, decPrincipal)** and press **Enter** twice.

8. Now remove any previous payments from the Payments box before displaying the current payments. Type **' clear the Payments box** and press **Enter**, then type **txtPayments.text = string.empty** and press **Enter** twice.

9. Step 3 in the algorithm begins with a pretest loop whose instructions should be processed for values from 2 through 5 in increments of 1. You will use the For...Next statement to code this counter loop. Type **' calculate and display the monthly payments** and press **Enter**. Type **for intTerm as integer = 2 to 5** and press **Enter**, then change the Next clause to **Next intTerm**.

10. The first instruction in the outer loop is to display the term in the txtPayments control. Click the **blank line** below the For clause, then enter the following two lines of code.

    txtPayments.text = txtPayments.text _
        & "Term: " & intTerm.tostring & controlchars.newline

11. The next instruction in the outer loop is another pretest loop; in this case, the loop instructions should be processed for values from 4% through 7% in increments of 1%. Here again, you will use the For...Next statement to code this counter loop. Type **for decRate as decimal = .04 to .07 step .01** and press **Enter**, then change the nested Next clause to **Next decRate**.

12. The two instructions in the nested loop should calculate and display the monthly payment amounts along with their corresponding annual interest rate. Click the **blank line** below the nested For clause, then enter the following lines of code, which completes the nested repetition structure.

    decPayment = -Financial.Pmt(decRate / 12, intTerm * 12, decPrincipal)
    txtPayments.Text = txtPayments.Text & decRate.ToString("P0") _
        & " -> " & decPayment.ToString("C2") _
        & ControlChars.NewLine

13. Click **after the last e** in the Next decRate clause, then press **Enter** to insert a blank line below the clause.

14. The last instruction in the outer loop should display a blank line in the Payments box. This will separate the current term's information from the previous term's information. In the blank line below the Next decRate clause, type **txtPayments.Text = txtPayments.Text & ControlChars.NewLine**.

15. Save the solution, then compare the code on your screen with the code shown in Figure 16-9.

```vb
Private Sub btnCalc_Click(ByVal sender As Object, _
    ByVal e As System.EventArgs) Handles btnCalc.Click
    ' calculates and displays monthly payment amounts
    ' using terms of 2 through 5 years and rates from 4% through 7%

    Dim decPrincipal As Decimal
    Dim decPayment As Decimal

    ' assign principal to a variable
    Decimal.TryParse(txtPrincipal.Text, decPrincipal)

    ' clear the Payments box
    txtPayments.Text = String.Empty

    ' calculate and display the monthly payments
    For intTerm As Integer = 2 To 5
        txtPayments.Text = txtPayments.Text _
            & "Term: " & intTerm.ToString & ControlChars.NewLine
        For decRate As Decimal = 0.04 To 0.07 Step 0.01
            decPayment = -Financial.Pmt(decRate / 12, intTerm * 12, decPrincipal)
            txtPayments.Text = txtPayments.Text & decRate.ToString("P0") _
                & " -> " & decPayment.ToString("C2") _
                & ControlChars.NewLine
        Next decRate
        txtPayments.Text = txtPayments.Text & ControlChars.NewLine
    Next intTerm
End Sub
```

Figure 16-9: Click event procedure for the btnCalc control

Now you will test the code to determine if it works correctly.

To test the Monthly Payment Calculator application:

1. Start the application. Type **12000** in the Principal box, then click the **Calculate Monthly Payments** button. The terms, rates, and monthly payments appear in the interface, as shown in Figure 16-10.

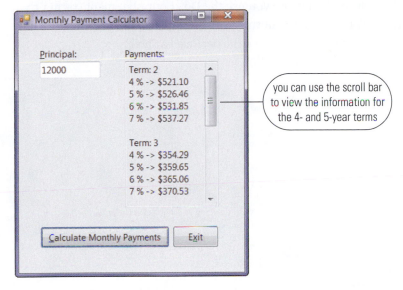

Figure showing Monthly Payment Calculator with callout: "you can use the scroll bar to view the information for the 4- and 5-year terms"

Figure 16-10: Interface showing the terms, rates, and payments

2. Use the scroll bar to view the monthly payments for the 4- and 5-year terms.

3. Delete the contents of the Principal box, then click the **Calculate Monthly Payments** button. A monthly payment of $0.00 appears for each rate within each term.

4. Click the **Exit** button. Close the Code Editor window, then close the solution.

BUT I WANT TO DO IT A DIFFERENT WAY

Rather than using two For...Next statements to code the Monthly Payment Calculator application, you also can use two Do...Loop statements or one For...Next statement and one Do...Loop statement. In the next set of steps, you will modify the Monthly Payment Calculator application so that it uses a Do...Loop statement to keep track of the annual interest rates.

To modify the Monthly Payment Calculator application:

1. Use Windows to make a copy of the Monthly Payment Solution-Version 1 folder. Save the copy in the ClearlyVB\Chap16 folder. Rename the copy Monthly Payment Solution-Version 2.

2. Open the **Monthly Payment Solution** (**Monthly Payment Solution.sln**) file contained in the Monthly Payment Solution-Version 2 folder. Open the designer window, then open the Code Editor window.

3. Locate the btnCalc control's Click event procedure. Modify the procedure's code as shown in Figure 16-11. Notice that when you use the Do...Loop statement (rather than the For...Next statement) to keep track of the annual interest rates, you must include instructions to declare, initialize, and update the decRate variable.

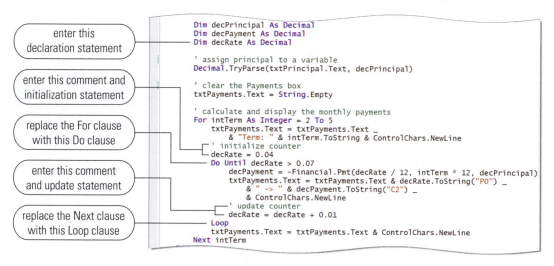

enter this declaration statement

enter this comment and initialization statement

replace the For clause with this Do clause

enter this comment and update statement

replace the Next clause with this Loop clause

```
Dim decPrincipal As Decimal
Dim decPayment As Decimal
Dim decRate As Decimal

' assign principal to a variable
Decimal.TryParse(txtPrincipal.Text, decPrincipal)

' clear the Payments box
txtPayments.Text = String.Empty

' calculate and display the monthly payments
For intTerm As Integer = 2 To 5
    txtPayments.Text = txtPayments.Text _
        & "Term: " & intTerm.ToString & ControlChars.NewLine
    ' initialize counter
    decRate = 0.04
    Do Until decRate > 0.07
        decPayment = -Financial.Pmt(decRate / 12, intTerm * 12, decPrincipal)
        txtPayments.Text = txtPayments.Text & decRate.ToString("P0") _
            & " -> " & decPayment.ToString("C2") _
            & ControlChars.NewLine
        ' update counter
        decRate = decRate + 0.01
    Loop
    txtPayments.Text = txtPayments.Text & ControlChars.NewLine
Next intTerm
```

Figure 16-11: Modified code contained in the btnCalc control's Click event procedure

4. Save the solution, then start the application. Type **12000** in the Principal box, then click the **Calculate Monthly Payments** button. The terms, rates, and monthly payments appear in the interface, as shown earlier in Figure 16-10. Click the **Exit** button. Close the Code Editor window, then close the solution.

MINI-QUIZ 1

1. Write the code to display the following pattern using two pretest loops along with the letter X. Use the Do...Loop statement for the outer loop. Use the For...Next statement for the nested loop. Display the pattern in the lblPattern control.

    XXXX

    XXXX

    XXXX

2. Rewrite the code from Question 1 using a For...Next statement for the outer loop and a Do...Loop statement for the nested loop.

3. For a text box to display scroll bars, its _____ property must be set to True.

    a. DisplayBars   b. Multiline

    c. Scrollable   d. ScrollBars

SUMMARY

» Repetition structures can be nested, which means you can place one repetition structure within another repetition structure.

» For a nested repetition structure to work correctly, it must be contained entirely within the outer repetition structure.

» When a text box's Multiline property is set to True, it can accept multiple lines of text.

» A text box's ScrollBars property determines whether scroll bars appear on the control. However, for the ScrollBars property to take effect, the text box's Multiline property must be set to True.

» You can prevent the user from editing the contents of a text box by setting the text box's ReadOnly property to True.

KEY TERMS

Multiline property—the text box property that specifies whether the text can span more than one line in the control

ReadOnly property—the text box property that specifies whether the contents of the text box can be edited by the user

ScrollBars property—the text box property that indicates whether scroll bars appear on the control; used in conjunction with the Multiline property

ANSWERS TO MINI-QUIZ

MINI-QUIZ 1

1.
```
Dim intOuter As Integer
intOuter = 1
Do While intOuter < 4
    For intNested As Integer = 1 To 4
        lblPattern.Text = lblPattern.Text & "X"
    Next intNested
    lblPattern.Text = lblPattern.Text & ControlChars.NewLine
    intOuter = intOuter + 1
Loop
```

2.
```
Dim intNested As Integer
For intOuter = 1 To 3
    intNested = 1
    Do While intNested < 5
        lblPattern.Text = lblPattern.Text & "X"
        intNested = intNested + 1
    Loop
    lblPattern.Text = lblPattern.Text & ControlChars.NewLine
Next intOuter
```

3. b. Multiline

REVIEW QUESTIONS

1. Which of the following will <u>not</u> display four asterisks on each of three lines in the lblAsterisks control?

   a. lblAsterisks.Text = "****" & ControlChars.NewLine & "****" & ControlChars.NewLine & "****"

   b. For intCounter As Integer = 1 To 3
         lblAsterisks.Text = lblAsterisks.Text & "****" & ControlChars.NewLine
     Next intCounter

   c. For intX As Integer = 1 To 4
         For intY As Integer = 1 To 3
            lblAsterisks.Text = lblAsterisks.Text & "*"
         Next intY
         lblAsterisks.Text = lblAsterisks.Text & ControlChars.NewLine
     Next intX

   d. For intX As Integer = 1 To 3
         For intY As Integer = 1 To 4
            lblAsterisks.Text = lblAsterisks.Text & "*"
         Next intY
         lblAsterisks.Text = lblAsterisks.Text & ControlChars.NewLine
     Next intX

2. How many times will the MessageBox.Show method in the following code be processed?

   For intX As Integer = 4 To 11 Step 3
       For intY As Integer = 1 To 3
           MessageBox.Show("Hello")
       Next intY
     Next intX

   a. 9   b. 10

   c. 11   d. None of the above.

3. What is the value in the intY variable when the nested loop in Review Question 2 ends?

   a. 0   b. 1

   c. 3   d. None of the above.

4. Which of the following will <u>not</u> display the number 123 on each of two lines in the lblNumbers control? (The intY variable was declared with the statement Dim intY As Integer.)

a. For intX As Integer = 1 To 2
    intY = 1
    Do
        lblNumbers.Text = lblNumbers.Text & intY.ToString
        intY = intY + 1
    Loop Until intY > 3
    lblNumbers.Text = lblNumbers.Text & ControlChars.NewLine
Next intX

b. intY = 1
Do Until intY > 2
    For intX As Integer = 1 To 3
        lblNumbers.Text = lblNumbers.Text & intX.ToString
        intY = intY + 1
    Next intX
    lblNumbers.Text = lblNumbers.Text & ControlChars.NewLine
Loop

c. For intX As Integer = 1 To 2
    intY = 1
    Do Until intY > 3
        lblNumbers.Text = lblNumbers.Text & intY.ToString
        intY = intY + 1
    Loop
    lblNumbers.Text = lblNumbers.Text & ControlChars.NewLine
Next intX

d. intY = 1
Do Until intY > 2
    For intX As Integer = 1 To 3
        lblNumbers.Text = lblNumbers.Text & intX.ToString
    Next intX
    intY = intY + 1
    lblNumbers.Text = lblNumbers.Text & ControlChars.NewLine
Loop

5. How can you prevent the user from editing the contents of a text box while an application is running?

   a. Set the text box's Editable property to False.

   b. Set the text box's Changeable property to False.

   c. Set the text box's ReadOnly property to True.

   d. Set the text box's WriteOnly property to False.

EXERCISES

1. In this exercise, you modify the Clock application coded in the chapter. Use Windows to make a copy of the Clock Solution folder. Save the copy in the ClearlyVB\Chap16 folder. Rename the copy Clock Solution-TRY THIS 1. Open the Clock Solution (Clock Solution.sln) file, which is contained in the ClearlyVB\Chap16\Clock Solution-TRY THIS 1 folder. Open the designer window, then open the Code Editor window. Modify the btnStart control's Click event procedure so that it uses Do...Loop statements rather than For...Next statements. Use the Until keyword in the Do clause. Save the solution, then start and test the application. Stop the application, then close the solution. (The answers to TRY THIS Exercises are located at the end of the chapter.)

    »TRY THIS

2. In this exercise, you modify the Clock application coded in the chapter. Use Windows to make a copy of the Clock Solution folder. Save the copy in the ClearlyVB\Chap16 folder. Rename the copy Clock Solution-TRY THIS 2. Open the Clock Solution (Clock Solution.sln) file, which is contained in the ClearlyVB\Chap16\Clock Solution-TRY THIS 2 folder. Open the designer window, then open the Code Editor window. Modify the btnStart control's Click event procedure so that it uses a posttest loop to display the number of minutes. Use the While keyword in the Loop clause. Save the solution, then start and test the application. Stop the application, then close the solution. (The answers to TRY THIS Exercises are located at the end of the chapter.)

    »TRY THIS

3. In this exercise, you modify one of the Monthly Payment Calculator applications coded in the chapter. Use Windows to make a copy of the Monthly Payment Solution-Version 1 folder. Save the copy in the ClearlyVB\Chap16 folder. Rename the copy Monthly Payment Solution-Version 1-MODIFY THIS. Open the Monthly Payment Solution (Monthly Payment Solution.sln) file contained in the Monthly Payment Solution-Version 1-MODIFY THIS folder. Open the designer window, then open the Code Editor window. Locate the btnCalc control's Click event procedure. Currently, the procedure displays the payments by rate within term. Change the procedure's code so it displays the payments by term within rate. Save the solution. Start and then test the application. Stop the application, then close the solution.

    »MODIFY THIS

»INTRODUCTORY

4. In this exercise, you code an application that displays a bar chart. The bar chart depicts the ratings for five hotels. Open the Hotel Solution (Hotel Solution.sln) file, which is contained in the ClearlyVB\Chap16\Hotel Solution folder. The Create Bar Chart button's Click event procedure should allow the user to enter the hotel rating for each of five hotels. The rating can be from 1 through 6 only. Use the InputBox function to get each rating. If the user enters an invalid rating, the procedure should display an appropriate message in a message box, and then ask the user for the hotel's rating again. In other words, the procedure should not accept an invalid rating. Use each hotel's rating to display the appropriate number of asterisks in the bar chart. Figure 16-12 shows a sample run of the application after the user enters the following ratings: 4, 6, 3, 8, 6, and 2. Save the solution. Start and then test the application. Stop the application, then close the solution.

Figure 16-12: Sample run of the Hotel Ratings application

»INTRODUCTORY

5. In this exercise, you modify one of the Monthly Payment Calculator applications coded in the chapter. Use Windows to make a copy of the Monthly Payment Solution-Version 2 folder. Save the copy in the ClearlyVB\Chap16 folder. Rename the copy Modified Monthly Payment Solution-Version 2. Open the Monthly Payment Solution (Monthly Payment Solution.sln) file contained in the Modified Monthly Payment Solution-Version 2 folder. Open the designer window, then open the Code Editor window. Locate the btnCalc control's Click event procedure. Change the procedure's code so it uses a Do...Loop statement to keep track of the terms. Save the solution. Start and then test the application. Stop the application, then close the solution.

»INTERMEDIATE

6. In this exercise, you modify the Clock application coded in the chapter. Use Windows to make a copy of the Clock Solution folder. Save the copy in the ClearlyVB\Chap16

folder. Rename the copy Modified Clock Solution. Open the Clock Solution (Clock Solution.sln) file contained in the Modified Clock Solution folder. Open the designer window. Currently, the interface and code display the number of hours and minutes. Modify the interface and code to also display the number of seconds. Use second values of 0 through 5 (rather than 0 through 59). Save the solution. Start and then test the application. Stop the application, then close the solution.

7. In this exercise, you code an application that displays a pattern of asterisks. Open the TwoToTenAsterisks Solution (TwoToTenAsterisks Solution.sln) file, which is contained in the ClearlyVB\Chap16\TwoToTenAsterisks Solution folder. The Display Asterisks button should display the pattern of asterisks shown below. The pattern contains 2 asterisks, 4 asterisks, 6 asterisks, 8 asterisks, and 10 asterisks. Display the pattern in the lblAsterisks control. Use a For...Next statement for the outer loop, and a Do...Loop statement for the nested loop. Save the solution, then start and test the application. Stop the application, then close the solution.

>> **INTERMEDIATE**

```
**

****

******

********

**********
```

8. In this exercise, you code an application for Cartwright Industries. Open the Cartwright Solution (Cartwright Solution.sln) file, which is contained in the ClearlyVB\Chap16\Cartwright Solution folder. The application should allow the user to enter the salesperson ID for any number of salespeople, as well as enter any number of sales amounts for a salesperson. Use the InputBox function to get the salesperson's ID and sales amounts. Total a salesperson's sales before moving on to the next salesperson. Display each salesperson's total sales, along with his or her ID, in the interface. When the user has finished entering data, display the company's total sales in the interface. Save the solution, then start and test the application. When you are finished testing the application, stop the application, then close the solution. Figure 16-13 shows a sample run of the application after the user enters the following IDs and sales amounts:

>> **ADVANCED**

ID	Sales amounts
AB2	300.35, 200.50, and 250.75
BN4	45.67 and 350.05
CR7	100.23, 67.45, and 35.85

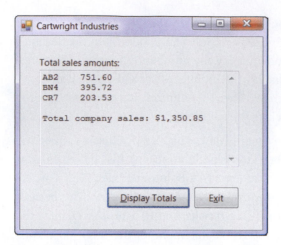

Figure 16-13: Sample run of the Cartwright Industries application

ADVANCED

9. In this exercise, you create an application that displays a table consisting of three rows and seven columns. The first column should contain the numbers 1 through 3. The second and subsequent columns contain the result of multiplying the number in the first column by the numbers 0 through 5. Open the Table Solution (Table Solution.sln) file, which is contained in the ClearlyVB\Chap16\Table Solution folder. Code the Display Table button's Click event procedure. Save the solution, then click the Display Table button. Figure 16-14 shows a sample run of the application. Stop the application, then close the solution.

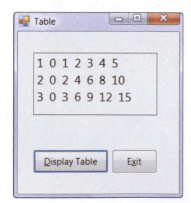

Figure 16-14: Sample run of the Table application

10. Open the FigureThisOut Solution (FigureThisOut Solution.sln) file, which is contained in the ClearlyVB\Chap16\FigureThisOut Solution folder. Open the Code Editor window and study the existing code. List the steps the computer takes when processing the code contained in the btnDisplay control's Click event procedure. What will be displayed by the btnDisplay control's Click event procedure? Start and then test the application. Stop the application, then close the solution.

11. In this exercise, you find an error in an application's code. Open the SwatTheBugs Solution (SwatTheBugs Solution.sln) file, which is contained in the ClearlyVB\Chap16\SwatTheBugs Solution folder. Open the Code Editor window and study the existing code. Start and then test the application. Notice that the application is not working correctly. To stop the application, click the Code Editor (or Designer) window, click Debug on the menu bar, and then click Stop Debugging. Locate and correct the error or errors in the code. Save the solution, then start and test the application again. Stop the application, then close the solution.

ANSWERS TO "TRY THIS" EXERCISES

1. See Figure 16-15.

```
Private Sub btnStart_Click(ByVal sender As Object, ByVal e As System.E
    ' displays hours and minutes

    Dim intHours As Integer
    Dim intMinutes As Integer

    Do Until intHours > 3
        lblHours.Text = intHours.ToString
        Do Until intMinutes > 9
            lblMinutes.Text = intMinutes.ToString
            Me.Refresh()
            System.Threading.Thread.Sleep(500)
            intMinutes = intMinutes + 1
        Loop
        intHours = intHours + 1
        intMinutes = 0
    Loop
End Sub
```

Figure 16-15

2. See Figure 16-16.

```vb
Private Sub btnStart_Click(ByVal sender As Object, ByVal e As System.E
    ' displays hours and minutes

    Dim intMinutes As Integer

    For intHours As Integer = 0 To 3
        lblHours.Text = intHours.ToString
        Do
            lblMinutes.Text = intMinutes.ToString
            Me.Refresh()
            System.Threading.Thread.Sleep(500)
            intMinutes = intMinutes + 1
        Loop While intMinutes <= 9
        intMinutes = 0
    Next intHours
End Sub
```

Figure 16-16

17

I HEAR YOU ARE BREAKING UP

After studying Chapter 17, you should be able to:

Create a sub procedure

Call a sub procedure

Pass data *by value* to a procedure

Pass data *by reference* to a procedure

WHAT'S THE PROPER PROCEDURE?

All of the procedures you have coded so far have been event procedures. Recall that an event procedure is a set of Visual Basic instructions that are processed when a specific event (such as the Click event) occurs. The Code Editor provides a code template for every event procedure. The code template contains the procedure's header and footer. As you know, an event procedure's header begins with the keywords Private Sub. The Private keyword indicates that the procedure can be used only within the current Code Editor window. The Sub keyword is an abbreviation of the term sub procedure, which is simply a block of code that performs a specific task. An event procedure always ends with the keywords End Sub. Figure 17-1 shows a sample Click event procedure for an Exit button.

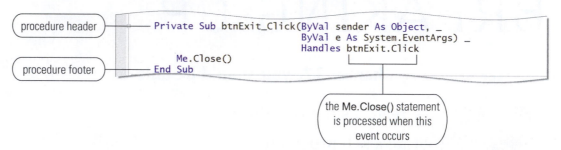

Figure 17-1: Sample Click event procedure for an Exit button

Event procedures are not the only sub procedures available in Visual Basic; you also can create your own sub procedures. The sub procedures you create are processed only when you call (invoke) them from code. But why would you want to create your own sub procedure? First, you can use a sub procedure to avoid duplicating code in different parts of a program. If a program needs to perform the same task several times, it is more efficient to enter the appropriate code once, in a procedure, and then call the procedure to perform its task when needed. Second, consider an event procedure that must perform many tasks. To keep the event procedure's code from getting unwieldy and difficult to understand, you can assign some of the tasks to a sub procedure. Lastly, procedures allow large and complex applications, which typically are written by a team of programmers, to be broken into small and manageable tasks. Each member of the team is assigned one or more tasks to code as a procedure. When each programmer completes his or her procedure, all of the procedures are gathered together into one application. Figure 17-2 shows the syntax for creating a sub procedure. It also includes an example of a sub procedure, as well as the steps you follow to enter a sub procedure in the Code Editor window. Where you enter the sub procedures is a matter of personal preference. Some programmers enter them above the first event procedure in the Code Editor window, while others enter them below the last event procedure. Still others enter them below the procedure from which they are called. In this book, you will enter the sub procedures above the first event procedure.

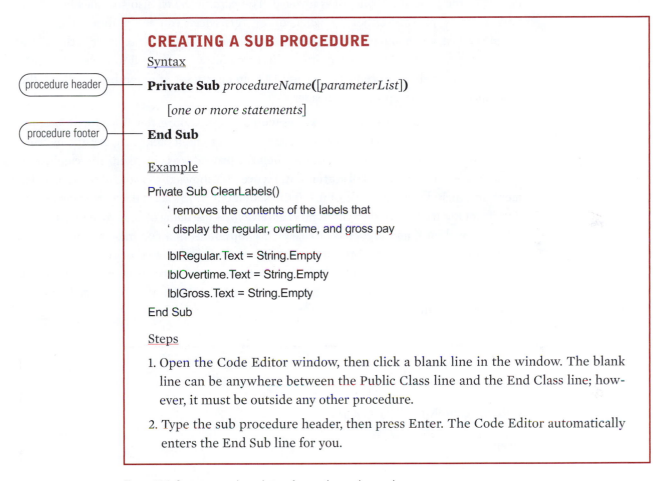

CREATING A SUB PROCEDURE

<u>Syntax</u>

procedure header → **Private Sub** *procedureName*(**[***parameterList***]**)

  [*one or more statements*]

procedure footer → **End Sub**

<u>Example</u>

```
Private Sub ClearLabels()
    ' removes the contents of the labels that
    ' display the regular, overtime, and gross pay

    lblRegular.Text = String.Empty
    lblOvertime.Text = String.Empty
    lblGross.Text = String.Empty
End Sub
```

<u>Steps</u>

1. Open the Code Editor window, then click a blank line in the window. The blank line can be anywhere between the Public Class line and the End Class line; however, it must be outside any other procedure.

2. Type the sub procedure header, then press Enter. The Code Editor automatically enters the End Sub line for you.

Figure 17-2: Syntax, example, and steps for creating a sub procedure

As indicated in Figure 17-2, sub procedures have both a procedure header and procedure footer. In most cases, the procedure header begins with the keywords Private Sub followed by the *procedureName*. The rules for naming a sub procedure are the same as those for naming variables and constants. The convention is to enter procedure names using Pascal case, which means capitalizing the first letter in the name and the first letter of each subsequent word in the name. You should select a descriptive name for the procedure; the name should indicate the task the procedure performs. It is a common practice to begin a procedure's name with a verb. For example, a good name for a sub procedure that clears the contents of the label controls in an interface is ClearLabels.

Following the *procedureName* in the procedure header is a set of parentheses that contains an optional *parameterList*. The *parameterList* lists the data type and name of one or more memory locations, called parameters. The **parameters** store the information passed to the procedure when it is invoked. The *parameterList* also specifies how each parameter is passed—either *by value* or *by reference*. You learn more about the *parameterList*, and about passing information *by value* and *by reference*, later in this chapter. If the procedure does not require any information to be passed to it, as is the case with the ClearLabels procedure in Figure 17-2, an empty set of parentheses follows the *procedureName* in the procedure header.

Unlike the procedure header, which varies with each procedure, the procedure footer for a sub procedure is always End Sub. Between the header and footer, you enter the instructions you want the computer to process when the procedure is invoked. You can invoke a sub procedure using the **Call statement**. Figure 17-3 shows the syntax of the Call statement and includes an example of using the statement to invoke the ClearLabels procedure from Figure 17-2. In the syntax, *procedureName* is the name of the procedure you are calling (invoking), and *argumentList* (which is optional) is a comma-separated list of arguments. An **argument** represents information that is passed to the procedure when it is invoked. If you have no information to pass to the procedure, as is the case with the ClearLabels procedure, you include an empty set of parentheses after the *procedureName* in the Call statement.

CALL STATEMENT

Syntax

Call *procedureName*(**[***argumentList***]**)

Example

Call ClearLabels()

Figure 17-3: Syntax and an example of the Call statement

You will use the ClearLabels procedure in the Weekly Pay application, which you view in the next section.

THE WEEKLY PAY APPLICATION

In the Weekly Pay application, employees are paid on an hourly basis and receive time and one-half for the hours worked over 40. The application calculates and displays an employee's regular pay, overtime pay, and gross pay.

To open the Weekly Pay application, and then test the application:

1. Start Visual Studio 2008 (or Visual Basic 2008 Express Edition). Open the **Weekly Pay Solution** (**Weekly Pay Solution.sln**) file, which is contained in the ClearlyVB\ Chap17\Weekly Pay Solution folder. If necessary, open the designer window.

2. Start the application. Type **41** in the Hours box and then type **9** in the Rate box. Click the **Calculate** button. The Calculate button's Click event procedure calculates and displays the regular pay, overtime pay, and gross pay. See Figure 17-4.

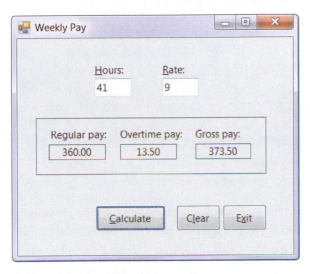

Figure 17-4: Interface showing the calculated amounts

3. Now change the number of hours from 41 to **4**, but don't click the Calculate button yet. Notice that the interface still shows the pay amounts for 41 hours; this is because the amounts aren't updated until you click the Calculate button. Click the **Calculate** button to update the pay amounts, then click the **Exit** button.

To avoid confusion, it would be better to remove the pay amounts from the interface whenever a change is made to either the number of hours in the txtHours control or the rate of pay in the txtRate control. You can do this by entering the three assignment statements lblRegular.Text = String.Empty, lblOvertime.Text = String.Empty, and lblGross.Text = String.Empty in each text box's TextChanged event procedure. A text box's **TextChanged event** occurs whenever a change is made to the contents of the text box. You also can remove the pay amounts by entering the assignment statements in a sub procedure, and then entering the appropriate Call statement in both TextChanged event procedures. You will use the latter approach, because entering the assignment statements in a sub procedure saves you from having to enter them more than once. In addition, if the application is modified—for example, if the user wants you to assign the string "N/A" rather than the empty string to the labels—you will need to make the change in only one place in the code.

To enter the ClearLabels sub procedure and Call statements, and then test the application:

1. Open the Code Editor window. Click the **blank line** below the Public Class frmMain line, then press **Enter**. Enter the ClearLabels procedure shown in Figure 17-5.

enter these comments and lines of code

```
Public Class frmMain

    Private Sub ClearLabels()
        ' removes the contents of the labels that
        ' display the regular, overtime, and gross pay

        lblRegular.Text = String.Empty
        lblOvertime.Text = String.Empty
        lblGross.Text = String.Empty
    End Sub

    Private Sub btnExit_Click(ByVal sender As Object, ByVal e As System.EventArgs) Ha
        Me.Close()
```

Figure 17-5: ClearLabels procedure entered in the Code Editor window

2. Open the code template for the txtHours control's TextChanged event procedure. Type **call ClearLabels()** and press **Enter**. Now open the code template for the txtRate control's TextChanged event procedure. Type **call ClearLabels()** and press **Enter**.

3. Save the solution, then start the application. Type **41** in the Hours box and then type **9** in the Rate box. Click the **Calculate** button. The regular pay, overtime pay, and gross pay amounts shown earlier in Figure 17-4 appear in the interface.

4. Now change the number of hours from 41 to **4**. Changing the number of hours causes the txtHours control's TextChanged event to occur. As a result, the computer processes the Call ClearLabels() statement entered in the event procedure. When processing the statement, the computer temporarily leaves the event procedure to process the code in the ClearLabels procedure. The assignment statements in the ClearLabels procedure remove the contents of three label controls in the interface. After processing the assignment statements, the computer processes the ClearLabels procedure's End Sub clause, which ends the procedure. The computer then returns to the txtHours control's TextChanged event procedure and processes the line of code located below the Call statement. In this case, the line below the Call statement is End Sub, which ends the event procedure.

5. Click the **Calculate** button, then change the rate of pay from 9 to **9.55**. Notice that the pay amounts are removed from the interface when you make a change to the rate. Click the **Calculate** button, then click the **Exit** button.

To complete the Weekly Pay application, you need to code the Clear button's Click event procedure. The procedure should remove the contents of both text boxes. It also should remove the pay amounts from the three label controls.

To code the Clear button's Click event procedure, then test the procedure:

1. Open the code template for the btnClear control's Click event procedure. Type **' clear text boxes and label controls** and press **Enter** twice.

2. Type **txtHours.text = string.empty** and press **Enter**, then type **txtRate.text = string.empty** and press **Enter**. You can use the ClearLabels procedure to remove the pay amounts from the label controls. Type **call ClearLabels()** and press **Enter**.

3. Save the solution, then start the application. Type **10** in the Hours box and then type **5** in the Rate box. Click the **Calculate** button. The values 50.00, 0.00, and 50.00 appear in the label controls. Click the **Clear** button to remove the contents of the text boxes and label controls, then click the **Exit** button.

4. Close the Code Editor window, then close the solution.

MINI-QUIZ 1

1. The items in the Call statement are referred to as _____.

   a. arguments   b. parameters

   c. passers   d. None of the above.

2. You can enter your sub procedures _____ in the Code Editor window.

   a. above the Public Class line

   b. above the first event procedure

   c. below the End Class line

   d. All of the above.

3. When the contents of a text box changes, the text box's _____ event occurs.

   a. ChangedText   b. ModifiedText

   c. TextModified   d. TextChanged

SEND ME SOMETHING

As mentioned earlier, a sub procedure can contain one or more parameters in its procedure header. Each parameter stores information that is passed to the procedure by the Call statement. The Call statement passes the information in its optional *argumentList*. The number of arguments in the Call statement should agree with the number of parameters in the procedure header. In addition, the data type and position of each parameter should agree with the data type and position of its corresponding argument. For example, if two arguments are passed to a procedure—the first one a String variable and the second one a Decimal variable—the first parameter should have a data type of String and the second parameter should have a data type of Decimal. Although you can pass a constant, keyword, or variable to a sub procedure, in most cases you will pass a variable.

Each variable declared in an application has both a value and a unique address that represents the location of the variable in the computer's internal memory. In Visual Basic, you can pass either the variable's value or its address to a procedure. Passing a variable's value is referred to as **passing by value**. Passing a variable's address is referred to as **passing by reference**. The method you choose (*by value* or *by reference*) depends on whether you want the receiving procedure to have access to the variable in memory. In other words, it depends on whether you want to allow the receiving procedure to change the contents of the variable. Although the idea of passing information *by value* and *by reference* may sound confusing at first, it is a concept with which you already are familiar. To illustrate, Rob (the mechanical man) has a savings account at a local bank. During a conversation with his friend Jerome, Rob mentions the amount of money he has in his account. Sharing this information with Jerome is similar to passing a variable *by value*. Knowing the balance in Rob's account does not give Jerome access to Rob's bank account. It merely gives Jerome information that he can use perhaps to compare to the amount he has saved. Rob's savings account example also provides an illustration of passing information *by reference*. To deposit money to or withdraw money from the account, Rob must provide the bank teller with his account number. The account number represents the location of Rob's account at the bank and allows the teller to change the account balance. Giving the teller the bank account number is similar to passing a variable *by reference*. The account number allows the teller to change the contents of Rob's bank account, similar to the way a variable's address allows a procedure to change the contents of a variable passed to it.

JUST GIVE ME ITS VALUE

To pass a variable *by value* in Visual Basic, you include the keyword ByVal before the variable's corresponding parameter in the receiving procedure's *parameterList*. When you pass a variable *by value*, the computer passes only the contents of the variable to the procedure. When only the contents are passed, the receiving procedure is not given access to the variable in memory; therefore, it cannot change the value stored inside the variable. You pass a variable *by value* when the receiving procedure needs to *know* the variable's contents, but the receiving procedure does not need to *change* the contents. Unless specified otherwise, variables are passed *by value* in Visual Basic. The Happy Birthday application, which you code in the next set of steps, passes two variables *by value* to a sub procedure.

To open the Happy Birthday application, and then code the application:

1. Open the **Birthday Solution** (**Birthday Solution.sln**) file, which is contained in the ClearlyVB\Chap17\Birthday Solution folder. If necessary, open the designer window. When the user clicks the Display Message button, the button's Click event procedure will prompt the user to enter a first name and age. It then will call a sub procedure to display the two input items in a birthday message, like this one: "Happy 18th Birthday, Rob!"

2. Open the Code Editor window. Locate the btnDisplay control's Click event procedure. The code prompts the user to enter the first name and age (in years), and it stores the values in the strName and strAge variables.

3. You will use a sub procedure named DisplayMessage to display the birthday message. The sub procedure will need to know the person's name and age, but it will not need to change either of those values. Therefore, you will pass the strName and strAge variables *by value*. First, enter the appropriate Call statement. Click the **blank line** above the End Sub clause in the btnDisplay control's Click event procedure, then type **call DisplayMessage(strName, strAge)** and press **Enter**. Don't be concerned about the jagged line that appears below DisplayMessage in the Call statement. The jagged line will disappear when you enter the DisplayMessage procedure in the Code Editor window.

4. Now enter the DisplayMessage procedure. The procedure will need two parameters to store the values passed to it by the Call statement. Because the Call statement passes two strings, both parameters must be String variables. Click the **blank line** below the Public Class frmMain line, then press **Enter** to insert another blank line. Type **private sub DisplayMessage(byval strPerson as string, byval strYears as string)** and press **Enter**. See Figure 17-6. Notice that the number, data type, and sequence of the arguments in the Call statement match the number, data type, and sequence of the corresponding parameters in the procedure header. Also notice that the names of the parameters do not need to be identical to the names of the corresponding arguments. In fact, to avoid confusion, it usually is better to use different names for the arguments and parameters.

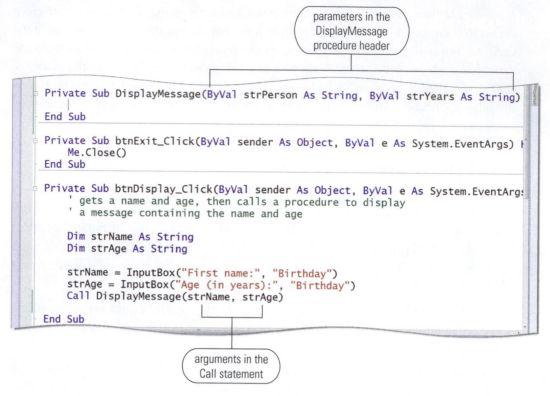

parameters in the DisplayMessage procedure header

```
Private Sub DisplayMessage(ByVal strPerson As String, ByVal strYears As String)

End Sub

Private Sub btnExit_Click(ByVal sender As Object, ByVal e As System.EventArgs)
    Me.Close()
End Sub

Private Sub btnDisplay_Click(ByVal sender As Object, ByVal e As System.EventArgs
    ' gets a name and age, then calls a procedure to display
    ' a message containing the name and age

    Dim strName As String
    Dim strAge As String

    strName = InputBox("First name:", "Birthday")
    strAge = InputBox("Age (in years):", "Birthday")
    Call DisplayMessage(strName, strAge)

End Sub
```

arguments in the Call statement

Figure 17-6: Call statement and DisplayMessage procedure header and footer

5. Type the comment and lines of code shown in Figure 17-7, then save the solution.

enter this comment and these lines of code

```
Private Sub DisplayMessage(ByVal strPerson As String, ByVal strYears As String)
    ' displays a message containing a name and age

    Dim strAddOn As String
    Dim intYears As Integer

    Integer.TryParse(strYears, intYears)

    Select Case intYears
        Case 1, 21, 31, 41, 51, 61, 71, 81, 91, 101
            strAddOn = "st"
        Case 2, 22, 32, 42, 52, 62, 72, 82, 92, 102
            strAddOn = "nd"
        Case 3, 23, 33, 43, 53, 63, 73, 83, 93, 103
            strAddOn = "rd"
        Case Else
            strAddOn = "th"
    End Select

    lblMessage.Text = "Happy " & strYears & strAddOn _
        & " Birthday, " & strPerson & "!"
End Sub
```

Figure 17-7: DisplayMessage procedure entered in the Code Editor window

Before testing the application, you will desk-check it using Rob as the name and 18 as the age. When the user clicks the Display Message button, the button's Click event procedure creates the strName and strAge variables. Next, the two InputBox functions prompt the user to enter the name and age. The functions store the name (Rob) and age (18) in the strName and strAge variables. Figure 17-8 shows the desk-check table before the Call statement is processed.

strName	strAge
Rob	18

Figure 17-8: Desk-check table before the Call statement is processed

Next, the Call statement is processed. The statement invokes the DisplayMessage procedure, passing it the strName and strAge variables *by value*, which means that only the contents of the variables are sent to the procedure. You know that the variables are passed *by value* because the keyword ByVal appears before each variable's corresponding parameter in the DisplayMessage procedure header. At this point, the computer temporarily leaves the Click event procedure to process the code in the DisplayMessage procedure. When processing the DisplayMessage procedure header, the computer creates the variables listed in the *parameterList*; in this case, it creates the strPerson and strYears variables. In those variables, it stores the name and age values received from the Call statement. The variables in a procedure header have procedure scope, which means they can be used only by the procedure in which they are declared. In this case, the strPerson and strYears variables can be used only by the DisplayMessage procedure. Figure 17-9 shows the desk-check table after the computer processes the Call statement and DisplayMessage procedure header.

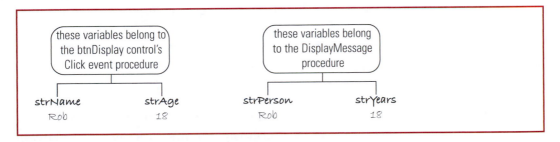

Figure 17-9: Desk-check table after the Call statement and procedure header are processed

Next, the computer creates the strAddOn and intYears variables declared in the DisplayMessage procedure. The TryParse method converts the string stored in the strYears variable to an integer and stores the result in the intYears variable. Because the intYears variable contains the number 18, the Case Else clause in the Select Case statement assigns "th" to the strAddOn variable. Figure 17-10 shows the desk-check table after the Select Case statement is processed.

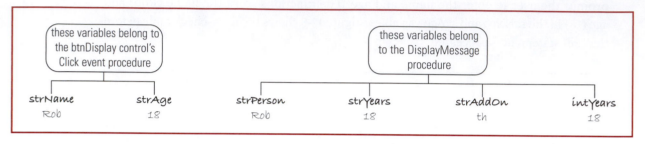

Figure 17-10: Desk-check table after the Select Case statement is processed

The last assignment statement in the sub procedure uses the values stored in the strPerson, strYears, and strAddOn variables to display the appropriate message. In this case, the statement displays the "Happy 18th Birthday, Rob!" message. The DisplayMessage procedure's End Sub clause is processed next. At this point, the computer removes the sub procedure's variables from internal memory, as illustrated in Figure 17-11. (Recall that a procedure-level variable is removed from the computer's memory when the procedure in which it is declared ends.)

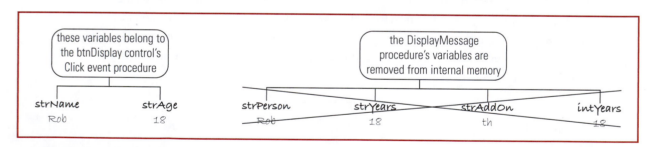

Figure 17-11: Desk-check table after the DisplayMessage procedure ends

After the DisplayMessage procedure ends, the computer returns to the line of code located below the Call statement in the btnDisplay control's Click event procedure. In this case, it returns to the End Sub clause, which marks the end of the event procedure. When the event procedure ends, the computer removes the strName and strAge variables from internal memory.

To test the Happy Birthday application:

1. Save the solution, if necessary, then start the application. Click the **Display Message** button. Type **Rob** and press **Enter**, then type **18** and press **Enter**. The birthday message appears in the interface, as shown in Figure 17-12.

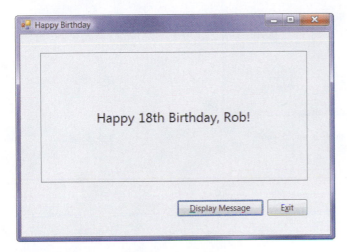

Figure 17-12: Birthday message displayed in the interface

2. Click the **Exit** button. Close the Code Editor window, then close the solution.

The Ch17-Sub Procedures video demonstrates sub procedures by stepping through the code.

WHERE DO YOU LIVE?

In addition to passing a variable's value to a procedure, you also can pass its address. In other words, you can pass its location in the computer's internal memory. As you learned earlier, passing a variable's address is referred to as passing *by reference* and it gives the receiving procedure access to the variable. You pass a variable *by reference* when you want the receiving procedure to change the contents of the variable. To pass a variable *by reference* in Visual Basic, you include the keyword ByRef before the variable's corresponding parameter in the receiving procedure's header. The ByRef keyword tells the computer to pass the variable's address rather than its contents. The Total Due Calculator application, which you code in this section, provides an example of passing a variable *by reference*. The application's interface and planning information are shown in Figures 17-13 and 17-14, respectively.

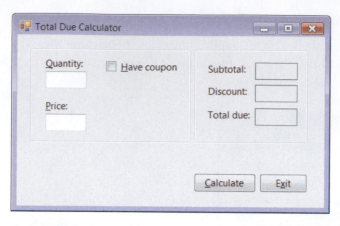

Figure 17-13: User interface for the Total Due Calculator application

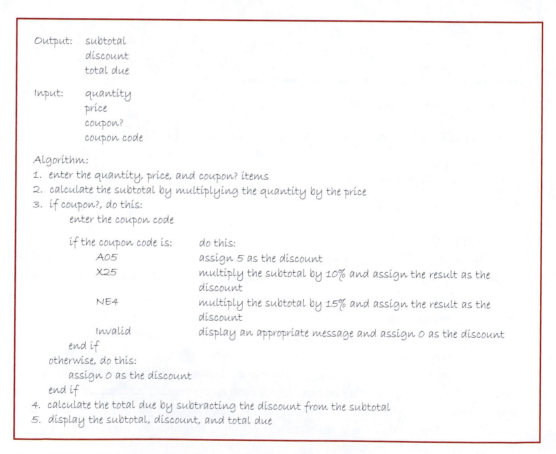

Output: subtotal
          discount
          total due

Input: quantity
          price
          coupon?
          coupon code

Algorithm:
1. enter the quantity, price, and coupon? items
2. calculate the subtotal by multiplying the quantity by the price
3. if coupon?, do this:
      enter the coupon code

      if the coupon code is: do this:
          A05   assign 5 as the discount
          X25   multiply the subtotal by 10% and assign the result as the
                                discount
          NE4   multiply the subtotal by 15% and assign the result as the
                                discount
          invalid   display an appropriate message and assign 0 as the discount
      end if
   otherwise, do this:
      assign 0 as the discount
   end if
4. calculate the total due by subtracting the discount from the subtotal
5. display the subtotal, discount, and total due

Figure 17-14: Planning information for the Total Due Calculator application

Now let's say it is Friday afternoon and you are anxious to leave work early. Before you can do so, however, you need to code and test the Total Due Calculator application. You decide to recruit Sandy, one of your co-workers, to help you with the coding. More specifically, you ask Sandy to code Step 3 in the algorithm as a sub procedure. Step 3's task is to assign the appropriate discount, so you and Sandy agree to name the sub procedure AssignDiscount. Both of you determine that the AssignDiscount procedure requires two items of information. First, it needs to know the value of the subtotal, because some of the discounts are based on that value. Second, it needs to know where to assign the discount. In other words, it needs to know the address of the variable that will store the discount.

To open the Total Due Calculator application, and then code the application:

1. Open the **Total Due Solution** (**Total Due Solution.sln**) file, which is contained in the ClearlyVB\Chap17\Total Due Solution folder. If necessary, open the designer window.

2. Open the Code Editor window. First, enter the Call statement. Locate the btnCalc control's Click event procedure. Click the **blank line** below the ' assign discount comment. The Click event procedure will need to pass the value stored in the decSubtotal variable and the address of the decDiscount variable. Type **call AssignDiscount(decSubtotal, decDiscount)** and press **Enter**.

3. Now enter the parameters in the AssignDiscount procedure header, which appears below the Public Class frmMain line. The parameters will need to accept a Decimal value followed by the address of a Decimal variable. Type the parameters shown in Figure 17-15, then save the solution.

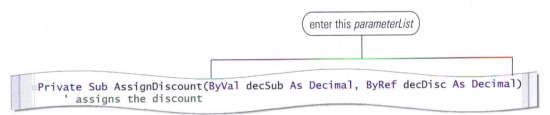

Figure 17-15: Parameters entered in the AssignDiscount procedure header

Before testing the application, you will desk-check it using 4 as the quantity, 15 as the price, and X25 as the coupon code. In addition, the Have coupon check box will be selected. When the user clicks the Calculate button, the computer creates the variables declared in the five Dim statements. The two TryParse methods store the quantity and price in the intQuantity and decPrice variables, respectively. Next, the decSubtotal = intQuantity * decPrice statement calculates the subtotal and stores the result in the decSubtotal variable. Figure 17-16 shows the desk-check table before the Call statement in the procedure is processed.

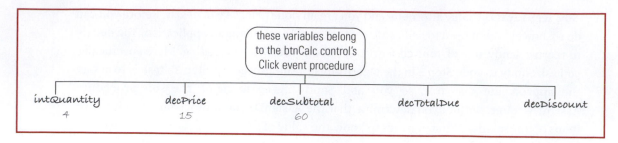

Figure 17-16: Desk-check table before the computer processes the Call statement

Next, the computer processes the Call AssignDiscount(decSubtotal, decDiscount) statement. At this point, the computer temporarily leaves the Click event procedure to process the code contained in the AssignDiscount procedure; the procedure header is processed first. The ByVal keyword indicates that the first parameter is receiving a value from the Call statement; as a result, the computer creates the decSub variable to store the value. In this case, the computer stores the value 60 in the decSub variable. The ByRef keyword, on the other hand, indicates that the second parameter is receiving the address of a variable. When you pass a variable's address to a procedure, the computer uses the address to locate the variable in its internal memory. It then assigns the parameter name to the memory location. In this case, for example, the computer locates the decDiscount variable in memory and assigns the name decDisc to it. At this point, the memory location has two names: one assigned by the btnCalc control's Click event procedure and the other assigned by the AssignDiscount procedure, as indicated in Figure 17-17. Notice that four variables in the table belong strictly to the Click event procedure, and one belongs strictly to the AssignDiscount procedure. One memory location, however, belongs to both procedures. Although both procedures can access the memory location, each procedure uses a different name to do so. The Click event procedure uses the name decDiscount, whereas the AssignDiscount procedure uses the name decDisc.

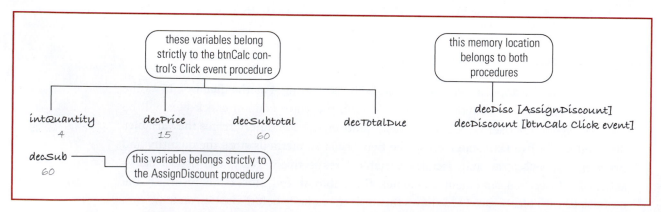

Figure 17-17: Desk-check table after the computer processes the Call statement and procedure header

After processing the AssignDiscount procedure header, the computer processes the code contained in the procedure. For this desk-check, the Have coupon check box is selected, so the computer follows the instructions in the selection structure's true path. The first instruction creates a variable named strCouponCode. Next, the InputBox prompts the user to enter the coupon code and stores the user's response (X25) in the strCouponCode variable. The Select Case statement is processed next. The instruction in the Case "X25" clause calculates the discount by multiplying the contents of the decSub variable (60) by 0.1; it then assigns the result (6) to the decDisc variable. Figure 17-18 shows the desk-check table after the Select Case statement is processed. Notice that when the contents of the decDisc variable changes, the contents of the decDiscount variable also changes. This happens because the names decDisc and decDiscount refer to the same location in the computer's internal memory.

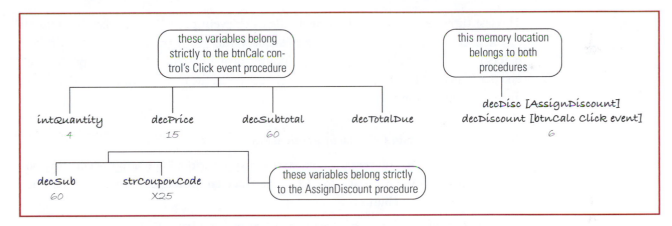

Figure 17-18: Desk-check table after the computer processes the Select Case statement

Next, the computer processes the AssignDiscount procedure's End Sub clause, which marks the end of the procedure. At this point, the computer removes the decSub and strCouponCode variables from memory. It also removes the decDisc name from the appropriate location in memory, as illustrated in Figure 17-19.

Figure 17-19: Desk-check table after the AssignDiscount procedure ends

After the AssignDiscount procedure ends, the computer returns to the line of code below the Call statement in the btnCalc control's Click event procedure. In this case, it returns to the decTotalDue = decSubtotal – decDiscount statement. Figure 17-20 shows the desk-check table after this statement is processed.

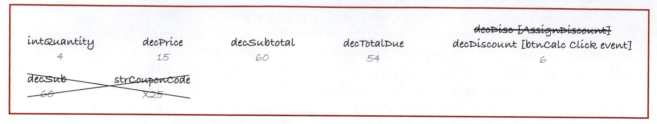

Figure 17-20: Desk-check table after the total due is calculated

The last three assignment statements in the Click event procedure display the contents of the decSubtotal, decDiscount, and decTotalDue variables (formatted with two decimal places) in the interface. Finally, the computer processes the Click event procedure's End Sub clause. When the Click event procedure ends, the computer removes the procedure's variables from memory.

To test the Total Due Calculator application:

1. Save the solution, if necessary, then start the application. Type **4** in the Quantity box and then type **15** in the Price box. Click the **Have coupon** check box to select it, then click the **Calculate** button.

2. Type **X25** as the coupon code, then press **Enter**. See Figure 17-21.

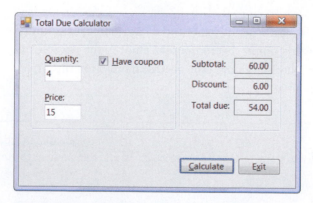

Figure 17-21: Subtotal, discount, and total due shown in the interface

3. Click the **Exit** button. Close the Code Editor window, then close the solution.

MINI-QUIZ 2

1. Which of the following is a valid procedure header for a procedure that receives the contents of a String variable followed by the contents of an Integer variable?

    a. Private Sub Display(ByRef strX As String, ByRef intY As Integer)

    b. Private Sub Display(ByVal strX As String, ByVal intY As Integer)

    c. Private Sub Display(strX As String, intY As Integer)

    d. None of the above.

2. Write a Call statement that invokes the Display procedure from Question 1. Pass the procedure the contents of the strName and intQuantity variables.

3. In the receiving procedure's header, you use the keyword _____ to indicate that a variable is being passed *by reference*.

For more examples of sub procedures, see the Sub Procedures section in the Ch17WantMore.pdf file.

SUMMARY

» You can create your own sub procedures in Visual Basic. Sub procedures allow you to avoid duplicating code in different parts of a program. They also allow you to split a program into small and manageable tasks.

» It is a common practice to begin a procedure name with a verb, and to enter the name using Pascal case.

» You can use the Call statement to invoke a sub procedure and (optionally) pass arguments to the procedure.

» When calling a procedure, the number of arguments listed in the Call statement's *argumentList* should agree with the number of parameters listed in the receiving procedure's *parameterList*. Also, the data type and position of each argument should agree with the data type and position of its corresponding parameter.

» You can pass information to a sub procedure either *by value* (using the ByVal keyword) or *by reference* (using the ByRef keyword). The procedure header indicates whether a variable is being passed *by value* or *by reference*.

» When you pass a variable *by value*, only the contents of the variable are passed. When you pass a variable *by reference*, the variable's address is passed.

» Variables that appear in a procedure header's *parameterList* have procedure scope, which means they can be used only by the procedure.

KEY TERMS

Argument—an item listed within parentheses in a Call statement; represents information passed to the receiving procedure

Call statement—the Visual Basic statement used to invoke a sub procedure

Parameters—the memory locations listed in a procedure header

Passing by reference—the process of passing a variable's address to a procedure

Passing by value—the process of passing a variable's contents to a procedure

TextChanged event—an event that occurs whenever a change is made to the contents of its associated text box

ANSWERS TO MINI-QUIZZES

MINI-QUIZ 1

1. a. arguments

2. b. above the first event procedure

3. d. TextChanged

MINI-QUIZ 2

1. b. Private Sub Display(ByVal strX As String, ByVal intY As Integer)

2. Call Display(strName, intQuantity)

3. ByRef

REVIEW QUESTIONS

1. To determine how a variable is being passed to a procedure—either *by value* or *by reference*—you will need to examine _____.

   a. the Call statement

   b. the procedure header

   c. the statements entered in the procedure

   d. Either a or b.

2. Which of the following statements can be used to call the CalcArea sub procedure, passing it two variables *by value*?

   a. Call CalcArea(dblLength, dblWidth)

   b. Call CalcArea(ByVal dblLength, ByVal dblWidth)

   c. Call CalcArea ByVal(dblLength, dblWidth)

   d. Call ByVal CalcArea(dblLength, dblWidth)

3. Which of the following is a valid header for a procedure that receives an integer followed by a number with a decimal place?

   a. Private Sub CalcFee(intBase As Integer, decRate As Decimal)

   b. Private Sub CalcFee(ByRef intBase As Integer, ByRef decRate As Decimal)

   c. Private Sub CalcFee(ByVal intBase As Integer, ByVal decRate As Decimal)

   d. None of the above.

4. Which of the following is false?

   a. In most cases, the number of arguments in a Call statement should agree with the number of parameters in the receiving procedure's header.

   b. The data type of each parameter should match the data type of its corresponding argument.

   c. The name of each parameter should be identical to the name of its corresponding argument.

   d. When you pass a variable to a sub procedure *by value*, the receiving procedure creates a procedure-level variable that it uses to store the value passed to it.

5. A sub procedure named CalcEndingInventory is passed four Integer variables named intBegin, intSales, intPurchases, and intEnding. The procedure's task is to calculate the ending inventory, based on the beginning inventory, sales, and purchase amounts passed to the procedure. The procedure should store the result in the intEnding memory location. Which of the following procedure headers is correct?

a. Private Sub CalcEndingInventory(ByVal intB As Integer, ByVal intS As Integer, ByVal intP As Integer, ByRef intFinal As Integer)

b. Private Sub CalcEndingInventory(ByVal intB As Integer, ByVal intS As Integer, ByVal intP As Integer, ByVal intFinal As Integer)

c. Private Sub CalcEndingInventory(ByRef intB As Integer, ByRef intS As Integer, ByRef intP As Integer, ByVal intFinal As Integer)

d. Private Sub CalcEndingInventory(ByRef intB As Integer, ByRef intS As Integer, ByRef intP As Integer, ByRef intFinal As Integer)

EXERCISES

»TRY THIS

1. In this exercise, you code an application that calculates and displays a bonus amount based on two sale amounts entered by the user. Open the Bonus Solution (Bonus Solution.sln) file, which is contained in the ClearlyVB\Chap17\Bonus Solution-TRY THIS 1 folder. Open the designer window, then open the Code Editor window. Use the algorithm shown in Figure 17-22 to code the btnCalc control's Click event procedure and the sub procedure. Save the solution, then start and test the application. Stop the application, then close the solution. (The answers to TRY THIS Exercises are located at the end of the chapter.)

```
                       1.  enter sale 1 and sale 2
                       2.  calculate the sum by adding together sale 1 and sale 2
                       3.  if the sum is greater than 1200, do this:
create a sub               calculate the bonus by multiplying the sum by 10%
procedure that         otherwise, do this:
will handle                calculate the bonus by multiplying the sum by 8%
Steps 3 and 4          end if
                       4.  display the bonus
```

Figure 17-22: Algorithm for the Bonus Solution-TRY THIS 1 application

2. In this exercise, you code an application that calculates and displays a bonus amount based on two sale amounts entered by the user. Open the Bonus Solution (Bonus Solution.sln) file, which is contained in the ClearlyVB\Chap17\Bonus Solution-TRY THIS 2 folder. Open the designer window, then open the Code Editor window. Use the algorithm shown in Figure 17-23 to code the btnCalc control's Click event procedure and the sub procedure. Save the solution, then start and test the application. Stop the application, then close the solution. (The answers to TRY THIS Exercises are located at the end of the chapter.)

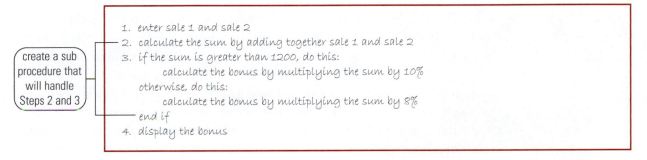

Figure 17-23: Algorithm for the Bonus Solution-TRY THIS 2 application

3. In this exercise, you modify the Total Due Calculator application coded in the chapter. Use Windows to make a copy of the Total Due Solution folder. Save the copy in the ClearlyVB\Chap17 folder. Rename the copy Total Due Solution-MODIFY THIS. Open the Total Due Solution (Total Due Solution.sln) file contained in the Total Due Solution-MODIFY THIS folder. Open the designer window, then open the Code Editor window. Create a sub procedure that clears the three payment amounts. Call the sub procedure when a change is made to the contents of either text box. Also call the sub procedure whenever the check box is clicked. Save the solution. Start and then test the application. Stop the application, then close the solution.

4. In this exercise, you code an application that displays a letter grade based on the average of three test scores. Open the Grade Solution (Grade Solution.sln) file, which is contained in the ClearlyVB\Chap17\Grade Solution folder. Code the application, using a sub procedure to both determine and display the letter grade. If the average is at least 90, the grade is A. If the average is at least 80 but less than 90, the grade is B. If the average is at least 70 but less than 80, the grade is C. If the average is at least 60 but less than 70, the grade is D. If the average is below 60, the grade is F. Save the solution. Start and then test the application. Stop the application, then close the solution.

» INTRODUCTORY

5. In this exercise, you modify the Grade application from Exercise 4. Use Windows to make a copy of the Grade Solution folder. Save the copy in the ClearlyVB\Chap17 folder. Rename the copy Modified Grade Solution. Open the Grade Solution (Grade Solution.sln) file contained in the Modified Grade Solution folder. Open the designer window, then open the Code Editor window. Currently, the sub procedure both determines and displays the letter grade. Modify the code so that the sub procedure determines but does not display the letter grade. The letter grade should be displayed by the btnDisplay control's Click event procedure. Save the solution. Start and then test the application. Stop the application, then close the solution.

» INTERMEDIATE

6. In this exercise, you modify the Happy Birthday application coded in the chapter. Use Windows to make a copy of the Birthday Solution folder. Save the copy in the ClearlyVB\Chap17 folder. Rename the copy Modified Birthday Solution. Open the Birthday Solution (Birthday Solution.sln) file contained in the Modified Birthday Solution folder. Open the designer window. The DisplayMessage procedure should use a sub procedure to assign the appropriate letters ("st", "nd", "rd", or "th"). Create the sub procedure, then modify the DisplayMessage procedure appropriately. Notice that a sub procedure can call another sub procedure. (Hint: If the Code Editor indicates that a String variable is being passed before it has been assigned a value, assign the String.Empty constant to the variable in the Dim statement.) Save the solution. Start and then test the application. Stop the application, then close the solution.

» INTERMEDIATE

7. In this exercise, you code an application that calculates a water bill. The clerk at the water department will enter the current meter reading and the previous meter reading in two text boxes. The application should calculate and display the number of gallons of water used and the total charge for the water. The charge for water is $2.05 per 1000 gallons, or .00205 per gallon. Use a sub procedure to make the calculations, then use another sub procedure to display the results. Call both sub procedures from the Calculate button's Click event procedure. Make the calculations only when the current meter reading is greater than or equal to the previous meter reading; otherwise, display an appropriate message in a message box.

   a. List the output and input items, as well as any processing items, then create an appropriate algorithm using pseudocode.

   b. Create a new Visual Basic Windows application. Name the solution, project, and form file Water Bill Solution, Water Bill Project, and frmMain.vb, respectively. Save the application in the ClearlyVB\Chap17 folder. If necessary, change the form's name to frmMain.

c. Create the interface shown in Figure 17-24, then code the application. Be sure to code each text box's KeyPress and TextChanged event procedures. Save the solution, then start and test the application. Stop the application, then close the solution.

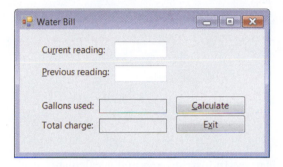

Figure 17-24: User interface for the Water Bill application

8. Sharon Barrow, the billing supervisor at Cable Direct (a local cable company) has asked you to create an application that she can use to calculate and display a customer's bill. The cable rates are shown in the following chart. Business customers must have at least one connection.

» ADVANCED

Residential customers:
  Processing fee: $4.50
  Basic service fee: $30
  Premium channels: $5 per channel
Business customers:
  Processing fee: $16.50
  Basic service fee: $80 for first 10 connections; $4 for each additional connection
  Premium channels: $50 per channel for any number of connections

a. Create a new Visual Basic Windows application. Name the solution, project, and form file Cable Direct Solution, Cable Direct Project, and frmMain.vb, respectively. Save the application in the ClearlyVB\Chap17 folder. If necessary, change the form's name to frmMain.

b. Create the interface shown in Figure 17-25, then code the application. Use one sub procedure to calculate the bill for a Residential customer, and another sub procedure to calculate the bill for a Business customer. Also include a sub procedure that clears the Total due box when a change is made to either text box, or when either radio button is clicked. Save the solution, then start and test the application. Stop the application, then close the solution.

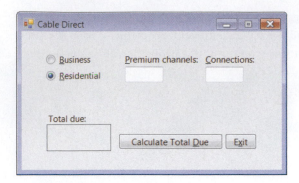

Figure 17-25: User interface for the Cable Direct application

>>ADVANCED

9. Khalid Patel, the payroll manager at Harvey Industries, manually calculates each employee's weekly gross pay, Social Security and Medicare (FICA) tax, federal withholding tax (FWT), and net pay—a very time-consuming process and one that is prone to mathematical errors. Mr. Patel has asked you to create an application that performs the payroll calculations both efficiently and accurately. Employees at Harvey Industries are paid every Friday. All employees are paid on an hourly basis, with time and one-half paid for the hours worked over 40. The amount of FICA tax to deduct from an employee's weekly gross pay is calculated by multiplying the gross pay amount by 7.65%. The amount of FWT to deduct from an employee's weekly gross pay is based on the employee's filing status—either single or married—and his or her weekly taxable wages. You calculate the weekly taxable wages by first multiplying the number of withholding allowances by $67.31 (the value of a withholding allowance for 2008), and then subtracting the result from the weekly gross pay. For example, if your weekly gross pay is $400 and you have two withholding allowances, your weekly taxable wages are $265.38. You use the weekly taxable wages, along with the filing status and the appropriate weekly Federal Withholding Tax table, to determine the amount of FWT to withhold. The weekly tax tables for the year 2008 are shown in Figure 17-26.

FWT Tables – Weekly Payroll Period				
Single person				
If the taxable wages are:	The amount of income tax to withhold is			
Over	**But not over**	**Base amount**	**Percentage**	**Of excess over**
	$ 51	0		
$ 51	$ 198	0	10%	$ 51
$ 198	$ 653	$ 14.70 plus	15%	$ 198
$ 653	$1,533	$ 82.95 plus	25%	$ 653
$1,533	$3,202	$ 302.95 plus	28%	$1,533
$3,202	$6,916	$ 770.27 plus	33%	$3,202
$6,916		$1,995.89 plus	35%	$6,916
Married person				
If the taxable wages are:	The amount of income tax to withhold is			
Over	**But not over**	**Base amount**	**Percentage**	**Of excess over**
	$ 154	0		
$ 154	$ 453	0	10%	$ 154
$ 453	$1,388	$ 29.90 plus	15%	$ 453
$1,388	$2,651	$ 170.15 plus	25%	$1,388
$2,651	$3,994	$ 485.90 plus	28%	$2,651
$3,994	$7,021	$ 861.94 plus	33%	$3,994
$7,021		$1,860.85 plus	35%	$7,021

Figure 17-26: Weekly Federal Withholding Tax tables

a. Create a new Visual Basic Windows application. Name the solution, project, and form file Harvey Industries Solution, Harvey Industries Project, and frmMain.vb, respectively. Save the application in the ClearlyVB\Chap17 folder. If necessary, change the form's name to frmMain.

b. Create the interface shown in Figure 17-27, then code the application. Use at least two sub procedures in the code: one to calculate the federal withholding tax and another to clear the contents of the Gross pay, FWT, FICA, and Net pay boxes. The four boxes should be cleared when a change is made to the Hours, Rate, or Allowances text boxes, or when one of the radio buttons is clicked. Code the KeyPress event procedures for the Hours, Rate, and Allowances text boxes. Also use the Math.Round method, which you learned about in Chapter 7's Advanced Exercises 8 and 9. Save the solution, then start and test the application. Stop the application, then close the solution.

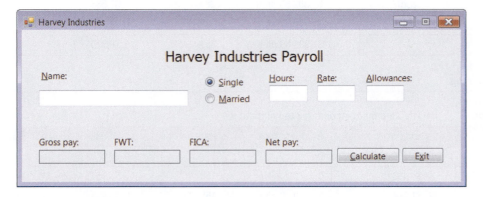

Figure 17-27: User interface for the Harvey Industries application

10. Open the FigureThisOut Solution (FigureThisOut Solution.sln) file, which is contained in the ClearlyVB\Chap17\FigureThisOut Solution folder. Open the Code Editor window and study the existing code. The first statement in the btnClear control's Click event procedure assigns the empty string to the txtSales control's Text property. As you learned in the chapter, when a change is made to the contents of a text box, the text box's TextChanged event occurs. In this case, the TextChanged event procedure calls the ClearLabels procedure to clear the contents of two label controls. Notice that the second statement in the btnClear control's Click event procedure also calls the ClearLabels procedure; your task is to determine whether the second statement is really necessary. Insert an apostrophe before the Call ClearLabels() statement in the btnClear control's Click event procedure to make the statement a comment. Save the solution, then start and test the application. Why is it necessary for the btnClear control to call the ClearLabels control? Stop the application. Delete the apostrophe you inserted. Save and then close the solution.

11. In this exercise, you find an error in an application's code. Open the SwatTheBugs Solution (SwatTheBugs Solution.sln) file, which is contained in the ClearlyVB\ Chap17\SwatTheBugs Solution folder. Open the Code Editor window and study the existing code. Start and then test the application. Notice that the application is not working correctly. Stop the application. Locate and correct any errors in the code. Save the solution, then start and test the application again. Stop the application, then close the solution.

ANSWERS TO "TRY THIS" EXERCISES

1. See Figure 17-28.

```
Public Class frmMain

    Private Sub CalcAndDisplayBonus(ByVal decTotal As Decimal)
        ' calculates and displays the bonus

        Dim decBonus As Decimal

        If decTotal > 1200 Then
            decBonus = decTotal * 0.1
        Else
            decBonus = decTotal * 0.08
        End If
        lblBonus.Text = decBonus.ToString("C2")
    End Sub

    Private Sub btnExit_Click ...

    Private Sub btnCalc_Click(ByVal sender As Object, ByVal e As System.EventArgs) Handle
        ' prompts the user to enter two sale amounts, then totals both amounts,
        ' and then calls a sub procedure to calculate and display the bonus

        Dim strInputSale1 As String
        Dim strInputSale2 As String
        Dim decSale1 As Decimal
        Dim decSale2 As Decimal
        Dim decSum As Decimal

        strInputSale1 = InputBox("First sale amount", "Bonus Solution")
        strInputSale2 = InputBox("Second sale amount", "Bonus Solution")

        Decimal.TryParse(strInputSale1, decSale1)
        Decimal.TryParse(strInputSale2, decSale2)
        decSum = decSale1 + decSale2
        Call CalcAndDisplayBonus(decSum)
    End Sub
End Class
```

Figure 17-28

2. See Figure 17-29.

```
Public Class frmMain

    Private Sub CalcBonus(ByVal decS1 As Decimal, _
                          ByVal decS2 As Decimal, _
                          ByRef decBonusAmt As Decimal)
        ' calculates the bonus

        Dim decSum As Decimal

        decSum = decS1 + decS2
        If decSum > 1200 Then
            decBonusAmt = decSum * 0.1
        Else
            decBonusAmt = decSum * 0.08
        End If
        lblBonus.Text = decBonusAmt.ToString("C2")
    End Sub

    Private Sub btnExit_Click ...

    Private Sub btnCalc_Click(ByVal sender As Object, ByVal e As System.EventArgs) Handle
        ' prompts the user to enter two sale amounts, then calls a
        ' sub procedure to calculate the bonus, then displays the bonus

        Dim strInputSale1 As String
        Dim strInputSale2 As String
        Dim decSale1 As Decimal
        Dim decSale2 As Decimal
        Dim decBonus As Decimal

        strInputSale1 = InputBox("First sale amount", "Bonus Solution")
        strInputSale2 = InputBox("Second sale amount", "Bonus Solution")

        Decimal.TryParse(strInputSale1, decSale1)
        Decimal.TryParse(strInputSale2, decSale2)
        Call CalcBonus(decSale1, decSale2, decBonus)
        lblBonus.Text = decBonus.ToString("C2")
    End Sub
End Class
```

Figure 17-29

18

TALK TO ME

After studying Chapter 18, you should be able to:

Explain the difference between a sub procedure
and a function procedure

Create a function procedure

Invoke a function procedure

WHAT'S THE ANSWER?

In addition to creating sub procedures, which you learned about in Chapter 17, you also can create function procedures. The difference between both types of procedures is that a **function procedure** returns a value after performing its assigned task, whereas a sub procedure does not return a value. Function procedures are referred to more simply as **functions**. Figure 18-1 shows the syntax for creating a function. The header and footer in a function are almost identical to the header and footer in a sub procedure, except the function's header and footer contain the Function keyword rather than the Sub keyword. Also different from a sub procedure header, a function's header includes the As *dataType* section. You use this section of the header to specify the data type of the value returned by the function. If the function returns a string, you enter As String at the end of the header; if the function returns a Double number, you enter As Double. As is true with a sub procedure, a function can receive information either *by value* or *by reference*. The information it receives is listed in the *parameterList* in the header. Between the function's header and footer, you enter the instructions you want the computer to process when the function is invoked. In most cases, the last statement within a function is Return *expression*, where *expression* represents the one and only value that will be returned to the statement that invoked the function. The data type of the *expression* in the Return statement must agree with the data type specified in the As *dataType* section of the header. In addition to the syntax, Figure 18-1 also includes an example of a function, as well as the steps you follow to enter a function in the Code Editor window. As with sub procedures, you can enter your functions above the first event procedure, below the last event procedure, or below the procedure from which they are invoked. In this book, you will enter the functions above the first event procedure. Like sub procedure names, function names are entered using Pascal case and typically begin with a verb. The name should indicate the task the function performs. For example, a good name for a function that returns a new price is GetNewPrice.

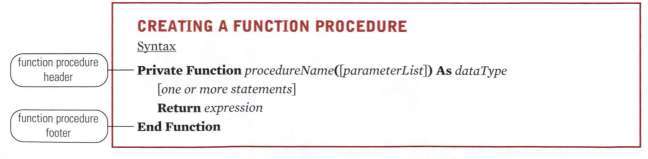

CREATING A FUNCTION PROCEDURE

Syntax

function procedure header — **Private Function** *procedureName*(**[***parameterList***]**) **As** *dataType*
    [*one or more statements*]
    Return *expression*
function procedure footer — **End Function**

Figure 18-1: Syntax, example, and steps for creating a function procedure (*continued on next page*)

```
Example

Private Function GetNewPrice(ByVal dblPrice As Double) As Double
    ' increases the current price by 5% and returns the new price

    dblPrice = dblPrice * 1.05
    Return dblPrice
End Function
```

Steps

1. Open the Code Editor window, then click a blank line in the window. The blank line can be anywhere between the Public Class line and the End Class line; however, it must be outside any other procedure.

2. Type the function procedure header, then press Enter. The Code Editor automatically enters the End Function line for you.

Figure 18-1: Syntax, example, and steps for creating a function procedure (*continued from previous page*)

After creating a function, you can invoke it from one or more places in an application's code. You invoke a function that you create in exactly the same way as you invoke one of Visual Basic's built-in functions, such as the InputBox function. You do this by including the function's name, along with any arguments, in a statement. The number, data type, and position of the arguments should agree with the number, data type, and position of the function's parameters. Usually the statement that invokes a function will assign the function's return value to a variable; however, it also may use the return value in a calculation or simply display the return value. Figure 18-2 shows examples of invoking the GetNewPrice function from Figure 18-1. The GetNewPrice(dblCurrentPrice) entry in each example invokes the function, passing it the value stored in the dblCurrentPrice variable. In Example 1, the function's return value is assigned to a variable. Example 2 shows how you can use the return value in a calculation, and Example 3 shows how you can display the return value in a label control.

INVOKING A FUNCTION PROCEDURE

Example 1 – assigning the return value to a variable

```
dblNewPrice = GetNewPrice(dblCurrentPrice)
```

Figure 18-2: Examples of invoking the GetNewPrice function (*continued on next page*)

Example 2 – using the return value in a calculation

dblTotalDue = intQuantity * GetNewPrice(dblCurrentPrice)

Example 3 – displaying the return value

lblNewPrice.Text = GetNewPrice(dblCurrentPrice).ToString("C2")

Figure 18-2: Examples of invoking the GetNewPrice function (*continued from previous page*)

You will use the GetNewPrice function in the Price Calculator application, which you view in the next section.

PRICE CALCULATOR APPLICATION

Figure 18-3 shows the Price Calculator application's user interface. The interface provides a text box for the user to enter the current price of an item. When the user clicks the Calculate button, the button's Click event procedure will use the GetNewPrice function to calculate and return the new price, which will be 5% more than the current price. The Click event procedure will then display the function's return value in the interface.

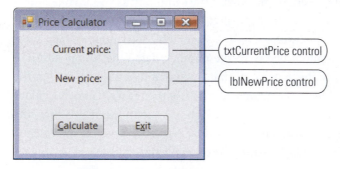

Figure 18-3: User interface for the Price Calculator application

To open the Price Calculator application, and then code and test the application:

1. Start Visual Studio 2008 (or Visual Basic 2008 Express Edition). Open the **Price Calculator Solution** (**Price Calculator Solution.sln**) file, which is contained in the ClearlyVB\Chap18\Price Calculator Solution folder. If necessary, open the designer window.

2. Open the Code Editor window. First, enter the GetNewPrice function. Click the **blank line** below the Public Class frmMain line, then press **Enter** to insert another blank line. Enter the GetNewPrice function shown in Figure 18-4.

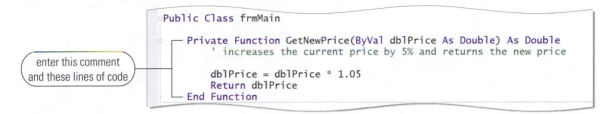

enter this comment
and these lines of code

```
Public Class frmMain

    Private Function GetNewPrice(ByVal dblPrice As Double) As Double
        ' increases the current price by 5% and returns the new price

        dblPrice = dblPrice * 1.05
        Return dblPrice
    End Function
```

Figure 18-4: GetNewPrice function entered in the Code Editor window

3. Now enter the statement to invoke the GetNewPrice function. Locate the btnCalc control's Click event procedure. The statement will pass the current price stored in the dblCurrentPrice variable to the function, and then store the function's return value in the dblNewPrice variable. Click the **blank line** below the ' get the new price comment. Type **dblNewPrice = GetNewPrice(dblCurrentPrice)** and press **Enter**.

4. Save the solution.

Before testing the application, you will desk-check it using $10 as the current price. When the user clicks the Calculate button, the button's Click event procedure creates the dblCurrentPrice and dblNewPrice variables. The TryParse method converts the contents of the txtCurrentPrice control to the Double data type and stores the result in the dblCurrentPrice variable. Figure 18-5 shows the desk-check table before the GetNewPrice function is invoked.

dblCurrentPrice   dblNewPrice
        10

Figure 18-5: Desk-check table before the GetNewPrice function is invoked

The dblNewPrice = GetNewPrice(dblCurrentPrice) statement is processed next. The statement invokes the GetNewPrice function, passing it the dblCurrentPrice variable *by value*. You know that the variable is passed *by value* because the keyword ByVal appears before the dblPrice parameter in the function's header. At this point, the computer temporarily leaves the Click event procedure to process the code in the function. When processing the function's header, the computer creates the dblPrice variable, and it stores the value passed to the function in the variable. The dblPrice variable can be used only by the GetNewPrice function because, like the variables in a sub procedure's header, the variables in a function's header have procedure scope. Next, the computer calculates the new price by multiplying the contents of the dblPrice variable by 1.05. It stores the new price in the dblPrice variable. Figure 18-6 shows the desk check table after the new price is assigned to the dblPrice variable.

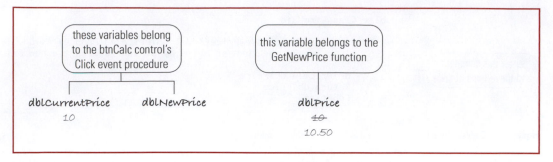

Figure 18-6: Desk-check table after the new price is assigned to the dblPrice variable

The function's Return dblPrice statement is processed next. The statement returns the contents of the dblPrice variable to the statement that invoked the function. That statement is the dblNewPrice = GetNewPrice(dblCurrentPrice) statement in the btnCalc control's Click event procedure. The End Function clause is processed next and ends the function. At this point, the computer removes the dblPrice variable from its internal memory and then returns to the btnCalc control's Click event procedure to finish processing the dblNewPrice = GetNewPrice(dblCurrentPrice) statement. The statement assigns the function's return value to the dblNewPrice variable. Figure 18-7 shows the desk-check table after the function ends and the new price is assigned to the dblNewPrice variable.

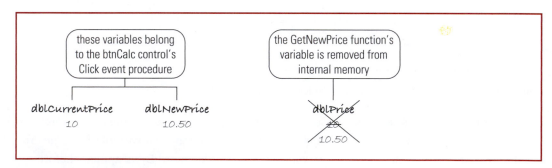

Figure 18-7: Desk-check table after the function ends and the new price is assigned to the dblNewPrice variable

The last assignment statement in the Click event procedure displays the new price (formatted with a dollar sign and two decimal places) in the interface. Finally, the computer processes the event procedure's End Sub clause. When the Click event procedure ends, the computer removes the dblCurrentPrice and dblNewPrice variables from its internal memory.

To test the Price Calculator application:

1. Save the solution, if necessary, then start the application. Type **10** in the Current price box, then click the **Calculate** button. $10.50 appears in the New price box.

2. Click the **Exit** button. Close the Code Editor window, then close the solution.

The Ch18-Functions video demonstrates function procedures by stepping through the code.

REVISITING THE TOTAL DUE CALCULATOR APPLICATION

Figure 18-8 shows the interface for the Total Due Calculator application from Chapter 17. As you may remember, you coded the application using a sub procedure to assign the discount amount. Figure 18-9 shows the code entered in both the AssignDiscount sub procedure and btnCalc control's Click event procedure in Chapter 17. Notice that the Call statement in the event procedure passes two items of information to the AssignDiscount sub procedure: the value stored in the decSubtotal variable and the address of the decDiscount variable. You passed the decSubtotal variable's value because the sub procedure required that information in two of the discount calculations. You passed the decDiscount variable's address to allow the sub procedure to set the variable's value.

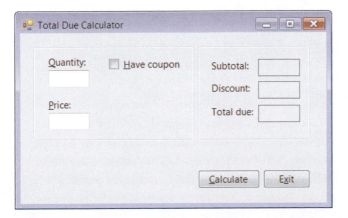

Figure 18-8: User interface for the Total Due Calculator application

the AssignDiscount sub procedure begins here

```vb
Private Sub AssignDiscount(ByVal decSub As Decimal, ByRef decDisc As Decimal)
    ' assigns the discount

    If chkCoupon.Checked = True Then
        Dim strCouponCode As String
        strCouponCode = InputBox("Coupon code:", "Total Due Calculator")
        Select Case strCouponCode.ToUpper
            Case "A05"
                decDisc = 5
            Case "X25"
                decDisc = 0.1 * decSub
            Case "NE4"
                decDisc = 0.15 * decSub
            Case Else
                MessageBox.Show("You entered an invalid coupon code.", _
                            "Total Due Calculator", MessageBoxButtons.OK, _
                            MessageBoxIcon.Information)
                decDisc = 0
        End Select
    Else
        decDisc = 0
    End If
End Sub
```

the btnCalc control's Click event procedure begins here

```vb
Private Sub btnCalc_Click(ByVal sender As Object, _
    ByVal e As System.EventArgs) Handles btnCalc.Click
    ' displays the subtotal, discount, and total due

    Dim intQuantity As Integer
    Dim decPrice As Decimal
    Dim decSubtotal As Decimal
    Dim decTotalDue As Decimal
    Dim decDiscount As Decimal

    Integer.TryParse(txtQuantity.Text, intQuantity)
    Decimal.TryParse(txtPrice.Text, decPrice)

    ' calculate subtotal
    decSubtotal = intQuantity * decPrice

    ' assign discount
    Call AssignDiscount(decSubtotal, decDiscount)

    ' calculate total due
    decTotalDue = decSubtotal - decDiscount
```

Call statement

Figure 18-9: Code entered in the AssignDiscount procedure and btnCalc control's Click event procedure (*continued on next page*)

```
' display subtotal, discount, and total due
lblSubtotal.Text = decSubtotal.ToString("N2")
lblDiscount.Text = decDiscount.ToString("N2")
lblTotalDue.Text = decTotalDue.ToString("N2")
End Sub
```

Figure 18-9: Code entered in the AssignDiscount procedure and btnCalc control's Click event procedure
(*continued from previous page*)

Rather than using a sub procedure to assign the discount amount, you can use a function instead. Consider the changes you will need to make to the code shown in Figure 18-9 in order to use a function. You will make the changes in the following set of steps.

To open the Total Due Calculator application, and then modify the code to use a function:

1. Open the **Total Due Solution** (**Total Due Solution.sln**) file, which is contained in the ClearlyVB\Chap18\Total Due Solution folder. If necessary, open the designer window.

2. Open the Code Editor window. Locate the btnCalc control's Click event procedure. The Call statement will need to be replaced with a statement that invokes the AssignDiscount function (rather than the AssignDiscount sub procedure). The statement will assign the function's return value, which is the discount amount, to the decDiscount variable. Like the sub procedure, the function will need the statement to pass the value stored in the decSubtotal variable, because the value is used in two of the discount calculations. However, it will not need the statement to pass the address of the decDiscount variable, because the statement itself will store the discount amount in the variable. Change the Call AssignDiscount(decSubtotal, decDiscount) statement to **decDiscount = AssignDiscount(decSubtotal)**. (Don't be concerned about the jagged line that appears below AssignDiscount(decSubtotal) in the statement. The jagged line will disappear after you complete Step 4 below.)

3. Locate the AssignDiscount sub procedure in the Code Editor window. First, change the Sub keyword in the procedure header to **Function**. The Code Editor automatically changes the Sub keyword in the footer to Function.

4. Next, delete **, ByRef decDisc As Decimal** from the function header. (Be sure to delete the comma.) Doing this causes a jagged line to appear below each occurrence of decDisc in the function. The jagged line indicates that the variable has not been declared. In order to use the decDisc variable, the function will need to declare it in a Dim statement. Click the **blank line** below the ' assigns the discount comment and press **Enter** to insert another blank line. Type **dim decDisc as decimal** and press **Enter**.

5. Recall that the data type of the function's return value is specified at the end of the function header. The AssignDiscount function returns a Decimal value. Click after the **)** in the function header, press the **Spacebar**, then type **As Decimal**.

6. Finally, you need to tell the function to return the discount amount, which is stored in the decDisc variable, to the statement that invoked the function. Click **after the letter f** in the End If clause, then press **Enter**. Type **return decDisc** and press **Enter**.

7. Save the solution. Figure 18-10 shows the code entered in the AssignDiscount function and in the btnCalc control's Click event procedure. The modified lines of code are shaded in the figure.

the AssignDiscount function begins here →

```
Private Function AssignDiscount(ByVal decSub As Decimal) As Decimal
    ' assigns the discount

    Dim decDisc As Decimal

    If chkCoupon.Checked = True Then
        Dim strCouponCode As String
        strCouponCode = InputBox("Coupon code:", "Total Due Calculator")
        Select Case strCouponCode.ToUpper
            Case "A05"
                decDisc = 5
            Case "X25"
                decDisc = 0.1 * decSub
            Case "NE4"
                decDisc = 0.15 * decSub
            Case Else
                MessageBox.Show("You entered an invalid coupon code.", _
                                "Total Due Calculator", MessageBoxButtons.OK, _
                                MessageBoxIcon.Information)
                decDisc = 0
        End Select
    Else
        decDisc = 0
    End If
    Return decDisc

End Function
```

the btnCalc control's Click event procedure begins here →

```
Private Sub btnCalc_Click(ByVal sender As Object, _
    ByVal e As System.EventArgs) Handles btnCalc.Click
    ' displays the subtotal, discount, and total due
```

Figure 18-10: Code entered in the AssignDiscount function and btnCalc control's Click event procedure (*continued on next page*)

```
            Dim intQuantity As Integer
            Dim decPrice As Decimal
            Dim decSubtotal As Decimal
            Dim decTotalDue As Decimal
            Dim decDiscount As Decimal

            Integer.TryParse(txtQuantity.Text, intQuantity)
            Decimal.TryParse(txtPrice.Text, decPrice)

            ' calculate subtotal
            decSubtotal = intQuantity * decPrice

            ' assign discount
            decDiscount = AssignDiscount(decSubtotal)

            ' calculate total due
            decTotalDue = decSubtotal - decDiscount

            ' display subtotal, discount, and total due
            lblSubtotal.Text = decSubtotal.ToString("N2")
            lblDiscount.Text = decDiscount.ToString("N2")
            lblTotalDue.Text = decTotalDue.ToString("N2")
        End Sub
```

invokes the function and assigns its return value to a variable

Figure 18-10: Code entered in the AssignDiscount function and btnCalc control's Click event procedure (*continued from previous page*)

To test the Total Due Calculator application:

1. Save the solution, if necessary, then start the application. Type **4** in the Quantity box and then type **15** in the Price box. Click the **Have coupon** check box to select it, then click the **Calculate** button.

2. Type **X25** as the coupon code, then press **Enter**. The values 60.00, 6.00, and 54.00 appear in the Subtotal, Discount, and Total due boxes, respectively.

3. Click the **Exit** button. Close the Code Editor window, then close the solution.

Now that you've seen two different ways of assigning the discount in the Total Due Calculator application—one using a sub procedure and the other using a function procedure—you may be wondering whether one way is better than the other. Comparing the sub procedure header in Figure 18-9 with the function header in Figure 18-10, you will notice that only the sub procedure is passed a memory location *by reference*. This is because the sub procedure is responsible for assigning a value to the memory location. After the computer processes the sub procedure header, the memory location has two different names (decDiscount and decDisc) and can be accessed by two different procedures (the AssignDiscount sub procedure and the btnCalc control's Click event procedure). Allowing more than one procedure to change the contents of a memory location can lead to subtle errors that are difficult to find, especially in large applications. As you learned in Chapter 9, fewer unintentional errors occur in applications when memory locations have the minimum scope needed. Therefore, using a function to assign the discount is the better way to code the Total Due Calculator application. Most programmers pass a variable *by reference* only when a procedure needs to produce more than one result. For example, a procedure may need to return the number of hours an employee worked and also whether the hours are valid.

MINI-QUIZ 1

1. An event procedure uses the statement dblBonusAmount = GetBonus(dblSales) to invoke the GetBonus function. The function multiplies the sale amount passed to it by 3% and then returns the result. Which of the following is the appropriate function header for the GetBonus function?

   a. Private Function GetBonus(ByVal dblSold As Double)

   b. Private Function GetBonus(ByRef dblSold As Double)

   c. Private Function GetBonus(ByVal dblSold As Double) As Double

   d. Private Function GetBonus(ByVal dblSold As Double, ByRef dblBonus As Double)

2. Write a Visual Basic statement that instructs the GetIncome function to return the contents of the decIncome variable.

3. Write a Visual Basic statement that invokes the GetSales function, passing it two Decimal variables named decSale1 and decSale2. The statement should multiply the function's return value by .08, and then assign the result to the decTax variable.

For more examples of functions, see the Function Procedures section in the Ch18WantMore.pdf file.

SUMMARY

» You can create your own function procedures, called functions, in Visual Basic. Unlike a sub procedure, a function returns a value after completing its task.

» Typically, the Return statement appears as the last statement in a function. A function returns only one value to the statement that invoked it.

» You invoke a function by including the function's name, along with any arguments, in a statement. The number of arguments listed in the statement should agree with the number of parameters listed in the function's *parameterList*. Also, the data type and position of each argument should agree with the data type and position of its corresponding parameter.

» The statement that invokes a function may assign the return value to a variable, use the return value in a calculation, or display the return value.

» Variables that appear in a function header's *parameterList* have procedure scope.

» In most cases, it is better to use a function rather than a sub procedure that passes a variable *by reference*.

KEY TERMS

Function procedure—a procedure that returns a value after completing its task; also referred to as a function

Functions—the term more commonly used when referring to function procedures

ANSWERS TO MINI-QUIZ

MINI-QUIZ 1

1. c. Private Function GetBonus(ByVal dblSold As Double) As Double

2. Return decIncome

3. decTax = GetSales(decSale1, decSale2) * .08

REVIEW QUESTIONS

1. Which of the following is false?

    a. A function can return one or more values to the statement that invoked it.

    b. A function can accept one or more items of data passed to it.

    c. The *parameterList* in a function header is optional.

    d. At times, a memory location inside the computer's internal memory may have more than one name.

2. Which of the following statements invokes the GetGross function and assigns its return value to the decGrossPay variable? The statement passes the contents of two Decimal variables to the function.

    a. decGrossPay = Call GetGross(decHours, decRate)

    b. Call GetGross(decHours, decRate, decGrossPay)

    c. decGrossPay = GetGross(decHours, decRate)

    d. decGrossPay = GetGross(ByVal decHours, ByVal decRate)

3. When the GetExpenses function completes its processing, it should send the value stored in the decTotalExpenses variable to the statement that invoked the function. Which of the following statements accomplishes this task?

    a. Return (ByVal decTotalExpenses)

    b. Send ByVal(decTotalExpenses)

    c. SendBack decTotalExpenses

    d. Return decTotalExpenses

4. Which of the following is false?

    a. A function can receive information *by value* and *by reference*.

    b. When a function ends, the computer processes the statement immediately following the one that invoked the function.

    c. The variables listed in a function's *parameterList* have procedure scope.

    d. When a function ends, the computer removes the function's variables from its internal memory.

5. A function named GetEnding is passed three Integer variables named intBegin, intSales, and intPurchases. The function's task is to calculate and return the ending inventory. Which of the following function headers is appropriate?

a. Private Function GetEnding(ByVal intB As Integer, ByVal intS As Integer, ByVal intP As Integer) As Integer

b. Private Function GetEnding(ByRef intB As Integer, ByRef intS As Integer, ByRef intP As Integer) As Integer

c. Private Function GetEnding(ByVal intB As Integer, ByVal intS As Integer, ByVal intP As Integer, ByRef intE) As Integer

d. Private Sub Function GetEnding(ByVal intB As Integer, ByVal intS As Integer, ByVal intP As Integer)

EXERCISES

1. In this exercise, you code an application that calculates and displays a bonus amount based on two sale amounts entered by the user. Open the Bonus Solution (Bonus Solution.sln) file, which is contained in the ClearlyVB\Chap18\Bonus Solution-TRY THIS 1 folder. Open the designer window, then open the Code Editor window. Use the algorithm shown in Figure 18-11 to code the btnCalc control's Click event procedure and the function. Name the function GetBonus. Save the solution, then start and test the application. Stop the application, then close the solution. (The answers to TRY THIS Exercises are located at the end of the chapter.)

» TRY THIS

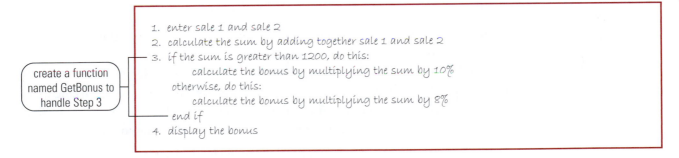

Figure 18-11: Algorithm for the Bonus Solution-TRY THIS 1 application

2. In this exercise, you modify the application from TRY THIS Exercise 1. Use Windows to make a copy of the Bonus Solution-TRY THIS 1 folder. Save the copy in the ClearlyVB\Chap18 folder. Rename the copy Bonus Solution-TRY THIS 2. Open the Bonus Solution (Bonus Solution.sln) file contained in the ClearlyVB\Chap18\Bonus Solution-TRY THIS 2 folder. Open the designer window, then change the form's Text

» TRY THIS

property to Bonus Solution-TRY THIS 2. Open the Code Editor window. The btnCalc control's Click event procedure should use a function to add together the two sale amounts and then return the sum. Create the GetSum function, then modify the event procedure's code. Save the solution, then start and test the application. Stop the application, then close the solution. (The answers to TRY THIS Exercises are located at the end of the chapter.)

» MODIFY THIS

3. In this exercise, you modify the Price Calculator application coded in the chapter. Use Windows to make a copy of the Price Calculator Solution folder. Save the copy in the ClearlyVB\Chap18 folder. Rename the copy Price Calculator Solution-MODIFY THIS. Open the Price Calculator Solution (Price Calculator Solution.sln) file contained in the Price Calculator Solution-MODIFY THIS folder. Open the designer window, then open the Code Editor window. Modify the code so that it uses a sub procedure rather than a function to calculate the new price. Save the solution. Start and then test the application. Stop the application, then close the solution.

» INTRODUCTORY

4. In this exercise, you code an application that displays a letter grade based on the average of three test scores. Open the Grade Solution (Grade Solution.sln) file, which is contained in the ClearlyVB\Chap18\Grade Solution folder. Code the application, using a function to determine and return the letter grade. If the average is at least 90, the grade is A. If the average is at least 80 but less than 90, the grade is B. If the average is at least 70 but less than 80, the grade is C. If the average is at least 60 but less than 70, the grade is D. If the average is below 60, the grade is F. Save the solution. Start and then test the application. Stop the application, then close the solution.

» INTRODUCTORY

5. In this exercise, you code an application that calculates and displays the amount of an employee's gross pay. Open the Gross Pay Solution (Gross Pay Solution.sln) file, which is contained in the ClearlyVB\Chap18\Gross Pay Solution folder. Code the application, using a function to calculate and return the gross pay. Employees working more than 40 hours receive time and one-half for the hours over 40. Save the solution. Start and then test the application. Stop the application, then close the solution.

» INTERMEDIATE

6. In this exercise, you modify the application you coded in Exercise 5.

   a. Use Windows to make a copy of the Gross Pay Solution folder. Save the copy in the ClearlyVB\Chap18 folder. Rename the copy Modified Gross Pay Solution.

   b. Open the Gross Pay Solution (Gross Pay Solution.sln) file contained in the Modified Gross Pay Solution folder. Open the designer window. The application should display the federal and state tax amounts and the net pay. Add label controls for displaying the three amounts.

c. Open the Code Editor window. Create a function that calculates and returns the federal tax. Also create a function that calculates and returns the state tax. For simplicity, use a rate of 25% for the federal tax and a rate of 5% for the state tax.

d. Modify the btnCalc control's Click event procedure to call both functions. The procedure also will need to calculate the net pay, as well as display the federal and state taxes and the net pay. (Use the Math.Round method, which you learned about in Chapter 7's Advanced Exercises 8 and 9.) Also modify both TextChanged event procedures.

e. Save the solution. Start and then test the application. Stop the application, then close the solution.

7. In this exercise, you code an application for the manager of Wallpaper Warehouse. The application calculates and displays the number of single rolls of wallpaper required to cover a room.

»INTERMEDIATE

a. Create a new Visual Basic Windows application. Name the solution, project, and form file Wallpaper Warehouse Solution, Wallpaper Warehouse Project, and frmMain.vb, respectively. Save the application in the ClearlyVB\Chap18 folder. If necessary, change the form's name to frmMain.

b. Create the interface shown in Figure 18-12.

c. Code the application. The text boxes should accept only numbers, the period, and the Backspace key. The Single rolls box should be cleared when a change is made to any of the four text boxes. Use a function to calculate and return the number of single rolls.

d. Save the solution, then start and test the application. Stop the application, then close the solution.

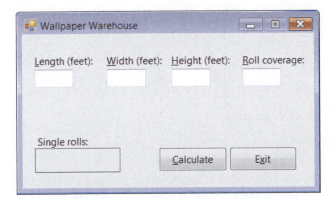

Figure 18-12: User interface for the Wallpaper Warehouse application

»ADVANCED

8. The Doughnut Shoppe sells four varieties of doughnuts: Glazed ($.65), Sugar ($.65), Chocolate ($.85), and Filled ($1.00). It also sells regular coffee ($1.80) and cappuccino ($2.50). The store manager wants an application that she can use to calculate and display a customer's subtotal, 3% sales tax, and total due.

    a. Create a new Visual Basic Windows application. Name the solution, project, and form file Doughnut Shoppe Solution, Doughnut Shoppe Project, and frmMain.vb, respectively. Save the application in the ClearlyVB\Chap18 folder. If necessary, change the form's name to frmMain.

    b. Create the interface shown in Figure 18-13.

    c. Code the application. Use one function to calculate and return the cost of the doughnut. Use another function to calculate and return the cost of the coffee. Use a third function to calculate and return the 3% sales tax. Use a sub procedure to clear the subtotal, sales tax, and total due amounts when a radio button is clicked.

    d. Save the solution, then start and test the application. Stop the application, then close the solution.

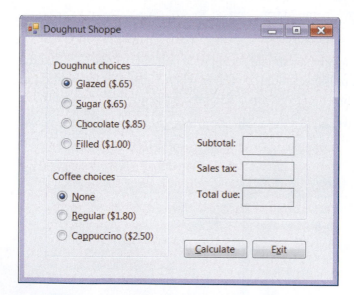

Figure 18-13: User interface for the Doughnut Shoppe application

»ADVANCED

9. In this exercise, you modify the Harvey Industries application created in Exercise 9 in Chapter 17. If you did not complete Chapter 17's Exercise 9, you will need to do so before you can complete this exercise. Use Windows to copy the Harvey Industries Solution folder from the ClearlyVB\Chap17 folder to the ClearlyVB\Chap18 folder. Open the Harvey Industries Solution (Harvey Industries Solution.sln) file contained in the

ClearlyVB\Chap18\Harvey Industries Solution folder. Change the sub procedure that calculates the federal withholding tax to a function. Also include a function to calculate the gross pay, and another function to calculate the FICA tax. Save the solution, then start and test the application. Stop the application, then close the solution.

10. Open the FigureThisOut Solution (FigureThisOut Solution.sln) file, which is contained in the ClearlyVB\Chap18\FigureThisOut Solution folder. Open the Code Editor window and study the existing code. Desk-check the function and Click event procedures' code using A, 75, and 83 as the operation, first number, and second number, respectively; then desk-check the code using M, 6, and 8. Save the solution, then start and test the application. Stop the application, then close the solution.

11. In this exercise, you find an error in an application's code. Open the SwatTheBugs Solution (SwatTheBugs Solution.sln) file, which is contained in the ClearlyVB\Chap18\SwatTheBugs Solution folder. Open the Code Editor window and study the existing code. Start and then test the application. Notice that the application is not working correctly. Stop the application. Locate and correct any errors in the code. Save the solution, then start and test the application again. Stop the application, then close the solution.

ANSWERS TO "TRY THIS" EXERCISES

1. Figure 18-14 shows the code for the GetBonus function and the btnCalc control's Click event procedure.

```vb
Private Function GetBonus(ByVal decTotal As Decimal) As Decimal
    ' calculates the bonus

    Dim decBonus As Decimal

    If decTotal > 1200 Then
        decBonus = decTotal * 0.1
    Else
        decBonus = decTotal * 0.08
    End If

    Return decBonus
End Function
```

Figure 18-14 (*continued on next page*)

```
Private Sub btnCalc_Click(ByVal sender As Object, _
    ByVal e As System.EventArgs) Handles btnCalc.Click
    ' prompts the user to enter two sale amounts, then totals both amounts,
    ' then calls a function to calculate the bonus, then displays the bonus

    Dim strInputSale1 As String
    Dim strInputSale2 As String
    Dim decSale1 As Decimal
    Dim decSale2 As Decimal
    Dim decSum As Decimal
    Dim decBonus As Decimal

    strInputSale1 = InputBox("First sale amount", "Bonus Solution")
    strInputSale2 = InputBox("Second sale amount", "Bonus Solution")

    Decimal.TryParse(strInputSale1, decSale1)
    Decimal.TryParse(strInputSale2, decSale2)
    decSum = decSale1 + decSale2
    decBonus = GetBonus(decSum)
    lblBonus.Text = decBonus.ToString("C2")
End Sub
```

Figure 18-14 (*continued from previous page*)

2. Figure 18-15 shows the code for the GetSum function. In the btnCalc control's Click event procedure, change the decSum = decSale1 + decSale2 statement to decSum = GetSum(decSale1, decSale2).

```
Private Function GetSum(ByVal decS1 As Decimal, _
                        ByVal decS2 As Decimal) As Decimal
    ' totals the sales amounts

    Return decS1 + decS2
End Function
```

Figure 18-15

19

A RAY OF SUNSHINE

After studying Chapter 19, you should be able to:

Explain the purpose of an array

Create a one-dimensional array

Store data in a one-dimensional array

Sort the contents of a one-dimensional array

Search a one-dimensional array

LET'S JOIN THE GROUP

All of the applications you have coded since Chapter 7 have used simple variables. A **simple variable**, also called a **scalar variable**, is one that is unrelated to any other variable in memory. At times, however, you will encounter situations where some of the variables in an application *are* related to each other. In those cases, it is easier and more efficient to treat the related variables as a group. You already are familiar with the concept of grouping. The clothes in your closet are probably separated into groups, such as coats, sweaters, shirts, dresses, and so on. Grouping your clothes in this manner allows you to easily locate your favorite sweater, because you just need to look through the sweater group rather than through the entire closet. You also probably have your CD (compact disc) collection grouped either by music type or artist. If your collection is grouped by artist, it will take only a few seconds to find all your Beatles CDs and, depending on the number of Beatles CDs you own, only a short time after that to locate a particular CD. When you group together related variables, the group is referred to as an array of variables or, more simply, an **array**. You might use an array of 12 String variables to store the names of the 12 months in a year. Or, you might use an array of 50 Decimal variables to store the sale amounts made in each of the 50 states. The most commonly used arrays in business applications are one-dimensional and two-dimensional. You will learn about one-dimensional arrays in this chapter and also in the next chapter. Two dimensional arrays are covered in Chapter 21.

Each variable in an array has the same name and data type. You distinguish one variable in a one-dimensional array from another variable in the array using a unique number, called a **subscript**. The subscript indicates the variable's position in the array and is assigned by the computer when the array is created in internal memory. The first variable in a one-dimensional array is assigned a subscript of 0, the second a subscript of 1, and so on. You refer to each variable in an array by the array's name and the variable's subscript, which is specified in a set of parentheses immediately following the array name. To refer to the first variable in a one-dimensional String array named strFriends, you use strFriends(0)—read "strFriends sub zero." Similarly, to refer to the third variable in the strFriends array, you use strFriends(2). Figure 19-1 shows this naming convention using the storage bin illustration from Chapter 7. The intAge, decRate, and strMonth variables included in the figure are scalar variables.

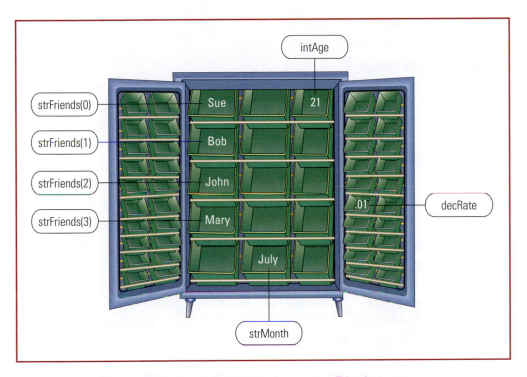

Figure 19-1: Illustration of the naming convention for the one-dimensional strFriends array

Figure 19-2 shows two versions of the syntax for declaring a procedure-level one-dimensional array in Visual Basic. In each syntax, *arrayName* is the name of the array and *dataType* is the type of data the array variables, referred to as elements, will store. Also included in the figure are examples of using both versions of the syntax.

DECLARING A PROCEDURE-LEVEL ONE-DIMENSIONAL ARRAY

Syntax—Version 1

Dim *arrayName*(*highestSubscript*) **As** *dataType*

Syntax—Version 2

Dim *arrayName*() **As** *dataType* = {*initialValues*}

Figure 19-2: Syntax versions and examples of declaring a procedure-level one-dimensional array (*continued on next page*)

> Example 1—Version 1's syntax
>
> Dim intNumbers(5) As Integer
> declares and initializes (to 0) a six-element Integer array named intNumbers
>
> Example 2—Version 2's syntax
>
> Dim strFriends() As String = {"Sue", "Bob", "John", "Mary"}
> declares and initializes a four-element String array named strFriends

Figure 19-2: Syntax versions and examples of declaring a procedure-level one-dimensional array (*continued from previous page*)

In Version 1 of the syntax, *highestSubscript* is an integer that specifies the highest subscript in the array. When the array is created, it will contain one element more than the number specified in the *highestSubscript* argument; this is because the first element in a one-dimensional array has a subscript of 0. As a result, the intNumbers array declared in Example 1 will contain six elements with subscripts of 0, 1, 2, 3, 4, and 5. When you use Version 1 of the syntax, the computer automatically initializes each element in the array when the array is created. The elements in a numeric array are initialized to the number 0. The elements in a String array, on the other hand, are initialized to the empty string.

Rather than having the computer use a default value to initialize each array element, you can use Version 2 of the syntax to specify each element's initial value when the array is declared. Assigning initial values to an array is often referred to as **populating the array**. You list the initial values in the *initialValues* section of the syntax, using commas to separate the values, and you enclose the list of values in braces ({}). Notice that Version 2's syntax does not include the *highestSubscript* argument; instead, an empty set of parentheses follows the array name. The computer automatically calculates the highest subscript based on the number of values listed in the *initialValues* section. Because the first subscript in a one-dimensional array is the number 0, the highest subscript is always one number less than the number of values listed in the *initialValues* section. The Dim strFriends() As String = {"Sue", "Bob", "John", "Mary"} statement, for instance, creates a four-element array with subscripts of 0, 1, 2, and 3. The computer assigns the string "Sue" to the strFriends(0) element, "Bob" to the strFriends(1) element, "John" to the strFriends(2) element, and "Mary" to the strFriends(3) element, as shown earlier in Figure 19-1.

The variables (elements) in an array can be used just like any other variables: you can assign values to them, use them in calculations, display their contents, and so on. Figure 19-3 shows examples of performing these tasks.

USING AN ELEMENT IN A ONE-DIMENSIONAL ARRAY

Example 1

```
Dim strCities() As String = {"Paris", "Rome", "Lisbon"}
strCities(0) = "Madrid"
```

assigns the string "Madrid" to the first element in the strCities array, replacing the string "Paris"

Example 2

```
Dim intSalaries() As Integer = {25000, 35000, 50000, 23000}
intSalaries(3) = intSalaries(3) + 2000
```

adds 2000 to the contents of the last element in the intSalaries array (23000), and then assigns the result (25000) to the element

Example 3

```
Dim decSales(10) As Decimal
Decimal.TryParse(txtSales.Text, decSales(2))
lblSales.Text = decSales(2).ToString("C2")
```

assigns the value returned by the TryParse method to the third element in the decSales array, then displays the value (formatted with a dollar sign and two decimal places) in the lblSales control

---

Figure 19-3: Examples of using an element in a one-dimensional array

The procedures you code in this chapter will demonstrate some of the ways one-dimensional arrays are used in an application. In most applications, the values stored in an array come from a file on the computer's disk and are assigned to the array after it is declared. However, so that you can follow the code and its results more easily, the applications in this chapter use the Dim statement to store the appropriate values in the array.

MINI-QUIZ 1

1. Write a Visual Basic statement that declares a 20-element one-dimensional Integer array named intQuantities.

2. The highest subscript in the intQuantities array from Question 1 is _____.

3. Write a Visual Basic statement that assigns the number 7 to the fourth element in the intQuantities array.

Before continuing, it may be helpful to view the Ch19-One-Dimensional Arrays video.

MY FRIENDS APPLICATION

The My Friends application will store four names in a one-dimensional String array named strFriends. It then will display the contents of the array in three label controls named lblOriginal, lblAscending, and lblDescending. In the lblOriginal control, the names will appear in the same order as in the array. In the lblAscending and lblDescending controls, the names will appear in ascending and descending order, respectively.

To open the Friends application, and then begin coding the application:

1. Start Visual Studio 2008 (or Visual Basic 2008 Express Edition). Open the **Friends Solution** (**Friends Solution.sln**) file, which is contained in the ClearlyVB\Chap19\ Friends Solution folder. If necessary, open the designer window.

2. Open the Code Editor window, then open the code template for the btnDisplay control's Click event procedure. Type ' **displays names in original, ascending, and descending order** and press **Enter** twice.

3. First, declare and initialize the strFriends array. Type **dim strFriends() as string = {"Sue", "Bob", "John", "Mary"}** and press **Enter** twice.

4. Now clear the contents of the three label controls. Type the following comment and three assignment statements. Press **Enter** twice after typing the last assignment statement.

```
' clear label controls
lblOriginal.Text = String.Empty
lblAscending.Text = String.Empty
lblDescending.Text = String.Empty
```

Next, you will display the contents of the array in the lblOriginal control. You can accomplish this task using a loop to access each element in the array, beginning with the element whose subscript is 0 and ending with the element whose subscript is 3. Because you want the loop instructions processed a precise number of times—in this case, from 0 to 3—you will code the loop using the For...Next statement. As you learned in Chapter 15, the For...Next statement provides a more convenient way to code a counter loop because, in addition to evaluating the loop condition, it also handles initializing and updating the counter variable. Figure 19-4 shows two versions of the appropriate code. Only the *endValue* in the For clause is different in each version. In Version 1, the *endValue* is 3 (the highest subscript in the array). In Version 2, the *endValue* is the expression strFriends.Length - 1. The expression uses the array's Length property, which contains an integer that represents the number of elements in the array; in this case, the Length property contains the number 4. To determine the highest subscript in the array, you simply subtract the number 1, as shown in the expression. Although both versions of code in Figure 19-4 will work, Version 2's code is the preferred one for several reasons. First, if you use the Length property, you won't have to count the number of array elements yourself. Second, the Length property is essential when you don't know the exact number of array elements; this may be the case when the array values come from a file. Finally, if the number of array elements changes in the future, the Length property's value will automatically adjust.

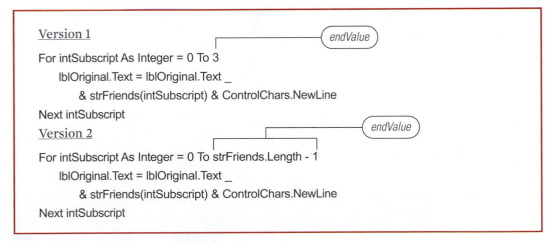

Figure 19-4: Two versions of the For...Next statement

To continue coding the My Friends application, and then test the code:

1. Type the comment and four lines of code indicated in Figure 19-5, then position the insertion point as shown in the figure.

```
Private Sub btnDisplay_Click(ByVal sender As Object, ByVal e As System
    ' displays names in original, descending, and ascending order

    Dim strFriends() As String = {"Sue", "Bob", "John", "Mary"}

    ' clear label controls
    lblOriginal.Text = String.Empty
    lblAscending.Text = String.Empty
    lblDescending.Text = String.Empty

    ' display in original order
    For intSubscript As Integer = 0 To strFriends.Length - 1
        lblOriginal.Text = lblOriginal.Text _
            & strFriends(intSubscript) & ControlChars.NewLine
    Next intSubscript


End Sub
```

enter this comment and these lines of code

position the insertion point here

Figure 19-5: Code to display the array contents in the original order

2. Before finishing the procedure's code, you will test it. Save the solution, then start the application. Click the **Display** button. The names Sue, Bob, John, and Mary appear in the lblOriginal control, as shown in Figure 19-6.

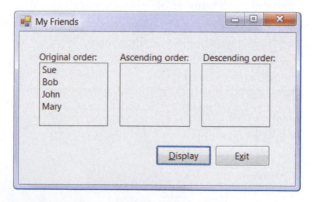

Figure 19-6: Array contents displayed in the Original order box

3. Click the **Exit** button.

Before displaying the array values in the lblAscending and lblDescending controls, you need to arrange the values in the appropriate order. Arranging data in a specific order is called **sorting**. To sort the values in a one-dimensional array in ascending order, you use the **Array.Sort method**. The method's syntax is **Array.Sort(***arrayName***)**. When an array is sorted in ascending order, the first element in the array contains the smallest value and the last element contains the largest value. To sort a one-dimensional array in descending order, you first sort the values in ascending order, and then use the **Array.Reverse method** to reverse the array elements. The method's syntax is **Array.Reverse(**arrayName**)**. When an array is sorted in descending order, the first element in the array contains the largest value and the last element contains the smallest value.

To complete the My Friends application, and then test the application:

1. Type the comments and lines of code indicated in Figure 19-7.

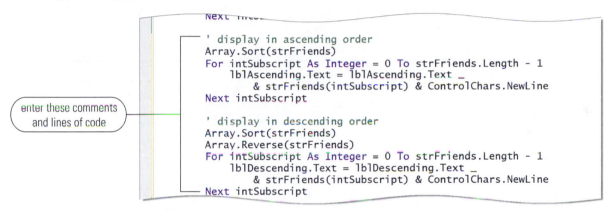

enter these comments and lines of code

```
Next intbu...

' display in ascending order
Array.Sort(strFriends)
For intSubscript As Integer = 0 To strFriends.Length - 1
    lblAscending.Text = lblAscending.Text _
        & strFriends(intSubscript) & ControlChars.NewLine
Next intSubscript

' display in descending order
Array.Sort(strFriends)
Array.Reverse(strFriends)
For intSubscript As Integer = 0 To strFriends.Length - 1
    lblDescending.Text = lblDescending.Text _
        & strFriends(intSubscript) & ControlChars.NewLine
Next intSubscript
```

Figure 19-7: Code to display the array contents in ascending and descending order

2. Save the solution, then start the application. Click the **Display** button. See Figure 19-8.

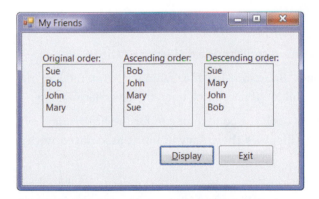

Figure 19-8: Array values displayed in the three label controls

3. Click the **Exit** button. Close the Code Editor window, then close the solution.

WANT MORE INFO

The Array.Sort method is not the only way to sort the contents of an array. To learn more about sorting arrays, see the Sorting Routines section in the Ch19WantMore.pdf file.

SALARY APPLICATION

The Salary application will store six salary amounts in a one-dimensional Integer array named intSalaries. Each salary amount corresponds to a salary code; the valid codes are the numbers 1 through 6. Code 1's salary is stored in the intSalaries(0) element in the array. Code 2's salary is stored in the intSalaries(1) element, and so on. Notice that the code is one number more than the subscript of its corresponding amount in the array. After storing the salary amounts in the array, the application will prompt the user to enter a salary code. It then will display the amount associated with the code. Figure 19-9 shows the planning information for the application.

Output: salary amount

Processing: 6-element one-dimensional array of salary amounts
                array subscript

Input: salary code (1 through 6)

Algorithm:
1. enter the salary code
2. calculate the array subscript by subtracting 1 from the salary code
3. use the array subscript to display (in a label control) the associated salary amount from the array

Figure 19-9: Planning information for the Salary application

To open the Salary application, and then code and test the application:

1. Open the **Salary Solution** (**Salary Solution.sln**) file, which is contained in the ClearlyVB\Chap19\Salary Solution folder. If necessary, open the designer window.

2. Open the Code Editor window, then open the code template for the btnDisplay control's Click event procedure. Type **' displays the salary amount associated with a code** and press **Enter** twice.

3. First, declare and initialize the intSalaries array. Also declare the necessary variables. Type the declaration statements shown in Figure 19-10, then position the insertion point as shown in the figure.

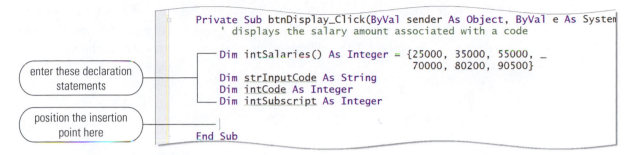

enter these declaration
statements

position the insertion
point here

```
Private Sub btnDisplay_Click(ByVal sender As Object, ByVal e As System
    ' displays the salary amount associated with a code

    Dim intSalaries() As Integer = {25000, 35000, 55000, _
                                    70000, 80200, 90500}
    Dim strInputCode As String
    Dim intCode As Integer
    Dim intSubscript As Integer


End Sub
```

Figure 19-10: Declaration statements entered in the procedure

4. The first step in the algorithm is to enter the salary code. Type **strInputCode = inputbox("Salary code (1-6)", "Salary")** and press **Enter**.

5. Step 2 in the algorithm is to calculate the array subscript by subtracting the number 1 from the salary code. Before you can do this, you need to convert the salary code from the String data type to the Integer data type. Type **integer.tryparse(strInputCode, intCode)** and press **Enter**. Type **' subtract 1 from the code to get the appropriate subscript** and press **Enter**, then type **intSubscript = intCode - 1** and press **Enter** twice.

6. Step 3 in the algorithm is to use the array subscript to display the appropriate salary amount from the array. Type **lblSalary.text = intSalaries(intSubscript).tostring** and press **Enter**.

7. Save the solution, then start the application. Click the **Display Salary** button. Type **1** as the salary code and press **Enter**. The salary amount stored in the intSalaries(0) element appears in the Salary box, as shown in Figure 19-11.

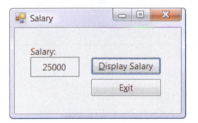

Figure 19-11: Interface showing the salary for code 1

8. Now you will observe the result of entering an invalid salary code. Click the **Display Salary** button. Type **8** and press **Enter**; doing this causes a runtime error. As a result, the Code Editor highlights the lblSalary.Text = intSalaries(intSubscript).ToString statement, and the help box indicates that the index (which is another term for subscript) is outside the bounds of the array.

9. Place your mouse pointer on intSubscript in the highlighted statement, as shown in Figure 19-12. The variable contains the number 7, which is one number less than the salary code you entered. The valid subscripts for the array, however, are the numbers 0 through 5 only.

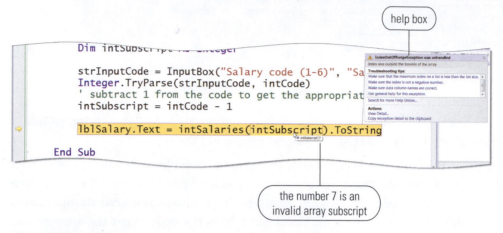

Figure 19-12: Result of the runtime error caused by an invalid array subscript

10. Click **Debug** on the menu bar, then click **Stop Debugging**.

Before accessing an array element, a procedure always should verify that the subscript is valid; in other words, that it is in range. If the subscript is not in the acceptable range, the procedure should not try to access the element because doing so results in a runtime error. Figure 19-13 shows the modified algorithm for the Salary application. Notice that Step 3 validates the array subscript, which must be greater than or equal to 0 but less than the number of array elements.

Algorithm:
1. enter the salary code
2. calculate the array subscript by subtracting 1 from the salary code
3. if the array subscript is greater than or equal to 0 but less than the number of array elements, do this:
       use the array subscript to display (in a label control) the associated salary amount from the array
    otherwise, do this:
       clear the label control that shows the salary amount
       display a message informing the user that the salary code is invalid
    end if

Figure 19-13: Modified algorithm for the Salary application

To complete the Salary application, and then code and test the application:

1. Enter the selection structure shown in Figure 19-14. You will need to move the lblSalary.Text = intSalaries(intSubscript).ToString statement into the selection structure's true path.

```
' subtract 1                    get the appropriate su
    intSubscript = intCode - 1

    If intSubscript >= 0 AndAlso intSubscript < intSalaries.Length Then
        lblSalary.Text = intSalaries(intSubscript).ToString
    Else
        lblSalary.Text = String.Empty
        MessageBox.Show("The salary code must be from 1 through 6.", _
                        "Salary", MessageBoxButtons.OK, _
                        MessageBoxIcon.Information)
    End If

End Sub
```

enter this selection structure

Figure 19-14: Selection structure entered in the procedure

2. Save the solution, then start the application. Click the **Display Salary** button. Type **1** as the salary code and press **Enter**. The number 25000 appears in the Salary box, which is correct.

3. Click the **Display Salary** button. Type **8** and press **Enter**. The message "The salary code must be from 1 through 6." appears in a message box. Press **Enter** to close the message box.

4. On your own, test the application using salary codes of 2 through 6. Also test it by clicking the OK button in the InputBox without entering any data. In addition, test it by clicking the Cancel button in the InputBox.

5. When you are finished testing the application, click the **Exit** button. Close the Code Editor window, then close the solution.

STATES APPLICATION

The States application stores the names of nine states in a one-dimensional String array named strStates. The names are stored in the order each was visited by the user. For example, the user visited Hawaii first, followed by Colorado. Therefore, "Hawaii" is stored in the strStates(0) element and "Colorado" is stored in the strStates(1) element. The application's interface provides a text box for the user to enter a state name. The application searches for the state name in the array, and then displays a message indicating whether the state name was found. Sample messages include "Hawaii is number 1 in the list of states you visited" and "You did not visit Illinois". Figure 19-15 shows the planning information for the application.

Output: message

Processing: 9-element one-dimensional array of state names
             array subscript
             found

Input: state name to search for

Algorithm:
1. enter the state name to search for, then convert the state name to uppercase
2. assign 0 to the array subscript
3. assign "N" to found
4. repeat until found = "Y" or the array subscript equals the number of array elements:
        if the contents of the current array element (converted to uppercase) is the same as the
        state name to search for, do this:
               assign "Y" to found
        otherwise, do this:
               add 1 to the array subscript
        end if
   end repeat
5. if found = "Y", do this:
        display the state name and visited rank in an appropriate message
   otherwise, do this:
        display the state name in an appropriate message
   end if

Figure 19-15: Planning information for the States application

To open the States application, and then code and test the application:

1. Open the **States Solution** (**States Solution.sln**) file, which is contained in the ClearlyVB\Chap19\States Solution folder. If necessary, open the designer window.

2. Open the Code Editor window, then locate the code template for the btnVisited control's Click event procedure. The procedure contains the statement to declare and initialize the strStates array.

3. First, declare the necessary variables. Click the **blank line** above the End Sub clause, then press **Enter**. Type the following three declaration statements. Press **Enter** twice after typing the last declaration statement.

Dim strSearchFor As String
Dim intSubscript As Integer
Dim strFound As String

4. First, assign the contents of the txtState control, in uppercase, to the strSearchFor variable. Type **strSearchFor = txtState.text.toupper** and press **Enter** twice. The strSearchFor variable now contains the name of the state to search for in the array.

5. The search will begin with the first array element. Type **intSubscript = 0** and press **Enter**. Before the search begins, the procedure will assume that the state is not contained in the array. Type **strFound = "N"** and press **Enter**.

6. Step 4 in the algorithm is a pretest loop that repeats its instructions until one of two conditions is true: either the state name has been found in the array or the subscript equals the number of array elements (which indicates there are no more elements to search). You will use the Do...Loop statement to code this loop. The For...Next statement is not appropriate in this case, because you don't know the exact number of times the loop instructions should be repeated. Type the Do...Loop statement shown in Figure 19-16.

```vb
Private Sub btnVisited_Click(ByVal sender As Object, ByVal e As System
    ' searches an array for the name of a state, then
    ' displays an appropriate message

    Dim strStates() As String = {"Hawaii", "Colorado", "Florida", _
                                 "California", "Georgia", "Idaho", _
                                 "North Carolina", "Texas", "New York"}

    Dim strSearchFor As String
    Dim intSubscript As Integer
    Dim strFound As String

    strSearchFor = txtState.Text.ToUpper

    intSubscript = 0
    strFound = "N"
    Do Until strFound = "Y" OrElse intSubscript = strStates.Length

    Loop
End Sub
```

enter this Do...Loop statement

Figure 19-16: Do...Loop statement entered in the procedure

7. The first instruction in the loop is a selection structure that compares the contents of the current array element (converted to uppercase) with the state name stored in the strSearchFor variable. If both names match, the selection structure's true path will assign "Y" to the strFound variable to indicate that the name was located in the array. If both names do not match, the selection structure's false path will increment the array subscript by 1; this will allow the loop to search the next element in the array. Type the selection structure shown in Figure 19-17, then position the insertion point as shown in the figure.

```
                    strFound...
        Do Until strFound = "Y" OrElse intSubscript = strStates.Length
            If strStates(intSubscript).ToUpper = strSearchFor Then
                strFound = "Y"
            Else
                intSubscript = intSubscript + 1
            End If
        Loop

        End Sub
```

enter this selection structure

position the insertion point here

Figure 19-17: Selection structure entered in the btnVisited control's Click event procedure

8. The contents of the **strFound** variable indicates whether the state name was located in the array, and it determines the appropriate message to display. Type the additional selection structure shown in Figure 19-18.

```
        Loop

        If strFound = "Y" Then
            lblMessage.Text = strSearchFor & " is number " _
                & (intSubscript + 1).ToString _
                & " in the list of states you visited"
        Else
            lblMessage.Text = "You did not visit " & strSearchFor
        End If
    End Sub
```

enter this selection structure

Figure 19-18: Additional selection structure entered in the procedure

9. Save the solution, then start the application. First, enter a state name that is contained in the array. Type **Texas** in the State box, then click the **Visited?** button. The appropriate message appears in the interface, as shown in Figure 19-19.

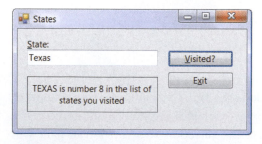

Figure 19-19: Interface showing the message for Texas

10. Now enter a state name that is not in the array. Type **Louisiana** in the State box, then click the **Visited?** button. The "You did not visit LOUISIANA" message appears in the interface.

11. On your own, test the application using different state names. When you are finished testing the application, click the **Exit** button. Close the Code Editor window, then close the solution.

MINI-QUIZ 2

1. Write a Visual Basic statement that sorts the strStates array in ascending order.

2. The integer stored in an array's _____ property represents the number of array elements.

3. If the decBonus array contains 10 elements, what will happen when the computer processes the decBonus(10) = 35.67 statement?

SUMMARY

» All of the variables in an array have the same name and data type.

» Each element in a one-dimensional array is identified by a unique subscript that appears in parentheses after the array's name. The first subscript is the number 0.

» When declaring a one-dimensional array, you provide either the highest subscript or the initial values.

» The number of elements in a one-dimensional array is one number more than its highest subscript.

» You refer to an element in a one-dimensional array using the array's name followed by the element's subscript.

» You can use array variables just like any other variable.

» A one-dimensional array's Length property contains an integer that represents the number of elements in the array.

» The Array.Sort method sorts the elements in a one-dimensional array in ascending order. The Array.Reverse method reverses the order of the elements in a one-dimensional array.

KEY TERMS

Array—a group of related variables that have the same name and data type

Array.Reverse method—reverses the order of the elements in a one-dimensional array

Array.Sort method—sorts the contents of a one-dimensional array in ascending order

Populating the array—refers to the process of assigning the initial values to an array

Scalar variable—another term for a simple variable

Simple variable—a variable that is unrelated to any other variable in memory; also called a scalar variable

Sorting—arranging data in a specific order

Subscript—an integer that indicates an element's position in an array

ANSWERS TO MINI-QUIZZES

MINI-QUIZ 1

1. Dim intQuantities(19) As Integer

2. 19

3. intQuantities(3) = 7

MINI-QUIZ 2

1. Array.Sort(strStates)

2. Length

3. A runtime error will occur.

REVIEW QUESTIONS

1. Which of the following creates a four-element one-dimensional String array named strLetters?

   a. Dim strLetters(3) As String

   b. Dim strLetters() As String = "A", "B", "C", "D"

   c. Dim strLetters(3) As String = {"A", "B", "C", "D"}

   d. Both a and c.

2. Which of the following statements assigns (to the lblCount control) the number of elements contained in the intItems array.

   a. lblCount.Text = intItems.Len.ToString

   b. lblCount.Text = intItems.Length.ToString

   c. lblCount.Text = Length(intItems).ToString

   d. None of the above.

3. The intItems array is declared using the Dim intItems(20) As Integer statement. The intSubscript variable keeps track of the array subscripts and is initialized to 0. Which of the following Do clauses tells the computer to process the loop instructions for each element in the array?

   a. Do While intSubscript > 20   b. Do While intSubscript < 20

   c. Do While intSubscript >= 20   d. Do While intSubscript <= 20

4. The decSales array is declared using the Dim decSales(4) As Decimal statement. Which of the following If clauses can be used to validate the array subscript stored in the intX variable?

   a. If decSales(intX) >= 0 AndAlso decSales(intX) < 4 Then

   b. If decSales(intX) >= 0 AndAlso decSales(intX) <= 4 Then

   c. If intX >= 0 AndAlso intX < 4 Then

   d. None of the above.

5. The decSales array is declared using the Dim decSales(4) As Decimal statement. Which of the following loops will correctly add 100 to each element in the array?

   a. intX = 0
      Do While intX <= 4
          decSales(intX) = decSales(intX) + 100
          intX = intX + 1
      Loop

   b. For intSubscript = 0 To 4
          decSales(intSubscript) = decSales(intSubscript) + 100
      Next intSubscript

   c. intX = 0
      Do
          decSales(intX) = decSales(intX) + 100
          intX = intX + 1
      Loop Until intX > 4

   d. All of the above.

EXERCISES

» TRY THIS

1. Open the Party List Solution (Party List Solution.sln) file, which is contained in the ClearlyVB\Chap19\Party List Solution folder. Open the designer window. The interface provides a text box for the user to enter a name. When the user clicks the Verify Invitation button, the button's Click event procedure should display (in a message box) either the message "*NAME* is invited." or "*NAME* is not invited." In each message, *NAME* is the name entered by the user. Open the Code Editor window, then open the code template for the btnVerify control's Click event procedure. Declare an array containing the following names: Jacob, Karen, Gregory, Jerome, Susan, Michele, Heather, Jennifer, and George. Code the procedure using the While keyword in the Do clause. Save the solution, then start and test the application. Stop the application, then close the solution. (The answers to TRY THIS Exercises are located at the end of the chapter.)

» TRY THIS

2. Open the Grades Solution (Grades Solution.sln) file, which is contained in the ClearlyVB\Chap19\Grades Solution folder. Open the designer window. The interface provides a text box for the user to enter a letter grade. When the user clicks the Count button, the button's Click event procedure should display (in a message box) the message "*Grade*: *number*", where *Grade* is the letter grade entered by the user and *number* is the number of times the student earned the grade. Open the Code Editor window, then open the code template for the btnCount control's Click event procedure. Declare an array containing the following letter grades: C, B, C, A, B, A, F, A, B, B, and C. Code the procedure using the For...Next statement. Save the solution, then start and test the application. Stop the application, then close the solution. (The answers to TRY THIS Exercises are located at the end of the chapter.)

» MODIFY THIS

3. In this exercise, you modify the Salary application coded in the chapter. Use Windows to make a copy of the Salary Solution folder. Save the copy in the ClearlyVB\Chap19 folder. Rename the copy Salary Solution-MODIFY THIS. Open the Salary Solution (Salary Solution.sln) file contained in the Salary Solution-MODIFY THIS folder. Open the designer window, then open the Code Editor window. Modify the btnDisplay control's Click event procedure to include a loop that increases each salary by $5000. Increase the salaries before prompting the user to enter the salary code. Save the solution. Start and then test the application. Stop the application, then close the solution.

» INTRODUCTORY

4. In this exercise, you code an application that displays the number of days in a month. Open the NumDays Solution (NumDays Solution.sln) file, which is contained in the ClearlyVB\Chap19\NumDays Solution folder. Open the code template for the btnDisplay control's Click event procedure. Declare a 12-element one-dimensional array. Use the number of days in each month to initialize the array. (Use 28 for February.) The procedure should display (in the lblDays control) the number of days corresponding

to the month number entered by the user. For example, if the user enters the number 1, the procedure should display 31 in the lblDays control, because there are 31 days in January. The procedure should display an appropriate message in a message box when the user enters an invalid month number. Code the application. Save the solution. Start and then test the application. Stop the application, then close the solution.

5. In this exercise, you code an application that displays the number of students earning a specific score. Open the Scores Solution (Scores Solution.sln) file, which is contained in the ClearlyVB\Chap19\Scores Solution folder. Open the code template for the btnDisplay control's Click event procedure. Declare a 20-element one-dimensional array, using the following numbers to initialize the array: 88, 72, 99, 20, 66, 95, 99, 100, 72, 88, 78, 45, 57, 89, 85, 78, 75, 88, 72, and 88. The procedure should prompt the user to enter a score from 0 through 100. It then should display (in a message box) the number of students who earned that score. Save the solution, then start the application. How many students earned a score of 72? How many earned a score of 88? How many earned a score of 20? How many earned a score of 99? Stop the application, then close the solution.

»**INTRODUCTORY**

6. In this exercise, you modify the application you coded in Exercise 5. Use Windows to make a copy of the Scores Solution folder, which is contained in the ClearlyVB\Chap19 folder. Save the copy in the ClearlyVB\Chap19 folder. Rename the copy Scores Solution-INTERMEDIATE 1. Open the Scores Solution (Scores Solution.sln) file contained in the Scores Solution-INTERMEDIATE 1 folder. Open the designer window, then open the Code Editor window. The btnDisplay control's Click event procedure should prompt the user to enter a minimum score and a maximum score. It then should display (in a message box) the number of students who earned a score in that range. Save the solution, then start the application. How many students earned a score from 70 through 79, inclusive? How many earned a score from 65 through 85, inclusive? How many earned a score from 0 through 50, inclusive? Stop the application, then close the solution.

»**INTERMEDIATE**

7. In this exercise, you modify the application you coded in Exercise 5. Use Windows to make a copy of the Scores Solution folder, which is contained in the ClearlyVB\Chap19 folder. Save the copy in the ClearlyVB\Chap19 folder. Rename the copy Scores Solution-INTERMEDIATE 2. Open the Scores Solution (Scores Solution.sln) file contained in the Scores Solution-INTERMEDIATE 2 folder. Open the designer window, then open the Code Editor window. Remove the existing code from the btnDisplay control's Click event procedure; however, leave the array declaration. Code the btnDisplay control's Click event procedure so that it displays (in a message box) the average score in the array. Save the solution, then start and test the application. Stop the application, then close the solution.

»**INTERMEDIATE**

»ADVANCED

8. JM Sales employs eight salespeople. The sales manager wants an application that allows him to enter a bonus rate. The application should use the rate, along with the eight sale amounts stored in an array, to calculate each salesperson's bonus amount. It also should calculate the total bonus paid to the salespeople. The application should display each salesperson's number (1 through 8) and bonus amount, as well as the total bonus paid, in the interface. Figure 19-20 shows a sample run of the application.

a. List the output and input items, as well as any processing items, then create an appropriate algorithm using pseudocode.

b. Create a new Visual Basic Windows application. Name the solution, project, and form file JM Sales Solution, JM Sales Project, and frmMain.vb, respectively. Save the application in the ClearlyVB\Chap19 folder. If necessary, change the form's name to frmMain.

c. Create the interface shown in Figure 19-20. The txtReport control's Font property is set to Courier New 10 point. Its Multiline and ReadOnly properties are set to True, and its ScrollBars property is set to Vertical.

d. Code the application. Use a one-dimensional array whose elements are initialized to the following sale amounts: 2400, 1500, 1600, 2790, 1000, 6300, 1300, and 2700. The txtRate control should accept only numbers, the period, and the Backspace key. The contents of the txtReport control should be cleared when a change is made to the contents of the txtRate control.

e. Save the solution, then start the application. Enter .1 as the bonus rate, then click the Create Report button. The interface should appear as shown in Figure 19-20. Test the application using your own data. Stop the application, then close the solution.

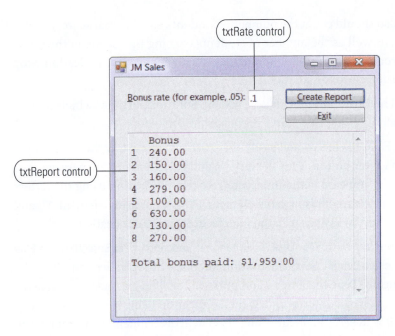

Figure 19-20: Sample run of the JM Sales application

9. In this exercise, you create an application that displays the highest and lowest values stored in an array.

»ADVANCED

a. Open the HighLow Solution, which is contained in the ClearlyVB\Chap19\ HighLow Solution folder. Open the designer window, then open the Code Editor window.

b. Locate the btnHighest control's Click event procedure. First, the procedure should sort the test scores to determine the highest score stored in the array. It then should count the number of students earning that score. Display the highest score, as well as the number of students earning that score, in the interface. Code the procedure. Save the solution, then start and test the application. Stop the application.

c. Locate the btnLowest control's Click event procedure. The procedure should determine the lowest score in the array without sorting the array. (Hint: Assign the first score to a variable, then compare the remaining array values with that score.)

The procedure also should count the number of students earning that score. Display the lowest score, as well as the number of students earning that score, in the interface. Code the procedure. Save the solution, then start and test the application. Stop the application, then close the solution.

10. Open the FigureThisOut Solution (FigureThisOut Solution.sln) file, which is contained in the ClearlyVB\Chap19\FigureThisOut Solution folder.

 a. Open the Code Editor window and study the existing code. Start the application. Click the Find a Letter button. Type the letter a and press Enter. The message "A is in array element 0" appears in the interface. Test the application using the letters b, c, and d. The messages "B is in array element 1", "C is in array element 2", and "D is not in the array" will appear in the interface. Stop the application.

 b. Change the Do clause to Do Until strLetters(intSubscript) = strSearchFor OrElse intSubscript = strLetters.Length. Save the solution, then start the application. Click the Find a Letter button. Type the letter a and press Enter. The message "A is in array element 0" appears in the interface. Test the application using the letters b and c. The messages "B is in array element 1" and "C is in array element 2" will appear in the interface. Click the Find a Letter button, then type the letter d and press Enter. A runtime error occurs. Click Debug on the menu bar, then click Stop Debugging.

 c. Why does a runtime error occur when the Do clause is Do Until strLetters(intSubscript) = strSearchFor OrElse intSubscript = strLetters.Length, but not when it is Do Until intSubscript = strLetters.Length OrElse strLetters(intSubscript) = strSearchFor?

 d. Change the Do clause to Do Until intSubscript = strLetters.Length OrElse strLetters(intSubscript) = strSearchFor. Save the solution, then start and test the application to verify that it is working correctly. Stop the application. Close the Code Editor window, then close the solution.

11. In this exercise, you find an error in an application's code. Open the SwatTheBugs Solution (SwatTheBugs Solution.sln) file, which is contained in the ClearlyVB\Chap19\SwatTheBugs Solution folder. Open the Code Editor window and study the existing code. Start and then test the application. Notice that the application is not working correctly. Stop the application. Locate and correct any errors in the code. Save the solution, then start and test the application again. Stop the application, then close the solution.

ANSWERS TO "TRY THIS" EXERCISES

1. See Figure 19-21.

```
Private Sub btnVerify_Click(ByVal sender As Object, _
    ByVal e As System.EventArgs) Handles btnVerify.Click
    ' searches the array for the name of a guest, then displays
    ' an appropriate message

    Dim strPartyList() As String = {"Jacob", "Karen", "Gregory", _
                            "Jerome", "Susan", "Michele", _
                            "Heather", "Jennifer", "George"}

    Dim strSearchFor As String
    Dim intSubscript As Integer
    Dim strFound As String

    strSearchFor = txtGuest.Text.ToUpper

    intSubscript = 0
    strFound = "N"
    Do While strFound <> "Y" AndAlso intSubscript < strPartyList.Length
        If strPartyList(intSubscript).ToUpper = strSearchFor Then
            strFound = "Y"
        Else
            intSubscript = intSubscript + 1
        End If
    Loop

    If strFound = "Y" Then
        MessageBox.Show(strSearchFor & " is invited.", _
                        "Party List", MessageBoxButtons.OK, _
                        MessageBoxIcon.Information)
    Else
        MessageBox.Show(strSearchFor & " is not invited.", _
                        "Party List", MessageBoxButtons.OK, _
                        MessageBoxIcon.Information)
    End If
End Sub
```

Figure 19-21

2. See Figure 19-22.

```vb
Private Sub btnCount_Click(ByVal sender As Object, _
    ByVal e As System.EventArgs) Handles btnCount.Click
    ' searches the array for a letter grade, then displays the
    ' number of times the letter grade appears in the array

    Dim strGrades() As String = {"C", "B", "C", "A", "B", "A", _
                                 "F", "A", "B", "B", "C"}

    Dim strSearchFor As String
    Dim intCounter As Integer   ' counter

    strSearchFor = txtLetterGrade.Text.ToUpper
    intCounter = 0

    For intSubscript As Integer = 0 To strGrades.Length - 1
        If strGrades(intSubscript) = strSearchFor Then
            intCounter = intCounter + 1
        End If
    Next intSubscript

    MessageBox.Show(strSearchFor & ": " & intCounter.ToString, _
                    "Grades", MessageBoxButtons.OK, _
                    MessageBoxIcon.Information)
End Sub
```

Figure 19-22

20

PARALLEL AND DYNAMIC UNIVERSES

After studying Chapter 20, you should be able to:

Create parallel one-dimensional arrays

Declare a module-level variable

Declare a module-level array

Utilize a dynamic one-dimensional array

WE SHARE THE SAME SUBSCRIPTS

In some applications, you may want to use an array to store items that are related but have different data types, such as employee IDs and salary amounts. The IDs are strings, whereas the salary amounts are numbers. But if all the data in an array must have the same data type, how can you store the employee items in an array? One solution is to use two parallel one-dimensional arrays: a String array to store the IDs and an Integer array to store the salaries. **Parallel arrays** are two or more arrays whose elements are related by their position in the arrays. In other words, the elements are related by their subscript. The strIds and intSalaries arrays illustrated in Figure 20-1 are parallel because each element in the strIds array corresponds to the element located in the same position in the intSalaries array. For example, employee A102's ID is stored in the first element in the strIds array, and his salary is stored in the first element in the intSalaries array. Likewise, employee C220's ID is stored in the strIds(1) element and her salary is stored in the intSalaries(1) element. The same relationship is true for the remaining elements in both arrays. To determine an employee's salary, you locate his or her ID in the strIds array and then view the corresponding element in the intSalaries array.

Figure 20-1: Illustration of two parallel one-dimensional arrays

You will use the strIds and intSalaries arrays in the Employee application, which you code in the next set of steps. The application's interface provides a text box for the user to enter an employee ID. The application will search for the ID in the strIds array. If it finds the ID, it will display the corresponding salary from the intSalaries array; otherwise, it will display the "Invalid ID" message. Figure 20-2 shows the planning information for the application.

Output: salary or "Invalid ID" message

Processing: 5-element one-dimensional IDs array
               5-element one-dimensional salaries array
               array subscript
               found

Input: ID to search for

Algorithm:
1. enter the ID to search for, then convert it to uppercase
2. assign 0 to the array subscript
3. assign "N" to found
4. repeat until found = "Y" or the array subscript equals the number of IDs array elements:
        if the contents of the current IDs array element is the same as the ID to search for, do this:
            assign "Y" to found
        otherwise, do this:
            add 1 to the array subscript
        end if
    end repeat
5. if found = "Y", do this:
        display the corresponding salary from the salaries array
    otherwise, do this:
        display the "Invalid ID" message
    end if

Figure 20-2: Planning information for the Employee application

To open the Employee application, and then code and test the application:

1. Start Visual Studio 2008 (or Visual Basic 2008 Express Edition). Open the **Employee Solution** (**Employee Solution.sln**) file, which is contained in the ClearlyVB\Chap20\ Employee Solution folder. If necessary, open the designer window.

2. Open the Code Editor window, then locate the code template for the btnDisplay control's Click event procedure. First, declare the two parallel arrays. Click the **blank line** below the ' declare parallel arrays comment. Enter the array declaration statements shown in Figure 20-3, then position the insertion point as shown in the figure.

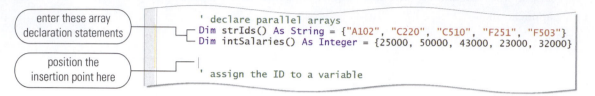

Figure 20-3: Parallel array declarations entered in the procedure

3. Now declare the remaining variables. Enter the following three declaration statements. The strSearchFor variable will store the ID entered by the user. The strFound variable will contain a letter (either N or Y) to indicate whether the ID is in the array. The intSubscript variable will keep track of the array subscripts while the strIds array is being searched.

Dim strSearchFor As String
Dim strFound As String
Dim intSubscript As Integer

4. Next, assign the employee ID (in uppercase) to the strSearchFor variable. Click the **blank line** below the ' assign the ID to a variable comment, then type **strSearchFor = txtId.Text.ToUpper** and press **Enter**.

5. The search will begin with the first element in the strIds array. Click the **blank line** immediately below the ' until the ID is found or the end of the array is reached comment. Type **intSubscript = 0** and press **Enter**.

6. Before the search begins, the procedure will assume that the ID is not contained in the strIds array. Type **strFound = "N"** and press **Enter**.

7. Step 4 in the algorithm is a pretest loop that repeats its instructions until one of two conditions is true: either the ID has been found in the strIds array or the subscript equals the number of array elements (which indicates there are no more elements to search). You will code the loop using the Do...Loop statement (rather than the For...Next statement), because you don't know the exact number of times the loop instructions should be processed. Type **Do Until strFound = "Y" OrElse intSubscript = strIds.Length** and press **Enter**.

8. The first instruction in the loop is a selection structure that compares the contents of the current element in the strIds array with the ID stored in the strSearchFor variable. If both IDs match, the selection structure's true path will assign "Y" to the strFound

variable to indicate that the ID was located in the array. If both IDs do not match, the selection structure's false path will increment the array subscript by 1; this will allow the loop to search the next element in the array. Type the selection structure shown in Figure 20-4.

```
' search the strIds array for the ID, continue searching
' until the ID is found or the end of the array is reached
intSubscript = 0
strFound = "N"
Do Until strFound = "Y" OrElse intSubscript = strIds.Length
    If strIds(intSubscript) = strSearchFor Then
        strFound = "Y"
    Else
        intSubscript = intSubscript + 1
    End If
Loop
```

enter this selection structure

Figure 20-4: Selection structure entered in the procedure

9. The letter stored in the strFound variable indicates whether the ID was located in the array, and it determines the appropriate information to display. Click the **blank line** below the ' determine whether the ID was found comment, then type the additional selection structure shown in Figure 20-5.

```
' determine whether the ID was found
If strFound = "Y" Then
    lblSalary.Text = intSalaries(intSubscript).ToString("C0")
Else
    lblSalary.Text = "Invalid ID"
End If
End Sub
```

enter this selection structure

Figure 20-5: Additional selection structure entered in the procedure

10. Save the solution, then start the application. First, enter a valid ID. Type **c510** in the Employee ID box. The ID appears in the strIds(2) element, and its corresponding salary amount (43000) appears in the intSalaries(2) element. Click the **Display Salary** button. The correct salary amount appears in the Salary box, as shown in Figure 20-6.

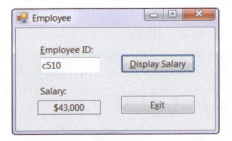

Figure 20-6: Salary amount displayed in the interface

11. Now enter an invalid ID. Type **c511** in the Employee ID box, then click the **Display Salary** button. The message "Invalid ID" appears in the Salary box.

12. Test the application several more times using valid and invalid IDs. When you are finished testing the application, click the **Exit** button. Close the Code Editor window, then close the solution.

WILL YOU SHARE THAT WITH ME?

In the applications you have coded so far, the variables and arrays were declared in procedures. This is because the memory locations were needed only by the procedure that declared them. At times, however, two or more procedures in an application may need to use the same variable or array. In those cases, you can declare the memory locations in the form's Declarations section, which begins with the Public Class line and ends with the End Class line in the Code Editor window. Variables and arrays declared in a form's Declarations section have **module scope** and are referred to as **module-level variables** and **module-level arrays**, respectively. As you learned in Chapter 7, scope refers to the area where a memory location is recognized by an application's code. Module-level memory locations are recognized by every procedure contained in the form's Code Editor window. Unlike a procedure-level memory location, which you declare using the Dim keyword, you declare a module-level memory location using the Private keyword. For example, when the Private intNumber As Integer statement is entered in the form's Declarations section, it creates a module-level variable named intNumber. Similarly, the Private decSales(4) As Decimal statement creates a module-level one-dimensional array named decSales. Module-level variables and arrays retain their values and remain in the computer's internal memory until the application ends. You will use both a module-level array and a module-level variable in the Test Scores application, which you code in the next set of steps. Figure 20-7 shows the application's user interface, and Figure 20-8 shows the planning information for the application. Notice that each algorithm uses a one-dimensional array of scores. The algorithm for the Enter Test Scores button fills the array with values. The algorithms for the Average Score and Highest Score buttons use the array values to determine the average score and highest score, respectively. For the array to be accessible by each button's Click event procedure, it will need to be declared as a module-level array. Rather than having each button's Click event procedure determine the number of elements in the array, you will assign the number of elements to a module-level variable that each procedure can use.

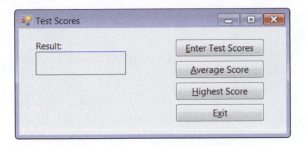

Figure 20-7: User interface for the Test Scores application

Output: average score or highest score

Processing: one-dimensional array of scores (module-level)
               number of array elements (module-level)
               array subscript
               total scores accumulator (start at 0)

Input: scores

Algorithm for the Enter Test Scores button:
1. repeat for array subscripts from 0 through the number of array elements – 1 in increments of 1:
        enter a score
        store the score in the current array element
    end repeat
2. clear the label control that displays the average score or highest score

Algorithm for the Average Score button:
1. assign 0 to the total scores accumulator
2. repeat for array subscripts from 0 through the number of array elements – 1 in increments of 1:
        add the contents of the current array element to the total scores accumulator
    end repeat
3. calculate the average score by dividing the total scores accumulator by the number of array elements
4. display the average score

Algorithm for the Highest Score button:
1. assign the contents of the first array element as the highest score
2. repeat for array subscripts from 1 through the number of array elements – 1 in increments of 1:
        if the contents of the current array element is greater than the highest score, do this:
            assign the contents of the current array element as the highest score
        end if
    end repeat
3. display the highest score

Figure 20-8: Planning information for the Test Scores application

To open the Test Scores application, and then code and test the application:

1. Open the **Test Scores Solution** (**Test Scores Solution.sln**) file, which is contained in the ClearlyVB\Chap20\Test Scores Solution folder. If necessary, open the designer window.

2. Open the Code Editor window. First, declare the module-level array and variable. For simplicity, you will use an array that can store only five scores. Click the **blank line** below the Public Class line. Notice that frmMain and (Declarations) appear in the Class Name and Method Name boxes, respectively; this is the Declarations section of the form. Press **Enter**, then type the comment and declarations shown in Figure 20-9.

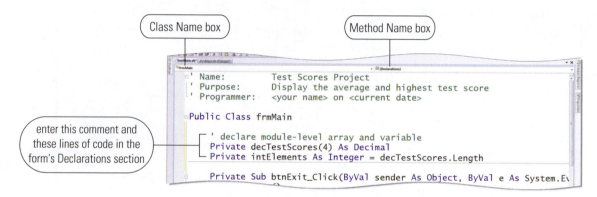

Figure 20-9: Module-level declarations entered in the form's Declarations section

3. Now code the algorithm for the Enter Test Scores button. Locate the btnEnter control's Click event procedure. Click the **blank line** below the comment, then press **Enter**. The procedure will use the InputBox function to prompt the user to enter a test score. You will need to declare a String variable to store the user's response. Type **dim strInputScore as string** and press **Enter** twice.

4. The first step in the algorithm is a pretest loop that repeats its instructions for array subscripts from 0 through the number of array elements minus 1. As you learned in Chapter 19, subtracting 1 from the number of array elements gives you the highest subscript in the array. You will code the loop using the For...Next statement, because you know the exact number of times the loop instructions should be processed. Type **for intSubscript as integer = 0 to intElements - 1** and press **Enter**, then change the Next clause to **Next intSubscript**.

5. The loop instructions should get a test score from the user and assign the test score to the current array element. Type the two statements indicated in Figure 20-10, then position the insertion point as shown in the figure.

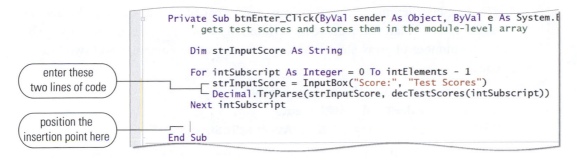

```
Private Sub btnEnter_Click(ByVal sender As Object, ByVal e As System.E
    ' gets test scores and stores them in the module-level array

    Dim strInputScore As String

    For intSubscript As Integer = 0 To intElements - 1
        strInputScore = InputBox("Score:", "Test Scores")
        Decimal.TryParse(strInputScore, decTestScores(intSubscript))
    Next intSubscript

    |
End Sub
```

enter these two lines of code → strInputScore = InputBox / Decimal.TryParse lines

position the insertion point here → blank line before End Sub

Figure 20-10: Loop instructions entered in the btnEnter control's Click event procedure

6. The last instruction in the algorithm is to clear the label that displays the average score or highest score. Type **' clear label control** and press **Enter**, then type **lblResult.text = string.empty** and press **Enter**.

7. Now code the algorithm for the Average Score button. Locate the code template for the btnAverage control's Click event procedure. Click the **blank line** below the comment, then press **Enter**. The procedure will use an accumulator variable to total the scores, as well as a variable to store the average score. Type **dim decTotal as decimal**, press **Tab** twice, then type **' accumulator** and press **Enter**. Type **dim decAverage as decimal** and press **Enter** twice.

8. Now accumulate the scores. Type **' accumulate the scores** and press **Enter**. First, assign 0 to the accumulator variable. Type **decTotal = 0** and press **Enter**. Now use a loop to add each score to the accumulator variable. Type the For...Next statement shown in Figure 20-11, then position the insertion point as indicated in the figure.

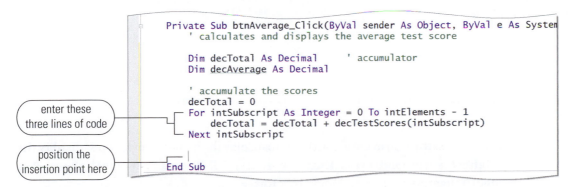

```
Private Sub btnAverage_Click(ByVal sender As Object, ByVal e As System
    ' calculates and displays the average test score

    Dim decTotal As Decimal        ' accumulator
    Dim decAverage As Decimal

    ' accumulate the scores
    decTotal = 0
    For intSubscript As Integer = 0 To intElements - 1
        decTotal = decTotal + decTestScores(intSubscript)
    Next intSubscript

    |
End Sub
```

enter these three lines of code → For...Next lines

position the insertion point here → blank line before End Sub

Figure 20-11: For...Next statement entered in the btnAverage control's Click event procedure

9. The last instructions in the algorithm are to calculate and display the average score. You calculate the average by dividing the value in the accumulator variable by the number of array elements. Enter the following comment and two lines of code.

' calculate and display the average score
decAverage = decTotal / intElements
lblResult.Text = "Average: " & decAverage.ToString("N1")

10. Finally, code the algorithm for the Highest Score button. Locate the code template for the btnHighest control's Click event procedure. Click the **blank line** below the comment, then press **Enter**. The procedure will use a variable to keep track of the highest score. Type **dim decHighest as decimal** and press **Enter** twice.

11. First, assign the contents of the first array element to the decHighest variable. Type **' determine highest score** and press **Enter**, then type **decHighest = decTestScores(0)** and press **Enter**.

12. Now use a loop to search the second through the last element in the array. You don't need to include the first element in the search because its value is already assigned to the decHighest variable. Type the For...Next statement shown in Figure 20-12, then position the insertion point as indicated in the figure.

```
Private Sub btnHighest_Click(ByVal sender As Object, ByVal e As System
        ' calculates and displays the highest test score

        Dim decHighest As Decimal

        ' determine highest score
        decHighest = decTestScores(0)
        For intSubscript As Integer = 1 To intElements - 1
            If decTestScores(intSubscript) > decHighest Then
                decHighest = decTestScores(intSubscript)
            End If
        Next intSubscript


    End Sub
```

enter these five lines of code

position the insertion point here

Figure 20-12: For...Next statement entered in the btnHighest control's Click event procedure

13. The last instruction in the algorithm is to display the highest score. Type **' display the highest score** and press **Enter**, then type **lblResult.text = "Highest: " & decHighest.tostring("N1")** and press **Enter**.

14. Save the solution, then start the application. First, enter five test scores. Click the **Enter Test Scores** button. Type the following five test scores, pressing **Enter** after typing each one: **80**, **75**, **90**, **63**, and **72**.

15. Now display the average and highest scores. Click the **Average Score** button. The message "Average: 76.0" appears in the Result box. Click the **Highest Score** button. The message "Highest: 90.0" appears in the Result box.

16. Click the **Exit** button. Close the Code Editor window, then close the solution.

MINI-QUIZ 1

1. The elements in parallel arrays are related by their subscripts and data type.

   a. True   b. False

2. The strState and strCapital arrays are parallel arrays. If Illinois is stored in the second element in the strState array, then Springfield is stored in the strCapital(2) element.

   a. True   b. False

3. Module-level variables are declared using the Private keyword.

   a. True   b. False

To learn more about module-level memory locations, see the Module-Level Memory Locations section in the Ch20WantMore.pdf file.

BUT I DON'T KNOW HOW MANY THERE ARE

At times, you may not know the precise number of array elements needed to store an application's data. In those cases, you can change the number of elements while the application is running; you do this using the **ReDim statement**. Although the ReDim statement allows you to make an array either larger or smaller, in most cases you will use it to increase the size of the array. Figure 20-13 shows the statement's syntax and includes examples of using the statement. The optional Preserve keyword in the syntax tells the computer to keep the current array values when the size of the array changes. For instance, the ReDim Preserve intNumbers(4) statement in Example 1 adds two elements to the end of the intNumbers array while preserving the contents of the first three array elements. The ReDim intNumbers(4) statement in Example 2 also adds two elements to the end of the intNumbers array; however, notice that the contents of the array are not saved.

As Example 3 indicates, if you use the ReDim statement to reduce the size of an array, the values in the truncated elements are not saved. When the number of elements in an array changes while an application is running, the array is referred to as a **dynamic array**.

REDIM STATEMENT

<u>Syntax</u>

ReDim [**Preserve**] *arrayName*(*highestSubscript*)

<u>Example 1</u>

Dim intNumbers() As Integer = {100, 120, 230}
ReDim Preserve intNumbers(4)

Result of Dim statement:

100
120
230

Result of ReDim statement:

100
120
230
0
0

<u>Example 2</u>

Dim intNumbers() As Integer = {100, 120, 230}
ReDim intNumbers(4)

Result of Dim statement:

100
120
230

Result of ReDim statement:

0
0
0
0
0

<u>Example 3</u>

Dim intNumbers() As Integer = {100, 120, 230}
ReDim Preserve intNumbers(1)

Result of Dim statement:

100
120
230

Result of ReDim statement:

100
120

Figure 20-13: Syntax and examples of the ReDim statement

You will use the ReDim statement in the ReDim application, which you code in the next set of steps.

Before completing the next set of steps, it may be helpful to view the Ch20-ReDim video.

To open the ReDim application, and then code the application:

1. Open the **ReDim Solution** (**ReDim Solution.sln**) file, which is contained in the ClearlyVB\Chap20\ReDim Solution folder. If necessary, open the designer window. The application's interface is shown in Figure 20-14. The application allows the user to enter as many sales amounts as needed, and it stores the sales amounts in an array. It then displays the sales amounts in the txtSales control.

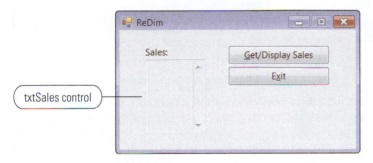

Figure 20-14: User interface for the ReDim application

2. Open the Code Editor window, then locate the code template for the btnDisplay control's Click event procedure. When the event procedure begins, the number of sales amounts to store in the array is unknown; therefore, you will declare an empty array named decSales. An empty array is an array that contains no elements and is declared using an empty set of braces. Click the **blank line** below the ' declare array comment. Type **dim decSales() as decimal = {}** and press **Enter**.

3. The procedure uses the InputBox function to get a sales amount from the user, and it stores the user's response in the strInputSales variable. The procedure's loop is processed as long as the variable does not contain the empty string, which indicates that the user clicked the Cancel button in the input box. In order to store the user's input in the decSales array, you first need to add an element to the array. Click the **blank line** below the ' add an element to the array comment. Type **redim preserve decSales(intSubscript)** and press **Enter**. The first time the ReDim statement is processed, the intSubscript variable will contain the number 0. As a result, the computer will change the size of the array to one element.

4. Now convert the sales amount to the Decimal data type and store it in the element added by the ReDim statement. Click the **blank line** below the ' store the sales amount in the

array comment. Type **decimal.tryparse(strInputSales, decSales(intSubscript))** and press **Enter**.

5. Finally, update the array subscript by adding the number 1 to the contents of the intSubscript variable. If the ReDim statement in the loop is processed a second time, the intSubscript variable will contain the number 1. As a result, the computer will change the size of the array to two elements. Click the **blank line** below the ' update the subscript comment. Type **intSubscript** = **intSubscript** + **1** and press **Enter**.

6. Save the solution. Figure 20-15 shows the code contained in the btnDisplay control's Click event procedure. The code you entered is shaded in the figure.

```vb
Private Sub btnDisplay_Click(ByVal sender As Object, _
    ByVal e As System.EventArgs) Handles btnDisplay.Click
    ' displays the sales amounts stored in an array

    'declare array
    Dim decSales() As Decimal = {}

    Const strPROMPT As String = "Enter a sales amount. Click Cancel to end."
    Dim strInputSales As String
    Dim intSubscript As Integer

    intSubscript = 0
    ' get a sales amount
    strInputSales = InputBox(strPROMPT, "ReDim")
    Do While strInputSales <> String.Empty
        ' add an element to the array
        ReDim Preserve decSales(intSubscript)

        ' store the sales amount in the array
        Decimal.TryParse(strInputSales, decSales(intSubscript))

        ' update the subscript
        intSubscript = intSubscript + 1

        ' get the next sales amount
        strInputSales = InputBox(strPROMPT, "ReDim")
    Loop

    ' display the sales amounts
    txtSales.Text = String.Empty
    For intX As Integer = 0 To decSales.Length - 1
        txtSales.Text = txtSales.Text & _
            decSales(intX).ToString & ControlChars.NewLine
    Next intX
End Sub
```

Figure 20-15: Code entered in the btnDisplay control's Click event procedure

To test the ReDim application:

1. Save the solution, if necessary, then start the application. First, enter two sales amounts. Click the **Get/Display Sales** button. Type **50** and press **Enter**, then type **100** and press **Enter**. Click the **Cancel** button. The numbers 50 and 100 appear in the txtSales control.

2. Now enter five sales amounts. Click the **Get/Display Sales** button. Enter the following five sales amounts, one at a time: **250.05**, **300**, **1000**, **25.67**, and **75**. Click the **Cancel** button. The five numbers appear in the txtSales control.

3. Click the **Exit** button. Close the Code Editor window, then close the solution.

SUMMARY

» You can use parallel arrays to store items of data that are related but have different data types.

» Module-level memory locations are declared in the form's Declarations section, which begins with the Public Class line and ends with the End Class line in the Code Editor window. You use the Private keyword to declare a module-level memory location.

» Module-level memory locations are recognized by every procedure contained in the form's Code Editor window.

» You can use the ReDim statement to change the size of an array while an application is running.

KEY TERMS

Dynamic array—an array whose number of elements changes while an application is running

Module scope—the scope of a memory location declared in the form's Declarations section; refers to the fact that the memory location can be used by any procedure in the form's Code Editor window

Module-level arrays—arrays declared in the form's Declarations section

Module-level variables—variables declared in the form's Declarations section

Parallel arrays—two or more arrays whose elements are related by their position (subscript) in the arrays

ReDim statement—the Visual Basic statement used to resize an array while an application is running

ANSWERS TO MINI-QUIZ

MINI-QUIZ 1

1. b. False

2. b. False

3. a. True

REVIEW QUESTIONS

1. The strMonth and intBonus arrays are parallel arrays. The strMonth array contains the names of the 12 months, and the intBonus array contains the bonus amounts paid for each month. If the string "June" is stored in the strMonth(5) element, which of the following assigns the June bonus amount, which is 34000, to the appropriate element?

   a. intBonus(4) = 34000   b. intBonus(5) = "34000"

   c. intBonus(5) = 34000   d. None of the above.

2. Which of the following declares a module-level variable named dblAmounts?

   a. Private dblAmounts As Double

   b. Module dblAmounts As Double

   c. Dim dblAmounts As Module Double

   d. None of the above.

3. Module-level arrays are declared in _____.

   a. an event procedure

   b. a sub procedure

   c. the form's Declarations section

   d. None of the above.

4. If elements are added to an array while an application is running, the array is referred to as _____ array.

   a. an expanding   b. a growing

   c. a parallel   d. None of the above.

5. To save the current contents of an array when elements are added to the array, you use the _____.

 a. Preserve keyword in the Dim statement

 b. Preserve keyword in the ReDim statement

 c. Save keyword in the ReDim statement

 d. None of the above.

EXERCISES

1. Open the Price List Solution (Price List Solution.sln) file, which is contained in the ClearlyVB\Chap20\Price List Solution folder. Open the designer window. The interface provides a text box for the user to enter a product ID. When the user clicks the Display Price button, the button's Click event procedure should display either the price associated with the product ID or the "Invalid product ID" message. Open the Code Editor window, then open the code template for the btnDisplay control's Click event procedure. Declare a String array containing the following five product IDs: BX35, CR20, FE15, KW10, and MM67. The prices corresponding to the product IDs are as follows: 13, 10, 12, 24, and 4. Store the prices in a parallel Integer array. Code the procedure appropriately. Save the solution, then start and test the application. Stop the application, then close the solution. (The answers to TRY THIS Exercises are located at the end of the chapter.)

» TRY THIS

2. Open the Temperature Solution (Temperature Solution.sln) file, which is contained in the ClearlyVB\Chap20\Temperature Solution folder. Open the designer window. When the user clicks the Get Temperatures button, the button's Click event procedure should prompt the user to enter 10 temperatures. Store the temperatures in an Integer array. When the user clicks the Display High/Low button, the button's Click event procedure should display the highest and lowest temperature contained in the array. Code the application. Save the solution, then start and test the application. Stop the application, then close the solution. (The answers to TRY THIS Exercises are located at the end of the chapter.)

» TRY THIS

3. In this exercise, you modify the Test Scores application coded in the chapter. Use Windows to make a copy of the Test Scores Solution folder. Save the copy in the ClearlyVB\Chap20 folder. Rename the copy Test Scores Solution-MODIFY THIS. Open the Test Scores Solution (Test Scores Solution.sln) file contained in the Test Scores Solution-MODIFY THIS folder. Open the designer window, then open the Code Editor window. Modify the application to allow the user to enter as many test scores as needed. Save the solution. Start and then test the application. Stop the application, then close the solution.

» MODIFY THIS

» INTRODUCTORY

4. In this exercise, you code an application that displays a grade based on the number of points entered by Professor Carver. The grading scale is shown in Figure 20-16. Open the Carver Solution (Carver Solution.sln) file, which is contained in the ClearlyVB\ Chap20\Carver Solution folder. Open the designer window. Open the Code Editor window, then open the code template for the btnDisplay control's Click event procedure. Store the minimum points in a five-element one-dimensional Integer array. Store the grades in a five-element one-dimensional String array. Both arrays should be parallel arrays. The procedure should display the grade corresponding to the number of points entered by the user. Code the procedure appropriately. Save the solution. Start and then test the application. Stop the application, then close the solution.

Minimum points	Maximum points	Grade
0	299	F
300	349	D
350	399	C
400	449	B
450	500	A

Figure 20-16: Grading scale

» INTRODUCTORY

5. In this exercise, you code an application that displays a shipping charge based on the number of items ordered by a customer. The shipping charge information is shown in Figure 20-17. Open the Laury Solution (Laury Solution.sln) file, which is contained in the ClearlyVB\Chap20\Laury Solution folder. Open the code template for the btnDisplay control's Click event procedure. Store the minimum order amounts in an Integer array. Store the shipping charge amounts in a different Integer array. Both arrays should be parallel arrays. The procedure should display the shipping charge corresponding to the number of items entered by the user. Save the solution, then start and test the application. Stop the application, then close the solution.

Minimum order	Maximum order	Shipping charge
1	10	15
11	50	10
51	100	5
101	No maximum	0

Figure 20-17: Shipping charge information

»**INTERMEDIATE**

6. Open the Magazine Solution (Magazine Solution.sln) file, which is contained in the ClearlyVB\Chap20\Magazine Solution folder. Open the designer window. When the user clicks the Get Names and Subscriptions button, the button's Click event procedure should prompt the user to enter a salesperson's name and the number of magazine subscriptions sold by the salesperson. Store the information in two five-element parallel arrays. When the user clicks the Display Number of Subscriptions button, the button's Click event procedure should prompt the user to enter a salesperson's name and then display the number of magazine subscriptions sold by the salesperson. (Hint: A runtime error will occur if you click the Display Number of Subscriptions button before clicking the Get Names and Subscriptions button. This is because the array you need to search will not contain any names. You should verify that the array contains data before you attempt to search it. You can do this by comparing the first element in the array to the empty string.) Code the application. Save the solution. Start and then test the application. Stop the application, then close the solution.

»**INTERMEDIATE**

7. In this exercise, you code an application that displays the name of either a food or animal corresponding to a letter entered by the user. Open the Letter Solution (Letter Solution.sln) file, which is contained in the ClearlyVB\Chap20\Letter Solution folder. Open the designer window. The interface provides a text box for the user to enter a letter. Open the Code Editor window. Declare a module-level String array. Initialize the array using the letters A, B, C, G, and K. Open the code template for the btnFood control's Click event procedure. Declare a parallel String array and initialize it using the following values: Apple, Banana, Carrot, Grape, and Kiwi. Code the procedure so that it displays the name of the food corresponding to the letter entered by the user. Open the code template for the btnAnimal control's Click event procedure. Declare a parallel String array and initialize it using the following values: Antelope, Bear, Camel, Goat, and Kangaroo. Code the procedure so that it displays the name of the animal corresponding to the letter entered by the user. Save the solution, then start and test the application. Stop the application, then close the solution.

»**ADVANCED**

8. In this exercise, you create an application that allows the user to enter as many rainfall amounts as needed. The application's user interface is shown in Figure 20-18. Each time the user enters a rainfall amount in the text box and then clicks the Add to Total button, the amount is added to the total rainfall amount, which is then displayed in the interface. In other words, the application keeps a running total of the rainfall amounts. When the user clicks the Calculate Average button, the button's Click event procedure calculates and displays the average rainfall amount. When the user clicks the Start Over button, the button's Click event procedure resets the counter and accumulator variables to 0 and also clears the total and average rainfall amounts from the labels.

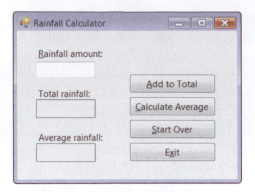

Figure 20-18: User interface for the Rainfall Calculator application

a. Create a new Visual Basic Windows application. Name the solution, project, and form file Rainfall Solution, Rainfall Project, and frmMain.vb, respectively. Save the application in the ClearlyVB\Chap20 folder. If necessary, change the form's name to frmMain.

b. Create the interface shown in Figure 20-18. Code the application without using an array. The text box should accept only numbers, the period, and the Backspace key. Display the average rainfall with two decimal places.

c. Save the solution, then start the application. Enter 3.5 in the Rainfall amount box, then click the Add to Total button. The number 3.5 appears in the Total rainfall box. Change the entry in the Rainfall amount box to 2, then click the Add to Total button. The number 5.5 appears in the Total rainfall box. Change the entry in the Rainfall amount box to 1.5, then click the Add to Total button. The number 7.0 appears in the Total rainfall box. Change the entry in the Rainfall amount box to 4, then click the Add to Total button. The number 11.0 appears in the Total rainfall box. Click the Calculate Average button. The number 2.75 appears in the Average rainfall box.

d. Click the Start Over button. Change the entry in the Rainfall amount box to 3, then click the Add to Total button. The number 3 appears in the Total rainfall box. Click the Calculate Average button. The number 3.00 appears in the Average rainfall box. Stop the application, then close the solution.

9. In this exercise, you create an application that displays the names of the students earning a specific grade.

» ADVANCED

   a. Open the Grade Solution, which is contained in the ClearlyVB\Chap20\Grade Solution folder. Open the designer window. The interface provides a text box for the user to enter a letter grade.

   b. Open the Code Editor window. The txtGrade control should accept only the following letters and the Backspace key: A, a, B, b, C, c, D, d, F, and f. The contents of the txtNames control should be cleared when the user changes the grade entered in the txtGrade control. Code the appropriate event procedures.

   c. Locate the btnDisplay control's Click event procedure. The procedure should search the entire strGrades array for the letter grade entered by the user. When the letter grade is found in the array, the procedure should store the corresponding name from the strNames array in a dynamic one-dimensional String array named strNamesFound. You will need to declare the strNamesFound array. After searching the strGrades array, the procedure should sort the contents of the strNamesFound array in ascending order, and then display the result in the interface. Save the solution, then start and test the application. Stop the application.

10. Open the FigureThisOut Solution (FigureThisOut Solution.sln) file, which is contained in the ClearlyVB\Chap20\FigureThisOut Solution folder. Open the Code Editor window and study the existing code. Start the application. Click the Calculate Average button. Why does a runtime error occur? How can you fix the problem? Click Debug, then click Stop Debugging. Modify the code to prevent the runtime error from occurring. Save the solution, than start the application. Click the Calculate Average button. No runtime error should occur. Stop the application. Close the Code Editor window, then close the solution.

11. In this exercise, you find an error in an application's code. Open the SwatTheBugs Solution (SwatTheBugs Solution.sln) file, which is contained in the ClearlyVB\Chap20\SwatTheBugs Solution folder. Open the Code Editor window and study the existing code. Start and then test the application. Notice that the application is not working correctly. Stop the application. Locate and correct any errors in the code. Save the solution, then start and test the application again. Stop the application, then close the solution.

ANSWERS TO "TRY THIS" EXERCISES

1. See Figure 20-19.

```
Private Sub btnDisplay_Click(ByVal sender As Object, _
    ByVal e As System.EventArgs) Handles btnDisplay.Click
    ' displays the price associated with the product
    ' ID entered by the user

    Dim strIds() As String = _
        {"BX35", "CR20", "FE15", "KW10", "MM67"}
    Dim intPrices() As Integer = {13, 10, 12, 24, 4}
    Dim strSearchFor As String
    Dim strFound As String
    Dim intSubscript As Integer

    ' assign the product ID to a variable
    strSearchFor = txtId.Text.ToUpper

    ' search the strIds array for the product ID
    ' continue searching until there are
    ' no more array elements to search or
    ' the product ID is found
    strFound = "N"
    Do Until intSubscript = strIds.Length _
        OrElse strFound = "Y"
        If strIds(intSubscript) = strSearchFor Then
            strFound = "Y"
        Else
                intSubscript = intSubscript + 1
        End If
    Loop

    ' determine whether the product ID
    ' was found in the strIds array
    If strFound = "Y" Then
        lblPrice.Text = intPrices(intSubscript).ToString("C0")
    Else
        MessageBox.Show("Invalid product ID", _
                        "Treasures Gift Shop", MessageBoxButtons.OK, _
                        MessageBoxIcon.Information)
    End If
End Sub
```

Figure 20-19

2. See Figure 20-20.

```
Public Class frmMain

    Private intTemps(9) As Integer
    Private intHighSub As Integer = intTemps.Length - 1

    Private Sub btnExit_Click(ByVal sender As Object, _
        ByVal e As System.EventArgs) Handles btnExit.Click
        Me.Close()
    End Sub

    Private Sub btnGet_Click(ByVal sender As Object, _
        ByVal e As System.EventArgs) Handles btnGet.Click
        ' gets the temperatures and stores them in the array

        Dim strInputTemp As String

        For intSubscript As Integer = 0 To intHighSub
            strInputTemp = InputBox("Temperature:", "Temperatures")
            Integer.TryParse(strInputTemp, intTemps(intSubscript))
        Next intSubscript

        lblHighest.Text = String.Empty
        lblLowest.Text = String.Empty
    End Sub

    Private Sub btnDisplay_Click(ByVal sender As Object, _
        ByVal e As System.EventArgs) Handles btnDisplay.Click
        ' display the highest and lowest temperature

        Dim intHigh As Integer
        Dim intLow As Integer

        intHigh = intTemps(0)
        intLow = intTemps(0)

        For intSubscript As Integer = 0 To intHighSub
            If intTemps(intSubscript) > intHigh Then
                intHigh = intTemps(intSubscript)
            End If
            If intTemps(intSubscript) < intLow Then
                intLow = intTemps(intSubscript)
            End If
        Next intSubscript

        lblHighest.Text = intHigh.ToString
        lblLowest.Text = intLow.ToString
    End Sub
End Class
```

Figure 20-20

21

TABLE TENNIS, ANYONE?

After studying Chapter 21, you should be able to:

Create a two-dimensional array

Store data in a two-dimensional array

Search a two-dimensional array

Sum the values in a two-dimensional array

LET'S TABLE THAT IDEA FOR NOW

As you learned in Chapter 19, the most commonly used arrays in business applications are one-dimensional and two-dimensional. You can visualize a one-dimensional array as a column of variables. A **two-dimensional array**, on the other hand, resembles a table in that the variables (elements) are in rows and columns. Each variable in a two-dimensional array is identified by a unique combination of two subscripts that the computer assigns to the variable when the array is created. The subscripts specify the variable's row and column position in the array. Variables located in the first row in a two-dimensional array are assigned a row subscript of 0. Variables in the second row are assigned a row subscript of 1, and so on. Similarly, variables located in the first column in a two-dimensional array are assigned a column subscript of 0. Variables in the second column are assigned a column subscript of 1, and so on. You refer to each variable in a two-dimensional array by the array's name and the variable's row and column subscripts, which are separated by a comma and specified in a set of parentheses immediately following the array name. To refer to the variable located in the first row, first column in a two-dimensional array named strProducts, you use strProducts(0, 0)—read "strProducts sub zero comma zero." You use strProducts(1, 2) to refer to the variable located in the second row, third column in the array. Figure 21-1 illustrates this naming convention. Notice that the row subscript is listed first within the parentheses.

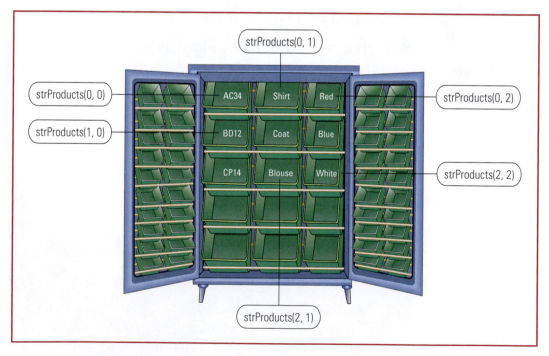

Figure 21-1: Names of some of the variable's contained in the strProducts array

Figure 21-2 shows two versions of the syntax you use to declare a two-dimensional array in Visual Basic. You use the Dim keyword to create a procedure-level array, and the Private keyword to create a module-level array. In each version of the syntax, *arrayName* is the name of the array and *dataType* is the type of data the array variables will store. In Version 1's syntax, *highestRowSubscript* and *highestColumnSubscript* are integers that specify the highest row and column subscripts in the array. When the array is created, it will contain one row more than the number specified in the *highestRowSubscript* argument, and one column more than the number specified in the *highestColumnSubscript* argument. This is because the first row subscript in a two-dimensional array is 0, and so is the first column subscript. When you declare a two-dimensional array using the syntax shown in Version 1, the computer automatically initializes each element in the array when the array is created. Now compare Version 1's syntax with Version 2's syntax. Notice that a comma appears within the parentheses that follow the array name in Version 2. The comma indicates that the array is a two-dimensional array. (Recall that a comma is used to separate the row subscript from the column subscript in a two-dimensional array.) You can use Version 2's syntax to specify each variable's initial value when the array is created. You do this by including a separate *initialValues* section, enclosed in braces, for each row in the array. If the array has two rows, then the statement that declares and initializes the array should have two *initialValues* sections. If the array has five rows, then the declaration statement should have five *initialValues* sections. Within the individual *initialValues* sections, you enter one or more values separated by commas. The number of values to enter corresponds to the number of columns in the array. If the array contains 10 columns, then each individual *initialValues* section should contain 10 values. In addition to the set of braces enclosing each individual *initialValues* section, Version 2's syntax also requires all of the *initialValues* sections to be enclosed in a set of braces. Figure 21-2 shows examples of using both syntax versions.

DECLARING A TWO-DIMENSIONAL ARRAY

Syntax - Version 1

{**Dim** | **Private**} *arrayName*(*highestRowSubscript*, *highestColumnSubscript*) **As** *dataType*

Syntax - Version 2

{**Dim** | **Private**} *arrayName*(,) **As** *dataType* = {{*initialValues*},...{*initialValues*}}

Example 1

Dim intScores(5, 3) As Integer
declares and initializes (to 0) a six-row, four-column array named intScores

---

Figure 21-2: Syntax and examples of declaring a two-dimensional array (*continued on next page*)

Example 2

```
Dim strProducts(,) As String = {{"AC34", "Shirt", "Red"}, _
                                {"BD12", "Coat", "Blue"}, _
                                {"CP14", "Blouse", "White"}}
```

declares and initializes a three-row, three-column array named strProducts; initializes the strProducts(0, 0) element to "AC34", strProducts(0, 1) to "Shirt", strProducts(0, 2) to "Red", strProducts(1, 0) to "BD12", strProducts(1, 1) to "Coat", strProducts(1, 2) to "Blue", strProducts(2, 0) to "CP14", strProducts(2, 1) to "Blouse", and strProducts(2, 2) to "White", as illustrated in Figure 21-1

Figure 21-2: Syntax and examples of declaring a two-dimensional array (*continued from previous page*)

The variables (elements) in a two-dimensional array can be used just like any other variables: you can assign values to them, use them in calculations, display their contents, and so on. Figure 21-3 shows examples of performing these tasks. If you need to access each element in a two-dimensional array, you typically do so using an outer loop and a nested loop: one loop for the row subscript and the other for the column subscript. If the outer loop controls the row subscript, as it does in Example 4, the array is filled with data, row by row. However, if the outer loop controls the column subscript, the array is filled with data, column by column.

USING AN ELEMENT IN A TWO-DIMENSIONAL ARRAY

Example 1

```
intScores(0, 1) = 95
```

assigns the number 95 to the element located in the first row, second column in the intScores array

Example 2

```
intSalaries(3, 0) = intSalaries(3, 0) + 2000
```

adds 2000 to the contents of the element located in the fourth row, first column in the intSalaries array, and then assigns the result to the element

Figure 21-3: Examples of using an element in a two-dimensional array (*continued on next page*)

Example 3

```
Decimal.TryParse(txtSales.Text, decSales(2, 1))
lblSales.Text = decSales(2,1).ToString("C2")
```
assigns the value returned by the TryParse method to the element located in the third row, second column in the decSales array, then displays the value (formatted with a dollar sign and two decimal places) in the lblSales control

Example 4

```
For intRow As Integer = 0 To 5
    For intColumn As Integer = 0 To 3
        intScores(intRow, intColumn) = 0
    Next intColumn
Next intRow
```
assigns the number 0 to each element in the six-row, four-column intScores array

Figure 21-3: Examples of using an element in a two-dimensional array (*continued from previous page*)

The procedures you code in this chapter will demonstrate some of the ways two-dimensional arrays are used in an application. As mentioned in Chapter 19, in most applications the values stored in an array come from a file on the computer's disk and are assigned to the array after it is declared. However, so that you can follow the code and its results more easily, the example applications in this chapter use the Dim statement to store the appropriate values in the array.

MINI-QUIZ 1

1. Write a Dim statement that declares a four-row, two-column Integer array named intQuantities.

2. The highest row subscript in the intQuantities array from Question 1 is _____.

3. Write a Visual Basic statement that assigns the number 7 to the element located in the third row, first column in the intQuantities array.

Before continuing, it may be helpful to view the Ch21-Two-Dimensional Arrays video.

REVISITING THE EMPLOYEE APPLICATION

You coded the Employee application in Chapter 20. As you may remember, the application stores the employee IDs and salaries in two parallel one-dimensional arrays. It then displays the salary corresponding to the ID entered by the user. Instead of storing the employee information in parallel one-dimensional arrays, you can store it in a two-dimensional array. However, to do this, you will need to treat the numeric salaries as strings. This is because the IDs are strings and all of the variables in an array must have the same data type. Figure 21-4 shows the planning information for the application, using a two-dimensional array.

Output: salary or "Invalid ID" message

Processing: two-dimensional employee information array
             row subscript
             number of rows
             found

Input: ID to search for

Algorithm:
1. enter the ID to search for, then convert it to uppercase
2. assign 0 to the row subscript
3. assign "N" to found
4. determine the number of rows in the two-dimensional employee information array
5. repeat until found = "Y" or the row subscript equals the number of rows in the array:
       if the ID in the first column of the current row is the same as the ID to search for, do this:
           assign "Y" to found
       otherwise, do this:
           add 1 to the row subscript
       end if
   end repeat
6. if found = "Y", do this:
       display the corresponding salary, which is located in the second column of the current row
   otherwise, do this:
       display the "Invalid ID" message
   end if

Figure 21-4: Planning information for the Employee application, using a two-dimensional array

To open the Employee application, and then begin coding the application:

1. Start Visual Studio 2008 (or Visual Basic 2008 Express Edition). Open the **Employee Solution** (**Employee Solution.sln**) file, which is contained in the ClearlyVB\Chap21\ Employee Solution folder. If necessary, open the designer window.

2. Open the Code Editor window, then locate the code template for the btnDisplay control's Click event procedure. First, declare the two-dimensional array. Click the **blank line** below the ' declare the two-dimensional array comment. Enter the array declaration statement shown in Figure 21-5, then position the insertion point as shown in the figure. Notice that each ID is stored in the first column of the array. The salary associated with the ID is stored in the corresponding row in the second column.

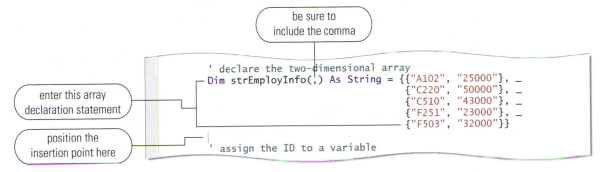

Figure 21-5: Two-dimensional array declaration entered in the procedure

3. Now declare the remaining variables. Enter the following four declaration statements. The strSearchFor variable will store the ID entered by the user. The strFound variable will contain a letter (either N or Y) to indicate whether the ID is in the array. The intRow variable will keep track of the row subscripts while the array is being searched. The intNumRows variable will store an integer that represents the number of rows in the array.

Dim strSearchFor As String
Dim strFound As String
Dim intRow As Integer
Dim intNumRows As Integer

4. Next, assign the employee ID (in uppercase) to the strSearchFor variable. Click the **blank line** below the ' assign the ID to a variable comment, then type **strSearchFor = txtId.Text.ToUpper** and press **Enter**.

5. The search will begin with the first row in the array. Click the **blank line** immediately below the ' row has been searched comment. Type **intRow = 0** and press **Enter**.

6. Before the search begins, the procedure will assume that the ID is not contained in the array. Type **strFound = "N"** and press **Enter**, then save the solution.

Before coding Step 4 in the algorithm, which is to determine the number of rows in the array, you will learn about an array's GetLowerBound and GetUpperBound methods.

THE GETLOWERBOUND AND GETUPPERBOUND METHODS

Both an array's **GetLowerBound method** and its **GetUpperBound method** return an integer that indicates the lowest subscript and highest subscript, respectively, in the specified dimension in the array. Figure 21-6 shows the syntax of both methods. In each syntax, *arrayName* is the name of the array, and *dimension* is an integer that specifies the dimension whose upper or lower bound you want to retrieve. In a one-dimensional array, the *dimension* argument will always be 0 (zero). In a two-dimensional array, the *dimension* argument will be either 0 or 1. The 0 represents the row dimension, and the 1 represents the column dimension. Figure 21-6 also includes examples of using both methods.

GETLOWERBOUND AND GETUPPERBOUND METHODS

Syntax - GetLowerBound method

arrayName.**GetLowerBound(***dimension***)**

Syntax - GetUpperBound method

arrayName.**GetUpperBound(***dimension***)**

Example 1

Dim intScores(5, 3) As Integer
intLowestColumnSub = intScores.GetLowerBound(1)
intHighestRowSub = intScores.GetUpperBound(0)
assigns the number 0 to the intLowestColumnSub variable, and assigns the number 5 to the intHighestRowSub variable

Example 2

Dim strCities (20) As String
intLowestSub = strCities.GetLowerBound(0)
intHighestSub = strCities.GetUpperBound(0)
assigns the number 0 to the intLowestSub variable, and assigns the number 20 to the intHighestSub variable

---

Figure 21-6: Syntax and examples of the GetUpperBound and GetLowerBound methods

Recall that Step 4 in the algorithm is to determine the number of rows in the strEmployInfo array. To do this, you first use the GetUpperBound method to get the highest row subscript; you then increase that value by 1. As mentioned earlier, the number of rows in a two-dimensional array is always one number more than the highest row subscript.

To continue coding the Employee application, and then test the application:

1. The insertion point should be positioned below the strFound = "N" statement. Type **intNumRows = strEmployInfo.GetUpperBound(0) + 1** and press **Enter**.

2. Step 5 in the algorithm is a pretest loop that repeats its instructions until one of two conditions is true: either the ID has been found in the first column of the array or the row subscript equals the number of rows in the array (which indicates there are no more rows to search). You will code the loop using the Do...Loop statement (rather than the For...Next statement), because you don't know the exact number of times the loop instructions should be processed. Type **Do Until strFound = "Y" OrElse intRow = intNumRows** and press **Enter**.

3. The first instruction in the loop is a selection structure that compares the ID stored in the first column of the current row in the array with the ID stored in the strSearchFor variable. If both IDs match, the selection structure's true path will assign "Y" to the strFound variable to indicate that the ID was located in the array. If both IDs do not match, the selection structure's false path will increment the row subscript by 1; this will allow the loop to search the next row in the array. Type the selection structure shown in Figure 21-7.

```
' search for the ID in the first column in the array
' continue searching until the ID is found or each
' row has been searched
intRow = 0
strFound = "N"
intNumRows = strEmployInfo.GetUpperBound(0) + 1
Do Until strFound = "Y" OrElse intRow = intNumRows
    If strEmployInfo(intRow, 0) = strSearchFor Then
        strFound = "Y"
    Else
        intRow = intRow + 1
    End If
Loop
```

enter this selection structure

Figure 21-7: Selection structure entered in the procedure

4. The letter stored in the strFound variable indicates whether the ID was located in the array, and it determines the appropriate information to display. If the ID was found, the procedure should display the salary stored in the second column of the current row in the array; otherwise, it should display the "Invalid ID" message. Click the **blank line** below the ' determine whether the ID was found comment, then type the additional selection structure shown in Figure 21-8.

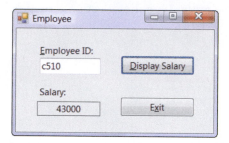

```
                        ' determine whether the ID was found
                     ┌─ If strFound = "Y" Then
   ┌──────────────┐  │      lblSalary.Text = strEmployInfo(intRow, 1)
   │  enter this  │  │  Else
   │ selection structure ├──┤      lblSalary.Text = "Invalid ID"
   └──────────────┘  └─ End If
                     End Sub
```

Figure 21-8: Additional selection structure entered in the procedure

5. Save the solution, then start the application. First, enter a valid ID. Type **c510** in the Employee ID box. The ID is located in the strEmployInfo(2, 0) element, and its associated salary is located in the strEmployInfo(2, 1) element. Click the **Display Salary** button. The correct salary amount appears in the Salary box, as shown in Figure 21-9. Notice that the salary amount is not formatted, as it was in Chapter 20's Employee application (see Figure 20-6).

Figure 21-9: Salary amount displayed in the interface

6. Click the **Exit** button.

In the Employee application in Chapter 20, the salary amounts were treated as numbers and stored in an Integer array. Because of this, you were able to use the ToString method to format the salary when it was displayed. In this chapter's Employee application, the salary amounts are strings and are stored in a String array. Before you can use the ToString method, you will need to convert the salary to a number.

To format the salary amount, and then test the application:

1. Modify the second selection structure as indicated in Figure 21-10.

enter these
two lines of code

modify this
line of code

```
' determine whether the ID was found
If strFound = "Y" Then
    Dim intSalary As Integer
    intSalary = strEmployInfo(intRow, 1)
    lblSalary.Text = intSalary.ToString("C0")
Else
    lblSalary.Text = "Invalid ID"
End If
```

Figure 21-10: Modified selection structure

2. Save the solution, then start the application. Type **c510** in the Employee ID box, then click the **Display Salary** button. The formatted salary amount ($43,000) appears in the Salary box.

3. Now enter an invalid ID. Type **c511** in the Employee ID box, then click the **Display Salary** button. The message "Invalid ID" appears in the Salary box.

4. Test the application several more times using valid and invalid IDs. When you are finished testing the application, click the **Exit** button. Close the Code Editor window, then close the solution.

CALENDAR ORDERS APPLICATION

The Calendar Orders application displays the total number of calendars ordered by three stores in each of six months. The number ordered each month by each store is stored in a three-row, six-column array. Each row in the array represents a store, and each column represents a month. To display the total number of calendars ordered, you will need to accumulate the values stored in the two-dimensional array.

To open the Calendar Orders application, and then code and test the application:

1. Open the **Orders Solution** (**Orders Solution.sln**) file, which is contained in the ClearlyVB\Chap21\Orders Solution folder. If necessary, open the designer window.

2. Open the Code Editor window, then locate the code template for the btnDisplay control's Click event procedure. First, declare the two-dimensional array. Click the **blank line** below the ' declare the two-dimensional array comment. Enter the array declaration statement shown in Figure 21-11, then position the insertion point as shown in the figure.

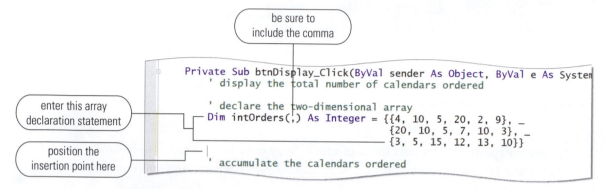

Figure 21-11: Array declaration entered in the procedure

3. The procedure will need an accumulator variable to total the orders. Type **dim intTotal as integer**, press **Tab**, then type **' accumulator** and press **Enter**.

4. To accumulate the values stored in the array, you will need to access each array element. As mentioned earlier, you do this using both an outer loop and a nested loop. You can access the elements either row by row or column by column; in this case, you will access them column by column. Click the **blank line** below the ' accumulate the calendars ordered comment. Enter the two repetition structures shown in Figure 21-12.

```
                         ' accumulate the calendars ordered
                      ┌─ For intColumn As Integer = 0 To intOrders.GetUpperBound(1)
enter these two       │    For intRow As Integer = 0 To intOrders.GetUpperBound(0)
repetition structures │      intTotal = intTotal + intOrders(intRow, intColumn)
                      │    Next intRow
                      └─ Next intColumn
```

Figure 21-12: Repetition structures entered in the procedure

5. Finally, display the total number of calendars ordered. Click the **blank line** below the ' display the number of calendars ordered comment. Type **lblTotal.text = intTotal.tostring** and press **Enter**.

6. Save the solution, then start the application. Click the **Display Total** button. The total number of calendars ordered appears in the Total ordered box, as shown in Figure 21-13.

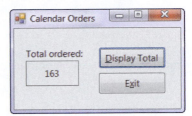

Figure 21-13: Interface showing the total number of calendars ordered

7. Click the **Exit** button. Close the Code Editor window, then close the solution.

To learn more about two-dimensional arrays, see the Two-Dimensional Arrays section in the Ch21WantMore.pdf file.

SUMMARY

» Each element in a two-dimensional array is identified by a unique combination of two subscripts: a row subscript and a column subscript. The subscripts appear in parentheses after the array's name. You list the row subscript first, followed by a comma and the column subscript.

» The first row subscript in a two-dimensional array is 0. The first column subscript also is 0.

» When declaring a two-dimensional array, you provide either the highest row and column subscripts or the initial values.

» The number of rows in a two-dimensional array is one number more than its highest subscript. Likewise, the number of columns is one number more than its highest column subscript.

» You refer to an element in a two-dimensional array using the array's name followed by the element's row and column subscripts, which are separated by a comma.

» You use both an outer loop and a nested loop to access each element in a two-dimensional array. One loop controls the row subscript and the other loop controls the column subscript.

» An array's GetLowerBound and GetUpperBound methods return the lowest subscript and highest subscript, respectively, in the array.

KEY TERMS

GetLowerBound method—returns an integer that represents the lowest subscript in an array

GetUpperBound method—returns an integer that represents the highest subscript in an array

Two-dimensional array—an array whose elements are identified by a unique combination of two numbers: a row subscript and a column subscript

ANSWERS TO MINI-QUIZ

MINI-QUIZ 1

1. Dim intQuantities(3, 1) As Integer

2. 3

3. intQuantities(2, 0) = 7

REVIEW QUESTIONS

1. Which of the following declares a two-dimensional String array named strLetters that contains four rows and two columns?

   a. Dim strLetters(3, 1) As String

   b. Private strLetters(3, 1) As String

   c. Dim strLetters(,) = {{"A", "B"}, {"C", "D"}, {"E", "F"}, {"G", "H"}}

   d. All of the above.

2. Which of the following statements assigns the highest column subscript in the array to the intHighCol variable?

   a. intHighCol = decSales.GetHighest(1)

   b. intHighCol = decSales.GetHighSub(1)

   c. intHighCol = decSales.GetUpper (0)

   d. intHighCol = decSales.GetUpperBound(1)

3. Which of the following statements assigns the string "Hawaii" to the variable located in the third column, fifth row in the strStates array?

   a. strStates(3, 5) = "Hawaii"

   b. strStates(5, 3) = "Hawaii"

   c. strStates(2, 4) = "Hawaii"

   d. strStates(4, 2) = "Hawaii"

4. Which of the following assigns the number 0 to each element in a two-row, four-column array named intSums?

   a. For intRow As Integer = 0 To 1
       For intColumn As Integer = 0 To 3
           intSums(intRow, intColumn) = 0
       Next intColumn
   Next intRow

   b. Dim intRow As Integer
   Dim intColumn As Integer
   Do While intRow < 2
       intColumn = 0
       Do While intColumn < 4
           intSums(intRow, intColumn) = 0
           intColumn = intColumn + 1
       Loop
       intRow = intRow + 1
   Loop

   c. For intRow As Integer = 1 To 2
       For intColumn As Integer = 1 To 4
           intSums(intRow - 1, intColumn - 1) = 0
       Next intColumn
   Next intRow

   d. All of the above.

5. Which of the following adds the number 100 to the contents of the variable located in the first row, second column of the array, and then assigns the result to the variable?

   a. intNum(0, 1) = intNum(0, 1) + 100

   b. intNum(1, 0) = intNum(1, 0) + 100

   c. intNum(1, 2) = intNum(1, 2) + 100

   d. intNum(2, 1) = intNum(2, 1) + 100

EXERCISES

»TRY THIS

1. Open the Price List Solution (Price List Solution.sln) file, which is contained in the ClearlyVB\Chap21\Price List Solution folder. Open the designer window. The interface provides a text box for the user to enter a product ID. When the user clicks the Display Price button, the button's Click event procedure should display either the price associated with the product ID or the "Invalid product ID" message. Open the Code Editor window, then open the code template for the btnDisplay control's Click event procedure. Declare a two-dimensional String array that contains the following product IDs and prices: BX35, 13, CR20, 10, FE15, 12, KW10, 24, MM67, and 4. Code the procedure appropriately. Save the solution, then start and test the application. Stop the application, then close the solution. (The answers to TRY THIS Exercises are located at the end of the chapter.)

»TRY THIS

2. Open the Inventory Solution (Inventory Solution.sln) file, which is contained in the ClearlyVB\Chap21\Inventory Solution folder. Open the designer window, then open the Code Editor window. Locate the btnDisplay control's Click event procedure. The procedure should add together the values stored in the intInventory array, and then display the total in the lblTotal control. Code the procedure. Save the solution, then start and test the application. Stop the application, then close the solution. (The answers to TRY THIS Exercises are located at the end of the chapter.)

»MODIFY THIS

3. In this exercise, you modify the Temperature application from Chapter 20's TRY THIS Exercise 2. Open the Temperature Solution (Temperature Solution.sln) file, which is contained in the ClearlyVB\Chap21\Temperature Solution folder. Open the designer window, then open the Code Editor window. Make the following modifications. When the user clicks the Get Temperatures button, the button's Click event procedure should prompt the user to enter the highest and lowest temperatures for seven days. Store the temperatures in a seven-row, two-column Integer array. The first column should contain the highest temperatures, and the second column should contain the lowest temperatures. When the user clicks the Display High/Low button, the button's Click event procedure should display the highest and lowest temperature contained in the array. Code the application. Save the solution, then start and test the application. Stop the application, then close the solution.

»INTRODUCTORY

4. In this exercise, you code an application that displays a grade based on the number of points entered by Professor Carver. The grading scale is shown in Figure 21-14. Open the Carver Solution (Carver Solution.sln) file, which is contained in the ClearlyVB\Chap21\Carver Solution folder. Open the designer window. Open the Code Editor window, then open the code template for the btnDisplay control's Click event procedure. Store the minimum points and grades in a five-row, two-column array. The procedure should display the grade corresponding to the number of points entered by

the user. Code the procedure appropriately. Save the solution. Start and then test the application. Stop the application, then close the solution.

Minimum points	Maximum points	Grade
0	299	F
300	349	D
350	399	C
400	449	B
450	500	A

Figure 21-14: Grading scale

5. In this exercise, you code an application that displays a shipping charge based on the number of items ordered by a customer. The shipping charge information is shown in Figure 21-15. Open the Laury Solution (Laury Solution.sln) file, which is contained in the ClearlyVB\Chap21\Laury Solution folder. Open the code template for the btnDisplay control's Click event procedure. Store the minimum order amounts and shipping charges in a four-row, two-column array. The procedure should display the shipping charge corresponding to the number of items entered by the user. Save the solution, then start and test the application. Stop the application, then close the solution.

»INTRODUCTORY

Minimum order	Maximum order	Shipping charge
1	10	15
11	50	10
51	100	5
101	No maximum	0

Figure 21-15: Shipping charge information

6. JM Sales employs 10 salespeople. The sales made by the salespeople during the months of January, February, and March are listed in Figure 21-16. The sales manager wants an application that allows him to enter the current bonus rate. The application should display each salesperson's number (1 through 10), total sales amount, and total bonus amount. It also should display the total bonus paid to all salespeople. Figure 21-17 shows a sample run of the application.

»INTERMEDIATE

a. Create a new Visual Basic Windows application. Name the solution, project, and form file JM Sales Solution, JM Sales Project, and frmMain.vb, respectively. Save the application in the ClearlyVB\Chap21 folder. If necessary, change the form's name to frmMain.

b. Create the interface shown in Figure 21-17. The txtReport control's Font property is set to Courier New 10 point. Its Multiline and ReadOnly properties are set to True, and its ScrollBars property is set to Vertical.

c. Code the application. Store the sales amounts in a 10-row, three-column Integer array. The txtRate control should accept only numbers, the period, and the Backspace key. The contents of the txtReport control should be cleared when a change is made to the contents of the txtRate control.

d. Save the solution, then start the application. Enter .1 as the bonus rate, then click the Create Report button. The interface should appear as shown in Figure 21-17. Test the application using your own data. Stop the application, then close the solution.

Salesperson	January	February	March
1	2400	3500	2000
2	1500	7000	1000
3	600	450	2100
4	790	240	500
5	1000	1000	1000
6	6300	7000	8000
7	1300	450	700
8	2700	5500	6000
9	4700	4800	4900
10	1200	1300	400

Figure 21-16: Monthly sales amounts for each salesperson

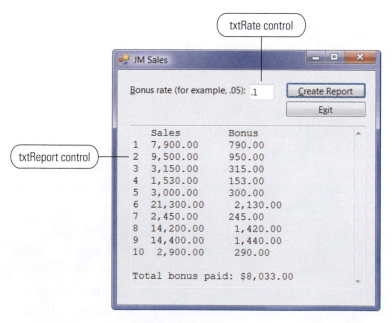

Figure 21-17: Sample run of the JM Sales application

7. In this exercise, you code an application that displays the number of times a value appears in a two-dimensional array. Open the Count Solution (Count Solution.sln) file, which is contained in the ClearlyVB\Chap21\Count Solution folder. Open the designer window, then open the Code Editor window. Code the btnDisplay control's Click event procedure to display the number of times each of the numbers from 1 through 9 appears in the intNumbers array. (Hint: Store the counts in a one-dimensional array.) Save the solution, then start and test the application. Stop the application, then close the solution.

» INTERMEDIATE

8. Conway Enterprises has both domestic and international sales operations. The company's sales manager wants an application that she can use to display the total domestic, total international, and total company sales made during a six-month period. The sales amounts are listed in Figure 21-18. Create a new Visual Basic Windows application. Name the solution, project, and form file Conway Solution, Conway Project, and frmMain.vb, respectively. Save the application in the ClearlyVB\Chap21 folder. If necessary, change the form's name to frmMain. Create the interface shown in Figure 21-19. Code the application using a six-row, two-column array to store the sales amounts. Save the solution, then start and test the application. Stop the application, then close the solution.

» ADVANCED

Month	Domestic	International
1	100,000	150,000
2	90,000	120,000
3	75,000	210,000
4	88,000	50,000
5	125,000	220,000
6	63,000	80,000

Figure 21-18: Sales amounts

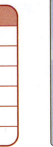

Figure 21-19: User interface for the Conway Enterprises application

9. Each year, Sabrina Cantrell, the owner of Waterglen Horse Farms, enters four of her horses in five local horse races. She uses a table similar to the one shown in Figure 21-20 to keep track of her horses' performances in each race. In the table, a 1 indicates that the horse won the race, a 2 indicates second place, and a 3 indicates third place. A 0 indicates that the horse did not finish in the top three places. Sabrina wants an application that displays a summary of each horse's individual performance, as well as the performances of all the horses. For example, the table shown in Figure 21-20 indicates that horse 1 won one race, finished second in one race, finished third in one race, and didn't finish in the top three in two races. Overall, Sabrina's

» ADVANCED

horses won four times, finished second three times, finished third three times, and didn't finish in the top three ten times. Create a new Visual Basic Windows application. Name the solution, project, and form file Waterglen Solution, Waterglen Project, and frmMain.vb, respectively. Save the application in the ClearlyVB\Chap21 folder. If necessary, change the form's name to frmMain. Create the interface shown in Figure 21-21. Code the application using a four-row, five-column array to store the race results. Save the solution, then start and test the application. Stop the application, then close the solution.

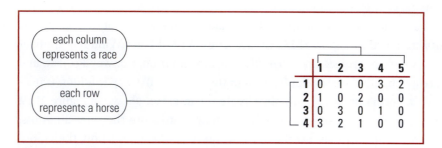

Figure 21-20: Horse race results

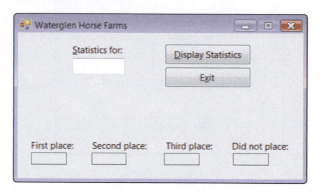

Figure 21-21: User interface for the Waterglen Horse Farms application

10. Open the FigureThisOut Solution (FigureThisOut Solution.sln) file, which is contained in the ClearlyVB\Chap21\FigureThisOut Solution folder. Open the Code Editor window, then locate the btnCount control's Click event procedure. You can determine the number of elements in a two-dimensional array by multiplying the number of rows by the number of columns. Code the procedure to display the number of array elements. Save the solution, than start and test the application. Stop the application. Close the Code Editor window, then close the solution.

11. In this exercise, you find an error in an application's code. Open the SwatTheBugs Solution (SwatTheBugs Solution.sln) file, which is contained in the ClearlyVB\ Chap21\SwatTheBugs Solution folder. Open the Code Editor window and study the existing code. Start and then test the application. Notice that the application is not working correctly. Click Debug, then click Stop Debugging. Locate and correct any errors in the code. Save the solution, then start and test the application again. Stop the application, then close the solution.

ANSWERS TO "TRY THIS" EXERCISES

1. See Figure 21-22.

```
Private Sub btnDisplay_Click(ByVal sender As Object, _
    ByVal e As System.EventArgs) Handles btnDisplay.Click
    ' displays the price associated with the product
    ' ID entered by the user

    Dim strPriceList(,) As String = {{"BX35", "13"}, _
                                     {"CR20", "10"}, _
                                     {"FE15", "12"}, _
                                     {"KW10", "24"}, _
                                     {"MM67", "4"}}
    Dim strSearchFor As String
    Dim strFound As String
    Dim intRow As Integer
    Dim intNumRows As Integer

    ' assign the product ID to a variable
    strSearchFor = txtId.Text.ToUpper

    ' search for the product ID in the first column of the array
    ' continue searching until there are no more rows to search or
    ' the product ID is found
    intRow = 0
    strFound = "N"
    intNumRows = strPriceList.GetUpperBound(0) + 1
```

Figure 21-22 (*continued on next page*)

```
        Do Until intRow = intNumRows OrElse strFound = "Y"
            If strPriceList(intRow, 0) = strSearchFor Then
                strFound = "Y"
            Else
                intRow = intRow + 1
            End If
        Loop

        ' determine whether the product ID
        ' was found in the array
        If strFound = "Y" Then
            Dim intPrice As Integer
            intPrice = strPriceList(intRow, 1)
            lblPrice.Text = intPrice.ToString("C0")
        Else
            MessageBox.Show("Invalid product ID", _
                            "Treasures Gift Shop", MessageBoxButtons.OK, _
                            MessageBoxIcon.Information)
        End If
    End Sub
```

Figure 21-22 (*continued from previous page*)

2. See Figure 21-23.

```
    Private Sub btnDisplay_Click(ByVal sender As Object, _
        ByVal e As System.EventArgs) Handles btnDisplay.Click
        ' displays the sum of the values stored in the array

        Dim intInventory(,) As Integer = {{34, 56}, _
                                          {75, 67}, _
                                          {5, 6}}

        Dim intTotal As Integer ' accumulator

        ' total the array values
        For intRow As Integer = 0 To intInventory.GetUpperBound(0)
            For intColumn As Integer = 0 To intInventory.GetUpperBound(1)
                intTotal = intTotal + intInventory(intRow, intColumn)
            Next intColumn
        Next intRow

        ' display the total
        lblTotal.Text = intTotal.ToString
    End Sub
```

Figure 21-23

22

BUILDING YOUR OWN STRUCTURE

After studying Chapter 22, you should be able to:

Create a structure

Declare and use a structure variable

Understand the advantages of using a structure

Pass a structure variable to a procedure

Create an array of structure variables

PUTTING THE PIECES TOGETHER

In previous chapters, you used only the data types built into Visual Basic, such as the Integer and Decimal data types. You also can create your own data types in Visual Basic using the **Structure statement**. Data types created using the Structure statement are referred to as **structures**. Similar to an array, you can use a structure to group together related items. However, unlike the items in an array, the items in a structure do not have to have the same data type. Because of this, you can group together items having the String data type (such as an employee's ID, first name, and last name) along with items having a numeric data type (such as a Decimal salary amount). Figure 22-1 shows the Structure statement's syntax. The name of the structure appears in the Structure clause. The convention is to enter structure names using Pascal case, which means capitalizing the first letter in the name and the first letter of each subsequent word in the name. Between the Structure and End Structure clauses, you define the members included in the structure. The members can be variables or procedures; however, in this book you will learn how to include variables only. This is because most programmers use the Class statement (rather than the Structure statement) to create data types that contain procedures. (You will learn about the Class statement in Chapter 27.) In most structures, the member variables are defined using the keyword Public followed by the variable's name, the keyword As, and the variable's *dataType*. The *dataType* identifies the type of data the variable will store. The *dataType* can be any of the standard data types available in Visual Basic; it also can be another structure. The Employee structure shown in Figure 22-1 contains four members: three String variables and one Decimal variable.

CREATING A STRUCTURE

<u>Syntax</u>

Structure *structureName*

    Public *memberVariableName1* **As** *dataType*

    [**Public** *memberVariableNameN* **As** *dataType*]

End Structure

Figure 22-1: Syntax and an example of creating a structure (*continued on next page*)

Example

Structure Employee
    Public strId As String
    Public strFirstName As String
    Public strLastName As String
    Public decSalary As Decimal
End Structure

Figure 22-1: Syntax and an example of creating a structure (*continued from previous page*)

In most applications, the Structure statement is entered in the form's Declarations section, which is the area between the Public Class and End Class lines in the Code Editor window. The Structure statement itself does not reserve any locations in the computer's internal memory. Rather, it provides the pattern for a data type that can be used to reserve a memory location. Variables declared using a structure are often referred to as **structure variables**. Figure 22-2 shows the syntax for creating a structure variable. You use the Dim keyword to declare a procedure-level structure variable, and the Private keyword to declare a module-level structure variable. The figure also includes an example of declaring a structure variable using the Employee structure from Figure 22-1.

DECLARING A STRUCTURE VARIABLE

Syntax

{**Dim** | **Private**} *structureVariableName* **As** *structureName*

Example

Dim manager As Employee
declares an Employee structure variable named manager; the structure variable contains four members

Figure 22-2: Syntax and an example of declaring a structure variable

Similar to the way the Dim intAge As Integer instruction declares an Integer variable named intAge, the Dim manager As Employee instruction declares an Employee structure variable named manager. However, unlike the intAge variable, the manager variable contains four members. In code, you refer to the entire structure variable by its name—in this case, manager. You refer to a member by preceding the member's name with the name of the structure variable, separating both names with the **dot member access operator** (a period). For example, to refer to the members within the manager structure variable, you use manager.strId, manager.strFirstName, manager.strLastName, and manager.decSalary. Figure 22-3 uses the storage bin analogy from Chapter 7 to illustrate the manager structure variable and its members.

Figure 22-3: Illustration of the manager structure variable

A structure variable's members can be used just like any other variables. You can assign values to them, use them in calculations, display their contents, and so on. Figure 22-4 shows various ways of using the members contained in the manager structure variable.

USING A MEMBER OF A STRUCTURE VARIABLE
<u>Example 1</u>

manager.strLastName = "Lopenski"
assigns the string "Lopenski" to the manager.strLastName member

---

Figure 22-4: Examples of using a member of a structure variable (*continued on next page*)

Example 2

manager.decSalary = manager.decSalary * 1.05
multiplies the contents of the manager.decSalary member by 1.05, and then assigns the
result to the member

Example 3

lblSalary.Text = manager.decSalary.ToString("C2")
formats the value contained in the manager.decSalary member and then displays the
result in the lblSalary control

Figure 22-4: Examples of using a member of a structure variable (*continued from previous page*)

The advantages of using structures will become more apparent as you code the applications in the next two sections.

Before continuing, it may be helpful to view the Ch22-Structures video.

WILLOW POOLS APPLICATION

The sales manager at Willow Pools wants an application that determines the amount of water required to fill a rectangular pool. To perform this task, the application will need to calculate the volume of the pool. You calculate the volume by first multiplying the pool's length by its width, and then multiplying the result by the pool's depth. Assuming the length, width, and depth are measured in feet, this gives you the volume in cubic feet. To determine the number of gallons of water, you multiply the number of cubic feet by 7.48, because there are 7.48 gallons in one cubic foot. Figure 22-5 shows a sample run of the Willow Pools application, and Figure 22-6 shows one way of coding the application without using a structure. (Only the CalcVolume function and btnCalc control's Click event procedure are shown in the figure.) Notice that the btnCalc control's Click event procedure passes three variables *by value* to the CalcVolume function. The function determines whether the three values it receives are greater than zero. If they are, the function uses the values to calculate the volume of the pool; otherwise, it assigns the number 0 as the pool's volume. The function returns the volume as a Decimal number to the Click event procedure, which assigns the value to the decPoolVolume variable.

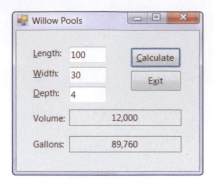

Figure 22-5: Sample run of the Willow Pools application

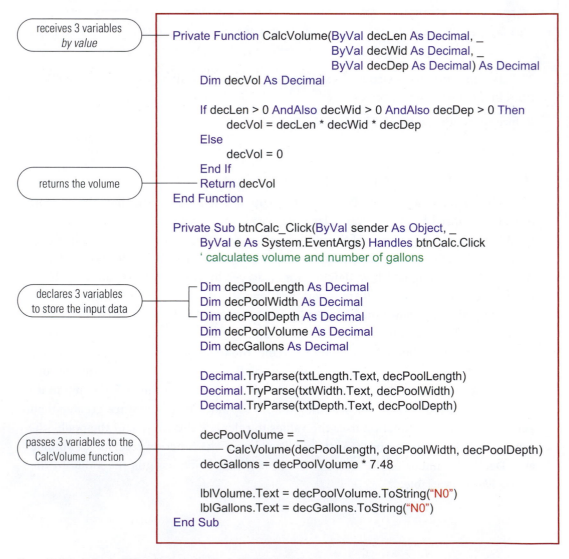

receives 3 variables
by value

returns the volume

declares 3 variables
to store the input data

passes 3 variables to the
CalcVolume function

```
Private Function CalcVolume(ByVal decLen As Decimal, _
                           ByVal decWid As Decimal, _
                           ByVal decDep As Decimal) As Decimal
    Dim decVol As Decimal

    If decLen > 0 AndAlso decWid > 0 AndAlso decDep > 0 Then
        decVol = decLen * decWid * decDep
    Else
        decVol = 0
    End If
    Return decVol
End Function

Private Sub btnCalc_Click(ByVal sender As Object, _
    ByVal e As System.EventArgs) Handles btnCalc.Click
    ' calculates volume and number of gallons

    Dim decPoolLength As Decimal
    Dim decPoolWidth As Decimal
    Dim decPoolDepth As Decimal
    Dim decPoolVolume As Decimal
    Dim decGallons As Decimal

    Decimal.TryParse(txtLength.Text, decPoolLength)
    Decimal.TryParse(txtWidth.Text, decPoolWidth)
    Decimal.TryParse(txtDepth.Text, decPoolDepth)

    decPoolVolume = _
        CalcVolume(decPoolLength, decPoolWidth, decPoolDepth)
    decGallons = decPoolVolume * 7.48

    lblVolume.Text = decPoolVolume.ToString("N0")
    lblGallons.Text = decGallons.ToString("N0")
End Sub
```

Figure 22-6: Code for the Willow Pools application (without a structure)

A more convenient way of coding the Willow Pools application is to use a structure to group together the length, width, and depth items. It's logical to group the three items because they are related: each represents one of the three dimensions of a rectangular pool. You will observe the advantage of using a structure in the next set of steps.

To open the Willow Pools application, and then modify the code to use a structure:

1. Start Visual Studio 2008 (or Visual Basic 2008 Express Edition). Open the **Pool Solution** (**Pool Solution.sln**) file, which is contained in the ClearlyVB\Chap22\Pool Solution folder. If necessary, open the designer window. The interface provides text boxes for the user to enter the pool's length, width, and depth.

2. Open the Code Editor window, which contains the code from Figure 22-6. First, declare the structure. Click the **blank line** below the Public Class frmMain line. As the Class Name and Method Name boxes indicate, this is the Declarations section of the form. The input items represent the pool's dimensions, so Dimensions would be a descriptive name for the structure. Press **Enter** to insert another blank line, then enter the Structure statement shown in Figure 22-7. The Dimensions structure contains three member variables named decLength, decWidth, and decDepth.

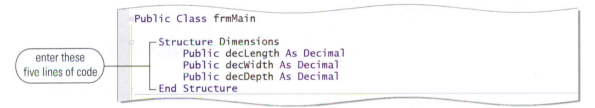

```
Public Class frmMain

        Structure Dimensions
            Public decLength As Decimal
            Public decWidth As Decimal
            Public decDepth As Decimal
        End Structure
```

enter these five lines of code

Figure 22-7: Dimensions structure entered in the form's Declarations section

3. Locate the code template for the btnCalc control's Click event procedure. The procedure will use a structure variable (rather than three scalar variables) to store the input items. Replace the three Dim statements that declare the decPoolLength, decPoolWidth, and decPoolDepth variables with the following Dim statement: **Dim poolSize As Dimensions**.

4. Now store each input item in its corresponding member in the structure variable. In the first TryParse method, change decPoolLength to **poolSize.decLength**. In the second TryParse method, change decPoolWidth to **poolSize.decWidth**. In the third TryParse method, change decPoolDepth to **poolSize.decDepth**.

5. Next, consider the changes you will need to make to the statement that invokes the CalcVolume function. Instead of sending three scalar variables to the function, you now need to send only one variable: the structure variable. When you pass a structure variable to a procedure, all of its members are passed automatically. Although passing one structure variable rather than three scalar variables may not seem like a great

advantage, consider the convenience of passing one structure variable rather than 10 scalar variables! Change the statement that invokes the CalcVolume function to **decPoolVolume = CalcVolume(poolSize)**. Don't be concerned about the jagged line that appears below CalcVolume(poolSize) in the statement. It will disappear when you modify the CalcVolume function in the next step.

6. Locate the CalcVolume function's code. The function will now receive a Dimensions structure variable rather than three Decimal variables. Like the Decimal variables, the structure variable will be passed *by value*. Change the function's header to **Public Function CalcVolume(ByVal pool As Dimensions) As Decimal**.

7. The function will need to use the members of the structure variable (rather than the scalar variables) in both the If clause and the statement that calculates the volume. Modify the If clause and the calculation statement as shown in Figure 22-8.

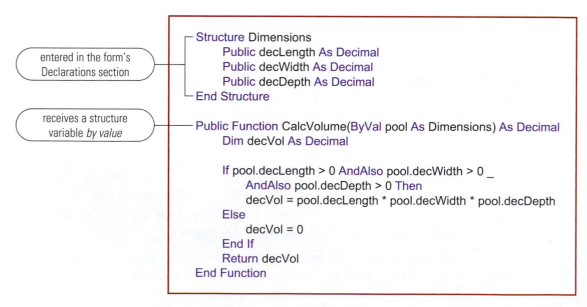

modify these lines of code

```
If pool.decLength > 0 AndAlso pool.decWidth > 0 _
    AndAlso pool.decDepth > 0 Then
    decVol = pool.decLength * pool.decWidth * pool.decDepth
Else
```

Figure 22-8: Modified If clause and calculation statement

8. Save the solution. Figure 22-9 shows the modified code, which uses a structure.

entered in the form's Declarations section

receives a structure variable *by value*

```
Structure Dimensions
    Public decLength As Decimal
    Public decWidth As Decimal
    Public decDepth As Decimal
End Structure

Public Function CalcVolume(ByVal pool As Dimensions) As Decimal
    Dim decVol As Decimal

    If pool.decLength > 0 AndAlso pool.decWidth > 0 _
        AndAlso pool.decDepth > 0 Then
        decVol = pool.decLength * pool.decWidth * pool.decDepth
    Else
        decVol = 0
    End If
    Return decVol
End Function
```

Figure 22-9: Modified code for the Willow Pools application (using a structure) (*continued on next page*)

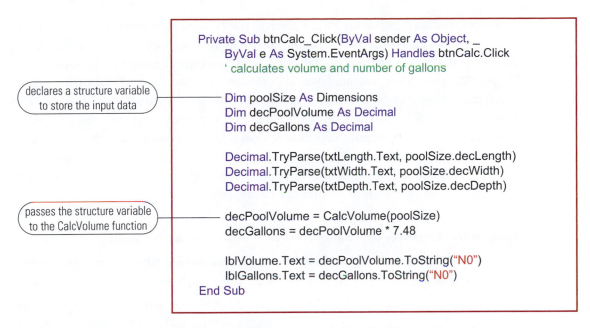

```
Private Sub btnCalc_Click(ByVal sender As Object, _
    ByVal e As System.EventArgs) Handles btnCalc.Click
    ' calculates volume and number of gallons

    Dim poolSize As Dimensions
    Dim decPoolVolume As Decimal
    Dim decGallons As Decimal

    Decimal.TryParse(txtLength.Text, poolSize.decLength)
    Decimal.TryParse(txtWidth.Text, poolSize.decWidth)
    Decimal.TryParse(txtDepth.Text, poolSize.decDepth)

    decPoolVolume = CalcVolume(poolSize)
    decGallons = decPoolVolume * 7.48

    lblVolume.Text = decPoolVolume.ToString("N0")
    lblGallons.Text = decGallons.ToString("N0")
End Sub
```

declares a structure variable to store the input data

passes the structure variable to the CalcVolume function

Figure 22-9: Modified code for the Willow Pools application (using a structure) (*continued from previous page*)

To test the Willow Pools application:

1. Save the solution, if necessary, then start the application. Type **100** in the Length box, **30** in the Width box, and **4** in the Depth box. Click the **Calculate** button. The numbers 12,000 and 89,760 appear in the Volume and Gallons boxes, as shown earlier in Figure 22-5.

2. Test the application several more times. When you are finished testing the application, click the **Exit** button. Close the Code Editor window, then close the solution.

The ability to pass a structure variable and its members as one unit is not the only advantage of using a structure. As you will learn in the next section, another advantage of using a structure is that a structure variable can be stored in an array, even when its members have different data types.

REVISITING THE EMPLOYEE APPLICATION...AGAIN!

You coded the Employee application in both Chapter 20 and Chapter 21. As you may remember, the application's interface provides a text box for the user to enter an employee ID. The application searches for the ID in an array. If it finds the ID, it displays the corresponding salary; otherwise, it displays the "Invalid ID" message. In Chapter 20, you stored the five employee IDs and corresponding salaries in two parallel one-dimensional arrays: a String array for the IDs and an Integer array for the salaries. In Chapter 21, you stored the employee information in a two-dimensional String array. Recall that, in order to do so, you had to treat the numeric salary amounts as strings. This is because the IDs are strings and all the elements in an array must have the same data type. Rather than using parallel one-dimensional arrays or a two-dimensional array, you also can use a one-dimensional array of structure variables. In the Employee application, the array will contain five structure variables, because there are five employees. Each structure variable will store an employee's ID and salary amount.

To open the Employee application, and then begin coding the application:

1. Open the **Employee Solution** (**Employee Solution.sln**) file, which is contained in the ClearlyVB\Chap22\Employee Solution folder. If necessary, open the designer window.

2. Open the Code Editor window. First, declare the structure in the form's Declarations section. The IDs and salaries represent employee information, so EmployInfo would be a descriptive name for the structure. Click the **blank line** below the Public Class frmMain line. Press **Enter** to insert another blank line, then enter the Structure statement shown in Figure 22-10. The EmployInfo structure contains two member variables named strId and intSalary.

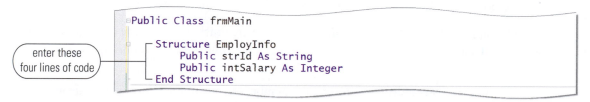

```
Public Class frmMain

    Structure EmployInfo
        Public strId As String
        Public intSalary As Integer
    End Structure
```

enter these four lines of code

Figure 22-10: EmployInfo structure entered in the form's Declarations section

3. Locate the code template for the btnDisplay control's Click event procedure. The procedure will store each employee's ID and salary in an EmployInfo structure variable. If the company had only one employee, you could declare the structure variable using the statement Dim employee As EmployInfo. However, because there are five employees, you need five structure variables—one for each employee. You can reserve five structure variables by declaring a five-element, one-dimensional array, using the EmployInfo structure as the data type. Click the **blank line** below the ' declare an array of structure variables comment. Type **dim employees(4) as EmployInfo** and press **Enter** twice.

4. Now declare the remaining variables. Enter the following three declaration statements. The strSearchFor variable will store the ID entered by the user. The strFound variable will contain a letter (either N or Y) to indicate whether the ID is in the array. The intSubscript variable will keep track of the subscripts while the array is being searched.

Dim strSearchFor As String
Dim strFound As String
Dim intSubscript As Integer

Next, you need to store the five IDs and salaries in the employees array. Keep in mind that each element in the array is a structure variable, and each structure variable contains two members: strId and intSalary. To access a member of a structure variable in an array, you use the syntax *arrayName(subscript).memberName*. For example, employees(0).strID refers to the strId member contained in the first array element. Likewise, employees(4). intSalary refers to the intSalary member contained in the last array element. Figure 22-11 illustrates this naming convention.

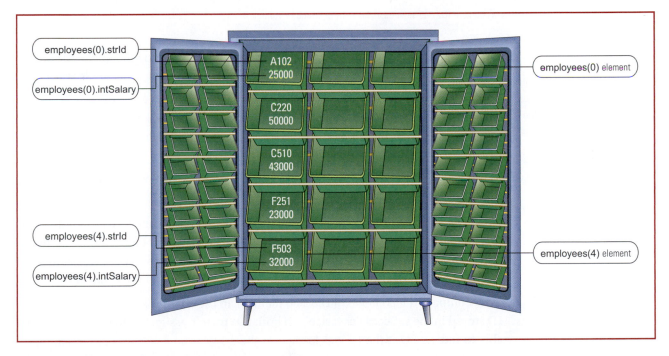

Figure 22-11: Illustration of the employees array of structure variables

To finish coding the btnDisplay control's Click event procedure, and then test the procedure:

1. Click the **blank line** below the ' assign the IDs and salaries to the array comment. Type the 10 assignment statements shown in Figure 22-12.

enter these 10 assignment statements

```
Dim strFound As String
Dim intSubscript As Integer

' assign the IDs and salaries to the array
employees(0).strId = "A102"
employees(0).intSalary = 25000
employees(1).strId = "C220"
employees(1).intSalary = 50000
employees(2).strId = "C510"
employees(2).intSalary = 43000
employees(3).strId = "F251"
employees(3).intSalary = 23000
employees(4).strId = "F503"
employees(4).intSalary = 32000

' assign the ID to a variable
```

Figure 22-12: Statements to assign the IDs and salaries to the array of structure variables

2. Now assign the employee ID entered by the user to a variable. Click the **blank line** below the ' assign the ID to a variable comment, then type **strSearchFor = txtId.Text.ToUpper** and press **Enter**.

3. The search will begin with the first element in the array. Click the **blank line** immediately below the ' row has been searched comment. Type **intSubscript = 0** and press **Enter**.

4. Before the search begins, the procedure will assume that the ID is not contained in the array. Type **strFound = "N"** and press **Enter**.

5. Next, enter a pretest loop that repeats its instructions until one of two conditions is true: either the ID has been found in the array or the subscript equals the number of array elements (which indicates there are no more elements to search). Type **do until strFound = "Y" orelse intSubscript = employees.length** and press **Enter**.

6. Now compare the contents of the strId member in the current array element with the ID stored in the strSearchFor variable. If both IDs match, assign "Y" to the strFound variable to indicate that the ID was located in the array. If both IDs do not match, increment the array subscript by 1; this will allow the loop to search the next element in the array. Type the selection structure shown in Figure 22-13.

```
str...
Do Until strFound = "Y" OrElse intSubscript = employees.Length
    If employees(intSubscript).strId = strSearchFor Then
        strFound = "Y"
    Else
        intSubscript = intSubscript + 1
    End If
Loop
```

enter this
selection structure

Figure 22-13: Selection structure entered in the procedure

7. The letter stored in the strFound variable indicates whether the ID was located in the array, and it determines the appropriate information to display. Click the **blank line** below the ' determine whether the ID was found comment, then type the additional selection structure shown in Figure 22-14.

```
' determine whether the ID was found
If strFound = "Y" Then
    lblSalary.Text = employees(intSubscript).intSalary.ToString("C0")
Else
    lblSalary.Text = "Invalid ID"
End If
```

enter this
selection structure

Figure 22-14: Additional selection structure entered in the procedure

8. Save the solution, then start the application. First, enter a valid ID. Type **f503** in the Employee ID box. The ID is stored in the employees(4).strId element, and its corresponding salary amount (32000) is stored in the employees(4).intSalary element. Click the **Display Salary** button. The correct salary amount appears in the Salary box, as shown in Figure 22-15.

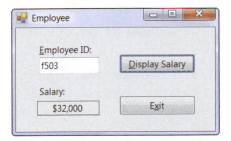

Figure 22-15: Salary amount displayed in the interface

9. Now enter an invalid ID. Type **f502** in the Employee ID box, then click the **Display Salary** button. The message "Invalid ID" appears in the Salary box.

10. Test the application several more times using valid and invalid IDs. When you are finished testing the application, click the **Exit** button. Close the Code Editor window, then close the solution.

As you observed by coding the Employee application in this chapter and in the previous two chapters, there are many different ways of solving the same problem. Most times, the "best" way is simply a matter of personal preference.

MINI-QUIZ 1

1. Most times, the code to define a structure is entered in the form's _____ section in the Code Editor window.

2. Write a Visual Basic statement that assigns the string "Maple" to the strStreet member of a structure variable named address.

3. An array is declared using the statement Dim inventory(4) As Product, where Product is the name of a structure. Write a Visual Basic statement that assigns the number 100 to the intQuantity member contained in the last array element.

 To learn more about structures, see the Structures section in the Ch22WantMore.pdf file.

SUMMARY

» You can use the Structure statement to create your own data types in Visual Basic. You typically enter the Structure statement in the form's Declarations section in the Code Editor window.

» After a structure is defined, you can use it to declare a structure variable. A structure variable contains one or more members, usually variables. You access a member using the structure's name followed by a period (the dot member access operator) and the member's name.

» The member variables in a structure variable can be used just like any other variables.

» A structure variable can be passed to a procedure.

» You can create a one-dimensional array of structure variables. You access a member in an array element using the array's name followed by the element's subscript enclosed in parentheses, a period (the dot member access operator), and the member's name.

KEY TERMS

Dot member access operator—a period; used to separate a structure variable's name from a member's name

Structure statement—used to create your own data type (structure) in Visual Basic

Structure variables—variables declared using a structure as the data type

Structures—data types created using the Structure statement

ANSWERS TO MINI-QUIZ

MINI-QUIZ 1

1. Declarations

2. address.strStreet = "Maple"

3. inventory(4).intQuantity = 100

REVIEW QUESTIONS

1. Which of the following declares a Country structure variable named england?

   a. Private england As Country   b. Dim england As Country

   c. Dim Country As england   d. Both a and b.

2. Which of the following statements assigns the string "London" to the strCity member of the Country variable from Question 1?

   a. england.strCity = "London"

   b. Country.strCity = "London"

   c. Country.england.strCity = "London"

   d. strCity.england = "London"

3. An application uses a structure named Product. Which of the following creates a five-element, one-dimensional array of Product structure variables?

   a. Dim items(5) As Product   b. Dim items(4) As Product

   c. Dim items As Product(5)   d. Dim items As Product(4)

BUILDING YOUR OWN STRUCTURE

4. Regarding the items array from Question 3, which of the following assigns the number 23 to the intPrice member contained in the first array element?

   a. items(0).intPrice = 23

   b. intPrice(0) = 23

   c. Product.items(1).intPrice = 23

   d. None of the above.

5. Regarding the items array from Question 3, which of the following increases by 100 the contents of the intPrice member located in the second array element?

   a. intPrice(1) = intPrice(1) + 100

   b. items.intPrice(2) = items.intPrice(2) + 100

   c. Product.items(1).intPrice = Product.items(1).intPrice + 100

   d. None of the above.

EXERCISES

» TRY THIS

1. In this exercise, you code an application that calculates and displays a commission amount.

   a. Open the Commission Solution (Commission Solution.sln) file, which is contained in the ClearlyVB\Chap22\Commission Solution folder. Open the designer window. The interface provides three text boxes for the user to enter the sales for three regions.

   b. Open the Code Editor window. Declare a structure named SalesInfo. The structure should contain three Decimal members to store the three sales amounts.

   c. Use a function named GetCommission to sum the three sales amounts and then return a 3% commission. The btnCalc control's Click event procedure should store the contents of the text boxes in a SalesInfo structure variable. It then should use the GetCommission function to calculate and return the commission. Finally, it should display the commission (formatted with a dollar sign and two decimal places) in the lblComm control. Code the function and Click event procedure.

   d. Save the solution, then start and test the application. Stop the application, then close the solution. (The answers to TRY THIS Exercises are located at the end of the chapter.)

» TRY THIS

2. Open the Price List Solution (Price List Solution.sln) file, which is contained in the ClearlyVB\Chap22\Price List Solution folder. Open the designer window. The interface provides a text box for the user to enter a product ID. When the user clicks the Display Price button, the button's Click event procedure should display either the price associated with the product ID or the "Invalid product ID" message. (Display the message in a message box.) Open the Code Editor window. Declare a structure named Item. The structure should contain two members: a String variable for the product ID and an Integer variable for the price. Locate the code template for the btnDisplay control's Click event procedure. Declare a five-element array of Item structure variables; name the array gifts. Assign the following IDs and prices to the gifts array: BX35, 13, CR20, 10, FE15, 12, KW10, 24, MM67, and 4. Finish coding the procedure. (You can use Figure 20-19 from Chapter 20 as a guide.) Save the solution, then start and test the application. Stop the application, then close the solution. (The answers to TRY THIS Exercises are located at the end of the chapter.)

» MODIFY THIS

3. In this exercise, you modify the application from TRY THIS Exercise 1. Use Windows to make a copy of the Commission Solution folder. Save the copy in the ClearlyVB\Chap22 folder. Rename the copy Commission Solution-MODIFY THIS. Open the Commission Solution (Commission Solution.sln) file contained in the ClearlyVB\Chap22\Commission Solution-MODIFY THIS folder. Open the designer window, then open the Code Editor window. Make the following modifications. The btnCalc control's Click event procedure should prompt the user to enter the commission rate. It then should pass the rate to the GetCommission function. Save the solution, then start and test the application. Stop the application, then close the solution.

» INTRODUCTORY

4. Open the Test Scores Solution (Test Scores Solution.sln) file, which is contained in the ClearlyVB\Chap22\Test Scores Solution folder. Open the designer window, then open the Code Editor window. Declare a structure that contains three Decimal members; each member represents a test score. Create a function that receives a structure variable. The function should sum the test scores and return the average score. The btnAverage control's Click event procedure should prompt the user to enter the test scores, and it should store the scores in a structure variable. It then should use the function to determine the average score. Finally, it should display the average score (formatted with one decimal place) in the lblResult control. Code the Click event procedure. Save the solution, then start and test the application. Stop the application, then close the solution.

» INTERMEDIATE

5. In this exercise, you modify the application from Exercise 4. If you did not complete Exercise 4, you will need to do so before completing this exercise. Use Windows to make a copy of the Test Scores Solution folder. Save the copy in the ClearlyVB\Chap22 folder. Rename the copy Modified Test Scores Solution. Open the Test Scores Solution (Test Scores Solution.sln) file contained in the ClearlyVB\Chap22\Modified Test Scores Solution folder. Open the designer window. Unlock the controls. Set the form's Size property to approximately 324, 220. Set the lblResult label's Size property to approximately 238, 65. Reposition the button controls, then lock the controls. Open the Code Editor window. Modify the btnAverage control's Click event procedure so it uses a three-element array of structure variables. Each element will contain the test scores for one student. The procedure should prompt the user for a student's three test scores, and then store the scores in one of the structure variables in the array. It then should use the function to determine the student's average score. Finally, it should display the student's number (1, 2, or 3) along with the average score (formatted with one decimal place) in the lblResult control. Save the solution, then start and test the application. Figure 22-16 shows a sample run of the application when the user enters the following scores: 100, 100, 100, 90, 85, 78, 73, 72, and 67. Stop the application, then close the solution.

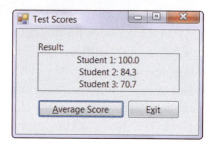

Figure 22-16: Sample run of the Test Scores application

» ADVANCED

6. In this exercise, you modify the Willow Pools application coded in the chapter. Use Windows to make a copy of the Pool Solution folder. Save the copy in the ClearlyVB\Chap22 folder. Rename the copy Modified Pool Solution. Open the Pool Solution (Pool Solution.sln) file contained in the ClearlyVB\Chap22\Modified Pool Solution folder. Currently, the application assumes that the entire pool has the same depth. Modify the interface and code so that the application displays the volume and number of gallons for a pool whose depth may vary. The formula for calculating the volume for such a pool is *length * width * (shallow end's depth + deep end's depth) / 2*. Modify the interface and code appropriately. Save the solution, then start and test the application. Stop the application, then close the solution.

7. Open the FigureThisOut Solution (FigureThisOut Solution.sln) file, which is contained in the ClearlyVB\Chap22\FigureThisOut Solution folder. Open the Code Editor window and study the existing code. What members are defined in the Structure statement? What is the purpose of the salesperson.decSales(0) = 2000 statement? Why does the procedure use salesperson.decSales(0) in the statement rather than salesperson(0).decSales? Start and test the application. Stop the application. Close the Code Editor window, then close the solution.

8. In this exercise, you find an error in an application's code. Open the SwatTheBugs Solution (SwatTheBugs Solution.sln) file, which is contained in the ClearlyVB\Chap22\ SwatTheBugs Solution folder. Open the Code Editor window and study the existing code. Correct the code to remove the jagged lines. Save the solution, then start and test the application. Notice that the application is not working correctly. Stop the application. Locate and correct any errors in the code. Save the solution, then start and test the application again. Stop the application, then close the solution.

ANSWERS TO "TRY THIS" EXERCISES

1. Figure 22-17 shows the code for the SalesInfo structure, GetCommission function, and btnCalc control's Click event procedure.

```
Structure SalesInfo
    Public decSale1 As Decimal
    Public decSale2 As Decimal
    Public decSale3 As Decimal
End Structure

Private Function GetCommission(ByVal company As SalesInfo) As Decimal
    ' calculates and returns the commission amount

    Dim decTotal As Decimal

    decTotal = company.decSale1 + company.decSale2 + company.decSale3
    Return decTotal * 0.03
End Function
```

Figure 22-17 (*continued on next page*)

```vb
Private Sub btnCalc_Click(ByVal sender As Object, _
    ByVal e As System.EventArgs) Handles btnCalc.Click
    ' displays the commission

    Dim companySales As SalesInfo
    Dim decCommission As Decimal

    Decimal.TryParse(txtRegion1.Text, companySales.decSale1)
    Decimal.TryParse(txtRegion2.Text, companySales.decSale2)
    Decimal.TryParse(txtRegion3.Text, companySales.decSale3)

    decCommission = GetCommission(companySales)
    lblComm.Text = decCommission.ToString("C2")
End Sub
```

Figure 22-17 (*continued from previous page*)

2. Figure 22-18 shows the code for the Item structure and the btnDisplay control's Click event procedure.

```vb
Structure Item
    Public strId As String
    Public intPrice As Integer
End Structure

Private Sub btnDisplay_Click(ByVal sender As Object, _
    ByVal e As System.EventArgs) Handles btnDisplay.Click
    ' displays the price associated with the product
    ' ID entered by the user

    ' declare an array of structure variables
    Dim gifts(4) As Item

    ' declare variables
    Dim strSearchFor As String
    Dim strFound As String
    Dim intSubscript As Integer
```

Figure 22-18 (*continued on next page*)

```
            ' assign IDs and prices to the array
            gifts(0).strId = "BX35"
            gifts(0).intPrice = 13
            gifts(1).strId = "CR20"
            gifts(1).intPrice = 10
            gifts(2).strId = "FE15"
            gifts(2).intPrice = 12
            gifts(3).strId = "KW10"
            gifts(3).intPrice = 24
            gifts(4).strId = "MM67"
            gifts(4).intPrice = 4

            ' assign the product ID to a variable
            strSearchFor = txtId.Text.ToUpper

            ' search the array for the product ID
            ' continue searching until there are
            ' no more array elements to search or
            ' the product ID is found
            strFound = "N"
            Do Until intSubscript = gifts.Length _
                OrElse strFound = "Y"
                If gifts(intSubscript).strId = strSearchFor Then
                    strFound = "Y"
                Else
                    intSubscript = intSubscript + 1
                End If
            Loop

            ' determine whether the product ID
            ' was found in the array
            If strFound = "Y" Then
                lblPrice.Text = gifts(intSubscript).intPrice.ToString("C0")
            Else
                MessageBox.Show("Invalid product ID", _
                            "Treasures Gift Shop", MessageBoxButtons.OK, _
                            MessageBoxIcon.Information)
            End If
        End Sub
```

Figure 22-18 (*continued from previous page*)

23

I'M SAVING FOR THE FUTURE

After studying Chapter 23, you should be able to:

Open and close a sequential access file

Write information to and read information from a sequential access file

Determine whether a sequential access file exists

Test for the end of a sequential access file

SEQUENTIAL ACCESS FILES

In addition to getting data from the keyboard and sending data to the computer screen, an application also can get data from and send data to a file on a disk. Getting data from a file is referred to as "reading from the file," and sending data to a file is referred to as "writing to the file." Files to which data is written are called **output files**, because the files store the output produced by an application. Files that are read by the computer are called **input files**, because an application uses the data in the files as input. Most input and output files are composed of lines of text that are both read and written sequentially—in other words, in consecutive order, one line at a time, beginning with the first line in the file and ending with the last line in the file. Such files are referred to as **sequential access files**, because of the manner in which the lines of text are accessed. Examples of text stored in sequential access files include an employee list, a memo, or a sales report. You will use a sequential access file in the Game Show Contestants application, which you code in the remaining sections of this chapter. Figure 23-1 shows the application's user interface. The interface provides a text box for entering a contestant's name. The Write to File button will write the name to a sequential access file. The Read from File button will read each name from the sequential access file and display each in the Contestants box. (The txtContestants control's Multiline and ReadOnly properties are set to True, and its ScrollBars property is set to Vertical.) You will code the Write to File button first.

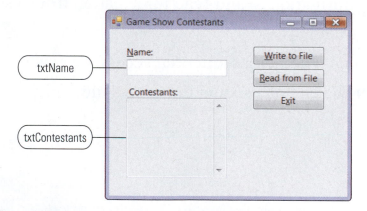

Figure 23-1: User interface for the Game Show Contestants application

WRITE THOSE LINES OF TEXT

An item of data—such as the string "Yolanda"—is viewed differently by a human being and a computer. To a human being, the string represents a person's name; to a computer, it is merely a sequence of characters. Programmers refer to a sequence of characters as a **stream of characters**. In Visual Basic, you use a **StreamWriter object** to write a stream of characters to a sequential access file. Before you create the StreamWriter object, you first declare a variable to store the object in the computer's internal memory. Figure 23-2 shows the syntax and an example of declaring a StreamWriter variable. The IO in the syntax stands for "Input/Output."

DECLARING A STREAMWRITER VARIABLE

<u>Syntax</u>

{**Dim** | **Private**} *streamWriterVariableName* **As IO.StreamWriter**

<u>Example</u>

Dim outFile As IO.StreamWriter
declares a StreamWriter variable named outFile

Figure 23-2: Syntax and an example of declaring a StreamWriter variable

To open the Game Show Contestants application, and then begin coding the application:

1. Start Visual Studio 2008 (or Visual Basic 2008 Express Edition). Open the **Contestant Solution** (**Contestant Solution.sln**) file, which is contained in the ClearlyVB\Chap23\ Contestant Solution folder. If necessary, open the designer window.

2. Open the Code Editor window, then locate the code template for the btnWrite control's Click event procedure. Click the **blank line** below the ' declare a StreamWriter variable comment. Type **dim outFile as io.streamwriter** and press **Enter**.

After declaring a StreamWriter variable, you can use the syntax shown in Figure 23-3 to create a StreamWriter object. As the figure indicates, creating a StreamWriter object involves opening a sequential access file using one of two methods: CreateText or AppendText. You use the **CreateText method** to open a sequential access file for output. When you open a file for output, the computer creates a new, empty file to which data can be written. If the file already exists, the computer erases the contents of the file before writing any data to it. You use the **AppendText method** to open a sequential access file for append. When a file is opened for append, new data is written after any existing data in the file. If the file does not exist, the computer creates the file for you. In addition to opening the file, both methods automatically create a StreamWriter object to represent the file in the application. You assign the StreamWriter object to a StreamWriter variable, which you use to refer to the file in code. Also included in Figure 23-3 are examples of using the CreateText and AppendText methods. When processing the statement in

Example 1, the computer searches for the pay.txt file in the ClearlyVB\Chap23 folder on the C drive. If the file exists, its contents are erased and the file is opened for output; otherwise, a new, empty file is created and opened for output. The statement creates a StreamWriter object and assigns it to the outFile variable. Unlike the *fileName* argument in Example 1, the *fileName* argument in Example 2 does not contain a folder path. Therefore, the computer will search for the file in the default folder, which is the current project's bin\Debug folder. In this case, if the computer locates the report.txt file in the default folder, it opens the file for append. If it does not find the file, it creates a new, empty file and then opens the file for append. Like the statement in Example 1, the statement in Example 2 creates a StreamWriter object and assigns it to the outFile variable.

CREATING A STREAMWRITER OBJECT BY OPENING A SEQUENTIAL ACCESS FILE

<u>Syntax</u>

IO.File.*method***(***fileName***)**

method	Description
CreateText	opens a sequential access file for output
AppendText	opens a sequential access file for append

<u>Example 1</u>

outFile = IO.File.CreateText("C:\ClearlyVB\Chap23\pay.txt")
opens the pay.txt file for output; creates a StreamWriter object and assigns it to the outFile variable

<u>Example 2</u>

outFile = IO.File.AppendText("report.txt")
opens the report.txt file for append; creates a StreamWriter object and assigns it to the outFile variable

---

Figure 23-3: Syntax and examples of creating a StreamWriter object by opening a file

When the user clicks the Write to File button in the Game Show Contestants application, the name entered in the Name box should be added to the end of the existing names in the file; therefore, you will need to open the sequential access file for append. A descriptive name for a file that stores the names of contestants is contestants.txt. Although it is not a requirement, the "txt" (short for "text") filename extension is commonly used when naming sequential access files; this is because the files contain text.

To continue coding the btnWrite control's Click event procedure:

1. Click the **blank line** below the ' open the file for append comment.

2. Type **outFile = io.file.appendtext("contestants.txt")** and press **Enter**.

After opening a file for either output or append, you can begin writing data to it. You can do this using either the **Write method** or the **WriteLine method**; however, in most cases you will use the WriteLine method. The difference between both methods is that the WriteLine method writes a newline character after the data. Figure 23-4 shows the syntax and an example of both methods. As the figure indicates, when using the Write method, the next character written to the file will appear immediately after the letter o in the string "Hello". When using the WriteLine method, however, the next character written to the file will appear on the line immediately below the string. Notice that you do not need to include the file's name in either method's syntax. This is because the data will be written to the file associated with the StreamWriter variable.

WRITING DATA TO A SEQUENTIAL ACCESS FILE

Syntax

streamWriterVariableName.**Write(***data***)**
streamWriterVariableName.**WriteLine(***data***)**

Example 1

outFile.Write("Hello")

Result

Hello| —————————— the next character will appear immediately after the letter o

Example 2

outFile.WriteLine("Hello")

Result

Hello
| —————————— the next character will appear on the next line

Figure 23-4: Syntax and examples of writing data to a sequential access file

Each contestant's name should appear on a separate line in the file, so you will use the WriteLine method to write each name to the file.

To continue coding the btnWrite control's Click event procedure:

1. Click the **blank line** below the ' write the name on a separate line in the file comment.

2. Type **outFile.writeline(txtName.text)** and press **Enter**.

You should use the **Close method** to close a sequential access file as soon as you are finished using it. This ensures that the data is saved and it makes the file available for use elsewhere in the application. The syntax to close a sequential access file associated with a StreamWriter object is *streamWriterVariableName*.**Close()**. Here again, notice that you use the StreamWriter variable to refer to the file in code.

To finish coding the btnWrite control's Click event procedure, and then test the code:

1. Click the **blank line** below the ' close the file comment, type **outFile.close()** and press **Enter**.

2. To make it more convenient for the user to enter the next name, you will clear the current name from the Name box and then send the focus to the box. Click the blank line below the ' clear the Name box, then set the focus comment. Type **txtName.text = string.empty** and press **Enter**. You can use a text box's Focus method to send the focus to the text box. Type **txtName.focus()** and press **Enter**. Figure 23-5 shows the code entered in the btnWrite control's Click event procedure.

```
Private Sub btnWrite_Click(ByVal sender As Object, ByVal e As System.E
    ' writes a name to a sequential access file

    ' declare a StreamWriter variable
    Dim outFile As IO.StreamWriter

    ' open the file for append
    outFile = IO.File.AppendText("contestants.txt")

    ' write the name on a separate line in the file
    outFile.WriteLine(txtName.Text)

    ' close the file
    outFile.Close()

    ' clear the Name box, then set the focus
    txtName.Text = String.Empty
    txtName.Focus()

End Sub
```

Figure 23-5: Code entered in the btnWrite control's Click event procedure

3. Save the solution, then start the application. Type **Hannah Jones** in the Name box, then click the **Write to File** button. Use the application to write the following four names to the file: **Clark Smith**, **Khalid Shaw**, **Joe Mendez**, and **Charise Jackson**.

4. Click the **Exit** button.

5. Now open the contestants.txt file to verify its contents. Click **File** on the menu bar, then click **Open File**. Open the project's bin\Debug folder. Click **contestants.txt** in the list of filenames, then click the **Open** button. The contestants.txt window opens and shows the five names contained in the file. See Figure 23-6.

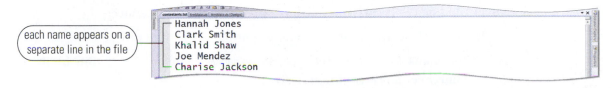

each name appears on a separate line in the file

```
Hannah Jones
Clark Smith
Khalid Shaw
Joe Mendez
Charise Jackson
```

Figure 23-6: Names contained in the contestants.txt file

6. Close the contestants.txt window by clicking its **Close** button.

MINI-QUIZ 1

1. Write the code to declare a variable that can be used to write data to a sequential access file. Name the variable outFile.

2. The AppendText method creates a _____ object.

3. Write a Visual Basic statement that sends the focus to the txtCity control.

NOW READ THOSE LINES OF TEXT

Next, you will code the Read from File button. In Visual Basic, you use a **StreamReader object** to read data from a sequential access file. Before creating the StreamReader object, you first declare a variable to store the object in the computer's internal memory. Figure 23-7 shows the syntax and an example of declaring a StreamReader variable. As mentioned earlier, the IO in the syntax stands for "Input/Output."

DECLARING A STREAMREADER VARIABLE

<u>Syntax</u>

{**Dim** | **Private**} *streamReaderVariableName* **As IO.StreamReader**

<u>Example</u>

Dim inFile As IO.StreamReader
declares a StreamReader variable named inFile

Figure 23-7: Syntax and an example of declaring a StreamReader variable

To begin coding the Read from File button's Click event procedure:

1. Locate the code template for the btnRead control's Click event procedure.

2. Click the **blank line** below the ' declare variables comment. Type **dim inFile as io.streamreader** and press **Enter**.

After declaring a StreamReader variable, you can use the **OpenText method** to open a sequential access file for input, which automatically creates a StreamReader object. When a file is opened for input, the computer can read the lines of text stored in the file. Figure 23-8 shows the OpenText method's syntax along with an example of using the method. The *fileName* argument in the example does not include a folder path, so the computer will search for the report.txt file in the current project's bin\Debug folder. If the computer finds the file, it opens the file for input; otherwise, a runtime error occurs, causing the application to end abruptly. You assign the StreamReader object created by the OpenText method to a StreamReader variable, which you use to refer to the file in code.

CREATING A STREAMREADER OBJECT BY OPENING
A SEQUENTIAL ACCESS FILE

<u>Syntax</u>

IO.File.OpenText(*fileName***)**

<u>Example</u>

inFile = IO.File.OpenText("report.txt")
opens the report.txt file for input; creates a StreamReader object and assigns it to the inFile variable

---

Figure 23-8: Syntax and an example of creating a StreamReader object by opening a file

You can use the Exists method to avoid the runtime error that occurs when the computer cannot locate the file you want opened for input. Figure 23-9 shows the method's syntax and includes an example of using the method. Here too, if the *fileName* argument does not include a folder path, the computer searches for the file in the current project's bin\Debug folder. The **Exists method** returns the Boolean value True if the file exists; otherwise, it returns the Boolean value False.

DETERMINING WHETHER A SEQUENTIAL ACCESS FILE EXISTS

<u>Syntax</u>

IO.File.Exists(*fileName***)**

<u>Example</u>

If IO.File.Exists("report.txt") = True Then

determines whether the report.txt file exists in the current project's bin\Debug folder

---

Figure 23-9: Syntax and an example of the Exists method

To continue coding the btnRead control's Click event procedure:

1. Click the **blank line** below the ' determine whether the file exists comment. Type **if io.file.exists("contestants.txt") = true then** and press **Enter**.

2. If the file exists, you will use the OpenText method to open the file. Type **' open the file for input** and press **Enter**, then type **inFile = io.file.opentext("contestants.txt")** and press **Enter** twice.

3. If the file does not exist, you will display an appropriate message. Type the additional lines of code shown in Figure 23-10, then save the solution.

```
                ' determine whether the file exists
                If IO.File.Exists("contestants.txt") = True Then
                    ' open the file for input
                    inFile = IO.File.OpenText("contestants.txt")

enter these     Else
lines of code       MessageBox.Show("Can't find the contestants.txt file", _
                            "Game Show Contestants", MessageBoxButtons.OK, _
                            MessageBoxIcon.Information)
                End If
```

Figure 23-10: Code entered in the selection structure's false path

After opening a file for input, you can use the **ReadLine method** to read the file's contents, one line at a time. A **line** is defined as a sequence (stream) of characters followed by the newline character. The ReadLine method returns a string that contains only the sequence of characters in the current line; the string does not include the newline character at the end of the line. In most cases, you assign the string returned by the ReadLine method to a String variable. Figure 23-11 shows the ReadLine method's syntax. The method does not require you to provide the file's name, because it uses the file associated with the StreamReader variable. Figure 23-11 also includes examples of using the ReadLine method to read a line of text from a sequential access file. The statement in Example 1 reads a line of text from the file associated with the inFile variable. It assigns the line, excluding the newline character, to a String variable named strMessage. In most cases, an application will need to read each line of text contained in a sequential access file, one line at a time. You can do this using a repetition structure along with the Peek method, as shown in Example 2 in Figure 23-11. The syntax of the Peek method is *streamReaderVariableName*.**Peek**. The **Peek method** "peeks" into the file to determine whether the file contains another character to read. If the file contains another character, the Peek method returns the character; otherwise, it returns the number -1. The Do Until inFile.Peek = -1 clause in Example 2 tells the computer to process the loop instructions until the Peek method returns the number -1, which indicates that there are no more characters to read. In other words, the Do clause tells the computer to process the loop instructions until the end of the file is reached.

READING DATA FROM A SEQUENTIAL ACCESS FILE

<u>Syntax</u>

streamReaderVariableName.**ReadLine**

<u>Example 1</u>

strMessage = inFile.ReadLine
reads a line from a sequential access file, and assigns the line (excluding the newline character) to a String variable named strMessage

<u>Example 2</u>

Do Until inFile.Peek = -1
    strLine = inFile.ReadLine
    MessageBox.Show(strLine)
Loop
reads the lines in a sequential access file, line by line, assigning the line (excluding the newline character) to the strLine variable and displaying the line in a message box

Figure 23-11: Syntax and examples of reading data from a sequential access file

To finish coding the btnRead control's Click event procedure:

1. First, declare a variable to store the string returned by the ReadLine method. Click the **blank line** below the Dim inFile As IO.StreamReader instruction. Each line in the contestants.txt file represents a name, so you will call the variable strName. Type **dim strName as string** and press **Enter**.

2. Click the **blank line** below the inFile = IO.File.OpenText("contestants.txt") statement. Type **' process the loop instructions until the end of the file** and press **Enter**, then type **do until inFile.peek = -1** and press **Enter**. (Be sure to type the hyphen before the number 1.)

3. Now read a line of text and assign it (excluding the newline character) to the strName variable. Type **' read a name** and press **Enter**, then type **strName = inFile.readline** and press **Enter**.

4. Now display the name in the Contestants box. Type **' display the name** and press **Enter**. Type **txtContestants.text = txtContestants.Text _** and press **Enter**. Press **Tab**, then type **& strName & ControlChars.NewLine**.

5. Finally, close the file. Click **after the letter p** in the Loop clause, then press **Enter** to insert a blank line. Type **' close the file** and press **Enter**, then type **inFile.Close()**. Figure 23-12 shows the code entered in the btnRead control's Click event procedure.

```
Private Sub btnRead_Click(ByVal sender As Object, _
    ByVal e As System.EventArgs) Handles btnRead.Click
    ' reads names from a sequential access file
    ' and displays them in the interface

    ' declare variables
    Dim inFile As IO.StreamReader
    Dim strName As String

    ' clear previous names from the Contestants box
    txtContestants.Text = String.Empty

    ' determine whether the file exists
    If IO.File.Exists("contestants.txt") = True Then
        ' open the file for input
        inFile = IO.File.OpenText("contestants.txt")
        ' process the loop instructions until the end of the file
        Do Until inFile.Peek = -1
            ' read a name
            strName = inFile.ReadLine
```

Figure 23-12: Code entered in the btnRead control's Click event procedure (*continued on next page*)

```
            ' display the name
            txtContestants.Text = txtContestants.Text _
                & strName & ControlChars.NewLine
        Loop
        ' close the file
        inFile.Close()
    Else
        MessageBox.Show("Can't find the contestants.txt file", _
                        "Game Show Contestants", MessageBoxButtons.OK, _
                        MessageBoxIcon.Information)
    End If
End Sub
```

Figure 23-12: Code entered in the btnRead control's Click event procedure (*continued from previous page*)

To test the btnRead control's Click event procedure:

1. Save the solution, then start the application. Click the **Read from File** button. The five names contained in the contestants.txt file appear in the Contestants box, as shown in Figure 23-13.

Figure 23-13: Contestant names appear in the Contestants box

2. On your own, use the Write to File button to add two more names to the file. Then use the Read from File button to display the seven names in the interface. Click the **Exit** button.

3. Now have the Exists method return the Boolean False. Change "contestants.txt" in the If clause to **"contestant.txt"**. Save the solution, then start the application. Click the **Read from File** button. The "Can't find the contestants.txt file" message appears in a message box. Click the **OK** button to close the message box, then click the **Exit** button.

4. Change "contestant.txt" in the If clause to **"contestants.txt"**. Save the solution, then start the application. Click the **Read from File** button, which displays the seven names in the interface. Click the **Exit** button. Close the Code Editor window, then close the solution.

MINI-QUIZ 2

1. Write the code to declare a variable that can be used to read data from a sequential access file. Name the variable inFile.

2. The OpenText method creates a _____ object.

3. The string returned by the ReadLine method contains the newline character.

   a. True   b. False

To learn more about sequential access files, see the Sequential Access Files section in the Ch23WantMore.pdf file.

To learn how to handle exceptions that occur when using sequential access files, view the Ch23-TryCatch video.

SUMMARY

» An application can both write data to and read data from a sequential access file. The data in a sequential access file is always accessed in consecutive order (sequentially) from the beginning of the file through the end of the file.

» You use a StreamWriter object to write a sequence (stream) of characters to a sequential access file. The StreamWriter object is created when you open a file for output or append. You use a StreamReader object to read a sequence (stream) of characters from a sequential access file. The StreamReader object is created when you open a file for input.

» You can use either the Write or WriteLine method to write data to a sequential access file. You use the ReadLine method to read a line of text from a sequential access file. The ReadLine method returns a string that includes only the characters on the current line; it does not include the newline character at the end of the line.

» You should use the Close method to close a sequential access file as soon as you are finished using the file.

» You can use a text box's Focus method to send the focus to the text box.

» The Exists method returns a Boolean value that indicates whether a sequential access file exists.

» If a file contains another character to read, the Peek method returns the character; otherwise, it returns the number -1.

KEY TERMS

AppendText method—used to open a sequential access file for append

Close method—used to close a sequential access file

CreateText method—used to open a sequential access file for output

Exists method—used to determine whether a file exists

Input files—files from which data is read

Line—a sequence (stream) of characters followed by the newline character

OpenText method—used to open a sequential access file for input

Output files—files to which data is written

Peek method—used to determine whether a file contains another character to read

ReadLine method—used to read a line of text from a sequential access file

Sequential access files—files composed of lines of text that are both read and written sequentially

Stream of characters—a sequence of characters

StreamReader object—used to read data from a sequential access file

StreamWriter object—used to write a sequence (stream) of characters to a sequential access file

Write method—used to write data to a sequential access file; differs from the WriteLine method in that it does not write a newline character after the data

WriteLine method—used to write data to a sequential access file; differs from the Write method in that it writes a newline character after the data

ANSWERS TO MINI-QUIZZES

MINI-QUIZ 1

1. Dim outFile As IO.StreamWriter

2. StreamWriter

3. txtCity.Focus()

MINI-QUIZ 2

1. Dim inFile As IO.StreamReader

2. StreamReader

3. b. False

REVIEW QUESTIONS

1. Which of the following opens the states.txt file and allows the computer to write new data to the end of the existing data in the file?

    a. outFile = IO.File.AddText("states.txt")

    b. outFile = IO.File.AppendText("states.txt")

    c. outFile = IO.File.InsertText("states.txt")

    d. outFile = IO.File.OpenText("states.txt")

2. If the file to be opened exists, the _____ method erases the file's contents.

    a. AppendText

    b. CreateText

    c. InsertText

    d. OpenText

3. Which of the following reads a line of text from a sequential access file and assigns the line (excluding the newline character) to the strText variable?

    a. inFile.Read(strText)   b. inFile.ReadLine(strText)

    c. strText = inFile.ReadLine   d. strText = inFile.Read(line)

4. The Peek method returns _____ when the end of the file is reached.

    a. -1

    b. 0

    c. the last character in the file

    d. the newline character

5. Which of the following can be used to determine whether the employ.txt file exists?

    a. If IO.File.Exists("employ.txt") = True Then

    b. If IO.File("employ.txt").Exists = True Then

    c. If IO.Exists("employ.txt") = True Then

    d. If IO.Exists.File("employ.txt") = True Then

EXERCISES

»TRY THIS

1. In this exercise, you code an application that both reads gross pay amounts from and writes gross pay amounts to a sequential access file. Open the Gross Pay Solution (Gross Pay Solution.sln) file, which is contained in the ClearlyVB\Chap23\Gross Pay Solution folder. Open the designer window. The interface provides a text box for entering a gross pay amount. The Save button should write the gross pay amount to a sequential access file named gross.txt. Save the file in the project's bin\Debug folder. The Display button should read the gross pay amounts from the gross.txt file and display each (formatted with a dollar sign and two decimal places) in the interface. Open the Code Editor window. Code the Click event procedures for the btnSave and btnDisplay controls. Save the solution, then start the application. Write the following 10 gross pay amounts to the file: 600, 1250, 750.67, 350.75, 2000, 450, 125.89, 560, 1400, and 555.78. Click the Display button to display the gross pay amounts in the interface. Stop the application, then close the solution. (The answers to TRY THIS Exercises are located at the end of the chapter.)

»TRY THIS

2. Open the Name Solution (Name Solution.sln) file, which is contained in the ClearlyVB\Chap23\Name Solution folder. Open the designer window, then open the Code Editor window. Open the names.txt file contained in the project's bin\Debug folder. The sequential access file contains five names. Close the names.txt window. The btnDisplay control's Click event procedure should read the five names contained in the names.txt file, storing each in a five-element one-dimensional array. The procedure should sort the array in ascending order, and then display the contents of the array in the lblFriends control. Code the procedure. Save the solution, then start and test the application. Stop the application, then close the solution. (If you need to recreate

the names.txt file, open the file in a window in the IDE. Delete the contents of the file, if necessary, then type the following five names, pressing Enter after typing each name: Jennifer, Zelda, Abby, Bruce, and Karen. The answers to TRY THIS Exercises are located at the end of the chapter.)

3. In this exercise, you modify an application from Chapter 19. Open the Salary Solution (Salary Solution.sln) file, which is contained in the ClearlyVB\Chap23\Salary Solution folder. Open the designer window. Open the Code Editor window and study the existing code. The btnDisplay control's Click event procedure stores six salary amounts in a one-dimensional Integer array named intSalaries. Each salary amount corresponds to a salary code from 1 through 6. Code 1's salary is stored in the intSalaries(0) element in the array. Code 2's salary is stored in the intSalaries(1) element, and so on. After storing the salary amounts in the array, the procedure prompts the user to enter a salary code. It then displays the amount associated with the code. Currently, the Dim statement assigns the six salary amounts to the array. Modify the procedure so that it reads the salary amounts from the salary.txt file, which is contained in the project's bin\Debug folder, and stores them in the array. Save the solution, then start and test the application. Stop the application, then close the solution.

   »MODIFY THIS

4. Open the Test Scores Solution (Test Scores Solution.sln) file, which is contained in the ClearlyVB\Chap23\Test Scores Solution folder. Open the designer window, then open the Code Editor window. The btnSave control's Click event procedure should allow the user to enter an unknown number of test scores, saving each score in a sequential access file. The btnCount control's Click event procedure should display (in a message box) the number of scores stored in the file. Code both procedures. Save the solution, then start and test the application. Stop the application, then close the solution.

   »INTRODUCTORY

5. In this exercise, you code an application that reads five numbers from a sequential access file and stores the numbers in a one-dimensional array. The application then increases each number by 1 and writes the numbers to the file. The application also displays the current contents of the sequential access file. Open the Numbers Solution (Numbers Solution.sln) file, which is contained in the ClearlyVB\Chap23\Numbers Solution folder. Open the designer window, then open the Code Editor window. Code the btnDisplay control's Click event procedure so it reads the five numbers stored in the numbers.txt file and displays the numbers in the lblNumbers control. The numbers.txt file is contained in the project's bin\Debug folder. Currently, the file contains the numbers 1 through 5. Code the btnUpdate control's Click event procedure so it reads the five numbers from the numbers.txt file and stores the numbers in an array. It then should increase each number in the array by 1 and write the array contents to an empty numbers.txt file. Save the solution, then start the application. Click the Display button. The numbers 1 through 5 appear in the interface. Click the Update button, then click the Display button.

   »INTERMEDIATE

The numbers 2 through 6 appear in the interface. Stop the application, then close the solution. (If you need to recreate the numbers.txt file, open the file in a window in the IDE. Delete the contents of the file, if necessary, then type the numbers 1 through 5, pressing Enter after typing each number.)

»ADVANCED

6. During July and August of each year, the Political Awareness Organization (PAO) sends a questionnaire to the voters in their district. The questionnaire asks the voter for his or her political party (Democratic, Republican, or Independent) and age. From the returned questionnaires, the organization's secretary tabulates the number of Democrats, Republicans, and Independents in the district. The secretary wants an application that she can use to save each respondent's information (political party and age) to a sequential access file. The application also should calculate and display the number of voters in each political party. Create a new Visual Basic Windows application. Name the solution, project, and form file PAO Solution, PAO Project, and frmMain.vb, respectively. Save the application in the ClearlyVB\Chap23 folder. If necessary, change the form's name to frmMain. Create the interface shown in Figure 23-14. The Party text box should accept only the Backspace key and the letters D, d, R, r, I, or i. The Age text box should accept only numbers and the Backspace key. Code the Click event procedures for the Write to File and Display Totals buttons. Save the solution, then start and test the application. Stop the application, then close the solution.

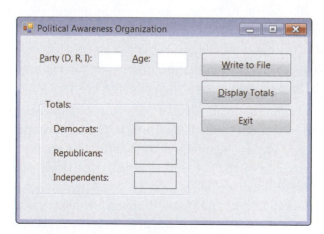

Figure 23-14: User interface for the PAO application

7. Open the FigureThisOut Solution (FigureThisOut Solution.sln) file, which is contained in the ClearlyVB\Chap23\FigureThisOut Solution folder. Open the Code Editor window and study the existing code. Why does the true path in the btnWrite control's Click event procedure open the sequential access file for output first, then close the file, and then open it for append? Start and test the application. Stop the application. Close the Code Editor window, then close the solution.

8. In this exercise, you find an error in an application's code. Open the SwatTheBugs Solution (SwatTheBugs Solution.sln) file, which is contained in the ClearlyVB\ Chap23\SwatTheBugs Solution folder. Open the Code Editor window and study the existing code. Start the application, then test it using Sue and 1000, and then using Pete and 5000. Click Debug, then click Stop Debugging. Open the bonus.txt file. Notice that the file is empty. Close the bonus.txt window. Locate and correct any errors in the code. Save the solution, then start and test the application again. Stop the application, then close the solution.

ANSWERS TO "TRY THIS" EXERCISES

1. Figure 23-15 shows the Click event procedures for the btnSave and btnDisplay controls.

```vb
Private Sub btnSave_Click(ByVal sender As Object, _
    ByVal e As System.EventArgs) Handles btnSave.Click
    ' writes a gross pay amount to a sequential access file

    ' declare a StreamWriter variable
    Dim outFile As IO.StreamWriter
    ' open the file for append
    outFile = IO.File.AppendText("gross.txt")
    ' write the amount on a separate line in the file
    outFile.WriteLine(txtGrossPay.Text)
    ' close the file
    outFile.Close()
    ' clear the Gross pay box, then set the focus
    txtGrossPay.Text = String.Empty
    txtGrossPay.Focus()
End Sub

Private Sub btnDisplay_Click(ByVal sender As Object, _
    ByVal e As System.EventArgs) Handles btnDisplay.Click
    ' reads gross pay amounts from a sequential access file
    ' and displays them in the interface

    ' declare variables
    Dim inFile As IO.StreamReader
    Dim strGrossPay As String
    Dim decGrossPay As Decimal
```

Figure 23-15 (*continued on next page*)

```
        ' clear previous amounts from the Gross pay box
        txtGrossPay.Text = String.Empty

        ' determine whether the file exists
        If IO.File.Exists("gross.txt") = True Then
            ' open the file for input
            inFile = IO.File.OpenText("gross.txt")
            ' process the loop instructions until the end of the file
            Do Until inFile.Peek = -1
                ' read an amount
                strGrossPay = inFile.ReadLine
                ' display the amount
                Decimal.TryParse(strGrossPay, decGrossPay)
                txtContents.Text = txtContents.Text _
                    & decGrossPay.ToString("C2") & ControlChars.NewLine
            Loop
            ' close the file
            inFile.Close()
        Else
            MessageBox.Show("Can't find the gross.txt file", _
                            "ABC Company", MessageBoxButtons.OK, _
                            MessageBoxIcon.Information)
        End If
    End Sub
```

Figure 23-15 (*continued from previous page*)

2. Figure 23-16 shows the Click event procedure for the btnDisplay control.

```
Private Sub btnDisplay_Click(ByVal sender As Object, _
    ByVal e As System.EventArgs) Handles btnDisplay.Click
    ' reads the 5 names from a sequential access file and stores
    ' them in an array, sorts the names and then displays them

    Dim strFriends(4) As String
    Dim inFile As IO.StreamReader
    Dim intSubscript As Integer

    ' clear previous names from the My friends box
    lblFriends.Text = String.Empty
```

Figure 23-16 (*continued on next page*)

```
' determine whether the file exists
If IO.File.Exists("names.txt") = True Then
    ' open the file for input
    inFile = IO.File.OpenText("names.txt")
    ' start the subscript at 0
    intSubscript = 0
    ' process the loop instructions until the
    ' end of the file or the array is filled
    Do Until inFile.Peek = -1 _
        OrElse intSubscript = strFriends.Length
        ' read a name and store it in the array
        strFriends(intSubscript) = inFile.ReadLine
        intSubscript = intSubscript + 1
    Loop
    ' close the file
    inFile.Close()

    Array.Sort(strFriends)

    For intSubscript = 0 To strFriends.Length - 1
        lblFriends.Text = lblFriends.Text _
            & strFriends(intSubscript) & ControlChars.NewLine
    Next intSubscript
Else
    MessageBox.Show("Can't find the names.txt file", _
                    "Friends", MessageBoxButtons.OK, _
                    MessageBoxIcon.Information)

End If
End Sub
```

Figure 23-16 (*continued from previous page*)

24

THE STRING SECTION

After studying Chapter 24, you should be able to:

Determine the number of characters in a string

Remove spaces from the beginning and end of a string

Replace characters in a string

Insert characters in a string

Search a string

Access characters in a string

Compare strings using pattern-matching

WORKING WITH STRINGS

Many times, an application will need to manipulate (process) string data in some way. For example, it may need to look at the first character in an inventory part number to determine the part's location in the warehouse. Or, it may need to search an address to determine the street name. In this chapter, you learn several ways of manipulating strings in Visual Basic. The first string manipulation technique shows you how to determine the number of characters in a string.

HOW MANY CHARACTERS ARE THERE?

If an application expects the user to enter a seven-digit phone number or a five-digit ZIP code, the application's code should verify that the user entered the required number of characters. The number of characters contained in a string is stored in the string's **Length property**. Not surprisingly, the value stored in the property is an integer. Figure 24-1 shows the syntax of the Length property and includes examples of using the property.

USING THE LENGTH PROPERTY

Syntax   Purpose

string.**Length**   stores the number of characters contained in a string

Example 1

```
strFullName = "Lee Thompson"
intNumChars = strFullName.Length
```
assigns the number 12 to the intNumChars variable

Example 2

```
Do
    strPhone = InputBox("7-digit phone number (no dashes)", "Phone")
Loop Until strPhone.Length = 7
```
gets a phone number from the user until the phone number contains exactly 7 characters

---

Figure 24-1: Syntax and examples of the Length property

GET RID OF THOSE SPACES

When entering data in a text box or input box, it's not unusual for a user to inadvertently press the spacebar after typing the data, thereby including an extraneous space character at the end of the data. You can use the **Trim method** to remove (trim) any spaces from both the beginning and end of a string. Figure 24-2 shows the method's syntax and includes an example of using the method. When processing the Trim method, the computer first makes a temporary copy of the *string* in memory. It then performs the necessary trimming on the copy only. In other words, the Trim method does not remove any characters from the original *string*. The Trim method returns a string that excludes any leading or trailing spaces.

USING THE TRIM METHOD

Syntax   Purpose

string.**Trim**   removes any spaces from both the beginning and end of a string

Example

strFullName = txtName.Text.Trim

assigns the contents of the txtName control, excluding any leading and trailing spaces, to the strFullName variable

---

Figure 24-2: Syntax and an example of the Trim method

You will use both the Length property and the Trim method in the Product ID application, which you code in the next section.

THE PRODUCT ID APPLICATION

The Product ID application displays (in a label control) a listing of the product IDs entered by the user. Each product ID must contain exactly five characters.

To open the Product ID application, and then code and test the application:

1. Start Visual Studio 2008 (or Visual Basic 2008 Express Edition). Open the **Product Solution** (**Product Solution.sln**) file, which is contained in the ClearlyVB\Chap24\ Product Solution folder. If necessary, open the designer window. The user interface provides a text box for entering the product ID.

2. Open the Code Editor window, then locate the code template for the btnAdd control's Click event procedure. Before verifying the product ID's length, you will remove any leading and trailing spaces from the ID. Click the **blank line** below the ' remove any leading and trailing spaces comment. Type **strId = txtId.text.trim** and press **Enter**.

3. Now determine whether the ID contains exactly five characters. Click the **blank line** below the ' verify length comment. Type **if strId.length = 5 then** and press **Enter**.

4. If the ID contains exactly five characters, the procedure should display the ID in the lblListing control; otherwise, it should display an appropriate message. Type the lines of code indicated in Figure 24-3.

```
Private Sub btnAdd_Click(ByVal sender As Object, ByVal e As System.Eve
    ' add product ID to listing

    Dim strId As String

    ' remove any leading and trailing spaces
    strId = txtId.Text.Trim

    ' verify length
    If strId.Length = 5 Then
        lblListing.Text = lblListing.Text & strId.ToUpper _
            & ControlChars.NewLine
    Else
        MessageBox.Show("The product ID must contain 5 characters.", _
                        "Product ID", MessageBoxButtons.OK, _
                        MessageBoxIcon.Information)
    End If

    txtId.Focus()
End Sub
```

enter these six lines of code

Figure 24-3: Completed Click event procedure for the btnAdd control

5. Save the solution, then start the application. First, enter an ID that contains four characters. Type **abc2** as the product ID, then click the **Add to List** button. A message box opens and displays the message "The product ID must contain 5 characters." Close the message box.

6. Now include two trailing spaces after the ID. Change the product ID to **abc23**, then press the **Spacebar** twice. Click the **Add to List** button. ABC23 appears in the listing of product IDs.

7. On your own, test the application using an ID that contains nine characters. Also test it using an ID that contains both leading and trailing spaces. When you are finished testing the application, click the **Exit** button. Close the Code Editor window, then close the solution.

LET'S MAKE A SUBSTITUTION

Visual Basic provides the **Replace method** for replacing a sequence of characters in a string with another sequence of characters, such as replacing area code "(800)" with area code "(877)" in a phone number. Figure 24-4 shows the syntax of the Replace method and includes examples of using the method. In the syntax, *oldValue* is the sequence of characters that you want to replace in the *string*, and *newValue* is the replacement characters. When processing the Replace method, the computer makes a temporary copy of the *string* in memory, and then replaces the characters in the copy only. The Replace method returns a string with *all* occurrences of *oldValue* replaced with *newValue*.

USING THE REPLACE METHOD

Syntax

string.**Replace(***oldValue*, *newValue***)**

Purpose

replaces every occurrence of *oldValue* with *newValue*

Example 1

strPhone = "(800) 111-2222"
strPhone = strPhone.Replace("(800)", "(877)")
assigns the string "(877) 111-2222" to the strPhone variable

Example 2

strWord = "latter"
strWord = strWord.Replace("t", "d")
assigns the string "ladder" to the strWord variable

Figure 24-4: Syntax and examples of the Replace method

I NEED TO FIT THIS IN SOMEWHERE

Rather than replacing characters in a string, an application may need to insert characters in a string. You insert characters using the **Insert method**. Possible uses for the method include inserting an employee's middle initial within his or her name, or inserting parentheses around the area code in a phone number. Figure 24-5 shows the Insert method's syntax.

In the syntax, *startIndex* specifies where in the *string* you want the *value* inserted. The *startIndex* argument is an integer that represents the character's index—in other words, its position in the string. The first character in a string has an index of 0, the second character an index of 1, and so on. To insert the *value* beginning with the fifth character in the string, you use a *startIndex* of 4, as shown in the example in Figure 24-5. When processing the Insert method, the computer makes a temporary copy of the *string* in memory, and then inserts the characters in the copy only. The Insert method returns a string with the appropriate characters inserted.

USING THE INSERT METHOD

Syntax	Purpose
string.**Insert(***startIndex***,** *value***)**	inserts characters in a string

Example

strName = "Rob Smith"
strFullName = strName.Insert(4, "T. ")
assigns the string "Rob T. Smith" to the strFullName variable

---

Figure 24-5: Syntax and an example of the Insert method

You will use the Replace and Insert methods in the Phone Numbers application, which you code in the next section.

THE PHONE NUMBERS APPLICATION

The Phone Numbers application saves (in a sequential access file) the phone numbers entered by the user. Each phone number is entered using 12 characters in the following format: 111-222-3333. Before writing a phone number to the file, the application removes the hyphens and then verifies that the phone number contains 10 characters (the original 12 characters minus the two hyphens). The application also displays the phone numbers contained in the file, both with and without the hyphens.

To open the Phone Numbers application, and then begin coding the application:

1. Open the **Phone Solution** (**Phone Solution.sln**) file, which is contained in the ClearlyVB\Chap24\Phone Solution folder. If necessary, open the designer window. The user interface provides a text box for entering the phone number.

2. Open the Code Editor window, then locate the code template for the btnSave control's Click event procedure. Before saving the phone number to the sequential access file, the procedure will replace the hyphens with the empty string. Click the **blank line** below the ' remove the hyphens comment. Type **strPhone = txtPhone.text.replace("-", string.empty)** and press **Enter**.

3. Save the solution, then start the application. First, enter an invalid phone number. Type **111-2222** as the phone number, then click the **Save** button. A message box opens and displays the "Invalid phone number" message. Close the message box.

4. Type **111-222-3333** as the phone number, then click the **Save** button. Type **222-333-4444** as the phone number, then click the **Save** button. Click the **Display** button. The button's Click event procedure reads each phone number from the phoneNumbers.txt file and displays each in the lblFileContents control. See Figure 24-6. Notice that the phone numbers do not contain any hyphens.

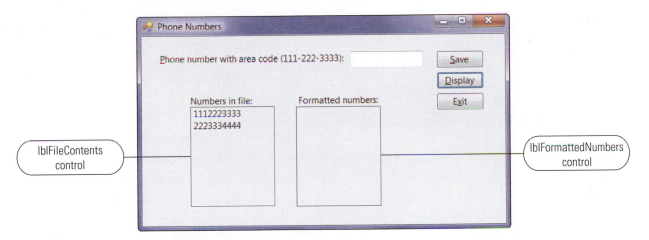

Figure 24-6: Contents of the phoneNumbers.txt file displayed in the lblFileContents control

5. Click the **Exit** button.

In addition to displaying the phone numbers contained in the file, the Display button also should insert the appropriate hyphens in each number and then display the formatted number in the lblFormattedNumbers control. You can insert the hyphens using the Insert method, as shown in Figure 24-7.

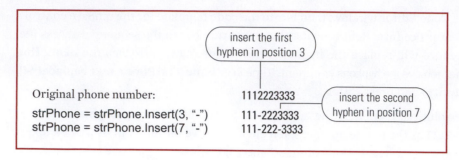

Figure 24-7: Statements needed to insert the two hyphens

To continue coding the Phone Numbers application, then test the application:

1. Locate the code template for the btnDisplay control's Click event procedure. Click the **blank line** below the ' insert hyphens, then display the phone number comment. Type the lines of code indicated in Figure 24-8.

```
                                    & strPhone & ControlChars.NewLine
                                ' insert hyphens, then display the phone number
                                strPhone = strPhone.Insert(3, "-")
enter these                     strPhone = strPhone.Insert(7, "-")
four lines of code              lblFormattedNumbers.Text = lblFormattedNumbers.Text _
                                    & strPhone & ControlChars.NewLine
                            Loop
                                                the file
```

Figure 24-8: Code to insert the hyphens and display the formatted numbers

2. Save the solution, then start the application. Click the **Display** button. The button's Click event procedure displays the numbers both with and without hyphens. See Figure 24-9.

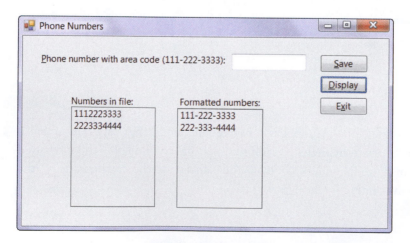

Figure 24-9: Numbers displayed both with and without hyphens

3. Click the **Exit** button. Close the Code Editor window, then close the solution.

MINI-QUIZ 1

1. Write the Visual Basic statement to remove the leading and trailing spaces from the txtAddress control.

2. Write a Visual Basic statement that uses the Insert method to change the contents of the strWord variable from "men" to "women".

3. Write the Visual Basic statement that uses the Replace method to change the contents of the strWord variable from "dog" to "frog".

WHERE DOES IT BEGIN?

You can use the **IndexOf method** to search a string to determine whether it contains a specific sequence of characters. Possible uses for the method include determining whether the area code "(312)" appears in a phone number, or whether "Elm Street" appears in an address. Figure 24-10 shows the syntax of the IndexOf method and includes examples of using the method. In the syntax, *subString* is the sequence of characters for which you are searching in the *string*, and *startIndex* is the index of the character at which the search should begin. In other words, *startIndex* specifies the starting position for the search. Recall that the first character in a string has an index of 0. The *startIndex* argument is optional in the IndexOf method's syntax; if omitted, the method begins the search with the first character in the *string*. The IndexOf method searches for the *subString* within the *string*, beginning with the character whose index is *startIndex*. If the IndexOf method does not find the *subString*, it returns the number -1. Otherwise, it returns the index of the starting position of the *subString* within the *string*. The IndexOf method performs a case-sensitive search, which means that the case of the *substring* must match the case of the *string*.

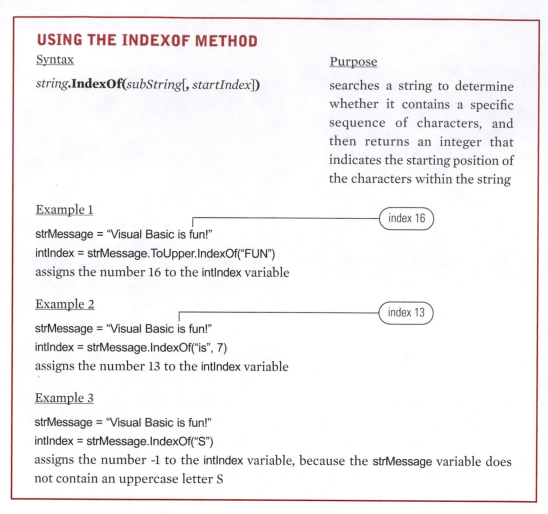

Figure 24-10: Syntax and examples of the IndexOf method

I JUST WANT A PART OF IT

In some applications, it is necessary to access one or more characters contained in a string. For instance, you may need to display only the string's first five characters, which identify an item's location in the warehouse. Visual Basic provides the **Substring method** for accessing any number of characters contained in a string. Figure 24-11 shows the method's syntax, which contains two arguments: *startIndex* and *count*. *StartIndex* is the index of the first character you want to access in the *string*. As you already know, the first character in a string has an index of 0. The optional *count* argument specifies the number of characters you want to access. The Substring method returns a string that contains *count* number of characters, beginning with the character whose index is *startIndex*. If you omit the *count* argument, the Substring method returns all characters from the *startIndex* position through the end of the string. Figure 24-11 also includes examples of using the Substring method.

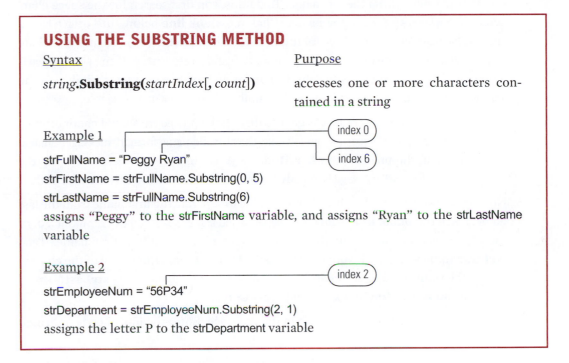

USING THE SUBSTRING METHOD

Syntax   Purpose

string.**Substring(***startIndex*[**,** *count*]**)**   accesses one or more characters contained in a string

Example 1

strFullName = "Peggy Ryan"
strFirstName = strFullName.Substring(0, 5)
strLastName = strFullName.Substring(6)
assigns "Peggy" to the strFirstName variable, and assigns "Ryan" to the strLastName variable

Example 2

strEmployeeNum = "56P34"
strDepartment = strEmployeeNum.Substring(2, 1)
assigns the letter P to the strDepartment variable

Figure 24-11: Syntax and examples of the Substring method

You will use the IndexOf and Substring methods in the Rearrange Name application, which you code in the next section.

THE REARRANGE NAME APPLICATION

The Rearrange Name application's user interface provides a text box for entering a person's first name followed by a space and the person's last name. The application rearranges the name so that the last name comes first, followed by a comma, a space, and the first name.

To open the Rearrange Name application, and then code and test the application:

1. Open the **Rearrange Name Solution** (**Rearrange Name Solution.sln**) file, which is contained in the ClearlyVB\Chap24\Rearrange Name Solution folder. If necessary, open the designer window.

2. Open the Code Editor window, then locate the code template for the btnRearrange control's Click event procedure. The procedure assigns the name entered by the user, excluding any leading or trailing spaces, to the strName variable.

3. Before you can rearrange the name stored in the strName variable, you need to separate the first name from the last name. To do this, you first search for the space character that appears between the names. Click the **blank line** below the ' search for the space in the name comment. Type **intIndex = strName.indexof(" ")** (be sure to include a space character between the quotation marks) and press **Enter**. If the strName variable contains a space character, the statement assigns the character's index to the intIndex variable; otherwise, it assigns the number -1 to the intIndex variable.

4. If the value in the intIndex variable is greater than -1, the procedure should continue rearranging the name; otherwise, it should display the "Invalid name format" message. Change the If clause in the procedure to **If intIndex > -1 Then**. The statement to display the "Invalid name format" message is already entered in the selection structure's false path.

5. Now use the value stored in the intIndex variable to separate the first name from the last name. Click the **blank line** below the ' separate the first and last names comment. All of the characters to the left of the space character represent the first name. Type **strFirstName = strName.substring(0, intIndex)** and press **Enter**. All of the characters to the right of the space character represent the last name. Type **strLastName = strName.substring(intIndex + 1)** and press **Enter**.

6. Finally, display the rearranged name in the interface. Enter the line of code indicated in Figure 24-12.

enter this line of code ─────

```
' assign the input to a variable
strName = txtName.Text.Trim

' search for the space in the name
intIndex = strName.IndexOf(" ")

' if the input contains a space
If intIndex > -1 Then
    ' separate the first and last names
    strFirstName = strName.Substring(0, intIndex)
    strLastName = strName.Substring(intIndex + 1)

    ' display last name, comma, space, and first name
    lblRearrangedName.Text = strLastName & ", " & strFirstName

Else    'processed when the name does not contain a space
    ...Box.Show("Invali...            ...nge Name"
```

Figure 24-12: Code to display the rearranged name

7. Save the solution, then start the application. Type **Veronica Chowski** as the name, then click the **Rearrange Name** button. The button's Click event procedure rearranges the name and displays it in the interface. See Figure 24-13.

Figure 24-13: Rearranged name shown in the interface

8. Click the **Exit** button. Close the Code Editor window, then close the solution.

MINI-QUIZ 2

1. If the strAddress variable contains the string "34 Elmset Street", the strAddress.IndexOf("Elm") method returns _____.

2. If the strAddress variable contains the string "34 Elmset Street", the strAddress.IndexOf("Elm", 4) method returns _____.

3. The strPartNum variable contains the string "ABCD34G". Write the Visual Basic statement that assigns the string "CD34" from the strPartNum variable to the strCode variable.

I LIKE THIS OPERATOR

The **Like operator** allows you to use pattern-matching characters to determine whether one string is equal to another string. Figure 24-14 shows the Like operator's syntax and includes examples of using the operator. In the syntax, both *string* and *pattern* must be String expressions; however, *pattern* can contain one or more of the pattern-matching characters listed in the figure. The last two pattern-matching characters contain a *charList*, which stands for *character list* and is simply a listing of characters. "[A9M]" is a *charList* that contains three characters: A, 9, and M. You also can include a range of values in a *charList*; you do this using a hyphen to separate the lowest value in the range from the highest value in the range. For example, to include all lowercase letters in a *charList*, you use "[a-z]". To include both lowercase and uppercase letters, you use "[a-zA-Z]" as the *charList*. The Like operator evaluates to True when the *string* matches the *pattern*; otherwise it evaluates to False.

USING THE LIKE OPERATOR

Syntax	Purpose
string **Like** *pattern*	compares two strings using pattern-matching characters

Pattern-matching characters	Matches in *string*
?	any single character
*	zero or more characters
#	any single digit (0-9)
[*charList*]	any single character in the *charList* (for example, "[AMT]" matches A, M, or T, whereas "[a-z]" matches any lowercase letter)
[!*charList*]	any single character not in the *charList* (for example, "[!a-z]" matches any character that is not a lowercase letter)

Example 1

If strFirstName.ToUpper Like "B?LL" Then

The condition evaluates to True when the string stored in the strFirstName variable (converted to uppercase) begins with the letter B followed by one character and then the two letters LL; otherwise, it evaluates to False. Examples of *strings* that would make the condition evaluate to True include "Bill", "Ball", "bell", and "bull". Examples of *strings* for which the condition would evaluate to False include "BPL", "BLL", and "billy".

Example 2

If strState Like "K*" Then

The condition evaluates to True when the string stored in the strState variable begins with the letter K followed by zero or more characters; otherwise, it evaluates to False. Examples of *strings* that would make the condition evaluate to True include "KANSAS", "Ky", and "Kentucky". Examples of *strings* for which the condition would evaluate to False include "kansas" and "ky".

Figure 24-14: Syntax and examples of the Like operator (*continued on next page*)

Example 3

Do While strId Like "###*"
The condition evaluates to True when the string stored in the strId variable begins with three digits followed by zero or more characters; otherwise, it evaluates to False. Examples of *strings* that would make the condition evaluate to True include "178" and "983Ab". Examples of *strings* for which the condition would evaluate to False include "X34" and "34Z5".

Example 4

If strFirstName.ToUpper Like "T[OI]M" Then
The condition evaluates to True when the string stored in the strFirstName variable (converted to uppercase) is either "TOM" or "TIM". When the strFirstName variable does not contain "TOM" or "TIM"—for example, when it contains "TAM" or "Tommy"—the condition evaluates to False.

Example 5

If strLetter Like "[a-z]" Then
The condition evaluates to True when the string stored in the strLetter variable is a lowercase letter; otherwise, it evaluates to False.

Example 6

```
For intIndex As Integer = 0 to strUserEntry.Length - 1
    If strUserEntry.Substring(intIndex, 1) Like "[!a-zA-Z]" Then
        intNonLetter = intNonLetter + 1
    End If
Next intIndex
```
Compares each character contained in the strUserEntry variable with the lowercase and uppercase letters of the alphabet, and counts the number of characters that are not letters.

Figure 24-14: Syntax and examples of the Like operator (*continued from previous page*)

MODIFYING THE PRODUCT ID APPLICATION

Earlier in the chapter, you coded the Product ID application, which displayed a listing of the product IDs entered by the user. As you may remember, each product ID contained exactly five characters. In the following set of steps, you will modify the application to ensure that the five characters are three letters followed by two numbers.

Before completing the next set of steps, it may be helpful to view the Ch24-Like operator video.

To modify the Product ID application, and then test the application:

1. Use Windows to make a copy of the Product Solution folder. Save the copy in the ClearlyVB\Chap24 folder. Rename the copy Modified Product Solution.

2. Open the **Product Solution (Product Solution.sln)** file contained in the ClearlyVB\Chap24\Modified Product Solution folder. Open the designer window.

3. Open the Code Editor window and locate the btnAdd control's Click event procedure. Change the ' remove any leading and trailing spaces comment to **' remove any leading and trailing spaces, then convert to uppercase**. Also change the strId = txtId.Text.Trim statement to **strId = txtId.Text.Trim.ToUpper**.

4. Change the ' verify length comment to **' verify that the ID contains 3 letters followed by 2 numbers**. Also change the If clause to **If strId Like "[A-Z][A-Z][A-Z]##" Then**.

5. In the statement below the If clause, change strId.ToUpper to **strID**. Finally, change the message in the MessageBox.Show method to **"Invalid product ID"**. Figure 24-15 shows the modified Click event procedure. The modified comments and code are shaded in the figure.

```vb
Private Sub btnAdd_Click(ByVal sender As Object, _
    ByVal e As System.EventArgs) Handles btnAdd.Click
    ' add product ID to listing

    Dim strId As String

    ' remove any leading and trailing spaces, then convert to uppercase
    strId = txtId.Text.Trim.ToUpper

    ' verify that the ID contains 3 letters followed by 2 numbers
    If strId Like "[A-Z][A-Z][A-Z]##" Then
        lblListing.Text = lblListing.Text & strId _
            & ControlChars.NewLine
    Else
        MessageBox.Show("Invalid product ID", _
                        "Product ID", MessageBoxButtons.OK, _
                        MessageBoxIcon.Information)
    End If

    txtId.Focus()
End Sub
```

Figure 24-15: Modified comments and code

6. Save the solution, then start the application. First, enter an invalid ID. Type **abc2f** as the product ID, then click the **Add to List** button. A message box opens and displays the "Invalid product ID" message. Close the message box.

7. Now enter a valid ID. Change the product ID to **abc23**, then click the **Add to List** button. ABC23 appears in the listing of product IDs.

8. On your own, test the application using different valid and invalid IDs. When you are finished testing the application, click the **Exit** button. Close the Code Editor window, then close the solution.

 To learn about other string manipulation techniques, see the String Manipulation Techniques section in the Ch24WantMore.pdf file.

SUMMARY

» A string's Length property stores an integer that represents the number of characters contained in the string.

» Visual Basic provides methods that allow you to manipulate strings. Each method covered in this chapter is listed in the Key Terms section.

» The first character in a string has an index of 0.

KEY TERMS

IndexOf method—determines whether a string contains a specific sequence of characters; returns an integer that indicates the starting position of the characters; its syntax is *string*.**IndexOf(***subString*[*, startIndex*]**)**

Insert method—inserts characters in a string; its syntax is *string*.**Insert(***startIndex, value***)**

Length property—one of the properties of a string; stores the number of characters contained in the string; its syntax is *string*.**Length**

Like operator—compares two strings using pattern-matching characters; its syntax is *string* **Like** *pattern*

Replace method—replaces all occurrences of a sequence of characters in a string with another sequence of characters; its syntax is *string*.**Replace(***oldValue, newValue***)**

Substring method—accesses one or more characters contained in a string; its syntax is *string*.**Substring(***startIndex*[*, count*]**)**

Trim method—removes spaces from both the beginning and end of a string; its syntax is *string*.**Trim**

ANSWERS TO MINI-QUIZZES

MINI-QUIZ 1

1. txtAddress.Text = txtAddress.Text.Trim

2. strWord = strWord.Insert(0, "wo")

3. strWord = strWord.Replace("d", "fr")

MINI-QUIZ 2

1. 3

2. -1

3. strCode = strPartNum.Substring(2, 4)

REVIEW QUESTIONS

1. Which of the following changes the string stored in the strName variable from "Mary Smyth" to "Mark Smyth"?

   a. strName = strName.Change("y", "k")

   b. strName = strName.Replace("y", "k")

   c. strName = strName.Replace(3, "k")

   d. None of the above.

2. Which of the following expressions evaluates to True when the strPart variable contains the string "123X45"?

   a. strPart Like "999[A-Z]99"

   b. strPart Like "######"

   c. strPart Like "###[A-Z]##"

   d. None of the above.

3. Which of the following changes the contents of the strCityState variable from "Boise Idaho" to "Boise, Idaho"?

   a. strCityState = strCityState.Insert(5, ",")

   b. strCityState = strCityState.Insert(6, ",")

   c. strCityState = strCityState.Insert(7, ",")

   d. None of the above.

4. If the strMessage variable contains the string "Today is Monday", which of the following assigns the number 9 to the intNum variable?

    a. intNum = strMessage.Substring("M")

    b. intNum = strMessage.Substring("M", 1)

    c. intNum = strMessage.IndexOf("M")

    d. intNum = strMessage.IndexOf(0, "M")

5. If the strName variable contains the string "John Jones", which of the following changes the contents of the variable to "John K. Jones"?

    a. strName = strName.Replace(" ", " K. ")

    b. strName = strName.Insert(5, "K. ")

    c. strName= strName.Insert(4, " K.")

    d. All of the above.

EXERCISES

1. The strAmount variable contains the string "3,123,560". Write the Visual Basic statement to change the contents of the variable to "3123560"; use the Replace method. Now that the strAmount variable contains the string "3123560", write the Visual Basic statements to change the variable's contents to "$3,123,560". (The answers to TRY THIS Exercises are located at the end of the chapter.)

   »TRY THIS

2. Open the Zip Solution (Zip Solution.sln) file, which is contained in the ClearlyVB\ Chap24\Zip Solution folder. Open the designer window. The Display Shipping Charge button's Click event procedure should display the appropriate shipping charge based on the ZIP code entered by user. To be valid, the ZIP code must contain exactly five digits, and the first three digits must be either "605" or "606". The shipping charge for "605" ZIP codes is $25. The shipping charge for "606" ZIP codes is $30. Display an appropriate message if the ZIP code is invalid. Code the procedure. Save the solution, then start the application. Test the application using the following ZIP codes: 60677, 60511, 60344, and 7130. Stop the application, then close the solution. (The answers to TRY THIS Exercises are located at the end of the chapter.)

   »TRY THIS

3. In this exercise, you modify the Phone Numbers application coded in the chapter. Use Windows to make a copy of the Phone Solution folder. Save the copy in the ClearlyVB\ Chap24 folder. Rename the copy Phone Solution-MODIFY THIS. Open the Phone Solution (Phone Solution.sln) file, which is contained in the ClearlyVB\Chap24\ Phone Solution-MODIFY THIS folder. Open the designer window. The btnSave

   »MODIFY THIS

control's Click event procedure should determine whether the user entered the phone number in the required format: three digits, a hyphen, three digits, a hyphen, and four digits. Display an appropriate message if the format is not correct. Modify the procedure appropriately. Save the solution, then start the application. Test the application using the following phone numbers: 1-234-567890 and 999-888-1111. Stop the application, then close the solution.

» INTRODUCTORY

4. Open the CityState Solution (CityState Solution.sln) file, which is contained in the ClearlyVB\Chap24\CityState Solution folder. Open the designer window. The interface provides a text box for entering the name of a city, followed by a comma, a space, and a state name. The Display Message button's Click event procedure should display the message "*cityName* is located in *stateName*", where *cityName* and *stateName* are the names of the city and state entered by the user. Code the procedure. Save the solution, then start and test the application. Stop the application, then close the solution.

» INTERMEDIATE

5. Open the Color Solution (Color Solution.sln) file, which is contained in the ClearlyVB\Chap24\Color Solution folder. Open the designer window. The Display Color button's Click event procedure should display the color of the item whose item number is entered by the user. All item numbers contain exactly five characters. All items are available in four colors: blue, green, red, and white. The third character in the item number indicates the item's color, as follows: a B or b indicates Blue, a G or g indicates Green, an R or r indicates Red, and a W or w indicates White. The procedure should display an appropriate message when the item number does not contain exactly five characters, or when the third character is not one of the valid color characters. Save the solution, then start the application. Test the application using 12b45 as the item number. The procedure should display the word "Blue" in the lblColor control. Test the application using the following valid item numbers: 99G44, abr55, and 78w99. Now test the application using the following invalid item numbers: 12x and 23abc. Stop the application, then close the solution.

» ADVANCED

6. Open the Jacobson Solution (Jacobson Solution.sln) file, which is contained in the ClearlyVB\Chap24\Jacobson Solution folder. Open the designer window. The interface provides a text box for entering a password. The text box's CharacterCasing property is set to Upper. The password can contain 5, 6, or 7 characters, but no space characters. The Display New Password button should create and display a new password using the following three rules. First, replace all vowels (A, E, I, O, and U) with the letter X. Second, replace all numbers with the letter Z. Third, reverse the characters in the password. Save the solution, then start and test the application. Stop the application, then close the solution.

7. Open the FigureThisOut Solution (FigureThisOut Solution.sln) file, which is contained in the ClearlyVB\Chap24\FigureThisOut Solution folder. Open the Code Editor window and study the existing code. What task is performed by the btnDisplay control's Click event procedure? Start and then test the application. Stop the application. Close the Code Editor window, then close the solution.

8. In this exercise, you find an error in an application's code. Open the SwatTheBugs Solution (SwatTheBugs Solution.sln) file, which is contained in the ClearlyVB\Chap24\ SwatTheBugs Solution folder. Open the Code Editor window and study the existing code. Start and then test the application. Notice that the application is not working correctly. Stop the application. Locate and correct any errors in the code. Save the solution, then start and test the application again. Stop the application, then close the solution.

ANSWERS TO "TRY THIS" EXERCISES

1. strAmount = strAmount.Replace(",", String.Empty)

   strAmount = strAmount.Insert(0, "$")
   strAmount = strAmount.Insert(2, ",")
   strAmount = strAmount.Insert(6, ",")

2. Figure 24-16 shows the Click event procedure for the btnDisplay control.

```
Private Sub btnDisplay_Click(ByVal sender As Object, _
    ByVal e As System.EventArgs) Handles btnDisplay.Click
    ' displays a shipping charge based on a ZIP code

    Dim strZip As String
    Dim intShipping As Integer

    strZip = txtZip.Text.Trim

    ' validate the ZIP code
    If strZip Like "605##" Then
        intShipping = 25
    ElseIf strZip Like "606##" Then
        intShipping = 30
    Else
        intShipping = 0
        MessageBox.Show("Invalid ZIP code.", "ZIP Code", _
                        MessageBoxButtons.OK, MessageBoxIcon.Information)
    End If

    ' display shipping charge and set the focus
    lblShipping.Text = intShipping.ToString("C0")
    txtZip.Focus()
End Sub
```

Figure 24-16

25

I'M SUFFERING FROM INFORMATION OVERLOAD

After studying Chapter 25, you should be able to:

Define the terms used when talking about databases

Connect an application to a Microsoft Access database

Bind table and field objects to controls

Customize a DataGridView control

Handle exceptions using the Try...Catch statement

Position the record pointer in a dataset

KEEPING GOOD RECORDS

In order to maintain accurate records, most businesses store information about their employees, customers, and inventory in computer databases. A **computer database** is an electronic file that contains an organized collection of related information. Many products exist for creating computer databases; such products are called database management systems (or DBMS). Some of the most popular database management systems are Microsoft Access, Microsoft SQL Server, and Oracle. You can use Visual Basic to access the data stored in databases created by these database management systems. This allows employees to use a standard interface (created in Visual Basic) to access information stored in a variety of database formats. Instead of learning each DBMS's user interface, the employee needs to know only one interface. The actual format of the database is unimportant and will be transparent to the user.

In this chapter, you learn how to access the data stored in Microsoft Access databases. Databases created using Microsoft Access are relational databases. A **relational database** stores information in tables composed of columns and rows, similar to the format used in a spreadsheet. The databases are called relational because the information in the tables can be related in different ways. Each column in a table represents a field, and each row represents a record. A **field** is a single item of information about a person, place, or thing—such as a name, a salary amount, a Social Security number, or a price. A **record** is a group of related fields that contain all of the necessary data about a specific person, place, or thing. The college you are attending keeps a student record on you. Examples of fields contained in your student record include your Social Security number, name, address, phone number, credits earned, and grades earned. The place where you are employed also keeps a record on you. Your employee record contains your Social Security number, name, address, phone number, starting date, salary or hourly wage, and so on. A group of related records is called a **table**. Each record in a table pertains to the same topic, and each contains the same type of information. In other words, each record in a table contains the same fields.

A relational database can contain one or more tables. A one-table database would be a good choice for storing information about the college courses you have taken. An example of such a table is shown in Figure 25-1. Each record in the table contains four fields: an ID field that indicates the department name and course number, a course title field, a number of credit hours field, and a grade field. In most tables, one of the fields uniquely identifies each record and is called the **primary key**. In the table shown in Figure 25-1, you could use either the ID field or the Title field as the primary key, because the data in those fields will be unique for each record.

ID	Title	Hours	Grade
CIS100	Intro to Computers	3	A
ENG100	English Composition	3	B
PHIL105	Philosophy Seminar	2	C
CIS201	Visual Basic 2008	3	A

Figure 25-1: Example of a one-table relational database

You might use a two-table database to store information about a CD (compact disc) collection. You would store the general information about each CD (such as the CD's name and the artist's name) in one table, and store the information about the songs on each CD (such as their title and track number) in the other table. You then would use a common field—for example, a CD number—to relate the records contained in both tables. Figure 25-2 shows an example of a two-table database that stores CD information. The first table is referred to as the **parent table**, and the second table is referred to as the **child table**. The CD_Number field is the primary key in the parent table, because it uniquely identifies each record in the table. The CD_Number field in the child table is used solely to link the song title and track information to the appropriate CD in the parent table. In the child table, the CD_Number field is called the **foreign key**. (Parent and child tables also are referred to as master and detail tables, respectively.)

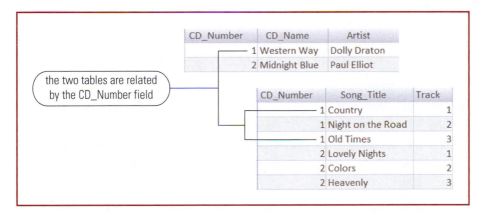

Figure 25-2: Example of a two-table relational database

Storing data in a relational database offers many advantages. The computer can retrieve data stored in a relational format both quickly and easily, and the data can be displayed in any order. The information in the CD database, for example, can be arranged by artist name, song title, and so on. You also can control the amount of information you want to view from a relational database. You can view all of the information in the CD database, or only the information pertaining to a certain artist, or only the names of the songs contained on a specific CD.

CONNECTING...CONNECTING

Raye Industries stores information about its employees in a Microsoft Access database named Employees. The Employees database is contained in the Employees.accdb file, which is located in the ClearlyVB\Chap25\Access Databases folder. The .accdb filename extension stands for Access Database and indicates that the database was created using Microsoft Access 2007. The Employees database contains one table, which is named tblEmploy. The seven fields and 12 records in the table are shown in Figure 25-3. The Emp_Number field is the primary key, because it uniquely identifies each record in the table. The Status field contains the employment status, which is either the letter F (for full-time) or the letter P (for part-time). The Code field identifies the employee's department: 1 for Accounting, 2 for Advertising, 3 for Personnel, and 4 for Inventory.

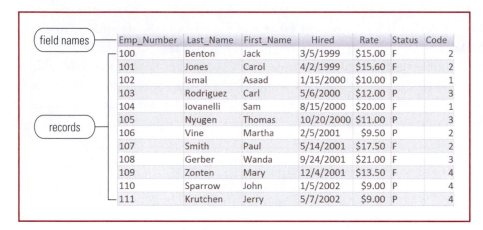

	Emp_Number	Last_Name	First_Name	Hired	Rate	Status	Code
	100	Benton	Jack	3/5/1999	$15.00	F	2
	101	Jones	Carol	4/2/1999	$15.60	F	2
	102	Ismal	Asaad	1/15/2000	$10.00	P	1
	103	Rodriguez	Carl	5/6/2000	$12.00	P	3
	104	Iovanelli	Sam	8/15/2000	$20.00	F	1
	105	Nyugen	Thomas	10/20/2000	$11.00	P	3
	106	Vine	Martha	2/5/2001	$9.50	P	2
	107	Smith	Paul	5/14/2001	$17.50	F	2
	108	Gerber	Wanda	9/24/2001	$21.00	F	3
	109	Zonten	Mary	12/4/2001	$13.50	F	4
	110	Sparrow	John	1/5/2002	$9.00	P	4
	111	Krutchen	Jerry	5/7/2002	$9.00	P	4

field names / records

Figure 25-3: Data contained in the tblEmploy table

For an application to access the data stored in a database, it needs to be connected to the database. The easiest way to connect an application to a database is using the Data Source Configuration Wizard.

Before completing Version 1 of the Raye Industries application, it may be helpful to view the Ch25-Database 1 video.

To open the Raye Industries application, and then connect the application to the Employees database:

1. Start Visual Studio 2008 (or Visual Basic 2008 Express Edition). Open the **Raye Industries Solution** (**Raye Industries Solution.sln**) file, which is contained in the ClearlyVB\Chap25\Raye Industries Solution-Version 1 folder. If necessary, open the designer window and auto-hide the Toolbox, Solution Explorer, and Properties windows.

2. Click **View** on the menu bar, then click **Server Explorer** (or **Database Explorer** if you are using the Express Edition) to open the Server (Database) Explorer window. The window lists the available data connections.

3. Click **Data** on the menu bar, then click **Show Data Sources** to open the Data Sources window. Click **Add New Data Source** in the Data Sources window to start the Data Source Configuration Wizard.

4. If necessary, click **Database** in the Choose a Data Source Type screen, then click the **Next** button. Click the **New Connection** button in the Choose Your Data Connection screen. The Add Connection dialog box opens. (If the Choose Data Source dialog box opens instead, click Microsoft Access Database File, then click the Continue button to open the Add Connection dialog box.)

5. If Microsoft Access Database File (OLE DB) does not appear in the Data source box, click the **Change** button to open the Change Data Source dialog box, then click **Microsoft Access Database File**, and then click the **OK** button to return to the Add Connection dialog box. (It may take a few seconds for the Add Connection dialog box to appear again.)

6. Click the **Browse** button in the Add Connection dialog box. Open the ClearlyVB\Chap25\Access Databases folder, then click **Employees.accdb** in the list of filenames. Click the **Open** button. Figure 25-4 shows the completed Add Connection dialog box. (The dialog box in the figure was widened to show the entire entry in the Database file name box. It is not necessary for you to widen the dialog box.)

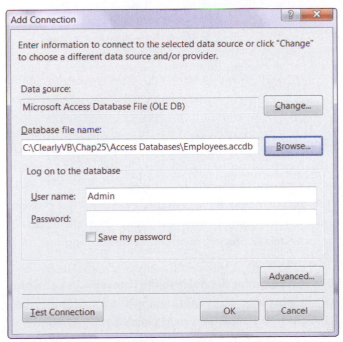

Figure 25-4: Completed Add Connection dialog box

7. Click the **Test Connection** button in the Add Connection dialog box. The "Test connection succeeded." message appears in a message box. Click the **OK** button to close the message box.

8. Click the **OK** button to close the Add Connection dialog box. Employees.accdb appears in the Choose Your Data Connection screen. It also appears below the Data Connections entry in the Server (Database) Explorer window. Click the **Next** button. A message similar to the one shown in Figure 25-5 appears in a message box. The message asks whether you want to include the database file in the current project. By including the file in the current project, you can more easily copy the application and its database to another computer.

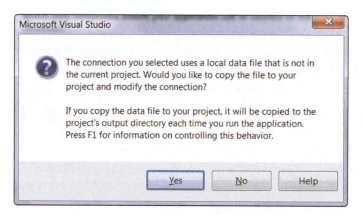

Figure 25-5: Message regarding copying the database file

9. Click the **Yes** button to add the Employees.accdb file to the current project. The file is added to the application's project folder.

10. The Save the Connection String to the Application Configuration File screen appears next and shows the default name for the connection string: EmployeesConnectionString. If necessary, select the **Yes, save the connection string as** check box. Click the **Next** button to display the Choose Your Database Objects screen. You can use this screen to select the table and/or field objects to include in the dataset, which is automatically named EmployeesDataSet. A **dataset** is a copy of the data (fields and records) the application can access from the database. The dataset is stored in the computer's internal memory while the application is running.

11. In this application, you need to include all of the fields in the dataset. Click the **plus box** next to Tables, then click the **plus box** next to tblEmploy. Click the **empty box** next to tblEmploy. Doing this selects the table and field check boxes, as shown in Figure 25-6.

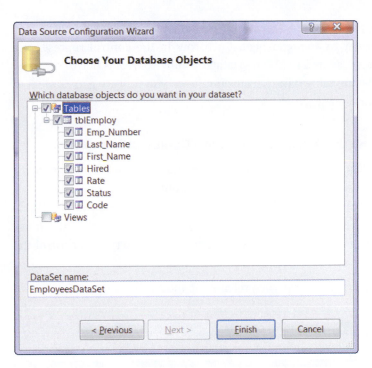

Figure 25-6: Objects selected in the Choose Your Database Objects screen

12. Click the **Finish** button. The computer adds the EmployeesDataSet to the Data Sources window. Click the **plus box** next to tblEmploy in the Data Sources window. The dataset contains one table and seven field objects.

13. Save the solution. Now preview the data contained in the dataset. Right-click **EmployeesDataSet** in the Data Sources window, then click **Preview Data** to open the Preview Data dialog box. Click the **Preview** button. The EmployeesDataSet contains the 12 records (rows) shown earlier in Figure 25-3. Each record is composed of seven fields (columns). Click the **Close** button to close the Preview Data dialog box.

LET THE COMPUTER DO IT

For the user to view the contents of a dataset while an application is running, you need to connect one or more objects in the dataset to one or more controls in the interface. Connecting an object to a control is called **binding**, and the connected controls are called **bound controls** (or data-aware controls). You can bind an object to a control that the computer creates for you; or, you can bind it to an existing control in the interface. In the next set of steps, you will have the computer create a DataGridView control and then bind the tblEmploy table object to it. A **DataGridView control** displays data in a row and columnar format, similar to a spreadsheet. Each row in the control represents a record, and each column represents a field. The DataGridView control is one of the most popular controls for displaying table data, because it allows you to view a great deal of information at the same time.

To have the computer bind the tblEmploy object to a DataGridView control:

1. Click **tblEmploy** in the Data Sources window. The icon that appears before an object's name in the Data Sources window indicates the type of control the computer will create when you drag the object to the form. The ⊞ icon indicates that a DataGridView control will be created when you drag the tblEmploy object to the form. (You can use the list arrow that appears next to an object's name to change the type of control the computer creates.)

2. Drag the **tblEmploy** object to the form, then release the mouse button. See Figure 25-7.

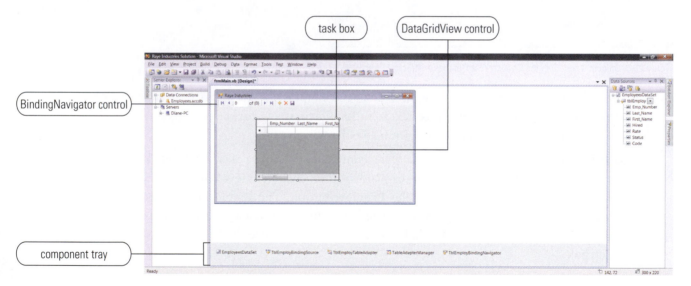

Figure 25-7: Result of dragging the tblEmploy object to the form

As Figure 25-7 shows, besides adding a DataGridView control to the form, the computer also adds a BindingNavigator control. While an application is running, you can use the **BindingNavigator control** to move from one record to the next in the dataset, as well as to add or delete a record and save any changes made to the dataset. The computer also places five objects in the component tray: a DataSet, BindingSource, TableAdapter, TableAdapterManager, and BindingNavigator. The **component tray** stores objects that do not appear in the user interface while an application is running. An exception to this is the BindingNavigator object, which appears as the BindingNavigator control during both design time and runtime. The **TableAdapter object** in the component tray connects the database to the **DataSet object**, which stores the information you want to access from the database. The TableAdapter is responsible for retrieving the appropriate information from the database and storing it in the DataSet. It also can be used to save to the database any changes made to the data contained in the DataSet. However, in most cases, you will use the **TableAdapterManager object** to save the changes, because it can handle saving data to multiple tables in the DataSet. The **BindingSource object** provides the connection between the DataSet and the bound controls on the form. The TblEmployBindingSource in Figure 25-7 connects the EmployeesDataSet to two bound controls: a DataGridView control and a BindingNavigator control. The TblEmployBindingSource allows the DataGridView control to display the data contained in the EmployeesDataSet. It also allows the BindingNavigator control to access the records stored in the EmployeesDataSet. Figure 25-8 illustrates the relationships among the database, the objects in the component tray, and the bound controls on the form.

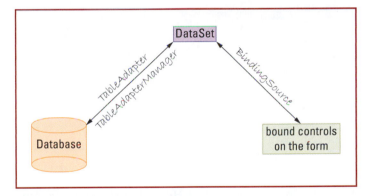

Figure 25-8: Illustration of the relationships among the database, the objects in the component tray, and the bound controls

You can use the DataGridView control's properties to customize the control. Some of the properties are listed only in the Properties window, while others can be set using either the Properties window or the control's task list.

To customize the DataGridView control, then start the application:

1. Click the **task box** on the DataGridView control. A list of tasks associated with the control appears. First, have the grid fill the interior of its parent container, which is the form. Click **Dock in parent container**.

2. Now change the header text for four of the columns. Click **Edit Columns** to open the Edit Columns dialog box. Emp_Number appears highlighted in the Selected Columns box. Click the **Alphabetical** button in the dialog box, then click **HeaderText**. Type **Employee Number** and press **Enter**. See Figure 25-9.

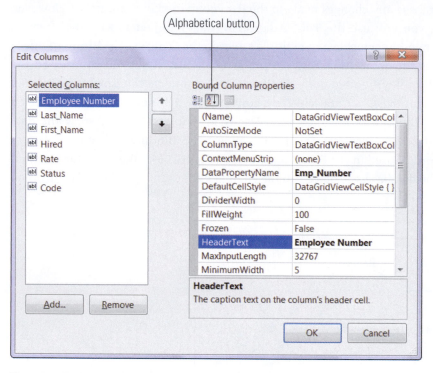

Figure 25-9: Edit Columns dialog box

3. Click **Last_Name** in the Selected Columns box. Click **HeaderText**, then type **Last Name** and press **Enter**. On your own, change the First_Name column's header text to **First Name**, and change the Rate column's header text to **Pay Rate**.

4. Now format the Pay Rate column. Click **DefaultCellStyle**, then click the **...** (ellipsis) button to open the CellStyle Builder dialog box. Click **Format** in the Behavior section, then click the **...** (ellipsis) button to open the Format String Dialog box. Click **Numeric**, then click the **OK** button to close the Format String Dialog box. The Format property now shows N2, which stands for Numeric format with two decimal places. Click the **OK** button to close the CellStyle Builder dialog box, then click the **OK** button to close the Edit Columns dialog box.

5. Click the **DataGridView** control to close its task list. Display the Properties window, then click **AutoSizeColumnsMode**. Click the **down arrow** in the Settings box, then

click **Fill**. The Fill setting automatically adjusts the column widths so that all of the columns exactly fill the display area of the control.

6. Save the solution, then start the application. See Figure 25-10.

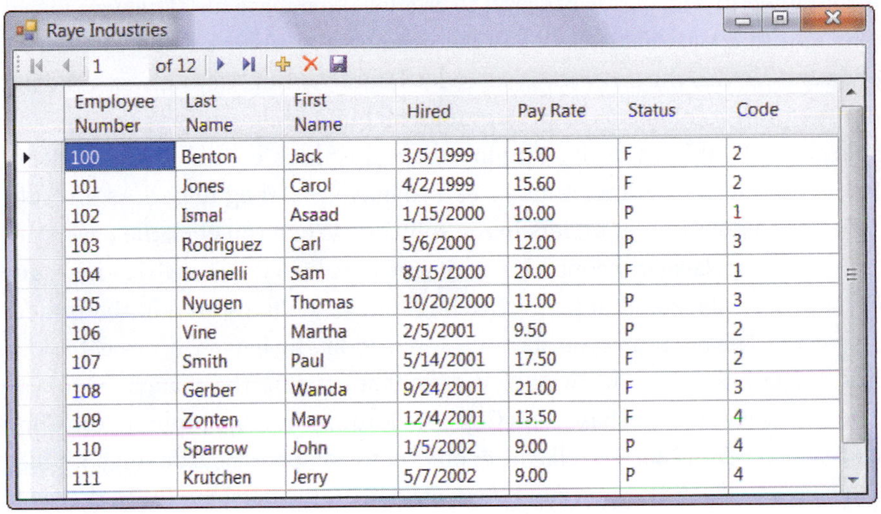

Employee Number	Last Name	First Name	Hired	Pay Rate	Status	Code
100	Benton	Jack	3/5/1999	15.00	F	2
101	Jones	Carol	4/2/1999	15.60	F	2
102	Ismal	Asaad	1/15/2000	10.00	P	1
103	Rodriguez	Carl	5/6/2000	12.00	P	3
104	Iovanelli	Sam	8/15/2000	20.00	F	1
105	Nyugen	Thomas	10/20/2000	11.00	P	3
106	Vine	Martha	2/5/2001	9.50	P	2
107	Smith	Paul	5/14/2001	17.50	F	2
108	Gerber	Wanda	9/24/2001	21.00	F	3
109	Zonten	Mary	12/4/2001	13.50	F	4
110	Sparrow	John	1/5/2002	9.00	P	4
111	Krutchen	Jerry	5/7/2002	9.00	P	4

Figure 25-10: Records shown in the customized DataGridView control

7. As is true in a spreadsheet, the intersection of a column and row in a DataGridView control is called a cell. You can use the arrow keys on your keyboard to move the highlight to a different cell. Press the **down arrow** key on your keyboard twice, then press the **right arrow** key three times.
8. The BindingNavigator control provides buttons for accessing the first and last records in the dataset, as well as accessing the previous and next records. Click the **Move first** button, then click the **Move last** button. Click the **Move previous** button, then click the **Move next** button.
9. You also can use the BindingNavigator control to access a record by its record number. The first record in a dataset has a record number of 1, the second a record number of 2, and so on. Change the number in the Current position box (which is located to the right of the Move previous button) to **3**, then press **Enter** to move the highlight to the third record.
10. Stop the application by clicking the **Close** button on the form's title bar.

The BindingNavigator control also provides buttons for adding and deleting records and saving the changes made to the records. The way changes are saved is controlled by the database file's Copy to Output Directory property.

THE COPY TO OUTPUT DIRECTORY PROPERTY

When the Data Source Configuration Wizard connects an application to a database, it adds the database file to the application's project folder. In this case, the Employees.accdb file was added to the Raye Industries application's project folder. A database file contained in a project is referred to as a local database file. The way Visual Basic saves changes to a local database file is determined by the file's **Copy to Output Directory property**. When the property is set to its default setting, Copy always, the file is copied from the project folder to the project folder's bin\Debug folder each time you start the application. In this case, the Employees.accdb file is copied from the Raye Industries Project folder to the Raye Industries Project\bin\Debug folder. As a result, the file will appear in two different folders in the solution. When you click the Save Data button 🔲 on the BindingNavigator control, any changes made in the DataGridView control are recorded in the file stored in the bin\Debug folder; the file stored in the project folder is not changed. The next time you start the application, the file in the project folder is copied to the bin\Debug folder, overwriting the file that contains the changes. One way to fix this problem is to set the database file's Copy to Output Directory property to "Copy if newer." The "Copy if newer" setting tells the computer to compare the dates on both files to determine which file has the newer (more current) date. If the database file in the project folder has the newer date, then copy it to the bin\Debug folder; otherwise, don't copy it.

To set the Copy to Output Directory property, then start and test the application:

1. Display the Solution Explorer window, then right-click **Employees.accdb**. Click **Properties**, then click **Copy to Output Directory**. Click the **down arrow** in the Settings box, then click **Copy if newer**.

2. Save the solution, then start the application. Press the **right arrow** key five times. When a cell is highlighted, you can modify its existing data by simply typing the new data. Type **P** and press **Enter** to change Jack Benton's status to part-time.

3. Click the **Add new** button ➕ on the BindingNavigator control to add a new row at the bottom of the DataGridView control. Click the empty cell in the new row's Employee Number column, type **999** and press **Tab**.

4. Click the **Save Data** button 🔲 on the BindingNavigator control, then stop the application by clicking the **Close** button on the form's title bar.

5. Start the application again. Notice that both the change you made to Jack Benton's status and the new record you added were saved. (You will need to scroll down to view the record you added.)

6. Click **999** in the Employee Number column, then click the **Delete** button ✖ on the BindingNavigator control to delete the record.

7. Change Jack Benton's status from P to **F**, then click the **Save Data** button 🖫.

8. Stop the application by clicking the **Close** button on the form's title bar. Start the application again to verify that the changes you made were saved, then stop the application.

MINI-QUIZ 1

1. In a table, a _____ is a single item of information about a person, place, or thing.

2. The _____ object connects a DataSet object to a bound control.

3. The process of connecting an object to a control is called _____.

HOW DOES VISUAL BASIC DO IT?

When a table or field object is dragged to the form, the computer adds the appropriate controls and objects to the application. It also enters two event procedures in the Code Editor window.

To view the code automatically entered in the Code Editor window:

1. Auto-hide the Server (Database) Explorer and Data Sources windows.

2. Open the Code Editor window. Figure 25-11 shows the two event procedures automatically entered by the computer. The two event procedures are the form's Load event procedure and the Save Data button's Click event procedure.

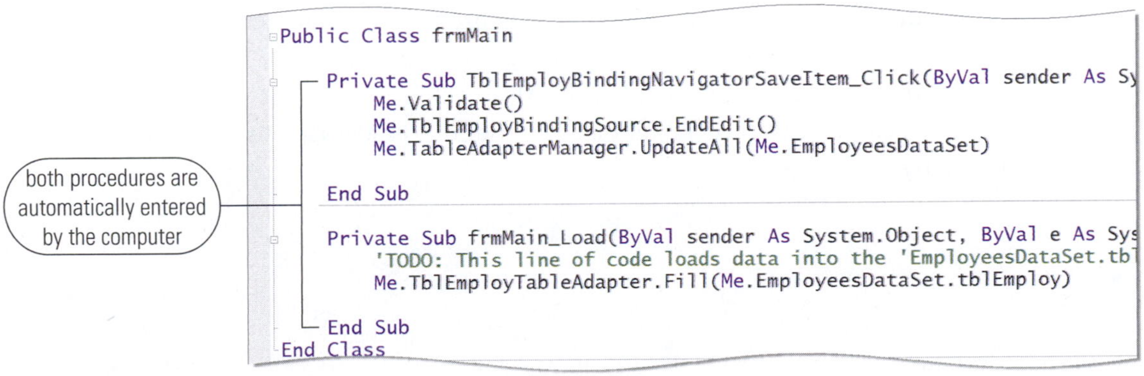

```
Public Class frmMain

    Private Sub TblEmployBindingNavigatorSaveItem_Click(ByVal sender As Sy
        Me.Validate()
        Me.TblEmployBindingSource.EndEdit()
        Me.TableAdapterManager.UpdateAll(Me.EmployeesDataSet)

    End Sub

    Private Sub frmMain_Load(ByVal sender As System.Object, ByVal e As Sys
        'TODO: This line of code loads data into the 'EmployeesDataSet.tb
        Me.TblEmployTableAdapter.Fill(Me.EmployeesDataSet.tblEmploy)

    End Sub
End Class
```

both procedures are automatically entered by the computer

Figure 25-11: Code automatically entered in the Code Editor window

A form's **Load event** occurs when the application is started and the form is displayed the first time. In the Load event procedure, you enter code you want processed before the form appears on the screen. The Load event procedure in Figure 25-11, for example, uses the TableAdapter object's Fill method to retrieve the appropriate data from the Employees database and store it in the DataSet object. In most applications, the code to fill a dataset with data belongs in the Load event procedure. However, if necessary, you can move the code to a different procedure or remove the code entirely. The TblEmployBindingNavigatorSaveItem_Click procedure, on the other hand, is processed when you click the Save Data button on the BindingNavigator control. The procedure's code validates the changes made to the data before saving the data to the database. Two methods are involved in the save operation: the BindingSource object's EndEdit method and the TableAdapterManager's UpdateAll method. The EndEdit method applies any pending changes (such as new records, deleted records, or changed records) to the dataset. The UpdateAll method commits the dataset changes to the database. Because it is possible for an error to occur when saving data to a database, it is a good programming practice to add error handling code to the Save Data button's Click event procedure.

THANK YOU FOR CATCHING MY ERRORS

As you learned in Chapter 15, an error that occurs while an application is running is called an exception. If you do not take deliberate steps in your code to handle the exceptions, Visual Basic "handles" them for you. Typically, it does this by displaying an error message and then abruptly terminating the application. You can prevent your application from behaving in such an unfriendly manner by taking control of the exception handling in your code; you can do this using the **Try...Catch statement**. Figure 25-12 shows the statement's basic syntax and includes examples of using the syntax. The basic syntax contains a Try block and a Catch block. Within the Try block you place the code that could possibly generate an exception. When an exception occurs in the Try block's code, the computer processes the code contained in the Catch block; it then skips to the code following the End Try clause. A description of the exception that occurred is stored in the Message property of the Catch block's ex variable. You can access the description using the code ex.Message, as shown in Example 2 in the figure.

USING THE BASIC SYNTAX OF THE TRY...CATCH STATEMENT

<u>Syntax</u>

Try

 one or more statements that might generate an exception

Catch ex As Exception

 one or more statements to execute when an exception occurs

End Try

<u>Example 1</u>

```
Private Sub btnDisplay_Click(ByVal sender As System.Object, _
    ByVal e As System.EventArgs) Handles btnDisplay.Click

    Try
        inFile = IO.File.OpenText("report.txt")
    Catch ex As Exception
        MessageBox.Show("Cannot find the report.txt file.", "File Error", _
                        MessageBoxButtons.OK, MessageBoxIcon.Information)
    End Try
End Sub
```

if an exception occurs when using the OpenText method to open a sequential access file, the code in the Catch block displays an appropriate message before the procedure ends

<u>Example 2</u>

```
Private Sub TblBooksBindingNavigatorSaveItem_Click _
    (ByVal sender As System.Object, ByVal e As System.EventArgs) _
    Handles TblBooksBindingNavigatorSaveItem.Click

    Try
        Me.Validate()
        Me.TblBooksBindingSource.EndEdit()
        Me.TableAdapterManager.UpdateAll(Me.BooksDataSet)
    Catch ex As Exception
        MessageBox.Show(ex.Message, "Book Sellers", _
                        MessageBoxButtons.OK, MessageBoxIcon.Information)
    End Try
End Sub
```

if an exception occurs when processing the code in the Try block, the code in the Catch block displays a description of the exception before the procedure ends

Figure 25-12: Basic syntax and examples of the Try...Catch statement

To enter a Try...Catch statement in the Save Data button's Click event procedure:

1. Click to the **immediate left of the letter M** in the Me.Validate() line, then press **Enter** to insert a blank line. Press the **up arrow** key, then type **try** and press **Enter**.

2. Modify the TblEmployBindingNavigatorSaveItem_Click event procedure as shown in Figure 25-13.

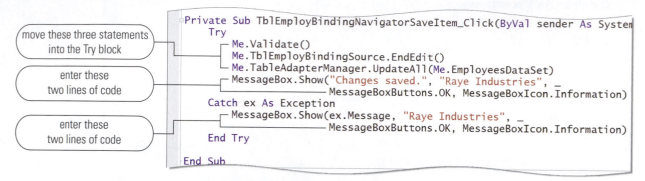

```
Private Sub TblEmployBindingNavigatorSaveItem_Click(ByVal sender As System
    Try
        Me.Validate()
        Me.TblEmployBindingSource.EndEdit()
        Me.TableAdapterManager.UpdateAll(Me.EmployeesDataSet)
        MessageBox.Show("Changes saved.", "Raye Industries", _
            MessageBoxButtons.OK, MessageBoxIcon.Information)
    Catch ex As Exception
        MessageBox.Show(ex.Message, "Raye Industries", _
            MessageBoxButtons.OK, MessageBoxIcon.Information)
    End Try

End Sub
```

move these three statements into the Try block

enter these two lines of code

enter these two lines of code

Figure 25-13: Try...Catch statement entered in the Save Data button's Click event procedure

3. Save the solution, then start the application. The statement in the form's Load event procedure retrieves the appropriate data from the Employees database and loads the data into the EmployeesDataSet. The data is displayed in the DataGridView control, which is bound to the tblEmploy table contained in the dataset.

4. Click the **Add new** button ✛ on the BindingNavigator control to add a new row at the bottom of the DataGridView control. Click the empty cell in the new row's Employee Number column, type **999** and press **Tab**.

5. Click the **Save Data** button 🖫 on the BindingNavigator control. The "Changes saved." message appears in a message box. Close the message box, then stop the application.

6. Start the application again. Click **999** in the Employee Number column, then click the **Delete** button ✕ on the BindingNavigator control to delete the record. Click the **Save Data** button 🖫. The "Changes saved." message appears in a message box. Close the message box, then stop the application.

7. Close the Code Editor window, then close the solution.

I'LL USE MY OWN CONTROLS, THANK YOU

As mentioned earlier, you can bind an object in a dataset to an existing control on the form. The easiest way to accomplish this is by dragging the object from the Data Sources window to the control.

Before completing Version 2 of the Raye Industries application, it may be helpful to view the Ch25-Database 2 video.

To open a different version of the Raye Industries application, and then bind the controls:

1. Open the **Raye Industries Solution** (**Raye Industries Solution.sln**) file, which is contained in the ClearlyVB\Chap25\Raye Industries Solution-Version 2 folder. If necessary, open the designer window. For your convenience, the application is already connected to the Employees.accdb database. You can verify the connection in the Server (Database) Explorer window.

2. Display the Data Sources window, then click the **plus box** that appears next to tblEmploy. A listing of field objects appears. Click **Emp_Number**, then drag the field object to the Number box, as shown in Figure 25-14. When you drag an object from the Data Sources window to an existing control, the computer does not create a new control; rather, it merely binds the object to the existing control.

lblNumber control

Emp_Number field object

field object being dragged to the lblNumber control

Figure 25-14: Emp_Number field object being dragged to the Number box

3. Release the mouse button. In addition to binding the Emp_Number object to the lblNumber control, the computer also adds DataSet, BindingSource, TableAdapter, and TableAdapterManager objects to the component tray. However, notice that when you drag an object to an existing control, the computer does not add a BindingNavigator control to the form or a BindingNavigator object to the component tray. (If you need to add a BindingNavigator control to the form, you can do so using the BindingNavigator tool in the Toolbox; doing this also adds a BindingNavigator object to the component tray. You then must set the BindingNavigator control's DataSource property to the name of the BindingSource object in the application. In this case, for example, you would set the DataSource property to TblEmployBindingSource.)

4. On your own, drag the Last_Name, Status, and Code field objects to the appropriate boxes in the interface.

5. Open the Code Editor window. When you drag an object from the Data Sources window to an existing control, the computer enters (in the Code Editor window) the Load event procedure shown earlier in Figure 25-11. (It does not enter the Save Data button's Click event procedure because the form does not contain a BindingNavigator control.)

6. Save the solution, then start the application. The first record in the dataset appears in the interface, as shown in Figure 25-15.

Figure 25-15: First record appears in the interface

7. The form does not contain a BindingNavigator control, so you will need to code the Next Record and Previous Record buttons to move from one record to the next in the dataset. Click the **Exit** button.

The BindingSource object uses an invisible record pointer to keep track of the current record in the dataset. The position of the record pointer is stored in the object's **Position property**. The first record is in position 0, the second in position 1, and so on. Figure 25-16 shows the Position property's syntax and includes examples of using the property. As Examples 2 and 3 indicate, you can use the Position property to move the record pointer to a record in the dataset.

THE BINDINGSOURCE OBJECT'S POSITION PROPERTY

<u>Syntax</u>

bindingSourceName.**Position**

<u>Example 1</u>

intRecordNumber = TblEmployBindingSource.Position
assigns the current record's position to the intRecordNumber variable

---

Figure 25-16: Syntax and examples of the BindingSource object's Position property (*continued on next page*)

Example 2

TblEmployBindingSource.Position = 4
moves the record pointer to the fifth record in the dataset

Example 3

TblEmployBindingSource.Position = _
   TblEmployBindingSource.Position + 1
moves the record pointer to the next record in the dataset

Figure 25-16: Syntax and examples of the BindingSource object's Position property (*continued from previous page*)

Rather than using the Position property to position the record pointer in a dataset, you also can use the BindingSource object's Move methods. The Move methods move the record pointer to the first, last, next, or previous record in the dataset. Figure 25-17 shows each Move method's syntax and includes an example of using the MoveFirst method.

THE BINDINGSOURCE OBJECT'S MOVE METHODS

Syntax

bindingSourceName.**MoveFirst()**

bindingSourceName.**MoveLast()**

bindingSourceName.**MoveNext()**

bindingSourceName.**MovePrevious()**

Example

TblEmployBindingSource.MoveFirst()
moves the record pointer to the first record in the dataset

Figure 25-17: Syntax and an example of the BindingSource object's Move methods

To code the Previous Record and Next Record buttons:

1. Auto-hide the Data Sources window, if necessary. Open the code template for the btnPrevious control's Click event procedure. Type **' moves the record pointer to the previous record** and press **Enter** twice. Type **TblEmployBindingSource. moveprevious()** and press **Enter**.

2. Open the code template for the btnNext control's Click event procedure. Type **' moves the record pointer to the next record** and press **Enter** twice. Type **TblEmployBindingSource.movenext()** and press **Enter**.

3. Save the solution, then start the application. Click the **Next Record** button several times, then click the **Previous Record** several times.

4. Click the **Exit** button. Close the Code Editor window, then close the solution.

MINI-QUIZ 2

1. If the BindingSource object's name is TblInventoryBindingSource, write the Visual Basic statement to move the record pointer to the first record in the dataset. Use the appropriate Move method.

2. A description of the exception that occurred is stored in the Message property of the Catch block's _____ variable.

3. When you drag a field object to an existing control in the interface, Visual Basic replaces the existing control with a new control.

   a. True   b. False

To learn more about connecting an application to a database, see the Database section in the Ch25WantMore.pdf file.

SUMMARY

» Databases created by Microsoft Access are relational databases. A relational database can contain one or more tables. Each table contains fields and records.

» The data in a relational database can be displayed in any order, and you can control the amount of information you want to view.

» Most tables contain a primary key that uniquely identifies each record.

» To access the data stored in a database, you first connect the application to the database. Doing this creates a dataset that contains objects, such as table objects and field objects.

» You display the information contained in a dataset by binding one or more of the dataset objects to one or more controls in the application's interface.

» The TableAdapter object connects a database to a DataSet object. A BindingSource object connects a DataSet object to the bound controls on a form.

» The DataGridView control displays data in a row and columnar format, similar to a spreadsheet.

» A database file's Copy to Output Directory property determines when and if the file is copied from the project folder to the project folder's bin\Debug folder each time the application is started.

» In most applications, the statement to fill a dataset with data is entered in the form's Load event procedure.

» You can use the Try...Catch statement to handle exceptions that occur while an application is running. A description of the exception is stored in the ex variable's Message property.

» The BindingSource object uses an invisible record pointer to keep track of the current record in a dataset. The location of the record pointer is stored in the BindingSource object's Position property. You can use the BindingSource object's Move methods to move the record pointer in a dataset.

KEY TERMS

Binding—the process of connecting an object in a dataset to a control on a form

BindingNavigator control—can be used to move the record pointer from one record to another in a dataset, as well as to add, delete, and save records

BindingSource object—connects a DataSet object to the bound controls on a form

Bound controls—the controls connected to an object in a dataset

Child table—a table linked to a parent table

Component tray—a special area in the IDE; it stores objects that do not appear in the user interface while an application is running

Computer database—an electronic file that contains an organized collection of related information

Copy to Output Directory property—a property of a database file; determines when and if the file is copied from the project folder to the project folder's bin\Debug folder

DataGridView control—displays table data in a row and columnar format

DataSet—a copy of the data (fields and records) that can be accessed by an application

DataSet object—stores the information you want to access from a database

Field—a single item of information about a person, place, or thing

Foreign key—the field used to link a child table to a parent table

Load event—occurs when an application is started and the form is displayed the first time

Parent table—a table linked to a child table

Position property—a property of a BindingSource object; stores the position of the record pointer

Primary key—a field that uniquely identifies each record in a table

Record—a group of related fields that contain all of the necessary data about a specific person, place, or thing

Relational database—a database that stores information in tables composed of fields and records

Table—a group of related records

TableAdapter object—connects a database to a DataSet object

TableAdapterManager object—handles saving data to multiple tables in a dataset

Try...Catch statement—used to handle exceptions that occur during runtime

ANSWERS TO MINI-QUIZZES

MINI-QUIZ 1

1. field

2. BindingSource

3. binding

MINI-QUIZ 2

1. TblInventoryBindingSource.MoveFirst()

2. ex

3. b. False

REVIEW QUESTIONS

1. A group of related fields is called a _____.

   a. database   b. record

   c. table   d. None of the above.

2. The _____ control contains buttons for moving from one record to another in a dataset.

   a. BindingNavigator   b. BindingSource

   c. TableAdapter   d. TableAdapterManager

3. The form's _____ event occurs before the form makes its initial appearance on the screen.

   a. Appearance   b. Initial

   c. Load   d. None of the above.

4. If the current record is the second record in the dataset, which of the following statements will position the record pointer on the first record?

   a. TblEmployBindingSource.Position = 0

   b. TblEmployBindingSource.Position = TblEmployBindingSource.Position - 1

   c. TblEmployBindingSource.MoveFirst()

   d. All of the above.

5. If an application contains the Catch ex As Exception clause, you can use _____ to access the exception's description.

   a. ex.Description   b. ex.Exception

   c. ex.Message   d. None of the above.

EXERCISES

1. Open the Morgan Solution (Morgan Solution.sln) file, which is contained in the ClearlyVB\Chap25\Morgan Solution folder. Open the designer window. Connect the application to the Employees database. The database is stored in the Employees.accdb file, which is located in the ClearlyVB\Chap25\Access Databases folder. After connecting the application to the database, click tblEmploy in the Data Sources window, then click the down arrow that appears next to tblEmploy. Click Details in the list. Drag the tblEmploy object to the form, then release the mouse button. Click Format

» TRY THIS

on the menu bar, point to Center in Form, then click Horizontally. Click Format on the menu bar, point to Center in Form, then click Vertically. Add a Try...Catch statement to the Save Data button's Click event procedure. Change the database file's Copy to Output Directory property to Copy if newer. Save the solution, then start and test the application. Stop the application, then close the solution.(The answers to TRY THIS Exercises are located at the end of the chapter.)

» MODIFY THIS

2. In this exercise, you modify one of the Raye Industries applications coded in the chapter. Use Windows to make a copy of the Raye Industries Solution-Version 2 folder. Save the copy in the ClearlyVB\Chap25 folder. Rename the copy Raye Industries Solution-Version 2-MODIFY THIS. Open the Raye Industries Solution (Raye Industries Solution.sln) file contained in the ClearlyVB\Chap25\Raye Industries Solution-Version 2-MODIFY THIS folder. Open the designer window. Modify the Click event procedures for the btnPrevious and btnNext controls to use the Position property rather than a Move method. Save the solution, then start and test the application. Stop the application, then close the solution.

» INTRODUCTORY

3. Open the Cartwright Solution (Cartwright Solution.sln) file, which is contained in the ClearlyVB\Chap25\Cartwright Solution folder. Open the designer window. Connect the application to the Items database. The database is stored in the Items.accdb file, which is contained in the ClearlyVB\Chap25\Access Databases folder. The database contains one table, named tblItems. The table contains 10 records, each composed of three fields. The ItemNum and ItemName fields contain text, and the Price field contains numbers. Display the records in a DataGridView control. Add a Try...Catch statement to the Save Data button's Click event procedure. Change the database file's Copy to Output Directory property. Save the solution, then start and test the application. Stop the application, then close the solution.

» INTERMEDIATE

4. Open the Playhouse Solution (Playhouse Solution.sln) file, which is contained in the ClearlyVB\Chap25\Playhouse Solution folder. Connect the application to the Play database. The database is contained in the Play.accdb file, which is located in the ClearlyVB\Chap25\Access Databases folder. The Play database contains one table named tblReservations. The table contains 20 records, each having three fields: a numeric field named Seat and two text fields named Patron and Phone. Drag the field objects to the appropriate label controls in the interface. Code the Click event procedures for the First Record, Last Record, Previous Record, and Next Record buttons. Save the solution, then start and test the application. Stop the application, then close the solution.

» ADVANCED

5. In this exercise, you modify the application from Exercise 4. Use Windows to make a copy of the Playhouse Solution folder, which is contained in the ClearlyVB\Chap25 folder. Save the copy in the ClearlyVB\Chap25 folder. Rename the copy Modified Playhouse Solution. Open the Playhouse Solution (Playhouse Solution.sln) file contained in the ClearlyVB\Chap25\Modified Playhouse Solution folder. Open the designer

window. Add another button to the interface. Name the button btnRecordNumber. Change the button's Text property to &Record Number. Code the button's Click event procedure so that it asks the user for a record number from 1 through 20, and then moves the record pointer to that record. Save the solution, then start and test the application. Stop the application, then close the solution.

6. Open the FigureThisOut Solution (FigureThisOut Solution.sln) file, which is contained in the ClearlyVB\Chap25\FigureThisOut Solution folder. Open the Code Editor window. What tasks are performed by the form's Load event procedure? Start and then test the application. What does the application do? (Hint: Refer to Figure 25-2.) Stop the application. Close the Code Editor window, then close the solution.

7. In this exercise, you find an error in an application's code. Open the SwatTheBugs Solution (SwatTheBugs Solution.sln) file, which is contained in the ClearlyVB\Chap25\ SwatTheBugs Solution folder. Open the Code Editor window. Correct the code to remove the jagged line, then save the solution. Start and then test the application. Notice that the application is not working correctly. Stop the application. Locate and correct any errors in the code. Save the solution, then start and test the application again. Stop the application, then close the solution.

ANSWERS TO "TRY THIS" EXERCISE

1. See Figures 25-18 through 25-20.

---

1. Click Data, then click Show Data Sources, and then click Add New Data Source.
2. If necessary, click Database in the Choose a Data Source Type screen, then click the Next button. Click the New Connection button in the Choose Your Data Connection screen.
3. If Microsoft Access Database File (OLE DB) does not appear in the Data source box, click the Change button, then click Microsoft Access Database File, and then click the OK button to return to the Add Connection dialog box. (It may take a few seconds for the Add Connection dialog box to appear again.)
4. Click the Browse button in the Add Connection dialog box. Open the ClearyVB\Chap25\Access Databases folder, then click Employees.accdb in the list of filenames. Click the Open button. Click the Test Connection button in the Add Connection dialog box. The "Test connection succeeded." message appears in a message box. Click the OK button to close the message box.
5. Click the OK button to close the Add Connection dialog box, then click the Next button. Click the Yes button to add the Employees.accdb file to the current project.
6. If necessary, select the check box in the Save the Connection String to the Application Configuration File screen, then click the Next button to display the Choose Your Database Objects screen.
7. Click the plus box next to Tables, then click the empty box next to tblEmploy. Click the Finish button.

Figure 25-18: Steps to connect the application to the database

```
Private Sub TblEmployBindingNavigatorSaveItem_Click _
    (ByVal sender As System.Object, ByVal e As System.EventArgs)
    Try
        Me.Validate()
        Me.TblEmployBindingSource.EndEdit()
        Me.TableAdapterManager.UpdateAll(Me.EmployeesDataSet)
        MessageBox.Show("Changes saved.", "Morgan Industries", _
                        MessageBoxButtons.OK, MessageBoxIcon.Information)
    Catch ex As Exception
        MessageBox.Show(ex.Message, "Morgan Industries", _
                        MessageBoxButtons.OK, MessageBoxIcon.Information)
    End Try
End Sub

Private Sub frmMain_Load(ByVal sender As System.Object, _
    ByVal e As System.EventArgs) Handles MyBase.Load
    'TODO: This line of code loads data into the 'EmployeesDataSet.tblEmploy' table.
    You can move, or remove it, as needed.
    Me.TblEmployTableAdapter.Fill(Me.EmployeesDataSet.tblEmploy)
End Sub
```

Figure 25-19: Morgan Industries application's code

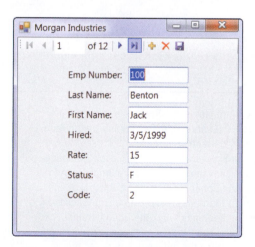

Figure 25-20: Sample run of the Morgan Industries application

26

THE MISSING "LINQ"

After studying Chapter 26, you should be able to:

Query a dataset using LINQ

Use the LINQ aggregate methods

ASKING QUESTIONS

In Chapter 25, you learned how to connect an application to a database, thereby creating a dataset. Recall that a dataset is a copy of the fields and records the application can access from the database. The dataset is stored in the computer's internal memory. You also learned how to display the fields and records by binding table and field objects to controls in the interface. In Chapter 25, all of the records were displayed in the order they appeared in the database. In this chapter, you learn how to display the records in a particular order, as well as how to display only records that meet specific criteria. The examples in this chapter use the Employees database from Chapter 25. The Employees database is shown in Figure 26-1. The database contains one table, which is named tblEmploy. The table contains seven fields and 12 records. The Emp_Number field is the primary key, because it uniquely identifies each record in the table. The Status field contains the employment status, which is either the letter F (for full-time) or the letter P (for part-time). The Code field identifies the employee's department: 1 for Accounting, 2 for Advertising, 3 for Personnel, and 4 for Inventory.

	Emp_Number	Last_Name	First_Name	Hired	Rate	Status	Code
field names							
	100	Benton	Jack	3/5/1999	$15.00	F	2
	101	Jones	Carol	4/2/1999	$15.60	F	2
	102	Ismal	Asaad	1/15/2000	$10.00	P	1
	103	Rodriguez	Carl	5/6/2000	$12.00	P	3
	104	Iovanelli	Sam	8/15/2000	$20.00	F	1
records	105	Nyugen	Thomas	10/20/2000	$11.00	P	3
	106	Vine	Martha	2/5/2001	$9.50	P	2
	107	Smith	Paul	5/14/2001	$17.50	F	2
	108	Gerber	Wanda	9/24/2001	$21.00	F	3
	109	Zonten	Mary	12/4/2001	$13.50	F	4
	110	Sparrow	John	1/5/2002	$9.00	P	4
	111	Krutchen	Jerry	5/7/2002	$9.00	P	4

Figure 26-1: Employees database

You use a **query** to specify the records to select in a dataset, as well as to specify the order in which to arrange (sort) the records. You can create a query in Visual Basic 2008 using a new language feature called **Language Integrated Query** or, more simply, **LINQ**. Figure 26-2 shows the basic syntax of LINQ when used to select and/or sort the records in a dataset. In the syntax, *variableName* and *elementName* can be any names you choose, as long as the name follows the naming rules for variables. Notice that the syntax does not require you to specify the variable's data type. Instead, the syntax allows the computer to infer the data type from the value being assigned to the variable. The Where and Order By clauses are optional parts of the syntax. You use the Where clause, which contains a *condition*, to limit the records you want to select. Similar to the *condition* in If...Then...Else and Do...Loop statements, the Where clause *condition* specifies a requirement that must be met for a record to be selected. The Order By clause is used to sort the records in either ascending (the default) or descending order by one or more fields. Also included in Figure 26-2 are examples of using the basic syntax. The statement in Example 1 selects all of the records in the dataset and assigns the records to the records variable. The statement in Example 2 performs the same task; however, the records are assigned in ascending order by the Code field. If you are sorting records in ascending order, you do not need to include the keyword Ascending in the Order By clause, because Ascending is the default. The statement in Example 3 assigns only the records for part-time employees to the records variable. The statement in Example 4 performs the same task; however, the records are assigned in descending order by the Code field. The statement in Example 5 uses the Like operator and the asterisk pattern-matching character to select only records whose First_Name field begins with the letter J. You learned about the Like operator and its pattern-matching characters in Chapter 24.

USING LINQ TO SELECT AND SORT RECORDS

Syntax

Dim *variableName* = **From** *elementName* **In** *dataset.table*
                    [**Where** *condition*]
                    [**Order By** *elementName.field1* [**Ascending**|**Descending**]
                             [**,** *elementName.fieldN* [**Ascending**|**Descending**]]]
                    Select *elementName*

Example 1

```
Dim records = From employee In EmployeesDataSet.tblEmploy _
         Select employee
```
selects all the records contained in the dataset

Example 2

```
Dim records = From employee In EmployeesDataSet.tblEmploy _
         Order By employee.Code _
         Select employee
```
selects all the records contained in the dataset, sorting the records in ascending order by the Code field

---

Figure 26-2: Basic syntax and examples of selecting and sorting records in a dataset (*continued on next page*)

Example 3

Dim records = From employee In EmployeesDataSet.tblEmploy _
        Where employee.Status.ToUpper = "P" _
        Select employee

selects only the part-time employee records

Example 4

Dim records = From employee In EmployeesDataSet.tblEmploy _
        Where employee.Status.ToUpper = "P" _
        Order By employee.Code Descending _
        Select employee

selects only the part-time employee records, sorting the records in descending order by the Code field

Example 5

Dim records = From employee In EmployeesDataSet.tblEmploy _
        Where employee.First_Name.ToUpper Like "J*" _
        Select employee

selects only the records whose first name begins with the letter J

Figure 26-2: Basic syntax and examples of selecting and sorting records in a dataset (*continued from previous page*)

REVISITING THE RAYE INDUSTRIES APPLICATION

You coded two versions of the Raye Industries application in Chapter 25. In the next set of steps, you will modify the second version to display records whose Last_Name field begins with one or more letters entered by the user.

Before completing the steps in this chapter, it may be helpful to view the Ch26-LINQ video.

To open the Raye Industries application, and then modify the application's code:

1. Start Visual Studio 2008 (or Visual Basic 2008 Express Edition). Open the **Raye Industries Solution** (**Raye Industries Solution.sln**) file, which is contained in the ClearlyVB\Chap26\Raye Industries Solution folder. If necessary, open the designer window. The interface was modified to display the First_Name field. It also includes two new buttons: Find Record and Calculate Average. See Figure 26-3.

Figure 26-3: Modified user interface for the Raye Industries application

2. Open the Code Editor window and locate the btnFind control's Click event procedure. First, use the InputBox function to prompt the user to either enter one or more letters or leave the input area empty. Click the **blank line** below the ' get user input comment. Type **strSearch = InputBox(strPROMPT, "Find Last Name").ToUpper** and press **Enter**.

3. Now enter the LINQ statement to select the appropriate records. Click the **blank line** below the ' select the appropriate records comment. Type **Dim records = From employee In EmployeesDataSet.tblEmploy _** and press **Enter**. Type **Where employee.Last_Name.ToUpper Like strSearch & "*" _** and press **Enter**, then type **Select employee** and press **Enter**. (If a jagged line appears below records in the Dim statement, click Tools on the menu bar, then click Options. Expand the Projects and Solutions entry, then click VB Defaults. Change Option Strict to Off.)

4. The LINQ statement merely selects the records and assigns them to the records variable. To view the records in the interface, you need to assign the contents of the records variable to the BindingSource object's DataSource property. By doing this, the label controls bound to the BindingSource object will display the appropriate data. Click the **blank line** below the ' display the records comment, then type **TblEmployBindingSource.DataSource = records** and press **Enter**.

5. Save the solution, then start the application. First, display the records of employees whose last name begins with the letter i. Click the **Find Record** button, then type **i** and press **Enter**. The LINQ statement in the button's Click event procedure selects the two records whose last name begins with the letter i: Asaad Ismal's record and Sam Iovanelli's record. Currently, Asaad Ismal's record appears in the interface. Click the **Next Record** button. Sam Iovanelli's record appears in the interface. Click the **Next Record** button again. Notice that Sam's record is the last record that meets the criterion. Click the **Previous Record** button to return to Asaad Ismal's record. Click the **Previous Record** button again. Notice that Asaad's record is the first record that meets the criterion.

6. Now display all of the records. Click the **Find Record** button, then click the **OK** button. Use the **Next Record** button to verify that all twelve records have been retrieved.

7. Click the **Exit** button.

MINI-QUIZ 1

1. Complete the Where clause in the following statement, which should select only records whose LastName field begins with an uppercase letter A.

   Dim records = From name In NamesDataSet.tblNames _
           Where _____ _
           Select name

2. Complete the following statement, which should arrange the records in descending order by the LastName field.

   Dim records = From name In NamesDataSet.tblNames _
           _____ _
           Select name

3. What does LINQ stand for?

ONE FOR ALL

In addition to using LINQ to sort and select the records in a dataset, you also can use it to perform arithmetic calculations on the fields in the records. The calculations are performed using the LINQ aggregate methods—namely, Average, Count, Max, Min, and Sum. Each **aggregate method** returns a single value from a group of values. The Sum method, for example, returns the sum of the values in the group, whereas the Min method returns the smallest value in the group. You include an aggregate method in a LINQ statement using the syntax shown in Figure 26-4. The figure also includes examples of using the syntax. The statement in Example 1 calculates the average of the values contained in the Rate field, assigning the result to the avgRate variable. The statement in Example 2 first selects only the part-time employee records. It then determines the highest value stored in the Rate field for those records. The statement assigns the result to the maxRate variable. Example 3's statement counts the number of employees in the Advertising department (Code = 2) and assigns the result to the counter variable.

USING THE LINQ AGGREGATE METHODS

Syntax

Dim *variableName* = **Aggregate** *elementName* **In** *dataset.table*
                     [**Where** *condition*]
                     Select *elementName.field*
                     Into *aggregateMethod*()

Example 1

```
Dim avgRate = Aggregate employee In EmployeesDataSet.tblEmploy _
            Select employee.Rate _
            Into Average()
```
calculates the average of the pay rates in the dataset and assigns the result to the avgRate variable

Example 2

```
Dim maxRate = Aggregate employee In EmployeesDataSet.tblEmploy _
            Where employee.Status.ToUpper = "P" _
            Select employee.Rate _
            Into Max()
```
finds the highest pay rate for a part-time employee and assigns the result to the maxRate variable

Example 3

```
Dim counter = Aggregate employee In EmployeesDataSet.tblEmploy _
            Where employee.Code = 2 _
            Select employee.Emp_Number _
            Into Count()
```
counts the number of employees whose department code is 2 and assigns the result to the counter variable

---

Figure 26-4: Syntax and examples of the LINQ aggregate methods

You will use the Average aggregate method to code the Calculate Average button's Click event procedure.

To code the Calculate Average button's Click event procedure, and then test the application:

1. Locate the btnAverage control's Click event procedure. First, enter the LINQ statement to calculate the average pay rate for all employees. Click the **blank line** below the ' calculate average pay rate comment. Type **Dim avgRate = Aggregate employee In EmployeesDataSet.tblEmploy** _ and press **Enter**, then type **Select employee.Rate Into Average()** and press **Enter**.

2. Now display the average pay rate in a message box. Click the **blank line** below the ' display average pay rate comment, then enter the MessageBox.Show method indicated in Figure 26-5.

```
Private Sub btnAverage_Click(ByVal sender As Object, ByVal e As System
    ' displays the average pay rate

    ' calculate average pay rate
    Dim avgRate = Aggregate employee In EmployeesDataSet.tblEmploy _
                    Select employee.Rate Into Average()

    ' display average pay rate
    MessageBox.Show("Average pay rate for all employees: " _
                    & avgRate.ToString("C2"), "Raye Industries", _
                    MessageBoxButtons.OK, MessageBoxIcon.Information)

    End Sub
```

enter these three lines of code

Figure 26-5: Calculate Average button's Click event procedure

3. Save the solution, then start the application. Click the **Calculate Average** button. A message box opens and displays the average pay rate for all employees: $13.59. Click the **OK** button to close the message box, then click the **Exit** button. Close the Code Editor window, then close the solution.

MINI-QUIZ 2

1. Complete the following statement, which should calculate the sum of the values stored in a numeric field named JanSales.

   Dim totalSales = Aggregate sales In SalesDataSet.tblSales _

        Select _____ _

        Into Sum()

2. Complete the following statement, which should calculate the average of the values stored in a numeric field named PointsEarned.

   Dim avgPoints = Aggregate points In PointsDataSet.tblPoints _

        _____ _

        _____

3. In LINQ, the _____ aggregate method returns the smallest value in the group.

 To learn more about LINQ, see the LINQ section in the Ch26WantMore.pdf file.

SUMMARY

» LINQ stands for Language Integrated Query. You can use LINQ to select and sort the records in a dataset, as well as to perform calculations on the fields in the records.

» LINQ provides the Average, Sum, Count, Min, and Max aggregate methods for performing calculations.

KEY TERMS

Aggregate method—a method that returns a single value from a group of values

Language Integrated Query—LINQ; the new query language in Visual Basic 2008

LINQ—Language Integrated Query

Query—specifies the records to select in a dataset, and the order in which to arrange the records

ANSWERS TO MINI-QUIZZES

MINI-QUIZ 1

1. name.LastName.ToUpper = "A*"

2. Order By name.LastName Descending

3. Language Integrated Query

MINI-QUIZ 2

1. sales.JanSales

2. Select points.PointsEarned
   Into Average()

3. Min

REVIEW QUESTIONS

1. Which of the following LINQ statements selects all of the records in the tblStates table?

   a. Dim records = From state In StatesDataSet.tblStates _
          Select All state

   b. Dim records = From state In StatesDataSet.tblStates _
          Select state

   c. Dim records = Select state From StatesDataSet.tblStates

   d. Dim records = From StatesDataSet.tblStates _
          Select tblStates.state

2. The tblCities table contains a numeric field named Population. Which of the following LINQ statements selects all cities having a population that exceeds 15,000?

   a. Dim records = From city In CitiesDataSet.tblCities _
                 Where Population > 15000 _
                 Select city

   b. Dim records = From city In CitiesDataSet.tblCities _
                 Select city.Population > 15000

   c. Dim records = From city In CitiesDataSet.tblCities _
                 Where city.Population > 15000 _
                 Select city

   d. Dim records = Select city.Population > 15000 From tblCities

3. The tblCities table contains a numeric field named Population. Which of the following LINQ statements calculates the total population of all the cities in the table?

   a. Dim total = Aggregate city In CitiesDataSet.tblCities _
              Select city.Population _
              Into Sum()

   b. Dim total = Sum city In CitiesDataSet.tblCities _
              Select city.Population _
              Into total

   c. Dim total = Aggregate CitiesDataSet.tblCities.city _
              Select city.Population _
              Into Sum()

   d. Dim total = Sum city In CitiesDataSet.tblCities.population

4. In a LINQ statement, the _____ clause limits the records that will be selected.

   a. Limit

   b. Order By

   c. Select

   d. Where

5. Which of the following LINQ statements arranges the records in ascending order by the LastName field, with records having the same last name arranged in descending order by the FirstName field?

a. Dim records = From name In NamesDataSet.tblNames _
          Order By name.LastName Ascending, _
          name.FirstName Descending _
          Select name

b. Dim records = From name In NamesDataSet.tblNames _
          Order By name.LastName, name.FirstName Descending _
          Select name

c. Dim records = Select name From NamesDataSet.tblNames _
          Order By name.FirstName Descending, name.LastName

d. Both a and b.

EXERCISES

»TRY THIS

1. Open the Magazine Solution (Magazine Solution.sln) file, which is contained in the ClearlyVB\Chap26\Magazine Solution-TRY THIS 1 folder. Open the designer window. The application is connected to the Magazines database, which is stored in the Magazines.accdb file. The database contains a table named tblMagazine; the table has three fields. The Cost field is numeric. The Code and MagName fields contain text. Start the application to view the records contained in the dataset, then stop the application. Open the Code Editor window. Code the btnSort control's Click event procedure so that it displays the records in descending order by the Cost field. Code the btnDisplayCode control's Click event procedure so that it displays the record whose Code field contains PG24. Code the btnDisplayName control's Click event procedure so that it displays only the Java record. Save the solution, then start and test the application. Stop the application, then close the solution. (The answers to TRY THIS Exercises are located at the end of the chapter.)

»TRY THIS

2. Open the Magazine Solution (Magazine Solution.sln) file, which is contained in the ClearlyVB\Chap26\Magazine Solution-TRY THIS 2 folder. Open the designer window. The application is connected to the Magazines database, which is stored in the Magazines.accdb file. The database contains a table named tblMagazine; the table has three fields. The Cost field is numeric. The Code and MagName fields contain text. Start the application to view the records contained in the dataset, then stop the application. Open the Code Editor window. Code the btnDisplayCost control's Click event procedure so that it displays records having a cost of $4 or more. Code the

btnDisplayName control's Click event procedure so that it displays only magazines whose name begins with the letter C (in either uppercase or lowercase). Code the btnAverage control's Click event procedure so that it displays the average cost of a magazine. Display the average in a message box. Save the solution, then start and test the application. Stop the application, then close the solution. (The answers to TRY THIS Exercises are located at the end of the chapter.)

3. In this exercise, you modify the Raye Industries application coded in the chapter. Use Windows to make a copy of the Raye Industries Solution folder. Save the copy in the ClearlyVB\Chap26 folder. Rename the copy Raye Industries Solution-MODIFY THIS. Open the Raye Industries Solution (Raye Industries Solution.sln) file contained in the ClearlyVB\Chap26\Raye Industries Solution-MODIFY THIS folder. Open the designer window, then open the Code Editor window and locate the btnAverage control's Click event procedure. Currently, the procedure displays the average pay rate for all employees. Modify the procedure so it displays three values in the message box: the average pay rate for part-time employees, the average pay rate for full-time employees, and the average pay rate for all employees. Save the solution, then start and test the application. Stop the application, then close the solution.

» MODIFY THIS

4. In this exercise, you code a different version of the Raye Industries application from the chapter. Open the Raye Industries Solution (Raye Industries Solution.sln) file, which is contained in the ClearlyVB\Chap26\Raye Industries Solution-INTRODUCTORY folder. Open the designer window, then open the Code Editor window. Code the btnDisplay control's Click event procedure so that it asks the user for the department code (1, 2, 3, or 4); use the InputBox function. The procedure should display only records matching that department code. If the user enters an invalid department code, display an appropriate message. If the user does not enter a department code, display all the records. Save the solution, then start and test the application. Stop the application, then close the solution.

» INTRODUCTORY

5. In this exercise, you modify the Raye Industries application coded in the chapter. Use Windows to make a copy of the Raye Industries Solution folder. Save the copy in the ClearlyVB\Chap26 folder. Rename the copy Raye Industries Solution-INTERMEDIATE. Open the Raye Industries Solution (Raye Industries Solution.sln) file contained in the ClearlyVB\Chap26\Raye Industries Solution-INTERMEDIATE folder. Open the designer window, then open the Code Editor window and locate the btnFind control's Click event procedure. Modify the procedure's code so that it displays (in a message box) the number of employees found. Save the solution, then start and test the application. Stop the application, then close the solution.

» INTERMEDIATE

6. In this exercise, you use a Microsoft Access 2007 database named Courses. The database is contained in the Courses.accdb file, which is located in the ClearlyVB\Chap26\Access Databases folder. The database contains one table named tblCourses. The table

» ADVANCED

has 10 records, each having four fields: ID, Title, CreditHours, and Grade. The CreditHours field is numeric; the other fields contain text. Open the College Courses Solution (College Courses Solution.sln) file, which is contained in the ClearlyVB\ Chap26\College Courses Solution folder. Open the designer window. Connect the application to the Courses database. Drag the table into the group box control, then dock the DataGridView control in its parent container. (In this case, the parent container is the group box control.) Use the task list to disable Adding, Editing, and Deleting. Change the DataGridView control's AutoSizeColumnsMode property to Fill. Remove the BindingNavigator control from the form by deleting the BindingNavigator object from the component tray. Open the Code Editor window. Delete the Save Data button's Click event procedure. Code the Next Record and Previous Record buttons. Code the Display button so it allows the user to display either all the records or the records matching a specific grade. Code the Calculate GPA button so it displays the student's GPA. (An A grade is worth 4 points, a B is worth 3 points, and so on.) Save the solution, then start and test the application. Stop the application, then close the solution.

7. Open the FigureThisOut Solution (FigureThisOut Solution.sln) file, which is contained in the ClearlyVB\Chap26\FigureThisOut Solution folder. Open the Code Editor window and study the existing code. What task is performed by the LINQ statement in the btnDisplay control's Click event procedure? Start and then test the application. Stop the application. Close the Code Editor window, then close the solution.

8. In this exercise, you find an error in an application's code. Open the SwatTheBugs Solution (SwatTheBugs Solution.sln) file, which is contained in the ClearlyVB\Chap26\ SwatTheBugs Solution folder. Open the Code Editor window and study the existing code. Start and then test the application. Notice that the application is not working correctly. Stop the application. Locate and correct any errors in the code. Save the solution, then start and test the application again. Stop the application, then close the solution.

ANSWERS TO "TRY THIS" EXERCISES

1. See Figure 26-6.

```vbnet
Private Sub btnSort_Click(ByVal sender As Object, _
    ByVal e As System.EventArgs) Handles btnSort.Click
    ' displays records in descending order by the Cost field

    Dim records = From magazine In MagazinesDataSet.tblMagazine _
                Order By magazine.Cost Descending _
                Select magazine
    TblMagazineBindingSource.DataSource = records
End Sub

Private Sub btnDisplayCode_Click(ByVal sender As Object, _
    ByVal e As System.EventArgs) Handles btnDisplayCode.Click
    ' displays the record whose Code field contains PG24

    Dim records = From magazine In MagazinesDataSet.tblMagazine _
                Where magazine.Code = "PG24" _
                Select magazine
    TblMagazineBindingSource.DataSource = records
End Sub

Private Sub btnDisplayName_Click(ByVal sender As Object, _
    ByVal e As System.EventArgs) Handles btnDisplayName.Click
    ' displays the record whose MagName field contains Java

    Dim records = From magazine In MagazinesDataSet.tblMagazine _
                Where magazine.MagName = "Java" _
                Select magazine
    TblMagazineBindingSource.DataSource = records
End Sub
```

Figure 26-6

2. See Figure 26-7.

```vb
Private Sub btnDisplayCost_Click(ByVal sender As Object, _
    ByVal e As System.EventArgs) Handles btnDisplayCost.Click
    ' displays magazines costing $4 or more

    Dim records = From magazine In MagazinesDataSet.tblMagazine _
                  Where magazine.Cost >= 4 Select magazine
    TblMagazineBindingSource.DataSource = records
End Sub

Private Sub btnDisplayName_Click(ByVal sender As Object, _
    ByVal e As System.EventArgs) Handles btnDisplayName.Click
    ' displays magazines whose name starts with C

    Dim records = From magazine In MagazinesDataSet.tblMagazine _
                  Where magazine.MagName Like "C*" _
                  Select magazine
    TblMagazineBindingSource.DataSource = records
End Sub

Private Sub btnAverage_Click(ByVal sender As Object, _
    ByVal e As System.EventArgs) Handles btnAverage.Click
    ' displays the average cost of a magazine

    Dim avgCost = Aggregate magazine In MagazinesDataSet.tblMagazine _
                  Select magazine.Cost Into Average()
    MessageBox.Show("Average cost of a magazine: " _
                  & avgCost.ToString("C2"), "Magazines", _
                  MessageBoxButtons.OK, MessageBoxIcon.Information)
End Sub
```

Figure 26-7

27

I LOVE THIS CLASS

After studying Chapter 27, you should be able to:

Define a class

Instantiate an object from a class that you define

Add Property procedures to a class

Include data validation in a class

Create a default constructor

Include methods in a class

THAT'S A REAL CLASSY OBJECT

Visual Basic 2008 is an object-oriented programming language, which is a language that allows the programmer to use objects to accomplish a program's goal. The objects used in an object-oriented program can take on many different forms. The text boxes, labels, and buttons included in most Windows programs are objects. An object also can represent something found in real life, such as a credit card receipt, a check, or even an employee. Every object is created from a **class**, which is a pattern or blueprint that the computer follows when creating the object. Using object-oriented programming (**OOP**) terminology, objects are **instantiated** (created) from a class, and each **object** is referred to as an **instance** of the class. A button control, for example, is an instance of the Button class, which is the class from which a button is instantiated. A text box, on the other hand, is an instance of the TextBox class. The class itself is not an object; only an instance of the class is an object. Every object has **attributes**, which are the characteristics that describe the object. Attributes are also called properties. Included in the attributes of buttons and text boxes are the Name and Text properties. DataGridView controls have a DataSource property as well as an AutoSizeColumnsMode property. In addition to attributes, every object also has behaviors. An object's **behaviors** include methods and events. **Methods** are the operations (actions) that the object is capable of performing. For example, a button control can use its Focus method to send the focus to itself. **Events** are the actions to which an object can respond. A button control's Click event, for instance, allows the button to respond to a mouse click. A class contains—or, in OOP terms, it **encapsulates**—all of the attributes and behaviors of the object it instantiates.

In previous chapters, you instantiated objects using classes that are built into Visual Basic, such as the TextBox and Label classes. You used the objects in a variety of ways in many different applications. In some applications, you used a text box to enter a name, while in other applications you used it to enter a sales tax rate or to display scrollable text. Similarly, you used label controls to identify text boxes and also to display the result of calculations. The ability to use an object for more than one purpose saves programming time and money—an advantage that contributes to the popularity of object-oriented programming. In addition to using the Visual Basic classes, you also can define your own classes and then create instances (objects) from those classes. Like the Visual Basic classes, your classes must specify the attributes and behaviors of the objects they create. You define a class using the **Class statement**, whose syntax is shown in Figure 27-1. Although it is not required by the syntax, the convention is to enter class names using Pascal case. Recall that Pascal case means you capitalize the first letter in the name and the first letter in any subsequent words in the name. The names of Visual Basic classes (for example, String and TextBox) also follow this naming convention. Within the Class statement, you define the attributes and behaviors of the objects the class will create. The attributes are represented by variables and Property procedures. You will learn about Property procedures in this chapter. The behaviors are represented by Sub and Function procedures, more commonly referred to as methods. (Some behaviors are represented by Event procedures; however, that topic is beyond the scope of this book.) Also included in Figure 27-1 is an example of a Class statement that defines a class named RectangularPool.

THE CLASS STATEMENT

Syntax

Public Class *className*
    attributes section (contains variables and Property procedures)
    behaviors section (contains Sub and/or Function procedures)
End Class

Example

Public Class RectangularPool
    attributes
    behaviors
End Class

Figure 27-1: Syntax and an example of the Class statement

You will use the Class statement in the Willow Pools application, which you begin coding in the next section.

REVISITING THE WILLOW POOLS APPLICATION

You coded the Willow Pools application in Chapter 22. As you may remember, the application calculates and displays both the volume of a rectangular pool and the amount of water required to fill the pool. The volume is calculated by multiplying the pool's length by its width, and then multiplying the result by the pool's depth. Assuming the length, width, and depth are measured in feet, this gives you the volume in cubic feet. To determine the number of gallons of water, you multiply the number of cubic feet by 7.48, because there are 7.48 gallons in one cubic foot. In Chapter 22, you used a structure to group together the pool's length, width, and depth measurements. Recall that it's logical to group the three items because they are related: each represents one of the three dimensions of a rectangular pool. Most of the application's code from Chapter 22 is shown in Figure 27-2. In this chapter, you will modify the code to use a class rather than a structure.

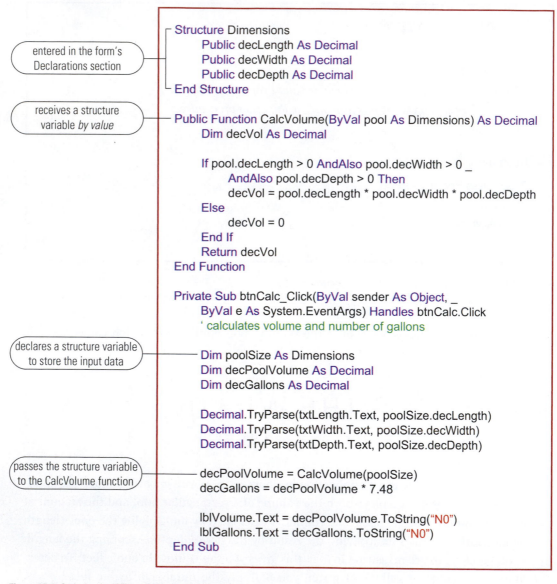

Figure 27-2: Code for the Willow Pools application using a structure

To open the Willow Pools application and then begin creating the class:

1. Start Visual Studio 2008 (or Visual Basic 2008 Express Edition). Open the **Pool Solution** (**Pool Solution.sln**) file, which is contained in the ClearlyVB\Chap27\Pool Solution folder. If necessary, open the designer window and display the Solution Explorer window.

2. First, you will use the Class statement to define a class named RectangularPool. You enter a Class statement in a class file. Click **Project** on the menu bar, then click **Add Class**. The Add New Item dialog box opens with Class selected in the Visual Studio installed templates box. Change the filename in the Name box to **RectangularPool.vb**, then click the **Add** button. The RectangularPool.vb window opens and shows the code template for the Class statement. In addition, the RectangularPool.vb filename appears in the Solution Explorer window. See Figure 27-3.

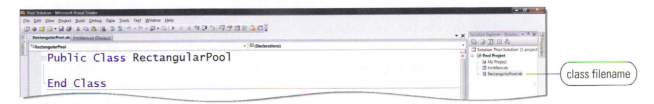

Figure 27-3: Class statement entered in the RectangularPool.vb window

In the context of OOP, a RectangularPool object has three attributes: a length, width, and depth. As mentioned earlier, the attributes in a class are represented by variables and Property procedures. The variables are entered first in the Class statement. In most cases, the variables are declared using the keyword Private. The Private keyword indicates that the variables can be used only within the class in which they are defined. When naming the Private variables in a class, many programmers use the underscore for the first character and then use camel case for the remainder of the name. In this case, you will use the variable names _decLength, _decWidth, and _decDepth.

To begin coding the RectangularPool class definition:

1. Auto-hide the Solution Explorer window, then click the **blank line** below the Public Class RectangularPool clause.

2. Enter the following three declaration statements. Press **Enter** twice after typing the last declaration statement.

Private _decLength As Decimal
Private _decWidth As Decimal
Private _decDepth As Decimal

WHO OWNS THAT PROPERTY?

When an application instantiates an object, only the Public members of the object's class are made available to the application. The application cannot access the Private members of the class. Using OOP terminology, the Public members are exposed to the application, whereas the Private members are hidden from the application. In this case, the _decLength, _decWidth, and _decDepth variables will be hidden from any application that contains an instance of the RectangularPool class. For an application to assign data to or retrieve data from a Private variable in a class, it must use a Public property. In other words, an application cannot directly refer to a Private variable in a class. Rather, it must refer to the variable indirectly, through the use of a Public property. You create a Public property using a **Property procedure**. The basic syntax of a Property procedure is shown in Figure 27-4. As the figure indicates, the header begins with the keywords Public Property followed by the name of the property. You should use nouns and adjectives to name a property and enter the name using Pascal case. Following the property name is a set of parentheses, the keyword As, and the property's *dataType*. The *dataType* must match the data type of the Private variable associated with the Property procedure. A Public Property procedure creates a property that is visible to any application that contains an instance of the class. A Property procedure ends with the procedure footer, which contains the keywords End Property. Between the Property procedure header and footer, you include a Get block of code and a Set block of code. The code contained in the **Get block** allows an application to retrieve the contents of the Private variable associated with the property. The code in the **Set block** allows an application to assign a value to the Private variable associated with the property. Also included in Figure 27-4 is an example of a Property procedure.

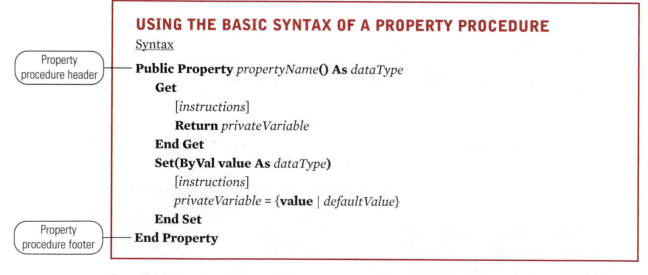

USING THE BASIC SYNTAX OF A PROPERTY PROCEDURE

<u>Syntax</u>

Property procedure header — **Public Property** *propertyName*() **As** *dataType*
    Get
        [*instructions*]
        Return *privateVariable*
    End Get
    Set(ByVal value As *dataType***)**
        [*instructions*]
        privateVariable = {**value** | *defaultValue*}
    End Set
Property procedure footer — **End Property**

Figure 27-4: Basic syntax and an example of a property procedure (*continued on next page*)

```
Example
Public Property Length() As Decimal
    Get
        Return _decLength
    End Get
    Set(ByVal value As Decimal)
        If value >= 0 Then
            _decLength = value
        Else
            _decLength = 0
        End If
    End Set
End Property
```

Figure 27-4: Basic syntax and an example of a property procedure (*continued from previous page*)

The Get block in a Property procedure contains the **Get statement**, which begins with the keyword Get and ends with the keywords End Get. Most times, you will enter only the Return *privateVariable* instruction within the Get statement. The instruction directs the computer to return the contents of the Private variable associated with the property. The Set block contains the **Set statement**, which begins with the keyword Set and ends with the keywords End Set. The Set keyword is followed by a parameter enclosed in parentheses. The parameter begins with the keywords ByVal value As. The keywords are followed by a *dataType,* which must match the data type of the Private variable associated with the Property procedure. The value parameter temporarily stores the value that is passed to the property by the application. You can enter one or more instructions within the Set statement. One of the instructions should assign the contents of the value parameter to the Private variable associated with the property. In the Set statement, you often will include instructions to validate the value received from the application before assigning it to the Private variable. The Set statement shown in the example in Figure 27-4 includes a selection structure that determines whether the value received from the application is valid. To be valid, the value must be greater than or equal to the number 0. If the value is valid, the _decLength = value instruction assigns the number stored in the value parameter to the Private _decLength variable; otherwise, the _decLength = 0 instruction assigns a default value (in this case, 0) to the variable. In the next set of steps, you will create a Public property for each Private variable in the RectangularPool class. Each Public property will allow an application indirect access to its associated Private variable.

To enter the Property procedures in the RectangularPool class definition:

1. The insertion point should be positioned two lines below the Private _decDepth As Decimal statement. First, enter a Public Property procedure for the _decLength variable. Type **public property Length as decimal** and press **Enter**. Notice that the Code Editor inserts a set of parentheses after the property name. Also notice that it enters the Get and Set statements for you, and positions the insertion point within the Get statement.

2. Recall that the Get block in a Property procedure simply returns the contents of the procedure's Private variable. Type **return _decLength**.

3. The Set block in a Property procedure should assign to the Private variable either the contents of the property's value parameter or a default value. In this case, you will assign the number contained in the value parameter only when the number is greater than or equal to 0; otherwise, you will assign the number 0. Click the **blank line** below the Set clause, then type the following selection structure.

   If value >= 0 Then
       _decLength = value
   Else
       _decLength = 0
   End If

4. Save the solution. Figure 27-5 shows the completed Length Property procedure, which is associated with the _decLength variable.

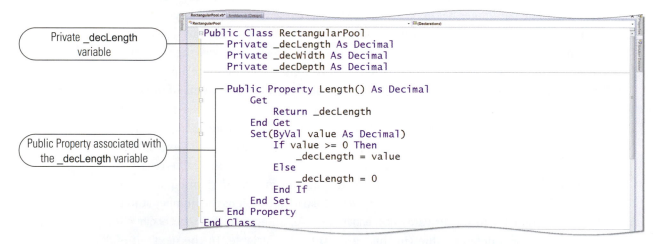

Figure 27-5: Completed Length Property procedure

5. Now enter the Property procedure for the _decWidth variable. Insert two blank lines below the End Property clause. Type **public property Width as decimal** and press **Enter**, then type **return _decWidth**. Click the **blank line** below the Set clause, then type the following selection structure.

   If value >= 0 Then
      _decWidth = value
   Else
      _decWidth = 0
   End If

6. Next, enter the Property procedure for the _decDepth variable. Insert two blank lines below the last End Property clause. Type **public property Depth as decimal** and press **Enter**, then type **return _decDepth**. Click the **blank line** below the Set clause, then type the following selection structure.

   If value >= 0 Then
      _decDepth = value
   Else
      _decDepth = 0
   End If

7. Save the solution.

MINI-QUIZ 1

1. OOP stands for _____.

2. Data validation code is entered in the _____ block of code in a Property procedure.

3. A Property procedure is associated with a Private variable named _strCity. What statement should you enter in the procedure's Get block of code?

CONSTRUCTIVE BEHAVIOR IS THE KEY TO SUCCESS

Besides having attributes, objects also have behaviors. As you learned earlier, behaviors include the operations (actions) that the object is capable of performing. A RectangularPool object will have three behaviors. First, it will be able to initialize its Private variables when it is instantiated. Second, it will be able to calculate and return its volume. Third, it will be able to calculate and return the number of gallons of water required to fill it. The first behavior—initializing the Private variables—requires a constructor. A **constructor** is a class method whose instructions are automatically processed by the computer when an object is instantiated. A constructor is responsible for creating the object and initializing the class's Private variables. The syntax of a constructor is shown in Figure 27-6. The syntax begins with the keywords Public Sub New followed by a set of parentheses that contains an optional *parameterList*; it ends with the keywords End Sub. Constructors never return a value, so they are always Sub procedures (rather than Function procedures). Within the constructor you enter the code to initialize the class's Private variables. The initialization occurs each time an object is instantiated from the class. A class can have more than one constructor. Each constructor will have the same name, New, but its parameters (if any) must be different from any other constructor in the class. A constructor that has no parameters is called the **default constructor**. A class can have only one default constructor. Figure 27-6 shows the default constructor for the RectangularPool class. The default constructor initializes the class's Private variables to the number 0.

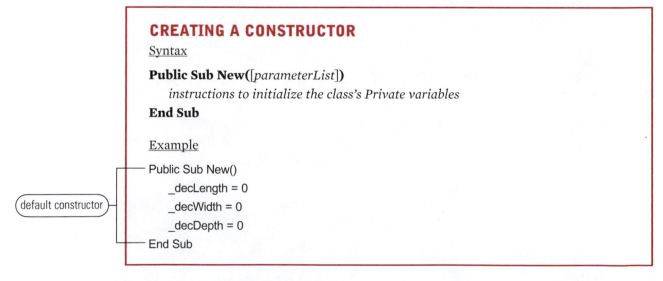

CREATING A CONSTRUCTOR

Syntax

Public Sub New([*parameterList*]**)**
   instructions to initialize the class's Private variables
End Sub

Example

```
Public Sub New()
    _decLength = 0
    _decWidth = 0
    _decDepth = 0
End Sub
```

default constructor

Figure 27-6: Syntax and an example of a constructor

To enter the default constructor in the RectangularPool class definition:

1. Insert two blank lines below the last End Property clause, then type **public sub New** and press **Enter**. Notice that the Code Editor adds a set of parentheses after the default constructor's name.

2. Type the following comment and lines of code.

    ' default constructor
    _decLength = 0
    _decWidth = 0
    _decDepth = 0

METHODS OTHER THAN CONSTRUCTORS

A class also can contain methods other than constructors. Except for constructors, which must be Sub procedures, the methods included in a class can be either Sub procedures or Function procedures. Recall from Chapter 18 that a Function procedure returns a value after performing its assigned task, whereas a Sub procedure does not return a value. Figure 27-7 shows the syntax of a method that is not a constructor. The {Sub | Function} in the syntax indicates that you can select only one of the keywords appearing within the braces. Like property names, method names should be entered using Pascal case. However, unlike property names, the first word in a method name should be a verb, and any subsequent words should be nouns and adjectives. The method name used in the example in Figure 27-7, GetVolume, follows this naming convention.

CREATING A METHOD THAT IS NOT A CONSTRUCTOR

<u>Syntax</u>

Public {Sub | Function} *methodName*(*[parameterList]*) **As** *dataType*
    instructions
End {Sub | Function}

<u>Example</u>

Public Function GetVolume() As Decimal
    Return _decLength * _decWidth * _decDepth
End Function

Figure 27-7: Syntax and an example of a method that is not a constructor

As mentioned earlier, a RectangularPool object should be able to calculate and return its volume, as well as calculate and return the number of gallons of water required to fill it. For a RectangularPool object to perform these tasks, you will need to include two additional methods in the class definition: GetVolume and GetGallons. Both methods will be Function procedures, because each will need to return a value to the application that contains the object.

To enter the GetVolume and GetGallons methods in the RectangularPool class definition:

1. Insert two blank lines below the End Sub clause, then type **public function GetVolume as decimal** and press **Enter**. Here again, the Code Editor inserts a set of parentheses after the function name. Type **return _decLength * _decWidth * _decDepth**.

2. Insert two blank lines below the End Function clause. Type **public function GetGallons as decimal** and press **Enter**.

3. Recall that you determine the number of gallons of water by multiplying the volume by 7.48. You can use the class's GetVolume method to get the volume. First, declare a variable to store the volume. Type **dim decVol as decimal** and press **Enter**. Then type **decVol = GetVolume** and press **Enter**. Notice that the Code Editor adds a set of parentheses after the method's name. Now type **return decVol * 7.48**, then click **a different line** in the Code Editor window.

4. Compare the code you entered with the code shown in Figure 27-8. Make any needed corrections, then save the solution.

```
Public Class RectangularPool
    Private _decLength As Decimal
    Private _decWidth As Decimal
    Private _decDepth As Decimal

    Public Property Length() As Decimal
        Get
            Return _decLength
        End Get
        Set(ByVal value As Decimal)
            If value >= 0 Then
                _decLength = value
            Else
                _decLength = 0
            End If
        End Set
    End Property
```

Figure 27-8: Completed RectangularPool class definition (*continued on next page*)

```vbnet
    Public Property Width() As Decimal
        Get
            Return _decWidth
        End Get
        Set(ByVal value As Decimal)
            If value >= 0 Then
                _decWidth = value
            Else
                _decWidth = 0
            End If
        End Set
    End Property

    Public Property Depth() As Decimal
        Get
            Return _decDepth
        End Get
        Set(ByVal value As Decimal)
            If value >= 0 Then
                _decDepth = value
            Else
                _decDepth = 0
            End If
        End Set
    End Property

    Public Sub New()
        ' default constructor
        _decLength = 0
        _decWidth = 0
        _decDepth = 0
    End Sub

    Public Function GetVolume() As Decimal
        Return _decLength * _decWidth * _decDepth
    End Function

    Public Function GetGallons() As Decimal
        Dim decVol As Decimal
        decVol = GetVolume()
        Return decVol * 7.48
    End Function
End Class
```

Figure 27-8: Completed RectangularPool class definition (*continued from previous page*)

USING THE PATTERN TO CREATE AN OBJECT

After defining a class, you then can use it to instantiate one or more objects. Figure 27-9 shows two versions of the basic syntax to accomplish this task. In both versions, *className* is the name of the class and *variableName* is the name of a variable that will store the object in the computer's internal memory. The difference between both versions relates to when the object is actually created. The computer creates the object only when it processes the statement containing the New keyword. As you learned earlier, New is the name of a class constructor. Recall that a constructor is responsible for creating the object and assigning initial values to the Private variables. Also included in Figure 27-9 is an example of using each version of the syntax. In Example 1, the Private pool As RectangularPool instruction creates a module-level variable named pool that can store a RectangularPool object; however, it does not create the object. The object isn't created until the computer processes the pool = New RectangularPool statement. The statement assigns the object to the pool variable. In Example 2, the Dim pool As New RectangularPool instruction creates a procedure-level variable named pool. It also instantiates a new RectangularPool object and assigns it to the variable.

INSTANTIATING AN OBJECT FROM A CLASS

Syntax—Version 1

{**Dim** | **Private**} *variableName* **As** *className*

variableName = **New** *class*

Syntax—Version 2

{**Dim** | **Private**} *variableName* **As New** *className*

Example 1—Version 1's syntax

Private pool As RectangularPool
pool = New RectangularPool
the first instruction declares a RectangularPool variable named pool; the second instruction instantiates a RectangularPool object, initializing its Private variables, and assigns the object to the pool variable

---

Figure 27-9: Basic syntax versions and examples of instantiating an object (*continued on next page*)

Example 2—Version 2's syntax

Dim pool As New RectangularPool
the instruction creates a RectangularPool variable named pool and also instantiates a
RectangularPool object, initializing its Private variables; it assigns the object to the
pool variable

Figure 27-9: Basic syntax versions and examples of instantiating an object (*continued from previous page*)

To modify the form's code to use a RectangularPool object rather than a structure:

1. If necessary, save the solution. Close the RectangularPool.vb window, then open the form's Code Editor window. The application will use the RectangularPool class rather than the Structure statement, so you can delete the Structure statement from the form's Declarations section. Select (highlight) the entire Structure statement, beginning with the Structure clause and ending with the End Structure clause, then press **Delete**.

2. You also can delete the CalcVolume function, because the volume will be calculated by the GetVolume method in the class. Select (highlight) the entire CalcVolume function, beginning with the Public Function clause and ending with the End Function clause, then press **Delete**.

3. Delete the blank lines, except for one, between the Public Class frmMain line and the procedure header for the btnCalc control's Click event procedure.

4. Now instantiate a RectangularPool object in the btnCalc control's Click event procedure. Change the Dim poolSize As Dimensions line to **Dim pool As New RectangularPool**.

5. Now use the object's properties to store the length, width, and depth measurements. Select (highlight) poolSize.decLength in the first TryParse method, then press **Delete**. Type **pool.** (be sure to type the period). If necessary, click the **Common** tab. A list of properties and methods for a RectangularPool object appears, as shown in Figure 27-10. The list shows the three properties and two of the three methods defined in the RectangularPool class. The only method that does not appear in the list is the default constructor (New).

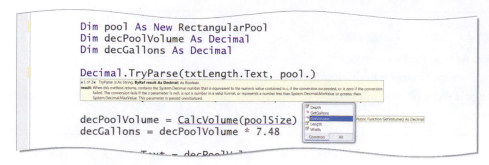

Figure 27-10: List of properties and methods for a RectangularPool object

6. Click **Length** in the list, if necessary, then press **Tab**. Click **another line** in the Code Editor window.

7. On your own, change poolSize.decWidth in the second TryParse method to **pool.Width**, and change poolSize.decDepth in the third TryParse method to **pool.Depth**.

8. Now use the class's GetVolume method to get the volume. Select CalcVolume(poolSize) in the statement below the last TryParse method, then type **pool.** (be sure to type the period). Click **GetVolume** in the list, then press **Tab**.

9. Finally, use the class's GetGallons method to get the number of gallons. On your own, change decPoolVolume * 7.48 to **pool.GetGallons**. Figure 27-11 shows the modified Click event procedure. The changes you made to the procedure are shaded in the figure.

```
Private Sub btnCalc_Click(ByVal sender As Object, _
    ByVal e As System.EventArgs) Handles btnCalc.Click
    ' calculates volume and number of gallons

    Dim pool As New RectangularPool
    Dim decPoolVolume As Decimal
    Dim decGallons As Decimal

    Decimal.TryParse(txtLength.Text, pool.Length)
    Decimal.TryParse(txtWidth.Text, pool.Width)
    Decimal.TryParse(txtDepth.Text, pool.Depth)

    decPoolVolume = pool.GetVolume
    decGallons = pool.GetGallons

    lblVolume.Text = decPoolVolume.ToString("N0")
    lblGallons.Text = decGallons.ToString("N0")
End Sub
```

Figure 27-11: Modified Click event procedure for the btnCalc control

In the next set of steps, you will test the application to verify that it is working correctly.

To test the application:

1. Save the solution, then start the application. Type **100** in the Length box, **30** in the Width box, and **4** in the Depth box. Click the **Calculate** button. The numbers 12,000 and 89,760 appear in the Volume and Gallons boxes, respectively.

2. Click the **Exit** button. Close the Code Editor window, then close the solution.

At this point, the advantage of creating a class and instantiating objects—in other words, the advantage of object-oriented programming—may not be apparent. After all, modifying the Willow Pools application to include a class required many more lines of code. The real advantage of object-oriented programming is the ability to reuse a class—for example, use it in a different way or in a different application. In the next section, you will use the RectangularPool class in the Pool Supplies application.

POOL SUPPLIES APPLICATION

Pool Supplies sells a water clarifier designed to combat a common problem in swimming pools: cloudy water. The company recommends one ounce of SoClear clarifier per 5000 gallons of water. The manager of Pool Supplies wants an application that calculates the number of gallons of water contained in a pool and the required number of ounces of clarifier. You can use the RectangularPool class that you created for the Willow Pools application. The RectangularPool.vb file is contained in the ClearlyVB\Chap27\Pool Solution\Pool Project folder.

To open the Pool Supplies application and then code and test the application:

1. Use Windows to copy the RectangularPool.vb file from the ClearlyVB\Chap27\ Pool Solution\Pool Project folder to the ClearlyVB\Chap27\Pool Supplies Solution\ Pool Supplies Project folder.

2. Open the **Pool Supplies Solution** (**Pool Supplies Solution.sln**) file, which is contained in the ClearlyVB\Chap27\Pool Supplies Solution folder. If necessary, open the designer window. The user interface provides text boxes for the user to enter the pool's dimensions.

3. First, add the RectangularPool.vb file to the project. Click **Project** on the menu bar, then click **Add Existing Item** to open the Add Existing Item dialog box. The Pool Supplies Project folder should be open. Click **RectangularPool.vb**, then click the

Add button. Temporarily display the Solution Explorer window to verify that it contains the RectangularPool.vb filename.

4. Open the Code Editor window. Locate the btnCalc control's Click event procedure, then click the **blank line** above its End Sub clause. First, instantiate a RectangularPool object. Type **dim pool as new RectangularPool** and press **Enter**.

5. Now declare variables to store the number of gallons of water and the number of ounces of clarifier. Type **dim decGallons as decimal** and press **Enter**, then type **dim decOunces as decimal** and press **Enter** twice.

6. Next, assign the input items to the RectangularPool object's properties. Enter the following three statements. Press **Enter** twice after typing the last statement.

   Decimal.TryParse(txtLength.Text, pool.Length)
   Decimal.TryParse(txtWidth.Text, pool.Width)
   Decimal.TryParse(txtDepth.Text, pool.Depth)

7. Now use the RectangularPool object's GetGallons method to get the number of gallons of water. Type **decGallons = pool.GetGallons** and press **Enter**.

8. You calculate the number of ounces of clarifier by dividing the number of gallons of water by 5000. Type **decOunces = decGallons / 5000** and press **Enter** twice.

9. Finally, display the number of gallons of water and the number of ounces of clarifier in the interface. Enter the two assignment statements indicated in Figure 27-12.

```
Private Sub btnCalc_Click(ByVal sender As Object, ByVal e As System.E
    ' calculates and displays the number of gallons in a pool
    ' and the number of ounces of clarifier needed

    Dim pool As New RectangularPool
    Dim decGallons As Decimal
    Dim decOunces As Decimal

    Decimal.TryParse(txtLength.Text, pool.Length)
    Decimal.TryParse(txtWidth.Text, pool.Width)
    Decimal.TryParse(txtDepth.Text, pool.Depth)

    decGallons = pool.GetGallons
    decOunces = decGallons / 5000

    lblGallons.Text = decGallons.ToString("N0")
    lblClarifier.Text = decOunces.ToString("N1")
End Sub
```

enter these two assignment statements

Figure 27-12: Completed Click event procedure for the btnCalc control

10. Save the solution, then start the application. Type **100** in the Length box, **30** in the Width box, and **4** in the Depth box. Click the **Calculate** button. See Figure 27-13. The interface shows that the pool contains 89,760 gallons of water and requires 18.0 ounces of clarifier.

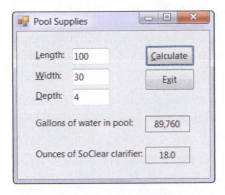

Figure 27-13: Output shown in the interface

11. Click the **Exit** button. Close the Code Editor window, then close the solution.

MINI-QUIZ 2

1. The name of the default constructor for a class named Animal is _____.

2. Write the statement to instantiate an Animal object, assigning the object to a procedure-level variable named dog.

3. A Private variable in a class can be accessed directly by a Public method in the same class.

   a. True   b. False

To learn more about classes, view the Ch27-Classes video.

To learn about overloading methods and inheritance, see the Overloading and Inheritance sections in the Ch27WantMore.pdf file.

SUMMARY

» The objects used in an object-oriented program are instantiated (created) from classes. A class encapsulates (contains) the attributes that describe the object it creates, and the behaviors that allow the object to perform tasks and respond to actions.

» You use the Class statement to define a class. Class names are entered using Pascal case. You enter a class definition in a class file, which you can add to the current project using the Project menu.

» When naming the Private variables in a class, many programmers begin the name with the underscore character. Subsequent characters in the name are entered using camel case.

» When an object is instantiated in an application, the Public members of the class are exposed to the application; the Private members are hidden from the application.

» When an application needs to assign data to or retrieve data from a Private variable in a class, it must use a Public property to do so. You create a Public property using a Property procedure. The names of the properties in a class should be entered using Pascal case. You should use nouns and adjectives in the name.

» In a Property procedure, the Get block allows an application to access the contents of the Private variable associated with the property. The Set block, on the other hand, allows an application to assign a value to the Private variable.

» A class can have one or more constructors. All constructors are Sub procedures that are named New. Each constructor must have a different *parameterList* (if any). A constructor that has no parameters is the default constructor. A class can contain only one default constructor.

» The names of the methods in a class should be entered using Pascal case. You should use a verb for the first word in the name, and nouns and adjectives for any subsequent words in the name.

KEY TERMS

Attributes—the characteristics that describe an object

Behaviors—includes an object's methods and events

Class—a pattern that the computer follows when creating (instantiating) an object

Class statement—the statement used to define a class in Visual Basic

Constructor—a method whose instructions are automatically processed each time the class instantiates an object; its purpose is to create the object and initialize the class's variables

Default constructor—a constructor that has no parameters

Encapsulates—an OOP term that means "contains"

Events—the actions to which an object can respond

Get block—the section of a Property procedure that contains the Get statement

Get statement—appears in a Get block in a Property procedure; contains the code that allows an application to retrieve the contents of the Private variable associated with the property

Instance—an object created from a class

Instantiated—the process of creating an object from a class

Methods—the actions that an object is capable of performing

Object—an instance of a class

OOP—an acronym for Object-Oriented Programming

Property procedure—creates a Public property that an application can use to access a Private variable in a class

Set block—the section of a Property procedure that contains the Set statement

Set statement—appears in a Set block in a Property procedure; contains the code that allows an application to assign a value to the Private variable associated with the property

ANSWERS TO MINI-QUIZZES

MINI-QUIZ 1

1. object-oriented programming

2. Set

3. Return _strCity

MINI-QUIZ 2

1. New

2. Dim dog As New Animal

3. a. True

REVIEW QUESTIONS

1. Which of the following statements is false?

   a. An example of an attribute is the _intMinutes variable in a Time class.

   b. An example of a behavior is the SetTime method in a Time class.

   c. A class is considered an object.

   d. An object created from a class is referred to as an instance of the class.

2. An application can access the Private variables in a class _____.

   a. directly

   b. using properties created by Property procedures

   c. through Private procedures contained in the class

   d. None of the above.

3. Which of the following creates an Animal object and assigns the object's address to the cat variable?

   a. Dim cat As Animal

   b. Dim cat As New Animal

   c. Dim cat As Animal
      cat = New Animal

   d. Both b and c.

4. An application instantiates an Animal object and assigns it to the cat variable. Which of the following invokes the Animal class's GetName method and assigns the return value to the strName variable?

   a. strName = Animal.GetName

   b. strName = cat.GetName

   c. strName = Animal.GetName.cat

   d. None of the above.

5. A constructor must be _____.

   a. a Function procedure

   b. a Sub procedure

   c. an Event procedure

   d. either a Function procedure or a Sub procedure

EXERCISES

1. Open the Area Solution (Area Solution.sln) file, which is contained in the ClearlyVB\Chap27\Area Solution folder. Open the designer window. Use the Project menu to add a class file named Square.vb to the project. Code the Square class. The class should have one attribute: a side measurement (which may contain a decimal place). It also should have two behaviors: a default constructor that initializes the class's Private variable and a function that calculates and returns the area of the square. Save the solution. Close the Square.vb window, then open the form's Code Editor window. Code the btnCalc control's Click event procedure. Save the solution, then start and test the application. Stop the application, then close the solution. (The answers to TRY THIS Exercises are located at the end of the chapter.)

» TRY THIS

2. In this exercise, you modify the Square class from Exercise 1. Use Windows to copy the Square.vb file from the ClearlyVB\Chap27\Area Solution\Area Project folder to the ClearlyVB\Chap27\Square Box Solution\Square Box Project folder. Open the Square Box Solution (Square Box Solution.sln) file contained in the ClearlyVB\Chap27\Square Box Solution folder. Open the designer window. Use the Project menu to add the Square.vb file to the project. Open the Square.vb file, then modify the Square class to include a method that calculates and returns the perimeter of a square. (To calculate the perimeter, you multiply the side measurement by 4.) Save the solution. Close the Square.vb window, then open the form's Code Editor window and code the btnDisplay control's Click event procedure. Save the solution, then start and test the application. Stop the application, then close the solution.

» MODIFY THIS

3. Open the Sweets Solution (Sweets Solution.sln) file, which is contained in the ClearlyVB\Chap27\Sweets Solution folder. Open the designer window. Add a class file named Salesperson.vb to the project. Code the Salesperson class. The class should have two attributes: a salesperson's ID and a sales amount. The ID may contain letters; the sales amount may contain a decimal place. The class should have one behavior: the default constructor. Save the solution. Close the Salesperson.vb window, then open the form's Code Editor window. The btnSave control's Click event procedure should save each salesperson's ID and sales amount to a sequential access file. Finish coding the procedure. Save the solution, then start and test the application. Stop the application, then close the solution.

» INTRODUCTORY

4. Open the Grade Solution (Grade Solution.sln) file, which is contained in the ClearlyVB\Chap27\Grade Solution folder. Open the designer window. Add a class file named CourseGrade to the project. Code the CourseGrade class. The class should have three attributes: the scores for three tests. It also should have two behaviors: the default constructor and a method that determines and returns the letter grade.

» INTERMEDIATE

The letter grade is based on the total score. If the total score is at least 270, the letter grade is A. If the total score is from 240 through 269, the letter grade is B. If the total score is from 210 through 239, the letter grade is C. If the total score is from 180 through 209, the letter grade is D. If the total score is less than 180, the letter grade is F. Save the solution. Close the CourseGrade.vb window, then open the form's Code Editor window. Code the btnDisplay control's Click event procedure. Save the solution, then start and test the application. Stop the application, then close the solution.

» ADVANCED

5. Shelly Jones, the manager of Pennington Book Store, wants an application that she can use to calculate and display the total amount a customer owes. Create a new Visual Basic Windows application. Name the solution, project, and form file Pennington Solution, Pennington Project, and frmMain.vb, respectively. Save the application in the ClearlyVB\Chap27 folder. If necessary, change the form's name to frmMain. Create the interface shown in Figure 27-14. A customer can purchase one or more books at either the same price or different prices. The application should keep a running total of the amount the customer owes, and display the total in the Total due box. For example, a customer might purchase two books at $6 and three books at $10. To calculate the total due, Shelly will need to enter 2 in the Quantity box and 6 in the Price box, and then click the Add to Sale button. The Total due box should display $12.00. To complete the order, Shelly will need to enter 3 in the Quantity box and 10 in the Price box, and then click the Add to Sale button. The Total due box should display $42.00. Before calculating the next customer's order, Shelly will need to click the New Order button. Add a class file named BookSale.vb to the project. Code the BookSale class. The class should have three attributes: a quantity, price, and total due. It also should have two behaviors: the default constructor and a method that keeps a running total of the amount the customer owes. Save the solution. Close the BookSale.vb window, then open the form's Code Editor window. Finish coding the application. Save the solution, then start and test the application. Stop the application, then close the solution.

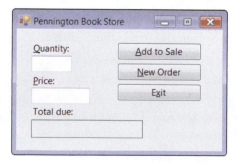

Figure 27-14: User interface for the Pennington Book Store application

6. Open the FigureThisOut Solution (FigureThisOut Solution.sln) file, which is contained in the ClearlyVB\Chap27\FigureThisOut Solution folder. Open the form's Code Editor window and the class's Code Editor window. Study the existing code. What is the difference between both constructors? Start and then test the application. Stop the application. Close the Code Editor window, then close the solution.

7. In this exercise, you find an error in an application's code. Open the SwatTheBugs Solution (SwatTheBugs Solution.sln) file, which is contained in the ClearlyVB\Chap27\SwatTheBugs Solution folder. Open the Code Editor window for the form and class. Correct the btnCalc_Click procedure to remove the jagged lines, then save the solution. Start and then test the application. Notice that the application is not working correctly. Stop the application. Locate and correct any errors in the code. Save the solution, then start and test the application again. Stop the application, then close the solution.

ANSWER TO "TRY THIS" EXERCISE

1. Figure 27-15 shows the Square class and the Click event procedure for the btnCalc control.

```vbnet
Public Class Square
    Private _decSide As Decimal

    Public Property Side() As Decimal
        Get
            Return _decSide
        End Get
        Set(ByVal value As Decimal)
            If value > 0 Then
                _decSide = value
            Else
                _decSide = 0
            End If
        End Set
    End Property

    Public Sub New()      ' default constructor
        _decSide = 0
    End Sub
End Class
```

Figure 27-15 (*continued on next page*)

```
    Public Function GetArea() As Decimal
        Return _decSide * _decSide
    End Function
End Class

Private Sub btnCalc_Click(ByVal sender As Object, _
    ByVal e As System.EventArgs) Handles btnCalc.Click
    ' calculates and displays the area of a square

    ' instantiate a Square object
    Dim mySquare As New Square

    ' declare a variable to store the area
    Dim decArea As Decimal

    ' assign input to the Square object's property
    Decimal.TryParse(txtSide.Text, mySquare.Side)

    ' call the Square object's method to calculate the area
    decArea = mySquare.GetArea

    ' display the area
    lblArea.Text = decArea.ToString

    txtSide.Focus()
End Sub
```

Figure 27-15 (*continued from previous page*)

DATA TYPES

Data type	Stores	Memory required
Boolean	a logical value (True, False)	2 bytes
Char	one Unicode character	2 bytes
Date	date and time information Date range: January 1, 001 to December 31, 9999 Time range: 0:00:00 (midnight) to 23:59:59	8 bytes
Decimal	a number with a decimal place Range with no decimal place: +/-79,228,162,514,264,337,593,543,950,335 Range with a decimal place: +/-7.9228162514264337593543950335	16 bytes
Double	a number with a decimal place Range: +/- $4.94065645841247 \times 10^{-324}$ to +/-$1.79769313486231 \times 10^{308}$	8 bytes
Integer	integer Range: -2,147,483,648 to 2,147,483,647	4 bytes
Long	integer Range: -9,223,372,036,854,775,808 to 9,223,372,036,854,775,807	8 bytes
Object	data of any type	4 bytes
Short	integer Range: -32,768 to 32,767	2 bytes
Single	a number with a decimal place Range: +/-1.401298×10^{-45} to +/-3.402834×10^{38}	4 bytes
String	text; 0 to 2 billion characters	

INDEX

D

V

W